Contents

KU-495-353

Introduction to
Florida

The aptly nicknamed "Sunshine State" is a land of alligators, orange groves, everglades, pelicans, Key lime pie, pink plastic lawn flamingos and miles and miles of gorgeous, sugary sands. You can party on the beach, kayak on blackwater rivers, feast on Apalachicola oysters, dive tropical reefs, swim in cool natural springs and take pics with Mickey Mouse in the Magic Kingdom. Within Florida's borders you have bucket-list attractions that range from Art Deco South Beach, NASA's space centre and the Daytona 500, to Hemingway's Key West and Jimmy Buffett's original Margaritaville. The beaches themselves can vary wildly – hordes of copper-toned partiers are often just a Frisbee's throw from a deserted, pristine strand. Look closer and you'll discover the influence of a vibrant blend of cultures – African, Spanish and Native American – in an array of ancient ruins, tantalizing restaurants and exuberant architecture.

Indeed, it's the sheer range of experiences on offer that often takes visitors by surprise, with the glitz of Hispanic Miami and the east coast a far cry from the traditional Southern culture on display in the Panhandle – parts of the Florida Keys and the Everglades can seem like completely different countries. Top of a long list are Florida's **natural attractions**, ranging from isolated keys and world-class wreck dives, to close encounters with dolphins, manatees and Key deer. Florida's state parks are especially well organized, supplementing nationally managed resources such as the Everglades with freshwater springs, dense forests and spectacular caverns.

   Culturally Florida is just as enticing, with a remarkable cache of **art** on display, largely thanks to donations over the years from its wealthier citizens – the Salvador Dalí and ale Chihuly collections in St Petersburg are truly exceptional. Native American culture presented by a small but vital community led by the Seminole tribe, while remnants anish rule – primarily old forts and missions – dot the northern half of the state. revalent is the stock of mansions and public buildings designed in lavish Italianate

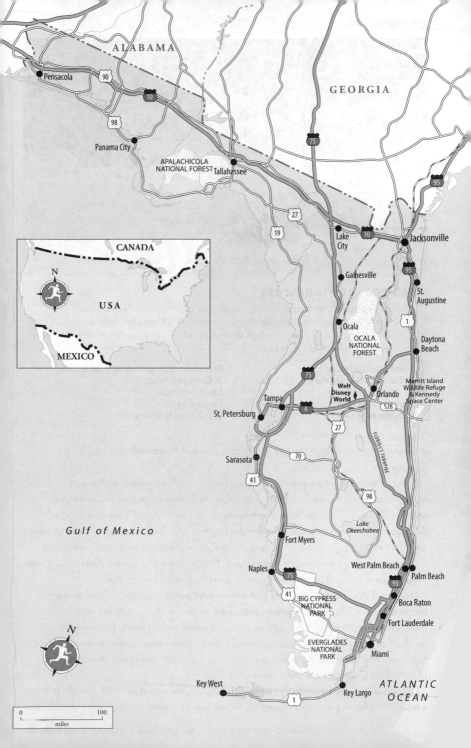

FLORIDA'S TOP 10 BEACHES

The Sunshine State takes great pride in its roughly 660 miles of clean, tidy and usually spellbinding **beaches**. Some of the most popular are around **Miami** on the Atlantic coast, although the best beaches lie on the **Gulf of Mexico**, where warm breezes, bone-white sands and spectacular sunsets are big draws.

Anna Maria Island p.233
Bahia Honda State Park p.125
Caladesi Island p.374
Fort de Soto Park p.370
Perdido Key p.443

St Andrew's State Park & Shell Island p.426
St George Island p.421
Sand Key Park p.374
Siesta Key p.227
South Beach, Miami p.50

or Spanish Revival style in the late nineteenth and early twentieth centuries, from St Augustine to Coral Gables.

Florida doesn't just attract tourists. The state boasts a vigorous **college sector**, best encapsulated by the fanatical support accorded to the University of Florida Gators sports teams in Gainesville, and the musical virtuosity of the Florida A&M University band in Tallahassee. Florida is also home to one of the biggest – and most influential – **Latin American communities** in the US (some 22 percent of the state population), with a well-established Cuban presence supplemented by Venezuelans, Puerto Ricans and Central Americans. Miami in particular is coloured by Latino culture, in everything from food to music.

Despite all this, Florida's **beaches and amusement parks** continue to drive tourism – for good reason. The mild climate – subtropical in the south – combined with mesmerizing white sands, especially on the Gulf coast, make Florida prime beach territory all year round. And while Orlando's theme parks won't appeal to everyone, it's hard not to be blown away by the sheer vastness, ingenuity and thrills on offer at the ˙kes of Walt Disney World and Universal Studios.

˙espite taking a hammering since the real-estate bubble burst in 2008, Florida remains ˙tively affluent place, with America's fourth largest economy. There are real problems,

ABOVE GULF COAST BEACH, ANNA MARIA ISLAND **RIGHT** DISNEY CANDY FOR SALE IN ORLANDO

of course: parts of Miami remain very poor and in 2013, over 3.5 million Floridians were living on food stamps. Immigrants are still coming, however, and like them you are bound to be won over by Florida's relentlessly sunny disposition, cultural diversity and awe-inspiring natural splendour.

Where to go

The essential stop in Florida is **Miami**, whose addictive, cosmopolitan vibe is enriched by its large Hispanic population, and where the much-photographed Art Deco district of **South Beach** provides an unmistakeable backdrop for the state's best nightlife.

From Miami, a simple journey south brings you to the **Florida Keys**: a hundred-mile string of islands, each with its own special draw, be it sportfishing, coral-reef diving, or a unique species of dwarf deer. The single road spanning the Keys comes to a halt at **Key West**, a blob of land that's legendary for its sunsets and anything-goes attitude. North from Miami, much of the **southeast coast** is an urbanized commuter strip, with a string of plush beach resorts running from **Fort Lauderdale** to **Boca Raton** and **Palm Beach**. Alongside the busy towns, beaches flow for many unbroken miles and finally escape the residential stranglehold along the **northeast coast**, where the **Kennedy Space Center** lies within a surprisingly rich wildlife reserve. Further north, **Daytona Beach** combines beaches with a world-famous speedway, while elegant **St Augustine** is the oldest city in America.

Orlando dominates central Florida, with a plethora of world-class theme parks such as **Walt Disney World** and **Universal Orlando** making this one of America's most visited cities. If you're not in the mood to indulge in this ingenious fix of escapist fun, skip

north to the untrammelled forests of the **Panhandle** – Florida's link with the Deep South – or to the artsy towns and ivory-white beaches of the **northwest and southwest coasts**. Visit time-warped **Cedar Key**, the manatee-rich waters of **Crystal River** and the dazzling art galleries of **St Petersburg** as you progress steadily south to **the Everglades**, a massive, alligator-filled swathe of sawgrass plain, mangrove islands and cypress swamp, which provides a definitive statement of Florida's natural beauty.

When to go

You'll have to take into account Florida's **climate** (see box below) – and, of course, what your goals are – when deciding on the best time for a visit. Florida is split into **two climatic zones**: subtropical in the south and warm temperate – like the rest of the southeastern US – in the north. These two zones determine the state's tourist seasons and can affect costs accordingly.

Anywhere **south of Orlando** experiences very mild winters (Nov–April), with pleasantly warm temperatures and a low level of humidity. This is the peak period for tourist activity, with prices at their highest and crowds at their largest. It also marks the best time to visit the inland parks and swamps. The southern summer (May–Oct) seems hotter than it really is – New York is often warmer – because of the extremely high humidity, relieved only by afternoon thunderstorms and sometimes even hurricanes (though the chances of being there during one are remote). Lower prices and fewer tourists are the rewards for braving the mugginess, though mosquitoes can render the natural areas off-limits.

Winter is the off-peak period **north of Orlando**; in all probability, the only chill you'll detect is a slight nip in the evening air, though it's worth bearing in mind that at this time of year the sea is really too cold for swimming, and snow has been known to fall in the Panhandle. The northern Florida summer is when the crowds arrive, and when the days – and the nights – can be almost as hot and sticky as southern Florida.

FLORIDA TEMPERATURES

	Jan	Feb	Mar	Apr	May	Jun	Jul	Aug	Sep	Oct	Nov	Dec
JACKSONVILLE												
Max/min (°C/°F))	12/53	13/55	17/62	20/68	23/74	27/80	28/82	28/82	26/78	21/70	17/62	13/56
KEY WEST												
Max °C/°F	21/70	21/70	23/74	25/77	27/81	28/83	29/85	29/84	28/83	27/80	24/76	22/72
MIAMI												
Max °C/°F	19/67	20/68	22/72	24/75	26/79	27/81	28/83	28/83	28/82	26/78	23/73	21/69
ORLANDO												
Max °C/°F	16/61	16/61	19/67	23/73	26/78	27/81	28/83	28/83	27/81	24/75	19/67	17/62
PENSACOLA												
Max °C/°F	11/51	12/54	16/60	19/67	24/75	27/80	28/82	28/82	26/78	21/69	16/61	12/54
TALLAHASSEE												
Max °C/°F	11/51	12/53	16/60	19/66	23/74	27/80	27/81	27/81	26/78	20/68	16/60	12/53
TAMPA												
Max °C/°F	16/60	16/61	19/67	22/71	25/77	27/81	28/82	28/82	27/81	24/75	20/68	17/63

Author picks

Our hard-travelling authors have visited every corner of the state to bring you some unique travel experiences.

Hip and hot nightlife South Beach remains one of the coolest nightlife 'hoods in the US; sample the *SkyBar* (p.98), the *Rose Bar* at the *Delano* (p.98) or the *Purdy Lounge* (p.98).

Oldest hotel The gorgeous *Florida House Inn*, Amelia Island, has been hosting the likes of Ulysses S. Grant and Cuban revolutionary José Martí since 1857 (p.349).

World-class art Enticing artistic gems include the Chihuly Collection (p.365) and Salvador Dalí Museum (p.366), both in St Petersburg, the Cummer Museum of Art in Jacksonville (p.341), the Ringling Museum in Sarasota (p.223) and the Pérez Art Museum Miami (p.66).

Native Florida Get a taster of Apalachee culture at stunning Mission San Luís (p.407), or learn about the Seminoles at the Ah-Tah-Thi-Ki Museum (p.68).

Waterside bars Top of a very crowded field are *Aunt Catfish's on the River* in Daytona Beach (p.324), *Boss Oyster* in Apalachicola (p.420), *Flora-Bama* on Perdido Key (p.443), *Mucky Duck* on Captiva Island (p.249) and *Alabama Jack's* in Key Largo (p.116).

Fish camps Some of the best of these cheap seafood shacks are *JB's* in New Smyrna (p.318) and *Owen's Fish Camp* (p.230), in downtown Sarasota.

Cuban coffee Get your heart thumping with a shot of *cafecito* at *Columbia* in Ybor City (p.357), and *Los Pinareños Frutería* (p.95) and *El Pub* (p.95) in Little Havana, Miami.

More manatees These loveable water giants are best seen at Lowry Park Zoo in Tampa (p.360), Homosassa Springs Wildlife State Park (p.382), Crystal River (p.384) and Lee County Manatee Park (p.241).

> Our author recommendations don't end here. We've flagged up our favourite places – a perfectly sited hotel, an atmospheric café, a special restaurant – throughout the Guide, highlighted with the ★ symbol.

RIGHT SALVADOR DALÍ MUSEUM

15

things not to miss

It's not possible to see everything that Florida has to offer in one trip – and we don't suggest you try. What follows, in no particular order, is a selective taste of the state's highlights: great beaches, outstanding national parks, spectacular wildlife – even good things to eat and drink. All highlights have a page reference to take you straight into the Guide, where you can find out more. Coloured numbers refer to chapters in the Guide section.

1

1 MIAMI ART DECO
Page 55
The pastel-shaded architecture of South Beach provides a gorgeous setting for Miami's most glamorous hotels and bars.

2 KENNEDY SPACE CENTER
Page 311
Everything you ever wanted to know about the history of the US space programme, and within sight of the launchpads on nearby Merritt Island.

3 FAMU MARCHING BAND
Page 407
See Florida A&M University's funky marching band in Tallahassee, a sublime, foot-stomping musical treat.

4 ALLIGATOR ENCOUNTERS
Pages 157 & 232
The "keepers of the Everglades", alligators are visible throughout the national park, particularly along the Anhinga Trail.

13

14

10 SALVADOR DALÍ MUSEUM
Page 366
One of the world's greatest stashes of Dalí paintings lies in a stunning gallery in downtown St Petersburg.

11 MIAMI BEACH
Page 50
With seven miles of wide, golden sands and a bar scene to match, Florida's most fashionable beach is perfect for swimming, jet-skiing or just lounging in the sun.

12 SWIMMING WITH MANATEES
Page 384
Take a dip with these gentle, endangered creatures in Crystal River, north of Tampa.

13 APALACHICOLA OYSTERS
Page 420
Seafood is king in Florida, but though stone crab claws come close, the tastiest delicacies are these slippery bivalves fished out of the Gulf.

14 ST AUGUSTINE'S OLD TOWN
Page 328
Explore the elegant narrow streets, preserved houses and centuries-old Spanish fortress of America's oldest city.

15 CANOEING IN THE EVERGLADES
Page 159
Florida has numerous creeks and swamps for canoeing, the most untouched and beautiful of which are in the Everglades.

Itineraries

Florida is not huge by US standards, but it is very long, meaning that driving from one end to another can take a couple of days – Key West is over 880 miles from Pensacola by road. The following itineraries cover the best the state has to offer, while taking into account distances between sights.

GRAND TOUR

This three-week tour focuses on the southern and central parts of the state – you'd need another couple of weeks to do the Panhandle.

❶ **Miami** Take three days to sample the bars, sands and Art Deco delights of South Beach, the Cuban culture in Little Havana, and the ornate architecture of Coral Gables. **See p.44**

❷ **Space Coast** Drive north to NASA's mind-blowing Kennedy Space Center, and the untrammelled wilderness of the surrounding Merritt Island Wildlife Refuge. **See p.308**

❸ **Orlando** Detour inland to sample the world's greatest theme parks, including Universal Studios and the granddaddy of them all, the city-size Walt Disney World. **See p.260**

❹ **St Augustine** Spend two days soaking up the historic charms of Spanish St Augustine, America's oldest city. **See p.326**

❺ **Tallahassee** Get a taster of the Panhandle at the genteel state capital of Florida, and visit the awe-inspiring Mission San Luís. **See p.402**

❻ **Cedar Key** Make a journey into Old Florida at this remote island, home to creaky "cracker" houses and delicious seafood. **See p.385**

❼ **St Petersburg** Hit the Gulf coast for the stunning art galleries and beaches of St Petersburg, spectacular Sand Key and untouched Fort de Soto Park. **See p.374 & p.370**

❽ **The Everglades** Sleepy Naples makes a fine base for forays into the alligator-rich Everglades, home to the Seminole tribe. **See p.154 & p.251**

❾ **Florida Keys** End your trip by driving US-1 across the shark- and ray-filled lagoons of the Keys to the Hemingway hideout, fishing capital and all-out party town of Key West. **See p.130**

KIDS' FLORIDA

You'll need at least two weeks to cover this itinerary – note that you'll find plenty of beach stops en route, too many to list here.

❶ **Coral Castle** This quirky favourite is guaranteed to amaze small kids. **See p.168**

❷ **Dolphin encounters, Florida Keys** It's not cheap, but gazing into the eyes of a dolphin is bound to be a trip highlight. **See p.111 & p.115**

❸ **Alligators in the Everglades** Seeing alligators lazing in the sun a few feet away is well worth the long drive out. **See p.157**

❹ **Sanibel Island** The most family-friendly Gulf coast island, with sandy beaches, fun restaurants and lots of colourful shells to collect. **See p.244**

❺ **Sarasota circuses** America's circus capital hosts touring companies in spring and autumn – the Walker Bros Circus is most fun. **See p.227**

❻ **Orlando** The theme-park capital of the universe is actually geared more to older teenagers and adults, but Disney's Magic Kingdom is a dream for younger kids. **See p.260**

ABOVE MIAMI; SEAWORLD, ORLANDO

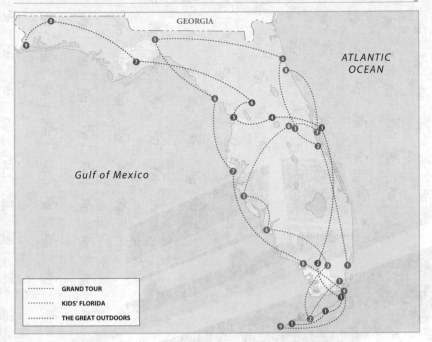

- - - - - - - GRAND TOUR
- - - - - - - KIDS' FLORIDA
- - - - - - - THE GREAT OUTDOORS

❼ Kennedy Space Center Budding scientists and sci-fi geeks of all ages will love this absorbing introduction to NASA and the space programme. **See p.311**

❽ Pirate & Treasure Museum, St Augustine Treasure hunts, electronic cannons and costumed pirates are on offer at this high-tech tribute to the buccaneers of the Caribbean. **See p.328**

THE GREAT OUTDOORS

Florida is home to exceptionally varied landscapes and ecosystems, but you can get a decent taster in two to three weeks.

❶ Florida Keys Highlights of this island chain include snorkelling and diving at the John Pennekamp Coral Reef State Park, visiting the Dolphin Research Center and spotting Key deer on Big Pine Key. **See p.112, p.111 & p.126**

❷ Everglades National Park Airboat rides and alligators await at this beautiful wilderness – spend at least two days here. **See p.154**

❸ Turtle-watching at Cape Canaveral Visit the northeast coast in June and July to see turtles crawling up the beach to lay eggs. **See p.315**

❹ Horseriding in the Ocala Forest Ocala's horse ranches offer myriad opportunities for riding and trekking through the woods; non-riders can tour the farms. **See p.391**

❺ Swim with manatees at Crystal River Crystal River is the only place in Florida where you are allowed to swim or dive with manatees – a captivating experience. **See p.384**

❻ Fresh springs Northwest Florida is studded with springs where you can swim and kayak through lush forest; the best are Rainbow Springs State Park, Alexander Springs and Wakulla Springs State Park. **See p.390, p.392 & p.412**

❼ Hiking in the Apalachicola National Forest Nowhere is more redolent of Old Florida than this vast undeveloped wilderness crisscrossed by hiking trails. **See p.418**

❽ Kayaking the Blackwater River State Forest The far northwest corner of the Panhandle is Florida's kayak capital. **See p.417**

❾ Gulf Islands National Seashore This national park encompasses some of Florida's most spectacular coast, including sections of Pensacola Beach and Perdido Key. **See p.441**

METROMOVER, MIAMI

Basics

Getting there

Florida is easily accessible by air, especially from Europe. Miami, Orlando and Tampa have international airports, and all the state's other cities and large towns – particularly Fort Lauderdale, Fort Myers and West Palm Beach – have frequent flights from other US cities and Canada.

Airfares depend on the **season**, and Florida is split into two climatic zones (see p.8). Flying on weekends is typically more expensive but in all cases you'll save a lot by booking months in advance; prices quoted below assume midweek travel.

Flights from the UK and Ireland

Although you can fly to the US from many of Britain's regional airports, the majority of nonstop scheduled flights to Florida are from **London**, and all of these land at Miami (via American, British Airways and Virgin), Orlando (British Airways and Virgin) and Tampa (British Airways). Delta flies nonstop between Manchester and Miami, while Virgin Atlantic also flies to Orlando nonstop from Manchester (and seasonally from Belfast and Glasgow). The flight time is around nine hours, usually leaving the UK around midday and arriving during the afternoon (local time). The return journey is slightly shorter, leaving in the early evening and flying through the night to arrive around breakfast time. A basic round-trip economy-class ticket (nonstop) from London to Miami will cost £450–500 for a midweek flight in low season and £600–700 in high season.

Assuming you book several months in advance, indirect flights via other US or European cities are unlikely to be much cheaper. Alternatively, you could take a flight to **New York** or another city on the northern US East Coast and travel on from there later – this won't save any money overall but is an option if you want to see more of the country before reaching Florida.

Travel agents can offer cut-price seats on direct **charter flights**. These are particularly good value if you're travelling from a British city other than London (Thomas Cook Airlines flies to Miami from

Manchester, for example, and to Orlando from Belfast, Birmingham, Cardiff and Glasgow), though they tend to be limited to the summer season and have fixed departure and return dates.

The cheapest and fastest options from **Dublin** to Miami also route through London (though Aer Lingus flies nonstop to Orlando). From Dublin you'll pay around the same rates in euro-equivalent as London to Miami.

Flights from the US and Canada

Of the **major US carriers**, Delta and American Airlines have the best links with the state's many smaller regional airports. Flying in to any of the three main airports, you can expect to pay between $150 and $250 one way from either **New York** or **Chicago**; from **LA**, the lowest fare will be around $260. You'll find a few excellent, low-cost airlines serving multiple Florida locations: JetBlue is especially good for flights to Orlando, Fort Lauderdale, Fort Myers, Jacksonville, Tampa, Sarasota and West Palm Beach. Carriers often run web-only specials, so be sure to check their sites before making a final purchase.

Frontier Airlines, Spirit Airlines, Southwest Airlines and Virgin America also offer flights from a number of western, southern, Midwestern and East Coast cities, while Allegiant Air serves Fort Lauderdale, Fort Myers, Tampa and Orlando's second airport at Sanford.

From **Toronto**, Air Canada flies direct to Miami, Orlando, Tampa and Fort Lauderdale, as well as Fort Myers and Sarasota in winter only; from **Montréal** the airline has direct flights to Orlando, Fort Lauderdale and Miami; and from **Vancouver**, they offer direct flights to Miami. Westjet flys direct to Fort Myers, Fort Lauderdale, Tampa and Orlando from Toronto, and offers seasonal direct flights to Key West and several cities from Montréal. From Toronto and Montréal, expect to pay at least Can$210 for a one-way flight to Miami, Can$275 from Vancouver. American Airlines often has competitive fares, with direct flights from Toronto and Montréal to Miami. It also flies to Miami from Vancouver (with a connection). Budget carriers Air Transat and Sunwing Airlines operate seasonal

---

FLY-DRIVE FLORIDA

If you intend to fly to Florida it's worth considering **fly-drive deals**, which give cut-rate (and sometimes free) car rental when buying your air ticket. They usually work out cheaper than renting on the spot (see p.22) and are especially good value if you intend to do a lot of driving. Most airlines – American Airlines, British Airways, Virgin Atlantic and many others – offer various holiday packages that include car rental.

A BETTER KIND OF TRAVEL

At Rough Guides we are passionately committed to travel. We believe it helps us understand the world we live in and the people we share it with – and of course tourism is vital to many developing economies. But the scale of modern tourism has also damaged some places irreparably, and climate change is accelerated by most forms of transport, especially flying. All Rough Guides' flights are carbon-offset, and every year we donate money to a variety of environmental charities.

flights between several regional Canadian airports and destinations in Florida.

Flights from Australia, New Zealand and South Africa

There are **no direct flights** to Florida from Australia or New Zealand. Most routes will require a change of plane in Los Angeles or Dallas, though it's rarely cheaper to buy separate tickets.

A basic round-trip economy-class ticket out of **Sydney or Melbourne** all the way to Miami will cost around Aus$1400 during the low season, Aus$3000 in high season, while from Auckland (to Miami) it will be around NZ$4500 (high season); add NZ$100 for departures from **Christchurch or Wellington**. Various coupon deals, valid within the continental US, are available with your main ticket.

Getting to Florida from **South Africa** will also involve a change of plane (typically in London via Virgin, or Atlanta via Delta). A return ticket to Miami from Johannesburg costs from around ZAR10,000 during the low season or ZAR15,000 in high season.

Round-the-world flights

If you intend to take in Florida as part of a world trip, a **round-the-world (RTW)** ticket offers the greatest flexibility. Qantas and Air New Zealand have allied themselves with one of three globe-spanning networks: the "Star Alliance", "One World" and "Skyteam". Fares depend on the number of segments required and the continents visited, but start at around Aus$3500 (low season) for a US–Europe–Asia and home itinerary. If this is more flexibility than you need, you can save Aus$200–300 by going with an individual airline (in concert with code-share partners) and accepting fewer stops.

Driving

Easily reachable by **car** for those living in the immediate region, Florida lies at the end of three major interstate highways: I-95, which runs up the East Coast to Maine; I-75, which winds through the south on the way to Ohio and Michigan; and I-10,

which stretches west across Texas and finally halts at Los Angeles.

How feasible it is to drive to Florida depends, of course, on exactly where you live (or arrive) and how much time you have. If you're aiming for the bustling tourist hot-spots like Orlando and Miami, you may enjoy the option of being able to spend a few days driving around the relaxing scenery of the southeast during your trip. From both New York City and Chicago, reckon on around twenty hours of actual driving to get to Miami; from Los Angeles you'll probably need around 45 hours behind the wheel.

Trains

Travelling to Florida on **Amtrak** trains (☎800 872 7245, ⓦamtrak.com) can be enjoyable and relaxing, if not particularly cheap.

From **New York**, the *Silver Meteor* and the *Silver Star* traverse the eastern seaboard daily to Miami via Orlando (the *Silver Star* detours to Tampa). Return fares vary wildly depending on when you go and how far you book in advance – the earlier you book the cheaper the rate. Return tickets start at around $280 online, or half that for a one-way ticket, and the journey from New York takes between 27 and 31 hours. To spare yourself a restless night, Amtrak offers various types of **sleeping accommodation**, which includes meals and en-suite cabins, and will set you back another $200–300 per trip.

If you really can't bear to be parted from your car and you live within driving distance of Lorton, Virginia (just south of Washington, DC), Amtrak's **Auto Train** will carry you and your vehicle to Sanford, near Orlando. The journey time is 17 hours 29 minutes and passenger fares range $127–250 each way depending on the time of year; the additional charge for a regular-sized car starts at around $186 each way. Cabins cost $200–300 extra.

Buses

Long-distance travel on **Greyhound** buses (☎800 231 2222, ⓦgreyhound.com) can be an endurance test but can be the cheapest form of public transport to the Sunshine State. Check the website or call the local Greyhound station for special fares, which are offered periodically, and remember that midweek travel is marginally cheaper than travelling on weekends.

For long-distance trips you are usually better off paying for a flight: special web round-trip bus fares from New York to Miami start at around $150 but take a day and a half; for refundable tickets you'll pay more than for most flights.

AIRLINES

Aer Lingus Ⓦ aerlingus.com
Air Canada Ⓦ aircanada.com
Air Transat Ⓦ airtransat.ca
Allegiant Air Ⓦ allegiantair.com
American Airlines Ⓦ aa.com
British Airways Ⓦ britishairways.com
Delta Air Lines Ⓦ delta.com
Frontier Airlines Ⓦ flyfrontier.com
JetBlue Ⓦ jetblue.com
Qantas Ⓦ qantas.com
Southwest Airlines Ⓦ southwest.com
Spirit Airlines Ⓦ spirit.com
Sunwing Airlines Ⓦ flysunwing.com
Thomas Cook Airlines Ⓦ thomascookairlines.com
United Airlines Ⓦ united.com
US Airways Ⓦ usairways.com
Virgin America Ⓦ virginamerica.com
Virgin Atlantic Airways Ⓦ virgin-atlantic.com
Westjet Ⓦ westjet.com

AGENTS AND OPERATORS

Contiki Tours ☎ 800 268 1835, Ⓦ contiki.com. Trips for the 18- to-35-year-old crowd, including the "Grand Southern", which runs between Los Angeles and New York, taking in St Augustine, Orlando, Miami, Cocoa Beach and Tallahassee (from $3844 for 26 days).

Creative Holidays Australia ☎ 1300 747 400, Ⓦ creativeholidays .com. Packages to Disney World.

Delta Vacations ☎ 800 654 6559, Ⓦ deltavacations.com. Good for package tours to Orlando, Miami, Daytona Beach and much more.

Monarch Holidays UK ☎ 0871 423 8568, Ⓦ monarch.co.uk. Operated by Cosmos Holidays (the UK's largest tour operator) and offering fly-drives, packages and flights to different parts of Florida.

North South Travel UK ☎ 01245 608 291, Ⓦ northsouthtravel .co.uk. Friendly, competitive travel agency, offering discounted fares worldwide. Profits are used to support projects in the developing world, especially the promotion of sustainable tourism.

STA Travel US ☎ 800 781 4040, UK ☎ 0871 2300 040, Australia ☎ 134 782, New Zealand ☎ 0800 474 400, South Africa ☎ 0861 781 781; Ⓦ statravel.com. Worldwide specialists in independent travel; also student IDs, travel insurance, car rental, rail passes and more. Good discounts for students and under-26s.

Thomas Cook UK ☎ 0871 895 0055, Ⓦ thomascook.com. Long-established one-stop travel agency for package holidays – including some good deals for Disney World – and scheduled flights, with bureaux de change issuing Thomas Cook travellers' cheques, and providing travel insurance and car rental.

Trailfinders UK ☎ 0845 058 5858, Republic of Ireland ☎ 01 677 7888, Australia ☎ 1300 780 212; Ⓦ trailfinders.com. One of the best-informed and most efficient agents for independent travellers.

AIR, RAIL AND BUS PASSES

AIR PASSES

The three global airline networks – Star Alliance (Ⓦ staralliance.com), One World (Ⓦ oneworld .com) and Skyteam (Ⓦ skyteam.com) – all sell their own North America **air passes** in conjunction with an international round-trip ticket. You must purchase at least two or three **coupons** (and up to a maximum of ten, or sixteen with Skyteam), each valid for a one-way flight in the US. Prices depend on factors such as the total number of coupons bought, the time of year, and the duration of each flight, but generally range from $130 to $350 per coupon.

AMTRAK RAIL PASS

Although rail travel can't get you around all of Florida, you might consider buying an Amtrak rail pass should you be planning on seeing more of the US than just the Sunshine State. The **US Rail Pass** entitles you to travel throughout the US, for fifteen, thirty or 45 days, for a price of $449, $679 or $879 respectively. Children aged 2–12 receive a fifty percent reduction. Passes can be bought online at Ⓦ amtrak.com and collected at any Amtrak station. You must pre-reserve trains – ideally as far in advance as possible (call ☎ 800 872 7245 from the US or ☎ +1 215 856 7953 from abroad). On production of a passport and one of these passes, your tickets will be issued.

GREYHOUND AND STUDENT ADVANTAGE

Greyhound no longer offers bus passes, but students can get up to twenty percent off regular tickets by applying for the Student Advantage card (Ⓦ studentadvantage.com; non-US-based students should visit Ⓦ cardnet ie). The card also gives ten percent off Amtrak tickets and a range of other discounts. Card prices start at $20 for one year.

Trek America ☎ 0845 330 6095, ⓦ trekamerica.com. Small-group camping adventure trips throughout the US, with a few long-distance tours which include Florida.

Virgin Holidays ☎ 0871 222 5825, ⓦ virginholidays.co.uk. Flights, fly-drive deals, tailor-mades and packages to almost anywhere in Florida.

Getting around

Travel in Florida is relatively easy, assuming you have a car. Crossing between the east and west coasts, for example, takes only a couple of hours, though travelling north–south can take considerably longer – driving from Miami to Pensacola is 677 miles and at least eleven hours on the road. Despite its size, flights within the state are surprisingly few (though things seem to be changing), and travelling by public transport requires adroit planning: cities and larger towns have bus links – and, in some cases, an infrequent train service – but many rural areas and some of the most enjoyable coastal sections are much harder to reach.

By car

As a major holiday destination, Florida is one of the cheapest places in the US in which to **rent a car**, thanks to a very competitive market. Drivers are supposed to have held their licences for at least one year (though this is rarely checked), and people under 25 may very well encounter problems or restrictions when renting, usually having to pay an extra $10–25 a day. If you're under 25, always call ahead. If you're under 21, you will not be able to rent a car at all. UK, Canadian, Australian and New Zealand nationals can drive in the US provided they have a full driving licence from their home country (International Driving Permits are not always regarded as sufficient).

Car rental companies will also expect you to have a **credit card**; if you don't have one, they may let you leave a hefty deposit (at least $300–500), but it's highly unlikely you'll be able to rent. Fly-drive deals are good value, though you can save up to sixty percent simply by booking in advance with a major firm (call their toll-free numbers for the best rates – most will try to beat the offers of their competitors, so it's worth haggling). Remember that standard rental cars have automatic transmissions.

Many airport car-rental branches also levy additional charges of up to ten percent onto the rental price – Miami doesn't, but most other Florida airports do. Always be sure to get free unlimited mileage and be aware that leaving the car in a different city than the one in which you rent it may incur a drop-off charge of as much as $200 – though most firms do not charge drop-off fees within Florida.

Insurance

Loss Damage Waiver (LDW) is a form of insurance that often isn't included in the initial rental charge, and without it you're liable for every scratch to the rental car – even those that aren't your fault. LDW usually costs $20–27 a day, although some credit card companies offer automatic LDW coverage to anyone using their card to pay in full for the rental.

Standard third-party liability (or supplemental liability) policies only cover you for the first $10,000 of the third party's liability claim against you (plus an additional $10,000 for property damage), a paltry sum in litigation-conscious America. Supplemental liability insurance will cost a further $10–16 a day, but indemnifies the driver for up to $1,000,000.

Breakdowns

If you **break down** in a rented car, call the emergency number pinned to the dashboard or on your keychain. If there isn't one, you should sit tight and wait for the Highway Patrol or State Police, who cruise by regularly. If in your own vehicle, call the American Automobile Association (**AAA**) (☎ 800 222 4357, ⓦ autoclubsouth.aaa.com). Note that if you're not an AAA member or affiliate, you'll have to become one to get service.

Raising the hood of your car is recognized as a call for assistance, though women travelling alone should, obviously, be wary of doing this.

Highways

The best roads for covering long distances quickly are the wide, straight and fast **interstate highways**, usually at least six lanes wide and always prefixed by "I" (for example I-95) – marked on maps by a red, white and blue shield bearing the number. Even-numbered interstates usually run east–west and those with odd numbers north–south. A grade down are the **state roads** and the **US highways** (eg US-1), sometimes divided into scenic off-shoots such as Hwy-A1A, which runs parallel to US-1 along Florida's east coast. Some major roads in cities are technically state or US highways but are better known by their local names. Part of US-1 in Miami, for instance, is more familiarly known as Biscayne

Boulevard. Rural areas also have much smaller **county roads**; their number is preceded by a letter denoting their county.

Toll roads

There are a number of **toll roads** in Florida, by far the longest being the 313-mile Florida's Turnpike. The problem for visitors is that cash toll booths have been phased out on most of these roads, replaced by an automatic system. It makes things faster on the road but can be a real headache for those driving rental cars. Tolls are collected either via the electronic **SunPass**, or by the **"Toll-By-Plate"** system, where cameras take a photo of your licence plate and you get charged later – in practice this means your rental company pays, which will then charge you an extortionate amount of fees for the inconvenience. If you are renting a car In Florida, you'll be given various options that include SunPass or electronic tolling, but make sure you understand the billing structure before you drive off. It's not worth installing a SunPass transponder yourself unless you expect to be driving on toll roads a lot or using your own car in Florida on a regular basis: the transponder costs $25 plus tax but you can now buy the SunPass Mini Sticker transponder for just $4.99 plus tax. Transponders are available online at ⓦsunpass.com. Both types require a minimum opening balance of $10.

You can, of course, simply avoid toll roads altogether, but that's almost impossible on some routes (Miami to the Florida Keys for example).

Rules of the road

Although the law says drivers must keep up with the flow of traffic, which is often hurtling along at 80mph, the official **speed limit** in Florida is 70mph on interstates, 65mph on a four-lane highway outside an urban area (with a population of 5000 or more), and 60mph on other state roads, with lower signposted limits – usually around 30–35mph – in built-up areas. A minimum speed limit of 40mph also applies on many interstates and highways. Apart from the obvious fact Americans **drive on the right**, various rules may be unfamiliar to foreign drivers. US law requires any **alcohol** be carried unopened in the boot (US trunk) of the car; it's illegal to make a U-turn on an interstate or anywhere where a single unbroken line runs along the middle of the road; it's also illegal to park on a highway, and for front-seat passengers to ride without fastened seatbelts. At intersections, you can **turn right on a red light** if there is no traffic approaching from the left; and some junctions are four-way stops: a crossroads where all traffic must stop before proceeding in order of arrival. It can't be stressed too strongly that **driving under the influence** (DUI) is a very serious offence. In some parts of the state the police are empowered to suspend your driving licence immediately. In Florida the fine for a first offence is $500–2000 along with fifty hours' community service (or $10 for each hour) and, in extreme cases, the possibility of a prison term of up to six or nine months. Your vehicle will be impounded for at least ten days regardless of the punishment.

Parking

You'll find, in cities at least, that **parking meters** are commonplace. Charges for an hour range from 25¢ to $1.50. **Car parks** (US "parking lots") generally charge $1.25–3 an hour, $6–12 per day. If you park in the wrong place (on the pavement/sidewalk, or within ten feet of a fire hydrant, for example) you will be fined ($23–47) or your car may also be towed away (in which case you'll have to pay upwards of $200 to get it back). Watch out for signs indicating the **street cleaning** schedule, as you mustn't park overnight before an early-morning clean. **Validated parking**, where your fee for parking in, say, a shopping mall's car park is waived if one of the stores has stamped your parking stub (just ask), is common, as is **valet parking** at even quite modest restaurants, for which a small tip is expected.

Whenever possible, park in the **shade**; if you don't, you might find the car too hot to touch when you return to it – temperatures inside cars parked in the full force of the Florida sun can reach 140°F (60°C).

Renting an RV

Recreational Vehicles (or **RVs**) – those huge juggernauts that rumble down the highway complete with multiple bedrooms, bathrooms and kitchens – are good for groups or families travelling together, but they can be quite unwieldy on the road and very pricey. A basic camper on the back of a pick-up truck can be rented from around $500 per week – the larger vehicles are much more expensive.

Rental outlets are not as common as you might expect, as people tend to own their own RVs. On top of the rental fees you have to take into account mileage charges, the cost of petrol (some RVs do twelve miles to the gallon or less), and any drop-off charges. In addition, it is rarely legal simply to pull up in an RV and spend the night at the roadside; you are expected to stay in designated **RV parks** – most of which charge $35–50 per night.

FLORIDA DISTANCES IN MILES

The figures shown on this chart represent the total distances **in miles** between major cities in Florida. They are calculated on the fastest available route by **major road**, rather than straight lines drawn on a map. For conversion, one mile is **1.6km**.

Daytona Beach	Daytona Beach								
Gainesville	97	Gainesville							
Jacksonville	89	71	Jacksonville						
Key West	420	484	505	Key West					
Miami	263	342	348	158	Miami				
Naples	260	289	356	267	128	Naples			
Orlando	55	115	140	394	238	200	Orlando		
Pensacola	444	345	357	882	677	619	449	Pensacola	
Tallahassee	253	154	166	642	486	433	259	196	Tallahassee
Tampa	140	133	200	400	260	166	86	468	274	Tampa

The National RV Dealers Association (@rvda.org) maintains a rental database on its website. One of the larger companies offering RV rentals is Cruise America (☎ 800 671 8042, @cruiseamerica.com).

By bus

Buses are normally the cheapest way to travel. The only long-distance service is **Greyhound**, which links all major cities and some smaller towns. In isolated areas buses are fairly scarce, sometimes only appearing once a day, if at all – so plot your route with care. Between the big cities, buses run to a fairly full timetable, stopping only for meal breaks (almost always fast-food dives) and driver changeovers. Any sizeable community will have a Greyhound station; in smaller places the local post office or petrol station doubles as the stop and ticket office.

Fares are relatively inexpensive – for example, $51 one way between Miami and Orlando – and can often be reduced to $18–23 if you buy on the website at least one week in advance. Student, child and senior discounts are also available – for more information, visit @greyhound.com, which also has an easy-to-use timetable and fare information; otherwise, contact the local terminals. The phone numbers for the larger Greyhound stations are given in the chapters.

Competition on the north–south route is provided by Red Coach (@redcoachusa.com), which offers cheap deals from Miami to West Palm Beach, Ocala, Orlando, Gainesville and Tallahassee.

By train

The **Amtrak rail network** in Florida is of limited scope, which makes the train a less viable way of getting around. Florida's railroads were built to service the boom towns of the 1920s and, consequently, some rural nooks have rail links as good as the modern cities. The actual trains are clean and comfortable, with most routes in the state offering two services a day. In some areas, Amtrak services are extended by buses, usable only in conjunction with the train. **Fares** can sometimes be cheaper than the bus – $43 one way between Miami and Orlando, for example. Student, child and senior discounts are available.

The Tri-Rail

Designed to reduce road traffic along the congested southeast coast, the elevated **Tri-Rail** system came into operation in 1989, ferrying commuters between Miami and West Palm Beach, stopping at places such as Fort Lauderdale and Boca Raton on the way. The single-journey fare is calculated on a zone basis, and ranges from $2.50 to $6.90; the majority of services tend to run around rush hours – meaning a very early start or an early-evening departure. There are fewer services (eight each way) on Saturdays and Sundays. All-day tickets, available on weekends and holidays, are only $5. Tickets must be bought at the station (not on the train), and those riding without them may be subject to hefty fines ($50–1000), arrest and/or removal from the train. For Tri-Rail information, call ☎ 800 874 7245 or check @tri-rail.com.

By air

Off-peak **plane travel** within Florida can work out to be only slightly more expensive than taking a bus or train – and will also, on the longer journeys at least, save you lots of time. The problem is that there are actually very few internal flights – many businesspeople end up changing planes in Atlanta when flying between points in Florida. Launched in 2011, Silver Airways (Ⓦsilverairways.com) has started to improve things with a roster of flights between hubs at Key West, Fort Lauderdale, Tampa, Pensacola and Orlando.

By bicycle

Cycling is seldom a good way to get around the major cities (with the exception of some sections of Miami), but many smaller towns are quiet enough to be pleasurably explored by bicycle. In addition, there are many miles of marked cycle paths along the coast, and long-distance bike trails crisscross the state's interior. Bikes can be **rented** for $15–30 a day, $40–80 a week, from many beach shops and college campuses, some state parks, and virtually any place where cycling is a good idea; outlets are listed in the chapters. The best cycling areas are in north central Florida, the Panhandle and in parts of the northeast coast. By contrast, the southeast coastal strip is heavily congested and many south-Florida inland roads are narrow and dangerous. Wherever you cycle, avoid the heaviest traffic – and the midday heat – by doing most of your pedalling before noon.

You can get many cycling maps online or from most youth hostels.

Hitching

Hitching is **illegal** in Miami and on the outskirts of many other cities and in whole counties. We advise you not to do it anywhere or at any time.

RIDE-SHARING SERVICES

Much to the chagrin of traditional taxi drivers, ride sharing is becoming big business in the US (shared car rides with independent drivers instead of taxis, typically arranged at very short notice – and paid for – with apps on smart phones). Uber (Ⓦuber.com) and Lyft (Ⓦlyft.com) launched in Miami in 2014, though at the time of writing Miami-Dade County officials had refused to license drivers. Despite a similar backlash in several cities Uber was available in Gainesville, Jacksonville, Orlando, Tallahassee and Tampa at the time of research. Lyft is available in Jacksonville, Orlando and Tampa. So far these companies have been a huge success with customers: safe, cheap and convenient.

Accommodation

Accommodation options in Florida range from youth hostels and the chain hotels and motels lining almost every highway, to the plush resorts found at the main tourist destinations. Most towns and cities also have more intimate bed and breakfasts, while camping is possible at Florida's many state parks.

Hotels and motels

While motels and hotels essentially offer the same things – double rooms with bathroom, TV and phone – **motels** are often one-off affairs run by their owners and tend to be cheaper (typically $55–75) than **hotels** ($75–150), which are likely to be part of a nationwide chain. Dependable **budget-priced chain hotels**, which, depending on location, can cost the same as a privately run motel, include *Days Inn*, *Econo Lodge* and *Super 8*. Higher up the scale are mid-range chains like *Best Western*, *Holiday Inn*, *Howard Johnson's* and *Hampton Inn*. Prices quoted by hotels and motels are almost always for the actual room rather than for each person using it – "singles" are typically double rooms at a slightly reduced rate – and most establishments will usually set up a third single bed for around $10 on top of the regular price, reducing costs for three people sharing. **Reservations** are only held until 5pm or 6pm unless you've told the hotel you'll be arriving late.

As for **facilities**, all but the cheapest motels and hotels have pools for guests' use and most offer cable TV, free local phone calls, and, usually, free wi-fi. Under $75, rooms tend to be similar in quality and features; spend over $75 in rural areas or $120 in the cities and you get more luxury – a larger room and often additional facilities such as a gym. Paying over $150 brings all of the above, plus probably a tennis court, golf course, an ocean view and some upmarket trappings.

Resorts

On your travels you'll also come across **resorts**, which are motels or hotels equipped with a restaurant, bar and private beach – on average these cost $100–200, with some establishments adding a "resort fee" of as much as $25 a day on top of the room rate; and **efficiencies**, which are motel rooms adapted to offer cooking facilities – ranging from a stove squeezed into a corner to a fully equipped kitchen – usually for $15–20 above the basic room rate.

There are of course – especially in cities – plenty of **high-end establishments**, which can cost just about any amount of money, depending on the level of luxury – we've pointed out which ones are worthwhile in the chapters. Bear in mind that the most upmarket establishments have all manner of services that may appear to be free but for which you'll be expected to **tip** in a style commensurate with the hotel's status.

Discount options

During **off-peak periods** many motels and hotels struggle to fill their rooms, and it's worth **haggling** to get a few dollars off the asking price. Staying in the same place for more than one night may bring further reductions. In addition, pick up the many **discount coupons** that fill tourist information offices and Welcome Centers (see p.42), and look out for the free *Traveler Discount Guide*. Read the small print, though: what appears to be an amazingly cheap room rate sometimes turns out to be a per-person charge for two people sharing and limited to midweek. **Websites** such as ⓦpriceline.com and ⓦhotwire.com offer especially good discounts for Florida – try the "name your own price" function at the former.

Bed and breakfasts

Bed and breakfast inns, or "**B&Bs**", are often restored buildings or homes in the smaller cities and more rural areas, and we've listed several throughout the chapters. B&Bs can offer a more personal experience than staying in a large and anonymous chain hotel – some enjoy the close interaction with one's hosts; others may find it a little overbearing.

While always including a huge and wholesome breakfast (five courses are not unheard of), **prices** vary greatly: anything from $60 to $250 depending on location and season; most cost between $80 and $120 per night for the cheapest double. Bear in mind most are booked well in advance, making it sensible to contact the inn directly at least a month ahead – longer in high season.

Hostels

At around $15–40 per night per person for a bed in a dormitory, hostels are clearly the cheapest accommodation option other than camping. In Florida there is just a smattering of independent hostels in tourist centres such as Miami, St Augustine and the Everglades. You can book a dorm bed or a private room ($35–75) at most of these establishments via their websites. Few hostels provide meals, but most have cooking facilities. Other **amenities** include communal areas, lockers, washing machines and free wi-fi access. Visit ⓦhostels.com for a current listing of Florida hostels. HI-Miami Beach is currently the only Hostelling International (ⓦhihostels.com/hostels/hi-miami-beach) affiliated establishment in the state.

Camping

Florida **campgrounds** range from the primitive (a flat piece of ground that may or may not have a water tap) in state parks, to others that are more like open-air hotels with shops, restaurants and washing facilities. Naturally, **prices** vary according to amenities, ranging from nothing at all for the most basic plots to around $35 a night for something comparatively luxurious. There are plenty of campgrounds but often plenty of people intending to use them: take special care over plotting your route if you're camping during public holidays or weekends, when many sites will be either full or very crowded. For camping in the wilderness or primitive camping in state parks (see below), there's usually a nightly charge of $5 or so payable at the area's administrative office.

Privately run campgrounds are everywhere, their prices ranging from $8 to $35, and the best are listed throughout the chapters. Note that these tend to attract more **RVs** than traditional campers. For a fuller list, check out the website of the Florida Association of RV Parks and Campgrounds (Ⓦ campflorida.com).

Primitive camping

Most hiking trails in Florida have areas designated for **primitive camping**, with either very limited facilities (a handpump for water, sometimes a primitive toilet) or none at all. Travelling by canoe, you'll often pass sandbars, which can make excellent overnight stops. It's preferable to **cook** by stove, but otherwise start fires only in permitted areas – indicated by signs – and use deadwood. Where there are no **toilets**, bury human waste at least four inches in the ground and a hundred feet from the nearest water supply and campground. Burn rubbish carefully, and what you can't burn, carry away. Never drink from rivers and streams, however clear and inviting they may look (you never know what unspeakable acts people – or animals – further upstream have performed in them), or from the state's many natural springs; **water** that isn't from taps should be boiled for at least five minutes or cleansed with an iodine-based purifier before you drink it. Always get advice, maps and a weather forecast from the park ranger's or wilderness area administration office – often you'll need to fill in a wilderness permit, too, and pay a small nightly camping fee.

State and national parks

State parks – there are over 150 in Florida – can be excellent places to camp and some of the more basic campgrounds in these parks will often be completely empty midweek. Sites usually cost $18–40 for up to four people sharing; visitors must make reservations a minimum of two days in advance. Bear in mind that some park gates close at sunset; you won't be able to camp there if you arrive later. Most state parks have information lines, listed in the chapters, but reservations can be made through ReserveAmerica (Ⓣ800 326 3521, Ⓦ reserveamerica.com). Similarly priced

TOP 5 FLORIDA STATE PARKS
John Pennekamp Coral Reef State Park
See p.112
Myakka River State Park See p.231
Paynes Prairie State Preserve See p.393
St Joseph Peninsula State Park See p.422
Wakulla Springs State Park See p.412

campgrounds exist in **national parks and national forests** – see the details throughout the Guide. For the Apalachicola, Ocala or Osceola national forests, contact the US Forest Service (Forest Supervisor's Office), 325 John Knox Rd, Suite F-100, Tallahassee, FL 32303 (Ⓣ850 523 8500, Ⓦ www.fs.usda.gov/florida).

However desolate it may look, much of undeveloped Florida is, in fact, **private land**, so never set up camp in what looks like a piece of wild countryside without checking in advance.

Food and drink

Floridian cuisine is as diverse as the state's population, ranging from authentic Cuban and Latin American influences in the south to Southern and New Orleans-inspired food in the north.

Fresh fish and **seafood** are abundant all over Florida, as is the high-quality produce of the state's cattle farms – served as ribs, steaks and burgers. Though the term is used sparingly, "Floribbean cuisine" has come to signify the blend of Latin American and Caribbean cuisines found primarily in the southern half of the state – anything from curried goat to mashed plantains and yucca. In the northern half of the state, the accent is on hearty cooking – traditional Southern dishes such as grits (a hot corn porridge), cornbread and fried chicken.

As for service and **tipping**, foreign visitors should note to top up the bill in restaurants by fifteen to twenty percent; $1 per drink is usual at a bar.

Breakfast

For the price (on average $5–10) **breakfast** makes a good-value, very filling start to the day. Go to a diner or café, both of which are very similar and usually serve breakfast until at least 11am (some continue all day) though there are special deals at earlier times, say 6am to 8am, when the price may be even less.

Lunch and snacks

Between 11.30am and 1.30pm, look for excellent-value **set menus** and **all-you-can-eat specials**. Most Cuban restaurants and fishcamps (see below) are exceptionally well priced all the time and you can get a good-sized lunch at either for $6–10. **Buffet restaurants** – most of which also serve breakfast and dinner – are found in most cities and towns; $10–15 lets you pig out as much as you can from a wide variety of hot dishes.

If it's a warm day and you can't face hot food, delis usually serve a broad range of **salads** for about $4–5 a pound. Frozen yogurt or **ice cream** may be all you feel like eating in the midday heat: look for exotic versions made with mango and guava sold by Cuban vendors.

Dinner

Even if it sometimes seems swamped by the more fashionable regional and international cuisines, traditional **American cooking** is found all over Florida. Portions are big and you start with **salad**, eaten before the main course arrives; look out for heart of palm salad, based around the delicious vegetable at the heart of the sabal palm tree (unfortunately for the tree, once the heart is extracted, the plant dies). Enormous steaks, burgers, piles of ribs or half a chicken tend to dominate **main dishes**, and often come with a vegetable and/or some form of potato.

Throughout the northern half of the state, **vegetables** such as okra, collard greens, black-eyed peas, fried green tomatoes and fried aubergine (US eggplant) are added to staples including fried chicken, roast beef and **hogjaw** – meat from the mouth of a pig. Meat dishes are usually accompanied by cornbread to soak up the thick gravy poured over everything; with fried fish, you'll get **hush puppies** – fried corn balls with tiny bits of chopped onion. Okra is also used in gumbo soups, a feature of **Cajun** cooking, which originated in nearby Louisiana as a way of using up leftovers. A few (usually expensive) Florida restaurants specialize in Cajun food but many others offer a few Cajun items (such as red beans and rice, and hot and spicy shrimp and steak dishes).

Alligator is on many menus: most of the meat comes from alligator farms, which process a certain number each year. The tails are deep-fried and served in a variety of styles – none of which makes much of a mark on the bland, chicken-like taste. **Frogs' legs** also crop up occasionally.

Regional **nouvelle cuisine** is largely too pretentious and expensive for the typical Floridian palate, although some restaurants in the larger cities do create small but beautifully presented affairs with local fish and the produce of the citrus farms for around $40–50 a head.

Almost wherever you eat you'll be offered **Key lime pie** as a dessert, a dish that began life in the Florida Keys, made from the small limes that grow there. The pie is similar to lemon meringue but with a sharper taste. Quality varies greatly; take local advice to find a good outlet and your taste buds will tell you why many swear by it.

Fish and seafood

Florida excels at **fish and seafood** – which is great news for non-meat-eaters. Even the shabbiest restaurant is likely to have an excellent selection, though fish comes freshest and cheapest at **fishcamps**: rustic places right beside a river or a lake where your meal was swimming just a few hours earlier; a fishcamp lunch or dinner will cost around $10–15. Grouper tends to top the bill, but you'll also find catfish, dolphin (the fish, not the mammal – sometimes known by its Hawaiian name, *mahi-mahi*), mullet, tuna and swordfish, any of which (except catfish, which is nearly always fried) may be boiled, grilled, fried or "blackened" (rubbed with zesty spices and charcoal-grilled). Of **shellfish**, the tender claws of **stone crabs**, eaten dipped in butter, raise local passions during the mid-October to mid-May season; spiny (or "Florida") **lobster** is smaller and more succulent than its more famous Maine rival; **oysters** can be extremely fresh (the best come from Apalachicola) and are usually eaten raw (though are best avoided during summer, when they carry a risk of food poisoning) – many restaurants have special "raw bars," where you can also consume meaty **shrimp**, in regular and jumbo sizes. Another popular crustacean is the very chewy **conch** (pronounced "konk"); abundant throughout the Florida Keys, they usually come deep-fried as fritters served up with various sauces, or as a chowder-like soup.

FLORIDA SPECIALITIES

Apalachicola oysters See p.420
The camel rider See p.343
Conch fritters See p.116 & p.145
Grits à Ya Ya See p.439
Key lime pie See p.146
Stone crab claws See p.167

FREE FOOD

Some **bars** are used as much by diners as drinkers, who fill up on the free **hors d'oeuvres** laid out by many city bars between 5 and 7pm Monday to Friday – an attempt to nab the commuting classes before they head off to the suburbs – and sometimes by beachside bars to grab beach-goers before they head elsewhere for the evening. For the price of a drink you can stuff yourself on chilli, seafood or pasta. Similarly, you may find your **hotel** lays on some sort of complimentary evening cocktail reception at around 6pm, featuring food, wine, beer and soft drinks.

Latin American cuisine

Thanks to Florida's large Latino population, Latin American cuisine here is some of the best in the US, and you'll find plenty of **Cuban food** in Miami. Most Cuban dishes are **meat**-based: frequently pork, less often beef or chicken, always fried (including the skin, which becomes a crispy crackling) and usually heavily spiced, served with a varying combination of yellow or white rice, black beans, plantains (a sweet, banana-like vegetable) and yucca (cassava) – a potato-like vegetable completely devoid of taste. **Seafood** crops up less often, most deliciously in thick soups, such as *sopa de mariscos* (shellfish soup). Unpretentious Cuban diners serve a filling lunch or dinner for under $10, though a growing number of upmarket restaurants will charge three times as much for identical food. In busy areas, many Cuban cafés have street windows where you buy a thimble-sized cup of sweet and rich *café Cubano* (Cuban coffee) or *cafécito*, strong enough to make your hair stand on end; also available is *café con leche* (coffee with warm milk or cream), though it's strictly for the unadventurous and regarded by Cubans as a children's drink. If you want a cool drink in Miami, look out for roadside stands offering **coco frio** – coconut milk sucked through a straw directly from the coconut – for $1.

Although nowhere near as prevalent as Cuban cooking, foods from other parts of the **Caribbean** and **Latin America** are easily found around Miami: Haitian, Argentinian, Colombian, Nicaraguan, Peruvian, Jamaican and Salvadoran restaurants also serve the city's diverse migrant populations – at very affordable prices.

International cuisine

American Chinese food (usually adapted from Cantonese cuisine) is everywhere in Florida and often very cheap; **Japanese** is more expensive; and **Italian** food is popular but can be expensive once you leave the simple pastas and explore the more gourmet-inclined Italian regional cooking in the major cities. **French** food, too, is widely available, though pricey. **Thai**, **Korean** and **Indonesian** cuisine is similarly city-based, though usually cheaper. More plentiful are well-priced, family-run **Greek** restaurants (especially in Tarpon Springs); and a smattering of **Minorcan** places, evidence of one of Florida's earliest groups of European settlers.

Drinking

Much **drinking** in Florida is done in restaurant or hotel lounges, at fishcamps (see p.28), or in "tiki bars" – open-sided straw-roofed huts beside a beach or hotel pool. Some beachside bars, especially in Panama City Beach, are split-level, multi-purpose affairs with discos and stages for live bands – and take great pride in being the birthplace of the infamous wet T-shirt contest.

LATIN AMERICAN FOOD TERMS

Ajiaco criollo Meat and root vegetable stew
Arroz Rice
Arroz con leche Rice pudding
Bocadillo Sandwich
Chicarones de pollo Fried chicken crackling
Frijoles Beans
Frijoles negros Black beans
Maduros Fried plantains
Masitoas de puerca Fried spiced pork
Morros y Cristianos Literally "Moors and Christians", black beans and white rice
Pan Bread
Pan con lechón Crispy pork sandwich
Picadillo Minced meat, usually beef, served with peppers and olives
Pollo Chicken
Puerca Pork
Sopa de mariscos Shellfish soup
Sopa de plantanos Meaty plantain soup
Tostones Fried mashed plantains
Vaca Beef

To buy and consume alcohol you need to be **21 or over** and could well be asked for ID even if you look much older; this is particularly common at family-orientated places such as Walt Disney World. Even elsewhere, recent clampdowns have resulted in bars "carding" anyone who looks 30 and under. Licensing laws and drinking hours vary from area to area, but generally alcohol can be bought and drunk in a bar, nightclub or restaurant any time between 10am and 2am. More cheaply, you can usually buy beer, wine or spirits in supermarkets and, of course, liquor stores, from 9am to 11pm Monday to Saturday and from 1pm to 11pm on Sundays. It is illegal to consume alcohol in a car, on most beaches, and in all state parks, with a possible fine of $100 or more.

Beer

Microbreweries are booming in Florida, with around 100 producers of small-batch tasty beers, though these are rarely sold beyond their own bars or restaurants. Otherwise discerning beer drinkers tend to stick to **imported brews**, the most widely available of which are the Mexican brands Bohemia, Corona and Dos Equis. Don't forget that in all but the more pretentious bars, you can save money by buying a quart or half-gallon pitcher of beer. If bar prices are a problem, you can stock up with six-packs from a supermarket for $9–12.

Wine and cocktails

If wine is more to your taste, try to visit one of the state's fast-improving **wineries**: several can be toured and their products sampled for free. In a bar or restaurant, however, beside a usually threadbare stock of European wines, you'll find a selection from Chile and California. A decent glass of wine in a bar or restaurant costs around $7–9, a bottle $15–30. Buying a bottle from a supermarket can cost as little as $10.

Cocktails are extremely popular, especially rich fruity ones consumed while gazing over the ocean or into the sunset. Varieties are innumerable, sometimes specific to a single bar or cocktail lounge, and most will cost $8–13. Cocktails and all other drinks come cheapest during **happy hours** (usually 5–7pm; sometimes much longer) when many are half-price.

The media

Florida ranks among the country's more media-savvy regions, with the range of media outlets the best in the southeastern US.

Newspapers

The best-read of Florida's **newspapers** is the *Tampa Bay Times,* while the *Orlando Sentinel*, the *South Florida Sun-Sentinel* in Fort Lauderdale and *The Miami Herald* are not far behind and, naturally enough, excel at reporting their own areas. The major national newspapers – *The New York Times, The Washington Post, USA Today* and *The Wall Street Journal* – are easily available, though **overseas newspapers** are usually a preserve of specialist bookshops.

Every community of any size has at least a few **free newspapers**, found in street distribution bins or just lying around in piles. It's a good idea to pick up a full assortment: some simply cover local goings-on; others provide specialist coverage of interests ranging from long-distance cycling to getting ahead in business. Many of them are also excellent sources for bar, restaurant and nightlife information, and we've mentioned the most useful titles in the chapters.

TV and radio

Florida **TV** is pretty much the standard network sitcom and talk-show barrage you get all over the country, with frequent interruptions for hard-sell commercials. Slightly better are the **cable networks**, to which you'll have access in most hotels. Especially in the south, Spanish-language stations provide services for the Hispanic communities.

Most of Florida's **radio stations** stick to the usual commercial format of retro-rock, classic pop, country or easy-listening. In general, except for news and chat, the occasional fire-and-brimstone preacher, and Latin and Haitian music, stations on the AM band are best avoided in favour of the FM band, in particular the public and college stations on the air in Tallahassee, Gainesville, Orlando, Tampa and Miami, found on the left of the dial (88–92FM). These invariably provide diverse and listenable programming, whether it be bizarre underground rock or abstruse literary discussions, and they're also good sources for local nightlife news.

> ## TOP 5 FLORIDA COCKTAILS
> **Bushwacker, Pensacola Beach** See p.443
> **Margarita, Key West** See p.147
> **Mojito, Miami** See p.97
> **Piña colada, Key West** See p.147
> **Pineapple Willy, Panama Beach City**
> See p.428

Sports and outdoor activities

Florida is fanatical about sports and outdoor activities, but what's surprising is that collegiate sports are often, especially among lifelong Floridians, more popular than their professional counterparts. This is because Florida's professional teams are comparatively recent additions to the sporting scene and have none of the traditions and bedrock support the state's college sides enjoy. In fact, it's common to find seventy thousand people attending a college football match. Given Florida's long and enticing coastline, it's no surprise that snorkelling and diving top the list of outdoor activities, though hiking and canoeing opportunities are also plentiful in the state's undeveloped regions.

Baseball

Until April 1993 Florida had no professional baseball team of its own – now, the state has two. In 1997, the first Florida team to come along, the **Florida Marlins** (since 2011 the **Miami Marlins**) became the youngest expansion team in history to win the World Series, shelling out millions of dollars to attract star-quality players. They won again in 2003, but the team subsequently slashed its budget, lost most of its big names, and is now a young, developing squad. The Miami Marlins play at Marlins Park, 1501 Marlins Way, Little Havana (2 miles west of downtown Miami). Tickets are available direct from the box office (☎877 627 5467, ⓦ miami.marlins .mlb.com).

Florida's other baseball team, the **Tampa Bay Rays**, were long considered to be one of the worst in the country. However, in the 2008 season they reached the World Series, losing eventually to the Philadelphia Phillies. Since then the team has continued to have moderate success, winning the AL East championship in 2010 and qualifying for the postseason tournament in 2011 and 2013.

The Rays play at Tropicana Field (☎727 825 3137, ⓦ tampabay.rays.mlb.com), which is actually located in St Petersburg.

The major-league **baseball season** runs from April to early October, with the league championships and the World Series, the final best-of-seven playoff, lasting through the end of that month.

Spring training

Even if the local pro team is slumping, Florida has long been the home of **spring training** (Feb & March) for a multitude of professional baseball clubs – and thousands of fans plan vacations so they can watch their sporting heroes going through practice routines and playing in the friendly matches of the Grapefruit League (the Cactus League plays in Arizona). Much prestige is attached to being a spring training venue and the local community identifies strongly with the team it hosts – in some cases the link goes back fifty years. Turn up at 10am to join the crowds watching the training (free); tickets to games range from $7 to $50. The fifteen sides that train in Florida include those below; for the training locations of all the teams, visit ⓦ springtrainingonline.com.

Atlanta Braves Champion Stadium, Disney's Wide World of Sports, Orlando ☎407 839 3900, ⓦ atlanta.braves.mlb.com.

Boston Red Sox JetBlue Park at Fenway South, Fort Myers ☎617 482 4SOX, ⓦ boston.redsox.mlb.com.

Detroit Tigers Joker Marchant Stadium, Lakeland ☎866 668 4437, ⓦ detroit.tigers.mlb.com.

NY Mets Tradition Field, 525 NW Peacock Blvd, Port St Lucie ☎772 871 2115, ⓦ newyork.mets.mlb.com.

NY Yankees Steinbrenner Field, 1 Steinbrenner Drive, Tampa ☎813 287 8844, ⓦ newyork.yankees.mlb.com.

Philadelphia Phillies Bright House Field, 601 Old Coachman Rd, Clearwater ☎215 463 1000, ⓦ philadelphia.phillies.mlb.com.

St Louis Cardinals Roger Dean Stadium, 4751 Main St, Jupiter ☎561 775 1818, ⓦ stlouis.cardinals.mlb.com.

Basketball

The state's two **professional basketball teams** have enjoyed plenty of success in the NBA. The **Miami Heat** won the NBA championship in 2006, 2012 and 2013 (reaching the finals four years in a row), and until 2014 fielded the "big three" of Chris Bosh, LeBron James and Dwyane Wade. The Heat play at the American Airlines Arena (☎786 777 1502, ⓦ nba .com/heat), while the **Orlando Magic** play at the Amway Center (☎407 896 2442, ⓦ nba.com/magic). Tickets for both teams are in the $10–115 range.

Top among the **college teams** are the **Florida University Gators** (☎352 375 4683 or ☎800 344 2867, ⓦ gatorzone.com) and the **Miami University Hurricanes** (☎800 462 2637, ⓦ hurricanesports .com).

Football (American)

Of the state's three **professional football teams**, the **Miami Dolphins** have been the most successful, appearing five times in the Super Bowl (winning twice) and, in 1972, enjoying the only undefeated season in NFL history. They play at Sun Life Stadium in the northern suburb of Miami Gardens (Ⓦmiamidolphins.com; tickets range $55–350). The **Jacksonville Jaguars**, who entered the league in 1995, have stolen a bit of the Dolphins' thunder; they've already been in the playoffs six times, twice coming within one game of the Super Bowl. They play at EverBank Field (Ⓣ877 452 7849, Ⓦjaguars.com; tickets $45–125). The **Tampa Bay Buccaneers** have also had success; after years of losing seasons, they won the Super Bowl in 2003. The Bucs play at Raymond James Stadium (Ⓣ813 879 2827 or Ⓣ800 795 2827, Ⓦbuccaneers.com; tickets $30–75; home tickets often sold out to season ticket holders).

Even greater fervour is whipped up by the **University of Florida Gators** (in Gainesville), the **Florida State University Seminoles** (in Tallahassee) and the **University of Miami Hurricanes**. All play around eleven games a season. Tickets to college games cost upwards of $40 and can be difficult to come by for the more competitive games. Further details are given in the chapters.

The **football season** for both the professional and collegiate levels begins in late summer and lasts until January.

Ice hockey

Florida boasts two teams in the NHL: the **Florida Panthers** (Ⓣ954 835 7825, Ⓦpanthers.nhl.com), who play at the BB&T Center in Sunrise near Fort Lauderdale, and the **Tampa Bay Lightning** (Ⓣ813 301 6600, Ⓦlightning.nhl.com), who play at the Amalie Arena in Tampa. The NHL **season** runs between October and June, and tickets for both teams range $25–270.

Snorkelling and diving

Even non-swimmers can quickly learn to **snorkel**, which is the best way to see one of the state's finest natural assets: the living coral reef curling around its southeastern corner and along the Florida Keys. Many guided snorkelling trips run to the reef, costing $35–50 – further details are given throughout the chapters. More adventurous than snorkelling is loading up with air tanks to go **scuba diving**. You'll need a diving licence to do this; if you don't already have one you'll be required to take the three-day Open Water Certification course, involving both water time and reading, and costing

from around $350 and up. Get details from diving shops, always plentiful near good diving areas, which can also provide equipment, maps and general information.

Surfing

The same reefs that make snorkelling and diving so much fun cause **surfing** to be less common than you might expect, limiting it to a few sections of the east coast. Florida's biggest waves strike land between Sebastian Inlet and **Cocoa Beach**, and surfing tournaments are held in the area during April and May. Lesser breakers are found at Miami Beach's First Street Beach, Boca Raton's South Beach Park, and around the Jacksonville beaches. Surfboards can be rented from local beach shops for $10–15 a day.

Fishing

Few things excite higher passions in Florida than **fishing**: the numerous rivers and lakes and the various breeds of catfish, bass, carp and perch inhabiting them bring eager fishermen from all over the US and beyond. Saltwater fishing is equally popular, with barely a coastal jetty in the state not creaking under the strain of weekend anglers. The most sociable way to fish, however, is from a "party boat" – a boatload of people putting to sea for a day of rod-casting and boozing; these generally cost $50–75 per person and are easily found in good fishing areas. Sportfishing – heading out to deep water to do battle with marlin, tuna and the odd shark – is much more expensive. In the prime sportfishing areas, off the Florida Keys and off the Panhandle around Destin, you'll need at least $550 a day for a boat and a guide. To protect fish stocks, a highly complex set of rules and regulations governs where you can fish and what you can catch. For the latest information, contact the Florida Fish and Wildlife Conservation Commission, Farris Bryant Building, 620 S Meridian St, Tallahassee, FL 32399-1600 (Ⓣ850 488 4676, Ⓦmyfwc.com).

Hiking

Almost all of Florida's state parks have undemanding nature trails intended for a pleasant hour's ramble; anything called a **hiking** or **backpacking trail** – plentiful in state and national parks, national forests and threading some unprotected land as part of the Florida National Scenic Trail – requires more thought and planning.

Many hiking trails can easily be completed in a day; the longer ones have rough camping sites at regular intervals (see p.27), and most periodically pass through fully equipped camping areas – giving the option of sleeping in comparative comfort. The best time to hike is from late autumn to early spring: this avoids the exhausting heat of the summer and the worst of the mosquitoes and reveals a greater variety of animals.

In some areas you'll need a **wilderness permit** (free or $5) from the local park ranger's or wilderness area administration office, where you should call anyway for maps, general information on the hike, and a weather forecast – sudden rains can flood trails in swampy areas. Many state parks run organized hiking trips, details of which are given throughout this book.

The 1300-mile **Florida National Scenic Trail**, stretching the length of the state, is about 85 percent completed. The loosely connected footpath extends from the Gulf Islands National Seashore in the northwest down to Big Cypress National Preserve in the Everglades. Those wanting to hike the trail end to end ("through-hike") must join the Florida Trail Association (see p.215), which arranges permissions and permits on hikers' behalf as some trail sections fall on private property.

While hiking, be extremely wary of the **poison-wood tree** (ask a park ranger how to identify it); any contact between your skin and its bark can leave you needing hospital treatment – and avoid being splashed by rainwater dripping from its branches. Besides food, carry plenty of drinking water, a first-aid kit, insect repellent and sunscreen.

For general hiking **information**, check the websites of the Florida Department of Environmental Protection (Wdep.state.fl.us) or the Florida Trail Association (Wfloridatrail.org). The latter gives details of most trails and is constantly updated. Two useful online hiking resources are Wtrailmonkey.com, which focuses on trails near the national parks and seashores, and Wtrails.com, a subscription service ($49.95 per year) that lets members download topographic maps and full trail descriptions.

Canoeing and kayaking

One way to enjoy natural Florida without getting blisters on your feet is by **canoeing** and **kayaking**. You can rent canoes and kayaks for around $25–45 a day wherever conditions are right: the best of Florida's rivers and streams are found in north central Florida and the Panhandle. Many state and national parks have canoe runs, too; the **Florida Canoe Trails System** comprises 36 marked routes along rivers and creeks, covering a combined distance of nearly a thousand miles.

Before setting off, get a canoeing **map** (you'll need to know the locations of access points and any rough camping sites) and check **weather conditions** and the river's **water level**: a low level can expose logs, rocks and other obstacles; a flooded river is dangerous and should not be canoed; coastal rivers are affected by tides. Don't leave the canoe to walk on the bank, as this will cause damage and is likely to be trespassing. When a **motorboat** approaches, keep to the right and turn your bow into the wake. If you're **camping**, do so on a sandbar unless there are designated rough camping areas beside the river. As with any hike you might do (see above), make sure you carry the usual outdoor essentials.

Several small companies run canoe and kayak trips ranging from half a day to a week; they supply the canoe and take you from the end of the route back to where you started. Details are given throughout this book.

Birdwatching

Florida's location on the north–south bird migration route means opportunities for **birdwatching** here are very good, and visitors are likely to spot many unfamiliar species in greater numbers than they would elsewhere. Commonly sighted birds include the **snowy egret** (entirely white, with bright yellow feet), the **brown pelican** (greyish-brown body with a white head and neck), and the **cormorant** and **anhinga** (both sleek, black fish-catchers), and though you stand a better chance of seeing them in the winter months, some species are present year-round.

Casual and experienced birders alike can take advantage of the **Great Florida Birding & Wildlife Trail** (T850 488 9478, Wfloridabirding trail.com), which links clusters of existing birding sites (such as parks, conservation areas and sanctuaries) via highways throughout the state using special highway signs and detailed maps. Overseen by the state's Fish and Wildlife Conservation Commission, the trail covers most of the state, from the east coast (Jacksonville area south to Fort Pierce) to the Panhandle and on the west coast as far south as Naples.

Travel essentials

Costs

For most foreign visitors, even when the **exchange rate** is at its least advantageous, you'll find virtually everything – accommodation, food, petrol, cameras, clothes and more – to be better value in the US than it is at home. If you're coming from elsewhere in the US, you'll probably not find Florida any more or less expensive, save in the resorts and big cities; hotels tend to be a lot cheaper in Florida than in the Northeast, however.

Accommodation is likely to be your biggest single expense. Few hotel or motel rooms in cities cost under $70 – around $85 is more usual for a halfway-decent room. Although hostels offering dorm beds – generally for $18–25 – exist, they are not widespread and in any case represent only a very small saving for two or more people travelling together. Camping, of course, is cheap (anywhere from $5 to perhaps $35 per night), but is rarely practical in or around the big cities.

As for **food**, $15–18 a day is enough to get you an adequate life-support diet, while for a daily budget of around $35 you can dine pretty well. Beyond this, everything hinges on how much sightseeing, taxi-taking, drinking and socializing you do. Much of any of these – especially in the major cities – and you're likely to go through upwards of $75 a day, excluding the other expenses mentioned above.

The rates for **travelling around** on buses, trains, and even planes, may look cheap on paper, but the distances involved mean costs soon mount. For a group of two or more, **renting a car** can be a very good investment (see p.22), not least because it enables you to stay in the ubiquitous budget motels along the highways instead of relying on expensive downtown hotels.

A **statewide sales tax** of six percent is added to virtually everything you buy in shops, except for groceries, but it isn't part of the marked price. Counties in Florida also charge an additional sales tax, which varies from 0.5 to 1.5 percent.

Crime and personal safety

No one could pretend Florida is trouble-free, though outside the urban centres crime rates are relatively low. Violent crime dropped sixty percent between 1993 and 2013 (even though the population rose some forty percent in the same period) and even the lawless reputation of Miami is in excess of the truth. Several clearly defined areas are strictly off limits, however, and at night you should always be cautious wherever you are. All the major tourist and nightlife areas in cities are invariably brightly lit and well policed. By being careful, planning ahead and taking good care of your possessions, you should, generally speaking, have few real problems.

Car crime

Given that many visitors get around by car in Florida, car crime is arguably the main danger to one's personal safety. When **driving**, under no circumstances stop in any unlit or seemingly deserted urban area – and especially not if someone is waving you down, suggesting there is something wrong with your car. Similarly, if you are "accidentally" rammed by the driver behind, do not stop immediately but drive on to the nearest well-lit, busy and secure area (such as a hotel, toll booth or petrol station) and phone the emergency number (☎911) for assistance. Keep your doors locked and windows never more than slightly open (as you'll probably be using air conditioning, you'll want to keep them fully closed anyway).

Always take care when planning your route, particularly through urban areas, and be sure to use GPS (sat nav) or a **reliable map** (see p.40). Particularly in Miami, local authorities add directions to tourist sights and attractions to road signs, thereby reducing the possibility of visitors unwittingly driving into dangerous areas. Aside from these problem areas, however, there is an easy-going and essentially safe atmosphere on roads throughout the state.

Street crime and hotel burglaries

After car crime, the biggest problem for most travellers in Florida is the threat of **mugging**. It's

---

LOST AND STOLEN CREDIT CARDS

American Express ☎800 992 3404
Diners Club ☎800 234 6377
MasterCard ☎800 627 8372
Visa ☎800 847 2911

impossible to give hard-and-fast rules about what to do if you're confronted by a mugger. Whether to run, scream or fight depends on the situation – the most common advice would be to offer no resistance and just hand over the money. There are a few **basic rules** worth remembering: don't flash money around; don't peer at your map (or this book) at every street corner, thereby announcing you're a lost stranger; avoid dark streets and never start to walk down one you can't see the end of; and in the early hours stick to the roadside edge of the sidewalk so it's easier to run into the road to attract attention.

If the worst happens, try to find a phone and dial ☎ 911, or head to the nearest police station. If you're in a big city, ring the local Travelers Aid (their numbers are listed in the phone book and at ⓦ travelersaid.org) for sympathy and practical advice.

Another potential source of trouble is having your **hotel room** broken into. Some Orlando-area hotels are notorious for this (it's been an on-again, off-again problem for years now, and also happens in Miami Beach), and many such break-ins appear to be inside jobs. Always store valuables in the hotel safe when you go out; when inside, keep your door locked and don't open it to anyone you don't trust; if they claim to be hotel staff and you don't believe them, call reception to check.

Electricity

US electricity is **110V AC** and most plugs are two-pronged. Unless they're dual voltage (most mobile phones, cameras, tablets, MP3 players and laptops are), all Australian, British, European, Irish, New Zealand and South African appliances will need a voltage transformer as well as a plug adapter (older hair-dryers are the most common problem for travellers).

Entry requirements

Under the Visa Waiver Program, citizens of Australia, Ireland, New Zealand and the UK do **not** require visas for visits to the US of ninety days or less. You will, however, need to obtain **Electronic System for Travel Authorization (ESTA)** online before you fly (see box below), which involves completing a basic immigration form in advance. You'll also need to present a machine-readable passport to Immigration upon arrival. With the new ESTA system, the only additional form you must fill in on arrival is the US Customs declaration (one per family/household), which airlines will provide en route (if you have an actual US visa you still need to fill-in form I-94). You should also be able to prove you have a return air ticket (if flying in) and enough **money** to support yourself while in the US; around $300–400 a week is usually considered sufficient – waving a credit card or two may do the trick. Anyone revealing the slightest intention of working while in the country is likely to be refused admission. You may also experience difficulties if you admit to being HIV-positive or having a criminal record.

Canadians now require a passport to cross the border, but can travel in the US for up to a year without a visa or visa waiver. For details on **customs**, check the US Customs and Border Protection website at ⓦ cbp.gov/travel.

US EMBASSIES AND CONSULATES ABROAD

Australia MLC Centre, Level 59, 19–29 Martin Place, Sydney ☎ 02 9373 9200, ⓦ sydney.usconsulate.gov.
Ireland 42 Elgin Rd, Ballsbridge, Dublin ☎ 01 668 8777, ⓦ dublin.usembassy.gov.
New Zealand 3rd Floor, Citigroup Building, 23 Customs St E, Auckland ☎ 09 303 2724, ⓦ newzealand.usembassy.gov.
South Africa 1 Sandton Drive, Sandhurst 2196, Johannesburg ☎ 11 290 3000, ⓦ southafrica.usembassy.gov.

ESTA CLEARANCE

The US government requires all travellers coming to or through the US under the Visa Waiver Program to apply for clearance via **ESTA** (Electronic System for Travel Authorization). This is not something to ignore – if you arrive at the airport without having done it, the airline won't allow you to check in. To apply for clearance visit ⓦ cbp.gov/travel/international-visitors/esta. There is a processing fee of $4, and a further $10 authorization fee once the ESTA has been approved (all paid via credit card online). Once given, authorizations are valid for multiple entries (of up to 90 days each visit) into the US for two years (or until your passport expires, whichever date is sooner) – it's recommended that you submit an ESTA application as soon as you begin making travel plans (in most cases the ESTA will be granted immediately, but it can sometimes take up to 72hr to get a response). Companies advertising assistance with ESTA clearance should be ignored, as no officially recognized bodies provide this service.

UK 24 Grosvenor Square, London W1A 1AE ☎ 020 7499 9000, ⓦ london.usembassy.gov; 3 Regent Terrace, Edinburgh EH7 5BW ☎ 0131 556 8315, ⓦ edinburgh.usconsulate.gov; Danesfort House, 223 Stranmillis Rd, Belfast BT9 5GR ☎ 028 9038 6100, ⓦ belfast .usconsulate.gov.

Extensions and leaving

The date stamped in your passport is the latest you're legally entitled to stay. Leaving a few days after may not matter, especially if you're heading home, but more than a week or so can result in a protracted – and generally unpleasant – interrogation from officials, which may cause you to miss your flight and be denied entry to the US in the future. For visa-holders it's essential to surrender your **I-94** (the white form stapled in your passport) to the authorities when you leave (sometimes the check-in staff will do this), to avoid similar complications on your next visit.

Note that if you visit the US under the Visa Waiver Program, you **cannot extend your stay** beyond the ninety days authorized on entry. If you have a visa and an I-94, you may be able to extend your stay by filing form I-539 online at ⓦ uscis.gov (the filing fee is $290). You may need to provide evidence of sufficient finances and, if possible, an upstanding American citizen to vouch for your worthiness. You'll also have to explain why you didn't plan for the extra time initially.

Festivals and public holidays

Someone, somewhere, is always celebrating something in Florida, though few festivities are shared throughout the region. Instead, there is a disparate multitude of local **annual events**: the most interesting of these are listed below and throughout the chapters. Festivals in Miami (see p.102) and Key West (see p.149) are especially worth attending.

The biggest annual event to hit Florida is **Spring Break** (see box below), while the biggest and most all-American of all the **public holidays** is **Independence Day** on July 4, when most of Florida grinds to

a standstill as people salute the flag and take part in firework displays, marches, beauty pageants and more. The large amusement parks, particularly Disney World, are completely swamped during this time. More sedate is **Thanksgiving Day**, on the fourth Thursday in November, which is essentially a domestic affair, when relatives return to the familial nest to stuff themselves with roast turkey.

On the **national public holidays** listed below (denoted by "**P**"), banks and offices are liable to be closed all day, and shops may reduce their hours. For other festivals, most things will be open as normal, but check with local tourist offices or your hotel.

FESTIVALS AND HOLIDAYS CALENDAR

January

(P) **New Year's Day** Jan 1.

(P) **Martin Luther King, Jr's Birthday** Third Mon in Jan.

Frog Leg Festival Fellsmere (near Vero Beach) ☎ 772 571 0250, ⓦ froglegfestival.com. Third week in Jan. Feast on frogs'-leg and gator-tail dinners over four days of events.

Gasparilla Pirate Festival Tampa ☎ 813 251 8844, ⓦ gasparillapiratefest.com. Last Sat in Jan. Since 1904 hundreds of costumed pirates have staged a mock invasion of Tampa aboard the *Jose Gasparilla*, accompanied by hundreds of boats. Parades and fireworks follow.

February

(P) **Presidents' Day** Third Mon in Feb.

Florida State Fair Florida State Fairgrounds, Tampa ☎ 813 621 7821, ⓦ floridastatefair.com. Late Feb. Huge showcase for the best of Florida agriculture, industry and entertainment over eleven days.

Lake Worth Street Painting Festival ☎ 561 582 4401, ⓦ streetpaintingfestivalinc.org. Last weekend in Feb. See the streets of downtown Lake Worth transformed by elaborate chalk paintings.

March/April

Daytona Beach Bike Week ⓦ officialbikeweek.com. Mid-March. One of America's most popular motorcycle festivals since 1937.

Miami International Film Festival ☎ 305 237 3456, ⓦ miamifilmfestival.com. March. Showcases the best of world cinema.

SPRING BREAK

Florida has been America's favourite **Spring Break** destination for decades, a six-week invasion (late Feb to early April) of tens of thousands of students seeking fun in the sun before knuckling down to their final exams. Times are changing, however: one traditional Spring Break venue, Fort Lauderdale, persuaded the students to go elsewhere; another, Daytona Beach, has had less success. **Panama City Beach**, though, welcomes the carousing collegiates with open arms, and **Key West** – despite its lack of beach – is a newer favourite Spring Break location. If you are in Florida during this time, it will be hard to avoid some signs of Spring Break – a mob of scantily clad drunken students is a tell-tale sign – and at the busier coastal areas you may well find accommodation costing three times the normal price; be sure to plan ahead.

Springtime Tallahassee ☎ 850 224 5012, ⓦ springtime
tallahassee.com. End March/early April. Huge festival that transforms
downtown Tallahassee with a parade, arts and craft market, live concerts,
seafood festival and beer garden.
Florida Film Festival ☎ 407 629 1088, ⓦ floridafilmfestival.com.
March & April. The best in cutting-edge current cinema held over ten
days in venues around central Florida (mostly Maitland and Winter Park).

May

(P) **Memorial Day** Last Mon in May.

June

Florida Dance Festival University of South Florida, Tampa ☎ 786
397 7717, ⓦ floridadanceassociation.org. Mid-June. World-class
dance classes and performances held at the University of South Florida.

July

(P) **Independence Day** July 4.

September

(P) **Labor Day** First Mon in Sept.
Pensacola Seafood Festival ☎ 850 433 6512,
ⓦ fiestaoffiveflags.com/pensacola-seafood-festival. Late Sept.
Live entertainment and mountains of seafood in historic downtown
Pensacola. Part of the Fiesta of Five Flags, an umbrella organization for
events held throughout the year.

October

(P) **Columbus Day** Second Mon in Oct.
Daytona Beach Biketoberfest ⓦ officialbikeweek.com.
Mid-Oct. Sister fest of the event held in March (see p.36).
Halloween Oct 31. Celebrated with special vigour at Florida's theme
parks. Mickey's Not-So-Scary Halloween Party at Disney's Magic
Kingdom; Universal Orlando's Halloween Horror Nights; Busch Gardens'
Howl-O-Scream event in Tampa; and SeaWorld's Halloween Spooktacular.

November

(P) **Veterans' Day** Nov 11.
Downtown Festival & Art Show Gainesville ☎ 352 334 5064,
ⓦ gvlculturalaffairs.org. Mid-Nov. See Gainesville morph into a vast
open-air art market, with food stalls and live music thrown in.
(P) **Thanksgiving Day** Fourth Thurs in Nov.
Festival of Trees Orlando Museum of Art, 2416 N Mills Ave,
Orlando ☎ 407 896 4231, ⓦ omart.org. Mid-Nov. Slightly kitsch but
seasonal celebration that sees the Orlando Museum of Art transformed
into a huge Santa's grotto, with hundreds of Christmas trees, wreaths and
gingerbread houses.
Nights of Lights St Augustine ☎ 800 653 2489,
ⓦ floridashistoriccoast.com/nights. Nov–Jan. Two-month-long
celebration of the holiday season that sees millions of white lights
illuminate colonial St Augustine, and a roster of special events.

December

(P) **Christmas Day** Dec 25.

Gay and lesbian Florida

The biggest gay and lesbian scene in Florida is in
Key West, at the very tip of the Florida Keys. The
island town's live-and-let-live tradition has made it a
holiday destination favoured by American gays and
lesbians for decades, and many arrivals simply never
went home: instead, they've taken up permanent
residence and opened guesthouses, restaurants
and other businesses – such as running gay and
lesbian snorkelling and diving trips.

In **Miami** and **Fort Lauderdale** the networks of
gay and lesbian resources, clubs and bars are quite
extensive – within certain areas – and it's not hard
to pick up on the scene. There are smaller levels of
activity in the other cities, and along developed
sections of the coast a number of motels and hotels
are specifically aimed at gay travellers – Fort
Lauderdale, for example, has over thirty gay hotels.
There are also active and relaxed gay scenes in
Pensacola and, to a lesser extent, **Tallahassee**.
Predictably, attitudes to gay and lesbian visitors get
progressively worse the further you go from the
populous areas. Being open about your sexuality in
the rural regions is likely to provoke an uneasy
response, if not open hostility.

For a complete rundown on local resources, bars
and clubs, see the individual city accounts. Online,
ⓦ gayosphere.com provides a wide range of useful
information about gay and lesbian travel in Florida.

CONTACTS AND RESOURCES

Damron Company ☎ 800 462 6654 or ☎ 415 255 0404,
ⓦ damron.com. Publishes pocket-sized listings of hotels, bars, clubs,
accommodation and resources for gay men and women.
Gayellow Pages ☎ 646 213 0263, ⓦ gayellowpages.com.
Directory of businesses in the US and Canada.
International Gay ⓦ gaytravel.co.uk Online gay and lesbian
travel guides – including Miami and Key West.
Lesbian Travel Association ☎ 954 630 1637, ⓦ iglta.org.
Provides a list of gay- and lesbian-owned or friendly travel agents,
accommodation and other travel businesses.

Health

For the average traveller, a case of sunburn is as
about as serious an injury that can be sustained
while in Florida. If you do get sick or have an
accident, things can get incredibly **expensive**;
organize **insurance** before your trip, just in case. It
will cost upwards of $100 to simply see a doctor or
dentist, and prescription drugs can be very pricey –
if you don't have US medical insurance (as opposed
to normal overseas travel insurance), you'll have to

cough up the money and make a claim when you get home.

Pharmacies such as Walgreens are easy to find all over Florida and often open 24 hours. Staff will recommend the most effective over-the-counter treatments, but don't assume that medicine you can buy at home without prescription will be similarly available in the US.

Should you find yourself requiring a doctor or dentist, ask if your hotel has links to a local practice, or look in the *Yellow Pages* under "Clinics" or "Physicians and Surgeons". Doctors often have long waiting lists however, and will be reluctant to see a new patient at short notice – if you have an accident or need immediate attention head to the **24-hour emergency rooms** at the nearest **hospital**. Should you be in a serious accident, an ambulance will pick you up and charge later. Note that basic emergency care will cost at least $200, ranging to several thousand dollars for serious trauma – that's in addition to fees for drugs, appliances, supplies and the attendant physician, who will charge separately.

Sunburn and mosquito bites

To avoid painful – and potentially dangerous – **sunburn**, apply liberal amounts of sunscreen whenever outside. Those with fair skin should wear a wide-brimmed hat and consider staying out of the sun entirely during its brightest period (11am–3pm).

From mid-May to November, **mosquitoes** – known as **"no see'ums"** – are a tremendous nuisance and virtually unavoidable in any area close to fresh water. During these months, insect repellent is essential, as is wearing long-sleeved shirts and trousers.

Dangerous animals

Florida's **snakes** don't go looking for trouble, but several species will retaliate if provoked – which you're most likely to do by standing on one. Two species are potentially deadly: the coral snake, which has a black nose and bright yellow and red

rings covering its body, and usually spends the daylight hours under piles of rotting vegetation; and the cottonmouth moccasin (sometimes called the water moccasin), dark-coloured with a small head, which lives around rivers and lakes. Less harmful, but still to be avoided, are two types of rattlesnake: the easily identified diamond-back, whose thick body is covered in a diamond pattern, and which turns up in dry, sandy areas and hammocks; and the gray-coloured pygmy, so small it's almost impossible to spot until it's too late. You're unlikely to see a snake in the wild and snake attacks are even more rare, but if bitten you should contact a ranger or a doctor immediately. It's a wise precaution to carry a snakebite kit, available for a couple of dollars from most camping shops.

The biggest surprises among Florida's wildlife may be the apparent docility of **alligators** – almost always they will back away if approached by a human (though this is not something you should put to the test). The only truly dangerous type of alligator is a mother guarding her nest or tending her young. Even then, she'll give you plenty of warning, by showing her teeth and hissing, before attacking.

MEDICAL RESOURCES FOR TRAVELLERS

CDC ⊕ 800 311 3435, ⓦ wwwnc.cdc.gov/travel. Official US government travel health site.

International Society for Travel Medicine ⊕ 770 736 7060, ⓦ istm.org. Has a full list of international travel health clinics, including an extensive list for Florida.

Insurance

Getting travel insurance is highly recommended, especially if you're coming from abroad and are at all concerned about your health – prices for medical attention in the US can be exorbitant (see p.37).

A typical travel insurance policy usually provides cover for the loss of baggage, tickets and – up to a certain limit – cash or cheques, as well as cancellation or curtailment of your journey. Most of them

---

ROUGH GUIDES TRAVEL INSURANCE

Rough Guides has teamed up with WorldNomads.com to offer great travel insurance deals. Policies are available to residents of over 150 countries, with cover for a wide range of adventure sports, 24hr emergency assistance, high levels of medical and evacuation cover and a stream of travel safety information. Roughguides.com users can take advantage of their policies online 24/7, from anywhere in the world – even if you're already travelling. And since plans often change when you're on the road, you can extend your policy and even claim online. Roughguides.com users who buy travel insurance with WorldNomads.com can also leave a positive footprint and donate to a community development project. For more information, go to ⓦ roughguides.com/travel-insurance.

exclude so-called **high-risk activities** unless an extra premium is paid: in Florida, this could mean scuba diving and windsurfing. If you need to make a claim, you should keep receipts for medicines and medical treatment, and in the event you have anything stolen, you must obtain an official theft report from the police.

Internet

You'll find **internet cafés** in most of Florida's cities and many towns, though their numbers are dwindling – **wi-fi** is king these days in the US, with numerous cafés, bars, shops and even whole towns offering it for free. Browse ⓦ wififreespot.com, which lists locations offering free wireless access throughout Florida and the rest of the US.

Laundry

All but the most basic hotels will wash **laundry** for you, but you can also do a wash (about $1.75–2) and tumble dry ($1.50–1.75) in the laundromats found everywhere; take plenty of quarters. Some hotels also have machines available for guests – ask when you check in.

Living in Florida

Far from being the land of the "newly wed and the nearly dead" as many comedians have described the state, Florida's immaculate climate has persuaded people from all over the US and the rest of the world to arrive in search of a subtropical paradise. Florida was hit hard by the 2008 financial crisis, though its unemployment rate finally lowered to national averages by 2014 (around six percent).

Finding work

For anyone looking for **short-term** work, the typical employment options are available – catering, restaurant and bar work – but if you're a foreigner, you start at a disadvantage. Unless you already have family in the US (in which case special rules may apply), you need a **work visa**, and these can be extremely difficult to get. The US visa system is one of the world's most complex, with a bewildering range of visa types to suit every circumstance – most people hire a lawyer to do the paperwork ($2000 and up). Essentially, you'll need a firm offer of work from a US company; however, unless you have a special skill, few companies will want to go through the hassle of sponsoring you. Since tourists are not supposed to seek work, legally you'll have to apply for jobs from overseas. Plenty of foreigners do manage to work for short periods illegally in Florida (typically cash-in-hand jobs, bar work or freelancing); be warned however that the penalties for doing so can be harsh (deportation and being barred from the US for up to ten years), and that if you repeatedly enter the country on a visa-waiver, you are likely to be severely questioned at immigration. For further visa information, go to ⓦ uscis.gov.

Agricultural work is always available on central Florida farms during the October-to-May citrus harvest; check with the nearest university or college, where noticeboards detail what's available. There are usually no problems with papers in this kind of labour, though you still run the risks of illegal work listed above and it often entails working miles from major centres in blistering heat. If you can stick it out, the pay is often good and comes with basic board and accommodation.

Publications and websites

Another pre-planning strategy for working abroad is to check websites such as ⓦ overseasjobs.com, part of a network of sites with worldwide job listings. Vacation Work (an imprint of Crimson Publishing, ⓦ crimsonpublishing .co.uk) also publishes books on summer jobs abroad and how to work your way around the world. Travel magazines like the reliable *Wanderlust* (ⓦ wanderlust.co.uk) have a Job Shop section that often advertises job opportunities with tour companies.

OPPORTUNITIES FOR FOREIGN STUDENTS

Foreign students wishing to **study in Florida** can either try the long shot of arranging a year abroad through their own university, or apply directly to a Florida university (be prepared to stump up the painfully expensive fees). The Student and Exchange Visitor Program, for which participants are given a J-1 visa enabling them to take a job arranged in advance through the programme, is not much use since almost all the jobs are at American summer camps – of which the state has none. If you're interested anyway, organizations to contact in the UK include BUNAC (see p.40).

STUDY AND WORK PROGRAMMES

Australians Studying Abroad Australia ☎ 800 645 755 or ☎ 03 9822 6899, Ⓦ asatours.com.au. Study tours focusing on art and culture.

BUNAC (British Universities' North America Club) UK ☎ 020 7251 3472, Ⓦ bunac.co.uk. Organizes working holidays in the US for students, typically at summer camps or training placements with companies.

Camp America US ☎ 0800 727 8233, Canada ☎ 902 422 1455, UK ☎ 020 7581 7373, Australia ☎ 1300 889 067, New Zealand ☎ 09 416 5337; Ⓦ campamerica.co.uk. Well-known company that places young people as counsellors or support staff in US summer camps.

Earthwatch Institute Europe ☎ 01865 318 838, US ☎ 1800 776 0188, Australia ☎ 1300 889 067; Ⓦ earthwatch.org. Scientific expedition project that spans over fifty countries with environmental and archeological ventures worldwide.

Mail

Ordinary mail within the US costs 49¢ for letters weighing up to an ounce, and 34¢ for postcards; addresses must include a **zip code** (post code) and a return address in the upper left corner of the envelope. International letters and postcards will usually take about a week to reach their destination; rates are currently $1.15 for letters and postcards to all other countries. To find a post office or check up-to-date rates, see Ⓦ usps.com or call ☎ 800 275 8777.

Maps

GPS (sat nav in the UK) is becoming a fairly common option when renting cars in the US (around $10–12/day extra), but if you'd rather not splash out, the excellent *Florida Official Transportation Map*, available for free at tourist offices, covers the state's roads in detail and also has plans of the principal cities and tourist areas. Otherwise, general-purpose road maps from publishers like the American Automobile Association (AAA), Rand McNally and Universal Map concentrate on providing information for drivers, although they may also include some tourist information or street plans. The detailed **Rough Guides' Florida map**, on waterproof, tearproof paper, highlights the main sights of interest. Some publishers (ITMB, Rand McNally, MapEasy) also do sectional maps just for the Gold Coast, Florida Keys, Central Florida and so on. You can pick up local **hiking maps** at ranger stations in state and national parks, and some camping shops carry a supply.

Members of the **AAA** and its overseas affiliates (such as the AA and the RAC in Britain) can also benefit from this organization's maps and general assistance. The AAA is based at 1000 AAA Drive,

Heathrow, FL 32746-5063 ☎ 407 444 4240, Ⓦ autoclubsouth.aaa.com); further offices all across the state are listed in local phone books or on the association's website.

Money

US **currency** comes in notes worth $1, $5, $10, $20, $50 and $100, plus various larger (and rarer) denominations. Confusingly, all are the same size and same green ' colour, making it necessary to check each note carefully. More recent $5, $10, $20 and $50 bills do have some added colour. The dollar is made up of 100 cents (¢) in coins of 1 cent (known as a penny), 5 cents (a nickel), 10 cents (a dime), and 25 cents (a quarter). **Change** (quarters are the most useful) is needed for buses, vending machines and telephones, so always carry plenty.

With an **ATM card**, you can withdraw cash from just about anywhere in Florida; transaction fees vary, but are usually $3–5 (plus what your own bank adds on). Foreign cash-dispensing cards linked to international networks, such as Plus or Cirrus, are also widely accepted. Check with your bank for details before leaving home.

Credit and debit cards

If you don't already have a **credit card**, you should think seriously about getting one before you set off. For many services, it's simply taken for granted that you'll be paying with plastic. When renting a car (or even a bike) or checking in to a hotel, you will be asked to show a credit card to establish your credit-worthiness – even if you intend to settle the bill in cash – or as security, or both; many hotels will require you to leave a huge cash deposit or simply refuse to check you in should you not have a credit card. **Debit cards** are OK for regular purchases and ATM machines, but not much better than cash for the larger expenses: most hotels and car rentals will accept them for payment at the end of your stay, but at the beginning of the rental period they will put a large hold on the debit card for security, which may freeze up your account.

Youth and student discounts

Full-time students are eligible for the **International Student ID Card** (ISIC; Ⓦ isic.org), which entitles the bearer to special air, rail and bus fares, and discounts at museums, theatres and other attractions. The card costs $25 for Americans; Can$20 for Canadians; Aus$30 for Australians; NZ$30 for New Zealanders; £12 in the UK; €15 in the Republic of Ireland; and ZAR100 in South Africa. For non-students, two other cards are available at the same prices as the ISIC card and offering the same benefits: you only have to be 13 to 30 to qualify for the **International Youth Travel Card**, while teachers are eligible for the **International Teacher Card**. All these cards are available from student-oriented travel agents in North America, Europe, Australia and New Zealand. Several other organizations and accommodation groups also sell their own cards, good for various discounts.

A university photo ID might open some doors, but is not as easily recognizable as the ISIC card; note that the latter is often not accepted as valid proof of age – in bars or liquor stores, for example. To prove your age, carry some form of government ID, such as a passport or driving licence.

Opening hours

Banking hours in Florida are generally 9am until 5pm or 6pm Monday to Friday and 9am to 1pm on Saturdays, while **post offices** are usually open Monday to Friday 9am to 5pm and Saturday 9am to noon. Most **shops** are open Monday to Saturday 9am to 6pm, and Sunday noon to 6pm, but times can differ considerably between cities and rural areas.

Phones

International visitors who want to use their **mobile phones** in Florida will need to check with their phone provider to make sure it will work, and what the call charges will be. In the US, AT&T and T-Mobile use the GSM standard, and most foreign companies partner with them to provide service to travelling customers. Note that unless you have a tri-band phone, it is unlikely that a mobile bought for use outside the US or Canada will work inside the States. If you have a Blackberry or iPhone these should work in the US, but you'll need to be extra careful about roaming charges, especially for data, which can be extortionate; even checking voicemail can result in hefty charges. Many travellers turn off voicemail and data roaming before they travel. Most phone companies will provide cheaper options for customers travelling to the US, so check in advance.

You can also rent mobile phones in the US via Phonerental (US ☎800 335 3705, international ☎1 619 446 6980, ⊚phonerentalusa.com); rates are around $1.50 per day (plus the cost of calls per minute).

Phone numbers throughout this book are given with the area code followed by the local number: for international calls dial the US international call

prefix (011), then the international access code of the country you are calling, followed by the local area code and phone number.

USEFUL PHONE NUMBERS

Emergencies ☎ 911. Ask for the appropriate emergency service: fire, police or ambulance.
Local directory information ☎ 411
Long-distance directory information
☎ 1- (area code) 555 1212
Directory enquiries for toll-free numbers ☎ 800 555 1212
Operator ☎ 0

Senior travellers

Along with being a popular place to retire to, people over the age of 62 can enjoy a tremendous variety of **discounts** when travelling in Florida. Both Amtrak and Greyhound, for example, and many US airlines, offer modest reductions on fares to older passengers. Museums, art galleries and even hotels offer small discounts as well, and since the definition of "senior" can drop as low as 55, it is always worth asking.

Any **US citizen** or **permanent resident** aged 62 or over is entitled to the **Senior Pass**, for which a one-time $10 fee is charged for a lifetime of free entry to national parks; it can be issued at any such site. This free entry also applies to any accompanying passengers in the car or, where a per person rather than a per vehicle fee is demanded, the passport-holder can bring in up to three additional adults free of charge. It also gives a fifty percent reduction on fees for camping, parking and boat launching.

CONTACTS AND RESOURCES

American Association of Retired Persons (AARP) 601 E St NW, Washington, DC 20049 ☎ 888 687 2277, ⊚ aarp.org. Can provide discounts on accommodation and vehicle rental. Membership open to anyone aged 50 or over for an annual fee of $16 (US residents), $17 (Canadian residents), or $28 (everyone else).

Road Scholar 11 Avenue de Lafayette, Boston, MA 02111 ☎ 877 454 5768, ⓦ roadscholar.org. Runs an extensive worldwide network of educational and activity programmes, cruises and homestays for people over 55 (companions may be younger). Programmes generally last a week or more and all-inclusive costs are around $120 per day. Florida destinations include Key Largo, St Augustine, Fernandina Beach and St Petersburg.

Saga Holidays The Saga Building, Enbrook Park, Folkestone, Kent CT20 3SE UK ☎ 0800 096 0089, ⓦ travel.saga.co.uk. The UK's biggest and most established specialist in tours and holidays aimed at older people. Offers several Florida packages.

Smoking

Since 2003, smoking has been **banned** in all enclosed workplaces in Florida, exempting private homes, tobacco shops, designated smoking rooms in hotels/motels, and most bars. See ⓦ tobaccofree florida.com.

Time

Most of Florida follows Eastern Standard Time, which is five hours behind Greenwich Mean Time. However, as you travel west through the Panhandle you'll eventually cross into the Central Time zone (at a point about 45 miles west of Tallahassee), which is an hour behind Eastern Time.

Tourist information

Florida's official tourism website (ⓦ visitflorida.com) is a reasonable starting point for advance information. Once you've arrived in the state, you'll find that most large towns have at least a Convention and Visitors Bureau ("CVB", usually open Mon–Fri 9am–5pm, Sat 9am–1pm), offering detailed information on the local area and discount coupons for food and accommodation; but they are unable to book accommodation.

In addition you'll find **Chamber of Commerce offices** almost everywhere; these are designed to promote local business interests, but are more than happy to provide travellers with local maps and information. Most communities have local free newspapers carrying news of events and entertainment – the most useful of which we've detailed throughout the book.

Drivers entering Florida will find **Welcome Centers** (daily 8am–5pm) fully stocked with information leaflets and discount booklets, at four points: on US-231 at Campbellton, near the Florida–Alabama border (☎ 850 263 3510); off I-75 four miles north of Jennings, just south of the Florida–Georgia line (☎ 386 938 2981); on I-10 sixteen miles west of Pensacola (☎ 850 944 0442); and for I-95 drivers, there's one seven miles north of Yulee (☎ 904 225 9182). There's another in the Capitol building in Tallahassee (see p.405).

Travellers with disabilities

The US has one of the best infrastructures in the world for disabled people, and travellers with mobility problems or other physical disabilities are likely to find Florida to be in tune with their needs. All public buildings must be wheelchair-accessible and have suitable toilets, many city street corners have dropped kerbs, and most city buses are able to "kneel" to make access easier and are built with space and handgrips for wheelchair users.

When organizing your holiday, read your **travel insurance** small print carefully to make sure that people with pre-existing medical conditions are not excluded. A **medical certificate** of your fitness to travel, provided by your doctor, is also extremely useful; some airlines or insurance companies may insist on it. Carry spares of any clothing or equipment that might be hard to find; if there's an association representing people with your disability, contact them early in the planning process.

On the ground, the **major car rental firms** can, given sufficient notice, provide vehicles with hand controls (though these are usually only available on the more expensive makes of vehicle). **Amtrak** will provide wheelchair assistance at its train stations and adapted seating on board, provided they have 72 hours' notice – and will give a fifteen percent discount on the regular fare. **Greyhound** buses, despite the fact that they lack designated wheelchair space, will allow a necessary helper to travel at a fifty percent discount.

TIPPING

You shouldn't depart a bar or restaurant without leaving a **tip** of at least fifteen to twenty percent (unless the service is utterly disgusting). If you're just drinking at a bar leave $1 per drink. About fifteen percent should be added to taxi fares – and round them up to the nearest 50¢ or dollar. Tip hotel porters roughly $1 per item for carrying your baggage to your room. When paying by credit or charge card, you're expected to add the tip to the total bill before filling in the amount and signing.

Many of Florida's **hotels and motels** have been built recently, and disabled access has been a major consideration in their construction. Rarely will any part of the property be difficult for a disabled person to reach, and often several rooms are specifically designed to meet the requirements of disabled guests.

The state's major **theme parks** are also built with disabled access in mind, and attendants are always on hand to ensure a disabled person gets all the necessary assistance and derives maximum enjoyment from their visit. Even in the Florida wilds, facilities are good: most **state parks** arrange programmes for disabled visitors; in Everglades National Park, all the walking trails are wheelchair-accessible, as is one of the backcountry camping sites.

CONTACTS AND RESOURCES

Access-Able Ⓦ access-able.com. Online resource for travellers with disabilities.

Florida Disabled Outdoors Association 2475 Apalachee Pkwy, Suite 205, Tallahassee ☎ 850 201 2944, Ⓦ fdoa.org. Information for the disabled sportsman on hunting, fishing, boating and a range of other adapted recreational activities.

Mobility International USA 132 E Broadway, Suite 343, Eugene, OR 97401 ☎ 541 343 1284 (voice and TDD), Ⓦ miusa.org. Information and exchange programmes for students with disabilities studying in the US.

Society for Accessible Travel & Hospitality (SATH) 347 Fifth Ave, Suite 605, New York, NY 10016 ☎ 212 447 7284, Ⓦ sath.org. Nonprofit educational organization that has actively represented travellers with disabilities since 1976.

Traveler's Aid ☎ 202 546 1127, Ⓦ travelersaid.org. Nonprofit organization with professional and volunteer staff who provide emergency assistance to disabled or elderly travellers at Orlando and Tampa airports.

Travelling with children

Much of Florida is geared toward child-friendly travel, what with the theme parks, water parks, beaches and so on, so you're unlikely to encounter too many problems with children in tow.

Hotels and **motels** usually welcome children; those in major tourist areas such as Orlando often have a games room and/or a play area, and allow children below a certain age (usually 14, sometimes 18) to stay for free in their parents' room.

In all but the most formal restaurants, young diners are likely to be presented with a **kids' menu**, plus crayons, drawing pads and assorted toys.

Most large towns have at least one child-orientated **museum** with plenty of interactive educational exhibits – often sophisticated enough to keep even adults amused for hours. Virtually all museums and other tourist attractions have reduced rates for children under a certain age.

Florida's **theme parks** may seem the ultimate in kids' entertainment, but in fact are much more geared toward entertaining adults than most people expect. Only Walt Disney World's Magic Kingdom is tailor-made for young kids (though even here, parents are warned some rides may frighten the very young); adolescents (and adults) are likely to prefer Disney's Hollywood Studios or the two parks at Universal Orlando.

Away from the major tourist stops, **natural Florida** has much to stimulate the young. In the many state parks and in Everglades National Park, park rangers specialize in tuning formative minds in to the wonders of nature – aided by an abundance of alligators, turtles and all manner of brightly coloured birds. A boat trip in dolphin-inhabited waters – several of these are recommended in this book – is another likely way to pique curiosity in the natural world.

On a more cautious note, adults should take great care not to allow young skin to be exposed to the Florida sun for too long: even a few minutes' unprotected exposure can cause serious **sunburn**.

A good idea in a major theme park is to show your child how to find (or how to recognize and ask uniformed staff to take them to) the "**Lost Kids Area**". This designated space not only makes lost kids easy to locate but also provides supervision, plus toys and games to keep them amused until you show up.

Children under 2 years old **fly** for free – though they will have to share your seat – and when aged from 2 to 12 they are usually entitled to reduced-price tickets, though even this is being phased out by most airlines.

If you're doing a fly-drive vacation, car rental companies can usually provide kids' **car seats** for around $5 a day. You would, however, be advised to take your own, as they are not always available.

Miami

MIAMI HOTEL POOLS

1

Miami

A gorgeous, gaudy city, part tropical paradise, part throbbing urban hub, Miami certainly lives up to its depiction in the holiday brochures: the bodies on the beach are as buff and tanned as you'd imagine, the nightlife raucous and raunchy, and the Art Deco hotels stylish. There are palm trees everywhere, and the temperature rarely dips below balmy. And though the climate and landscape may be near perfect, it's the people who give Miami its depth and diversity: two-thirds of the city's population of over two million is of Hispanic origin. Spanish is the main language in most areas, and news from Havana, Caracas or Bogotá frequently gets more attention than the latest word from Washington.

Miami is a city of wildly diverse districts, jigsawed into a vast urban corridor from two technically separate cities (though most amenities are shared): mainland **Miami** and the huge sandbar known as **Miami Beach**. Distances between its neighbourhoods can be large, so if you're planning on exploring the whole city, it's worth renting a car. If you're sticking to the most popular areas in Miami Beach and downtown, though, you can zip around easily by bus and on foot. Either way, it pays to remember that, though the crime-spattered Miami of the 1980s is a distant memory, there are still some rough areas where visitors should exercise caution – we've noted them in the text.

Most people spend their time in **South Beach**, a fairly small area at the southern end of the sandbar, where you'll find many of Florida's leading art galleries, trendsetting restaurants, and much of its boisterous club scene. Heading north, **Central Miami Beach** was where 1950s screen stars had fun in the sun and helped cement Miami's international reputation as a glamorous holiday spot.

Surprisingly few tourists venture beyond Miami Beach, and so miss out on some of the most enticing parts of the city. To see these, a good place to start is **downtown Miami**, where an astonishing construction boom has seen the waterfront crammed with ostentatious skyscrapers. It also hosts excellent history and cultural centres, including the showy new **Pérez Art Museum**. On the waterfront, Bayside Marketplace is the staging post for **boat tours** of Miami's most exclusive offshore keys.

To the north sits the city's buzziest neighbourhood, the strip of land along and around Biscayne Boulevard, known as the **Biscayne Corridor**; it includes the dazzling

YAMBO CAFÉ, LITTLE HAVANA

Highlights

❶ South Beach Enjoy the beach and the nightlife, but don't miss the fabulous array of Art Deco buildings, mostly hotels, from the 1930s and 1940s. **See p.50**

❷ Boat and kayak tours of Biscayne Bay Go sailing around the celebrity mansions of Biscayne Bay, or soak up the stellar views from a kayak. **See p.63**

❸ Pérez Art Museum Miami Spectacularly sited, this world-class art museum is the jewel in downtown's crown and a symbol of the city's resurgence. **See p.66**

❹ Art Walk Miami is one of the most dynamic art centres in the world, best experienced on a monthly Art Walk through the graffiti-wrapped galleries of Wynwood. **See p.68**

❺ Little Havana A true slice of Latin America, this lively neighbourhood is the place to come for gut-busting Cuban fare and heady *café con leche*. **See p.71**

❻ Venetian Pool, Coral Gables Coral Gables' civic amenities don't come better than this – a converted quarry that's both inviting and historic. **See p.77**

HIGHLIGHTS ARE MARKED ON THE MAP ON P.48

1

Performing Arts Center, the art galleries and showrooms of **Wynwood** and the **Design District**, and even the grubby but thrilling immigrant neighbourhood known as **Little Haiti**.

The first of Miami's Cubans settled southwest of downtown, just across the Miami River, in **Little Havana**. This is still one of the most intriguing parts of the city, rich with Latin American looks and sounds, though it's less solidly Cuban than it used to be. Immediately south, Little Havana's grid gives way to the spacious boulevards of **Coral Gables**. South of the downtown area is **Coconut Grove**, the oldest settlement in the area and once an arty, bohemian place, but nowadays known for its shopping and cafés. The large island visible off the coast of Coconut Grove is **Key Biscayne**, linked to the mainland via the massive Rickenbacker Causeway. This classy, secluded island community offers exquisite beaches and bike trails, only five miles from downtown.

MIAMI AREA

HIGHLIGHTS

1. South Beach
2. Boat and kayak tours of Biscayne Bay
3. Pérez Art Museum, Miami
4. Art Walk
5. Little Havana
6. Venetian Pool, Coral Gables

Beyond Coconut Grove and Coral Gables, lacklustre **South Miami** fades into farming territory toward Homestead (see p.168), a good base for exploring the Everglades.

Brief history

Little has been recorded of the area's indigenous inhabitants: the **Tequesta** people were virtually wiped out by the **Spanish** conquistadors led by Juan Ponce de León, who arrived in 1513. The new invaders had no interest in developing southern Florida, being far more concerned with Cuba, and built only a few small settlements along the Miami River and around Biscayne Bay. The whole of the region was finally sold by Spain to the British in 1763, and until two centuries ago Miami was a swampy outpost where some one thousand mosquito-tormented settlers commuted by boat between a trading post and a couple of coconut plantations. The first mention of the "**Village of Miami**" comes after the Second Seminole War in 1842, when one William English re-established a plantation once owned by his uncle and started selling plots of land. Cleveland natives **William Brickell** (who set up a trading post on the Miami River in 1871) and **Julia Tuttle** (the "mother of Miami") are credited with founding the modern city; much of today's downtown area was a citrus farm owned by Tuttle in the 1890s, and it was thanks to her efforts that oil tycoon **Henry Flagler** was persuaded to extend his railroad south (though only after he'd been given vast swathes of land in return).

The completion of the railroad in 1896 gave Miami its first fixed land link with the rest of the country, and literally cleared the way for the 1920s property boom. Entire communities, such as George Merrick's **Coral Gables**, sprang up almost overnight and formed the basis of the city that stands today; the land here was hawked to sun-seeking northerners who swarmed down to enjoy Florida's climate.

The development of Miami Beach

The most popular part of the city remains **Miami Beach**. Three miles offshore, sheltering Biscayne Bay from the Atlantic Ocean, Miami Beach was an ailing fruit farm in the 1910s when its Quaker owner, John Collins, formed an unlikely partnership with a flashy entrepreneur named Carl Fisher. With Fisher's money, Biscayne Bay was dredged, and the muck raised from its murky bed provided the landfill that transformed it into the sculptured landscape of palm trees, hotels and tennis courts that – by and large – it is today. During the 1950s, Miami Beach established itself as a celebrity-filled resort, while at the same time – and with much less fanfare – thousands of Cubans fleeing the successive Batista and Castro regimes began arriving in mainland Miami. The 1960s and 1970s brought decline, as Miami Beach's celebrity cachet waned and it became a haven for retirees. The city's tourist industry was damaged still further by the Liberty City Riot of 1980, which marked a low point in Miami's black–white relations.

Miami Vice years: the 1980s

Miami has cleaned itself up considerably since the 1980s, when it was plagued by the highest murder rate in America. The city has since grown rich as a key gateway for US–Latin American trade, to which its string of expensively designed banks and financial institutions bears witness. Strangely enough, another factor in Miami's revival was the mid-1980s cop show *Miami Vice*, which was less about crime than designer clothes and subtropical scenery.

Miami today

Today, with the strengthening of Latin American economic links and a younger, more cosmopolitan breed of visitor energizing Miami Beach, the city is enjoying a surge of affluence and optimism. Away from the beaches, Miami has gained a reputation as one of the foremost centres for **contemporary art** in the US, with areas like the Wynwood

1

Arts District studded with galleries and studios, and an annual December art show, **Art Basel**, that draws thousands of artists, dealers and fans. Miami's downtown bears witness to this resurgence: once a no-man's land, it's now a thriving residential area filled with restaurants, parks and attractive new hotels.

South Beach

Undoubtedly, Miami's most exciting area is **SOUTH BEACH**, which occupies the southernmost three miles of Miami Beach. Filled with pastel-coloured Art Deco buildings, up-and-coming art galleries, modish diners and suntanned beach addicts, it's often celebrated as one of the hippest places in the world. Socially, South Beach has an unbeatable buzz. Here, Latin, black and white cultures happily collide, gay and straight tourists soak up the sun together, and Cuban cafés and chic boutiques sit side by side. Though elsewhere Miami's cultural schizophrenia may cause friction, here it's at its riotous, cocktail-clinking best.

More than anywhere else in the city, you can wander safely in South Beach day or night. The only time the streets are empty is early morning, when most of Miami Beach is still sleeping off the excesses of the night before. This is also the perfect time to grasp South Beach's allure for photographers and take in the sheer beauty of its Art Deco buildings; try to turn in early one night and wake up for a stroll at dawn – the lucid white light and wave-lapped tranquillity are striking.

Ocean Drive

Much of South Beach falls within the **Art Deco District**, an area of around 1100 protected Art Deco gems recognized by the National Register and bounded roughly by 5th and 23rd streets and Ocean Drive and Lenox Avenue. The best place to start exploring this rich architectural legacy is **Ocean Drive**, the main drag that hugs the gloriously wide beach. You can admire the exquisite Art Deco on display by simply wandering the streets around here, and though few buildings are open to the public, all the **hotels** listed below are generally tolerant of small groups of tourists taking a quick peek at the lobby. You can always stop for a drink or something to eat – worth considering, as the interiors are often even more exuberant than the outsides. You could also take a **walking tour** (see box, p.86), a fun way to see the key buildings and hear the colourful stories behind their construction and preservation.

Park Central

640 Ocean Drive • ☎ 305 538 1611, ⓦ theparkcentral.com

One of the area's earliest renovations was **Park Central**: completed in 1937 by **Henry Hohauser** (one of Miami's most lauded architects), it's a geometric tour de force, with ten-sided windows, terrazzo floors and sharp vertical columns in the facade, part of the signature Art Deco "rule of three": a strong central section supported by two complementary side sections.

Beach Patrol Station and Art Deco Welcome Center

1001 Ocean Drive • Daily 9.30am–5pm (Thurs till 7pm), gift shop open till 7pm • ☎ 305 672 2014, gift shop ☎ 305 531 3484, ⓦ mdpl.org

In Lummus Park (the grassy patch that separates Ocean Drive from the beach), right in the heart of South Beach, stands the boat-shaped **Beach Patrol Station**, still the base of local lifeguards. Unmistakeable for its vintage oversized date-and-temperature sign, its panels were digitized in 2011, though the structure retains its antique frame. Inside the complex is the useful **Art Deco Welcome Center** and **gift shop**, a great place to procure flamingo lawn ornaments, and the starting point for architectural tours of the area (see box, p.55).

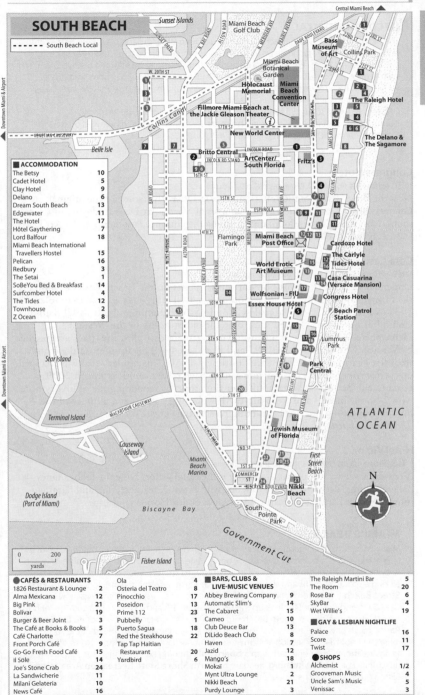

Central Miami Beach

SOUTH BEACH

- - - - - South Beach Local

Sunset Islands

Miami Beach
Golf Club

Bass
Museum
of Art

Collins Park

W. 20TH ST

Miami Beach
Botanical
Garden

Holocaust
Memorial

Miami
Beach
Convention
Center

The Raleigh Hotel

Fillmore Miami Beach at
the Jackie Gleason Theater

VENETIAN CAUSEWAY

Belle Isle

Collins Canal

17TH ST

New World Center

The Delano &
The Sagamore

Britto Central

LINCOLN ROAD

ArtCenter/
South Florida

Fritz's

LINCOLN RD STAND
16TH ST

15TH ST

ESPAÑOLA WAY

Flamingo
Park

Miami Beach
Post Office

Cardozo Hotel

14TH ST

The Carlyle
Tides Hotel

World Erotic
Art Museum

Casa Casuarina
(Versace Mansion)

Wolfsonian - FIU

Congress Hotel

Essex House Hotel

Beach Patrol
Station

Lummus
Park

Park
Central

Star Island

MACARTHUR CAUSEWAY

Terminal Island

Jewish Museum
of Florida

ATLANTIC
OCEAN

Causeway
Island

Dodge Island
(Port of Miami)

Miami
Beach
Marina

First
Street
Beach

Nikki
Beach

Biscayne Bay

South
Pointe
Park

Government Cut

N

Downtown Miami & Airport

0   200
yards

Fisher Island

ACCOMMODATION

The Betsy	10
Cadet Hotel	5
Clay Hotel	9
Delano	6
Dream South Beach	13
Edgewater	11
The Hotel	17
Hôtel Gaythering	7
Lord Balfour	18
Miami Beach International Travellers Hostel	15
Pelican	16
Redbury	3
The Setai	1
SoBeYou Bed & Breakfast	14
Surfcomber Hotel	4
The Tides	12
Townhouse	2
Z Ocean	8

● CAFÉS & RESTAURANTS

1826 Restaurant & Lounge	2
Alma Mexicana	12
Big Pink	21
Bolívar	19
Burger & Beer Joint	3
The Café at Books & Books	5
Café Charlotte	7
Front Porch Café	9
Go-Go Fresh Food Café	15
Il Sole	14
Joe's Stone Crab	24
La Sandwicherie	11
Milani Gelateria	10
News Café	16

Ola	4
Osteria del Teatro	8
Pinocchio	17
Poseidon	13
Prime 112	23
Pubbelly	1
Puerto Sagua	18
Red the Steakhouse	22
Tap Tap Haitian Restaurant	20
Yardbird	6

■ BARS, CLUBS & LIVE-MUSIC VENUES

Abbey Brewing Company	9
Automatic Slim's	14
The Cabaret	15
Cameo	10
Club Deuce Bar	13
DiLido Beach Club	8
Haven	7
Jazid	12
Mango's	18
Mokaï	2
Mynt Ultra Lounge	1
Nikki Beach	21
Purdy Lounge	3

The Raleigh Martini Bar	5
The Room	20
Rose Bar	6
SkyBar	4
Wet Willie's	19

■ GAY & LESBIAN NIGHTLIFE

Palace	16
Score	11
Twist	17

● SHOPS

Alchemist	1/2
Grooveman Music	4
Uncle Sam's Music	5
Venissac	3

1

DECO BIKE RENTAL

The best way to tour South Beach is by renting a **Deco Bike** (W decobike.com). Located at one hundred stations across the island (from the southernmost tip up to Surfside), these cushy new bikes come complete with baskets and a bell. Bicycles can be returned to any station, and switched for another at any point during the rental period (useful if you don't want to deal with locks). Upon return, make sure you hear a beep from the station, signifying your bike's acceptance into the system.

Rates are $4 for 30min, $6 for an hour, $10 for 2hr, $18 for 4hr and $24 for 24hr. Unfortunately, stations do not provide **helmets**. Note that bikes aren't allowed on the wooden boardwalk that runs from 22nd to 47th streets.

Congress Hotel

1052 Ocean Drive • ☎ 305 534 6820, W congresshotelsouthbeach.com

Near the Beach Patrol Station, back on Ocean Drive, the facade of the original **Congress Hotel** is one of the purest examples of Miami Art Deco (today it's just a shop). Notice the "frozen fountains" framing the entrance, another popular Art Deco feature, based on fanciful Mayan imagery.

Casa Casuarina

1116 Ocean Drive • ☎ 305 576 8003, W thevillabybartong.com

Undeniably one of the most popular tourist sights on the Beach, **Casa Casuarina** is the former home of murdered fashion designer Gianni Versace. It was completed in 1930 as a replica of the Alcázar de Colón in Santo Domingo, built by Christopher Columbus's son in 1510, and said to be the oldest house in the Western Hemisphere. After a time as a run-down apartment complex, the space was rescued by Versace, who bought it in 1992 and lived here until his murder on the front steps five years later. After Versace's untimely demise, his opulent pad was snapped up by developer Peter Loftin, who's said to have paid around $19m. In 2009, restaurateur Barton G. Weiss took over the property, reopening it as a luxury hotel with 24-hour butlers and a mosaic-tiled swimming pool. Get a glimpse of the building's dazzling interior by making reservations at the on-site restaurant, *The Villa by Barton G* (see p.92).

Hotel Victor

1144 Ocean Drive • ☎ 305 779 8700, W hotelvictorsouthbeach.com

A few doors down from *Casa Casuarina* is the **Hotel Victor**. Note the lobby's fancy hanging lamps, decorative white peacock with flowing, feathered tail and flamingo mural by artist Earl LaPan, featuring a typical South Florida landscape.

MIAMI'S BEACHES

Miami Beach boasts gorgeous Art Deco buildings and a glittering nightlife, but the core of its appeal remains its fabulous strip of clean, bone-white sands. With twelve miles of calm waters, swaying palms and famous candy-coloured **lifeguard towers**, you can't go wrong when picking a spot (restrooms and showers line the beach at regular intervals). To the south, **First Street Beach** is favoured by families and surfers alike, and is especially convivial at weekends. The young and the beautiful soak up the rays between 5th and 21st streets, a convenient hop from the bars and cafés of South Beach. From 6th to 14th streets, the area around **Lummus Park** – much of whose sand was shipped in from the Bahamas – is the heart of the scene; there's an unofficial gay section at 12th Street (rainbow flags mark the spot). North of 21st, things are more family-oriented, with a **boardwalk** running between the shore and the hotels up to 46th. For good **swimming**, head up to **North Shore State Recreation Area** around 85th, a quiet stretch just south of Surfside.

The Tides

1220 Ocean Drive • ☎ 305 604 5070, ⓦ tidessouthbeach.com

The Tides Hotel was designed by master architect L. Murray Dixon, its tall and imposing facade completed in 1936 from blocks of oolitic limestone quarried from Key Largo. Take a look inside the lobby, one of the most mesmerizing spaces on South Beach: the luxurious interior looks like a giant piece of installation art, a sophisticated blend of earthy browns and beiges with rattan, wood and leather furnishings. The hotel's fancy restaurant is decorated with giant tortoise shells and metallic gold palms.

The Carlyle and the Cardozo Hotel

The facade of **The Carlyle**, 1250 Ocean Drive, featured in the movie *Birdcage* (1996), and a decade later was converted from a hotel into nineteen condos going for $1 million and above. The **Cardozo Hotel** at no. 1300 is another Hohauser masterpiece, finished in 1939 and now owned by Gloria and Emilio Estefan. Featuring a rounder, softer style, the *Cardozo* housed the original offices of Barbara Capitman (see box, p.55) and appeared in the movie *There's Something About Mary* (1998).

Collins Avenue

The Art Deco theme continues on Collins Avenue, one block west of Ocean Drive, lined with mid-range hotels and a swanky shopping strip between 5th and 7th streets; it runs along the coast all the way to Fort Lauderdale.

The Hotel

801 Collins Ave • ☎ 305 531 2222, ⓦ thehotelofsouthbeach.com

The pick of several architectural highlights here is the former **Tiffany Hotel** at no. 801, now just *The Hotel*. Designed by L. Murray Dixon, its 1939 terrazzo floors and mosaic mirrors have been faithfully restored, but its most iconic feature is the futuristic spire on top; head up to the funky *Spire Bar* on the roof for a closer look – and stupendous views of the Atlantic.

Essex House Hotel

1001 Collins Ave • ☎ 305 534 2700, ⓦ essexhotel.com

The **Essex House Hotel** is a real treat; built by Hohauser in 1938, the lobby features another mural by LaPan, this time featuring a Seminole tribesman fishing in the Everglades. Look for the arrows set into the terrazzo floor, a not-so-subtle legacy of illegal gambling in the 1940s – gamblers would follow the arrows and place their bets at the back.

Washington Avenue and around

On **Washington Avenue**, the area's main commercial artery, small, Cuban-run supermarkets stand alongside local boutiques and nightclubs. Its everyday vibe is pleasantly refreshing after the plucked-and-tweezed perfection closer to the beach.

Hotel Astor

956 Washington Ave • ☎ 305 531 8081, ⓦ hotelastor.com

Take a peek inside the **Hotel Astor**, designed by T. Hunter Henderson in 1936. The decorative elements of the facade, crafted from oolitic limestone, have been beautifully maintained, while the lobby features the original Vitrolite wall panels. The hotel's handsome restaurant, *The Downstairs*, is also a fun sight: modernist chairs and long, grey couches dot a dining room hung with showy white lights.

1

Wolfsonian-Florida International University museum

1001 Washington Ave • Mon, Tues & Sat 10am–6pm, Thurs & Fri 10am–9pm, Sun noon–6pm • $7, free admission Fri 6–9pm •
☎ 305 531 1001, ⓦ wolfsonian.org

Just across the street from the *Astor* sits the handsome **Wolfsonian-FIU museum**. Some 70,000 decorative arts and crafts items from Europe and the Americas have been assembled in this florid Mediterranean-Revival building by Mitchell Wolfson Jr, a local businessman. Anyone with an interest in interior design, architecture or politically inspired art will find something of note in the displays, whose exceptional galleries are the Beach's cultural must-visit. Friday nights are surprisingly quiet despite the free admission, and make for an inviting date spot or pre-clubbing activity.

World Erotic Art Museum

1205 Washington Ave • Mon–Thurs 11am–10pm, Fri & Sun 11am–midnight • $15 • ☎ 305 532 9336, ⓦ weam.com

At the corner of 12th Street and Washington Avenue, you'll find one of the quirkier sights in South Beach, the **World Erotic Art Museum**. It's home to the $10-million collection of erotic ephemera amassed by a filthy-minded rich widow – Miami's philanthropic answer to Dr Ruth – who's put on show everything from cheeky bottom-baring Victorian figurines to *The Pillow Book*, Japan's calligraphic version of the *Kama Sutra*.

Miami Beach Post Office

1300 Washington Ave • Mon–Fri 8am–5pm, Sat 8.30am–2pm • ☎ 305 672 2447, ⓦ usps.com

On the corner of 13th Street is the charming **Miami Beach Post Office**, a squat dome built in the Depression Moderne style. Duck into the rotunda to see its flashy **geometric mural** of Spanish conquistadors Ponce de León and De Soto, and a depiction of a treaty being signed between the US Army and the Seminoles – sadly, a fictional event.

Española Way

Between Washington and Jefferson aves

At the northern end of Washington Avenue, sandwiched between 14th Place and 15th Street, stands **Española Way**, a pedestrian strip built by Carl Fisher, who disliked the prevalent Art Deco style and made this Mediterranean-Revival development his pet project. Completed in 1925, it was grandly envisaged as an artists' colony – today it's lined with commercial art galleries, gift shops and alfresco restaurants. Though the architecture is certainly novel and there are a couple of enticing places to eat here, you won't miss much by skipping it.

Lincoln Road Mall

Between Alton Rd and Washington Ave

Between 16th and 17th streets, the pedestrianized **Lincoln Road Mall** was considered the flashiest shopping precinct outside of New York during the 1950s, its jewellery and clothes stores earning it the label "Fifth Avenue of the South". Store-dresser-turned-architect Morris Lapidus (see p.58) was the genius behind its pedestrianization – then a revolutionary idea – and also designed the space-age structures that serve as sunshades. Though its fortunes plummeted alongside the rest of South Beach in the 1970s and 1980s, it's now a sparkling shopping strip lined with clothing stores and dozens of pavement cafés; the Sunday-afternoon stroll here is a ritual not to be missed.

ArtCenter/South Florida

800 Lincoln Rd • Mon–Thurs noon–9pm, Fri & Sat 11am–10pm, Sun 11am–9pm • Free • ☎ 305 674 8278, ⓦ artcentersf.org

It's worth stopping by the **ArtCenter/South Florida**, an artists' collective that has been here since 1984, to see the work of more than fifty local painters, sculptors and photographers, displayed in revolving exhibitions.

Britto Central

818 Lincoln Rd • Mon–Thurs & Sun 10am–11pm, Fri & Sat 10am–midnight • Free • ☎ 305 531 8821, ⓦ britto.com

Art lovers should also check out **Britto Central**, showcasing the flamboyant pop art of Brazilian Romero Britto, Miami's best-known artist. Britto's colourful, city-defining installations pepper the town: everything from the Miami Children's Museum (see p.60) to downtown's psychedelic parking meters and the bow-tied *Welcome* sculpture by the Dadeland North metrorail station are the product of his exuberant palette. Since 1993, Britto's gallery has been here on Lincoln Road, exhibiting original canvases as well as photographs and mementos in its all-white interior.

The Delano, Sagamore and Raleigh hotels

1685, 1671 & 1775 Collins Ave

On **Collins Avenue**, just east of Lincoln Road Mall, it's worth rounding off a tour of Art Deco South Beach with a look at some of the most opulent hotels on the strip. The **Delano** at no. 1685 (see p.89) was the tallest building in Miami Beach when it opened in 1947; check out Philippe Starck's recently added drape-lined lobby, and the fabulous pool at the back. Pop into the **Sagamore** at no. 1671 to admire the vivid contemporary art displayed in the lobby and immaculate all-white bar areas; while one block to the north, the **Raleigh Hotel** at no. 1775, another jewel designed by L. Murray Dixon (finished in 1940), is the place to end your stroll with a cocktail by its gorgeous palm-fringed Modernist pool.

DECODING ART DECO

Miami became a haven for **Art Deco** in large part due to the wrecking power of South Florida's hurricanes. In 1926, the city was levelled by a devastating storm, and its wooden buildings were replaced with concrete structures in the newly modish Art Deco style.

Art Deco (1930s–1940s) is easily identifiable by its signature features. Look for "eyebrows" above the windows that provide shade as well as decoration, elements in groups of three, porthole windows, stepped rooflines and a symmetry in the facade. **Streamline Moderne** (1930s–1940s), prevalent in Miami Beach today, bridges the simplicity of early Deco and the playfulness of Miami Modern or **MiMo** (1945–69). As with many MiMo structures (see p.58), all elements of Streamline buildings are designed to give a feeling of movement, and the hard edges are rounded off. The simpler **Depression Moderne** was a sub-style of Streamline, often used for government buildings, such as the Post Office (see p.54); it was less ostentatious and ornamental than Miami Deco, and money was spent subtly on interior spaces, like murals and ironwork. Though Deco dominated building in Miami for more than twenty years, there was a contemporary alternative, known as **Mediterranean Revival** (1915–30), whose asymmetry and ramshackle design were intended to give the impression of age. Many at the time sniffed that this was how gangsters and movie stars – ie, those with more money than taste – liked to commission houses; even so, almost one-third of the structures in the so-called Art Deco District are classified under this style.

It's a sobering thought that Miami Beach almost lost all of these significant structures. In the mid-1970s, the **Miami Design Preservation League** – whose first meeting drew just six people – was born with the aim of saving the buildings and raising awareness of their architectural and historical importance. The league's success has been dramatic – a major turning point was convincing the buck-hungry developers of the earning potential of such a unique area. The driving force of the movement was the late **Barbara Capitman**, but it was her preservation partner, interior designer **Leonard Horowitz**, who came up with the now-trademark palette of sherbet yellows, pinks and blues – "a palette of Post Modern cake-icing pastels now associated with *Miami Vice*", in the words of disgruntled Florida architecture chronicler Hap Hatton. Originally, most Deco buildings were painted white with their features picked out in navy or dark brown – a rare surviving example of this colour scheme is the City Hall in Coconut Grove.

The League's ninety-minute **Art Deco walking tours** (see box, p.86) are a Miami must-do.

1

Jackie Gleason Theater
1700 Washington Ave • ☎ 305 673 7300, ⓦ fillmoremb.com

Immediately north of Lincoln Road Mall, the 2600-seat **Fillmore Miami Beach at the Jackie Gleason Theater** is worth a visit for Pop artist Roy Lichtenstein's expressive *Mermaid* sculpture at the front, and for its classical concerts (see p.100). However, it is best known to elderly Americans as the home of entertainer Jackie Gleason's immensely popular TV show, *The Honeymooners*, which began in the 1950s and ran for twenty years.

New World Center
500 17th St • Tours Tues & Thurs at 4pm, Fri & Sat at noon; 30–45min; reservations required • Tours $5 • ☎ 305 673 3331, ⓦ newworldcenter.com

Across the street from the Jackie Gleason Theater, Frank Gehry's spectacular **New World Center**, built in 2011, is the cultural darling of Miami Beach and the only full-time orchestral academy in the US. Home to the **New World Symphony orchestra**, its glass facade reveals a cavernous interior that's hung with sweeping, curved white panels that look like a massive, cracked eggshell. Its open design is most intriguing in the sound-proofed atrium, which enables passers-by to watch rehearsals from outside the building. The Center also projects movies and live performances (generally Fri or Sat at 7.30 or 8pm; free) onto its 7000-square-foot exterior, popular and fun events that take place on its front lawn – a 2.5-acre park. Check the website for information on reserving a seat in the acoustically perfect, 756-seat performance hall.

The Holocaust Memorial
1933–1945 Meridian Ave • Daily 9.30am–sunset • Free; $2 donation for brochure • ☎ 305 538 1663, ⓦ holocaustmemorialmiamibeach.org

It's impossible not to be moved by Kenneth Treister's **Holocaust Memorial**, just northwest of the New World Center. Completed in 1990 and dedicated to Elie Wiesel, the monument depicts a 42ft-high bronze arm tattooed with an Auschwitz number reaching toward the sky. Life-sized figures of emaciated, tormented people attempt to climb this wrenching sculpture. The black marble walls around it are etched with names of the dead as well as some shockingly graphic photographs of Nazi atrocities.

Miami Beach Botanical Garden
2000 Convention Center Drive • Tues–Sun 9am–5pm • Free • ☎ 305 673 7256, ⓦ mbgarden.org

Framing the Holocaust Memorial, this small, 2.6-acre **botanical garden** is alive with orchids, spiky palms and hot pink bromeliads. Easy-going trails visit a Japanese garden, stone sculptures and a pond filled with water lilies. Though it's not Miami's grandest horticultural attraction (that honour goes to Fairchild Tropical Garden; see p.83), this tiny greenspace makes for a lovely escape in busy Miami Beach.

Bass Museum of Art
2100 Collins Ave • Wed–Sun noon–5pm • $8 • ☎ 305 673 7530, ⓦ bassmuseum.org

The only fine-art museum on Miami Beach, the **Bass Museum of Art** is housed in an angular, white 1930s building designed by Russell Pancoast, the architect son-in-law of beach pioneer John Collins. What began as the local public library became a museum to house the private collection of local socialites John and Johanna Bass, which was donated to the city in 1963. The museum unveiled a showy expansion by Japanese architect Arata Isozaki in 2002 – the white box he grafted onto the original building along Park Avenue tripled its exhibition space. It's a shame, then, that the holdings, mainly contemporary works, are so hit-and-miss. The permanent collection holds a number of gems, notably the stunning Flemish tapestry *The Salute before the Tournament*, and a sampling of works by Rubens and Bol.

South of Fifth Street ("SoFi")

The last chunk of South Beach to undergo gentrification lies south of Fifth Street, where bars and restaurants are slowly spreading downward and bringing the tourist crowds with them. This area was originally the Jewish enclave on the beach, since Fifth Street marked the northernmost point where Jews could buy housing. By the 1980s, though, the area had collapsed into a shabby, no-go area, spurred by the arrival of undesirables in the wake of the Mariel boatlift (see box, p.72). The most obvious sign of the current upswing is an influx of new residents, drawn to what local estate agents have taken to calling "SoFi" (South of Fifth), especially at the southern tip known as South Pointe. The high-rises here – like the luxury 26-storey **South Pointe Towers** that leap skyward from South Pointe Park (see below) – dwarf the area, which has a quiet, residential feel. Come for the Jewish Museum or some of South Beach's hottest restaurants, such as *Prime 112* (see p.92).

Jewish Museum of Florida

301 Washington Ave • Tues–Sun 10am–5pm • $6, free on Sat • ☎ 305 672 5044, ⓦ jmof.fiu.edu

During the 1920s and 1930s, South Beach became a major destination for Jewish tourists escaping the harsh northeastern winters. In response, many businesses placed "Gentiles Only" signs at their reception desks, and the slogan "restricted clientele" was used in hotel brochures. Despite this, by the 1940s South Beach had a largely Jewish population and for a time it was home to the second largest community of Holocaust survivors in the country. The **Jewish Museum of Florida** bears testimony to Jewish life not only in Miami Beach, but in all of Florida, since the earliest days of European settlement.

The permanent collection is exhaustive, and there are visiting exhibitions on Jewish life in general – make sure to chat with one of the volunteers when wandering around as they're enthusiastic and knowledgeable. The museum itself is housed in an elegant 1929 Art Deco **building** – now lavishly restored – that served as an Orthodox synagogue for Miami Beach's first Jewish congregation.

South Pointe

Below 5th St, between Ocean Drive and the Atlantic Ocean

The best route to beautiful **South Pointe**, Miami Beach's southernmost tip, is the mile-long shorefront boardwalk that begins near the southern end of Lummus Park and finishes by the 300ft-long jetty off First Street Beach, the only **surfing beach** in Miami and packed with tanned, athletic bodies even when the waves are calm. You can swim and snorkel here, too, plus there's a nice vantage point for watching the big cruise ships pass by on their way out to sea.

The boardwalk skirts **South Pointe Park** (daily 8am–sunset), whose dog-friendly lawns and tree-shaded picnic tables were given a handsome refurbishment in 2009, and now sport an inviting playground and splashing fountains. The park is a good place to be on Friday evenings when its open-air stage is the venue for enjoyable free **music events** (ⓦweb.miamibeachfl.gov), and you can admire the sea views and cruise ships over a cold beer at *Smith & Wollensky* steakhouse.

Central Miami Beach

Art Deco gives way to massive tower blocks as South Beach settles into the more sedate area known as **CENTRAL MIAMI BEACH**. Collins Avenue charts a five-mile course through the area, between Indian Creek and the swanky **hotels** around which the Miami Beach high life revolved during the glamorous 1950s. These often madly ostentatious establishments are the main attraction here, with little in the way of traditional sights; the strand itself is largely the preserve of families and older folk,

1

and is backed by a long and lovely boardwalk that stretches alongside the premium beachfront for over a mile from 21st Street. Arthur Godfrey Road (41st St), the main drag in these parts and a connector to the mainland, is notable as being a hub of Jewish culture and restaurants: a great place to score a pastrami sandwich before hunkering down on the sand.

Russian & Turkish Baths

5445 Collins Ave (in the Castle Beach Club) • Daily noon–midnight • $35 • ☎ 305 867 8313, ⓦ russianandturkishbaths.com

Established in 1892, this co-ed bathhouse has been pleasing a nice cross-section of Miamians – couples, retirees, hungover club kids and families – for ages. Admission provides access to the *shvitz*, or wooden steam room (complete with buckets of ice-cold water), a saltwater jacuzzi, a chilly "polar bear" sauna and an aromatherapy steam room, among other delights. While it certainly isn't a five-star spa – it's pretty care-worn – R&T is a unique and rejuvenating Miami experience.

The Fontainebleau

4441 Collins Ave • ☎ 305 538 2000, ⓦ fontainebleau.com

Before Central Miami Beach became a celebrities' playground, the nation's rich and powerful built rambling shorefront mansions here. One of them, the winter home of tyre-baron Harvey Firestone, was demolished in 1953 to make room for the **Fontainebleau**, a dreamland of over-the-top design cooked up by architect **Morris Lapidus** that defined the Miami Beach of the late 1950s and 1960s. Gossip-column perennials, such as Joan Crawford, Joe DiMaggio, Lana Turner and Bing Crosby, were Fontainebleau regulars, as was crooner Frank Sinatra who, besides starting a scrambled-egg fight in the coffee shop, shot many scenes here as the private-eye hero of the 1967 film *Tony Rome*. The interior has been brutally remodelled several times since Lapidus first designed it, but its 2008 restoration returned many of his elegant touches, including ripping up carpet to reveal the bowties (Lapidus's trademark) embedded in the lobby's terrazzo floor.

The Eden Roc

4525 Collins Ave • ☎ 305 531 0000, ⓦ edenrocmiami.com

The *Fontainebleau*'s opulent sister, the **Eden Roc**, next door, is another love child of designer Morris Lapidus (see above) and a Miami Beach icon. Completed in 1956, in its heyday the hotel courted a perpetual string of celebrity pearls: Elizabeth Taylor, Lucille Ball and the Rat Pack all hung their hats in the *Mona Lisa Room* restaurant, Katharine Hepburn and Groucho Marx danced in *Harry's American Bar* (although probably not with each other), and Harry Belafonte sang in *Café Pompeii*. The hotel underwent an extensive renovation in 2008, which saw the addition of lobby bar with rosewood columns, infinity pools and a tropical garden (see p.90).

North Miami Beach

Collins Avenue continues up through **North Beach** between 63rd Street and 87th Terrace, the latest beachfront enclave to be eyed by preservationists, thanks to its heavy concentration of playful mid-century **MiMo** buildings. The *Fontainebleau*'s Morris Lapidus was one of the best known proponents of this style, which emphasizes swooping movement and speedy touches like rooftop fins, as well as decorative, non-functioning elements like cheesehole (holes bored through concrete like bubbles in Swiss cheese).

North Beach Resort Historic District

Eight blocks of the eastern side of Collins Avenue, from 63rd to 71st streets, were designated the North Beach Resort Historic District in 2004: this area includes masterpieces like the **Sherry Frontenac** hotel at 65th and Collins, with its jazzy neon signs, and the (currently closed) stone-grill-fronted **Golden Sands** at 69th and Collins. Though neither is particularly noteworthy for its rooms, both make ideal photo ops.

Normandy Isle

For more MiMo buildings, head west along 71st Street onto **Normandy Isle** (by way of Normandy Drive), rapidly becoming a trendy hub for hipsters priced out of South Beach, as well as a cluster of expat Argentinians who've earned the area its nickname of Little Buenos Aires. It's a great neighbourhood for sampling Latin cuisine, with most of the area's restaurants clustered along Collins Avenue between 69th and 74th streets (see p.93).

Surfside and Bal Harbour

The low-rise buildings of the **Surfside** neighbourhood retain an appealing old-fashioned ambience; the **beach**, between 91st and 95th streets, is the main reason to spend an afternoon here. Directly north, **Bal Harbour** – its aspirations of "Olde Worlde" elegance reflected in its anglicized name – is similar in size to Surfside but entirely different in character: an upmarket area filled with the carefully guarded homes of some of the nation's wealthiest people.

Bal Harbour Shops

9700 Collins Ave • Mon–Sat 10am–9pm, Sun noon–6pm • ☎ 305 866 0311, ⓦ balharbourshops.com • Bus #H

The exclusive **Bal Harbour Shops**, packed with expensive designer stores, sets the tone for the area; ironically, given its upmarket aspirations, the town's origins lie in a soldiers' training camp that once stood here during World War II.

Haulover Beach Park

10800 Collins Ave • ☎ 305 947 3525, ⓦ miamidade.gov/parks • Take bus #H or #S up Collins Ave and get off at the coastguard station ("Marine Center"), where there are also parking facilities ($6)

The most notorious local attraction is two miles north of Bal Harbour, the **Haulover Beach Park**. This is Miami's only nude beach, but the furore over the clothing-free bathing eclipses its other upsides – the sands are wide enough to never feel crowded, there are ample picnic tables, showers and restrooms, and it's only a twenty-minute drive from South Beach. From the coastguard station turn right for the regular beach or left for the "clothing optional" one, which starts at beach watch-station 24 and ends at watch-station 29, predominantly a gay area.

Sunny Isles Beach and Golden Beach

The main draw in the resort town of **Sunny Isles Beach** is (you guessed it) the sumptuous beach; to combat erosion, it's regularly replenished by sand dredged from the ocean floor. By the time you reach **Golden Beach**, the northernmost community of Miami Beach, much of the traffic pounding Collins Avenue has turned inland on the Lehman Causeway (192nd St), and the string of hotels has given way to quiet shorefront homes. Collins Avenue, as Hwy-A1A, continues north to Hollywood and Fort Lauderdale (see p.177).

1

Ancient Spanish Monastery

16711 W Dixie Hwy, North Miami Beach • Mon–Sat 10am–4.30pm, Sun 11am–4.30pm • $10 • ☎ 305 945 1461, ⓦ spanishmonastery.com

Visitors may be surprised to learn that an **Ancient Spanish Monastery**, built in Segovia, Spain, in 1141, lurks just off West Dixie Highway, four miles northwest of Haulover Beach. A monastery for seven hundred years, it shuttered in the 1830s because of a social revolution. The grounds remained boarded up until it was spotted by travelling newspaper magnate William Randolph Hearst, who bought the whole kit-and-kaboodle in 1925 and had it sent back to the States for reconstruction. Soon after, Hearst went bust, and the structure (which was shipped over in an impressive 11,000 crates) wasn't reassembled until 1954, when it was purchased and rebuilt in Miami to the tune of $1.5 million.

Now an Episcopal church, the cloisters are a beguiling place, with lush foliage and a meditative garden. Take note of the chapel's beautiful, telescopic stained-glass windows, which date to the twelfth century.

Downtown Miami and around

For years **DOWNTOWN MIAMI** was the chaotic, Latin heart of the city, but while a few Cuban coffee counters remain, those days are largely gone. The whole area, from Brickell in the south to the Omni mall north of I-395, is being transformed by one of the largest construction booms in the United States. Vast, shimmering towers of glass and steel line the waterfront: a mixture of offices, hotels and, above all, flashy condos. While it has retained its commercial core, downtown is quickly becoming an upmarket residential area.

Downtown's best attractions are **HistoryMiami** and the absorbing modern art round-up at the **Pérez Art Museum Miami**, but you should also make time for a boat tour of **Biscayne Bay** from **Bayside Marketplace**. The main artery is **Flagler Street**, largely given over to cut-price electronics, clothes and jewellery stores. Most of the new development lies along the bay; a few blocks inland change is proceeding more slowly, where older neighbourhoods – and roughness – remain. Wandering downtown on foot is manageable and safe enough during the day, though the Metromover (see p.88) is a handy way to jump between the main sights.

WATSON ISLAND

Travelling between Miami Beach and downtown it's worth stopping at **Watson Island**, midway along the MacArthur Causeway as you cross Biscayne Bay. Here you'll find **Jungle Island** (Mon–Fri 10am–5pm, Sat & Sun 10am–6pm; $34.95, parking $10; ☎ 305 400 7000, ⓦ jungleisland.com), a wildlife park that features a flamingo lake, serpentarium, parrot bowl and even a tiger compound, all hidden within a lushly landscaped jungle habitat. One of the best areas is the Manu Encounter, modelled on a Peruvian mountaintop, where you can wander among free-flying macaws. Next door, the renovated **Ichimura Miami-Japan Garden** (daily 9am–6pm; free; ⓦ friendsofjapanesegarden.com) was established in the 1950s, but given a smart makeover in 2006, making for a delightful, if tiny, place to stroll.

Opposite the garden and Jungle Island sits the **Miami Children's Museum** (daily 10am–6pm; $18; ☎ 305 373 5437, ⓦ miamichildrensmuseum.org), housed in a jagged building designed by Arquitectonica (see p.67). It's a quirky place, ideal to amuse restive kids for an afternoon or so: among other interactive exhibits, there's a mini supermarket and television studio, and even a bank where you can design your own currency. The Castle of Dreams indoor playground is terrific for any tykes who need to burn off excess energy.

There's plentiful **parking** on the island if you're coming by car (the car park near the museum is $1/hr); otherwise, you can catch bus #S or #C from either downtown or South Beach.

Flagler Street

Busy **Flagler Street**, the traditional heart of downtown Miami, has seen great change in the past five years. Once a scruffy mix of panhandling and discount stores, it has renewed itself with sidewalk cafés, restaurants and bars – and become an emblem of downtown's liveability.

Gusman Center for the Performing Arts

174 E Flagler St • ☎ 305 374 2444, ⓦ gusmancenter.org

The **Gusman Center for the Performing Arts** began life in 1926 as the vaudeville **Olympia Theater**, and also hosts the Downtown Welcome Center (see p.86). It's worth a look at the lobby for a taster of the exquisitely kitsch trappings inside, though to experience the Moorish-inspired auditorium (complete with a twinkly starscape ceiling) you'll have to see a performance.

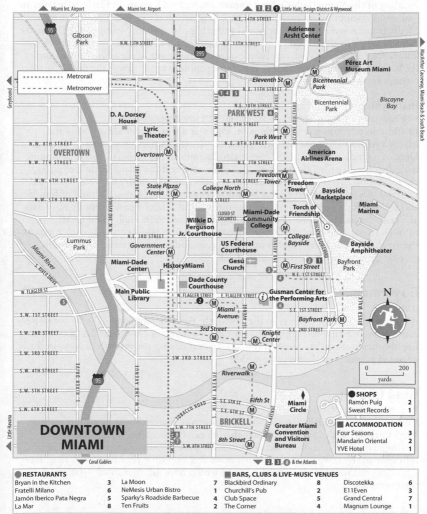

● RESTAURANTS				
Bryan in the Kitchen	3	La Moon	7
Fratelli Milano	6	NeMesis Urban Bistro	1
Jamón Iberico Pata Negra	5	Sparky's Roadside Barbecue	4
La Mar	8	Ten Fruits	2

■ BARS, CLUBS & LIVE-MUSIC VENUES			
Blackbird Ordinary	8	Discotekka	6
Churchill's Pub	2	E11Even	3
Club Space	5	Grand Central	7
The Corner	4	Magnum Lounge	1

● SHOPS	
Ramón Puig	2
Sweat Records	1

■ ACCOMMODATION	
Four Seasons	3
Mandarin Oriental	2
YVE Hotel	1

1

Dade County Courthouse
73 W Flagler St

Six forbidding Doric columns mark the entrance to the handsome **Dade County Courthouse**. Completed in 1928 on the site of an earlier courthouse – where public hangings used to take place – this was Miami's tallest building (360ft) for 44 years, and at night, it projected lights showing off its distinctive stepped-pyramid peak, beaming out a symbolic warning to wrongdoers all over the city. Little inside the courthouse is worth passing the security check for.

Miami-Dade Cultural Center
101 W Flagler St

From Dade County Courthouse, cross SW First Avenue toward the air-raid-shelter-like building of the **Miami-Dade Cultural Center**, entered via a ramp off Flagler. This was an ambitious attempt by renowned architect Philip Johnson to create a postmodern Mediterranean-style piazza, a congenial gathering place where Miami could display its cultural side. The theory almost worked: a superb historical museum and a major library frame the courtyard, but Johnson forgot the power of the south Florida sun. Rather than pausing to rest and gossip, most people scamper across the open space towards the nearest shade.

HistoryMiami
101 W Flagler St • Mon–Sat 10am–5pm, Sun noon–5pm • $8 • ☎ 305 375 1492, ⊛ historymiami.org

In addition to temporary exhibitions on topics as diverse as Florida cartoons and Miami's African Diaspora, the **HistoryMiami** museum houses a permanent "Tropical Dreams" section upstairs, a well-chronicled account of the region's history. Beginning with displays on early Native American inhabitants and the **Miami Circle** (see p.67), the exhibition covers early European colonization and the rivalry between Spain and England. Also well charted are the Seminole Wars; the fluctuating fortunes of Key West and its "wrecking", sponge and cigar industries; and Miami Beach, from its early days as a celebrity vacation spot – with amusing photos of 1920s Hollywood greats – through to the renovation of the Art Deco district. The exhibition ends with a look at the arrival of Cuban and Haitian immigrants, including two genuine refugee rafts, shockingly small given their passenger load.

Government Center
11 NW 1st St

Adjoining the Cultural Center to the north, the **Government Center** chiefly comprises county government offices, notable as the place where, on November 22, 2000, young Republicans stormed the Stephen P. Clark Center to stop the **recount** of votes in the disputed presidential election (see p.458).

Gesù Church
118 NE 2nd St • ☎ 305 379 1424, ⊛ gesuchurch.org

Commercial activity falls away as you head north of Flagler Street. Look out for the 1925 Catholic **Gesù Church**, its peach-sherbet exterior adorned with foamy lemon-meringue touches. The stout, dimly lit interior usually hums with private prayers and is brightened by lavish stained-glass windows and imposing marble *retablo* (altarpiece) – it's designed without pillars so the Jesuits would have uninterrupted sightlines for their sermons.

US Federal Courthouse

300 NE 1st Ave • ☎ 305 523 5100

North along First Avenue is Miami's courthouse district. The old **US Federal Courthouse** (now the David W. Dyer Federal Building), with its Neoclassical design and Corinthian columns, was finished in 1931. Sadly, in 2008 the deterioration of the building (the mould in the basement is said to have been a serious health hazard) forced its closure.

Bayside Marketplace

401 Biscayne Blvd • Mon–Thurs 10am–10pm, Fri & Sat 10am–11pm, Sun 11am–9pm • Free • ☎ 305 577 3344, ⓦ baysidemarketplace.com

Typical Miamian consumerism is on display at the **Bayside Marketplace**, a large, pink shopping mall providing pleasant waterfront views from its terraces. The seascapes are reason enough to stop by, though you'd be remiss not to take one of the **boat tours** around **Biscayne Bay** that leave from the dock here (see box below).

Bayfront Park

Bayside Marketplace caps the northern end of **Bayfront Park**, a pleasant enough green space that is home to the John F. Kennedy Memorial **Torch of Friendship**. It was designed in 1960 to symbolize good relations between the US and its southern neighbours, with a pointed space left for the Cuban national emblem among the alphabetically sorted crests of each country.

BISCAYNE BAY'S MILLION-DOLLAR MANSIONS

America's rich and famous have been coming to Miami for years, hiding away within ostentatious palm-smothered mansions on the keys that lie between the city and Miami Beach. With the exception of Fisher Island, all of these can be reached by road (from the causeways that cross Biscayne Bay), but the only way to get a good look at the houses is to take a **boat tour** from **Bayside Marketplace**. These are unashamedly touristy, but provide fabulous views of the city, and include a narrated jaunt around some of the most exclusive keys (which must seriously irritate their affluent inhabitants). Guides will point out the opulent mansions of Shaquille O'Neal, Sean Combs (aka Diddy) and Gloria Estefan on Star Island, Oprah Winfrey's palace on Fisher Island and Al Capone's former abode on Palm Island, among numerous others.

You can also tour the same islands by **kayak**, though it pays to take the boat tour first so you know which celebrity backyard you're paddling past. Be sure to stop at **Flagler Memorial Island**, which is topped with a 110ft obelisk honouring oil baron and Miami pioneer Henry Flagler, and has picnic tables and a short strip of sand, though it can get mobbed at the weekends.

BOAT TOURS

Heritage of Miami II ☎ 305 358 7600, ⓦ miami aquatours.com. For a sedate voyage around the bay, try this elegant cruise ship that makes multiple, 1hr 15min circuits (Mon–Sat 11.30am, 12.30pm, 1.30pm, 2.30pm, 4.30pm, 5.30pm & 6.30pm) for $27.

Island Queen Cruises ☎ 305 379 5119, ⓦ island queencruises.com. Daily boat tours (10.30am–7pm; at 10.30am and then on the hour; 1hr 30min) cost $28, or $24 if purchased online.

Thriller Speed Boat ☎ 305 373 7001, ⓦ thriller miami.com. Offers 45min powerboat tours (daily 11am, 12.30pm, 2pm, 3.30pm and 5pm) for $36.

WATER TAXI

Water Taxi Miami ☎ 305 600 2511, ⓦ water taximiami.com. This convenient service (daily 11am–7pm) zips between Bayside Market-place and Alton Rd, on the southwest side of Miami Beach (a 15min walk to the sand). $15 one way, $25 round trip.

KAYAK TRIPS

South Beach Kayak 1771 Purdy Ave, Miami Beach, near the Venetian Causeway ☎ 305 975 5087, ⓦ southbeachkayak.com. Mon–Fri 10.30am–6pm, Sat & Sun 9am–6pm; rentals $25/2hr, $40/4hr.

1

American Airlines Arena

601 Biscayne Blvd • Miami Heat tickets $10–400 • ☏ 786 777 1000, ⊛ aaarena.com

Adjacent to Bayfront Park and situated on Biscayne Bay, the **American Airlines Arena** is home to the city's much-loved **Miami Heat basketball team**. After a period of stagnation following their 2006 National Basketball Championship win, the Heat catapulted back into the spotlight in 2010 with the acquisition of LeBron James and Chris Bosh, who, combined with Dwyane Wade, formed what the media dubbed "The Big Three" – a superstar triumvirate that created a major buzz for the team and helped snag further titles in 2012 and 2013.

North of downtown

The once impoverished area of waterfront north of downtown Miami is being transformed by a spate of new condos, hotels and cultural projects, notably **Museum Park** and its gorgeous **Pérez Art Museum Miami**, the revitalization of the Omni shopping mall on Biscayne Boulevard between 15th and 17th streets, and the astonishing César Pelli-designed Performing Arts Center, a sprawling Modernist masterpiece.

Freedom Tower

600 Biscayne Blvd • Wed–Sun noon–5pm, open till 8pm first Fri of the month • Free • ☏ 305 577 3344, ⊛ mdcmoad.org

There's one notable attraction on Biscayne Boulevard, across from Bayside Marketplace: the 225ft **Freedom Tower**, originally home to the now-defunct *Miami Daily News*. It earned its current name by housing the Cuban Refugee Center, which began operations in 1962. Most of those who left Cuba on the "freedom flights" got their first taste of US bureaucracy here: between 1965 and 1972, ten empty planes left Miami each week to collect Cubans allowed by Fidel Castro to leave the island. The 1925 building isn't the only one in Miami that was modelled on the Giralda bell tower in Seville, Spain; so was the *Biltmore Hotel* in Coral Gables (see p.77). Today the tower is owned by Miami-Dade College and is used as an art exhibition space.

Park West

Beyond the Freedom Tower lies **Park West**, a warehouse district that the city has cannily designated a nightlife zone – it's also called the "downtown nightclub district" – granting 24-hour alcohol licences to a cluster of clubs along 11th Street (see p.99) with the idea that it will draw traffic away from South Beach's choked bars.

Adrienne Arsht Center for the Performing Arts

1300 Biscayne Blvd • Tours Mon & Sat noon • ☏ 305 949 6722, ⊛ arshtcenter.org

Masterminded by architect César Pelli, the enormous **Adrienne Arsht Center for the Performing Arts** opened in 2006 as the second-largest performing arts centre in the US, after New York's Lincoln Center. The one historic landmark on the site, the octagonal, medieval-fortress-like Art Deco tower next to the opera house, was once part of the now-demolished 1929 Sears flagship building, and now houses a *Books & Books* café (see p.103).

The best way to appreciate Pelli's grand vision is to take a **free one-hour tour** from the Ziff Ballet Opera House, which includes all the theatres, as well as a peek into star dressing rooms, private rooms and lounges not open to the public. It's a thrill to attend a performance at one of the three main venues (see p.100); the **John S. and James L. Knight Concert Hall** is a 2200-seat shoebox-design space intended to maximize acoustics; the slightly larger **Ziff Ballet Opera House** is devoted to opera, dance and Broadway-style shows; and the tiny **Carnival Studio Theater**, with a flexible 200-seat auditorium, is available to local arts groups.

1

The centre has two resident companies: the Florida Grand Opera and Miami City Ballet. The superb Cleveland Orchestra has also signed on for a ten-year residency, during which it will stage a three-concert series in south Florida every winter.

Pérez Art Museum Miami (PAMM)

1103 Biscayne Blvd • Tues–Sun 10am–6pm, Thurs 10am–9pm • $16, free every first Thurs and second Sat of the month • ☎ 305 375 3000, ⓦ pamm.org

On the edge of Biscayne Bay, the **Pérez Art Museum Miami (PAMM)** has a stunning location and an intelligently curated permanent collection. Formerly the Miami Art Museum, it was rechristened in 2013 and moved from the Metro-Dade Cultural Center into a showy new three-storey building in Museum Park. Galleries contain a notable selection of post-1940 artworks (particularly strong on Latin American artists) and showcases outstanding international travelling exhibits (the first focused on the work of Ai Weiwei). The museum's most exceptional feature, however, is its setting – views reach across Biscayne Bay to the MacArthur Causeway and twinkling Miami Beach, and the wide front plaza is landscaped with a forest of tropical foliage and incredible hanging plant installations, nearly as tall as the building itself.

Overtown

From the earliest days, Coloredtown, as **OVERTOWN** was previously known, was divided by train tracks from the white folks of downtown Miami: cordoned off from the rest of the population, the black community here thrived – during the 1930s, jazz clubs crammed NW Second Avenue between Sixth and Tenth streets (then variously known as Little Broadway, The Strip or even The Great Black Way), thrilling multiracial audiences. By World War II, though, the area was in decline, accelerated rapidly in the 1960s by the construction of the I-95 freeway through the neighbourhood, which displaced some 20,000 residents and isolated it from local amenities. Overtown came to be synonymous with Miami's every ill, from drugs to violence, and though today it's clawing its way back to economic health, it can still be a dangerous place for visitors even during the day. If you're curious to visit this historic part of Miami, make sure to do so on an organized tour (see p.86) – preferably one that includes the **Overtown Historic District**.

D.A. Dorsey House

250 NW 9th St

Though it's now dirty and rubbish-strewn, there are a few remnants of Overtown's glory days still standing here, notably the **D.A. Dorsey House**. This white, two-storey clapboard home is an exact replica of the one built in 1914 by the first African-American millionaire in Miami (fittingly, given today's construction boom, Dana Albert Dorsey made his money in property). The house is a private home with no public access.

Lyric Theater

819 NW 2nd Ave • ☎ 305 636 2390, ⓦ theblackarchives.org

Close to the Dorsey House, on a deserted strip, is the regal **Lyric Theater**, where the likes of Nat King Cole and Lena Horne were once regular performers. A beautiful renovation of the structure began in 2004, which included the addition of a glass atrium to its northern side to expand the theatre's capacity. The theatre anchors one of several ambitious projects to regenerate the district, given the umbrella title **Overtown Folklife Village**.

The Miami Circle

1

401 Brickell Ave • Daily sunrise–sunset • Free, tours $30; reservations required • Tours ☎ 305 375 5792, ⊛ historymiami.org

Fifteen minutes' walk south along SE Second Avenue from Flagler Street, the **Miami River** marks the southern limit of downtown, now totally hemmed in by skyscrapers. As you cross the Brickell Bridge, glance across to the tip of the southern bank; you should be able to make out the mysterious ring of 24 holes cut into the limestone bedrock known as the **Miami Circle**. The developer who bought this land for a condo complex was shocked when in 1998 archeologists monitoring the demolition unearthed the circle, along with prehistoric remains such as shell tools and pottery shards, carbon-dated to be 1700 to 2000 years old; after a heated legal contest and local protests, the developer agreed to sell the site to the state (for a tidy profit of just over $18 million), and today it's a beautiful park that remains conspicuously condo-free. No one knows much about the circle's true purpose, though it seems reasonable to assume that it was constructed by the ancestors of the Tequesta people. **HistoryMiami**, which has a permanent exhibit on the circle (see p.62), took over management of the site in 2008, and offers historical walking tours of the area. There are also free video and audio tours at ⊛ historymiami.org.

Brickell

In the 1870s, "father of Miami" William Brickell established a trading post on the south side of the Miami River, in an area now known as **BRICKELL** (rhymes with pickle). Beginning immediately across the Brickell Bridge and running to Coconut Grove (see p.78), its main thoroughfare, **Brickell Avenue**, was *the* address in 1910s Miami, easily justifying its "millionaires' row" nickname. While the original grand homes have largely disappeared, money is still Brickell Avenue's most obvious asset: over the bridge begins a half-mile parade of **condominiums and banks**, whose imposing forms are softened by forecourts filled with sculptures, fountains and palm trees. Far from being places to change travellers' cheques, these institutions are bastions of international high finance. From the late 1970s, Miami emerged as a corporate banking centre, cashing in on political instability in South and Central America by offering a secure home for Latin American money, some of which needed laundering.

Four Seasons Hotel and Espírito Santo Plaza

1435 Brickell Ave • ☎ 305 358 3535, ⊛ fourseasons.com/miami

At 789ft, the seventy-storey **Four Seasons Hotel** is one of the city's loftiest buildings. The posh bars and restaurants inside (enhanced by a modern sculpture collection worth over $3.5 million) make for a luxurious if expensive pit stop, though you won't get higher than the twentieth floor (the upper levels are private condos). Highlights include the massive **Fernando Botero** bronze sculpture in the lobby, *Seated Woman, 2002*.

Don't miss the sparkling glass tower of **Espírito Santo Plaza**, nearby at 1395 Brickell Ave, a local favourite for its scintillating 36-storey curving facade.

The Atlantis

2025 Brickell Ave

South of the *Four Seasons Hotel* (and best seen from a car or bus window), pricey condo towers now overshadow the building that most defined Miami in the 1980s: the **Atlantis**. Finished in 1983, the Atlantis crowned several years of innovative construction by a small architectural firm called **Arquitectonica**, whose style – variously termed "beach-blanket Bauhaus" and "ecstatic modernism" – fused postmodern thought with a strong sense of Miami's eclectic architectural heritage. The building's focal point is a gaping square hole through its middle where a palm tree, a jacuzzi and a red-painted spiral staircase tease the eye.

1

The Biscayne Corridor

On Miami's north side lie sections of the city that have only recently appeared on visitor itineraries, in an area known as the **Biscayne Corridor**, after its main artery, Biscayne Boulevard. The most noteworthy example of its rebirth is in the southernmost area, where neighbourhoods are being transformed by the migration of **contemporary art galleries**. The **Wynwood Arts District**, famed for its astonishing murals, has become a haven for artists. Further north is the more upscale **Design District**, while **Little Haiti** is a great place to try cheap, tasty Caribbean food. Art fans should also make the trek up to North Miami for the overlooked **Museum of Contemporary Art**, the city's arresting showcase for the avant-garde.

Wynwood Arts District

Bound between NW 20th and NW 37th sts, I-95 and N Miami Ave • Art Walk second Sat of the month 6–10pm • ⓦ wynwoodmiami.com • Bus #2 runs through the heart of the district

The **Wynwood Arts District** is home to one of the largest and most dynamic concentrations of **art galleries** in the city. Most of the seventy or so exhibition spaces occupy an area of mural-emblazoned warehouses, boutiques and coffee shops. It's great fun to wander around: nearly all the buildings, and even the car parks, are wrapped in gorgeous swathes of graffiti art, collectively transforming what was once a scruffy corner of Miami into a grandiose string of world-class art.

Margulies Collection at the Warehouse

591 NW 27th St • Nov to late April Wed–Sat 11am–4pm • $10 • ☎ 305 576 1051, ⓦ margulieswarehouse.com

If you're visiting in season, be sure to make a stop at the **Margulies Collection at the Warehouse**, a beautifully presented ensemble of video, sculpture and a particularly fine collection of twentieth-century photography, with work by Walker Evans and Cindy Sherman.

Rubell Collection

95 NW 29th St • Jan–July & Dec Tues–Sat 10am–6pm, Sun 10am–4pm • $10 • ☎ 305 573 6090, ⓦ rfc.museum

The **Rubell Collection** is a massive modern-art collection housed in an old warehouse once used by the Drug Enforcement Agency for storing evidence. A comprehensive survey of the last forty years in modern art, the collection sets acknowledged masterpieces alongside lesser-known, more experimental work, including early photography from Cindy Sherman, postmodern sculpture from Jeff Koons, and graffiti canvases by the late Keith Haring.

ART WALK

On the second Saturday of every month Wynwood's galleries and studios open their doors to the public for **Art Walk**: a festive evening of art, music and refreshments (6–10pm), and the neighbourhood comes alive with swarms of stylish fans – it's really not to be missed. You can get details from any of the galleries listed here, or check out ⓦ wynwoodmiami.com (the "walk" is an open evening rather than an organized guided tour). Most of the action centres on NW Second Avenue, where parking can get very tight during Art Walk – it's a good idea to leave your car further out (try NW 5th Ave).

Highlights include **Emerson Dorsch** (151 NW 24th St; Tues–Sat noon–5pm; ☎ 305 576 1278, ⓦ dorschgallery.com), a warehouse crammed with tantalizing canvases and avant-garde multimedia, and **Wynwood Walls** (167 NW 25th St; Wed–Sat noon–10pm; ☎ 305 722 8959, ⓦ thewynwoodwalls.com), whose grassy courtyard, encircled by an eye-opening collection of graffiti art, functions as the pulsing, neon heart of Art Walk, complete with cocktails, live bands and an enthusiastic crowd that mills about and soaks up the scene until the wee hours.

1

Bakehouse Art Complex
561 NW 32nd St · Daily noon–5pm · Free · ☎ 305 576 2828, ⓦ bacfl.org

Art appreciators should be sure to check out the contemporary works cooked up by residents at the **Bakehouse Art Complex**, which comprises two galleries, ceramic kiln, woodworking and welding areas, and seventy individual artist studios.

Midtown
Bounded by 32nd and 36th sts, Midtown Blvd and N Miami Ave · ⓦ midtownmiami.com

Located in the northeastern corner of Wynwood (just before I-195 and the Design District), Midtown Miami is a stylish shopping centre comprising restaurants, a Target department store, boutiques, chain stores and art galleries. While it's currently pretty nondescript, the area is definitely up-and-coming, exemplified by its food scene – Midtown plays host to some of the buzziest eateries in town (see p.94).

The Design District
Bounded by 38th and 42nd sts, N Miami Ave and Biscayne Blvd · Most shops open Mon–Sat 11am–5pm · ⓦ miamidesigndistrict.net · Bus #9 and #10 zip up and down NE 2nd Ave from downtown ($2.25); metered parking is available everywhere for $1.50/hr

Miami's flourishing **Design District** was originally a pineapple plantation owned by Theodore Moore, the "Pineapple King of Florida". On a whim, he opened a furniture showroom on NE 40th Street, and had soon created what became known as **Decorators' Row**. During Miami's Art Deco building boom of the 1920s and 1930s, this was the centre of the city's design scene, filled with wholesale interiors stores selling furniture and flooring.

By the early 1990s, though, the factory-filled district was deserted and crime-ridden. Savvy developer Craig Robins, one of the masterminds behind the gentrification of South Beach, spotted the potential here and started buying buildings, enticing high-end showrooms like Knoll and Kartell. Robins has overseen the regeneration of the area, including an emphasis on public art and sculpture.

The Design District can be an intriguing area for a stroll, though note that the main emphasis (obviously) is on designer furniture and art galleries. Robins' initial plans have been revamped somewhat, and now the district's twenty art galleries and around seventy design showrooms have been joined by luxury retailers like Prada, Hermès, and Louboutin, trendy **restaurants** (see p.94) and jazzy, mid-rise condo towers. Most of the action takes place on 39th and 40th streets between NE Second Avenue and N Miami Avenue.

Living Room Building
4000 N Miami Ave, at NW 40th St

One of Robins' best-known projects is the whimsical **Living Room Building**. The entranceway to this squat office block has been turned inside out, and features a giant black concrete sofa and two standard lamps, as well as floral wallpaper walls – in other words, a witty, irresistible photo opportunity (though it's been marred slightly by graffiti).

Locust Projects
3852 N Miami Ave · Tues–Sat 10am–5pm · Free · ☎ 305 576 8570, ⓦ locustprojects.org

Relocated from the Wynwood Arts District (where it was a catalyst for the neighbourhood's rejuvenation), **Locust Projects** is a well-respected, avant-garde gallery that always has something interesting going on, be it a splashy mural, billboard or multimedia installation.

Haitian Heritage Museum
4141 NE 2nd Ave, #105C · Tues–Fri 10am–5pm, second Sat of each month 7–10pm · $10 · ☎ 305 371 5988, ⓦ haitianheritagemuseum.org

The **Haitian Heritage Museum** showcases Haitian visual arts and Haitian literary works. Founded in 2004, its small but intriguing gallery space is powered by charismatic staff who aim to "give people a taste of Haiti" through lectures, cultural workshops and art.

1

Little Haiti

Coming from the Design District, take the Little Haiti Connection (bus #202; $2.25)

About 200,000 Haitians live in Miami, forming one of the city's major ethnic groups – albeit it far smaller than the Cuban population – and roughly a third of them live in **LITTLE HAITI**, a district running along the bay from 40th to 85th streets. There are few specific sights in Little Haiti, so it's best to wander along the main drag, NE Second Avenue (known here as "Felix Morisseau-Leroy Avenue"), and enjoy the Caribbean colours, music and smells. Almost all Miami's Haitians speak English as a third language after Creole and French, so you'll see trilingual signage throughout. Though it's relatively safe to explore, the area remains dodgy at night and caution should be taken.

Caribbean Marketplace and Little Haiti Cultural Center

It's easy enough to spot one of the area's landmarks, the **Caribbean Marketplace** at 5927 NE Second Ave (Thurs–Sun 11am–8pm), with its brightly coloured woodwork modelled after the Iron Market in Port-au-Prince, Haiti. After years of neglect, the market was completely renovated in 2009 as part of the **Little Haiti Cultural Center** behind it at 212–260 NE 59th Terrace (☎305 960 2969, ⊛littlehaiticulturalcenter .com), which serves as a theatre/auditorium, dance facility, community meeting room and gallery space.

Libreri Mapou

5919 NE 2nd Ave • Daily 11am–7pm • ☎305 757 9922, ⊛librerimapou.com

For a taste of Caribbean music, head to **Libreri Mapou**, a bookstore that's packed with a wide assortment of reading materials and CDs in addition to bottles of the owner's home-made "Kremas Mapou" drink mix – a boozy blend of rum, caramel, milk, Haitian spices and coconut.

SANTERÍA: SAINTS AND SACRIFICES

Estimated numbers of those practicing the Caribbean religion of **Santería** worldwide vary wildly, anywhere from 60,000 up to 5 million; regardless, it has a hidden but influential role in Miami society, as many people are at least part-time believers. A secretive religion with an oral tradition, Santería was one of the many spiritual hybrids created under colonial rule. Slaves, many of them Yoruba from West Africa, were forcibly baptized and converted to Christianity, but this conversion proved to be largely cosmetic: to preserve their own religions, gods or **orishas** in the African pantheon were "translated" into Christian saints, so that they could be worshipped without fear of being caught. In fact, the name Santería itself began as slang, when colonial Spaniards noticed how greatly their African slaves venerated the saints rather than Christ.

Much like the gods in Ancient Greece, *orishas* have flaws and favourites: each is identified with a given colour, food and number, and requires animal sacrifices and human praise for nourishment. Altars in Santería temples are covered with offerings of cigarettes or designer perfume – the *orishas* are all too human in their vulnerability to flattery and expensive gifts. Religious services, conducted in secret by a priest or priestess, involve channelling the gods through dance and trance. Its practitioners can get *orishas* to give aid and guidance through plant, food or animal sacrifices offered during chants and dancing initiations.

Wandering around Miami, you'll see signs of **Santería activity** if you look hard enough – streetside offerings, usually found by holy kapok trees, are common in Little Havana and Haiti. There is also much sensationalist reporting when Santería offerings are discovered near local courthouses, supposedly attempts by family members to invoke the *orishas'* help during trials. Despite opposition to the religion – much of it from animal-rights activists – a court case in Miami's Hialeah district in 1993 confirmed the constitutional rights of adherents to practice their religion.

1

Dupuis Building
Southeast corner of NE 2nd Ave and 62nd St

A short walk north of Libreri Mapou sits one of the oldest buildings in the area. Built in 1902 in what was once the heart of Lemon City, the now-derelict **Dupuis Building** served as a pharmacy and a post office before being abandoned several decades ago. While you can't go inside, the facade is attractive enough, and offers a glimpse into what life was like in Little Haiti nearly a century ago.

Toussaint L'Ouverture statue
Intersection of N Miami Ave and 62nd St

A few blocks northwest of the neighbourhood's centre you'll find the striking 13.5ft bronze statue of the father of Haitian independence, **Toussaint L'Ouverture**, erected in 2005. Born a slave in 1743, the self-educated Toussaint went on to galvanize the people of Haiti (the country was then known as Saint-Domingue) into a force that overthrew its French colonizers on New Year's Day, 1804.

Northeast 54th Street
If you're in the area, be sure to make a detour down **NE 54th Street** (particularly near its intersection with NE 2nd Ave), the heart of Miami's *voudou* and Santería culture (see box, p.70), which has a handful of **botánicas**, stores where believers can purchase ritual potions, candles and statuettes. Almost all will permit a casual visitor to browse their merchandise but it goes without saying that photographing the racks of gaudy statuary and glass jars packed with herbs could cause offence.

Museum of Contemporary Art
770 NE 125th St • Tues–Sun 11am–5pm • $5 • ☎ 305 893 6211, ⊛ mocanomi.org • Take bus #16, #10 or #G to the corner of NE 125th St and NE 8th Ave

Ten miles north of downtown, Biscayne Boulevard leads into **North Miami**, another neighbourhood noted for its Haitian community. The main reason for visiting this blue-collar community is the small but absorbing **Museum of Contemporary Art**. Temporary exhibits here feature young and emerging local and international talent – expect extremely innovative multimedia work blending film and installations with traditional art forms. You may also see pieces from the museum's permanent collection, with art by Yoko Ono, John Baldessari, Dan Flavin, Louise Nevelson and Gabriel Orozco. At research time, the museum was in the midst of a dispute with North Miami officials, and there was a discussion about splitting the collection with a new space in the Design District.

Little Havana

The impact of **Cubans** – unquestionably the largest ethnic group in Miami – on the city over the last four decades has been incalculable. Unlike most Latino immigrants to the US, Miami's first Cuban arrivals in the late 1950s had already tasted affluence in their home country. They rose quickly through the social strata and nowadays wield considerable clout in the running of the city, and indeed the state.

Cubans first settled a few miles west of downtown Miami in what became known as **LITTLE HAVANA**, a quiet district of sherbet-coloured houses where you're more likely to see newspaper boxes selling *El Nuevo Herald* than the English-language *Miami Herald*, and statues of Cuba's patron saint, the Virgin Mary, in front gardens. Only the neighbourhood's main strip, SW 8th Street, or **Calle Ocho**, offers more than houses: street-side counters serve up tiny cups of sweet Cuban coffee; the odours of baking bread and cigars being rolled waft across the sidewalk; shops sell Santería

1

ephemera (see box, p.70) beside 6ft-high models of Catholic saints; and you'll spot the only branch of *Dunkin' Donuts* with guava-filled doughnuts. Though there are few official sights, most people come here to gorge themselves on the delicious, gut-busting Cuban food in one of the local restaurants and to wander around the monuments on Cuban Memorial Boulevard (see p.73). For all the reminders of the area's fierce connection to Cuba, Little Havana is increasingly a misnomer: as the successful Cuban community decamps to wealthier neighbourhoods like Coral Gables, they're gradually replaced by Latin American immigrants from Honduras, Colombia and Nicaragua (the eastern portion of Little Havana is often referred to as Little Managua).

Be sure to check out the **Calle Ocho Festival** in March (see p.102), and at other times of year the **Viernes Culturales** (Cultural Fridays), an arts, music and culture fair held every last Friday night of the month (7–11pm) along Calle Ocho between 13th and 17th avenues (ⓦviernesculturales.org).

Calle Ocho and around

Little Havana's main drag, **Calle Ocho**, is a vibrant stretch packed with tantalizing restaurants and the bulk of the area's commercial offerings, including shops selling music, cigars and souvenirs. At the corner of SW 15th Avenue, you'll spot a charming 1926 Art Deco **theatre** that's still in use by movie-goers today (see p.102).

THE CUBAN QUESTION

Proximity to Cuba has long made Florida a refuge for its activists and economic migrants. A raft from Cuba's northern shore can take four days to arrive in south Florida. However, until comparatively recent times, New York, not Miami, was the centre of Cuban émigré life in the US.

During the mid-1950s, when opposition to the Batista dictatorship began to assert itself, a trickle of Cubans started arriving in the predominantly Jewish section of Miami called Riverside. The trickle became a flood when **Fidel Castro** came to power, and as Cuban businesses sprang up on SW 8th Street and Cubans began making their mark on Miami life, the area began to be known as **Little Havana**.

These Cubans were derived largely from the affluent middle classes and stood to lose the most under communism. Many regarded themselves as the entrepreneurial sophisticates of the Caribbean. Stories are plentiful of formerly high-flying Cuban capitalists who arrived penniless and, over the course of two decades – and aided by a network of old expats – toiled, wheeled and dealed their way to positions of power and influence.

The second great Cuban influx into Miami was of a quite different social nature: the **Mariel boatlift**, which in May 1980 brought 125,000 islanders from the Cuban port of Mariel to Miami. These arrivals were largely poor and uneducated; a percentage of them fresh from Cuban jails – incarcerated for criminal rather than political crimes. Most "Marielitos" settled in South Beach, where they proceeded to terrorize the local community, becoming a source of embarrassment for Miami's longer-established, determinedly respectable Cubans.

Local division gives way to fervent agreement when discussing Castro: he's universally detested. But despite failing to depose the Cuban leader, Cuban-Americans (who have a seventy percent turn-out rate at elections) have been far more successful at influencing the US government. Ronald Reagan gained immense popularity among Miami Cubans for his support of the Nicaraguan Contras – and for his conservative policies in general – in the 1980s (12th Ave is dubbed "Ronald Reagan Blvd"). Cubans have been vociferous supporters of the **Republican Party** ever since, though things are changing; in the landmark 2008 presidential election, 55 percent of Miami Cuban-Americans aged 29 or younger voted for Barack Obama. And with **Raúl Castro** formally replacing his ailing brother as Cuban president in 2008, the US Cuban community is planning for the post-Fidel era and the eventual end of the **US embargo of Cuba** (imposed in 1962).

Brigade 2506 Memorial

1

SW 8th St and SW 13th Ave

The defining events and heroes of the Cuban-American community are honoured along **Cuban Memorial Boulevard** (SW 13th Ave, just south of Calle Ocho), of which the **Brigade 2506 Memorial** is the best known. Inscribed with the brigade crest and topped by an eternal flame, this simple stone pillar remembers those who died at the Bay of Pigs on April 17, 1961, during the attempt by a group of US-trained Cuban exiles to invade the island and wrest control from Castro. Depending on who tells the story, the outcome was the result of either ill-conceived plans, or the US's lack of commitment to Cuba (JFK withheld air support that may have changed the battle's outcome) – to this day, sections of the Cuban community hate Kennedy only slightly less than they do Fidel Castro. Every anniversary, veterans clad in combat fatigues and carrying assault rifles gather here to make pledges of patriotism throughout the night.

The Cuban map monument and bust of Antonio Maceo

SW 13th Ave and SW 10th St

Near the Brigade 2506 Memorial lies a 16ft raised **map of Cuba** bearing a worn inscription by independence hero José Martí: *La patria es agonía y deber* ("The homeland is agony and duty"). The massive **tree** looming over the monuments is a beautiful kapok, sacred to the Santería religion (see box, p.70), and as such you'll sometimes find candles and offerings – such as candy and teddy bears – placed amid its knobbly roots. Further along is a simple bust of Cuban independence fighter **Antonio Maceo**, and a statue of the Virgin Mary, often with bouquets of flowers at her feet.

Los Pinareños Frutería

1334 SW 8th St • Mon–Sat 6am–6pm, Sun 6am–3pm • ☎ 305 285 1135

On the corner of Calle Ocho and the Memorial Boulevard is one of the oldest and best open-air coffee counters in the area, *Los Pinareños Frutería*. Order a potent *cafecito*, *batido de níspero* (loquat smoothie), sugar cane juice or *coco frío* (coconut water), served straight out of the shell. The place doubles as a small tropical-fruit stall.

El Titan de Bronze Cigars and Little Havana To Go

Walk east for one of the area's treasures, **El Titán de Bronze Cigars** at 1071 SW 8th St near SW 11th Avenue (Mon–Sat 9am–5pm; ☎ 305 860 1412, ⊛ eltitancigars.com), the home of hand-crafted, Cuban-style cigars. For general souvenirs try **Little Havana To Go** at 1442 SW 8th St (daily 10am–5pm; ☎ 305 857 9720), a store that sells Cuban flags, paintings, music, dolls, T-shirts and other paraphernalia.

Máximo Gómez Park – Domino Club

Corner of SW 15th Ave and SW 8th St • Daily 9am–6pm

At the heart of the neighbourhood lies **Máximo Gómez Park**; access to its open-air tables is (quite illegally) restricted to men over 55, and this is one place where you really will see old men playing dominoes. Be aware that they don't take kindly to snapshot-happy tourists.

Bay of Pigs Museum

1821 SW 9th St • Mon–Fri 9am–4pm • Free • ☎ 305 649 4719, ⊛ bayofpigs2506.com

You can't get a more up-close-and-personal account of the Bay of Pigs invasion (see above) than the one offered at this two-room museum, staffed by soldiers and former pilots who were there on April 17, 1961. One volunteer was a political prisoner for eighteen years – he'll even show you an eye-opening exit wound he received from a rifle bullet. While the exhibits are simply a compilation of memorabilia

1

under glass (as well as heartbreaking photographs of Brigade 2506 members who died during the invasion), it's worth making a visit here just to chat with the stalwart staff. Take note of the golden flag in the back room: carried into battle for the invasion, it was given as a gift in 1962 to President John F. Kennedy, who in turn promised the banner's return to a "free Havana". When this didn't occur, the flag ended up in storage and veterans successfully sued for its return in the 1970s.

Woodlawn Park Cemetery

3260 SW 8th St • Daily 7.30am–5.30pm • ☎ 305 445 5425

To the west of the district, the peaceful greenery of **Woodlawn Park Cemetery** belies the scheming and skulduggery that some of its occupants indulged in during their lifetimes. Two former Cuban heads of state are buried here: Gerardo Machado, ousted from office in 1933, is in the mausoleum, while one of the protagonists in his downfall, Carlos Prío Socarras, president from 1948 to 1952, lies just outside. Also interred in the mausoleum (and marked only by his initials) is **Anastasio Somoza**, dictator of Nicaragua until overthrown by the Sandinistas in 1979, and later killed in Paraguay. George Merrick, founder of Coral Gables (see below), is also buried here.

Coral Gables

Though all of Miami's constituent cities are quick to assert their individuality, none has a greater case than **CORAL GABLES**, south of Little Havana. Encompassing twelve square miles of broad boulevards and leafy streets lined by elaborate Spanish- and Italian-style architecture, the city was the pet project of one man, **George Merrick**. Taking Mediterranean Europe as his inspiration, he envisaged a lavish Venetian settlement (albeit with Spanish street names) steeped in old-world grandeur to inspire civic pride among its residents. He enlisted his artist uncle, Denman Fink, and architect Phineas Paist to plan the plazas, fountains and carefully aged stucco-fronted buildings that would sit on the three thousand acres of citrus groves and pineland he inherited from his father.

Merrick's true flair, however, was in publicity, and he staged countless stunts to attract attention and residents – including sending fleets of coral-coloured buses across Florida to ferry potential customers down to the site. Of the $150 million he made in the five years following the first sale in 1921, he funnelled one third into publicity and advertising. The layout and buildings of Coral Gables quickly took shape, but the sudden end of Florida's property boom in 1926 (see p.455) wiped Merrick out. He ran a fishing camp in the Florida Keys until that was destroyed by a hurricane, and ended up as Miami's postmaster until his death in 1942.

Coral Gables, however, was built with longevity as well as beauty in mind. Despite successive economic crises, it has never lost its good looks, and these days, boosted equally by a host of multinational companies working out of renovated office buildings and its very image-conscious residents, Coral Gables is as well-to-do and well kept as ever.

The liveliest time to be here is on the first Friday of every month, when the Coral Gables Gallery Association (☎ 305 444 4493) organizes **Gables Gallery night** (6–10pm), and free shuttle buses link the area's fine-art galleries and studios.

The Miracle Mile and around

Coral Gables' main commercial drag is SW 22nd Street, which is known downtown as the **Miracle Mile** (though only half a mile long). In the past ten years it has recharged its retail batteries by luring casual cafés and shops back to the main street.

GETTING AROUND CORAL GABLES

Ponce de León Boulevard is serviced frequently by the free **Coral Gables trolley bus** (Mon–Fri 6.30am–8pm; ☎305 460 5070, 🌐coralgables.com), which terminates at Douglas Road Metrorail and Metrobus station; but to really tour the whole area you'll need a **car**.

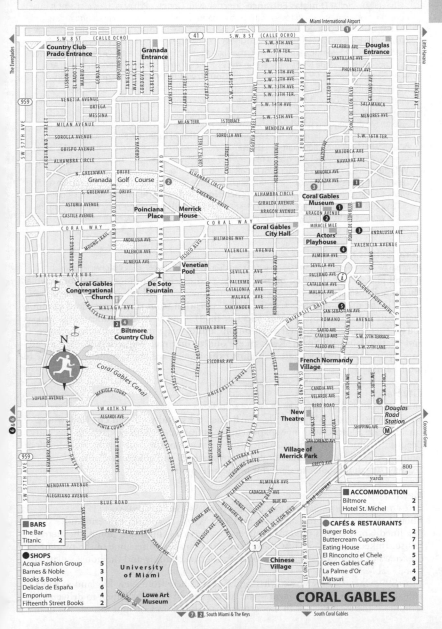

CORAL GABLES

1

CORAL GABLES: ENTRANCES AND VILLAGES

To make a strong first impression on visitors to Coral Gables, founder George Merrick planned eight grand **entrances** on the main access roads, of which only four were completed before he went bust. The three most impressive are along a two-and-a-half-mile stretch of SW 8th Street, and well worth seeking out.

The million-dollar **Douglas Entrance** (junction with Douglas Rd) was the most ambitious, consisting of a gateway and tower with two expansive wings of shops, offices and artists' studios. During the 1960s it was almost bulldozed to make room for a supermarket, but survived to become a well-scrubbed business area, still upholding Merrick's Mediterranean themes in its architecture. Further west, the sixty-foot-high vine-covered **Granada Entrance** (junction with Granada Blvd) is based on the entrance to the city of Granada in Spain. An even better appetizer for Coral Gables is the **Country Club Prado Entrance** (junction with Country Club Prado), the expensive re-creation of a formal Italian garden bordered by freestanding stucco-and-brick pillars topped by ornamental urns and lamps with wrought-iron brackets.

To revive the flagging housing market, which began to soften in the 1920s, Merrick hit on another architectural gimmick, the so-called **International Villages**, which were clusters of houses around town, each built in a different style. Though fourteen were planned, only seven were built before Merrick ran out of money. The most eye-popping of these is the **Chinese Village**, just south of US-1 on Riviera Drive: its red and yellow chinoiserie, complete with carved balconies and dragons, is gaudy and irresistible. Also worth a look are the brown and white timber-beamed cottages of the **French Normandy Village**, on the 400 block of Vizcaya Avenue at Le Jeune Road, and the **French City Village**, on the 1000 block of Hardee Road, where the front gardens of the neat townhouses are boxed in by high walls.

Coral Gables Museum

285 Aragon Ave • Tues–Fri noon–6pm, Sat 11am–5pm, Sun noon–5pm • $7 • ☎ 305 603 8067, ⓦ coralgablesmuseum.org

A good place to get oriented on the history of the neighbourhood is the **Coral Gables Museum**, housed in the city's one-time courthouse, jail and fire station. Established in 2011, the museum tracks Coral Gables' transition from rugged pineland to family grapefruit farm – run by the Merricks (see p.74) – to the Mediterranean villa you see today. There are also temporary exhibitions and displays on the area's architecture and relationship with Spain. Keep an eye out for original design details, such as jail bars repurposed as gallery gates (the first exhibition space you'll come to was once the local slammer).

City Hall

405 Biltmore Way • Mon–Fri 8am–5pm • ☎ 305 446 6800, ⓦ coralgables.com

Heading west on the Miracle Mile, you'll reach the grandly pillared **City Hall**, whose corridors are adorned with newspaper clippings from the 1920s advertising the "City Beautiful", which bear witness to the property mania of the time. From the third-floor landing you can view Denman Fink's impressive blue and gold mural of the Four Seasons, which decorates the interior of the bell tower.

Merrick House

907 Coral Way • By 45min tour only; Sun & Wed 1pm, 2pm & 3pm • $5 • ☎ 305 460 5361, ⓦ coralgables.com

About half a mile west of City Hall, on Coral Way – a typically peaceful and tree-lined Coral Gables residential street – is Merrick's childhood home, the **Merrick House**. In keeping with its restrictive hours, the museum offers one of the pithiest overviews of the area's past, via its focus on Merrick's family and the house's place in Coral Gables history.

In 1899, when George was 12, his family arrived here from New England to run a 160-acre fruit and vegetable farm – and, in the case of George's father, to deliver sermons at the local Plymouth Congregational Church in Coconut Grove. The farm was so successful that the house quickly grew from a wooden shack into a modestly elegant dwelling of coral rock and gabled roof line (the inspiration behind the name of the city that later grew up around the family farm). The dual blows of the property crash and a citrus blight led to the gradual deterioration of the house, until restoration began in the 1970s. The place now showcases several of Denman Fink's chocolate-box-like canvases as well as quirky Merrick memorabilia.

Poinciana Place
937 Coral Way

A few houses west of the Merrick House, at the corner of Granada Boulevard, stands **Poinciana Place**, one of the earliest structures in the city. Merrick built this ranch-style home, with its low-slung terracotta tiling, close to his family's base when he married Eunice Peacock in 1916.

De Soto Boulevard and south

A short drive west of Coral Gables' centre, curvy De Soto Boulevard links some of George Merrick's best-known designs, including the enchanting Venetian Pool (see below). The southwestern edge of this swimmer's delight (at Granada Blvd) is marked by the opulent **De Soto Fountain**, named for conquistador Hernando de Soto, who led an expedition to Florida from Cuba in 1539.

The Venetian Pool
2701 De Soto Blvd • Normally daily 11am–5pm but hours fluctuate wildly; call for an update • April–Sept $11.50 • ☎ 305 460 5306, Ⓦ coralgables.com

Just north of the De Soto Fountain lies one of Merrick's grandest achievements. While his property-developing contemporaries left ugly scars across the city after digging up the local limestone, Merrick had the foresight – and the help of Denman Fink – to turn his biggest quarry into a sumptuous swimming pool. **The Venetian Pool**, an elaborate conglomeration of palm-studded paths, Venetian-style bridges and coral-rock caves, was opened in 1924. Despite its ornamentation, the pool was never designed with the social elite in mind; admission was cheap and open to all, and even today local residents get a special discount.

Coral Gables Congregational Church
3010 De Soto Blvd • ☎ 305 448 7421, Ⓦ gablesucc.org

Follow De Soto Boulevard south of the fountain for a few minutes and you come to the **Coral Gables Congregational Church**, a Spanish Revival flurry topped by a barrel-tiled roof and enhanced by Baroque features, built on land donated by Merrick. The building has excellent interior acoustics that make it a popular venue for jazz and classical **concerts**; ask for details at the church office, just inside the entrance.

Biltmore Hotel
1200 Anastasia Ave • Daily afternoon tea 2pm & 3.30pm; $29.50 • Free building tours Sun 1.30pm & 2.30pm • ☎ 855 311 6903, Ⓦ biltmorehotel.com

Merrick's crowning achievement – aesthetically if not financially – was the **Biltmore Hotel**. The hotel's 26-storey tower can be seen across much of low-lying Miami: if it seems similar to the Freedom Tower (see p.64), it's because they're both modelled on the Giralda bell tower of Seville Cathedral in Spain. The *Biltmore* was hawked as "the last word in the evolution of civilization", and everything about it was outrageous: 25ft-high frescoed walls, vaulted ceilings, a wealth of imported marble and tiles, immense fireplaces, custom-loomed rugs, and the biggest hotel pool in the continental United States.

1

Although high-profile celebrities, such as Bing Crosby, Judy Garland and Ginger Rogers, kept the *Biltmore* on their itineraries, the end of the Florida land boom and the start of the Depression meant that the hotel was never the success it might have been. After decades of decline the hotel reopened in 1993 after a multimillion-dollar refit. Now once again it's back to its glorious beginnings; you can step inside to admire the elaborate architecture or take **afternoon tea** in the lobby. There are also free **historical tours** every Sunday in the main hall, but these can be hit and miss – the best way to absorb the hotel's grandeur is just to amble through its spacious common areas.

Biltmore Country Club

1200 Anastasia Ave • ☎ 305 460 5364, ⓦ biltmorehotel.com/golf

Next to the *Biltmore Hotel*, the **Biltmore Country Club** has fared better. You can poke your head inside for a closer look at its painstakingly renovated Beaux Arts features, but most people turn up to knock a ball along the lush fairways of the **Biltmore Golf Course**, a par-71 course that was designed in 1925 and which, in the glory days of the hotel, hosted the highest-paying golf tournament in the world. It's now home to an upmarket Golf Academy which offers various lesson packages – call or check the website for details.

Lowe Art Museum

1301 Stanford Drive • Tues–Sat 10am–4pm, Sun noon–4pm • $10 • ☎ 305 284 3535, ⓦ lowemuseum.org

One of the few parts of Coral Gables where Mediterranean-style architecture doesn't prevail is on the campus of the **University of Miami**, home of the first-rate **Lowe Art Museum**. Established in 1950, the Lowe underwent major renovation and extension work in 1995 and is now one of the largest museums in Florida, with holdings covering everything from Old Master paintings to tantalizing Native American, African and East Asian artefacts. In 2008 it added a sunlit pavilion shot through with the mesmerizing colours and swirls of contemporary glass arts. Among the museum's holdings, its **permanent collection** boasts *The Barge and the Boat*, a rural waterfront scene by Gauguin, and Monet's *Waterloo Bridge*, a pinkish meditation on a fogged-out River Thames. One standout gallery is the museum's modern art collection, which includes photographs by Nan Goldin and a lifelike football player sculpted in polyvinyl resin by Duane Hanson.

Coconut Grove

A stomping ground of down-at-heel artists, writers and lefties throughout the 1960s and 1970s, **COCONUT GROVE** is better known these days for its sidewalk cafés, two shopping plazas and a slew of condo towers with stunning waterfront views. Though it may have lost its counter-culture edge, Coconut Grove has retained its vinegary character: many locals still treat it as distinct from the rest of Miami, which annexed it in the late nineteenth century. It owes its personality in part to the unique mix of settlers who first called it home: Bahamian immigrant labourers lived alongside New England intellectuals who came here searching for spiritual fulfilment, and together created a fiercely independent community. Nowadays, the city is just a pleasant, fairly posh enclave, dripping with palms – turn down any side street and you'll find it thick with gorgeous vegetation. The **Coconut Grove Chamber of Commerce** (see p.86) has free leaflets and maps of the area.

Central Coconut Grove

Central Coconut Grove is compact and walkable, with a movie theatre, shops and restaurants – including two of the city's best-known malls, CocoWalk and Streets of

Mayfair – and plentiful parking. An inviting place for Sunday brunch, the neighbourhood is also a University of Miami hangout.

Barnacle Historic State Park

3485 Main Hwy • **Park** Mon & Wed–Sun 9am–5pm • $2 • **The Barnacle** same hours; tours depart at 10am, 11.30am, 1pm & 2.30pm from the porch • $3 (plus $2 park entry fee) • ☎ 305 442 6866, ⓦ floridastateparks.org/thebarnacle

Heading south down Main Highway from CocoWalk mall, a short, tree-shaded track on the left leads to the tranquil Bayside **Barnacle Historic State Park**. The Barnacle is the park's most striking feature, a house built by "Commodore" Ralph Middleton Munroe in 1891, a sailor and brilliant yacht designer. The pagoda-like structure was ingeniously put together with local materials and tricks learned from nautical design. Raising the structure eight feet off the ground in 1908 improved air circulation and prevented flooding, a covered veranda enabled windows to be opened during rainstorms, and a skylight allowed air to be drawn through the house – all major innovations that alleviated some of the discomforts of living all year in the heat and humidity of south Florida. More inventive still, when Munroe needed additional space for his family he simply jacked up the single-storey structure and added a new floor underneath.

Only with the **guided tour** can you see inside the house, where many original furnishings remain alongside some of Munroe's intriguing photos of pioneering Coconut Grovers. You are free to explore the **park**, however, on your own. The lawn extends to the shore of Biscayne Bay, while behind the house are the last remnants of the tropical hardwood hammock that once extended throughout the Miami area.

A.C.'s Icees

David Kennedy Park car park, 2200 S Bayshore Drive • Daily 11am–6pm • Icees $3–6

A vestige of Coconut Grove's bohemia lives on at **A.C.'s Icees**, located in Kennedy Park, a little over a mile from the Barnacle. Shaggy-haired and charming, A.C. has been purveying his all-natural **frozen lemonade** from a little white truck here since 1978, long enough for it to become a Coconut Grove rite of passage. A sweet solution to Miami's blazing temperatures, the cherry-lemon icee is particularly good, but half the fun is just watching enthusiastic locals turn up for a slushy – some longstanding regulars who came here as kids now arrive with their own families.

Kampong Garden

4013 Douglas Rd • Mon–Fri 9am–4pm; reservations required • **Guided tours** Jan–June & Sept–Dec Wed & Sat 10.30am & noon • $20 • ☎ 305 442 7169, ⓦ ntbg.org/gardens/kampong.php

One of the city's best undiscovered sights is the eleven-acre **Kampong Garden**, an exuberant collection of more than two thousand tropical flowers, fruit trees and plants. These were collected by famed plant explorer and horticulturalist **David Fairchild** – one of the masterminds behind the Fairchild Tropical Garden (see p.83) – who lived on the waterfront estate here with his wife from 1928 to 1954. The result is an eclectic, far-reaching botanical display with an emphasis on Asia: look for the wide-leafed philodendra, whose enormous, waxy fronds are used as impromptu umbrellas. The Kampong is a mile or so southwest of downtown Coconut Grove and can be a little hard to find – look for the semicircular entrance and tiny street-number sign along a stretch of residential mansions.

South Miami Avenue

Skirting Biscayne Bay between Brickell and Coconut Grove, the rumbling stretch that is South Miami Avenue passes over the Rickenbacker Causeway – which leads to Key Biscayne (see p.80) – and I-95 entrance ramps before quickly arriving at the Vizcaya Museum and Gardens, and the Miami Science Museum.

1

Vizcaya Museum and Gardens

3251 S Miami Ave • Mon & Wed–Sun 9.30am–4.30pm; ask for tour times at Main House • $18, tours $5 • ☎ 305 250 9133, ⓦ vizcaya.org •
Short walk from the Vizcaya Metrorail station (or bus #12 and #48), but most people drive – it's too far to walk from downtown Coconut Grove

In 1914, farm-machinery mogul James Deering followed his brother, Charles – of Charles Deering Estate fame (see p.84) – to south Florida and spent an eye-opening $15 million re-creating a sixteenth-century Italian villa within the belt of vegetation between Miami and Coconut Grove, now preserved as the **Vizcaya Museum and Gardens**. Deering's lavish **art collection** and his belief that the villa should appear to have been inhabited for four hundred years resulted in a melee of Baroque, Renaissance, Rococo and Neoclassical fixtures and furnishings. The rooms are dazzling, but may get overwhelming en masse – you can wander on your own, but **tours** provide a more structured introduction. Be sure to roam the landscaped **gardens**, trimmed with musing statuary, fountains and labyrinthine shrubs.

Miami Science Museum

3280 S Miami Ave • Daily 10am–6pm • $14.95 • ☎ 305 646 4200, ⓦ miamisci.org

Straight across South Miami Avenue from Villa Vizcaya is the family-friendly **Miami Science Museum**. Its interactive exhibits provide a good two-hour diversion, though a stronger reason to visit is the collection of **wildlife** at the museum's rear. Vultures and owls are among a number of injured birds seeing out their days here, a variety of snakes can be viewed at disturbingly close quarters, and the resident tarantula is happy to be handled. The adjoining **planetarium** has the usual trips-around-the-cosmos shows; check the website or from the ticket office for details. The museum is scheduled to relocate downtown in 2016, as part of the Museum Park project (see p.66).

Ermita de la Caridad

3609 S Miami Ave • Daily 8am–9pm • ☎ 305 854 2404, ⓦ ermitadelacaridad.org

Five minutes' walk south of the Miami Science Museum, look for signs down a winding side road (at the "3601 Block") to the **Ermita de la Caridad**, perched on the waterfront in the shadows of the massive Mercy Hospital. Looking like a large, angular meringue half-dipped in chocolate, the Modernist church was built on 10¢ donations from Miami Cubans and dedicated to Our Lady of Charity, an incarnation of the Virgin Mary dating back to seventeenth-century Cuba; the statue inside is a replica of the revered original from the shrine in El Cobre, Cuba, brought into the US via the Panamanian embassy in 1961. The church is the religious heart of expat Cuban life and its architecture and design are highly symbolic: the columns represent the six traditional provinces of Cuba, while beneath the altar there's Cuban soil, sand and rock, cast together with water from a refugee boat. There's also a lovely sepia mural behind the altar, tracing the island's history.

Key Biscayne and Virginia Key

A compact, immaculately manicured community just five miles off the Miami shore, **Key Biscayne** is a different world to downtown Miami and South Beach. Seeking relaxation and creature comforts away from life in the fast lane, the moneyed of Miami

---

GETTING TO KEY BISCAYNE

Without a private yacht, the only way onto Key Biscayne is via **Rickenbacker Causeway**, a four-mile-long continuation of SW 26th Road just south of downtown Miami; it soars above Biscayne Bay, allowing ships to glide underneath, and provides a scintillating view of the Brickell Avenue skyline. Drivers have to pay a $1.75 toll (no charge coming back), collected electronically by SunPass transponders (available at Publix supermarkets) – no cash is accepted; otherwise you can cross the causeway by bus (#B) or bike, or even on foot.

HITTING THE WATER IN KEY BISCAYNE

If you'd like to test your skills out on the water, visit **Sailboards Miami** on the Rickenbacker Causeway (☎ 305 892 8992, ⊛ sailboardsmiami.com), which guarantees to teach you to windsurf in just two hours ($79). They also rent **kayaks** ($15/hr, $40/3hr) and windsurf boards ($30/hr).

---

fill the island's upmarket homes and condos: even Richard Nixon had his presidential winter house here.

This elite enclave got its start in the decades after World War I, when the Matheson family – who made millions with its chemical dye business – moved in to manage a huge coconut plantation, but it wasn't until the opening of Rickenbacker Causeway in 1947 that large-scale development began. In the 1960s the island came to be known as a place where the rich could live undisturbed. More recently, many wealthy Europeans and Latin Americans have bought second homes here, and it's estimated two-thirds of Key Biscayne's population is Hispanic. For visitors, Key Biscayne and the smaller island to the north, **Virginia Key**, offer a number of inviting beaches, a third of them inside a state park, a chance to see some wildlife without leaving the city, and a fabulous cycling path running the full length of the island. **Rent bikes** from Mangrove Cycles in Key Biscayne village (see p.88) or at the car park in Baggs Cape Florida State Recreation Area (daily 10am–sunset; $5/hr; ☎ 305 361 5811).

Virginia Key

After the causeway, the first land you'll hit is the unexceptional and sparsely populated **VIRGINIA KEY**. Although most people speed through on the way to Key Biscayne, those who stop will find a pleasant park equipped with a merry-go-round and miniature train at weekends.

Virginia Key Beach Park

Daily 7am–7pm (sunrise to sunset); toy train and carousel Sat & Sun only • Mon–Fri cars $5, Sat & Sun $6; toy train $1, carousel $1 • ☎ 305 960 4600, ⊛ virginiakeybeachpark.net

The island's main point of interest is **Virginia Key Beach Park**, reached by a two-mile lane that winds through a cluster of woodland. During the years of segregation, this was set aside for Miami's black community, but in 2008 it reopened after a major renovation, with a toy train for kids at weekends, a historic carousel and nature trails; a museum of black history is also in the works.

Miami Seaquarium

4400 Rickenbacker Causeway • Daily 9.30am–6pm, box office closes 4.30pm; show times vary, but are most frequent 9.30am–noon • $42.99, kids 3–9 $33.99; Dolphin Encounter programme $150, kids 5–9 $110; parking $8 • ☎ 305 361 5705, Dolphin Encounter programme ☎ 305 365 2501, ⊛ miamiseaquarium.com

The **Miami Seaquarium** marine park is a bustling place where you can while away three or four hours watching the usual roster of performing seals and dolphins. Be sure not to miss Lolita, the 8000-pound star of the spectacular **killer whale** show. You can also swim with **dolphins** as part of the Dolphin Harbor programme, but you need to call in advance. The park's most important work – undertaking breeding programmes to preserve Florida's endangered sea life and serving as a halfway house for injured manatees and sea turtles – goes on behind the scenes. Contrary to this mission, in recent years the Seaquarium has found itself at the centre of an animal rights battle for larger living pens and better training facilities.

1

Key Biscayne

Follow the Rickenbacker Causeway (which becomes Crandon Blvd) past the Miami Seaquarium to enter the upmarket village of **KEY BISCAYNE**, home to the area's commercial centre, in addition to an enticing beach and nature preserve.

Crandon Park Beach

6747 Crandon Blvd • Daily sunrise–sunset • Parking $7 • ☎ 305 361 5421, ⓦ miamidade.gov/parks

Not content with living in one of the best natural settings in Miami, the people of Key Biscayne also possess one of the finest landscaped beaches in the city – **Crandon Park Beach**, a mile along Crandon Boulevard (the main road that continues beyond the causeway from Virginia Key). Three miles of golden beach fringe the park, and you can wade out in knee-deep water to a sandbar far from shore. Filled with the sounds of boisterous kids and sizzling barbecues on weekends, the park at any other time is disturbed only by the occasional jogger or holiday-maker straying from a posh hotel nearby.

Biscayne Nature Center

6767 Crandon Blvd, at the northern end of Crandon Park • Daily 9am–4pm • Parking $7 • ☎ 305 361 6767, ⓦ biscaynenaturecenter.org

Other than the beach, the main attraction at Crandon Park is the **Biscayne Nature Center**, which is especially fun for kids. Exhibition rooms, videos and mini-aquariums provide an insight into the marine and wildlife found on the island, and the centre also organizes special programmes featuring kayaking, snorkelling and guided hikes – check the website for details.

Key Biscayne's residential section

Besides its very green, manicured looks and some excellent places to eat, the **residential section** of Key Biscayne (known simply to locals as "the village"), beginning with an abrupt wall of apartment buildings at the southern edge of Crandon Park Beach, has little to offer visitors. You'll need to pass through, however, on the way to the rewarding Bill Baggs Cape Florida State Recreation Area (see below), and while doing so should pick up information on the area at the **Chamber of Commerce** (see p.86).

Bill Baggs Cape Florida State Recreation Area

1200 S Crandon Blvd • Daily 8am–sunset • Cars $8 (2–8 people), $4 individual driver, pedestrians and cyclists $2 • ☎ 305 361 5811, ⓦ floridastateparks.org/capeflorida

Crandon Boulevard terminates at the entrance to the 440-acre **Bill Baggs Cape Florida State Recreation Area**, which covers the southern extremity of Key Biscayne. An excellent swimming **beach** lines the Atlantic-facing side of the park, and four

---

KEY BISCAYNE WILDLIFE

The most notorious inhabitants of Key Biscayne are its fast-multiplying **green iguanas** – descendants of pets released into the wild – which grow to be lumbering six-foot orange-and-black giants. Most environmentalists want to control the population, though locals remain divided; some find them cute (the golf club promotes them as a unique obstacle), while others find the pool-lounging creatures unbearable. You should see plenty basking on the sides of roads or on the bike paths; look for them in the trees near *Boater's Grill*. In cooler weather, you might see them literally falling from the trees (they actually seize up). Another striking yet common island native is the **white ibis** – the birds tend to congregate at the junction of East Enid Street and Crandon Boulevard, but you'll see them all over the place. The beaches are also rich in marine life; **spotted eagle rays** and **dolphins** are particularly common offshore. In the summer months **loggerhead turtles** lay eggs on the Atlantic beaches, and nests are marked off with yellow tape – ask at the Biscayne Nature Center (see above) for special tours and volunteer programmes.

boardwalks cut around the wind-bitten sand dunes and angle towards the **Cape Florida Lighthouse** (Mon & Thurs–Sun 9am–5pm; tours 10am & 1pm; free), built in 1825 and one of the oldest structures in south Florida. The lighthouse was severely damaged in 1836 (during the Second Seminole War), but rebuilt and extended in 1855. Climb the 95ft-high structure (109 steps) for mesmerizing views of the whole island, downtown Miami, and the last few remaining houses of Stiltsville (see below). For more detailed information, take a ranger-led tour and check out the exhibits and video in the **lighthouse keeper's cottage**, a 1970 replica of the nineteenth-century original.

Stiltsville
Ⓦ stiltsvilletrust.org
Looking out from Bill Baggs park across the bay, you'll spy the grouping of fragile-looking houses known as **Stiltsville**. Held above water by stilts, these wooden dwellings were built and occupied by fishermen in the 1930s, becoming a haven for illegal alcohol joints and gambling in the 1950s. Stiltsville's demise was compounded by the destruction wrought by Hurricane Andrew in 1992; only seven of the houses are still standing. Thanks to aggressive local attempts to secure funding for preservation, the buildings are now overseen and being restored by **Biscayne National Park** (see p.168). Until restoration is complete they remain sadly off-limits; whether the rickety structures can survive many more of Florida's increasingly fierce hurricane seasons remains to be seen.

South Miami

South of Coral Gables and Coconut Grove, monotonous middle-class suburbs consume almost all of **SOUTH MIAMI**, an expanse of cosy family homes reaching to the edge of the Everglades, interrupted only by golf courses, mini-malls and a few contrived tourist attractions along US-1. You can't avoid this route entirely, but from south Coral Gables a better course is **Old Cutler Road**, which makes a pleasing meander from Coconut Grove through a thick belt of woodland between Biscayne Bay and the suburban sprawl. While in this vicinity, you should take advantage of the excellent **Tropical Everglades Visitor Information Center** (see p.86).

Fairchild Tropical Garden
10901 Old Cutler Rd • Daily 7.30am–4.30pm; free tram tours Mon–Fri on the hour 10am–3pm, Sat & Sun 10am–4pm • $25 • ☎ 305 667 1651, Ⓦ fairchildgarden.org
Dividing Coconut Grove and South Miami, **Fairchild Tropical Garden** is the largest tropical botanical garden in the continental United States, and a treasured Miami landmark. Dotted with velvety lawns, flowerbeds and pristine lakes, this fascinating green space is also known for its large-scale **art installations** – sculptures by big names like Chihuly and Lichtenstein are set up amid the foliage here between December and May, resulting in an incredible hybrid of nature and design. A good way to begin exploring the 83-acre site is to hitch a ride on the free **tram** for a 45-minute trip along the trails, with live commentary on the variegated flora. Don't miss the "Windows to the Tropics", a hothouse filled with the most delicate, exotic plants, as well as the *Amorphophallus titanum*, nicknamed "Mr Stinky", whose rare blooms are renowned for their rotting-flesh smell.

The garden is named for David Fairchild, an esteemed, early twentieth-century plant explorer and Miami resident (see p.79) who travelled to every continent (minus Antarctica) to import hundreds of plants such as nectarines, palms and mangoes – even Washington, DC's famous cherry blossom trees – for study and conservation. Continuing this legacy of research, the garden works with scientists all over the world to preserve ecological diversity. Many of the species here, such as Cape Sable whiteweed and *Alvaradoa*, are extinct in their original environment, and efforts have been made to re-establish them at the source.

Charles Deering Estate

16701 SW 72nd Ave • Daily 10am–5pm, last ticket sold at 4pm; tours of the interior daily 10.30am & 3pm; tours of the grounds Oct–May daily at 12.30pm • $12, including tour • ☎ 305 235 1668, ⓦ deeringestate.com

Long before modern highways scythed through the city, Old Cutler Road was the sole road between Coconut Grove and Cutler, a small town that went into decline in the 1910s after being bypassed by the new Flagler railroad. A wealthy industrialist and amateur botanist, Charles Deering – brother of James, the owner of Villa Vizcaya (see p.80) – was so taken with the natural beauty of the area that he purchased all of Cutler and, with one exception, razed its buildings to make way for the **Charles Deering Estate**, completed in 1922.

Richmond Cottage

The one building that Deering preserved was Richmond Cottage, Cutler's only hotel, which he turned into his own living and dining quarters. Its pleasant wooden form now stands in marked contrast to the limestone mansion he erected alongside, whose interior – echoing halls, dusty chandeliers and checker-board-tile floors – is Mediterranean in style but carries a Gothic spookiness. Though Deering's daughters sold off many of the opulent furnishings after his death, the estate has gradually been seeking the return of some of his key works of art (many donated by the family), including 340 historic books and two vigorous paintings by Ramon Casas i Carbó. The ticket price includes a free one-hour historical tour of the interior.

The grounds

Make time to amble around the tranquil, 444-acre **grounds**; signs of human habitation dating back 10,000 years have been found amid the pine woods, mangrove forests and tropical hardwood hammocks. The ticket price includes various tours of the grounds, led by extremely knowledgeable rangers – be sure not to miss out.

Zoo Miami

12400 SW 152nd St • Mon–Fri 10am–5pm, Sat & Sun 9.30am–5.30pm, last admission 4pm • $17.95, children 3–12 $13.95 • ☎ 305 251 0400, ⓦ zoomiami.org

An extensive display of wildlife is on view at **Zoo Miami**, a vast compound that organizes animals by continent, and mixes in unusual creatures like anoa (which resemble small buffalo) alongside the giraffes and lions. The zoo uses moats and other natural barriers rather than cages, and the educational plaques flagging each species are highly informative. Come early in the day, as the baking noonday sun makes most of the animals sluggish.

Fruit and Spice Park

24801 SW 187th Ave • Daily 9am–5pm; tours daily at 11am, 1.30pm & 3pm • $8, children 6–11 $2 • ☎ 305 247 5727, ⓦ fruitandspicepark.org

The subtle fragrances wafting out of the 37-acre **Fruit and Spice Park** tickle your nostrils as soon as you enter. Star fruit and the aptly named Panama candle tree are the highlights of a host of tropical curiosities, grouped together by species or by theme (look for the bizarre banana plantation where dozens of misshapen varieties are grown together). Labelling at the park is erratic, however, so unless you're an avid gardener it's best to hop on one of the tram tours, led by expert guides.

Monkey Jungle

1

14805 SW 216th St • Daily 9.30am–5pm, last admission 4pm • $29.95, children 3–9 $23.95 • ☎ 305 235 1611, ⓦ monkeyjungle.com

South toward Homestead, **Monkey Jungle** is one of the few preserves in the US for endangered primates. Covered walkways keep visitors in closer confinement than the monkeys and lead through a steamy hammock where baboons, orangutans, gorillas and 35 species of monkey move through the vegetation. Despite initial impressions, plenty of the monkeys are in cages and signage is infrequent, making it far from the eco-utopia its owners claim. However, it's a fun place to visit – be sure to bring plenty of quarters to buy sunflower seeds to feed the monkeys, who have devised ingenious ways of accessing food.

ARRIVAL AND DEPARTURE   MIAMI

All points of entry are within a few miles of the centre, and public transport links are generally reliable. All trains and buses (including Amtrak and Greyhound services) arrive at the **Miami Intermodal Center** (ⓦ micdot.com) next to the airport. Connecting the airport to the Intermodal Center is the **MIA Mover**, a 1.25-mile elevated tram.

BY PLANE

All passenger flights land at Miami International Airport (☎ 305 876 7000, ⓦ miami-airport.com), a glistening complex at 2100 NW 42nd Ave, 6 miles west of downtown. **Car rental** With the opening of the new Miami Intermodal Center (see above) flyers now get their rental wheels (see p.87) at the spacious Rental Car Center, located at 3900 NW 25th St, and accessed from the airport via the MIA Mover, a 1.25-mile elevated tram that shuttles between the Rental Car Center and Miami Central Station (the airport's train and bus hub).

Buses Local buses leave from Miami Central Station (☎ 305 891 3131, ⓦ miamidade.gov/transit); take #7 ($2.25; Mon–Fri 5.46am–8.56pm, Sat & Sun 5.54am–7.01pm; every 30min) to downtown Miami (40–50min), or the #J bus ($2.25; Mon–Fri 4.43am–11.45pm, Sat & Sun 4.39am–11.45pm; every 20–40min) for the slightly longer journey to Miami Beach (50min–1hr at peak times). There is also an express bus route to South Beach (#150; daily 6am–11pm; $2.65), which runs down Collins Ave to 16th St. Shuttle buses also leave from the airport bus station to the nearby Tri-Rail station, with onward services to Palm Beach. Beginning in 2015, Greyhound buses will leave from Miami Central Station, reached via the MIA Mover tram.

Metrorail The airport is linked to Miami Central Station via Metrorail ($2.25; ☎ 305 891 3131, ⓦ miamidade.gov/transit), which connects with the Earlington Heights station, and continues on downtown.

SuperShuttle Quicker, if more expensive, than public transport, the blue-and-yellow SuperShuttle minivans (☎ 305 871 2000, ⓦ supershuttle.com) run around the clock and will deliver you to any address in or around Miami, with per-person rates ranging from $18 one way for downtown and Coconut Grove to $21 one way for South Beach. Their representatives are easy to spot as you leave the baggage claim area.

Taxis Taxis are in plentiful supply outside the airport building. There are flat rates from the airport: $24 to the cruise terminals, $32 to South Beach, and $37–52 to areas in northern Miami Beach. Downtown and Coconut Grove should be around $22 (for full fare information, see ⓦ miami-airport.com/hotel_shuttles.asp).

BY BUS

Of several Greyhound terminals in the Miami area, the busiest is the one near the airport at 4111 NW 27th St (☎ 305 871 1810). In 2015, Greyhound will move into Miami Central Station, linked to the airport by the MIA Mover tram.

Destinations Daytona Beach (5 daily; 8hr 30min); Fort Lauderdale (11 daily; 45min); Fort Myers (4 daily; 4hr); Fort Pierce (7 daily; 3hr–3hr 50min); Jacksonville (6 daily; 8hr 50min–14hr 10min); Key West (2 daily; 4hr 30min); Orlando (8 daily; 5hr 20min–6hr 10min); St Petersburg (3 daily; 7hr–7hr 50min); Tampa (6 daily; 7hr 40min–10hr 45min); West Palm Beach (8 daily; 1hr 50min–2hr 25min).

BY TRAIN AND TRI-RAIL

Amtrak station The Amtrak train station, 8303 NW 37th Ave, is 7 miles northwest of downtown Miami, with plenty of taxis waiting outside; you can also take bus #L from here to central Miami Beach. In 2015, Amtrak's new station at the airport's Intermodal Center (see above) should be up and running.

Destinations New York (2 daily; 26hr 45min–31hr 30min); Ocala (via Lakeland; 1 daily; 7hr 15min); Orlando (2 daily; 5hr–7hr 20min); Sebring (2 daily; 3hr 10min); Tampa (1 daily at 11.50am; 5hr 15min); Washington, DC (2 daily; 23hr–27hr 30min); Winter Haven (2 daily; 3hr 50min).

Tri-Rail station Just north of the airport lies the Tri-Rail Miami Airport Station, at 1200 SE 11th Ave, serving Tri-Rail, the cheap commuter service running between Miami and West Palm Beach (see p.201). Three miles north, Tri-Rail connects with Metrorail, which has service ($2.25) to downtown Miami (see p.88).

1

MIAMI TOURS

If you've had enough of the beach, sign up for one of the standout **tours** listed below to expand your cultural horizons. There's also a variety of boat tours to choose from (see box, p.63).

Art Deco Walking Tour ☎305 672 2014, ⓦmdpl .org. In South Beach, don't miss the Art Deco Walking Tour. A perfect introduction to the area's phenomenal architecture, the tour runs Mon–Wed & Fri–Sun at 10.30am (1hr 30min; Thurs additional tour at 6.30pm) from the Art Deco Welcome Center at 1001 Ocean Drive (at 10th St). The shop also offers a self-guided audio walking tour of the district (available daily 9.30am–5pm; 1hr 30min; $20). Walking tour $25.

David Brown ☎305 416 6868, ⓦmiamicultural tours.com. For less-visited parts of the city, try David Brown, who specializes in Miami's African-American neighbourhoods, including Liberty City and Little Haiti.

Dr Paul George's Walking Tours ☎305 375 5792, ⓦhistorymiami.org. For an informative and entertaining stroll, take one of Dr Paul George's Walking Tours, which are offered in conjunction with the HistoryMiami museum and take in a number of areas, including downtown Miami, Coconut Grove, Coral Gables, Little Havana and South Beach. There are numerous other itineraries, each lasting around two to three hours, though he tends to organize just three to four tours per month (usually at the weekends; no tours July & Aug). The museum also offers bike, boat and eco-history tours. Tours cost $30 and up; reservations required.

Eco Adventures ☎305 365 3018, ⓦmiamidade .gov/ecoadventures. Wildlife enthusiasts should contact Eco Adventures, a Miami-Dade Parks initiative providing a variety of guided excursions to Biscayne Bay (kayaking and snorkelling; $70), Key Biscayne (by kayak; $40), and further afield into the Everglades.

Miami Culinary Tours ☎855 642 3663, ⓦmiamiculinarytours.com. Eat your way across town with the affable guides at Miami Culinary Tours, who run tasting safaris in Little Havana (2hr 30min; Thurs–Sun 12.30pm; $59), South Beach (daily at noon & 5pm; $59) and Wynwood (Fri & Sat at 12.30pm; $69).

Destinations Mon–Fri 25 daily, Sat & Sun 8 daily: Boca Raton (1hr); Delray Beach (1hr 10min); Fort Lauderdale (40min); Hollywood (25min); West Palm Beach (1hr 35min).

BY CAR

Most of the major roads into Miami take the form of elevated expressways that – accidents and rush hours permitting – make getting into the city simple and quick. From the north, I-95 (also called the North-South Expressway) streaks over the downtown streets before joining US-1 (also called South Dixie 1), an ordinary road that continues on through South Miami. Unless you're taking the slower, scenic coastal route from Hollywood and Fort Lauderdale (Hwy-A1A), the fastest way to South Beach is to take I-395 east off I-95, which merges with US-41 at the MacArthur Causeway. Crossing the Everglades from the west coast on US-41 (also called the Tamiami Trail), you'll save time by turning off north along Florida's Turnpike then heading east along Hwy-836, which rejoins US-41 (via I-395) at the MacArthur Causeway.

INFORMATION

TOURIST INFORMATION

Airport Tourist information at Concourse E, level 2 (daily 6am–10pm; ☎305 876 7000).

Coconut Grove 2889 McFarlane Rd (Tues–Thurs 11am–4pm; ☎305 444 7270, ⓦcoconutgrovechamber .com).

Coral Gables 224 Catalonia Ave (Mon–Thurs 9am–5pm, Fri 9am–4pm; ☎305 446 1657, ⓦcoralgableschamber.org).

Downtown The Miami Convention & Visitors Bureau, Suite 2700, inside the Bank of America building at 701 Brickell Ave (Mon–Fri 8.30am–6pm; ☎305 539 3000, ⓦmiamiandbeaches.com), is great for drop-ins; the Downtown Welcome Center in the lobby of the Olympia Theater is another asset (174 E Flagler St; Mon noon–5pm, Tues–Sat 10am–5pm; ☎305 448 7488, ⓦdowntownmiami.com).

Key Biscayne Inside the Village Hall at 88 W McIntyre St (Mon–Fri 9am–5pm; ☎305 361 5207, ⓦkeybiscayne chamber.org). They have an excellent 24hr information room stocked with leaflets and maps.

Miami Beach The Visit Miami Beach information centre, located in Hall C of the conference centre (1901 Convention Center Drive; daily 10am–4pm; ☎786 276 2763, ⓦmiamibeachguest.com), is crammed with leaflets and staffed by helpful locals.

South Beach The snazzy Art Deco Welcome Center (daily 9.30am–5pm), located at 1001 Ocean Drive (in front of the Beach Patrol Station), offers plenty of information on Art Deco and South Beach. The Miami Design Preservation League (☎305 672 2014, ⓦmdpl.org) runs lauded Art Deco tours from here (see box above).

South Miami and Everglades Tropical Everglades Visitor

MIAMI ADDRESSES AND ORIENTATION

Miami's **street naming and numbering system** may seem confusing at first but won't take long to get used to. On the mainland, the city splits into quadrants (northeast, southeast, northwest and southwest), divided by Flagler Street and Miami Avenue, which intersect downtown; numbers rise as you move away from this intersection in any direction. Meanwhile, within each quadrant, Roads, Avenues, Courts and Places run north–south, while everything else runs east–west.

In some areas the pattern varies, most obviously in Coral Gables, where streets have names instead of numbers, and avenues are numbered in sequence from Douglas Road. In Miami Beach, most avenues run north–south and streets run east–west.

Information Center (Mon–Sat 8am–5pm, Sun 10am–2pm; ☎ 305 245 9180, ⓦ tropicaleverglades.com), located at 160 US-1, close to the junction with Hwy-9336 (344th St), offers a wealth of information on attractions around South Miami, but is particularly strong on the Everglades.

NEWSPAPERS

Miami Herald Miami's daily newspaper, the *Miami Herald* (35¢ weekdays, $1 Sun; ⓦ miamiherald.com), provides acclaimed coverage of state, national and world events. The best day to pick up a copy is Friday when a free and informative entertainment supplement is included.

Sun Sentinel The *Sun Sentinel* newspaper (50¢ weekdays, $1.50 Sun; ⓦ sun-sentinel.com) focuses largely on south Florida.

EVENTS LISTINGS

The following are the best sources of up-to-date entertainment and arts listings; most can be picked up free around town and at hotels.

Miami New Times ⓦ miaminewtimes.com. The best weekly listings paper in Miami covers food, drink, entertainment and the arts. Published Thurs (free).

Ocean Drive ☎ 305 532 2544, ⓦ oceandrive.com. Glossy magazine available in every hotel that follows the Beautiful People on the local scene; otherwise for sale at bookshops and newsstands ($6.99).

Scene in the Tropics ⓦ http://blogs.herald.com/scene _in_the_tropics. Local gossip maven, nightlife connoisseur and all-round connected scenester Lesley Abravanel writes this amusing, spot-on blog for the *Miami Herald*.

GETTING AROUND

While designed for cars, Miami is an easily navigable city boasting a comprehensive public transport system that provides a sound alternative for **daytime travel**. An integrated network of buses, trains and a monorail run by Metro-Dade Transit covers Miami (☎ 305 891 3131, ⓦ miamidade.gov/transit), making the city easy – if time-consuming – to get around by day. **Night travel** is much harder, especially away from South Beach. For free route maps and timetables, go downtown to the Transit Service Center inside the Government Center Metrorail station, 111 NW 1st St (Mon–Fri 7am–6pm), or log on to ⓦ miamidade.gov/transit.

BY CAR

Driving around Miami is practical and reasonably easy. Traffic in and out of Miami can be heavy, but the city's expressways (see opposite) will carry you swiftly from one area to another. Driving between Miami and Miami Beach is straightforward using one of seven causeways; each is well marked and quickly accessed from the main arteries.

Car rental Most of the major car rental companies have booking desks at the airport. Many companies also have offices along Collins Ave in South Beach: Alamo, 4332 Collins Ave, suite #104 (☎ 888 826 6893); Avis, 99 SE 2nd St, 8330 S Dixie Hwy, 3655 SW 22nd St (at Douglas Rd in Coral Gables) & 2318 Collins Ave (☎ 800 831 2847); Budget, 6742 Collins Ave & 665 SW 8th St (☎ 800 527 0700); Hertz, 229 SE 2nd St & 1619 Alton Rd (☎ 800 654 3131); Thrifty, 1520 Collins Ave (☎ 877 283 0898). Charges – including taxes – are around $35–50/day or $150–300/week for an economy car, with an insurance premium of $25–40 per day depending on the type of cover. Before you book, it's worth investigating travel websites like ⓦ hotwire.com or

MAJOR MIAMI BUS ROUTES

Metro-Dade Transit (☎ 305 770 3131, ⓦ miamidade.gov/transit) runs the following bus services from downtown Miami to:

Biscayne Corridor #3
Coconut Grove #48
Coral Gables #24
Key Biscayne #B
Little Havana #8
Miami Beach #C or #S
Miami International Airport #150 or #7

1

ⓦ priceline.com, which offer cut-rate deals on car rental.

Parking There is plenty of provision for street parking in Miami, though actually finding an empty space can prove difficult, particularly on South Beach. Parking meters are everywhere and cost $1/hr (if you're south of 23rd Street on Miami Beach, it's $1.75/hr). The coin system is starting to get phased out, however; many meters now take credit or debit cards (it's still a good idea to stock up on coins until the transition is complete). Parking at public parks and beaches normally costs $6/day; car parks are pricier – the most convenient on South Beach is the municipal garage on 13th St between Ocean Drive and Collins Ave, which costs $1/hr, with $20 as the maximum daily rate. For downtown and Bayside Marketplace the best option is the College Station parking garage on 190 NE 3rd St (at NE 2nd Ave), which costs a maximum of $16 (24hr) Mon–Fri, $5 Sat & Sun. Parking in a marked residential area will incur a ticket, and meter times are strictly enforced on Miami Beach.

BY BUS

Routes and tickets Bus routes (☎ 305 770 3131, ⓦ miamidade.gov/transit) cover the entire city, most emanating from downtown Miami, and run from 4am to 2.30am daily. The flat-rate one-way bus fare is $2.25, payable on board by exact change. If you're planning on using lots of public transport, it's a good idea to buy the seven-day unlimited pass ($29.25), which covers all bus and Metrorail services, and is available for sale at any Metrorail station or online at ⓦ miamidade.gov/transit.

South Beach Local One way to get around South Beach is via the South Beach Local – an air-conditioned shuttle that runs on electricity. The route runs almost the entire length of Washington Ave before cutting up Meridian Ave (past the Holocaust Memorial), then looping back down West Ave and Alton Rd (Mon–Sat 7.40am–1.20am, Sun 10am–1am; every 13–20min; 25¢, exact change only; ☎ 305 770 3131, ⓦ miamidade.gov/transit).

BY METRORAIL

Metrorail (☎ 305 770 3131, ⓦ miamidade.gov/transit) is an elevated railway that links the northern suburbs with South Miami. Trains run every 5–20min between 5am and midnight. Useful stops are Government Center (for downtown), Vizcaya, Coconut Grove, and Douglas Road or University (for Coral Gables). Stations do, however, tend to be awkwardly situated, and you'll often need to use Metrorail services in conjunction with a bus. One-way Metrorail fares are $2.25, and require the purchase of an Easy Card or Easy Ticket, for sale at every station (or online at ⓦ miamidade.gov/transit). Note that you must also tap your card out when exiting a station.

BY METROMOVER

Downtown Miami is ringed by the Metromover (sometimes called the "People Mover"), a monorail loop that is fast and clean, if a little limited – but a great way to get your bearings on arrival (daily 5am–midnight, later during major events at American Airlines Arena; free; ☎ 305 770 3131, ⓦ miamidade.gov/transit).

BY TAXI

Taxis are abundant and often the only way to get around at night without a car. Fares are $2.50 for the first sixth of a mile and 40¢ for each additional sixth of a mile. An empty cab will stop if the driver sees you waving, but if you want to pre-book, Central Cab (☎ 305 532 5555) is reliable. If you have a smartphone, sign up for the free ⓦ uber.com app, which brings drivers to your door and seamlessly charges your credit card. In South Beach, Swoop (daily 1pm–2am; ☎ 305 409 6636, ⓦ theswoopride.com) is a fun, frugal option: this cadre of electric golf carts zips everywhere south of 23rd St, and only charges the price of a tip for its service (though you should tip generously).

BY BIKE

If you're keen to cycle around, downtown is not your best option – there are few cycle lanes and traffic is a hassle. Instead, follow the 14-mile path down to South Miami from Coconut Grove; or opt for a jaunt round the leafy parks of Key Biscayne. South Beach, where car parking's pricey, is also bike-friendly: try an oceanfront cycle along Ocean Drive (see box, p.88).

Bike rental You can rent a bike from several outlets including: DecoBike, which has stations throughout Miami Beach (see box, p.88); Mangrove Cycles, The Square Mall, 260 Crandon Blvd in Key Biscayne (Tues–Sun 9.30am–6pm; $25/day, $50/3 days; ☎ 305 361 5555, ⓦ mangrovecycles .com); and the Miami Beach Bicycle Center, 601 5th St, South Beach (Mon–Sat 10am–7pm, Sun 10am–5pm; $8/hr, $24/24hr; ☎ 305 531 4161, ⓦ bikemiamibeach.com). Aside from DecoBikes (which do not provide them at all), helmets are usually included in the price, though you may have to pay an extra $1/day for the lock.

Bike tours Dr Paul George (see box, p.86) often leads cycle tours to and around historical points of interest.

ROLLERBLADING SOUTH BEACH

Rollerblading is still popular in Miami, especially in South Beach. **Fritz's Skate, Bike & Surf Shop**, at 1620 Washington Ave (Mon–Sat 10am–9pm, Sun 10am–8pm; ☎ 305 532 1954, ⓦ fritzsmiamibeach.com), sells and rents out rollerblades and safety gear. Rentals cost $10/hr, $24/day; bike rentals are also available at the same rates.

BY BOAT

Boat rental Club Nautico (📞305 216 8879, 🌐clubnauticomiami.com) on North Miami Beach, 7910

West Drive and 4000 Crandon Blvd, Key Biscayne (📞305 361 5421), rents powerboats from $399 for a half-day.

ACCOMMODATION

Areas The lion's share of hotels and motels are in South Beach, an ideal base for nightlife, beachlife and seeing the city. Though it can be great fun to stay in one of the numerous Art Deco South Beach hotels, note that they were built in a different era, and, as such, rooms can be tiny. While there are pleasant enough places in Coconut Grove or Coral Gables, there's no compelling reason to stay in either neighbourhood. With the addition of a Miami Beach water taxi (see p.63), downtown now offers the convenience of the seashore matched with the pull of a civic centre and its accompanying restaurants and museums.

Rates and seasons Finding a place to stay in Miami is only a problem over Art Basel and important holiday weekends such as Memorial Day and Labor Day. Prices vary from $35 to $500, but you can anticipate spending at least $110 per night during the summer and $160 during the winter (or upwards of $250 in the increasing number of ultra-luxe South Beach hotels). During the winter you'd be well advised to reserve ahead, especially during peak times like Art Basel. Prices below are for high season – in other words, winter; expect lower rates from May to September. Note that parking fees hover at around $30/day, and are not included in the rates.

SOUTH BEACH

★**The Betsy Hotel** 1440 Ocean Drive 📞305 531 6100, 🌐thebetsyhotel.com; map p.51. On a quiet stretch of Ocean Drive, rooms here are turned out in soothing marble white and marigold, and have plenty of in-room amenities, such as bespoke furniture and a television in the bathroom. The rooftop deck, dotted with bamboo fronds and chaise loungers, overlooks the tempting shorefront. **$245**

★**Cadet Hotel** 1701 James Ave 📞305 672 6688, 🌐cadethotel.com; map p.51. Tranquil boutique hotel, with a fresh, clean look enhanced by bamboo floors and a patio-garden where you can enjoy a glass of wine; the fresh strawberries and chocolate in the rooms upon arrival are nice touches. **$170**

Clay Hotel 1438 Washington Ave 📞305 534 2988, 🌐clayhotel.com; map p.51. This beautiful converted monastery serves as the city's best budget hotel. The location's great, and the *Clay* is a terrific place to meet other travellers – just see a room before you commit, since some are cleaner and more welcoming than others. **$115**

Delano 1685 Collins Ave 📞305 672 2000, 🌐morganshotelgroup.com; map p.51. One of South Beach's chicest (and most expensive) lodgings mixes Art Deco with minimalist modernism (lots of white) and all-round luxury. Gauzy white curtains billow in the lobby and

the stunning pool features underwater music. **$380**

Dream South Beach 1111 Collins Ave 📞305 673 4747, 🌐dreamhotels.com; map p.51. Guestroom light switches at this imaginative hotspot turn on everything, from the vanity mirror to the beaded chandelier, and the turquoise low-lights around the bedframe. New in 2011, *Dream* has established itself as one of South Beach's "it" spots, with stellar service and a killer rooftop pool. Note that rooms are on the small side. **$229**

Edgewater South Beach 1410 Ocean Drive 📞786 517 6200, 🌐edgewatersouthbeach.com; map p.51. At the northern end of Ocean Drive, this Mediterranean Revival property pampers guests with free beach chair and umbrella use and complimentary breakfasts on the roof – complete with tremendous ocean views. No pool, but better rates as a payoff. **$170**

★**The Hotel** 801 Collins Ave 📞305 531 2222, 🌐thehotelofsouthbeach.com; map p.51. Designer Todd Oldham oversaw every element in the renovation of this hotel, and his colourful yet thoughtful makeover makes it one of the best luxury options on the beach. Don't miss the rooftop pool, shaped like a gemstone in honour of the hotel's original name, preserved in the "Tiffany" sign on the turret. **$190**

Hôtel Gaythering 1409 Lincoln Rd 📞786 284 1176, 🌐gaythering.com; map p.51. Don't sweat the strange name – this well-priced, arty boutique hotel, catering largely to gay men (it's self-proclaimed as "hetero friendly") is one of the best new places to stay in Miami. Though it's a bit of a hike from the beach (15min on foot), the location, on the western side of the island, is quite cool – the designer shops and restaurants of Lincoln Road are just steps away. **$109**

Lord Balfour 350 Ocean Drive 📞305 290 3108, 🌐lordbalfourmiami.com; map p.51. From the inscribed ceiling in the lobby to the wall-sized photos of tattooed women hanging above guestroom beds, *Lord Balfour* pops with colour and fun design quirks. Kindly staff members will point you in the direction of the beach – it's just across the street. **$185**

Miami Beach International Travellers Hostel 236 9th St 📞305 534 0268, 🌐hostelmiamibeach.com; map p.51. If you're in town to party and aren't bothered by occasional dinginess, you'll have a great time at this very popular hostel, centrally positioned in South Beach. Six-person dorms start at $35, and there are also private rooms from $80. Offers free meals, laundry, occasional language lessons, a comfortable movie lounge and also books tours. Dorms **$35**, rooms **$80**

1

Pelican 826 Ocean Drive ☎305 673 3373, ⓦpelicanhotel.com; map p.51. Irreverent Italian jeanswear company Diesel owns this hotel, so the quirky, campy decor of the rooms should come as no surprise. Each is individually themed and named – try the lush red bordello known as the "Best Whorehouse" room. **$219**

Redbury 1776 Collins Ave ☎305 604 1776, ⓦtheredbury.com/southbeach; map p.51. The hip, easy vibe of this Hollywood transplant is exemplified by its music collection – each guestroom comes with its own record player and hand-picked selection of vinyl. Wall art ranges from punchy psychedelic posters to black-and-white photographs of 1920s Miami. Even better than the rooftop's swimming area is access to *The Raleigh*'s gorgeous mid-century pool and cabana deck, across the street. **$199**

The Setai 2001 Collins Ave ☎888 625 7500, ⓦthesetaihotel.com; map p.51. Condo-tower-cum-hotel that's known for its celeb-heavy clientele (Lenny Kravitz bought a penthouse complete with recording studio in the building) as much as for its pricey, vaguely Asian-themed rooms. Splurge for the snob appeal and the best views on the beach. **$600**

SoBeYou Bed & Breakfast 1018 Jefferson Ave ☎305 534 5247, ⓦsobeyou.us; map p.51. Cosy, centrally located bed and breakfast with ten bright white rooms clustered around an Art Deco-era swimming pool, fringed with palms. You'll find cheerful Britto prints (see p.55) throughout. Gourmet breakfasts and cheap parking ($10/day) add to the value. Very friendly staff. **$170**

Surfcomber Hotel 1717 Collins Ave ☎305 532 7715, ⓦsurfcomber.com; map p.51. A classic Art Deco exterior swathes plush, distinguished guestrooms at this pet-friendly hotel with a private slip of beach. The oversized turquoise pool, framed by cabanas and swaying palm trees, is sure to please; an added perk is the complimentary wine hour that's held daily 5–6pm. **$240**

★**The Tides** 1220 Ocean Drive ☎305 604 5070, ⓦtidessouthbeach.com; map p.51. Spectacularly situated on Ocean Drive, with enormous floor-through rooms featuring ocean and city views; Kelly Wearstler is behind the glamorous design, with plush beds and linens and tech amenities like iPod docking stations and espresso machines. **$310**

Townhouse 150 20th St ☎305 534 3800, ⓦtownhousehotel.com; map p.51. From the small but beautifully designed white rooms to the chatty, cheerful staff and the relaxing roof deck filled with cushy chaise loungers, this boutique hotel aims to please – and the prices are surprisingly low, too. **$140**

Z Ocean 1437 Collins Ave ☎305 672 4554, ⓦzoceanhotelsouthbeach.com; map p.51. One of the few newly built hotels in South Beach, this all-suite spot was designed by Arquitectonica (see p.67) and surrounds a spacious outdoor courtyard; note the lobby's cut-out "skylights" – the base of the pool is lined in glass, so you'll see people swimming overhead. Many of the large, subtly decorated rooms also have private hot tubs as well as patios. The brunch restaurant *Front Porch Café* (see p.92) is just outside its lobby. **$225**

CENTRAL MIAMI BEACH

Canyon Ranch 6801 Collins Ave ☎305 514 7000, ⓦcanyonranch.com/miamibeach. If massage treatments feature heavily in your Miami fantasy, and you relish organic food and unspooled hours on a private beach, look no further than *Canyon Ranch*, a world-class spa consortium that opened here in 2008. An all-suiter, the spacious rooms come with soaking tubs and full kitchens. Unlimited free exercise classes included. **$495**

Circa 39 3900 Collins Ave ☎305 538 4900, ⓦcirca39.com. Another mid-range Miami Beach hotel given the boutique makeover: the rooms here are white with mandarin accents, and feature teak furniture and flat-screen TVs. The common areas are especially playful, with bright Modernist furniture scattered throughout the lobby as well as a handy, well-priced onsite café; incredibly cheap rates in the off season. **$120**

Courtyard Cadillac 3925 Collins Ave ☎305 538 3373, ⓦhotelcadillacmiamibeach.com. This historic Art Deco hotel, dating to 1940, was given a thorough makeover in 2013 – a flashy, 93-room tower was added to its oceanfront digs. Overlooking the boardwalk and beach, the *Courtyard* boasts two pools, a tiki bar and soothing rooms with balconies and modern art. **$179**

Eden Roc 4525 Collins Ave ☎305 531 0000, ⓦedenrocmiami.com. A Miami Beach landmark since the 1950s, *Eden Roc* was given a huge makeover in 2008 – expect infinity pools, tropical fountains, a stunning 1950s lobby and rooms enhanced by iPod docks, HDTVs and marble bathrooms. **$275**

Fontainebleau 4441 Collins Ave ☎305 538 2000, ⓦfontainebleau.com. Once the last word in glamour, this Miami icon reopened in 2008 after a lavish renovation which saw the addition of two new, luxury all-suite towers with kitchenettes and spacious balconies overlooking the Atlantic. There's a stunning pool, plus eleven restaurants and lounges and a giant spa. **$299**

Freehand Hostel 2727 Indian Creek Drive ☎305 531 2727, ⓦthefreehand.com. Set in a historic Art Deco hotel that's a 2min walk from the beach, this boutique property – with a landscaped pool, bike rental and trend-setting cocktail bar (see p.98) and restaurant – is elevating the standard for hostels everywhere. Dorms **$22**, doubles **$99**

DOWNTOWN MIAMI

Four Seasons 1435 Brickell Ave ☎305 358 3535, ⓦfourseasons.com/miami; map p.61. There are over two hundred polished chambers at this skyline-defining business hotel perched beside the waters of Biscayne Bay. Handsome guestrooms are decked out with marble bathrooms and pale wood accents and offer incredible city views. **$389**

Mandarin Oriental 500 Brickell Key Drive, Brickell Key ☎ 305 913 8288, ⓦ mandarinoriental.com/miami; map p.61. The pick of the luxury chains downtown for unbeatable service and jaw-dropping views across Biscayne Bay. Modern Asian-themed rooms come with marble bathrooms and cherry-wood furnishings, and the spa, pool deck, bar and restaurants (see p.93) are all world-class. **$259**

YVE Hotel 146 Biscayne Blvd ☎ 888 325 5017, ⓦ yvehotelmiami.com; map p.61. A sign of things to come downtown, this contemporary property has a central location just off the waterfront, and all the perks of a mid-range hotel: plush guestrooms, fitness centre and a top-notch restaurant. **$125**

CORAL GABLES

Biltmore 1200 Anastasia Ave ☎ 855 311 6903, ⓦ biltmorehotel.com; map p.75. A landmark,

BEST BUDGET EATS
Bryan in the Kitchen p.93
Burger Bobs p.96
El Palacio de los Jugos p.95
La Sandwicherie p.92
Lemoni Café p.95

Mediterranean-style hotel that has been pampering the rich and famous since 1926. The rooms, furnished in peach and cream tones, are reminiscent of a Spanish villa, but it's the massive chevron-shaped pool that proves the main draw. **$299**

Hotel St Michel 162 Alcazar Ave ☎ 305 444 1666, ⓦ hotelstmichel.com; map p.75. A small, romantic hotel just off the Miracle Mile, with modernized rooms, striped bedding and copious European antiques. Rates include a continental breakfast. **$129**

EATING

Miami does **Cuban food** best – think rice and beans, fried plantains and shredded pork sandwiches. You'll also want to try Cuban coffee: choose between *café Cubano*, strong, sweet and frothy, or *café cortadito*, a smaller version of *café con leche* (with steamed milk). **Haitian cooking** is also popular, and the restaurants in Little Haiti, just north of downtown, are the most authentic places in which to sample it. **Argentine, Colombian and Peruvian restaurants** bear witness to the city's strong Caribbean and Latin American elements. **Seafood** is abundant: succulent grouper, yellowfin tuna and wahoo, a local delicacy, are among five hundred species of fish that thrive offshore. **Stone-crab claws** (served Oct–May) are another South Florida speciality.

Opening hours As with their nightlife, Miamians tend to eat late – restaurants get quite buzzy around 8pm – and many places keep long hours to satisfy the city's cadre of partying night owls.

Tipping Always check your bill, especially on South Beach, where restaurants often add an eighteen-percent gratuity. You can cross this off if you're not happy with the service (but remember that it is customary to tip 15–20 percent in the US).

SOUTH BEACH

★ **1826 Restaurant & Lounge** 1826 Collins Ave ☎ 305 763 8860, ⓦ 1826collins.com; map p.51. For a splash-out meal, look no further than *1826*, fronted by star chef Luke Bergman and with an interior that looks like James Bond is behind things – leather banquettes, swivelling metallic chairs and a duo of lamps made from gilded machine guns. The New American menu ranges from leek croquettes ($10) to marinated burrata ($18) and short ribs with grilled artichoke ($29). Tues–Thurs 6pm–1am, Fri & Sat 6pm–3am.

Alma Mexicana 1344 Washington Ave ☎ 305 695 0880, ⓦ almamexicanamiamibeach.com; map p.51. Authentic, cheap and quick, this friendly hole-in-the-wall is the place to go for the Beach's best Mexican fare. *Alma*

delivers, so you can satisfy your late-night cravings poolside. Daily 10am–11pm.

Big Pink 157 Collins Ave ☎ 305 532 4700, ⓦ mylesrestaurantgroup.com; map p.51. Futuristic diner decked out in pink Lucite and aluminium that serves massive portions of all-American favourites – try the novel TV dinners presented on old-fashioned trays ($14.50) or the lush red-velvet cake ($10.95). The long tables are good for getting to know your fellow diners. Mon–Wed & Sun 8am–midnight, Thurs 8am–2am, Fri & Sat 8am–5am.

Bolívar 661 Washington Ave ☎ 305 305 0801, ⓦ bolivarmiamibeach.com; map p.51. Superb Latin restaurant firing off classic dishes from across South America. Prices are fair (*bandeja paisa* with steak, pork, plantains and corn cakes, $16), servers are stellar and there's live music and traditional dancing on Saturday nights. Mon–Sat 11am–11pm, Sun 11am–6pm.

Burger & Beer Joint 1766 Bay Rd ☎ 305 672 3287, ⓦ bnbjoint.com; map p.51. On the western outskirts of South Beach (near the Venetian Causeway), this popular hangout grills monster-sized burgers like the "Hotel California", topped with guacamole, coriander (cilantro) sour cream, cheddar cheese and a fried egg ($14). The duck fat fries ($6) and cheese gratin ($7) are also recommended. Good beer menu. Daily 11.30am–midnight.

1

The Café at Books & Books 927 Lincoln Rd ☎ 305 695 8898, ⓦ cafeatbooksandbooks.com; map p.51. A lovely hybrid: Miami's best independent bookstore, paired with a creative, largely vegetarian menu that's served under sidewalk café umbrellas. Great for eyeing the Lincoln Road scene. Mon–Thurs 10am–10pm, Fri 10am–11pm, Sat 9.30am–11pm, Sun 9.30am–10pm.

Café Charlotte 1497 Washington Ave ☎ 305 535 1522; map p.51. Don't be put off by the no-frills ambience at this tiny, Argentine-Italian hybrid a couple of blocks from the beach – *Café Charlotte* is a gem, with mouthwatering comfort food like skirt steak ($11.95), sweet plantains ($3.50), and chicken in wine and cream sauce ($13.95). The adjacent bakery is great for picking up *empanadas*, stuffed with savouries from ham and cheese to spicy beef and black olives. Mon–Sat noon–11pm, Sun noon–10pm.

Front Porch Café 1458 Ocean Drive ☎ 305 531 8300, ⓦ frontporchoceandrive.com; map p.51. This local hangout is refreshingly low-key given its touristy location: the delicious, dinner-plate-sized pancakes will double as both breakfast and lunch, as will the overstuffed sandwiches. Main courses hover around $15 (happy hour 4–7pm). Daily 7am–11pm.

Go-Go Fresh Food Café 926 Alton Rd ☎ 305 673 3137, ⓦ gogomiamibeach.com; map p.51. Recover from South Beach bacchanalia at this quick and healthy lunch counter serving veggie burger plates, soups and delicious salads like "SoBe shrimp" – garlicky shrimp, baby spinach, avocado, toasted almonds and coriander (cilantro) for $10.70. The flaky pastry pies, such as Nutella and banana ($2.50), are also excellent. Mon–Fri 11.30am–10pm, Sat & Sun 11.30am–9pm.

Il Sole at the Villa by Barton G 1116 Ocean Drive ☎ 305 576 8003, ⓦ thevillabybartong.com; map p.51. Unless you're staying in the on-site hotel, this exclusive restaurant is the only way for the public to satisfy its curiosity and get past the gate at *Casa Casuarina* (see p.52), Gianni Versace's former mansion (he was murdered on its steps). The dining room is opulent, the limited menu is Continental, the wine list is extensive and the prices are exorbitant. Reservations are a must. Tues–Thurs & Sun noon–2pm & 7–10pm, Fri & Sat noon–2pm & 7–11pm.

Joe's Stone Crab 11 Washington Ave ☎ 305 673 0365, ⓦ joesstonecrab.com; map p.51. Expect long lines of tourists waiting (usually a couple of hours) to pay $20 or more for a succulent plateful. Florida stone crabs are in season mid-Oct to mid-May; *Joe's* is closed Aug–Sept. Sun & Mon 5–10pm, Tues–Thurs 11.30am–2.30pm & 5–10pm, Fri & Sat 11.30am–2.30pm & 5–11pm.

★**La Sandwicherie** 229 14th St ☎ 305 532 8934, ⓦ lasandwicherie.com; map p.51. This outdoor café serves sandwiches stuffed with gourmet ingredients – prosciutto, cornichons, imported cheeses and the like – that make others look miniature in comparison, from $5.60

to $10.80. Mon–Thurs 8am–5am, Fri & Sat 8am–6am.

★**Milani Gelateria** 436 Española Way ☎ 305 532 8562, ⓦ milanigelateria.com; map p.51. Hands down, Miami Beach's best gelato, scooped from a wheel of authentic Italian flavours – both the Nutella and strawberry are to die for. Fun location too, fronted by ice-cream-cone chairs, and set in the heart of Española Way. Mon–Thurs 12.30pm–12.30am, Fri–Sun 12.30pm–1am.

News Café 800 Ocean Drive ☎ 305 538 6397, ⓦ newscafe.com; map p.51. Pavement café/brasserie with an extensive mid-price breakfast, lunch and dinner menu, and front-row seating for the South Beach promenade. Not the scene it once was, but still a local favourite. Open 24hr.

Ola 1745 James Ave, at the Sanctuary Hotel ☎ 305 695 9125, ⓦ olamiami.com; map p.51. Helmed by superstar chef Horacio Rivadero, this hot spot has decamped to a prime South Beach hotel. Highlights of the pricey pan-Latin menu include a vast range of ceviches (try the oyster or Ecuadorian shrimp) as well as some knockout mojitos. Daily 6–11pm.

★**Osteria del Teatro** 1443 Washington Ave ☎ 305 538 7850, ⓦ osteriadelteatromiami.com; map p.51. A fine-dining experience – set within a stunning Art Deco exterior – that has built its reputation on highly attentive service and some of the best Italian fare in South Beach. No wonder it comes at a premium. Pastas, such as *spaghetti puttanesca*, cost around $19, while veal *pizzaiola* is $34. Mon–Thurs & Sun 6–11pm, Fri & Sat 6pm–midnight.

Pinocchio 760 Ocean Court ☎ 305 672 3535; map p.51. In a pocket of South Beach that's low on good eats, enter this affordable Italian deli with friendly counter service and copious *tchotchkes* devoted to the eponymous puppet. Try a crisp salad tossed with mixed greens, mozzarella, provolone, mushrooms, artichokes and corn ($8.50). Excellent cappuccinos, too. Daily 8.30am–7pm.

Poseidon 1131 Washington Ave ☎ 305 534 4434, ⓦ poseidonmiami.com; map p.51. Sublime Greek restaurant with great service and a renowned seafood menu – all the fish is flown in fresh from the Aegean Sea. Order the swordfish, doused in lemon and oregano ($25), and an assortment of dips and pitta for the table ($14). Mon–Thurs noon–11pm, Fri noon–midnight, Sat & Sun 5pm–midnight.

Prime 112 112 Ocean Drive ☎ 305 532 8112, ⓦ mylesrestaurantgroup.com; map p.51. Housed in a converted 1915 hotel, this trendy spot features a dining room that pops with white leather chairs and pale walls and has waiters decked out in butcher aprons. The steak-heavy menu is pricey but tasty – and the $25 Kobe-beef hot dog is more than splurge worthy. Reservations recommended. Mon–Thurs noon–3pm & 5.30pm–midnight, Fri noon–3pm & 5.30pm–1am, Sat 5.30pm–1am, Sun 5.30pm–midnight.

★**Pubbelly** 1131 Washington Ave ☎305 532 7555, ⓦ pubbellyboys.com; map p.51. Located in South Beach's northwestern corner (dubbed "Sunset Harbour") this wildly popular gastropub offers decadent duck and pumpkin dumplings ($14) and pork and Gruyère sandwiches ($6) in a hip dining room filled with exposed brick and dangling lamps. Tues–Thurs & Sun 6pm–midnight, Fri & Sat 6pm–1am.

Puerto Sagua 700 Collins Ave ☎305 673 1115; map p.51. Where local Cubans meet gringos over excellent espresso, coffee, beans and rice. Cheap, filling breakfasts, lunches and dinners – the *ropa vieja* (shredded beef) is $10.95 and sandwiches $6–9. Daily 7.30am–2am.

Red the Steakhouse 119 Washington Ave ☎305 534 3688, ⓦ redthesteakhouse.com; map p.51. Feast upon creamed spinach ($12), truffle mashed potatoes ($16) and prime cuts of succulent steak (around $45) from a cushy black-leather banquette at this buzzy hotspot favoured by Miami Heat players. Mon–Thurs 5.30pm–midnight, Fri & Sat 5.30pm–1am.

★**Tap Tap Haitian Restaurant** 819 5th St ☎305 672 2898, ⓦ taptapmiamibeach.com; map p.51. Some of the tastiest and most attractively presented Haitian food in Miami – the goat in a peppery tomato broth is a knockout – at reasonable prices, most under $18. Wander around the restaurant to admire the Haitian murals. Daily noon–11am.

★**Yardbird** 1600 Lenox Ave ☎305 538 5220, ⓦ runchickenrun.com; map p.51. This hip, Southern crowd-pleaser, just off Lincoln Rd, serves its drinks in mason jars, has sublime desserts and does a mean fried green tomato BLT ($14). Don't leave town without ordering the fried chicken with biscuits, a sweet and savoury tower slathered with pepper jelly and home-made pickles ($14). Mon–Thurs 11.30am–11pm, Fri 11.30am–midnight, Sat 9.30am–midnight, Sun 9.30am–11pm

CENTRAL MIAMI BEACH AND NORTH

The Forge 432 41st St ☎305 538 8533, ⓦ theforge .com. Dining at this Miami Beach institution is an unmissable experience, not for the staggeringly huge wine cellar, the hearty and traditional steaks and chops (around $45), or the kitschy 1930s gilt decor, but rather for the vibrant scene, where you'll find hip locals eating alongside 60-something old-school Miami Beachers. Mon–Thurs & Sun 6–11pm, Fri & Sat till midnight.

★**Indomania** 131 26th St ☎305 535 6332, ⓦ indomaniarestaurant.com. An Indonesian restaurant owned by a Dutch couple (the husband works the front of the house while his wife cooks) that serves *rijsttafel* – platter-style small portions of rice-based dishes (a cuisine developed by Dutch colonials in the West Indies). Chicken

BEST LATE-NIGHT EATS

1826 Restaurant & Lounge p.91
The Corner p.98
La Moon p.94
La Perrada de Edgar p.93
Versailles p.96

in coconut curry, spiced aubergine (eggplant) stew, and fried fish in banana leaves are a sampling of what awaits. $26–30 per platter. Tues–Sun 6–10.30pm.

La Perrada de Edgar 6976 Collins Ave ☎305 866 4543, ⓦ laperradadeegdar.com. This wild and wacky hot-dog landmark serves 24 varieties of wieners, including the Colombian – topped with mozzarella cheese, onion, potato sticks and special sauce ($4.99). There's also the infamous "Edgar Special", slathered with mozzarella, pineapple, blackberry and plum sauces and whipped cream ($5.99). Mon–Fri noon–midnight, Sat & Sun noon–3am.

★**Moises Bakery** 7310 Collins Ave ☎305 868 0548, ⓦ moisesbakery.com. Gourmet bakery in the Argentinean expat hub that serves glistening handmade tarts, breads and *empanadas*, as well as coffee and a mouthwatering selection of fruit-topped cakes. Daily 6am–10pm.

DOWNTOWN

★**Bryan in the Kitchen** 104 NE 2nd Ave ☎305 371 7777, ⓦ bryaninthekitchen.com; map p.61. Cute little café in the heart of downtown with citrus-coloured walls and fresh cupcakes ($2.25) topped with Earl Grey, rose, *lemoni* and Nutella icing. The menu – which emphasizes organic ingredients – ranges from oatmeal with smashed banana ($4.50), to power salads with walnuts ($7) and artisanal grilled cheeses, stuffed with the likes of figs and Brie ($8). Mon–Fri 8.30am–6pm, Sat 8.30am–4pm.

★**Fratelli Milano** 213 SE 1st St ☎305 373 2300, ⓦ ristorantefratellimilano.com; map p.61. Twin brothers re-create Milan – or at least the flavour of it – in downtown with a well-regarded menu at competitive prices. The crowd-pleasing *contadina* pizza with sausage, mushroom and peppers is a mere $13, while the creamy seafood risotto rings in at $21. Mon–Thurs 11am–10pm, Fri & Sat 11am–11pm.

Jamón Iberico Pata Negra 10 SW South River Drive ☎305 324 1111, ⓦ ibericopatanegra.com; map p.61. A little tricky to find, this authentic Spanish tapas joint feels like it was airlifted from Madrid and dropped into the bottom floor of a shiny condominium tower. Pig legs dangle from the ceiling above diners savouring small plates of manchego cheese, *chorizo* and squid ink paella. Tues–Thurs noon–10pm, Fri & Sat noon–11pm, Sun noon–9pm.

La Mar 500 Brickell Key Drive, in the Mandarin Oriental ☎305 913 8358, ⓦ mandarinoriental.com; map p.61.

1

Toast someone special with a tangy *pisco* sour – the house's signature drink – at this Peruvian trailblazer with a stunning location on Biscayne Bay. Start your meal with a *nikei* ceviche to share (tuna, avocado, daikon and cucumber; $18) and finish it with chocolate mousse, topped with caramelized quinoa ($11). Daily 11.30am–3.30pm & 5.30–11pm.

★**La Moon** 97 SW 8th St ☎305 379 5617, ⓦlamoon restaurantmiami.com; map p.61. Morning, noon and night this hopping restaurant sells gut-busting fare like the "Supermoon Perro" – smoked sausage topped with bacon and egg, plus cheese chips and a choice of five sauces. Other menu highlights include traditional Colombian *arepas* (corn pancakes filled with cheese, chicken or beef) and hefty mains such as steak with rice and beans. Mon–Wed 10am–midnight, Thurs 10am–6am, Fri & Sat 9am–6am, Sun 9am–midnight.

NeMesis Urban Bistro 1035 N Miami Ave ☎305 415 9911, ⓦnemesisbistro.com; map p.61. *Haute cuisine* is the name of the game at this stylish newcomer, located in a somewhat dodgy part of town. The top-notch, diverse menu – which ranges from leek and fig braised potstickers to ostrich carpaccio – was inspired by a round-the-world trip taken by the owner. The restaurant's modern ambience is an added treat – bright white walls are overlaid with exposed pipes, black-and-white photographs and upturned umbrellas. Tues–Thurs 6–10pm, Fri & Sat 6–11pm.

Sparky's Roadside Barbecue 204 NE 1st St ☎305 377 2877, ⓦsparkysroadsidebarbecue.com; map p.61. Right in the centre of things, this casual barbecue joint with checked napkins and scuffed teal walls does the Southern culinary tradition proud – the pulled pork plate sets you back $13.75, and includes sides like mac and cheese and sweet potato mash. Mon–Thurs 11am–9pm, Fri 11am–10pm, Sat & Sun noon–10pm.

★**Ten Fruits** 143 NE 3rd Ave ☎305 373 7678, ⓦtenfruitsmiami.com; map p.61. Jumpstart your day with a coconut acai bowl ($10) or wholewheat waffles dotted with berries ($8.50) and a watermelon smoothie ($8) at this contemporary, all-white café with a devoted clientele. Mon–Fri 7am–7pm, Sat 8am–5pm.

THE BISCAYNE CORRIDOR

★**Andiamo!** 5600 Biscayne Blvd ☎305 762 5751, ⓦandiamopizzamiami.com. Half the fun of a meal at this pizzeria is the ambience: what looks a bit like a spaceship is actually a converted 1950s gas station with a busy brick oven and chrome-and-concrete dining room. The food should not be overlooked, however: this is Miami's best pizza, topped with everything from fresh basil and ricotta to cured pancetta and sweet pineapple. Mon–Thurs & Sun 11am–11pm, Fri & Sat 11am–midnight.

WYNWOOD

Panther Coffee 2390 NW 2nd Ave ☎305 677 3952, ⓦpanthercoffee.com. This arty little coffee shop is Wynwood's heartbeat. In many ways, the neighbourhood grew up around *Panther*, but the two have a symbiotic relationship and fuel each other. Inside you'll find home-roasted beans, excellent espresso drinks and gourmet pastries. Free wi-fi. Mon–Sat 7am–9pm, Sun 8am–9pm.

Zak the Baker 405 NW 26th St ⓦzakthebaker.com. Miami's best breads, with tempting aromas to greet you at the door. Kosher, artisanal loaves and a quirky, limited selection of vegetarian eats, such as roast beet and feta on toast, quiche and kale salad with roasted squash. There's a hip-yet-rustic ambience, with a chalkboard menu, picture windows and hand-carved tables. 9am–4pm; closed Sat.

MIDTOWN MIAMI

The Cheese Course 3451 NE 1st Ave, Unit 100 ☎786 220 6681, ⓦthecheesecourse.com. Dairyheads go crazy for this gourmet cheese shop and bistro with a sun-dappled patio and overstuffed sandwiches filled with prosciutto and fresh mozzarella or roast turkey with chutney and smoked cheddar. Come back at night for cheese plates to share and good deals on wine. Casual. Mon–Wed & Sun 8am–9pm, Thurs 8am–10pm, Fri & Sat 8am–11pm.

★**Sugarcane** 3252 NE 1st Ave ☎786 369 0353, ⓦsugarcanerawbargrill.com. When this raw bar opened its doors in 2011, it effectively sanctified Midtown as Miami's new foodie hotspot. Run by the masterminds behind Manhattan's *Sushi Samba*, the small-plates menu is filled with oysters, crab legs and clams ($2–30), but you can also enjoy bacon-wrapped dates ($11) and grilled Japanese aubergine (eggplant) ($6). Mon–Wed 11.30am–midnight, Thurs 11.30am–1am, Fri 11.30am–2am, Sat 10am–2am, Sun 10am–midnight.

THE DESIGN DISTRICT

★**Buena Vista Bistro** 4582 NE 2nd Ave ☎305 456 5909, ⓦbuenavistabistro.com. Outside the hustle and bustle of the Design District's heart, this neighbourhood restaurant, decked out with French posters, burgundy leather booths and specials scribbled on a wall-sized mirror, cooks up bistro classics like *bouillabaisse* and jumbo scallops *provençale* (mains $13–27). A few doors down (no.

BEST PLACES TO BLOW THE BUDGET

1826 Restaurant & Lounge p.91
The Forge p.93
La Palme d'Or p.96
Osteria del Teatro p.92
Prime 112 p.92

4590), you can grab gorgeous pastries and breads from its sister business, the *Buena Vista Deli*. Sunday brunch is stellar – don't miss the crispy French toast ($10). Service can be slow. Daily 11am–midnight.

Crumb on Parchment 3930 NE 2nd Ave ☎ 305 572 9444. Though it's set in a shopping centre, this café feels quite cosy. There's a chic country-cottage motif – mismatched chairs and lots of floral and gingham – all holding court in a sunny atrium. From the rotating menu, expect sundries such as rotisserie chicken sandwiches with goat's cheese ($10), and butter lettuce salad with jalapeño ranch dressing ($9). It's a casual place – order at the counter and the meal is brought to your table – but, given the neighbourhood, it's packed with smart dressers. Mon–Fri 9am–4pm.

Lemoni Café 4600 NE 2nd Ave ☎ 305 571 5080, ⊛ mylemonicafe.com. Short on space but long on charm, this corner café, just outside the Design District, serves up flavourful, casual fare like veggie *quesadillas* with peppers, spinach and spicy guacamole ($10) and melted Brie toasts with dates and drizzled honey ($9). Portions are mighty. Mon–Sat 11am–10.30pm, Sun 11am–5pm.

Mandolin Aegean Bistro 4312 NE 2nd Ave ☎ 305 749 9140, ⊛ mandolinmiami.com. Bring a date and feast on grilled octopus ($18), *kefte* (lamb meatballs; $14) and white sangria with rosewater ($36/pitcher) at this romantic, convivial backyard patio filled with bright blue chairs and umbrellas. The menu is hit or miss, especially for the price – it's more about the ambience. Mon–Sat noon–11pm, Sun noon–10pm.

★ **Michael's Genuine Food** 130 NE 40th St ☎ 305 573 5550, ⊛ michaelsgenuine.com. One of the hottest restaurants in the Design District, with seasonal, local ingredients whipped into eclectic creations by lauded chef Michael Schwartz. The menu features pizza and steak along with wood-roasted onion stuffed with lamb and crispy beef cheek, in sizes that range small to extra large (medium and large mains $14–29). Mon–Thurs 11.30am–11pm, Fri 11.30am–midnight, Sat 5.30pm–midnight, Sun 11am–2.30pm & 5.30–10pm.

LITTLE HAITI

Chez Le Bébé 114 NE 54th St ☎ 305 751 7639. Cheap and authentic Haitian food, with a short, basic menu of classics; try the tender *griot* (fried pork) and aromatic stewed goat. Every main meat dish comes with rice, beans, plantains and salad. Portions are massive but you'll rarely pay more than $10. Mon–Sat 8am–midnight, Sun 8am–11pm.

Soyka 5556 NE 4th Court ☎ 305 759 3117, ⊛ soykarestaurant.com. This upmarket restaurant, among the first of its kind to open in the area, serves tasty, Italian-inflected dishes (including fantastic crispy, wafer-thin pizzas) in a raw, spacious concrete hall. Lunch is much

more reasonable ($12–21 per dish) than dinner. Mon–Thurs & Sun 11am–11pm, Fri & Sat 11am–midnight.

LITTLE HAVANA

Azucar Ice Cream Company 1503 SW 8th St ☎ 305 381 0369, ⊛ azucaricecream.com. Unmissable with its hot-pink neon sign topped with an enormous, colourful cone, this ice-cream shop has addictive, Latin-inspired flavours like *café con leche*, *platano maduro* and, everyone's favourite, *abuela maria* – tangy guava, cream cheese and butter cookies folded into sweet vanilla ice cream. Mon–Wed 11am–9pm, Thurs–Sat 11am–11pm, Sun 11am–10pm.

El Cristo 1543 SW 8th St ☎ 305 643 9992, ⊛ elcristorestaurant.com. This casual Cuban restaurant has the sort of inviting atmosphere that can only be found at family-run establishments. Opened in 1972, the extensive menu has top-notch takes on *bistec de palomilla* (steak with rice, beans and plaintains; $10.99) and *masitas de puerco* (fried pork with yucca; $9.99). Located on a quiet section of the main drag removed from the hustle and bustle. Daily 8am–10pm.

★ **El Palacio de los Jugos** 5721 W Flagler St ☎ 305 264 1503, ⊛ elpalaciodelosjugos.com. A handful of tables at the back of a Cuban produce market, where the pork sandwiches and shellfish soup from the takeaway stand are the tastiest for miles. Be sure to try one of the namesake *jugos* (juices) for $2–3; orange-carrot and *guanabana* are both outstanding. Mon–Sat 8am–9pm, Sun 8am–8pm.

El Pub 1548 SW 8th St ☎ 305 642 9442. Stepping into this long-standing Cuban haunt – plastered with newspaper clippings and filled with Latin music – is like being transported to a café in Havana. While the food isn't the neighbourhood's best, *El Pub* is worth visiting for ambience and exceptional *café con leche* ($1.50). Note the colourful rooster sculpture out front, which was stolen (and returned) by pranksters in 2011. Daily 7am–midnight.

El Rey de las Fritas 1821 SW 8th St ☎ 305 644 6054, ⊛ elreydelasfritas.com. Regulars come here for one thing: the tangy *frita*, or Cuban hamburger (less than $4), smothered with home-made shoestring fries, though the batidos (shakes) are also good. Mon–Sat 8am–10.30pm.

★ **Exquisito** 1510 SW 8th St ☎ 305 643 0227, ⊛ elexquisitomiami.com. Authentic Cuban diner run by émigrés since the 1970s, and the most convenient spot for lunch if you're touring the main Little Havana drag, Calle Ocho. Hearty roast meats and sandwiches cost $6–13. Daily 7am–11pm.

Los Pinareños Frutería 1334 SW 8th St ☎ 305 285 1135. Atmospheric *frutería* stretched along the southern side of Little Havana's main drag: for $5 you'll snag a flagon

1

of juice squeezed to order. Even better, you'll rub elbows with the old-timers from the neighbourhood who hang out here during the day. Mon–Sat 6am–6pm, Sun 6am–3pm.

Versailles 3555 SW 8th St ☎305 444 0240, ⓦversaillesrestaurant.com. Gorge on inexpensive, authentic Cuban food amid a kitschy decor of chandeliers and mirrored walls (hence the name) and a buzzing neighbourhood atmosphere (you may see politicians doing deals over plates of rice and beans) – the takeaway coffee window is said to serve over a thousand *cafécitos* daily. Mon–Thurs 8am–1am, Fri 8am–2.30am, Sat 8am–3.30am, Sun 9am–1am.

Yambo 1643 SW 1st St ☎305 649 0203. For less than $6 a plate you can feast on Nicaraguan specialities like *puerca asada* (grilled pork), but the real draw is the atmosphere: a slice of Central America, with mosaic-encrusted tables, Spanish-language radio blaring from the kitchen, and a Virgin Mary shrine. Open 24hr.

CORAL GABLES

Burger Bobs 2001 Granada Blvd ☎305 567 3100; map p.75. Tucked away in the clubhouse of the public Granada Golf Course, this homespun café, with its red vinyl chairs, white plastic tables, yellow mustard bottles and nostalgic radio tunes (think Patsy Cline) is a no-frills but tasty hideaway: try the cheeseburger, a steal at $4.20. Cash only. Daily 6am–3pm.

Buttercream Cupcakes 1411 Sunset Drive ☎305 669 8181, ⓦbuttercreamcupcakes.com; map p.75. Divine hazelnut, chocolate Oreo and guava – the cupcakes here are as rich and tasty as they are beautifully presented. Makes a great gift (if you can restrain yourself from eating them before delivery). Mon–Thurs 11am–9pm, Fri & Sat 11am–10pm, Sun noon–9pm.

★**Eating House** 804 Ponce de León Blvd ☎305 448 6524, ⓦeatinghousemiami.com; map p.75. Resembling a funky ski lodge, *Eating House* has a casual ambience that belies its skill in the kitchen – the American fusion fare, such as chicken and waffles with candied bacon ($15) and pasta with truffles ($23), is some of the area's best. The "dirt cup" dessert, a tempting blend of Nutella, cookie crumbs and pretzels ($9), wins rave reviews. Seating is limited; reservations recommended for dinner. Mon 11.30am–3pm, Tues–Thurs 11.30am–3pm & 6–10.30pm, Fri 11.30am–3pm & 6–11.30pm, Sat 6–11.30pm, Sun 11am–4pm.

El Rinconcito el Chele 3791 Bird Rd ☎305 444 0700; map p.75. The lunchtime hub of Miami's power Cuban scene: within a derelict-looking building are two lunch counters and a couple of tables, with whiteboards on the wall listing the day's offerings – try the juicy *croqueta preparada* (Cuban sandwich). Also great for breakfast. Daily 7am–10pm.

Green Gables Café 327 Alhambra Circle ☎305 445 7015, ⓦgreengablescafe.com.com; map p.75. Superlative vegetarian, vegan and just plain nutritious fare that will satisfy even the pickiest carnivores. Try the coriander (cilantro) salad with chicken, avocado and citrus aioli ($12) or the black bean burger ($15), a house speciality. Mon–Fri 7.30am–4.30pm.

La Palme d'Or 1200 Anastasia Ave, in the Biltmore Hotel ☎305 913 3201, ⓦbiltmorehotel.com; map p.75. Exquisite bistro inside the opulent *Biltmore Hotel*. In the 1920s, Ginger Rogers laid down her head here, Al Capone went to galas, and Judy Garland toured the property in a gondola. You don't have to be a celebrity to reserve a table, but the impeccable service and best-in-town French fare, served beneath frescoed ceilings and twinkling chandeliers, will make you feel like a starlet. Very pricey: expect to spend $125 per person. Tues–Sat 6–10.30pm.

Matsuri 5759 Bird Rd ☎305 663 1615; map p.75. *Matsuri* flouts its humble strip-mall location by dishing up the best sushi in town. Regulars flock to the modern dining room, backed by a striking image of bamboo strands, for melt-in-your-mouth *sashimi* comprised of tuna, salmon and eel. Rolls $4–15. Tues–Thurs 11.30am–2.30pm & 5.30–10pm, Fri 11.30am–2.30pm & 5.30–11pm, Sat 5.30–11pm, Sun 5.30–10pm.

COCONUT GROVE

★**A.C.'s Icees** Kennedy Park car park, 2200 S Bayshore Drive. A.C. has been knocking out delicious frozen lemonade from his white van since 1978, long enough to become a Coconut Grove institution; the frosted drinks cost $3–6, and he also serves hot dogs. Cash only. Daily 11am–6pm.

Bombay Darbar 3195 Commodore Plaza ☎305 444 7272, ⓦbombaydarbarrestaurant.com. Perpetually packed, but for good reason – the Indian food at this Coconut Grove favourite is bar none. Classic dishes such as butter chicken ($17) and lamb *vindaloo* ($17) are well represented, but the excellent service is what makes the meal. Reservations recommended. Mon & Wed 6–10pm, Thurs & Sun noon–3pm & 6–10pm, Fri & Sat noon–3pm & 6–11pm.

Daily Bread Marketplace 2400 SW 27th St ☎305 856 0363, ⓦdailybreadmarketplace.com. Middle Eastern grocery store and restaurant where you can pick up salads, falafel and pitta sandwiches filled with fragrant ingredients. Also delicious are the spinach pie and the sticky pistachio *baklava*. Mon–Sat 9am–8pm, Sun 11am–5pm.

El Carajo 2465 SW 17th Ave ☎305 856 2424, ⓦel-carajo.com. Don't be fooled by the exterior: this Spanish restaurant shares space with a petrol station, but it's still a stellar place for tapas. Iberian delights like shrimp in garlic sauce ($13.50) and fried chickpeas ($8) are small-plates favourites; heartier appetites might feast on *tabla de carne*, a wooden platter loaded with cuts of beef, pork, chicken and lamb ($35). The extensive wine list means there's always a good match for your palate. Fill 'er up. Mon–Thurs noon–10pm, Fri & Sat noon–11pm, Sun 1–9pm.

Greenstreet Café 3468 Main Hwy ☎305 444 0244, ⓦ greenstreetcafe.net. Quaint pavement café with an eclectic assortment of low- to mid-priced cuisine ranging from Middle Eastern to Italian, including lamb burgers with goat's cheese ($16) or duck salad ($16). The terrific, hearty egg breakfasts make this spot a real scene at weekends. Mon, Tues & Sun 7.30am–1am, Wed–Sat 7.30am–3am.

Jaguar Ceviche 3067 Grand Ave ☎305 444 0216, ⓦ jaguarhg.com. The ceviche here is legendary and comes in spoon-sized, $2 portions (in addition to full-sized bowls), allowing the curious to sample broadly. Start your meal off right by ordering a table-sized round of the ceviche oriental – tuna swimming in ginger, soy, jalapeño, lime, avocado and sesame seeds ($18). Mon–Thurs 11.30am–11pm, Fri 11.30am–11.30pm, Sat 11am–11pm, Sun 11am–10pm.

Scotty's Landing 3381 Pan American Drive ☎305 854 2626, ⓦ sailmiami.com/scottys.htm. Tasty, inexpensive seafood and fish'n'chips served at marina-side picnic tables in a simple setting. You'll find it hard to spend more than $15 a head on food. It's somewhat difficult to find as it's tucked away on the water by City Hall – ask for directions. Daily 11am–11pm.

KEY BISCAYNE

Donut Gallery 83 Harbor Drive ☎305 361 9985, ⓦ donutgallerydiner.com. With its red vinyl stools and faded Formica tables, this noisy old-time diner is a great place to indulge a craving for chocolate-chip pancakes and other greasy spoon fare. Don't go expecting doughnuts however – the name remains from a former business. Daily 5.30am–3pm.

Oasis Sandwich Shop 19 Harbor Drive ☎305 361 9009. In south Florida, where anyone with two slices of bread will tell you they can make an outstanding Cuban, here's an addictive, off-the-radar place that's worth checking out on a trip through Key Biscayne. Regulars practically need an intervention from the *pan con bistec* (steak) sandwich. Daily 6am–9pm.

SOUTH MIAMI

Shorty's Bar-B-Q 9200 S Dixie Hwy ☎305 670 7732, ⓦ shortys.com. Sit at a picnic table, tuck a napkin in your shirt, and graze on barbecued ribs (full rack $17.99), chicken (wings with blue cheese dip are a steal at $8.99), and corn on the cob – pausing only to gaze at the cowboy memorabilia on the walls. Mon–Thurs & Sun 11am–10pm, Fri & Sat 11am–11pm.

Whip 'n Dip Ice Cream Shoppe 1407 Sunset Drive ☎305 665 2565, ⓦ whipndipicecream.com. This is the best ice cream in the city, with a roster of constantly changing flavours and plenty of extra sweet treats: chocolate-covered bananas, ice cream cannoli, and frozen cakes. It's a short drive off US-5, in the southern section of Coral Gables. Mon–Thurs 11am–10.30pm, Fri & Sat 11am–11.30pm, Sun noon–10.30pm.

DRINKING

For a city renowned for its nightlife, Miami is not a hard-drinking town. Its upmarket **lounges** and louche **bars** are places where you can linger all evening over a cocktail or two; most **restaurants** will also have a small bar area, as will the hipper **hotels** (in fact, the hotel bars here are often the trendiest pit stops). There are also a few old-time dive bars left where anyone determined to drink to oblivion can happily – and more cheaply – do so. Bear in mind that the dividing lines between bars, restaurants and clubs can be blurry, so check the "Nightlife" listings (see p.99) for additional suggestions. **South Beach** has the largest selection of drinking spots, though you'll find a few places worth a detour scattered around the city: the burgeoning **Biscayne Corridor** enclave on the mainland is increasingly lively in the evenings, a number of hotspots have popped up **downtown**, and there's a locals-heavy scene in **Coconut Grove** and in **Brickell**.

ESSENTIALS

Opening times Most places where you can drink don't really get going until about 10pm – before then, there's little atmosphere anywhere – and they keep serving until at least 2am. It's also worth remembering that most bars will be buzzing every night of the week, and it's often best to avoid the hippest places at weekends, when they'll be choked with partiers.

SOUTH BEACH

Abbey Brewing Company 1115 16th St ☎305 538 8110, ⓦ abbeybrewinginc.com; map p.51. Small, unpretentious, pub-like microbrewery serving the best beers on SoBe,

acclaimed for its creamy Oatmeal Stout. Daily 1pm–5am.

Automatic Slim's 1216 Washington St ☎305 672 2220, ⓦ automatic-slims.com; map p.51. Wild rock 'n' roll bar that's trashy fun, with neon-coloured shots in test tubes administered by bargirls in crop tops and plaid skirts. Tues–Sat 10pm–5am.

Club Deuce Bar 222 14th St ☎305 531 6200; map p.51. Raucous neighbourhood dive bar open until 5am, with a jukebox, pool table, and a wide-ranging clientele – everyone from cops to drag queens, artists and models. Its low prices are a major plus. Daily 8am–5am.

DiLido Beach Club Ritz Carlton South Beach, 1 Lincoln Rd ☎786 276 4000, ⓦ ritzcarlton.com; map p.51.

1

Dreamy beachfront club, with a large blue-tiled bar and day-beds scattered throughout the gardens. It's worth trying the refreshing house special, frozen mojitos, though just one costs over $20 when tax and gratuity are factored in. Daily noon–8pm.

Haven 1237 Lincoln Rd ☏305 987 8885, ⓦhaven lounge.com; map p.51. Remarkably inviting considering its ultra-hip decor. The walls, bar and ceiling at this spacious lounge are retrofitted with tiny lights that constantly morph into intoxicating chromatic schemes. The avant-garde menu features *pisco*-watermelon cocktails ($16) alongside *gyro* sliders with *tzatziki* ($10). Daily 6pm–5am.

★**Purdy Lounge** 1811 Purdy Ave ☏305 531 4622, ⓦpurdylounge.com; map p.51. An unheralded gem, this large neighbourhood bar on the less-touristed western side of South Beach pulls a loyal contingent of locals along with savvy out-of-towners. Mon–Fri 3pm–5am, Sat & Sun 6pm–5am.

The Raleigh Martini Bar 1775 Collins Ave, in the Raleigh Hotel ☏305 534 6300, ⓦraleighhotel.com; map p.51. This elegant 1940s hotel bar, with its lushly restored wood panelling, is a throwback to the heyday of cocktail culture. Mon–Thurs & Sun 6–10pm, Fri & Sat 6–11pm.

The Room 100 Collins Ave, at 1st St ☏305 531 6061; map p.51. Tiny, low-lit Miami outpost of the minimalist NYC wine and beer bar, with raw concrete floors and industrial metal tables. Daily 7pm–5am.

Rose Bar 1685 Collins Ave, in the Delano Hotel ☏305 674 5752, ⓦmorganshotelgroup.com; map p.51. Spilling onto the hotel's white gauze-draped lobby, this appropriately pinkish spot features ornate chandeliers and a long, candlelit bar. Mon–Thurs & Sun noon–2am, Fri & Sat noon–3am.

SkyBar 1901 Collins Ave, in the Shore Club ☏305 695 3100, ⓦmorganshotelgroup.com; map p.51. Sprawling outdoor bar arranged around the hotel pool, with giant overstuffed square seats and a great SoBe scene. Check out the smaller *Redroom* attached to it, with fine views of the beach and ocean, and the *Rumbar*, with 75 types of rum on offer. Mon–Wed & Sun 4pm–2am, Thurs–Sat 4pm–3am.

Wet Willie's 760 Ocean Drive ☏305 532 5650, ⓦwetwillies.com; map p.51. There's something irresistibly uncool about this fratboy-packed bar: chug one of the frozen drinks, served from washing-machine-sized mixers, on its upstairs terrace. Mon–Thurs 11am–3am, Fri & Sat 11am–4am, Sun till 3am.

CENTRAL MIAMI BEACH

Broken Shaker 2727 Indian Creek Drive, in the Freehand Hostel ☏305 531 2727, ⓦthefreehand.com. Muddled, shaken or stirred, the cocktails here are some of the freshest (many ingredients are plucked straight from

the garden) and most innovative in town. Split a punch bowl with friends, or order a kale pineapple caipirinha ($11) and hang out by the pool. Mon–Fri 6pm–2am, Sat & Sun 2pm–2am.

★**Cecconi's** 4385 Collins Ave, in the Soho Beach House ☏786 507 7902, ⓦcecconismiamibeach.com. Beautifully designed, the wooden terraces of this alfresco bar and upscale Italian restaurant are interspersed with buttonwood trees festooned in hundreds of tiny white lights. Patrons sip champagne cocktails ($14) and strike *Mad Men* poses on the powder-blue and white striped tiles. Mon–Thurs & Sun 7am–11pm, Fri & Sat 7am–midnight.

DOWNTOWN AND NORTH

Blackbird Ordinary 729 SW 1st Ave, Brickell ☏305 671 3307, ⓦblackbirdordinary.com. Just across the river from downtown, this hip tavern pleases a nice cross-section of Miamians with its potent but well-priced drinks and sexy ski-club ambience – think black banquettes, cherry-wood panelling, and a DJ booth bursting with painted blackbirds. Mon–Fri 3pm–5am, Sat & Sun 5pm–5am.

Churchill's Pub 5501 NE 2nd Ave, Little Haiti ☏305 757 1807, ⓦchurchillspub.com; map p.61. A British enclave, with big-screen live soccer matches and UK beers on tap. Look out for the enormous Union Jack emblazoned on the side of the building. There's live music too. Daily 11am–3am.

★**The Corner** 1035 N Miami Ave, downtown ☏305 961 7887, ⓦthecornermiami.com; map p.61. A porcelain-topped bar, candlelit corners, and cocktails mixed with bitters give this downtown favourite a bygone-era feel. If you're peckish, try a salad topped with tabouli, tomato and feta ($9.50) or the famed *croque madame* sandwich ($10), which oozes with egg and béchamel sauce ($10). One caveat: it's in a ropey neighbourhood. Mon–Thurs 4pm–5am, Fri & Sat 4pm–8am, Sun 7pm–5am.

Magnum Lounge 709 NE 79th St, Biscayne Corridor ☏305 757 3368; map p.61. This out-of-the-way restaurant-bar feels more like a bordello or a speakeasy, with its lush red banquettes and hidden entrance. The food's so-so, but the campy sing-alongs around the piano and stiff cocktails make it a fun detour for a drink or two. Tues–Thurs 5pm–midnight, Fri & Sat 5pm–2am.

CORAL GABLES

The Bar 172 Giralda Ave ☏305 442 2730, ⓦgablesthebar.com; map p.75. Established in 1946, this inviting hole-in-the-wall has a friendly atmosphere and well-worn wooden booths positioned on its checkerboard floor. Ladies score free drinks at Friday's happy hour (5.30–7.30pm). Daily 11.30am–3am.

Titanic 5813 Ponce de León Blvd ☎305 668 1742, ⓦtitanicbrewery.com; map p.75. Excellent micro-brewery, serving draught stouts and ales brewed on the premises (pints $5); the boiler-room nut-brown ale is magnificent. Very popular with students. Frequent live jazz and blues. Mon–Thurs & Sun 11.30am–1am, Fri & Sat 11.30am–2am.

NIGHTLIFE

Miami is a city with a flexible concept of what makes a club or a restaurant or a bar: you could end up dancing almost anywhere, since aside from a few megaplexes (see below) almost every dancefloor is attached to a bar or restaurant. And while Miami's nightlife scene may have sobered up slightly since the debauched and celebrity-studded 1990s, there's still plenty of choice and – especially away from the beach – some intriguing options. Many of the major clubs (like *Space*) are located in **Park West**, a warehouse district just north of downtown, though there's little to do here other than dance. Earlier in the evening, you're better off sticking to **South Beach** and one of the better bars for dancing, like *Mynt*. Otherwise, if you're feeling adventurous, skip the hard house and techno beats, and check out one of the city's salsa or merengue clubs, hosted by Spanish-speaking DJs, and mainly found in **South Beach** and **Little Havana**.

ESSENTIALS

Club nights The best place for up-to-date listings is the free-sheet *New Times* (published Thurs) or the website ⓦcooljunkie.com.

Cover charges and entry restrictions Expect a cover charge of around $25, and a minimum age of 21 (it's normal for ID to be checked). In a city as VIP-conscious as Miami, it also pays to remember that the downright scruffy will be turned away at almost every door.

Gay clubs Many of the clubs below present gay nights during the week, but there are plenty of gay-and-lesbian-specific clubs too (see p.103).

Opening times Most places open at 10pm, but don't even think of turning up before midnight as they only hit a peak between then and 2am – although some continue until 7 or 8am. However, Miami Beach's alcohol laws prohibit drinks from being served after 5am – past this you'll need to head to the mainland, where there's no such proscription on partying. Note that clubs open and close with alarming regularity in Miami, so call ahead before you jump in a taxi.

MIAMI BEACH

Cameo 1445 Washington Ave ☎305 587 2272, ⓦcameomiami.com; map p.51. Once the hardest-partying club on the Beach, the word on the street is that *Cameo*'s star is on the wane. Expect to pay $20 for well drinks, dress nicely and get ready to shake it up to hip-hop beats. Tues, Fri & Sat 11pm–5am.

LIV 4441 Collins Ave, in the Fontainebleau hotel ☎305 674 4680, ⓦlivnightclub.com; map p.51. The city's one-stop clubbing utopia – a throbbing, sprawling dancefloor with all the elements in play: gruff bouncers, high heels, short skirts, dapper men, very expensive cocktails, flashing neon lights, a beautiful crowd, and even the occasional celebrity. In the city that made partying an art form, *LIV* is located inside its most outrageous establishment – the legendary *Fontainebleau* (see p.58). Wed–Sun 11pm–5am.

Mansion 1235 Washington Ave ☎305 695 8411, ⓦmansionmiami.com; map p.51. Sprawling theatre-cum-nightclub complex, with six VIP areas, nine bars and five dancefloors, each with its own style of music; hip-hop and sets by big-name DJs are the most popular. Mon & Wed–Sat 11pm–5am.

Mokaï 235 23rd St ☎305 673 1409, ⓦmokaimiami.com; map p.51. This enormous, moody lounge fills with a glossy, dressy crowd who don't mind paying for bottle service. The incomprehensible name's a nod to its inspiration, a vast canyon in New Zealand used to film *Lord of the Rings*. If you're peckish, there's a snack menu served until 5am. Mon, Fri & Sat 11pm–5am.

Mynt Ultra Lounge 1921 Collins Ave ☎305 532 0727, ⓦmyntlounge.com; map p.51. Lounge/dance club washed in green light, with a vast bar, large black leather sofas and backlit Perspex tables for bottle service. It's becoming more mainstream after several years as the hottest nightspot in town, but expect a tough door policy any night of the week. Thurs–Sat midnight–5am.

★**Nikki Beach** 1 Ocean Drive ☎305 538 1111, ⓦnikkibeachmiami.com; map p.51. Right on the sand, this massive club, featuring loungers, beds and palm trees, offers an iconic South Beach experience. The food is passable, but the host of international and local DJs is the main reason to show up. Mon–Thurs noon–6pm, Fri & Sat noon–11pm, Sun 11am–5am.

MAINLAND

Club Space 34 NE 11th St, Park West ☎305 375 0001, ⓦclubspace.com; map p.61. This downtown warehouse pioneer has a rough decor and highly regarded resident DJs, spinning a mix of house and hip-hop. Most people migrate here when the other venues shut down, for after-hours dancing until dawn. Fri 10pm–Sat 10am, Sat 10pm–Sun 4pm.

Discotekka 950 NE 2nd Ave, Park West ☎305 371 3773, ⓦdiscotekka.com; map p.61. A night at this venue, sprawling across 35,000 square feet, is a five-for-one deal, with distinct clubs and music styles in each of its different rooms, from the Egypt-themed *Allure* to Asian-inspired *Discotekka*. Fri & Sat 10pm–5am.

E11Even 29 NE 11th St, Park West ☎ 305 829 2911, ⊛ 11miami.com; map p.61. State-of-the-art, Las Vegas-style venue known for its wild live performances (think burlesque meets contortion). Open 24hr.

LIVE MUSIC

Live music can be a bit hit-and-miss in Miami, though it's not hard to find **rock, jazz, reggae and Latin bands** playing somewhere in town. If you're hoping to catch some good **Cuban music**, Little Havana has the best options.

Ticket prices Other than for megastar performers (who charge at least $50 a ticket), expect to pay $25 and upwards to see a band you've heard of; for a local act, admission will be $5–10 or free.

LATIN

★ **Hoy Como Ayer** 2212 SW 8th St, Little Havana ☎ 305 541 2631, ⊛ hoycomoayer.us. A hidden gem, this dark, smoky joint is a superb place to discover funky, emerging Latin talent. The walls are plastered with black-and-white photos of Cuban crooners past, and the dancefloor's always filled with a happy crowd. Cover $7–35. Wed–Sat 9am–3am.

Mango's 900 Ocean Drive, South Beach ☎ 305 673 4422, ⊛ mangos.com; map p.51. Shamelessly tacky and gloriously over-the-top, with mainstream, Latin-inflected music spilling out onto the pavement. Best on weekdays when the crowd's more local. Cover $5–20 after 8pm. Daily noon–4am.

ROCK, JAZZ, REGGAE AND HIP-HOP

The Cabaret South Beach 233 12th St, South Beach ☎ 305 763 8799, ⊛ thecabaretsouthbeach.com. Convivial jazz, burlesque and piano-playing venue where servers and bartenders double as astounding songbirds. No cover. Daily 7pm–2am.

Churchill's Pub 5501 NE 2nd Ave, Little Haiti ☎ 305 757 1807, ⊛ churchillspub.com. This pub (see p.61) is a good place to hear local hopeful rock, indie and jazz bands. Cover usually $8–15.

Electric Pickle 2826 N Miami Ave, Wynwood ☎ 305 456 5613, ⊛ electricpicklemiami.com. Smoky, divey venue known for its solid array of electronica DJs and local rock bands. Dance under the massive disco ball upstairs, or kick back and play groupie on the outdoor patio. Cover about $15. Wed–Sat 10pm–5am.

Grand Central 697 N Miami Ave, downtown ☎ 305 377 2277, ⊛ grandcentralmiami.com; map p.61. This spacious nightclub-cum-live-music-venue books notable rock and hip-hop acts like Lauryn Hill, Ladytron and The Rapture. Located in a dodgy neighbourhood, *Grand Central* is pulling in regulars and helping to revitalize downtown. Check online for schedule.

★ **Jazid** 1342 Washington Ave, South Beach ☎ 305 673 9372, ⊛ jazid.net; map p.61. An alternative to the relentless house music heard on South Beach's main clubbing drag, *Jazid* showcases a blend of Latin, reggae, hip-hop and jazzy funk – live bands backed up by DJs most nights. Daily 9pm–5am.

Luna Star Café 775 NE 125th St, North Miami ☎ 305 799 7123, ⊛ lunastarcafe.com. This largely vegetarian café hosts an eclectic range of live bands and folk concerts, usually from 8pm on, but phone before you go. There is a $10 minimum per person charge (for drinks/food) on live nights, and sometimes a cover ($10). Tues–Sat 4pm–midnight.

★ **The Stage** 170 NE 38th St, Design District ☎ 305 576 9577, ⊛ thestagemiami.com. Under-the-radar gem with a great outdoor patio and a modish interior hung with local art and geometric chandeliers. Plenty of bands rock out here, and patrons are low-key and fun. Satisfy your late-night cravings at the food truck parked out back. Tues 10pm–2am, Wed 9pm–2am, Fri & Sat 9pm–5am, Sun 2pm–2am.

CLASSICAL MUSIC, DANCE AND OPERA

In the past decade, Miami has transformed its classical music scene by unveiling two extraordinary performance spaces: the **Adrienne Arsht Center for the Performing Arts** in downtown and the **New World Center** on Lincoln Road. **Tickets** generally cost $20–150, with opera tickets at the upper end of the range. For dance, one to watch is the **Ballet Flamenco La Rosa** (☎ 305 899 7730, ⊛ balletflamencolarosa.com), devoted to exploring new and avant-garde styles based on traditional Flamenco and Latin dance; call for schedules and prices (tickets about $30). To find out what's on, check the **listings** in the free *New Times* (published on Thurs).

Adrienne Arsht Center for the Performing Arts 1300 Biscayne Blvd, downtown ☎ 305 949 6722, ⊛ arshtcenter.org. Premier arts venue in Miami, with three main performance spaces (see p.64). It's home to the Florida Grand Opera (⊛ fgo.org), which brings impressive

names to the area to perform a varied repertoire, and the Miami City Ballet (⊛ miamicityballet.org), two of the city's foremost performing arts companies.

The Fillmore Miami Beach at the Jackie Gleason Theater 1700 Washington Ave, South Beach

1

☎ 305 673 7300, ⓦ fillmoremb.com. Biggest venue in Miami Beach, with acts tending more towards pop and rock music, but with occasional dance and classical concerts.

Gusman Concert Hall, Frost School of Music 1314 Miller Drive, University of Miami ☎ 305 284 2438, ⓦ music.miami.edu. The Frost School puts on concerts year-round by guest artists as well as university ensembles (which are usually free).

Miami-Dade County Auditorium 2901 W Flagler St, downtown ☎ 305 547 5414, ⓦ miamidade.gov/parks. Huge, county-owned venue hosting opera, symphony orchestras, theatre, concerts and ballets.

New World Center 500 17th St, South Beach ☎ 305 673 3330, ⓦ nws.edu. A beautiful 756-seat venue (see p.56) on Lincoln Road that's home to the New World Symphony Orchestra (ⓦ nws.edu), and offers concert experience to some of the finest graduate classical musicians in the US.

Olympia Theater at Gusman Center 174 E Flagler St, downtown Miami ☎ 305 374 2444, ⓦ olympiatheater .org. Historic and atmospheric venue with an eclectic line-up of ballet, opera, rock, folk and classical music.

THEATRE

Miami has a strong, lively **theatre** scene. Spanish speakers should make a point of visiting one of the city's **Spanish-language** theatres, whose programmes are listed in *El Nuevo Herald* (the Spanish-language version of the *Miami Herald* newspaper). For **listings**, check the free *New Times* (published on Thurs).

Actors' Playhouse 280 Miracle Mile, Coral Gables ☎ 305 444 9293, ⓦ actorsplayhouse.org. There are three stages here – a 100-seat black-box raw space for experimental work, the 300-seat Balcony Theater, and the main stage, which is twice the size. Often part of the Off-Broadway tryout circuit for major new shows, as well as showy local stagings of favourites such as *Grease* or *Les Misérables*. Tickets $35–50.

The New Theatre South Miami-Dade Cultural Arts Center, 10950 SW 211 St, South Miami ☎ 786 573 5300, ⓦ new-theatre.org. Sitting neatly between mainstream and alternative, this intimate theatre company often produces the best work in the city; the Pulitzer-winning *Anna in the Tropics* was commissioned through them.

Performs in a flashy space designed by Arquitectonica (see p.67). Tickets $35–40.

Olympia Theater at the Gusman Center 174 E Flagler St ☎ 305 374 2444, ⓦ olympiatheater.org. Classical and contemporary plays, music and dance are staged here from October to June. The only way to check out the elaborate interior is by taking in a show. Tickets vary dramatically according to performances, from $8 to $150.

Teatro de Bellas Artes 2173 SW 8th St ☎ 305 325 0515, ⓦ teatrodebellasartes.com. A Spanish-language theatre that's good for plays and musicals.

Teatro Trail 3715 SW 8th St ☎ 305 443 1009, ⓦ teatrotrail.com. The best Spanish-language theatre for comedies.

FILM

The choice of movies in Miami is vibrant and wide ranging. The **Miami Film Festival** (☎ 305 237 3456, ⓦ miamifilmfestival.com) is ten days and nights of new films from far and wide in March held at various locations across the city. There's also a superb **Gay & Lesbian Film Festival** in April (see p.102). In fact, at one point in American history, Florida rivalled Hollywood as the film capital of the world (see p.467).

CINEMAS

There are plenty of multi-screen cinemas inside shopping malls showing first-run American features.

Coral Gables Art Cinema 260 Aragon Ave, Coral Gables ☎ 786 385 9689, ⓦ gablescinema.com. Newish theatre with an intriguing roster of art-house, independent and silent films. Great location – right in the heart of the neighbourhood – that's nicely sited for dinner and a movie. Tickets $11.50.

Cosford Cinema University of Miami campus, Memorial Building, Coral Gables ☎ 305 284 4861, ⓦ cosfordcinema.com. Shows classic and new indie movies. Tickets $9.

Miami Beach Cinematique 1130 Washington Ave, South Beach ☎ 305 673 4567, ⓦ mbcinema.com. Excellent line-up of art-house films – tickets usually $11.

★**O Cinema** 90 W 29th St, Wynwood Arts District ☎ 305 571 9970, ⓦ o-cinema.org. Cool little independent theatre with charismatic owners and home-made snacks; wine and beer also served. Get there early to snag one of the coveted love seats at the front. New location on Miami Beach at 500 71st Ave. Tickets $11.

Paragon Grove 13 3015 Grand Ave, Coconut Grove ☎ 305 446 6843, ⓦ paragontheaters.com. Multiplex cinema sporting the latest in technology, and the best option for downtown, Key Biscayne and Coconut Grove. Tickets $11.50.

Regal South Beach 18 1120 Lincoln Rd, South Beach ☎ 305 673 6766, ⓦ regmovies.com. The only multiplex in South Beach, showing all the main Hollywood blockbusters. Tickets $15.

★**Tower Theater** 1508 SW 8th St, Little Havana

1

☎305 643 8706, ⊛towertheatermiami.com. Handsome 1926 Art Deco theatre screening international and Spanish-language films (subtitles in English). Tickets $10.

FESTIVALS

Miami likes to party, and the city puts on a wide variety of festivals year-round. **Art festivals** have become increasingly in vogue in recent years, with major events like Art Basel (see p.50) complemented by monthly Art Walks in Wynwood (see box, p.68).

JANUARY
Art Deco Weekend ☎305 672 2014, ⊛artdecoweekend.com. Talks and free events along Ocean Drive, focusing on South Beach architecture. Generally held the second weekend of Jan.

Homestead Championship Rodeo ☎305 247 3515, ⊛homesteadrodeo.com. Professional rodeo cowboys compete in steer wrestling, bull riding, calf roping and bareback riding. Final weekend.

FEBRUARY
Coconut Grove Arts Festival ☎305 447 0401, ⊛cgaf .com. Hundreds of talented unknowns display their works along South Bayshore Drive in Coconut Grove and on nearby streets. Third weekend.

MARCH
Carnaval Miami/Calle Ocho Festival ☎305 644 8888, ⊛carnavalmiami.com. A nine-day celebration of Latin culture, with Hispanic-themed events across the city culminating in the huge Calle Ocho street party in Little Havana, with food kiosks and live music. First week of March.

The Fair ☎305 223 7060, ⊛thefair.me. A celebration of southern Florida's agricultural traditions, including home-made crafts, music and amusement rides at the Fair Expo Center on Coral Way. Last week of March, continuing into the first week of April.

Miami International Film Festival ☎305 237 3456, ⊛miamifilmfestival.com. Art-house and mainstream films from the US and overseas are shown across the city at venues including the Regal Theater on South Beach and the Gusman Center in downtown Miami. First week of March.

Miami Open ☎305 442 3367, ⊛miamiopen.com. Men and women compete in the world's largest tennis tournament held at the Crandon Park Tennis Center in Key Biscayne. Last week of March.

Winter Music Conference ☎954 563 4444, ⊛wintermusicconference.com. This convention brings together music promoters, producers, managers and well-known DJs who perform at local clubs. Third week of March.

APRIL
Miami Gay and Lesbian Film Festival ☎305 751 6305, ⊛mglff.com. Amateur and professional submissions are shown at different Miami Beach venues, including the botanical garden. End of April.

JUNE
Goombay Festival ☎305 446 0643, ⊛goombayfestivalcoconutgrove.com. A spirited bash in honour of Bahamian culture, in and around Coconut Grove's Peacock Park. Early June.

JULY
America's Birthday Bash ☎305 358 7550, ⊛miami4thofjuly.com. Music, fireworks and a laser-light show celebrate Independence Day at Bayfront Park in downtown Miami.

OCTOBER
Festival Miami ☎305 284 4940, ⊛festivalmiami .com. Four weeks of performing and visual arts events organized by the University of Miami, mostly taking place at the Adrienne Arsht Center for the Performing Arts and the university.

Columbus Day Regatta ⊛columbusdayregatta.net. Florida's largest watersports event is a race commemorating Columbus's historic voyage. At Key Biscayne. Second Mon of Oct.

NOVEMBER
Miami Book Fair International ☎305 237 3258, ⊛miamibookfair.com. A wealth of volumes from across the world spread across the campus of Miami-Dade College in downtown Miami. Second week of Nov.

The White Party ⊛whiteparty.org. Huge HIV/AIDS fundraiser held over the Thanksgiving weekend, with parties held across the city culminating in the outrageous White Party costumed ball. Last week of Nov.

DECEMBER
Art Basel Miami Beach ⊛artbasel.com. One of the most important art festivals in the US, combining top galleries with a programme of special exhibitions, parties and events featuring music, film, architecture and design. Exhibition sites are located throughout South Beach and Wynwood. Generally the first weekend in Dec.

King Mango Strut ☎305 582 0955, ⊛kingmangostrut .org. A very alternative New Year's Eve celebration, with tonnes of wild and wonderful costumes (think "Cuban Eye for the Gringo Guy") parading through Coconut Grove.

GAY AND LESBIAN MIAMI

Miami has long been viewed as a prime destination by **gay and lesbian tourists** – a welcoming place with an "anything goes" Caribbean vibe. Now, though, the pace has slowed somewhat as mainstream tourism has taken over the beach – the number of gay-targeted bars and clubs has dwindled as gay or lesbian locals have migrated further up the coast to Fort Lauderdale (see p.177). Even as the population shifts, there's little evidence of discrimination or discomfort with gay and lesbian tourists anywhere in the city, though outside of **South Beach** same-sex couples are less likely to stroll hand-in-hand.

RESOURCES

Gay South Beach ⓦsobegayinfo.com. Useful website with advice, travel tips and plenty of listings.

Hot Spots Magazine ⓦhotspotsmagazine.com. Covers the whole of the state, with a heavy focus on the party scene; better for men's information than for women's.

Miami Dade Gay & Lesbian Chamber of Commerce 1130 Washington Ave, First Floor (North) Corridor, South Beach ⓣ305 673 4440, ⓦgogaymiami.com. Can advise on accommodation, beachlife and nightlife.

Wire Magazine ⓦwireweekly.com. South Beach-centric weekly freesheet available in bars, record stores and clubs that's good for clubs and other nightlife listings. Published every Thurs.

BARS AND CLUBS

Palace 1200 Ocean Drive, South Beach ⓣ305 531 7234, ⓦpalacesouthbeach.com; map p.51. Friendly, welcoming bar-café opposite the beach, with a diverse clientele – old and young, buff and less so. Widely loved for its drag shows (Sat & Sun at 11.30am & 2pm). Daily 11am–1am.

Score 1437 Washington Ave, South Beach ⓣ305 535 1111, ⓦscorebar.net; map p.51. This video bar and dancing magnet attracts a dressed-up, mostly male crowd. Upstairs is the swishy, dressier *Crème Lounge*. Cover for club nights $7–20. Daily 3pm–5am.

SoBe Social Club ⓣ305 535 6696, ⓦsobesocialclub .com. Gay promoter Edison Farrow runs this roaming party, which shuttles between different venues every day of the week; the crowd's youngish and friendly, making most of the parties great fun. Check website for schedule.

Twist 1057 Washington Ave, South Beach ⓣ305 538 9478, ⓦtwistsobe.com; map p.51. A South Beach institution, it's a party gone wild, with a maze of seven rooms (each with a different vibe), an outdoor terrace and two techno dancefloors. There's a separate building toward the back of the patio where go-go boys perform. No cover. Daily 1pm–5am.

FESTIVALS

Gay culture utterly subsumes straight culture twice a year: during the White Party at Thanksgiving (see opposite), and at the Winter Party (ⓦwinterparty.com) in March, the biggest gay beach party in North America.

SHOPPING

There are plenty of opportunities to exercise your credit card in Miami, where balmy temperatures make store browsing particularly enjoyable. Music buffs will be well satisfied here, especially anyone interested in Latin culture. For clothing boutiques and chains, head to **Lincoln Road** (see p.54), an alfresco, pedestrian-only stretch on South Beach. Luxury labels – such as Dior, Louboutin and Hermès – can be found in the **Design District**.

BOOKS

Barnes & Noble 152 Miracle Mile, Coral Gables ⓣ305 446 4152; map p.75. The only centrally located branch of this mega-chain within reach of downtown Miami or Miami Beach, stocking the usual wide mix of books and records. Daily 9am–11pm.

Books & Books 265 Aragon Ave, Coral Gables ⓣ305 442 4408, ⓦbooksandbooks.com; map p.75. Excellent stock of general titles but especially strong on Floridian art and design, travel and new fiction; also has author signings and talks. Branches: 927 Lincoln Rd, South Beach (ⓣ305 532 3222), and 9700 Collins Ave, Bal Harbour (ⓣ305 864 4241). Mon–Thurs & Sun 9am–11pm, Fri & Sat 9am–midnight.

The Bookstore in the Grove 3390 Mary St, Coconut Grove ⓣ305 443 2855, ⓦthebookstore.co. A

bookworm's treasure-trove overflowing with titles from every literary genre. There's a nice café on-site too, serving sandwiches, coffee and snacks like carrot cake and *empanadas*. Mon–Thurs & Sun 7.30am–8pm, Fri & Sat 7.30am–9pm.

Fifteenth Street Books 296 Aragon Ave, Coral Gables ⓣ305 442 2344; map p.75. Run by the original founder of Books & Books, this highly browsable secondhand store is strong on art books and old hardcovers in prime condition. Mon–Sat 11am–7pm.

Libreri Mapou 5919 NE 2nd Ave, Little Haiti ⓣ305 757 9922, ⓦlibrerimapou.com. Go-to Haitian bookstore with helpful staff and an extensive collection of Creole books and CDs, T-shirts and even a home-brewed cocktail mix (see p.70). Daily 11am–7pm.

1

CLOTHES AND THRIFT STORES

★**Acqua Fashion Group** 3138 Ponce de Léon Blvd, Coral Gables ☎305 447 1490. Jewel box of a shop that runs the clothing gamut, from summery dresses and eventwear to skinny jeans and tailored shirts. The best part of a visit here is spending time with the owner, whose sharp eye rarely fails when selecting customer try-ons. Great prices. Mon–Sat noon–8pm.

Alchemist 1109 Lincoln Rd and 1111 Lincoln Rd (level 5), South Beach ☎305 531 4653 and 305 531 4815, ⓦshopalchemist.com; map p.51. This industrial space is like an art museum for clothes. Located on the fifth floor of a car park (of all places), there are mirrored ceilings and slim racks of pricey items. It's worth a visit for the views alone. The original shop (no. 1109) is a high-end boutique with fancy candles, gifts and haute labels like Proenza Schoeler and Alaïa. Daily 10am–10pm.

Emporium 2606 Ponce de Léon Blvd, Coral Gables ☎786 268 0689, ⓦshopemporiummiami.com; map p.75. Sweet, baby-blue gift boutique with a great selection of kids' clothes, jewellery, fun homeware and well-priced, stylish womenswear. Mon–Fri 11am–7pm, Sat noon–7pm.

Ramón Puig 5840 SW 8th St, Little Havana ☎305 266 9683, ⓦramonpuig.com. Pick up one of the billowy Cuban shirts known as *guayaberas* here; the cheapest cost around $40, while a custom-made design starts at $250. Second location downtown at 24 W Flagler St. Mon–Sat 10am–7pm, Sun 10am–4pm.

★**Venissac** 1627 Washington Ave, South Beach ☎305 672 8111, ⓦvenissac.com; map p.51. Like a seersucker suit or a martini served poolside, Venissac is a Miami classic: men's *guayaberas*, linen trousers and shoes, women's halter dresses, silk scarves and bright beach bags, all designed with the label's signature "tropical elegance" look. Mon–Sat 11am–9pm, Sun 11am–8pm.

DEPARTMENT STORES AND MALLS

Bal Harbour Shops 9700 Collins Ave, Miami Beach ☎305 866 0311, ⓦbalharbourshops.com. Packed with designer names like Gucci and Prada, this upmarket mall is always crowded, but great fun to browse in. Mon–Sat 10am–9pm, Sun noon–6pm.

CocoWalk 3015 Grand Ave, Coconut Grove ☎305 444 0777, ⓦcocowalk.net. In the heart of Coconut Grove, this open-air complex has a relatively small range of stores and some good places to eat. Mon–Thurs & Sun 10am–10pm, Fri & Sat 10am–11pm.

The Falls US-1 and SW 136th St, South Miami ☎305 255 4570, ⓦshopthefalls.com. Sit inside a gazebo and contemplate the waterfalls and the rainforest that prettify suburban Miami's classiest set of shops. Mon–Sat 10am–9pm, Sun noon–7pm.

Mary Brickell Village 901 S Miami Ave ☎305 381 6130, ⓦmarybrickellvillage.com. Located in the heart of Miami's financial district, this fancy mall offers plenty of bars and restaurants as well as shops: Village Humidor, Sowinski Jewelers, Studio LX and Mogra among them. Mon–Thurs 11am–9pm, Fri & Sat 11am–10pm, Sun noon–6pm.

Premium Outlets 250 E Palm Drive, Florida City ☎305 248 4727, ⓦpremiumoutlets.com. On the Florida's Turnpike and US-1, conveniently located for people travelling to the Keys or Everglades. Dedicated shoppers will find huge savings on name brands. Mon–Sat 10am–9pm, Sun 11am–6pm.

Village of Merrick Park Ponce de León Blvd and US-1, Coral Gables ☎305 529 0200, ⓦvillageofmerrickpark .com. Fairly recent upmarket rival to long-established Bal Harbour Shops: amid the open-air walkways, you'll find a branch of the sumptuous Elemis Spa, as well as fashions from Burberry, Diane von Furstenberg and Jimmy Choo. Mon–Sat 10am–9pm, Sun noon–6pm.

FOOD

Delicias de España 4016 SW 57th Ave, Coral Gables ☎305 669 4485, ⓦdeliciasdeespana.com; map p.75. An Old World trading post in the middle of subtropical Miami. There are huge bottles of olive oil, Serrano ham – sold either whole hog or sliced paper-thin – wineskins and paella pans. There's also a café for grazing on tapas and a bakery peddling fresh pastries. It's like having all the vendors of a traditional Spanish market holding court under one roof. Mon–Wed 7am–9pm, Thurs–Sat 7am–10pm, Sun 7am–4pm.

MUSIC

Grooveman Music 1543 Washington Ave, South Beach ☎305 535 6257, ⓦshop.groovemanmusic.com; map p.51. A DJ's dream, stocking an ample selection of house and trance. Daily noon–10pm.

Lily's Records 1419 SW 8th St, Little Havana ☎305 856 0536. Unsurpassed stock of salsa, merengue and other Latin sounds, as well as guitars and DVDs. Daily 9am–8pm.

★**Sweat Records** 5505 NE 2nd Ave, Little Haiti ☎786 693 9309, ⓦsweatrecordsmiami.com. Indie hangout next to *Churchill's Pub* (see p.61) with artfully compiled stacks of CDs and records. Also has a vegan café, wi-fi, free concerts, comedy nights, and even the occasional waffle breakfast. Tues–Sat noon–10pm, Sun noon–5pm.

Uncle Sam's Music 939 Washington Ave, South Beach ☎305 532 0973, ⓦunclesamsmusic.net; map p.51. Established in 1984, this Miami landmark peddles techno, trance and rock, with a solid collection of vinyl in addition to CDs. Central location, near the beach, and just a few blocks down from Grooveman Music (see above). Mon–Sat 10am–10pm, Sun 11am–10pm.

CIGARS

Little Havana Cigar Factory 1106 SW 8th St, Little Havana ☎305 858 4162, ⊛lhcfstore.com. One of the best smokeshops in the city, with rows of cigar boxes, freshly brewed Cuban coffee, and soft leather seats to relax with them both. Mon & Sun 10am–6pm, Tues–Sat 10am–7pm.

DIRECTORY

Consulates Canada, 200 S Biscayne Blvd, Suite 1600, downtown Miami (☎305 579 1600); France, 1395 Brickell Ave, Suite 1050, downtown Miami (☎305 403 4150); Germany, Suite 2200, 100 N Biscayne Blvd, downtown Miami (☎305 358 0290); Netherlands, 701 Brickell Ave, 5th floor, downtown Miami (☎786 866 0480); UK, 1001 Brickell Bay Drive, Suite 2800, wntown Miami (☎305 400 6400).

Hospitals In Miami: Jackson Memorial Hospital, 1611 NW 12th Ave (☎305 585 1111, ⊛jacksonhealth.org); Mercy Hospital, 3663 S Miami Ave (☎305 854 4400, ⊛mercymiami.com). In Miami Beach: Mt Sinai Medical Center, 4300 Alton Rd (☎305 674 2121, ⊛msmc.com). All have casualty departments/emergency rooms.

Police Non-emergency: ☎305 673 7900 (Miami Beach Police); emergency: ☎911. If you are robbed anywhere on Miami Beach, report it at the station at 1100 Washington Ave; the report (for insurance purposes) can usually be collected within 3–5 days (records office Tues–Fri 8am–3pm; ☎305 673 7100).

Post offices In Miami Beach, 1300 Washington Ave (☎305 672 2447); in downtown Miami, 500 NW 2nd Ave (☎305 373 7562); in Coral Gables, 20 Miracle Mile & 251 Valencia Ave (☎305 443 2532); in Coconut Grove, 3191 Grand Ave (☎305 529 6700). All open Mon–Fri 8.30am–5pm, Sat 8.30am–2pm, or longer hours.

1

The Florida Keys

BAHIA HONDA STATE PARK

The Florida Keys

Trailing from Florida's southern tip, the Florida Keys are a string of over ten thousand small islands of which fewer than fifty are inhabited, a hundred-mile-long arc petering out to within ninety miles of Cuba. The Keys (named after the Spanish "cayo", meaning small islet or coral bank) are best known for the Florida Reef, a great band of living coral just a few miles offshore, whose range of colour and dazzling array of ocean life – including dolphins and loggerhead turtles – are exceptional sights. Throughout the Keys, and especially for the first sixty-odd miles, fishing, snorkelling and diving dominate, making it one of the country's best places to partake in watersports.

Here and there, houses built around the turn of the nineteenth century by Bahamian settlers and seedy waterside bars run by refugees from points north hint at the islands' history. And while there are some stunning natural areas and worthwhile ecology tours, the whole stretch is primarily a build-up to Key West, the real pearl on this island strand.

Heading down the chain from the mainland, the first place to visit on the reef is **John Pennekamp State Park**, the standout feature of **Key Largo** on the **Upper Keys**. Like **Islamorada**, further south, Key Largo is rapidly being populated by suburban Miamians, drawn by the sailing and fishing yet reliant on amenities like shopping centres and upmarket restaurants. Islamorada is the best base for fishing, and also has some natural and historical points of note – as does the next major settlement, **Marathon**, which is at the centre of the **Middle Keys** and thus makes a useful short-term base. Thirty miles on, the **Lower Keys** get fewer visitors and less publicity than their neighbours, but in many ways they're the most unusual and appealing of the chain. Covered with scrubby forest, they are home to a tiny and endangered species of Key deer, and, at **Looe Key**, offer a tremendous departure point for trips to the Florida Reef. **Key West** is the end of the road in every sense: shot through with an intoxicating aura of abandonment, but also an immensely vibrant place. Here, there are old homes and museums to explore and plenty of bars in which to while away the hours. The part of the Keys with the strongest sense of history, Key West was once – unbelievably – the richest town in the US and the largest settlement in Florida. It also has an illustrious literary heritage: this was the town where novelist Ernest Hemingway, playwright Tennessee Williams and poet Elizabeth Bishop (among others) chose to lay down roots in the mid-twentieth century. Today, visitors will discover that the town is still imbued with a dynamic creative spirit.

CHRIST OF THE DEEP STATUE, JOHN PENNEKAMP STATE PARK

Highlights

❶ John Pennekamp Coral Reef State Park
Dive or snorkel this rich undersea preserve, with a long stretch of the Florida Reef teeming with tropical fish, barracuda and the occasional shark. **See p.112**

❷ Indian Key The ruins of the settlement that once thrived here are spooky and evocative, overrun by untamed greenery. **See p.117**

❸ No Name Pub This oddball gem encapsulates the cranky charm of the Keys better than almost anywhere else. **See p.126**

❹ Key West Soak up the Caribbean vibes in America's southernmost town, with weathered conch cottages, absorbing museums and a famously raucous nightlife. **See p.130**

❺ Key lime pie and conch fritters Every restaurant in the Keys has a take on these fine local specialities, with the best cooked up in Key West. **See p.146**

❻ Dry Tortugas Spend a day or two at this cluster of islands at the western end of the Keys. The coral reef is stunning, and there's a bird sanctuary and an old fort to explore on land. **See p.150**

HIGHLIGHTS ARE MARKED ON THE MAP ON P.109

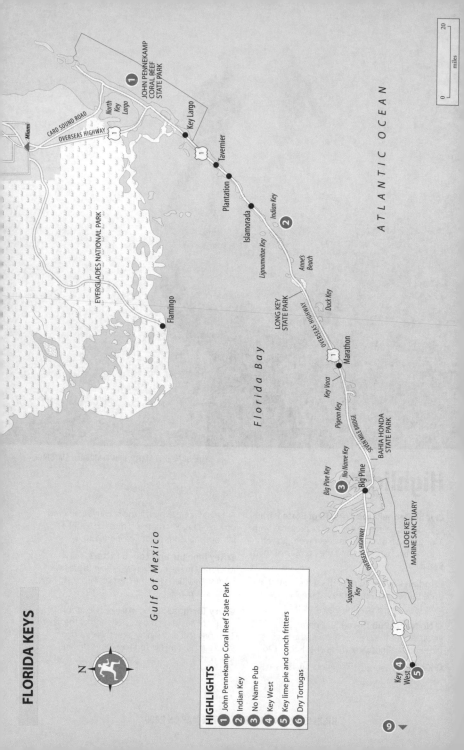

FLORIDA KEYS

N

Gulf of Mexico

Florida Bay

ATLANTIC OCEAN

EVERGLADES NATIONAL PARK

Miami

CARD SOUND ROAD

OVERSEAS HIGHWAY

North Key Largo

JOHN PENNEKAMP CORAL REEF STATE PARK

Key Largo

Tavernier

Plantation

Islamorada

Indian Key

Lignumvitae Key

Anne's Beach

Duck Key

LONG KEY STATE PARK

OVERSEAS HIGHWAY

Marathon

Key Vaca

Pigeon Key

SEVEN-MILE BRIDGE

BAHIA HONDA STATE PARK

Big Pine Key

No Name Key

Big Pine

LOOE KEY MARINE SANCTUARY

Sugarloaf Key

OVERSEAS HIGHWAY

Key West

Flamingo

0   20
         miles

HIGHLIGHTS

1 John Pennekamp Coral Reef State Park
2 Indian Key
3 No Name Pub
4 Key West
5 Key lime pie and conch fritters
6 Dry Tortugas

9 ▼

TURNPIKE TOLLS FROM MIAMI TO KEY WEST

In 2011, Florida implemented an all-electronic toll system on the Florida's Turnpike between Miami and Florida City. For road trippers, this means that the drive between Miami and Key West no longer has booths with human toll-takers; instead, cars will be charged via a registered Sunpass that's placed on the dashboard, ordered online at ⓦ sunpass.com (see p.23), or tolled electronically by registration plate (which is more expensive). Car rental companies have outfitted their cars to use Sunpass lanes but charge a fee for the service.

2

Beaches are rarely found in the Keys owing to the reef, though the sands at **Bahia Honda State Park** are pretty good. What the islands do offer in abundance are spectacular **sunsets**; as the nineteenth-century ornithologist John James Audubon once rhapsodized: "a blaze of refulgent glory streams through the portals of the west, and the masses of vapor assume the semblance of mountains of molten gold".

GETTING TO AND AROUND THE KEYS

BY PLANE

Key West International Airport (EYW), at 3491 S Roosevelt Blvd (☎ 305 809 5200, ⓦ monroecounty-fl .gov), is a small but useful airport with frequent flights, although most come by way of Miami. There is also an airport in Marathon (☎ 305 743 4222), which is utilized only by local carriers.

Shuttle buses Keys Shuttle (☎ 305 289 9997, ⓦ keys shuttle.com) runs a door-to-door minibus service from Miami and Fort Lauderdale airports to anywhere in the Keys six times a day; Miami rates are $60 to Key Largo and $90 to Key West.

BY CAR

Overseas Highway Travelling through the Keys could hardly be easier as there's just one route all the way through to Key West: the beautiful Overseas Highway (US-1), which follows the path of Henry Flagler's old railway – destroyed in a 1935 hurricane (see p.123). This is punctuated by mile markers (MM) – small

green-and-white signs on which mileage is posted, starting with MM127, just south of Homestead, and finishing with MM0, in Key West at the junction of Fleming and Whitehead streets. Almost all places of business use mile markers as an address, and throughout this chapter they are tagged with an "MM" (for example, "the Holiday Inn, at MM100"). We've also followed the local convention of indicating whether buildings sit on the Bayside (Key West-bound) or Oceanside (Miami-bound) side of the freeway.

Road information To keep up with closures and potential problems on US-1, tune to US-1 Radio (104.1FM; ⓦ us1radio.com) or Island 107.1FM (ⓦ island107.com); call the local sheriff's office at ☎ 305 293 7300 or ☎ 305 293 7311; or check ⓦ monroecounty-fl.gov for updates.

BY BUS

Greyhound Two daily Greyhound buses run between Miami and Key West (departing 12.25pm & 5.45pm from Miami and 8.15am & 5.45pm from Key West; $45 one way,

SWIMMING WITH DOLPHINS

Dolphins are a common sight around the Florida Keys and the star attraction of marine parks – though watching them perform somersaults in response to human commands gives just an inkling of their potential. In the region, you will find attempts at preservation: the **Dolphin Research Center**, MM59-Bayside in Marathon (daily 9am–4.30pm; ☎ 305 289 1121, ⓦ dolphins.org), provides a home to 23 dolphins and other sea mammals that cannot be re-released into the wild. Dolphins here also participate in therapeutic programmes for people with disabilities and recovering soldiers, displaying exceptional patience and gentleness from their residence in a natural seawater lagoon. A leader in dolphin cognition research, the centre offers narrated behaviour sessions and educational presentations on these remarkable – and still barely understood – mammals (daily 9am–4pm, every 30min; $25, children 4–11 $20).

The Dolphin Research Center is also one of five places in the Florida Keys where you can **swim with dolphins** ($199 for around 20min); call at least a month ahead (six weeks in high season; ☎ 305 289 0002) to book a session (although limited walk-in appointments are offered). You can also visit **Dolphins Plus** and **Dolphin Cove** in Key Largo (see p.114), and **Theater of the Sea** in Islamorada (see p.117).

discounted tickets online; ☎ 800 231 2222, ⓦ greyhound .com). The bus stops at: Key Largo (MM99.6); Islamorada (*Burger King*, 82201 Overseas Hwy); Marathon (Marathon Airport, MM52); Big Pine Key (across from Keys Federal Credit Union, MM30); and Key West (3535 S Roosevelt Blvd, Key West International Airport ☎ 305 296 9072). Journey

times from Miami are as follows: Key Largo (1hr 30min); Islamorada (2hr 5min); Marathon (3hr 10min); Big Pine Key (3hr 35min); Key West (4hr 30min).

Local buses There's a local bus service between Key West and Marathon (9 daily 5.30am–10pm; $4; ⓦ kwtransit.com).

ACCOMMODATION IN THE KEYS

Prices Accommodation is abundant but more expensive than on the mainland. Prices are always much cheaper in the wetter summer months, but remember that underwater visibility is often poor at this time, and

hurricanes are a possibility.

Camping Camping is considerably less expensive year-round, and is well catered for throughout the Keys.

The Upper Keys

The northernmost portion of the Florida Keys, the **UPPER KEYS** are roughly made up of three major communities – Key Largo, Tavernier and Islamorada – between which lies a scattering of small islands, most accessible only by boat. **Key Largo** is the biggest of the Keys, though not the most picturesque, and boasts the **John Pennekamp Coral Reef State Park**, an excellent diving centre. Lower down the island, the little town of **Tavernier** is really just a place to pass through (though it does offer some good restaurants) on the way to bigger and livelier **Islamorada**, which comprises a string of state parks.

Key Largo

Thanks to the 1948 film in which Humphrey Bogart and Lauren Bacall grappled with what were then Florida's best-known features – crime and hurricanes – almost everybody has heard of **KEY LARGO**. Yet the main section of the island can be a disappointing introduction to the Keys, since most of its beauty is underwater; on land, it's largely chain development. Scratch a little beneath the surface, though, and you'll find plenty of local flavour, accommodating residents and outstanding slices of Key lime pie. Ironically, the film's title was chosen for no other reason than it suggested somewhere warm and exotic, and, though set here, *Key Largo* was shot almost entirely in Hollywood. Links with Hollywood (and Bogart) are maintained today by the steam-powered boat *The African Queen*, used in the 1951 movie of the same name and displayed at the marina of the *Holiday Inn*, MM100-Oceanside (it's no longer taken out on tours).

There are some good restaurants in town, but it's John Pennekamp Coral Reef State Park and the offshore islands that are the best reasons to stay for a night or two: the magnificent scuba and fishing opportunities the Keys are known for begin here in earnest.

John Pennekamp Coral Reef State Park

MM102.5-Oceanside • Daily 8am–sunset • $8 per car plus 50¢ per person; pedestrians and cyclists $2.50 • ☎ 305 451 6300, ⓦ pennekamppark.com

The one essential stop as you approach the centre of Key Largo is the **John Pennekamp Coral Reef State Park**. At its heart is a protected 78-square-mile section of living coral reef three to eight miles off Key Largo, part of a chain running from here to the Dry Tortugas (see p.150). Just a few decades ago, great sections of the reef were dynamited or hauled up by crane to be broken up and sold as souvenirs. These days, collecting Florida coral is illegal, and any samples displayed in tourist shops have probably been imported from the Philippines. Despite the damage wrought by ecologically unsound tourism, experts still rate this as one of the most beautiful reef systems in the world. Whether you opt to visit the reef here or elsewhere in the Keys, such as Looe Key (see p.127), make sure you do visit it – the eulogistic descriptions you'll hear are rarely exaggerations.

SEEING THE REEF

Since most of the park lies underwater, the best way to see it is with a **tour** arranged by on-site concessionaire Coral Reef Park Company. Take a **snorkelling tour** (9am, 10.15am, noon, 1.15pm, 3pm & 4.15pm; 1hr 30min; $29.95, plus $9 for equipment; ☎305 451 6300, ⓦpennekamppark.com) or, if you're qualified, a two-tank **guided scuba dive** (9am & 1.30pm; 2hr; $55, plus $29 for full equipment; diver's certificate required; ☎305 451 6322). If you prefer to stay dry, a remarkable amount of the reef can be enjoyed on the **glass-bottom-boat tour** (9.15am, 12.15pm & 3pm; 2hr 30min; $24; ☎305 451 6300); note that the tours don't visit the Elbow or the *Christ of the Deep* statue. You can also **rent a canoe** ($20/hr), **double kayak** ($17/hr) or **powerboats** (from $160/4hr; ☎305 451 6325).

To be sure of a space on a dive or tour, make a **reservation**; if there's no room, try one of the numerous local dive outfits along US-1 (see box, p.114).

THREE WAYS YOU CAN PREVENT REEF DAMAGE

While snorkelling and dive boats do their best to educate visitors on proper reef etiquette, it doesn't hurt to be better informed about this extremely fragile ecosystem before donning flippers and heading beneath the surface.

• Look but don't touch: a single graze can irreparably damage and kill live coral by making it vulnerable to disease.
• Be sunblock-aware. Studies have found solid links between coral bleaching and chemical sunscreen; to be safe, douse yourself in the most environmentally friendly block that money can buy.
• Urine can have an extremely destructive impact on coral, so hold it in until you're back on the boat.

To find out more about what you can do to help save coral reefs, log on to ⓦreefrelief.org.

Another option for exploring the park is to rent a **canoe or kayak** (see box above) and glide around the mangrove-fringed inner waterways.

The reef

The **reef** shelters a multitude of crazy-coloured fish and exotic marine life, and even from the glass-bottom boat you're virtually guaranteed to spot lobsters, angelfish, eels and wispy jellyfish shimmering through the current, as well as shoals of minnows stalked by angry-faced barracudas, and many more, less easily identified, aquatic curiosities.

Despite looking like a big lump of rock, the reef itself is a delicate living thing, composed of millions of minute coral polyps that extract calcium from the seawater and grow from one to sixteen feet every thousand years. Coral takes many shapes and forms, resembling anything from stag horns to a bucket, and comes in a paint-box variety of colours due to the plants – *zooxanthellae* – living within the coral tissues. Sadly, it's far easier to spot signs of death than life on the reef: white patches show where a carelessly dropped anchor or a diver's hand have scraped away the protective mucus layer and left the coral susceptible to lethal disease.

This destruction got so bad at the horseshoe-shaped **Molasses Reef**, about seven miles out, that the authorities sank two obsolete coastguard cutters nearby to create an alternative attraction for divers. The plan worked and today you can enjoy some great snorkelling around the reef and the cutters. If you prefer diving older wrecks, head for **the Elbow**, a section of the reef a few miles northeast of Molasses, where a number of intriguing, barnacle-encrusted nineteenth-century specimens lie; like most of the Keys' diveable wrecks, these were deliberately brought here to bolster tourism in the 1970s.

By far the strangest thing at the reef is the **Christ of the Deep**, a 9ft bronze statue of Christ intended as a memorial to perished sailors. The algae-coated creation, 20ft down at Key Largo Dry Rocks, is a replica of Guido Galletti's *Christ of the Abyss*, similarly submerged off the coast of Genoa, Italy – and is surely the final word in Florida's long-time fixation with Mediterranean art and architecture.

2

The visitor centre

MM102.5-Oceanside • Daily 8am–5pm • ☎ 305 451 6300, ⓦ pennekamppark.com

Provided you visit the reef early, there'll be plenty of time left to enjoy the terrestrial portion of the park. The ecological displays at the **visitor centre** provide an inspiring introduction to the flora and fauna of the Keys, especially its **aquarium**, replete with pristine corals, hogfish and queen angels. You'll also gain a practical insight into the region's transitional zones: the vegetation changes dramatically within an elevation of just a few feet.

Hiking trails

Short **hiking trails** cut through the park's fine tropical **hardwood hammock** – a pocket of woodland able to flourish where the ground elevation rises a few feet above the surrounding wetlands – and meander through red mangroves, pepper trees and graceful frangipani. Raccoon, heron and fiddler crab tracks are everywhere, and hairy-legged, golden orb spiders dangle from many a branch.

The beaches

John Pennekamp Coral Reef State Park also boasts some small but fine artificial **beaches** (you'll find very few others – artificial or not – until Bahia Honda), but note that the coral is very unforgiving to bare feet.

Dolphins Plus

31 Corrine Place; south on Ocean Bay Drive off US-1, just beyond the *Holiday Inn* (MM100-Oceanside) • Daily 8am–5pm • 30min structured swim $195, or $10 to observe; natural swim $150 • ☎ 305 451 1993 or ☎ 866 860 7946, ⓦ dolphinsplus.com

You'll find two spots on Key Largo where you can swim with **dolphins**. The first is **Dolphins Plus**, a dolphin education and research facility where you can engage in a "dolphin encounter" with one of twelve friendly creatures. You can partake in a "structured" half-hour swim with the dolphins, or just observe, and there is also a "natural" option, during which participants snorkel alongside wild dolphins – though with the latter, contact is not guaranteed.

SNORKELLING, FISHING AND KAYAKING OFF KEY LARGO

The reef and tiny, uninhabited **islands** off Key Largo provide glorious opportunities for snorkelling and fishing, and if you can't make the official boat trips in the state park (see p.113), there's no shortage of alternatives along US-1. The most reliable **snorkelling** options are Keys Diver at MM100-Oceanside ($29.95 for 1hr trip; ☎ 305 451 1177, ⓦ keysdiver.com) and Sundiver III at MM103-Bayside ($34.95 for 1hr 30min in the water; ☎ 305 451 2220, ⓦ snorkelingisfun .com).

Sailor's Choice, also at the *Holiday Inn* marina at MM100-Oceanside, runs family-friendly **fishing** trips ($40; ☎ 305 451 1802, ⓦ sailorschoicefishingboat.com), though serious fishing aficionados should get in touch with Key Largo Fishing Adventures (same location; half-day trips from $625 with up to six people; ☎ 305 923 9293, ⓦ keyssportfishing.com).

To explore on your own, make for Florida Bay Outfitters at MM104-Bayside (☎ 305 451 3018, ⓦ kayakfloridakeys.com), which offers **canoe** ($45) and **kayak** rentals ($40), as well as lauded ecotours (from $60), or try Boat Rental Florida Keys at MM90.8-Bayside (☎ 305 896 2219, ⓦ boatrental411.com), which rents **powerboats** from $220 a day.

If a **glass-bottom-boat tour** is more up your alley, head to the *Holiday Inn* docks at MM100-Oceanside, where the *Key Largo Princess* makes two-hour cruises around the John Pennekamp Coral Reef State Park (daily 10am, 1pm & 4pm; $35; ☎ 305 451 4655, ⓦ keylargoprincess.com). Caribbean Watersports at MM97-Bayside (☎ 305 852 4707, ⓦ caribbeanwatersports.com) offers knowledgeable backcountry "enviro-tours" of the area ($60), as well as two-hour champagne cruises ($225 for up to six people), parasailing ($70) and other aquatic activities.

Dolphin Cove

MM101.9-Bayside · **Structured swims** 9am, 10.30am, 1pm & 3pm · $195 **Shallow water encounter** Times vary · $165 · **Natural swim** 8.30am & 2pm · $150 · **Paint with dolphins** Times vary · $125 · **Sea lion encounter** Times vary · $140 · ☎ 305 451 4060, ⓦ dolphinsplus.com

Set in a five-acre marine environment research centre, swims at **Dolphin Cove** begin with a 30–45-minute educational talk, and end with participants taking turns to interact with dolphins in a lagoon that opens onto the bay. There's also a "shallow water encounter", ideal for young children; a natural swim, where you snorkel alongside the dolphins but aren't guaranteed contact; and a painting experience, where you assist and observe a dolphin "painting" a canvas for you. If you can't afford a close encounter, $10 gets you in as a non-swimming observer. Alternatively, you can get up close and personal with the resident sea lion, Wono.

ARRIVAL AND INFORMATION
KEY LARGO

By bus Two daily Greyhound buses run from Miami to Key Largo (see p.111).

Tourist information Stop in at the Key Largo Visitor Center, MM106-Bayside (daily 9am–6pm; ☎ 305 451 6226 or ☎ 800 822 1088), for details on scuba diving and fishing, plus other general information.

ACCOMMODATION

You'll usually have no problem finding reasonably priced accommodation in Key Largo – it has some of the widest range of choices in the Keys, although it can veer into pricier territory than some of the hostelries in the Middle and Lower Keys.

Azul del Mar MM104.3-Bayside ☎ 305 451 0337, ⓦ azulkeylargo.com. Six contemporary bungalows done up in beachy hues of white and blue and accented by dark wood furniture. Each has a modern kitchenette and access to a small private beach, barbecue setups, and a DVD library. No children. $189

★ **Coconut Palm Inn** MM92-Bayside ☎ 305 852 3017, ⓦ coconutpalminn.com. This simple but stylish waterfront hotel is great value, with twenty rooms and suites beautifully decked out with modern wooden beds and cooling tile floors. Amenities include a small but attractive pool, tiki huts, a marina and a white sand beach with hammocks. $149

Dove Creek Lodge 147 Seaside Ave ☎ 305 852 6200, ⓦ dovecreeklodge.com. This nineteen-room oceanfront getaway has the perks of a luxury hotel with the hospitality of a B&B. Rooms are a smart blend of tropical colours, Floridian furniture and fluffy white bedding, and come with fridges, flat-screen TVs, pool access and shaded parking spots. Great for families. $169

Ed & Ellen's Economy Efficiency MM103.3-Oceanside ☎ 305 451 9949, ⓦ ed-ellens-lodgings .com. On the corner of Snapper Ave, this five-room motel is hidden from the main road by a leafy sea-grape grove. It's a terrific low-cost option: rooms are basic but clean, and three have a small kitchenette and private bathroom. $79

John Pennekamp Coral Reef State Park MM 102.5-Oceanside ☎ 305 451 1202, ⓦ floridastateparks .org. The cleanest and cheapest of the many campgrounds in and around Key Largo has full hook-up sites for RVs, as well as tent sites. Book several months ahead for high season (Nov–Feb). Tent sites $43

Jules' Undersea Lodge 51 Shoreland Drive ☎ 305 451 2353, ⓦ jul.com. This tiny hotel, 21ft below the ocean's surface, is always booked well in advance; the two-bedroom lodgings are perfectly safe and linked to land by an intercom system. Just remember your diver's certificate – otherwise you'll have to take the hotel's 3hr crash course ($150) before you'll be allowed to unpack. Very costly, but one of a kind: those on a budget can still experience it during a 3hr visit to watch a movie or eat lunch ($150 per person). $675

★ **Kona Kai Resort** MM97.8-Bayside ☎ 305 852 7200, ⓦ konakairesort.com. A breathtaking place: the chalets here are huge and stylish, a dozen strains of banana grow in the botanic garden, and the hotel has its own art gallery, private beach, tennis court, jacuzzi and pool. No children. $299

Tarpon Flats Inn & Marina 29 Shoreland Drive, MM103.5-Bayside ☎ 305 453 1313, ⓦ tarponflats.com. Laidback, hidden gem on Largo Sound. Each of the four suites has a veranda overlooking the ocean, and comes with a full kitchen and daily breakfast basket. Chartered boats can whisk you away right from the dock, where it's common to spot manatees. Pet friendly. $160

EATING AND DRINKING

Far enough south for great Caribbean cuisine, but close enough to the Everglades for a taste of 'gator, Key Largo is a fine place for eating out. Surprisingly, many of the best restaurants are down the way in little Tavernier (see p.116). Some of the following also double as casual drinking dens.

2

★**Alabama Jack's** 58000 Card Sound Rd ☎305 248 8741. If you'd like to relax with some good conch fritters and a beer while a jam band plays in the background, stop off here, just north of the toll booth on the Card Sound Road (Hwy-905A) before you enter the Keys proper. It's a local tradition and a perfect introduction. Daily 11am–7pm.

Ballyhoo's MM97.8 in the median ☎305 852 0822, ⓦballyhoosrestaurant.com. Run by the same family for two generations, this small shack-like diner features a wide selection of grilled food, salads and drinks, with a Friday night fish fry and all-you-can-eat stone crab, in season (Oct–May). Opposite *Kona Kai Resort*. Daily 11am–10pm.

The Caribbean Club MM104-Bayside ☎305 451 4466. The place for a lively drink, provided you're not daunted by the sight of bikers in leather jackets and tropical shorts. Carl Fisher, of Miami Beach fame, built the club in 1938, although the claim that *Key Largo* was shot here is dubious. Nice bayside porch and jukebox. Cash only. Daily 7am–4am.

Fish House Encore MM102.4-Oceanside ☎305 451 0650, ⓦfishhouse.com. For a splash-out seafood meal, this is as dressy a spot as you'll find in Key Largo. Fish of the day is offered in various styles, from traditional blackened or broiled to more adventurous options like Matecumbe (with capers, tomatoes and shallots; $25) or Jamaican Jerk (from $23.99), in addition to sushi and shellfish dishes. Daily 5–10pm.

Harriette's MM95.7-Bayside ☎305 852 8689. Best place for a filling, diner-style breakfast, set in a modest but cosy shack just off the highway. Try the massive Key lime muffin, and order the tasty biscuit instead of toast. Daily 6am–3pm.

★**Mrs Mac's Kitchen** MM99.5-Bayside ☎305 451 3722, ⓦmrsmackskitchen.com. Adorable no-frills diner festooned with licence plates, which cooks up home-style food at reasonable prices. The fresh fish and home-made chilli are highlights, but the crab cakes, Key lime pie and conch fritters have to be tried; look out for all-you-can-eat catfish on Tuesday nights. Mon–Sat 7am–9.30pm.

Tavernier

Huddled at the southern end of Key Largo is **TAVERNIER** (Tav-uh-NEE-uh), a small, sleepy town that was once the first stop on the Flagler railway. There's not a whole lot here, although a number of enticing restaurants make it worth a pit stop.

Florida Keys Wild Bird Center

MM93.6-Bayside • Daily sunrise–sunset • $5 donation • ☎305 852 4486, ⓦfkwbc.org

Just before crossing into Tavernier is the **Florida Keys Wild Bird Center**, an inspirational place where volunteers rescue and rehabilitate birds that have been orphaned or have met with other common catastrophes such as colliding with cars or power lines. A wooden walkway is lined with huge enclosures, and signs detail the birds' histories – watch out for the great horned owl, dubbed "Junior", who sustained a partial amputation to his wing and now makes his permanent home at the centre because he can no longer fly.

Harry Harris Park

MM 93.5-Oceanside • Daily 7.30am–sunset • Non-residents $5 on weekends and public holidays • ☎305 852 7161

If you drop into **Harry Harris Park**, at the end of long, snaking Burton Drive, on a weekend, you could well find an impromptu party and live music – locals sometimes come by with instruments and station themselves on picnic tables for jam sessions. Otherwise, during the week, it's a fine place to lounge since there's a wide, sandy beach.

ACCOMMODATION AND EATING TAVERNIER

Made 2 Order MM90.6-Oceanside ☎305 852 3251, ⓦmade2orderonline.com. Dock your boat and head in for a terrific waterfront meal at this buzzing, breakfast-all-day hub that grills peerless tropical French toast ($7.50), Brie and avocado omelettes ($9.50) and dolphin melts on buttered rye ($12.95). Endearingly dog-friendly. Daily 8am–3pm.

Sunrise Restaurant MM91.8-Oceanside ☎305 852 7216. If you're in the mood for a delicious, dark *café cubano* for just 90¢, stop by *Sunshine Restaurant*, a top-notch, low-key café next to a supermarket. You can also dig in to a piled-high plate of Cuban food: a juicy sandwich is just $7, while grilled fresh fish meals cost under $14. Daily 5am–9pm.

Islamorada

Fishing is headline news in beautiful **ISLAMORADA** (meaning "purple island" and pronounced "eye-lah-more-RAH-da"). Tales of monstrous tarpon and blue marlin

SPORTFISHING, SNORKELLING AND DIVING AT ISLAMORADA

Islamorada claims to be the sportfishing capital of the world, so as you'd expect it's easy to charter **fishing** boats ($950/day), or, for much less, join a fishing party boat from any of the local marinas (around $65). The biggest docks are at Bud 'n' Mary's Fishing Marina, MM79.8-Oceanside (☎800 742 7945, ⓦbudnmarys.com), and the Holiday Isle, MM84.5-Oceanside (fishing charters ☎305 433 9942; boat rentals ☎305 664 9425, ⓦholidayisle.com).

There are notable **snorkelling** and **diving** opportunities in the area, too. Crocker and Alligator reefs, a few miles offshore, both have near-vertical sides, whose cracks and crevices provide homes for a lively variety of crab, shrimp and other small creatures that in turn attract bigger fish looking for a meal. Nearby, the wrecks of the *Eagle* and the *Cannabis Cruiser* provide a home for families of gargantuan amberjack and grouper. Get full snorkelling and diving details from the marinas or any dive shop on the Overseas Highway (such as Conch Republic Divers, MM90.8-Bayside; ☎305 852 1655, ⓦconchrepublicdivers.com) – expect to pay $45–50 for a half-day of snorkelling.

2

captured off the coast are legendary, and there's no end to the smaller prey routinely hooked by total novices. You reach Islamorada by crossing Tavernier Creek: the "town" is actually a twenty-mile strip of separate islands, including Plantation, Windley, and Upper and Lower Matecumbe, collectively dubbed Islamorada.

Upper Matecumbe Key and around

Long considered Islamorada's "downtown", **Upper Matecumbe Key** is a built-up island with a couple of mildly interesting diversions along its relatively busy commercial strip.

Theater of the Sea

MM84.5-Oceanside on Windley Key • Daily 9.30am–5pm • $31.95, kids 3–10 $21.95; swimming with dolphins $185, stingrays $65, sea lions $145, sharks $85 • ☎305 664 2431, ⓦtheaterofthesea.com

You could pass a couple of hours at the **Theater of the Sea**, but only if you're not planning to visit any of the other marine parks in Florida – such as SeaWorld – which are more state of the art. Here, you'll find the usual dolphin and sea lion shows and marine exhibits, and kids will enjoy swimming with dolphins, stingrays, sea lions and sharks, though considering the prices, parents may not be so keen.

History of Diving Museum

MM83-Bayside • Daily 10am–5pm • $12 • ☎305 664 9737, ⓦdivingmuseum.org

The **History of Diving Museum** boasts an odd but absorbing collection of rare diving helmets and suits, as well as exhibits highlighting the three-thousand-year history of diving and the role of undersea treasure-seekers in south Florida.

Hurricane Monument

MM81.6-Oceanside

A short drive south from the Diving Museum, the Art Deco **Hurricane Monument** marks the grave of the 1935 Labor Day hurricane's 425 victims, many killed when a tidal wave hit the train attempting to evacuate them. It's estimated that many more people died in the storm, but exact numbers will never be known.

Indian Key and Lignumvitae Key

Indian Key and **Lignumvitae Key** – two state parks at the southern end of Islamorada – offer a broader perspective of the area than just fishing and diving. The former reveals a near-forgotten chapter of the Florida Keys' history, the latter an enchanting virgin forest.

2

TOURS AND ACTIVITIES IN INDIAN KEY AND LIGNUMVITAE KEY

Tours to Indian and Lignumvitae keys are organized Friday to Sunday (Nov–March only) at 8.30am; at least six people are needed to run boats ($47 per person, including tour) from Robbie's Marina, MM77.5-Bayside (☎ 305 664 9814, ⊛ robbies.com). Indian Key is the first stop, which visitors explore for an hour on their own. Captains then steer enthusiasts over to Lignumvitae, for an hour-long, ranger-guided tour. Lignumvitae has a second ranger-led tour (Fri–Sun) at 2pm, but outside of the aforementioned weekend jaunt, the only way to visit either island is by renting kayaks or boats: Robbie's rents **powerboats** from $135/ half-day, and you can get **kayaks** from the Kayak Shack ($20/hr, $50/day; ☎ 305 664 4878), also at the marina.

At Robbie's you can also feed the monstrous **tarpons** (entry $1): buy a bucket of herring for $3.30 and toss chunks from the pier to get the fish leaping out of the shallow waters.

Indian Key Historic State Park

Daily sunrise–sunset • ☎ 305 664 2540, ⊛ floridastateparks.org/indiankey

You'd never guess from the highway that **Indian Key Historic State Park**, one of many small, mangrove-skirted islands off Lower Matecumbe Key, was once a busy trading centre, given short-lived prosperity – and notoriety – by a nineteenth-century New Yorker named Jacob Housman (see box below). The trip here is well worth it for the **ruins**, which are an evocative, if crumbling, reminder of early settler life in the Keys – especially the grassy paddock that was once the town square – and the observation tower's spectacular views across the island's lush and jumbled foliage. Look, too, for **Housman's grave** – his body was brought here after he died in 1841, working on a wreck off Key West.

Lignumvitae Key Botanical State Park

Mon & Thurs–Sun 8am–5pm; tours Fri–Sun 10am & 2pm (see box above) • ☎ 305 664 2540, ⊛ floridastateparks.org/lignumvitaekey

By the time you finish the one-hour tour of **Lignumvitae Key Botanical State Park** (see box above), you'll know a strangler fig from a gumbo limbo and be able to recognize many more of the fifty or so species of tropical tree in this 280-acre hammock. The key is named after the lignumvitae tree (Latin for "wood of life") that's common here and whose extraordinary wood has been prized for centuries – denser and tougher than iron, it's almost impossible to wear out and has been used for everything from ship rigging to false teeth. The trail through the forest was forged by wealthy Miamian **W.J. Matheson**, who made millions supplying mustard gas to the government during

THE LEGEND OF JACOB HOUSMAN

After stealing one of his father's ships, **Jacob Housman** sailed to Key West in 1825 looking for a piece of the lucrative wrecking (or "shipwreck salvaging") business. Ostracized by the close-knit Key West community, he retreated to **Indian Key**, which he bought as a base for his own wrecking operation in 1831. In the first year, Housman made vast sums of money and furnished the eleven-acre island with streets, a store, warehouses, a hotel, more than two dozen homes and a population of around fifty. However, some of his income was not honestly gained, and he eventually lost his licence for salvaging in 1838. That same year, Housman sold Indian Key to plant-mad doctor Henry Perrine, who had been cultivating species in the Keys with an eye to their commercial potential (one of his abortive schemes centred on growing mulberry trees to kick-start a silk industry). Perrine's plans were thwarted after the Seminoles launched a midnight attack in August 1840, burning every building to the ground and ending the island's habitation. A number of people died in the raid; Housman was lucky, surviving by hiding in the water behind his cottage, but Perrine was discovered in the cupola of his house, hacked to death. The doctor's **plants** still thrive today, though, and the island is now choked with sisal, coffee, tea and mango plants.

World War I, and purchased the island for only $1 (and "valuable consideration" – posited to be $100,000, under the table) in 1919. The **limestone house** he built that year is the island's only sign of habitation and shows the deprivations of early island living, even for the well-off; the house actually blew away in the 1935 hurricane, but was rebuilt after the storm.

Lignumvitae Key is considered the best remaining example of a Florida Keys tropical hammock (oddly, thanks to its location in the Gulf of Mexico and its thick forest of trees, the temperature here is usually at least ten degrees cooler than on the main islands). The island is ravaged by mosquitoes, so make sure to bring long-sleeved shirts and trousers, plus plenty of repellent.

Long Key State Park

MM67.4-Oceanside • Daily 8am–sunset • $4.50 per car and driver, plus $1.50 for first passenger, 50¢ for each additional passenger; pedestrians and cyclists $2.50; kayak rental $17/2hr • ☎ 305 664 4815, ⓦ floridastateparks.org/longkey

You can spot many of the tree species found on Lignumvitae Key at **Long Key State Park**. A nature trail leads along the shoreline and on a boardwalk over a mangrove-lined lagoon or, better still, you can rent a kayak and follow the simple **canoe trail** through the tidal lagoons in the company of mildly curious wading birds. It's also possible to **camp** in the park (see p.120).

Anne's Beach

MM73-Oceanside • Daily sunrise–sunset • Free • ☎ 305 664 4503

Tranquil **Anne's Beach** is named after local environmentalist Anne Eaton, who advocated for the Keys. You won't find many waves, but there's a gentle boardwalk peppered with wooden pavilions and shaded picnic tables, a mellow beach and, at low tide, a sweep of tidal flats, great for little beachcombers.

ARRIVAL AND INFORMATION	ISLAMORADA

By bus Two daily Greyhound buses run from Miami to Islamorada (see p.111).
Tourist information Islamorada Visitors Center,

MM87-Bayside (Mon–Fri 9am–5pm, Sat 9am–4pm, Sun 9am–3pm; ☎ 305 664 4503, ⓦ islamoradachamber.com).

ACCOMMODATION

In general, you're unlikely to find accommodation in Islamorada for under $150 a night, although there are a handful of bargain motels listed below. Included in the price is access to some of the Keys' best restaurants and bars, however.

★ **Casa Morada** MM82.2-Bayside, 136 Madeira Rd ☎ 305 664 0044, ⓦ casamorada.com. Walk through *Casa Morada's* small but bright tropical garden, past its winsome bocce-ball court, and cross the short white bridge to what must be one of the most beautiful little bars in the world, which overlooks Florida Bay and the Everglades and courts only the hotel's handful of guests. The rest of the property is exceptional as well: a choice waterfront pool, yoga classes, sumptuous breakfasts, and sixteen contemporary suites brightened by orchids. $329

Cheeca Lodge & Spa MM82-Oceanside ☎ 305 664 4651, ⓦ cheeca.com. This lavish lodge was built on a historic spot – the first guest at the inn's predecessor was none other than President Harry Truman – and the property has been refurbished to reflect its swanky beginnings. There's a private beach, kayaks, bikes, on-site spa, Jack Nicklaus-designed golf course, and simple, country-club-style rooms – be prepared for the hefty $39/

day resort fee, though. $240

★ **Drop Anchor** MM85-Oceanside ☎ 305 664 4863, ⓦ dropanchorresort.com. A little out of town, this upmarket, boutiquey motel has an oceanside pool and is dotted with loungers, picnic tables and swaying palm trees; the spacious plantation-style rooms have ceiling fans, verandas and furniture from Indonesia and the Philippines. The waterfront views are stunning. $149

Islander Resort MM82.1-Oceanside ☎ 305 664 2031, ⓦ guyharveyoutpostislamorada.com. Hands down, the best pool around – in fact, two: one huge freshwater spot and another saltwater dipping pool. It's also family-friendly, with bungalow rooms dotting a large campus; all of them have screened-in verandas where you can lounge, mosquito-free, in the evenings. Other appealing touches include the on-site tiki bar, watersports facility, 24hr fishing pier and the fact that the local strip of restaurants is just a short walk away. $229

2

Key Lantern/Blue Fin Inn MM82.1-Bayside ☎305 664 4572 and ☎305 664 8709, ⊕keylantern.com. These twinned motels are true budget gems in the Keys. The *Blue Fin* has fourteen basic rooms; the ten spots at the *Key Lantern* are better. With naturally cooling coral-rock walls and terrazzo floors, plus pastel-coloured vintage bathrooms, they're pristine examples of a mid-century motel (rooms 2 and 7 are the largest). The same owner is also responsible for the equally well-priced *Sunset Inn* nearby (MM82.2; ☎305 664 3454, ⊕sunsetinnkeys.com), so ask about availability there if these two are full. **$55**

Long Key State Park ☎305 664 4815, ⊕florida stateparks.org. Picturesque, waterfront campsites with showers, electricity, boardwalks and nature trails. **$36**

Pines & Palms MM80.4-Oceanside ☎305 664 4343, ⊕pinesandpalms.com. This old-style Keys throwback (floral sofas and wicker furniture) has 25 bright, plush rooms, each with a kitchenette. Groups can snag a bargain at the two-bedroom condo complete with dining room, jacuzzi and washer-dryer – it sleeps six people, starting at $399 per night. The views from the oceanfront pool are spectacular. **$159**

Ragged Edge Resort MM86.5-Oceanside, 243 Treasure Harbor Rd, Plantation Key ☎305 852 5389, ⊕ragged-edge.com. Rooms right on the ocean, offering cosy cottages or efficiencies with kitchenettes and new bathrooms; the furnishings are a bit dated, but all rooms are spotless. Friendly owners, great service and terrific fishing off the pier, plus complimentary bike use. **$99**

EATING AND DRINKING

Green Turtle Inn MM81.2-Oceanside ☎305 664 2006, ⊕greenturtlekeys.com. Easy to spot with its blinking neon turtle sign, this local favourite has two personalities: down-home breakfast joint and, come nightfall, upmarket bistro with renowned wine list. Breakfast is particularly recommended, though, for the French toast grilled on challah bread, pancakes studded with fresh fruit and omelettes scrambled with spinach and artichokes. Tues–Thurs & Sun 7am–9pm, Fri & Sat 7am–10pm.

★**Hungry Tarpon** MM77.5-Bayside ☎305 664 0535, ⊕hungrytarpon.com. This converted 1940s bait shop is tucked away in Robbie's Marina (see box, p.118) – look for it by the bridge at the north end of the key. It serves killer breakfasts like burritos (from $9), French toast ($8) and huge pancakes ($6), all dished up with piles of crispy hash browns. Ask for a table out back on the wooden jetty. Daily 6.30am–9pm.

Islamorada Restaurant & Bakery MM81.6-Bayside ☎305 664 8363, ⊕bobsbunz.com. Known locally as *Bob's Bunz* and famous for its gooey cinnamon and sticky buns, this bakery opens at 6am for early risers, and usually fills with families; there are some plastic tables inside if you want to linger, as well as a few picnic tables outside on the shaded porch. Daily 6am–2pm.

Lorelei MM82-Bayside ☎305 664 4338, ⊕loreleicabanabar.com. Investigate the nightly drink specials at this popular waterfront bar, where sunset celebrations reel in the crowds. It also has a large beachside eating area, where you can eat breakfast, lunch and dinner; try the cracked conch sandwich ($12.95) or yellowtail snapper ($22.95). Daily 7am–11pm.

Morada Bay Beach Café MM81.6-Bayside ☎305 664 3225, ⊕moradabay.com. The perfect choice for a splurge or a romantic dinner on the beach, with fire-lit tiki huts and mesmerizing sunsets. Everything on the seafood-heavy menu (main courses $24–33) is top-notch, but the shrimp ceviche ($15) and chunky home-made coconut sorbet ($7) are standouts. Round out the experience with a drink at neighbouring *Pierre's*, whose mahogany bar and decor is reminiscent of Morocco, while its plush, plantation-house veranda is delightfully bygone-era American South. Daily 11.30am–10pm.

Spanish Gardens Café MM80.9-Oceanside, at the Galleria Plaza mall ☎305 664 3999, ⊕spanish gardenscafe.com. Crisp salads, soup *del día* and seasonal tapas are fired off at this little Iberian gem serving pressed sandwiches at lunchtime and exceptional Mediterranean small plates and seafood paella ($50 for two) come nightfall. Manages to shine despite its location in a strip mall. Dinner for two $35–45. Tues–Sun 11.30am–9.30pm.

Tiki Bar Postcard Inn Beach Resort (MM84.5-Oceanside) ☎305 664 2321, ⊕holidayisle.com. When it comes to nightlife, many people get no further than the landmark *Tiki Bar*, which throbs most nights to the sound of rock and pop bands; it also claims to have invented the rumrunner, a mind-bending concoction of Bacardi, banana, blackberry brandy and lime juice. Mon–Thurs & Sun noon–midnight, Fri & Sat 11am–2am.

★**Ziggie and Mad Dog's** MM83-Bayside ☎305 664 3391, ⊕ziggieandmaddogs.com. Once part of a pineapple plantation, then a legendary restaurant and gambling hangout (it's said that even Al Capone laid down his cards here), landmark *Ziggie's* stakes its claim as the best steakhouse in the Upper Keys, grilling up mouthwatering ribeyes and pairing them with truffled mac and cheese, pistachio creamed spinach, and fresh bread with honey butter that you'll dream about for months. Mains $28–38. Reservations recommended. Mon–Thurs & Sun 5.30–10pm, Fri & Sat 5.30–11pm.

The Middle Keys

The Long Key Bridge (alongside the old Long Key Viaduct) points south from Long Key and leads to the **Middle Keys**, which stretch from Duck Key to Pigeon Key. Highlights of a visit here include the sweeping **Seven Mile Bridge** (see p.123) – a historic span that was once a railroad track and now lends itself to long strolls sandwiched by nothing but ocean and sky.

2

Marathon

The largest of the Middle Keys islands is Key Vaca – once a shantytown of railway workers – which holds the area's major settlement, **MARATHON**, a blue-collar town said to be named for the back-breaking shifts that workers endured as they raced to finish the Seven Mile Bridge (see p.123).

Crane Point

Turn right at MM50.5-Bayside (opposite the K-Mart) • Mon–Sat 9am–5pm, Sun noon–5pm • $12.50 • ☎ 305 743 9100, ⓦ cranepoint.net

If you didn't get your fill of tropical trees at Lignumvitae Key (see p.117), head for the 63 steamy acres of subtropical forest at **Crane Point**. At the entrance, the park's excellent **Museum of Natural History of the Florida Keys** offers a thought-provoking rundown of the area's history – starting with the Calusa tribe (who had a settlement on this site until they were wiped out by disease brought by European settlers in the 1700s) and continuing with the story of early Bahamian and American settlers. A large section of the museum features interactive displays designed to introduce kids to the wonders of the Keys' subtropical ecosystems, including the hardwood hammocks and reefs.

Crane Point nature trail

The Museum of Natural History has a free booklet that gives details of the hardwood trees you'll find along the 1.5-mile **nature trail** from here; halfway along you'll pass **Adderley House**, built in 1903 by Bahamian immigrants and giving a vivid impression of what life was like for them, with its simple construction and

---

WATERSPORTS IN THE MIDDLE KEYS

The choice locale for the pursuits of **snorkelling** and **scuba diving** is around **Sombrero Reef**, marked by a 142ft high nineteenth-century lighthouse, whose nooks and crannies provide a safe haven for thousands of darting, brightly coloured tropical fish – the best time to go out is in the morning when the reef is most active. The pick of local dive shops is Captain Hook's Marina and Dive Center (☎ 305 743 2444 or ☎ 800 278 4665, ⓦ captainhooks.com), at MM53-Bayside. Day-long introductory diving courses cost $210, while night diving, wreck diving and certificate courses are available to the experienced. Once certified, you can rent equipment and join a dive trip ($195 for six dives, including equipment). Spirit Snorkeling at MM47.5-Bayside (☎ 305 289 0614, ⓦ spiritsnorkeling.net) runs a catamaran out to the reef for its popular snorkelling trips (daily 9am & 1pm; $30).

Around Marathon, **spearfishing** is permitted a mile offshore (there's a three-mile limit elsewhere), and the town hosts four major **fishing tournaments** each year: tarpon (May), dolphin fish (May), bonefish (Sept) and sailfish (April). Entering costs several hundred dollars and only the very top anglers participate, but if you feel inspired to put to sea yourself, wander along one of the marinas and ask about chartering a boat. Boats take up to six people and charge between $600 and $1000 for a full day's fishing (8am–4pm), including bait and equipment. If you can't get a group together, join one of the countless group boats for about $60 per person for a full day – remember, though, it's easier to catch fish with fewer people aboard. A reliable option for **fishing charters** is Catch 'Em All at MM47.5-Bayside (☎ 305 481 4568, ⓦ catch-em-all.com).

barebones amenities. Towards the end of the trail, near the coast, the **Wild Bird Center** (same hours as Crane Point) rehabilitates injured birds – you may see pelicans, cormorants and even ospreys here.

Sombrero Beach

2150 Sombrero Beach Rd • Daily 7am–dusk • Free parking • Follow the signs for Sombrero Beach Road or Marathon High School, turning off the Overseas Hwy near K-Mart Plaza, MM50-Oceanside (opposite Crane Point)

If you have a leisurely day in mind, head to **Sombrero Beach**. A couple of miles along Sombrero Beach Road there's a slender, well-kept strip of sand, with full facilities including showers, a kids' playground, volleyball net and picnic tables, plus a bit of shade from pavilions and lush palms.

Turtle Hospital

MM48.5-Bayside • Tours daily on the hour from 9am–4pm, reservations recommended • $18 • ☎ 305 743 2552, ⊕ turtlehospital.org

Not far from Crane Point, the **Turtle Hospital** mounts often heart-breaking efforts to save injured or sick turtles picked up all over the Caribbean; boat hits, oil spills and a virus that causes crippling tumours are typical problems. The guided tour includes a look at the turtle rehabilitation area, a short slide show and a chance to feed some of the loveable permanent residents.

Dolphin Research Center

MM59-Bayside • Daily 9am–4.30pm • ☎ 305 289 1121, ⊕ dolphins.org

Just east of Marathon is the **Dolphin Research Center**, offering dolphin encounters (see box, p.111). At about 7ft in length, dolphins look disconcertingly large at close quarters – and will lose interest in you long before you tire of their company – but if you do get the opportunity to join them, it's an unforgettable experience.

ARRIVAL AND INFORMATION   MARATHON

By bus Two daily Greyhound buses run from Miami to Marathon (see p.111).

Tourist information For information on the Middle Keys area and accommodation, head to the Marathon Chamber of Commerce at MM53.5-Bayside (daily 9am–5pm; ☎ 305 743 5417 or ☎ 800 262 7284, ⊕ floridakeysmarathon .com).

ACCOMMODATION

Anchor Inn MM51.3-Oceanside ☎ 305 743 2213, ⊕ anchorinnkeys.com. The seven blue-and-white rooms at this delightful nautically themed budget motel vary in size and amenities: if you want to cook, ask for room no. 3, 6 or 7, each of which has a full kitchenette (the others just have microwaves and fridges). There's a BBQ grill for guests, as well as an on-site laundry. $89

Curry Hammock State Park MM56-Oceanside ☎ 305 289 2690, ⊕ floridastateparks.org. This campground is made up of a group of small islands centring on Little Crawl Key and has picnic tables, grills and showers. Pitches $36

★**Ranch House Motel** MM51-Oceanside ☎ 305 743 2217. Very well-maintained roadside 1950s motel run by a darling little lady who line-dries her sheets and occasionally bakes pie for guests. One efficiency, and nine basic but spotless rooms (some even have original Dade County pine walls). All come with fridge and microwave. Wi-fi reaches the Adirondack chairs, perfect for catching rays. $125

Sea Dell MM49.8-Bayside ☎ 305 743 5161, ⊕ seadellmotel.com. The bright white- and- turquoise rooms are simply furnished but immaculately clean, making this a great budget option in the Keys. It's also well located for local nightlife and has a freshwater heated pool. $109

Seascape Motel and Marina 1275 76th St East (MM52-Oceanside) ☎ 305 743 6212, ⊕ seascape motelandmarina.com. Hospitable, no-frills, eleven-room inn located on four acres of idyllic oceanfront property. The varied layout accommodates everyone from singles to groups of six (some rooms come with full kitchens), and there's a pool with terrific water views, fishing and on-site boat rental. $125

★**Tranquility Bay** MM48.5-Bayside ☎ 305 289 0888, ⊕ tranquilitybay.com. You'll want to make this unabashedly well-appointed resort your permanent home. Comprised of two- and three-bedroom beach houses, all facing the Gulf of Mexico, its stylish interiors are enlivened by contemporary art and come with state-of-the-art kitchens, plasma-screen TVs and porches. Just outside your door lie two elongated pools, a small man-made beach, a watersports department, tiki bar and restaurant. $249

EATING AND DRINKING

Marathon will definitely be your base for eating in this stretch of the Middle Keys. The town does go to sleep early, though; for nightlife, you're best joining the standard locals' pub crawl starting at the *Hurricane Grille* (see below). All of the places below can be found on Key Vaca.

Castaway 1406 Oceanview Ave, off 15th St, at MM47.5-Oceanside ☎305 743 6247, ⓦjonesn4sushi .com. No-nonsense local restaurant with several different dining areas: a screened-in porch overlooking the water, a cosy lounge and a casual café facing the jetty that doubles as a buzzy bar in the evenings. The restaurant is best known for its plates of peel-it-yourself beer-steamed shrimp ($25, second plate free); every dinner includes a visit to the huge salad bar and a basket of hot, honey-drenched doughnut-style buns. Daily 11am–10pm.

ChikiTiki Bar & Grille 1200 Oceanview Ave, at MM47.5-Oceanside ☎305 743 9204. Large, thatched-roof bar-restaurant on the waterfront (part of Burdines Marina), with terrific views from the outdoor lounge on the second floor. The food is Mex-inflected American, with dishes such as a green chilli cheeseburger and taco salad, but they also do fried Key lime pie (seriously); most dishes are under $12. To reach it, turn towards the ocean down 15th St from US-1 (you'll pass *Castaway*). Daily 11.30am–9pm.

The Hurricane Grille MM49.5-Bayside ☎305 743 2220, ⓦhurricaneblues.com. Classic roadside American bar with nightly live music on a small stage in the back. This is an early stop on the daily pub crawl that concludes around 4am in the *Brass Monkey*, MM50-Oceanside in nearby K-Mart Plaza (☎305 743 4028). Daily 11am–2am.

Keys Fisheries 3502 Gulf View Ave, MM49-Bayside ☎305 743 4353, ⓦkeysfisheries.com. It's a culinary rite of passage to order the signature lobster Reuben ($14.95) at this takeout window with a sense of humour (you tell them your favourite car, Disney character or college, for example, and they call it out with your order). Located inside a marina, patrons dine on baskets of ultra-fresh seafood at covered picnic tables with terrific views of the bay. Daily 11am–9pm.

★**Lazy Days South** 725 11th St Ocean, MM47.3-Oceanside ☎305 289 0839, ⓦlazydayssouth.com. Arguably the best seafood in Marathon is the "*Lazy Days*-style" catch *du jour* – fresh fish sautéed in panko bread crumbs and cooked with diced tomatoes, spring onions, parmesan cheese and Key lime butter sauce ($24.99). The banana bread ($2.99) is also a must. Great ocean views from its casual outdoor seating. Reservations recommended. There's another location in Islamorada at MM79.9-Oceanside (☎305 664 5256). Mon–Thurs & Sun 11am–9.30pm, Fri & Sat 11am–10pm.

The Seven Mile Grill MM47.5-Bayside ☎305 743 4481, ⓦ7-mile-grill.com. It may not look like much – the decoration's limited to some old beer cans and pictures of fans in *Seven Mile Grill* T-shirts in front of world landmarks – but locals flock here for fine conch chowders ($3.25) and shrimp steamed in beer ($9.95), not to mention the silky Key lime pie, said to be the best outside Key West ($3.25). The home-made peanut butter pie is nearly as addictive. Daily 6.30am–9pm.

★**Stuffed Pig** MM49-Bayside ☎305 743 4059, ⓦthestuffedpig.com. Squeeze into the casual dining room or relax under a tiki hut at this inexpensive, aptly named breakfast hub with lobster omelettes, decadent crab-cake Benedicts and $2.50 mimosas. Expect long waiting times at weekends. Cash only. Mon–Sat 5am–noon, Sun 6am–noon.

The Seven Mile Bridge

In 1905, **Henry Flagler**, whose railway opened up Florida's east coast (see p.453), undertook the extension of its tracks to Key West. The Overseas Railroad, as it became known (though many called it "Flagler's folly"), was a monumental task that took seven years to complete and was marked by the appalling treatment of the railworkers.

Bridging the Middle Keys gave Flagler's engineers some of their biggest headaches. North of Marathon, the two-mile-long Long Key Viaduct, a still-elegant structure of nearly two hundred individually cast arches, was Flagler's personal favourite and was widely pictured in advertising campaigns. Yet a greater technical accomplishment was the **Seven Mile Bridge** (built from 1908 to 1912) to the south, linking Marathon to the Lower Keys. At one point, every US-flagged freighter on the Atlantic was hired to bring in materials – including German concrete impervious to saltwater seepage – while floating cranes, dredges and scores of other craft set about a job that eventually cost the lives of 700 labourers. When the trains eventually started rolling, passengers were treated to an incredible panorama: a broad sweep of sea and sky, sometimes streaked by luscious red sunsets or darkened by storm clouds.

2

The Flagler bridges were strong enough to withstand everything the Keys' volatile weather could throw at them, except for the calamitous 1935 Labor Day hurricane, which tore up the railway. The bridges were subsequently adapted to accommodate a road: the original Overseas Highway. Tales of hair-raising bridge crossings (the road was only 22ft wide), endless tailbacks as the drawbridges jammed – and the roadside parties that ensued – are part of Keys folklore. The later bridges, such as the $45-million new **Seven Mile Bridge** between Key Vaca and Bahia Honda Key that opened in the early 1980s, certainly improved traffic flow but also ended the mystique of travelling the old road.

Pigeon Key

Visitor centre MM47-Oceanside • Daily 9am–5pm, last ferry at 3.45pm • $12 • ☎ 305 743 5999, ⓦ pigeonkey.net

The old Seven Mile Bridge – intact, though missing its middle section to prevent vehicle access – now serves as extraordinarily long fishing piers and jogging strips. The section that begins in Marathon traces the old road up to **Pigeon Key** (a distance of 2.2 miles). The island, accessible by ferry (see below), was a railway work camp from 1909 to 1912, and later served as home to a small village of workers maintaining the bridges till 1982. Today its primary function is to host school science trips, but its seven original wooden buildings have been restored and opened to visitors as **Historic Pigeon Key**, whose small **museum** reveals the hardships routinely suffered by the workers. It's also one of the few places you can study the original bridge up close; the rail bridge was unnervingly slim, before being widened slightly in 1938 to allow cars to pass.

ARRIVAL AND INFORMATION   PIGEON KEY

By ferry Visitors can take a 10–15min ferry from the visitor centre, which is included in the entry price. Ferries are met by enthusiastic volunteers, who give illuminating 1hr 30min tours of Pigeon Key. Afterwards, you're welcome to hang out all day on the island (snorkelling around the piers is good year-round) – be sure to confirm there'll be room for you on the next boat back. Ferries depart from the visitor centre at 10am, noon and 2pm. Return trips from Pigeon Key are usually available 20min after each arrival, with a final departure at 3.45pm.

By bike or on foot The ferry is the only way to reach Pigeon Key; however, many folks walk or cycle the 2.2 miles that come up beside the island. It's a nice trip – giant stingrays and loggerhead turtles are often easy to spot from the bridge.

Tourist information The visitor centre is on Knight's Key at MM47-Oceanside (daily 9.30am–4pm; ☎ 305 743 5999, ⓦ pigeonkey.net), in a converted 1915 dining car that once plied the railway to Key West.

ACCOMMODATION

Pigeon Key Foundation ☎ 305 743 5999. The Pigeon Key Foundation rents out the island – bedding included

– for $55/person, with a fifteen-person minimum. Note that there are no eating facilities on the island.

The Lower Keys

Starkly different from their northerly neighbours, the **LOWER KEYS** are quiet, heavily wooded and predominantly residential. Unlike the Upper and Middle Keys, they are aligned north–south rather than east–west, and rest on a base of limestone, not coral reef. These islands have flora and fauna that are very much their own; species like the endangered Key deer, the Lower Keys cotton rat and the Cudjoe Key rice rat live here, though mainly tucked away miles from the Overseas Highway. Most visitors speed through the area on the way to Key West, just forty miles further on, but the area's lack of major tourism and easily found seclusion make this a good place to linger for a day or two.

LOWER KEYS UNDERWATER MUSIC FESTIVAL

If you're visiting the Looe Key Marine Sanctuary around the second Saturday in July, you may want to don your flippers and check out the annual **Lower Keys Underwater Music Festival** (☎ 305 872 9100, ⓦ us1radio.com). The music is broadcast via special speakers suspended beneath boats positioned above the reef, and there's quite a carnival atmosphere, with most of the divers dressing up before they go down. There's no actual charge, though you'll have to pay for the boat and diving equipment at the sanctuary office.

2

Bahia Honda State Park

MM37-Oceanside • Daily 8am–sunset; snorkelling trips daily 9.30am & 1.30pm • $4.50 car and driver, $8.50 car and up to seven passengers; $2 pedestrians and cyclists; snorkelling $29.95, full equipment rental $8; kayak rental $10/hr, $30/half-day • ☎ 305 872 2353, snorkelling ☎ 305 872 3210, ⓦ bahiahondapark.com

While not officially part of the Lower Keys, the first place of consequence you'll hit after crossing the Seven Mile Bridge is the 500-acre **Bahia Honda State Park**, boasting the Keys' best **beaches** and inviting, two-tone ocean waters.

Facilities in the park include a campground and cabins, a snack bar and a concession offering **snorkelling trips** twelve miles out to the Looe Key Marine Sanctuary (see p.127), and **kayak rental**.

Sandspur Beach

Turn left after the park entrance • Nature walk Mon & Wed at 10am

Delightful **Sandspur Beach** has scattered plants growing in the sand and all the usual amenities; while here, take a ramble on the **nature trail**, which loops from the shoreline through a hammock of silver palms, sea grape and buttonwood trees, passing rare plants, such as dwarf morning glory and spiny catesbaea. Keep a lookout for white-crowned pigeons, great white herons, roseate spoonbills and giant ospreys (whose bulky nests are plentiful throughout the Lower Keys, often atop telephone poles). Of the ranger-run programmes offered throughout the year, the **nature walk** is by far the best, but it's all pleasant enough without a guide.

Calusa Beach

At the park's northwestern tip

Near the marina and concession, **Calusa Beach** is more family friendly than Sandspur Beach, with plenty of shady pavilions, though the occasional ripe seaweed aroma may be off-putting to some.

Loggerhead Beach

On the south side of the island

Facing the ocean on the other side of the concession, **Loggerhead Beach** is a gloriously isolated strip of golden sand – though it has little shade to offer. The waters here are good for swimming, as well as for snorkelling, diving and especially windsurfing – rent equipment from the marina concession. You'll see small spotted eagle rays frolicking in the thick seaweed beds here, along with large jackfish and the occasional nurse shark.

Old Bahia Honda Bridge and the Sun and Sea Nature Center

Near Calusa Beach, a path leads from the road through the undergrowth towards the two-storey **Old Bahia Honda Bridge**, where you can gaze down on huge stingrays gliding through the channel. The unusually deep waters here (Bahia Honda is Spanish for "deep bay") made this the toughest of the old railway bridges to construct, and widening it for the road proved impossible; the solution was to put the highway on a higher tier. Nearby, the tiny **Sand and Sea Nature Center** at the end of the main car park (daily 10am–4pm; free; ☎ 305 872 9807) has displays on the local flora and fauna.

Big Pine Key and around

Daily sunrise–sunset

The eponymous trees on **Big Pine Key** are less of a draw than its **Key deer** (see box below), delightfully tame creatures that enjoy the freedom of the island; don't feed them (it's illegal and will cost you $250 in fines), and be cautious when driving – signs alongside the road state the number of known deaths to date during the year.

Blue Hole and around

At the intersection of Key Deer Blvd and Higgs Rd

The **Blue Hole** is a freshwater quarry with a healthy population of soft-shelled turtles and several alligators, which now and then emerge from the cool depths to sunbathe – parts of the quarry-side path may be closed if they have staked out a patch for the day. Should the alligators get your adrenaline pumping, take a calming stroll along two **nature trails** a quarter of a mile to the north: the Watson Trail (0.6 miles) cuts through tropical hardwood hammock, while the Mannillo Trail (800ft) is wheelchair-accessible and takes in pine rocklands and a freshwater wetland slough.

No Name Pub

30813 N Watson Blvd • ☎ 305 872 9115, ⓦ nonamepub.com • Head north along Key Deer Blvd to Watson Blvd and turn right; follow this curving road for 2 miles through a residential neighbourhood until the pub appears on the left

East of the Blue Hole, the rollicking **No Name Pub** is well worth the circuitous detour for a sight of the rather unusual wallpaper: dollar bills covering every inch of wall and ceiling inside, worth some $200,000 by the owners' account. If you fancy adding a bill or two, just ask the staff for the house staple gun. Built in 1936, the premises served time as a general store, brothel and fishing shop before opening as a restaurant and pub in the 1950s (see p.128). The pub lies just before the bridge leading to **No Name Key**, home to a few settlers living off solar power and septic tanks, but better known as the staging ground for the Bay of Pigs invasion (see p.456).

The Torch Keys and Ramrod Key

An even more peaceful atmosphere prevails on the Lower Keys south of Big Pine Key, despite the efforts of property developers. **The Torch Keys**, so-named for their forests of torchwood – used for kindling by early settlers, since it burns even when green – can be swiftly bypassed on the way to **Ramrod Key**, where you can access Looe Key Marine Sanctuary and the offshore coral reef.

KEY DEER

Key deer are a relatively small subspecies of the North American white-tailed deer and arrived long ago when the Keys were still joined to the mainland. For many years, sailors and Key West residents hunted them, but this and the destruction of their natural habitat led to near-extinction by the late 1940s. The **National Key Deer Refuge**, established in 1957 to safeguard the animals and their environment, has helped the population grow to around 800, thanks to rigorous preservation tactics including specially excavated tunnels beneath the roads so that the deer can cross in safety. Pick up information on the deer (and maps showing where to see them) from the **refuge visitor centre**, tucked away in the Big Pine Key Shopping Plaza off Key Deer Boulevard, just north of US-1 at MM30 (Mon–Fri 9am–4pm; call ahead, as lack of volunteers can mean shorter hours; ☎ 305 872 2239, ⓦ fws.gov /nationalkeydeer). To see the creatures, drive to the end of Key Deer Boulevard or turn east onto No Name Key. You should spot a few; the best time is at sunrise or sunset, when the deer come out to forage.

Looe Key Marine Sanctuary

Keen underwater explorers should head for **Looe Key Marine Sanctuary**, named after HMS *Looe*, a British frigate that sank here in 1744. This five-square-mile area of protected crystal-clear waters and reef formations creates an unforgettable spectacle: showy elkhorn and star coral, as well as rays, octopus and a multitude of gaily coloured fish flit between tall coral pillars. The water, which ranges from eight to 35 feet deep, will appeal to novice and experienced snorkellers alike, but anyone wanting to catch sight of the HMS *Looe* will be disappointed – it has long since disintegrated.

The **Florida Keys National Marine Sanctuary office** in Key West (33 East Quay Rd; Mon–Fri 8am–5pm; ☎305 809 4700, ⍵floridakeys.noaa.gov) offers basic information; you should also pop in to the Florida Keys Eco-Discovery Center in Key West (see p.138). You can only visit the reef on a trip organized by one of the many diving shops throughout the Keys; the nearest to the reef is the **Looe Key Reef Resort & Center** (☎305 872 2215 or ☎877 816 3483, ⍵diveflakeys.com), which also offers accommodation (see p.128), MM27.5-Oceanside (on Ramrod Key), which runs five-hour trips (daily 7.30am & 12.15pm) for snorkelling ($39) and diving (two dives $69). You can also visit the sanctuary from the Bahia Honda State Park (see p.125).

Perky's Bat Tower

Sugarloaf Key, 11 miles west of Ramrod Key, at MM17-Bayside

The 35ft **Perky's Bat Tower** stands as testimony to one man's misguided belief in the mosquito-killing powers of bats. A get-rich-quick book of the 1920s, *Bats, Mosquitoes and Dollars*, led Richter C. Perky, a property speculator who had recently purchased Sugarloaf Key, into thinking bats would be the solution to the Keys' mosquito problem. With much hullabaloo, he erected this brown cypress lath tower in 1929 and dutifully sent away for the costly "bat bait", which he was told would lure an army of bats to the tower. It didn't work: the bats didn't show up, the mosquitoes stayed healthy, and Perky went bust soon after (in fact, if he'd imported the bats himself, it might have worked, as a single bat will eat its own weight in insects each night). The background story is far more interesting than the actual tower, but if the tale tickles your fancy, drive down the narrow road between the air strip and the sprawling *Sugarloaf Lodge*.

ARRIVAL AND INFORMATION   THE LOWER KEYS

By bus Two daily Greyhound buses run from Miami to Big Pine Key (see p.111).

Tourist information The Lower Keys Chamber of Commerce, at MM31-Oceanside in the main settlement of Big Pine (Mon–Fri 9am–5pm, Sat 9am–3pm; ☎305 872 2411 or ☎800 872 3722, ⍵lowerkeyschamber.com), is packed with information on the area.

ACCOMMODATION

Accommodation options here are more limited than further north in the Keys, and many of the motels are pricey for the few amenities they offer; below are some worthwhile exceptions.

Big Pine Key Fishing Lodge MM33-Oceanside ☎305 872 2351. Family-run and -maintained, this popular lodge offers sixteen spotless efficiencies, some from the 1950s that have basic interiors but personal boat docks outside, and others from the 1990s that are refurbished with modern bathrooms and bedding. It's also one of the best choices for budget camping, with full hook-ups, heated pool, convenience store, and great access for fishing and diving. Camping $39, efficiencies $109

Deer Run Bed & Breakfast MM33-Oceanside, 1997 Long Beach Drive ☎305 872 2015, ⍵deerrunfloridabb .com. Eco-minded, four-room bed and breakfast with organic bedding, reclaimed tiles and furniture and gauzy drapes ingeniously reborn from plastic bottles. An organic vegan breakfast is included in the rate, as well as bike and kayak use. Off the beaten path, *Deer Run's* tranquil waterfront property is dotted with ambrosial strains of mango, banana and avocado. No children. Closed mid-Aug to mid-Oct. $235

Little Palm Island Resort & Spa MM28.5-Oceanside,

2

off Little Torch Key ☎305 872 2524, ⓦlittlepalmisland .com. The thirty thatched cottages – each with its own outdoor bamboo shower – are the ultimate splurge, set in lush gardens a few feet from the beach on an idyllic private islet. It also has a fantastic – though expensive – fish restaurant, often rated by critics as the best in the Keys. No children. **$790**

Looe Key Reef Resort MM27.5-Oceanside, Ramrod Key ☎305 872 2215, ⓦdiveflakeys.com. Especially convenient for visiting the marine sanctuary (see p.127). The decor is early 1980s but this super-clean, two-storey motel offers terrific value for its location. Guests can also rent kayaks and snorkel gear, and there's a swimming pool and tiki bar on-site. Cheaper single rates available. **$115**

Parmer's Resort 565 Barry Ave, Little Torch Key,

off US-1 at MM28.5-Bayside ☎305 872 2157, ⓦparmersresort.com. This friendly inn offers a range of good-value options, from standard motel rooms to one- or two-bedroom apartments with kitchens. Made up of a complex of buildings set in lush, green gardens, it has an old Keys vibe, thanks to its tropical bedspreads and the hammocks strewn about the property. There's a little putting green, heated pool, an on-site coin-operated laundry and free breakfast, plus every room comes with a veranda. Doubles **$159**, apartments **$214**

Sugar Loaf Key KOA MM20-Oceanside, 251 State Rd 939 ☎305 745 3549, ⓦkoa.com. This leafy campground is tucked away down a long winding road and has ample facilities, including plenty of picnic tables for eating alfresco. Tent sites without hook-ups **$55**

EATING AND DRINKING

You'll find a few good eating options in the Lower Keys, especially around the settlement on Big Pine Key. As for nightlife, locals who want to live it up generally head for Key West. Otherwise, try the *No Name Pub* (see below & p.126) or the *Looe Key Reef Resort* (see above) for weekend drinking.

Baby's Coffee MM15-Oceanside ☎305 744 9866, ⓦbabyscoffee.com. Unbeatable, warehouse-like coffee shop, serving six delicious home-roasted blends ($1 a cup) as well as gourmet cakes, Key lime pie and sandwiches; they also sell T-shirts, and even wine by the bottle, and you can buy house blends by the pound to take home (a great Keys souvenir). Mon–Sat 6.30am–8pm, Sun 7am–5pm.

Bobalu's Southern Café MM10-Bayside ☎305 296 1664. A brightly painted café that makes for a terrific pre-Key West pit stop for hearty soul food at lunch or dinner, though it also does some of the best pizzas (from $12) in the Keys – New Haven style (with a thin, bitter crust), thanks to the Connecticut owners. Otherwise sample specials like a fried conch sandwich ($11) or fried green tomatoes ($4.99) along with belly-busting sides like sweet potato casserole ($2). Cash only. Tues–Sat 11am–9.30pm.

Coco's Kitchen MM30-Bayside, 283 Key Deer Blvd, Big Pine Key Shopping Plaza ☎305 872 4495, ⓦcocoskitchen.com. The stools have been spinning since 1969 at this family-run lunch counter that serves exceptional American, Nicaraguan and Cuban food like *picadillo* (ground beef in a tomato sauce with raisins; $10) and roast pork in lime marinade with beans and rice ($10). Wonderfully cheap (the garden burger is only $5). Located in a shopping centre by the Key Deer Refuge visitor centre. Wed–Sat 7am–2pm & 4.30–7pm.

Good Food Conspiracy MM30.2-Oceanside ☎305 872 3945, ⓦgoodfoodconspiracy.com. After a week of fried fish and booze, you'll feel your cells revitalize when you bite into a *Good Food* "everything" wrap – tuna, cashews, avocado, cheddar cheese, sprouts and a "rainbow of veggies" ($8). There are also daily soups, fresh smoothies

and juices. Really just a small health-food store, seating is very limited. Unmissable with its turquoise-painted exterior and huge yin-yang sign. Mon–Sat 9.30am–7pm, Sun 11am–5pm.

★**No Name Pub** 30813 N Watson Blvd, Big Pine Key ☎305 872 9115, ⓦnonamepub.com. In addition to its oddball dollar-bill "wallpaper" (see p.126), it's also worth ducking in to the oldest pub in the Keys for their knockout thin-crust "gourmet" pizzas for $19–25, like the delicate, spicy Caribbean Chicken or the Mexican, loaded down with chilli, cheddar cheese, sour cream and salsa. Beer drinkers should enjoy the No Name Pub Amber ($3.50). Daily 11am–11pm.

★**Square Grouper** MM22.5-Oceanside ☎305 745 8880, ⓦsquaregrouperbarandgrill.com. Humorously named for the bales of marijuana locals fished offshore in the '70s and '80s (abandoned by drug trafficking boats fearful of investigation), this hopping bar and grill has an expansive menu that successfully touches on everything from rice bowls with cashews ($18), to baked goat cheese with honey and fig ($10), seared scallops with bacon-mushroom vinaigrette ($29) and "magical brownies" ($9). No reservations taken, so get there early or expect a wait. Tues–Sat 11am–10pm.

★**Sugarloaf Food Company** MM24-Bayside ☎305 744 0631. This lemon-yellow sweet-tooth oasis pops up on the final stretch to Key West. There's an excellent chalkboard sandwich menu (home-made meatloaf on sourdough bread; $8.25), crisp Cobb salads with avocado ($9.95), and espresso. Chocolate-cherry cookie, or Key lime pistachio? Such are the agonizing decisions that await. Mon–Sat 7.30am–3pm.

Key West

Closer to Cuba than mainland Florida, **KEY WEST** often seems very far removed from the rest of the US. Famed for their tolerant attitudes and laidback lifestyles, its 30,000 islanders seem adrift in a great expanse of sea and sky. Despite the million tourists who arrive each year, the place resonates with an anarchic and individualist spirit that hits you the instant you arrive. Long-term residents here, known as Conchs (pronounced "konk") after the giant sea snails eaten by early settlers, ride bicycles everywhere, shoot the breeze on street corners, and smile at complete strangers.

Yet as wild as it may at first appear, Key West today is far from being the misfits' paradise it once was. Much of the sleaziness has been brushed away through restoration and revitalization – it takes a lot of money to buy a house here now – paving the way for a sizeable holiday industry that at times seems to revolve around party boats and heavy drinking. Not that Key West is near to losing its special identity. The liberal attitudes have attracted a large influx of gay people, estimated at two in five of the population, who take an essential role in running the place, and sink thousands of dollars into its future.

For many tourists a trip to Key West boils down to just two things: **fishing**, and its notoriously bacchanalian **nightlife**. There's much more to the town, however; while Key West's knack for tourism can be gaudy, it's quite easy to bypass the commercial traps and discover an island as unique for its present-day society as for its remarkable past.

The tourist epicentre is on **Duval Street**, whose northern end is marked by **Mallory Square**, a historic landmark now home to a brash chain of bars that entirely ignores the whimsical, freethinking spirit of the island. But just a few steps east of here is the historic section, a network of streets teeming with rich foliage and brilliant blooms draped over curious architecture. This area boasts many of the best guesthouses and lots of restaurants and wacky galleries, while to the west lies **Bahama Village**, a neighbourhood of dusty lanes where cockerels wander, stray cats lounge and birds screech into the night.

Brief history

Piracy was the main activity around Key West (known in Spanish as Cayo Hueso), before Florida joined the US and the navy established a base here in 1823. This cleared

---

THE CONCH REPUBLIC

The story behind Key West's nickname, the "**Conch Republic**", offers a telling example of the town's political savvy and its sense of humour. In April 1982, the US Border Patrol set up a roadblock on US Highway 1 at the **Last Chance Saloon** in Florida City, ostensibly to prevent illegal aliens from entering the US mainland; while local residents were suspected of smuggling Cuban refugees, drugs were also thought to be a target. The roadblock effectively cut off the Florida Keys at the confluence of the only two roads out to the mainland, leading to seventeen-mile tailbacks and a sudden, sharp decline in tourist numbers – as well as causing massive disruption to basic services. The mayor of Key West (with the backing of other community leaders), after failing to remove the checkpoint through legal means, formed the "Conch Republic" and **seceded from the US** in Mallory Square on April 23 – and declared war on Washington for good measure. The first "shots" fired were of stale Cuban bread broken over the head of a man dressed in an admiral's uniform – though some claim there were more concrete targets in the form of federal spies who had quickly descended on the town. The mayor-turned-prime-minister then surrendered to the US Navy – and demanded US foreign aid and war reparations of one billion dollars. Washington didn't respond directly (at least with an aid package), though it did quietly remove the offending checkpoint. A publicity stunt, but one that worked, and the event is now celebrated annually at the **Conch Republic Independence Celebration** (see box, p.149), a great excuse for a week-long party. There's a small brass plaque commemorating the event outside the visitor centre in Mallory Square.

2

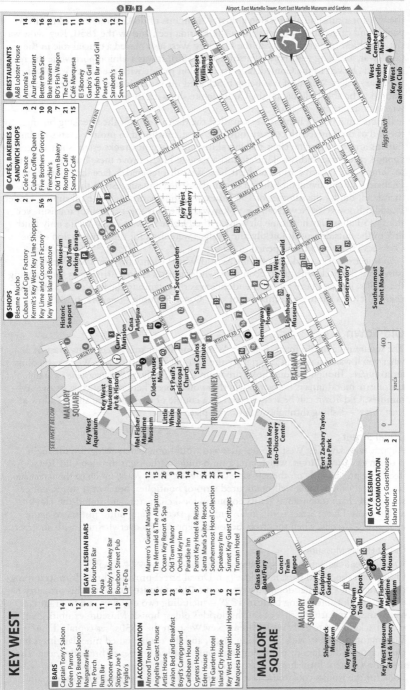

KEY WEST

● BARS

Captain Tony's Saloon	14
Green Parrot	5
Hog's Breath Saloon	12
Margaritaville	3
The Porch	2
Rum Bar	11
Schooner Wharf	1
Sloppy Joe's	13
Virgilio's	4

■ GAY & LESBIAN BARS

801 Bourbon Bar	8
Aqua	6
Bobby's Monkey Bar	9
Bourbon Street Pub	7
La-Te-Da	10

● SHOPS

Bésame Mucho	4
Cuban Leaf Cigar Factory	2
Kermit's Key West Key Lime Shopper	1
Key Lime and Coconut Factory	5/6
Key West Island Bookstore	3

● CAFÉS, BAKERIES & SANDWICH SHOPS

Cole's Peace	3
Cuban Coffee Queen	2
Five Brothers Grocery	10
Frenchie's	20
Old Town Bakery	7
Rooftop Café	21
Sandy's Café	15

● RESTAURANTS

A&B Lobster House	1
Antonia's	14
Azur Restaurant	8
Better than Sex	16
Blue Heaven	18
BO's Fish Wagon	5
Café Marquesa	13
The Café	11
El Siboney	19
Garbo's Grill	4
Hogfish Bar and Grill	9
Paseo's	6
Sarabeth's	12
Seven Fish	17

■ ACCOMMODATION

Almond Tree Inn	18
Angelina Guest House	16
Artist House	10
Avalon Bed and Breakfast	23
Boyd's Campground	8
Caribbean House	19
Cypress House	5
Eden House	4
The Gardens Hotel	13
Island City House	6
Key West International Hostel	22
Marquesa Hotel	11
Marrero's Guest Mansion	12
The Mermaid & The Alligator	15
Ocean Key Resort & Spa	26
Old Town Manor	9
Orchid Key Inn	20
Paradise Inn	14
Parrot Key Hotel & Resort	7
Santa Maria Suites Resort	24
Southernmost Hotel Collection	25
Speakeasy Inn	21
Sunset Key Guest Cottages	1
Truman Hotel	17

■ GAY & LESBIAN ACCOMMODATION

Alexander's Guesthouse	3
Island House	2

the way for a substantial **wrecking industry**. Millions of dollars were earned by lifting people and cargo off shipwrecks along the Florida reef, and by the 1850s Key West was the wealthiest (per capita) city in the US. Key West also played a crucial role in the Civil War, as, along with Fort Jefferson (see p.150), it was a Union port while the rest of Florida hewed to the Confederacy. Its decision to side with the North wasn't wholly voluntary – Key West port was being blockaded into submission, since the Union wanted to be able to liquidate the Confederate ships it captured at Key West's lucrative wreckers' auctions.

The building of reef lighthouses sounded the death knell for the wrecking business by the end of the nineteenth century, but Key West continued to prosper even so. Many **Cubans** arrived, bringing **cigar-making** skills, and migrant **Greeks** established a lucrative **sponge** enterprise. Industrial unrest and a sponge-blight drove these businesses north to Tampa and Tarpon Springs and left Key West ill-prepared to face the **Depression**. Diehard Conchs, living on fish and coconuts, defied any suggestion they move to the mainland, but by the summer of 1934 they were finally driven into bankruptcy. Under Franklin Roosevelt's New Deal, Key West was tidied up and readied for tourism, yet the 1935 Labor Day hurricane blew away the Flagler railway – Key West's only land link to the outside world. Luckily, the bridges were used for the construction of the Overseas Highway, which opened in 1938.

An injection of naval dollars during World War II eventually saved Key West by providing the backbone for its economy, while **tourists** started arriving in force during the 1980s, just as a taste for independence was rising among the locals and a strange chain of events led to the formation of the "**Conch Republic**" (see box, p.130).

Old Town

The square mile of **Old Town** (between White and Front streets) contains most of what you'll want to see and is certainly the best place to absorb Key West's easygoing atmosphere. Though visitors choke the main streets, only blocks away the casually hedonistic mood infects everyone, whether you've been here twenty years or twenty minutes. Old Town can be seen on foot in a couple of days, but you should allow at least three – dashing through won't do the place justice.

Duval Street

Anyone who saw Key West two decades ago would now barely recognize the main promenade, **Duval Street**, which cuts a mile-long swathe right through Old Town. Teetering precariously on the safe side of seedy for many years, much of the street has been transformed into a well-manicured strip of boutiques, beachwear stores, coffee shops and chain restaurants. Yet its colourful local characters and round-the-clock action mean Duval Street is still an interesting place to hang out – just try to avoid cruise-ship arrivals, when the street becomes depressingly overwhelmed with shoppers.

Oldest House Museum

322 Duval St • Mon & Tues, Thurs–Sat 10am–4pm, last entry 3.45pm • Free • ☎ 305 294 9501, ⊛ oirf.org

Other than shops and bars, few places on Duval Street provide a break from tramping the pavement. One that does, however, is the **Oldest House Museum**. This property has withstood a lot since being built in 1829 – including two city fires and five raging hurricanes – to earn the title of south Florida's oldest house. Museum exhibits give some background to early settler life in Key West. In the 1830s, sea captain Francis Watlington moved in with his young bride, and the couple raised nine daughters here without the aid of indoor plumbing, and only tropical breezes to break the heat. The museum's current furnishings, many original to the Watlingtons, all date to the 1840s. Look for the wonky cookhouse in the back garden, built separately from the main house to reduce the risk of fire.

St Paul's Episcopal Church
401 Duval St • Daily 9am–5.30pm • Free organ concert daily at noon • ☎ 305 296 5142, ⓦ stpaulschurchkeywest.org

One block south of the Oldest House Museum, **St Paul's Episcopal Church** dates from 1912 and is worth a quick look for its richly coloured stained-glass windows. Aim to visit at noon, when daily concerts fill the cavernous chambers with the sumptuous sounds of organ hymns.

San Carlos Institute
516 Duval St • Mon–Wed & Sun 11am–5pm, Thurs–Sat 11am–9pm • Free, $3 suggested donation • ☎ 305 294 3887, ⓦ institutosancarlos.org

The imposing **San Carlos Institute** has played a leading role in Cuban exile life since it opened on nearby Anne Street in 1871. It was here in 1892 that Cuban Revolution hero José Martí wielded the exiles into a force that would achieve the island's independence from Spain ten years later. The current building, which dates from 1924, was financed by an $80,000 grant from the Cuban government after a hurricane wrecked the original building. Cuban architect Francisco Centurión designed the two-storey structure in the **Cuban Baroque** style of the period, noticeable in the wrought-iron balconies and creamy facade. The soil on its grounds was taken from Martí's farm (he was killed in Cuba in 1895), and a cornerstone from a colonial wall in Havana. Today it contains a passable permanent **exhibition** focusing on Martí and his men, mostly consisting of old newspaper clippings and letters, exhibits on Cuban presidents from 1902 to 1958, and a section on Cuban immigrants; you can also watch absorbing DVDs, on demand, on Martí's life and a host of other subjects including Cuban music.

Butterfly Conservatory
1316 Duval St • Daily 9am–5.30pm, last ticket sold at 4.30pm • $12 • ☎ 305 296 2988, ⓦ keywestbutterfly.com

A worthy diversion on the lower Duval drag is the surprisingly charming **Butterfly Conservatory**. Race through the entrance hall – a gift shop and waiting room – and head straight for the enormous conservatory. It's a dazzling experience to be surrounded by flocks of tame butterflies that dive-bomb or land on you without hesitation – an odd, almost creepy sensation. It's essential that the butterflies here don't breed – caterpillars consume such huge volumes of greenery they'd devastate the foliage within days – so there are no plants here that are used by any species' caterpillar as their sole source of food. Instead, the pupae are shipped in and hatched on-site in a special standalone nursery – you can see rows of the chrysalises dangling in its glass windows like an alien hatchery.

The southernmost point
You'll know when you get near the southern end of Duval Street because, whether it's a motel, a petrol station or a pharmacy, everything sprouts a "southernmost" epithet. The true **southernmost point** in Key West, and consequently in the continental US, is at the intersection of Whitehead and South streets: it's only ninety miles from Cuba and flagged by a squat red, black and yellow marker.

Mallory Square and around
In the early 1800s, thousands of dollars' worth of marine salvage was landed at the piers, stored in the warehouses, and sold at the auction houses on **Mallory Square**, just west of the northern end of Duval Street. Nowadays the spacious waterfront section contrasts with the hubbub of the area behind it (alongside Wall St), as thousands of cruise-ship passengers and other tourists flock here by day for the souvenir market selling ice cream, trinkets and T-shirts; it's a constant jam of shuttles, trolleys and tour buses.

2

SUNSET CELEBRATION

Mallory Square's bustle doesn't let up in the evening, thanks to the touristy **Sunset Celebration** (Ⓦ sunsetcelebration.org), started in the 1960s by local hippies but now stage-managed by the Key West Cultural Preservation Society. Jugglers and fire-eaters are on hand to create a merry backdrop for the sinking of the sun, and though the event's charms are rather overrated, it's worth experiencing at least once – some of the entertainers are real characters, and their performances are certainly enhanced by the plastic cups of beer and cocktails sold at the stands nearby.

Historic Sculpture Garden

Between Wall St and Mallory Square • Daily 7.30am–9pm • Free • ☎ 305 294 2587, Ⓦ keywestsculpturegarden.org

In front of the Waterfront Playhouse theatre is the **Historic Sculpture Garden**, anchored by the heroic *Wreckers*, a striking monument symbolizing the spirit of Key West. The rest of this tiny, offbeat walled garden houses cast-iron busts of a varied selection of local heroes, most of whom look as if they'd be more at home in a waxwork chamber of horrors than this supposedly stirring tribute. Aside from heavyweights like Hemingway, Truman and Henry Flagler, look for the scions of several local families whose names – like Whitehead and Mallory – now grace streets and squares round town.

Key West Aquarium

1 Whitehead St • Daily 10am–6pm, guided tours and feedings 11am, 1pm, 3pm & 4.30pm • $14, valid for two days • ☎ 888 544 5927, Ⓦ keywestaquarium.com

More entertaining than Mallory Square's daytime scene is the small gathering of sea life in the adjacent Art Deco **Key West Aquarium**. Built in 1934 as an open-air attraction, it's been enclosed and enlarged since then without compromising its superb design. These days the aquarium is home to four species of sea turtle, fascinating creatures such as porcupine fish and longspine squirrel fish who leer from behind glass, and sharks (the smaller kinds such as blacknose and bonnethead) that are known to jump out of their open tanks out back during the half-hour **guided tours and feedings**. If you intend to eat conch you might change your mind after seeing the live ones here – they're not the world's prettiest crustaceans.

Shipwreck Museum

1 Whitehead St • Daily 9.40am–5pm; shows every 20min until 4.40pm • $15 • ☎ 305 292 8990, Ⓦ keywestshipwreck.com

Housed in a towering wooden plank structure opposite the aquarium is the kitschy **Shipwreck Museum**. Enthusiastic guides throw out dozens of creaky gags while introducing an informative, if careworn, movie on the wrecking industry. On the two upper storeys are several exhibits of cargo from the *Isaac Allerton*, which sank in 1856 and remained untraced until 1985: the most arresting items are feathery lace gloves, still intact after more than a century in the sea, and silverware ornamented with crusty coral. Better still is the panoramic view of Key West seen from the top of the rickety 65ft tower.

Mel Fisher Maritime Museum

200 Greene St • Mon–Fri 8.30am–5pm, Sat & Sun 9.30am–5pm • $12.50 • ☎ 305 294 2633, Ⓦ melfisher.org

Not all the ships that foundered off Key West were salvaged when they sank – some early galleons, which plied the trade route between Spain and its New World colonies during the sixteenth and seventeenth centuries, held onto their treasure until only a few decades ago when advanced technology enabled treasure hunters to locate them. You can see a lavish selection of such rescued cargo at the **Mel Fisher Maritime Museum**, including a chunky emerald cross, massive cannons, and a "poison cup" said to neutralize toxins, all salvaged from two seventeenth-century wrecks. In 1980, after years of searching, treasure hunter Mel Fisher discovered the *Santa Margarita*, and five years later, the *Nuestra Señora de Atocha*, both sunk during a hurricane in 1622, forty miles southeast of Key West – they yielded a haul said to be worth at least $200 million. Though it's easy to get sidetracked by the monetary value of such finds – the *Atocha* yielded 1041 silver bars and 77 gold bricks – the collection has immense historic importance, offering a window into the early years of Spanish colonization of America. Inca symbols as well as European technology and an incredibly eclectic range of items from jewellery, cookware and ceramics to weaponry, medicinal items and even rat bones were discovered – there's also a sobering display dedicated to the slave ship *Henrietta Marie* (which sank in 1700).

Upstairs, the La Plata del Mar exhibit includes silver from fleets sunk in 1715 and 1733. The first floor previously displayed a 74oz gold bar that visitors were actually allowed to lift – and lift it someone did: two thieves stole the precious brick (valued at $550,000) as the museum closed for the day on August 18, 2010 (a hawk-eyed guard now oversees the room). The suspects were caught on camera, but despite a reward (and a clear image of the modern-day pirates) the historic bullion has yet to be returned.

KEY WEST BEACHES AND WATERSPORTS

Key West is not a **beach** resort, but if you're really desperate, the beach at **Fort Zachary Taylor** (see p.138) is fine for a few hours of lounging, while tiny **Higgs Beach** at the end of Reynolds Street has a decent strip of sand (though the water isn't that enticing), with a cheap café and bar nearby. Further east, along South Roosevelt Boulevard, **Smathers Beach** is the weekend parade ground of Key West's most toned physiques and a haunt of windsurfers and parasailers – this one-mile stretch of fine sand usually has plenty of beach chairs, windsurfers, jet skis and kayaks to rent.

Key West is far better known as a **watersports** and **fishing** centre. You'll find most charters in the Seaport (see p.137).

Andy Griffiths Charters By the Hogfish Bar and Grill (see p.147) at 6810 Front St, Stock Island (on the north side of the bridge before entering Key West) ☎305 296 2639, ⓦfishandy.com. This experienced local fisherman arranges three-day fishing excursions out to the Dry Tortugas (from $3600). Check the website for the more affordable 4hr trips for parties of up to six anglers ($100 per person).

Blue Planet Kayak Tours leave from Fort East Martello Museum (call and they'll pick you up) ☎305 294 8087 (rentals), ☎305 809 8110 (tour reservations), ⓦblue-planet-kayak.com. Rent a kayak ($30) or take an exhilarating tour through mangrove tunnels (2hr 30min; $50) alive with osprey, coral and stingray. Reservations essential.

Dive Key West 3128 N Roosevelt Blvd ☎800 426 0707, ⓦdivekeywest.com. Divers should contact this highly acclaimed outfit, which runs two trips daily (9am & 2pm), both to a wreck and reef; snorkellers pay $59, divers $75–99 (not including equipment).

Fury Glass Bottom Boat Sails from the Pier House Resort dock at 2 Duval St ☎888 976 0899,

ⓦfurycat.com. Modern glass-hulled catamaran that makes 2hr trips over the reef for those unwilling to get wet ($41). The same outfit also offers snorkelling and watersports rentals.

Jolly II Rover Foot of Greene and Elizabeth sts ☎305 304 2235, ⓦschoonerjollyrover.com. Live out your pirate fantasies on this square-rigged schooner – a gorgeous tall ship; daily 2hr trips for $35. Reservations recommended.

Sebago Watersports 205 Elizabeth St, Seaport ☎800 507 9955, ⓦkeywestsebago.com. Offers sunset cruises ($69, includes champagne and appetizers), snorkelling ($49, includes wine and beer), parasailing ($49), jet-ski tours ($125, includes drinks and meals) and all-inclusive ecotours ($99, combines sailing, snorkelling and kayaking).

Western Union Schooner End of William St, Seaport ☎305 292 1208, ⓦschooner westernunion.org. Built in Key West in 1939, the romantic tall ship that once ministered Western Union cable lines (it's also the city's flagship vessel) was under repair at research time, but its sunset cruises should be up and running by 2016.

Key West Museum of Art & History

281 Front St • Daily 9.30am–4.30pm • $9 • ☎ 305 295 6616, ⓦ kwahs.com

Across the road from the maritime museum, the handsome, rust-brown Romanesque **Customs House** was built in 1891 and used as a post office, customs office and federal courthouse until meeting its current incarnation as the **Key West Museum of Art & History**. Permanent exhibits include displays dedicated to Hemingway, and sections on Key West's nineteenth-century history, with an impressive 7ft diorama of the town in its bustling 1850s heyday. There is also a compelling gallery devoted to Henry Flagler's overseas railroad (see p.123): visitors watch video clips inside a re-created train car and peruse displays chock-a-block with railway-related postcards, uniforms and quotes from former passengers, one of whom remarked: "Climbing aboard the [train] was like entering a magical side door to paradise … Passengers had an aerial view of molten sea, distant mangrove keys … and flaming cloud formations." Throughout the museum, you'll find temporary displays of local art.

Audubon House and Tropical Gardens

205 Whitehead St • Daily 9.30am–5pm, last tour 4.15pm • $12, gardens only $7.50 • ☎ 305 294 2116, ⓦ audubonhouse.com

Renovated in 1958, the **Audubon House and Tropical Gardens** was the first of Key West's elegant Victorian-style properties to get a thorough restoration. The wealthy Wolfson family, who purchased the place to prevent its demolition, set about returning the house to its original grandeur, using furniture and decorative arts culled from European auctions and estate sales.

The house takes its name from famed ornithologist John James Audubon, who was so taken with the property's tropical garden that, during his six-week expedition to the Keys in 1832, he made it his alfresco studio, using it as a workspace for painting regional birds. Audubon spent his visit to the region ambling around mangroves, looking for the birdlife he later portrayed in his highly regarded *Birds of America* folio. During the trip – in which he also spent time in the Dry Tortugas – Audubon came across 22 birds he hadn't previously seen, some of which, such as the flamingo and the brown pelican, comprise his most famous works. Twenty-eight of his original lithographs (including the latter two) now line the house's dignified walls and staircase. Look closely at the white crowned pigeon print – it's said that the branches on which the pair rests are that of the front yard's Geiger tree.

The man who actually owned and built the property (in 1830) was a wrecker named John Geiger. In addition to twelve children of their own, Geiger and his wife took in others from shipwrecks and broken marriages. **Guided tours** provide a ten-minute introduction to Audubon and the home, after which you're free to explore the property's three floors and one-acre garden.

Caroline and Greene streets

Walk along **Caroline Street** or **Greene Street**, and you'll come across numerous examples of late-1800s "**conch houses**", built in a mix-and-match style fusing elements of Victorian, Colonial and Tropical architecture. The houses were raised on coral slabs and rounded off with playful "gingerbread" wood trimming. Erected quickly and cheaply, conch houses were seldom painted, but many here are bright and colourful, evincing their recent transformation in the last fifteen years from regular dwellings to sophisticated winter homes. The reason such houses have lasted so long is that many were put up by shipwrights using boat-building techniques, so they sway in high winds and weather extremes of climate well.

Curry Mansion

511 Caroline St • Daily 9am–5pm • $5 • ☎ 305 294 5349 or ☎ 800 253 3466, ⓦ currymansion.com

In marked contrast to the tiny conch houses, the grand three-storey **Curry Mansion** (now a B&B) was first built in 1869 as the abode of William Curry, Florida's first millionaire (who made his loot by selling salvaged goods in the 1840s). The current structure dates from 1899, when Curry's son Milton inherited and expanded the property. Exhaustively restored, the house is an awkward hybrid of museum and inn; inside, amid a riot of antiques and oddities, is a stash of strange and stylish fittings such as Henry James's piano and a hanging light designed by Frank Lloyd Wright. The real reason to stop by, however, is the **Widow's Walk** (a tiny lookout on the roof where sailors' wives watched for their husbands' return), which affords an impressive view across Old Town.

Historic Seaport
Starting at the end of Front Street, the Harbor Walk follows the marina to Margaret Street, where the Seaport (also called the Key West Bight) has been spruced up into a shopping and eating strip (see p.149). Here you'll find numerous **fishing, diving and watersport charters**, plus ferries to the **Dry Tortugas** (see p.150).

Key West Turtle Museum
On the dock at 200 Margaret St • Tues–Sat noon–4pm • Admission by donation • ☎ 305 294 0209, Ⓦ keywestturtlemuseum.org

Located on a short pier in the heart of the Seaport, the **Key West Turtle Museum** was once one of three turtle canneries in Key West, and is now an annexe of the Mel Fisher Maritime Museum (see p.134) that commemorates Key West's nineteenth- and mid-twentieth-century heritage as the centre of the grim turtle-processing industry. In the cannery's 1950–60s heyday, ships would capture two- to seven hundred green turtles in the Caribbean, and hold them here in waterfront pens (called "kraals"); the turtles were then minced and made into soup (the cannery slaughtered about 25–30 turtles a day). Overfishing led to catch-size regulations in 1971, and the end of the turtle fishing industry – currently, all six species of sea turtle found in US waters are protected under the Endangered Species Act. The small museum, housed in a wooden clapboard shack, has displays on turtle fishing techniques, ephemera such as turtle soup cans, postcards of the kraals (once a tourist attraction), and even a 1963 picture of pin-up and former Key Wester Bettie Page astride a reptilian beauty. Peer outside the window for a glimpse of one of the museum's remaining turtle kraals, located in the water to the side of the building.

Casa Antigua
314 Simonton St • Daily 9.30am–6pm • $2, or free with a $10 purchase at the Pelican Poop Shoppe • ☎ 305 292 9955, Ⓦ pelicanpoopshoppe.com

Tucked behind the unfortunately named Pelican Poop Shoppe, **Casa Antigua** was Hemingway's first residence in Key West: "Papa" and his wife were graciously hosted at the hotel that stood here in 1928 when the car they'd ordered was late in its delivery to the property's auto dealership. The Hemingways were so taken with the island that this seven-week waiting period stretched into three years at the hostelry, and Ernest completed his novel *A Farewell to Arms* on-site. The building's history is now retold via a kooky six-minute tape that's piped through speakers overhanging the beautiful bricked atrium, lined with dense palms, tropical blooms and a pool with spouting fountains. That's all the sightseeing you'll get from the Casa, however; for a more detailed look at the writer's life and times in Key West, head to the Ernest Hemingway Home and Museum on Whitehead Street (see p.139).

The Truman Annex
Between Whitehead St and the Atlantic Ocean • Daily 8am–6pm • Free

The old naval storehouse containing the Fisher trove (see p.134) was once part of the **Truman Annex**, a decommissioned naval base established in 1822. Some of the buildings subsequently erected on the base, which spans a hundred acres between Whitehead Street and the sea, were – and still are – among Key West's most distinctive.

In 1986, the Annex passed into the hands of a property developer who encouraged redevelopment by opening up the **Presidential Gates** on Caroline Street to the public (previously it was only accessible to heads of state); a smart move which defused much local suspicion and anxiety. The complex is now the site of some of the most luxurious private homes in Key West – pick up a free **map** from one of the boxes at the complex entrances. The buildings' interiors, unfortunately, are closed to the public.

2

Harry S. Truman Little White House Museum

111 Front St, at Caroline St • Daily 9am–4.30pm; admission by guided tour only (tours run every 20min) • $15 • ☎ 305 294 9911, ⓦ trumanlittlewhitehouse.com

The most famous among the private homes in the Truman Annex is the 9000-square-foot **Harry S. Truman Little White House Museum**. Built in 1890, this house earned its name by being the favourite holiday spot of President Harry S. Truman, who first visited in 1946 and allegedly spent his vacations playing poker, entertaining guests at the piano, and practising his "Missouri dog paddle" swimming style. The house is now a museum chronicling the Truman years with an immense array of memorabilia; there's nothing especially compelling about the interior (though ninety percent of the furniture is original to the house), but the affable tour guides' encyclopedic knowledge enlivens the visit considerably.

Florida Keys Eco-Discovery Center

35 East Quay Rd • Tues–Sat 9am–4pm • Free • ☎ 305 809 4750, ⓦ floridakeys.noaa.gov

The Truman Annex provides access, via Southard Street, to the waterfront **Florida Keys Eco-Discovery Center**, which offers a comprehensive introduction to the flora and fauna of the Keys. Among the compelling hands-on exhibits inside is a mock-up of Aquarius, the world's only underwater ocean laboratory (currently located near the reef off Key Largo), an interactive weather kiosk, a movie theatre, a vivid living-reef exhibit and a special display on the Dry Tortugas (see p.150).

Fort Zachary Taylor Historic State Park

601 Howard England Way • Daily 8am–sunset; tours daily at noon • $4.50 per car and driver, plus $2.50 for first passenger, 50¢ for each additional passenger; pedestrians and cyclists $2.50; tours free • ☎ 305 295 0037, ⓦ fortzacharytaylor.com

Walk southeast toward the ocean from the Truman Annex and you'll find **Fort Zachary Taylor Historic State Park**, built in 1845 and later used in the blockade of Confederate shipping during the Civil War. Yet within fifty years, the fort was made obsolete, thanks to the invention of the powerful rifled cannon, and over ensuing decades the structure simply disappeared under sand and weeds. Recent excavation work has gradually revealed much of historical worth, though it's hard to comprehend the full importance without joining the free 45-minute **guided tour**. Most locals pass by the fort on the way to the best **beach** in Key West – a place yet to be discovered by tourists, just a few yards beyond, with picnic tables, public grills, a café and plenty of trees for shade. Be aware the beach is a mix of crushed coral, sand and pebbles, and the craggy sea bottom can be tough on your feet, so bring waterproof sandals.

Key West Cemetery

701 Passover Lane • Daily: winter sunrise–6pm; summer 7am–7pm; tours Tues & Thurs 9.30am • Free; tours $15; reservations essential • ☎ 305 292 6718, ⓦ historicfloridakeys.org

Leaving the waterfront and heading a mile inland along Angela Street will take you to the **Key West Cemetery**, which dates back to 1847. Many residents are buried in vaults above ground, as the city's solid coral-rock foundation prevents the traditional six-feet-under interment. There may be a lack of celebrity stiffs here, but by wandering through this massive graveyard you'll notice the impact of immigration on Key West – the cemetery is filled with people from across the country and abroad. Most visitors amble about without a guide (you can usually grab a **free map** at the entrance, under the historic marker), but a far better plan is to join one of the chatty, low-key one-hour tours run by the Historic Florida Keys Foundation. If you decide to explore on your own, start at the plot dedicated to the **USS Maine** near the entrance, usually marked by US flags (though two British airmen are also buried here); survivors of the *Maine's* mysterious destruction – which started the Spanish–American War in 1898 – were brought back to Key West from Havana, and many died here from their injuries.

Several individual plots are worth seeking out, including those of Edwina Lariz, whose stone reads "devoted fan of singer Julio Iglesias"; B.P. Roberts, who continues to carp from beyond the grave "I told you I was sick"; and Thomas Romer, a Bahamian born in 1783 who died 108 years later and was "a good citizen for 65 of them". Look out also for the fenced grave of Dr Joseph Otto, whose family home is now the *Artist House* guesthouse. Included on the plot is the grave of the family's pet Key deer, Elfina, and three Yorkshire terriers, one of whom is described as being "a challenge to love".

Tennessee Williams' house

1431 Duncan St

A fifteen-minute walk from the cemetery is the modest two-storey clapboard house kept by **Tennessee Williams**, who arrived in 1941 and died in 1983. Unlike his more flamboyant counterparts, Williams – Key West's longest residing literary figure, made famous by his steamy evocations of Deep South life in plays such as *A Streetcar Named Desire*, which he wrote while living in town – kept a low profile during his thirty-odd years here. In fact, this house was originally situated downtown on Bahama Street but Williams was so keen for seclusion he had it moved here, which at the time was a swampy backwater outside town. The building itself, which isn't open to the public, is still a fine example of a Bahamian-style home, though it's only worth a pilgrimage if you're a devoted fan – nothing marks the famous association. To view a great selection of Williams memorabilia, including his typewriter, pop into the Key West Business Guild (see box, p.148), which hosts a small exhibit on the author.

The Secret Garden

518 Elizabeth St • Daily 10am–3pm • $10 • ☎ 305 294 0015, ⓦ nancyforrester.com

Make time for Nancy Forrester's **Secret Garden**, just off Simonton Street, a tranquil spot with a typically unconventional Key West background. Local artist Nancy Forrester and friends began working on the garden in the 1970s, transforming a one-acre group of lots behind her home on Elizabeth Street into a leafy, tropical escape that "nourishes the spirit and soul", opening it to the public in 1994 (city dwellers will be amused to note that Forrester considers modern Key West a "concrete jungle"). Her efforts have produced a truly magnificent botanical garden, with numerous orchids, bromeliads, aroids, ferns, a family of macaws and over 150 different species of palm.

Ernest Hemingway Home and Museum

907 Whitehead St • Daily 9am–5pm; tours leave every 10–30min and last approx 30min • $13 • ☎ 305 294 1136, ⓦ hemingwayhome.com

Home to one of America's literary giants for almost ten years, the fascinating **Ernest Hemingway Home and Museum** is Key West's top tourist draw. After spending three years at Casa Antigua (see p.137), Hemingway bought this house in 1931, thanks to an $8000 gift from the rich uncle of his then wife, Pauline. Originally one of the grander (and hurricane-resistant) Key West homes, built in 1851 for a wealthy merchant, the dwelling was seriously run-down by the time the Hemingways arrived. It soon acquired luxuries such as a 60ft turquoise swimming pool, carved out of solid coral and costing more than twice the price of the house to build; to this day, it's still one of the city's largest.

Hemingway produced some of his most acclaimed work in the deer-head-dominated **study**, located in an outhouse, which the author entered by way of a home-made iron walkway (now long gone). Here he penned the short stories *The Snows of Kilimanjaro* and *The Short and Happy Life of Francis Macomber*; and the novels *For Whom the Bell Tolls* and *To Have and Have Not*, the latter describing Key West life during the Depression.

The tour

To see inside the house you have to join the half-hour **guided tour**, though at quiet times you'll be allowed to wander around unattended. Tours provide a brief intro-duction to the author, enhanced by numerous old photos and stories of him and his four wives. In the garden, a water trough for the cats is supposedly a urinal from *Sloppy Joe's* (now *Captain Tony's Saloon*; see p.147), where the big man downed many a drink. When Hemingway divorced Pauline in 1940, he boxed up his manuscripts and moved them to a back room at *Sloppy Joe's* before heading off to a house in Cuba with his new wife, journalist Martha Gellhorn (it's said they met when she dressed up and staked him out at the same legendary bar).

After the tour, you're free to roam at leisure and pat some of the forty-odd **cats**, presumed to be descendants from a feline family that lived in Hemingway's day; several of these famous kitties have paws with extra toes.

Lighthouse Museum

938 Whitehead St • Daily 9.30am–5pm • $10 • ☎ 305 294 0012, ⓦ kwahs.com

From the Hemingway House, you'll easily catch sight of the 86ft **Lighthouse Museum** – one of Florida's first beacons, raised in 1847, and still functioning. Start at the **keeper's quarters**, a simple white house in the gardens, with furnishings and other bits and pieces dating to the 1910s, as well as a more absorbing DVD about the lighthouse and some of the people who served here – including the remarkable women who took over from their temporarily injured husbands for prolonged periods. Afterwards, it's possible to climb the 88 steps to the top of the tower, though the views of Key West are actually better from the top-floor bar of the Shipwreck Museum (see p.134) or the Curry Mansion (see p.136). Most of the pictures taken here are not of the lighthouse but of the majestic banyan tree at the base. You can ogle the lighthouse's huge lens – a 12ft-high, dizzying honeycomb of glass, from the ground floor.

Bahama Village

The narrow streets around the lighthouse and to the west of Whitehead Street constitute **Bahama Village**, which still has the feel of old Key West. Many of the small buildings – some of them former cigar factories – are a little run down, and make a refreshing counterbalance to the elegant restoration found elsewhere in Old Town. The Caribbean vibe here is authentic, dating back to the many Bahamians working in the salvage trade who eventually settled in Key West, and noticeable in the lilting music playing in cafés and the laidback attitude of locals. For now, the place is still relatively untouched. Though you may see chickens on the street everywhere in Key West, you're likely to see the largest number here. The descendants of Cuban fighting cocks, they are protected from harm by law, especially as their appetite for scorpions helps keep the arthropods' population down.

The eastern section

There's not much more to Key West beyond its compact Old Town. Most of the **eastern section** of the island – encircled by the north and south sections of Roosevelt Boulevard – is residential, but Key West's longest **beach** is located here (see p.135), and there are several minor points of botanical, natural and historical interest.

Fort East Martello Museum and Gardens

3501 S Roosevelt Blvd • Daily 9.30am–4.30pm • $9 • ☎ 305 296 3913, ⓦ kwahs.com

The most worthwhile sight in the eastern part of the island, just beyond the airport, is the **Fort East Martello Museum and Gardens**, the second of two Civil War lookout posts that complemented Fort Zachary Taylor (see p.138). The solid, vaulted casements now store a fascinating assemblage on local history, plus the wild junk-sculptures of legendary Key Largo scrap dealer Stanley Papio and the Key West scenes created in wood by a Cuban-primitive artist named Mario Sanchez. There are also displays on local writers and **Robert the Doll**, a creepy sailor-suited doll said to be haunted; owned by Key West artist Robert Eugene Otto in the late nineteenth century, it was so scary it was locked in an attic until the 1970s. Today Robert is said to ruin photographs and cause unexplained events – typically, he's become something of a Key West mascot.

Key West Garden Club and West Martello Tower

1100 Atlantic Blvd, where White St meets the ocean • Daily 9.30am–5pm • Admission by donation • ☎ 305 294 3210, ⓦ keywestgardenclub.com

If partying in Old Town has given you a headache, seek sanctuary at the **Key West Garden Club and West Martello Tower**, once one of three Key West Civil War forts (see p.138), and since 1955 refurbished as a tranquil 1.5-acre botanical garden next to Higgs Beach (see p.135). Here, tropical blooms drape a crumbling military structure (and seem to make a victorious statement about man versus nature), geckos dart along cobbled brick paths, and short trails are fringed with bread fruit, old man palm, strangler fig and screwpine; the latter look like an assemblage of giant broomsticks. Pause at the little white gazebo, perched on a small hill, for ocean vistas.

African Cemetery at Higgs Beach

Next to the Key West Garden Club; White St at the Atlantic Ocean • Daily 24hr • Free • ☎ 305 294 4633, ⓦ africanburialgroundathiggsbeach.org

Before visiting the soft sands of Higgs Beach (see p.135), take time to peruse the artwork and historic marker denoting the **African Cemetery**, adjacent to the Key West Garden Club. This monument to a little-known, grievous chapter in American history commemorates the 294 African men, women and children who died and were buried here in 1860 as a result of the slave trade. During that summer, the US Navy rescued 1432 slaves from three American-owned ships headed to Cuba for illegal trading. The freed slaves were given temporary residence in Key West, but after having suffered intolerable conditions during the crossing, nearly three hundred of them perished here from disease. Those who survived were provided with a return passage to Liberia, in West Africa.

Don't expect to see any tombstones, however – West Martello Tower was built on top of the unmarked graves. The memorial consists of a cartographic mural that depicts the path of the ships and the community's return to Africa, led by a soaring dove.

ARRIVAL AND DEPARTURE   KEY WEST

BY AIR

Four miles east of Old Town at 3491 S Roosevelt Blvd is the small Key West International Airport (☎ 305 809 5200, ⓦ monroecounty-fl.gov). Silver Airways (☎ 800 229 9990, ⓦ silverairways.com) has direct flights into Key West from a number of Florida cities (Tampa, Fort Myers, Orlando and Fort Lauderdale), while American Airlines (☎ 800 433 7300, ⓦ aa.com) flies to Miami five times daily. Most of Key West's car rental firms have offices at the airport (see above), and city buses ($2; ☎ 305 809 3910 or ☎ 305 600 1455, ⓦ kwtransit.com) make the journey into town from

the east end of the terminal. With groups of two or more, taxis charge $8 per person for trips to and from the airport; solo travellers pay by the meter (around $16 into town). Heading back to the airport, try Friendly Cab (☎ 305 292 0000) or Key Lime Taxi (☎ 305 292 6128).

BY BUS

There are two daily buses to Key West from Miami (see p.111). The terminus for Greyhound buses in Key West is at the airport (☎ 305 296 9072; $45 one way to Miami; tickets purchased online have discounted fares).

2

BY CAR

Driving into Old Town on US-1 is straightforward enough, and most hotels have parking arrangements. Metered parking ($2.50/hr) on the street is available but hard to find in Old Town, and nonresidents will be towed if they use spaces marked "Residential Parking", so it's best to aim for the Old Town Parking Garage at the corner of Caroline and Grinnell streets (24hr access; $2/hr, $13/day; ☎305 809 3910) – your parking ticket can be used to claim free rides on all city buses throughout the day.

BY FERRY

A passenger-only ferry service operated by Key West Express (☎888 539 2628, ⓦseakeywestexpress.com) runs from Key West across to Fort Myers or Marco Island on the Gulf of Mexico side of mainland Florida (see "Sarasota and the southwest" chapter). The ferry leaves from the terminal in the Seaport at 100 Grinnell St, and is a good way of getting to Florida's west coast without zigzagging back across the Keys and through the Everglades. The ferry runs daily to Fort Myers – weather permitting – at 6pm ($89 single, $149 return; 3hr 30min), and daily in season (usually Dec–April) at 5pm to Marco Island (same prices; 3hr 30min).

INFORMATION

Tourist information The Key West Chamber of Commerce, behind *Sloppy Joe's* at 510 Greene St (Mon–Fri 8am–6pm, Sat & Sun 9am–6pm; ☎305 294 2587 or ☎800 527 8539, ⓦkeywestchamber.org), offers plenty of tourist pamphlets and discount vouchers. Online, the Keys region's official website, ⓦfla-keys.com, offers useful information, as does local blog ⓦkeysvoices.com.

Newspapers The local newspaper is the *Key West Citizen* (50¢; ⓦkeysnews.com), whose comprehensive entertainment supplement, *Paradise*, is bundled with the main paper on Thursdays. *Solares Hill,* a publication that lists current events, is published in the Sunday edition.

GETTING AROUND

On foot For getting around the narrow, pedestrian-filled streets of Old Town, you're far better off walking than driving. If street signs appear curiously absent, you'll find them painted vertically on the base of each junction lamppost, though many are peeling off.

By bike and scooter A great way to get around flat-as-a-pancake Key West is by renting a bike. Try the friendly Eaton Bikes at 830 Eaton St ($18/day; ☎305 294 8188, ⓦeatonbikes.com), which also offers hotel delivery. The Bike Shop ($12/day, $60/week; ☎305 294 1073, ⓦthebikeshopkeywest.com), near the cemetery at 1110 Truman Ave, is another standout option. The Moped Hospital (601 Truman Ave; ☎866 296 1625, ⓦmopedhospital.com) rents scooters (single $45/day, $155/week; doubles $70/day, $260/week) as well as bikes ($12/day, $40/week).

By bus Remarkably, there is a bus service ($2; ☎305 809 3910 or ☎305 600 1455, ⓦkwtransit.com) in Key West: two routes, clockwise and anticlockwise, loop around the tiny island, and make pickups roughly every 15min between 6am and 10pm.

By car Renting a car is only worth it if you're heading off to see the other Keys or driving back to the mainland after a one-way flight. All companies are based at the airport: Avis (☎305 296 8744); Budget (☎305 294 8868); Dollar/Thrifty (☎305 296 9921); Hertz (☎305 294 1039).

By pedicab and electric car The pedicabs that are wheeled around charge $1.50/min – that's about $20 from one end of Duval St to the other. Otherwise, if you're feeling

KEY WEST TOURS

The oft-plugged, ninety-minute guided tours of the island's main sights might seem a tourist-ready rip-off, but the best known, the **Conch Tour Train** (hop on at Mallory Square; every 20–30min 9am–4.30pm; $31; ☎888 916 8687, ⓦconchtourtrain.com), is astonishingly informative and its drivers' commentary far from rote or robotic. A similar alternative is the **Old Town Trolley** (board at any of the marked stops around Old Town; every 30min 9am–4.30pm; $31; ☎888 910 8687, ⓦtrolleytours.com).

For some kitschy fun, take one of the ninety-minute **Ghost Tours** (daily 9pm; $18; reservations recommended; ☎305 292 2040, ⓦkeywestghostandmysterytour.com), a guided walking tour that starts at the Porter Mansion at 429 Caroline St, and takes in some of the numerous haunted homes and ghost legends of Key West. **Lloyd's Tropical Bike Tour** (☎305 304 4700, ⓦlloydstropicalbiketour.com) offers two-hour pedals around the island ($39, includes bike rental) with a true Key West character who visits other celebrity Conchs and takes the time to sample coconuts, mangoes and sapodilla. **Key Lime Bike Tours** (tours 2hr 30min; $39; ☎305 340 7834, ⓦkeylimebiketours.com) is another acclaimed outfit.

flush or lazy, try one of the nifty mini electric cars that can be rented from Tropical Rentals, 1300 Duval St (two-seaters from $59/2hr, four-seaters from $79/2hr; ☎ 305 294 8136, ⓦ tropicalrentacar.com).

ACCOMMODATION

Accommodation **rates** in Key West are always high – particularly from January to April when the simplest motel room will be in excess of $150 per night. Prices drop considerably at other times, but expect to pay at least $100 wherever you stay. Genuine budget options are limited to the seaside (but out of town) *Boyd's Campground* (see p.145) or the *Key West International Hostel* (see p.145). You'll find cheaper **motels** along US-1 at the northern end of the island, but any savings on the room will be eaten up by the cost of parking in town. You're better off checking into one of the centrally located hotels or guesthouses listed below. Wherever you stay, a **reservation** is essential from November to April, and would be a sensible precaution for weekends at any other time. If you arrive in October during Fantasy Fest, expect a hike in room cost and a multi-night minimum stay. Many of the restored villas operating as guesthouses in the historic district are **gay-run**, and while most welcome all adults, few accept young children. A handful (we've noted which ones) are exclusively gay male.

HOTELS AND MOTELS

Cypress House 601 Caroline St ☎ 305 294 6969, ⓦ historickeywestinns.com. Historic nineteenth-century property whose original cypress and pine exterior strikes a nice balance with the interior's modern renovation – guestrooms have tufted leather headboards, striped rugs and citrus-coloured throws. $189

Ocean Key Resort & Spa Zero Duval St ☎ 305 296 7701, ⓦ oceankey.com. Perched by the ocean at the tip of Duval St, this is one of the plushest hotels in the city, though you'll pay for the convenience and views. The lavish rooms are brightly furnished in tropical prints, and many have balconies. $270

Orchid Key Inn 1004 Duval St ☎ 305 296 9915, ⓦ orchidkeyinn.com. Right in the heart of Duval St and yet worlds away, tranquillity-wise, this hip hotel has 24 rooms clustered around a white sundeck, heated pool and jacuzzi, with original art throughout. Savour a nightcap at the inn's pearlescent bar – there are seats for just seven lucky tipplers. $260

★ **Parrot Key Hotel & Resort** 2801 N Roosevelt Blvd ☎ 305 809 2200, ⓦ parrotkeyresort.com. One of the most luxurious resorts in town, with four swimming pools, onsite watersports and tranquil Conch-style houses (one-, two- and three- bedroom) with back porches and full kitchens. Set in lush gardens on Florida Bay, with a narrow white-sand beach, a short taxi ride from Old Town. $179

Santa Maria Suites Resort 1401 Simonton St ☎ 305 296 5678, ⓦ santamariasuites.com. Thirty-five grandiose, pampered suites with state-of-the-art kitchens (think sub-zero fridges, full stoves and wine chillers), in-room laundry, nightly turn-down service, and rooms turned out in linen, rattan and marble. Chilled pool towels, doled out by a beach attendant, are another luxurious extra. $319

★ **Southernmost Hotel Collection** 1319 Duval St ☎ 305 296 6577, ⓦ southernmost resorts.com. Comprising three separate, luxe hotel properties right by tiny South Beach (where Tennessee Williams is said to have swum every morning), guestrooms here have luxury linens, iPod docks, balconies and marble bathrooms; there are three pools (including one on the ocean) and a beachfront restaurant. Free parking (some in the shade – a big plus in these parts). $220

Speakasy Inn 1117 Duval St ☎ 305 296 2680, ⓦ speakeasyinn.com. This nineteenth-century property – once the home of a noted rumrunner – offers excellent budget lodgings three blocks from the Hemingway House. Rooms come with fridges and microwaves, and there's a lively bar in the lobby (see p.149). Note the bottle and heart "gingerbread" on the second floor patio, a nod to the property's speakeasy days. $129

Sunset Key Guest Cottages 245 Front St ☎ 305 292 5300, ⓦ westinsunsetkeycottages.com. A 10min ferry ride from the *Westin Key Resort*, where you check in (guests share facilities), this luxurious, car-free, manmade island – just 40 years old – features 37 elegant standalone cottages that are like private homes with maid service. Try to nab one of the cottages on the northwest side for the best sunset views. $635

★ **Truman Hotel** 611 Truman Ave ☎ 305 296 6700 or ☎ 866 487 8626, ⓦ trumanhotel.com. Boldly decorated with zebra-striped rugs and punchy contemporary art, this small hotel with a hip clientele has the feel of a sophisticated pool party. Turn-down service, shaded parking spots and breakfast pastries are all included. $199

GUESTHOUSES

★ **Almond Tree Inn** 512 Truman Ave ☎ 305 296 5415, ⓦ almondtreeinn.com. Falling somewhere between an inn and a sophisticated bed and breakfast, this 22-room lodging offers turndown service, complimentary breakfast and an afternoon wine hour. There's a cascading swimming pool bordered by orchids and a tropical garden. Great location, too, at the corner of Duval St, in the heart of Old Town. No children. $269

★ **Angelina Guest House** 302 Angela St ☎ 305 294 4480, ⓦ angelinaguesthouse.com. A charming

2

LIVING LIKE A LOCAL IN KEY WEST

For longer stays and larger groups, **renting an apartment** can be an economic alternative to Key West's hotels and guesthouses; Historic Hideaways (☎800 654 5131, ⚙historichideaways .com) and Rent Key West (☎305 294 0990, ⚙rentkeywest.com) are good places to start, with weekly rates starting at $1000 for studios and $1800 for two bedrooms. Airbnb (⚙airbnb.com), the undisputed champion of international apartment rental, also has a number of affordable in-town options (rates start at around $100 a night).

guesthouse, with a cool, Caribbean feel, tucked away in the backstreets of Bahama Village. One of the best deals in town (even the shared bathrooms are lovely), with fourteen simple rooms (no phones or TVs) decorated in pastel yellow or blue. The small pool is a great place to enjoy the owners' cinnamon rolls at breakfast. No children. **$109**

Artist House 534 Eaton St ☎305 296 3977, ⚙artisthousekeywest.com. Lovely lavender Victorian – famed as Robert the Doll's (see p.141) house – with four-poster beds, walnut furniture, wallpapered halls and a turret enclosing an octagonal suite. Complimentary continental breakfast is served on the patio. **$185**

Avalon Bed and Breakfast 1317 Duval St ☎305 294 8233, ⚙avalonbnb.com. Romantic B&B with gauzy canopy beds, wicker furniture and welcoming staff near the southernmost point marker. In the nineteenth century, the house was used as a meeting spot for Cuban revolutionaries; while the ambience is decidedly more relaxed these days, the owners have been careful to maintain the historical integrity of the building. **$169**

Caribbean House 226 Petronia St ☎305 296 0999, ⚙caribbeanhousekw.com. Offering good value in a central location, the ten colourful, smallish, spotless chambers at this Bahama Village guesthouse come with free coffee and cable TV. The charming owner speaks English, Spanish and French. Pet-friendly. **$129**

★**Eden House** 1015 Fleming St ☎305 296 6868, ⚙edenhouse.com. Recently renovated, this guesthouse is a gem, run by the Eden family for over thirty years. Rooms are decorated in the usual pastels and pale woods, though most overlook the pool. Best of all, there's free off-street parking and a daily happy hour at 4–5pm (plus a beer at check-in). **$250**

★**The Gardens Hotel** 526 Angela St ☎305 294 2661, ⚙gardenshotel.com. One of the swishest hotels in town, this graceful inn has only seventeen rooms, decked out in an airy Bahamian plantation style with flat-screen TVs, fresh flowers and enormous beds. The honeymoon-worthy luxury is ramped up by the namesake groves of greenery and orchids enveloping the building, swathing it from prying eyes. **$220**

Island City House 411 William St ☎305 294 5702, ⚙islandcityhouse.com. This massive mansion, built in the 1880s for a Charleston merchant family, claims to be the oldest in town (it's been welcoming paying guests since 1912). The luxurious studios and one- or two-bedroom apartments overlook the pool and tropical gardens, and are accessed by a shady tunnel from the main street; choose from suites in the main house (Victorian), Cigar House (old Florida plantation), and Arch House (modernized antique). **$230**

Marquesa Hotel 600 Fleming St ☎305 292 1919, ⚙marquesa.com. A grand guesthouse built in 1884 with a formal clientele and lush green surroundings including its own on-site waterfall and swimming pools. The spotless rooms are smart and modern, with marble bathrooms and relaxing patios. No children under 14. **$325**

Marrero's Guest Mansion 410 Fleming St ☎305 294 6977, ⚙marreros.com. Reputedly haunted, this antique-crammed old mansion is an opulent place to stay – ghost-hunters should ask for room 18 ($220 per night), where most paranormal activity has been reported. Note that the pool is clothing optional. Two rooms have a shared bath and a cheaper rate. **$130**

★**The Mermaid & the Alligator** 729 Truman Ave ☎305 294 1894, ⚙kwmermaid.com. This 1904 mansion has a rich colour scheme and beautiful design details like cathedral ceilings, wraparound balconies and French doors leading to the small pool. The garden is filled with palms, pink hibiscus and fragrant jasmine, and the TV-free setup, gourmet breakfasts and evening wine hour make for a deeply relaxing stay. No children under 16. **$248**

Old Town Manor 511 Eaton St ☎305 292 2170, ⚙oldtownmanor.com. Fun, affordable, pet-friendly option right in the heart of things. Guestrooms are done up in cheery hues like apricot and lime, and there's a complimentary breakfast buffet with local bagels, boiled eggs and fruit from the garden. **$135**

Paradise Inn 819 Simonton St ☎305 293 8007, ⚙theparadiseinn.com. This unique property consists of two Bahamian-style houses and three historic Conch cottages, used by Cuban cigar makers in the mid-1850s, and now refurbished with jacuzzi tubs and dignified tropical decor. Lodgings are decked out with marble bathrooms and sundecks. Outside, koi fish dart in the lily pond, and palms and red ginger sway around the swimming pool. **$199**

EXCLUSIVELY GAY GUESTHOUSES

★**Alexander's Guesthouse** 1118 Fleming St ☎305 294 9919, ⓦalexanderskeywest.com. The antithesis of most antique-filled B&Bs, this sleek, gay-only spot has white modernist furniture in its large lobby, a big on-site pool (where happy hour is held daily 5.30–7.30pm), and roomy suites, most with king-size beds, done up in stark white style. No kids, pets or smoking. $175

Island House 1129 Fleming St ☎305 294 6284, ⓦislandhousekeywest.com. Men-only, clothing-optional resort that's one of the few remaining cruisey accommodation options in town: there's a sauna, video room and large pool-cum-sundeck (in fact, guests need only wear clothes when using the exercise equipment in the gym). The sophisticated rooms have overstuffed leather chairs and crisp white linens; the largest suites are poolside.

Even if you're not staying here, you can buy a pass to use the hotel's amenities ($25/day). $195

CAMPING AND HOSTEL

Boyd's Campground 6401 Maloney Ave ☎305 294 1465, ⓦboydscampground.com. Out of town on Stock Island, this seaside campsite has a heated swimming pool, showers, RV hook-ups and a bus stop outside its front door. Tent sites $63

Key West International Hostel 718 South St ☎305 296 5719, ⓦkeywesthostel.com. The cheapest digs in town are these grubby dorms, run by a friendly owner who provides bikes for rent. They also run the basic, dim *Sea Shell Motel* next door. The decor isn't much, but there's a nice communal spirit about the place. Dorms $44, doubles $129

EATING

While you'll find some excellent **restaurants** and **snack stands** along the main streets, it's difficult to eat cheaply in Key West. There's no shortage of chic venues for fine French, Italian and Asian cuisine, but if you want really good, inexpensive food, your best bet is to head for the **Cuban sandwich shops**, which offer filling, tasty meals at a fraction of the price of a main-street pizza. Those same cafés also serve up thimble-sized shots of sweetened espresso, known as a *cafecito* elsewhere but nicknamed a *bucci* in Key West. Most menus, not surprisingly, feature fresh **seafood**, and you should sample **Key lime pie** and **conch fritters** – Key West specialities – at least once.

CAFÉS, BAKERIES AND SANDWICH SHOPS

★**Cole's Peace** 1111 Eaton St ☎305 292 0703, ⓦcolespeace.com. Renowned bakery that crams gobs of fantastic sandwich fillings onto home-made bread – the mouthwatering "cobba-lotta" is piled with roast turkey, bacon, avocado, blue cheese and boiled egg on a fresh ciabatta roll ($8.98). Away from Old Town, and hidden inside a commercial strip, *Cole's* is a handy stop before a beach or boat trip. Mon–Fri 8am–4pm, Sat 8am–2pm.

★**Cuban Coffee Queen** 284 Margaret St ☎305 294 7787, ⓦcubancoffeequeen.com. The colossal "Greetings from Key West" mural on the side of this revered takeaway stand is a beacon for those in search of the island's best *café con leche* ($1.95), *bucci* ($1) and iced java, kept cold with frozen coffee cubes ($2.95). They also serve pressed sandwiches ($7), rice and beans ($7), and smoothies ($6). Daily 6.30am–sunset.

★**Five Brothers Grocery** 930 Southard St ☎305 296 5205. Expect long lines at this age-old grocery store, a real locals' favourite for its strong Cuban coffee and cheap Cuban sandwiches ($6). It's also crammed with provisions, plus pots and pans dangling from the ceiling. There are a few benches out front if you want to stay awhile. Look out for *Five Brothers Grocery Two* on Ramrod Key (MM27 ☎305 872 0702). Mon–Fri 6am–4pm, Sat 6am–3pm.

Frenchie's 529 United St ☎305 396 7124. Aptly named, this superb café has some of the best and most affordable French-style breakfasts in town – fresh croissants, quiche lorraine with bacon and rich *croque monsieur*. Excellent

coffee, too. Wonderful staff, but limited seating. Daily 7am–3pm.

★**Old Town Bakery** 930 Eaton St ☎305 396 7450, ⓦoldtownbakery.com. Exquisite patisserie with a beautiful, white, French-style interior. *Old Town Bakery* peddles strong coffee and fresh-from-the-oven croissants, fruit tarts, crusty baguettes and rosemary loaves. Daily 7am–5pm.

Sandy's Café Inside the M&M Laundry, 1026 White St ☎305 295 0159, ⓦkwsandyscafe.com. A basic counter serving terrific Cuban sandwiches. Try the Cuban-mix sandwich ($8) or shots of potent *cortadito* ($2), settle onto a stool at the counter outside, and watch the locals milling round you. Daily 24hr.

RESTAURANTS

A&B Lobster House 700 Front St ☎305 294 5880, ⓦaandblobsterhouse.com. There could hardly be a more scenic setting than this harbourside restaurant, which is actually two separate venues originally opened by a pair of fishermen in 1947. Downstairs is an upmarket spot for a luxury seafood dinner including seared Key West shrimp pasta ($30.50) or a saffron-heavy *bouillabaisse* ($33.75). If you find the prices too rich (or are here during lunch), head to the adjacent *Alonzo's Oyster Bar* where the simpler dishes cost about half the price. Daily 11am–11pm.

Antonia's 615 Duval St ☎305 294 6565, ⓦantonias keywest.com. This inviting, upmarket spot has two very different dining rooms; ask for a table in the old front

2

KEY LIME PIE

Hands down, Key West's best-known culinary export is **Key lime pie**, a tangy, sweet-crusted slab made from the tiny, yellow citrus fruits every local seems to grow in their backyard. Nearly every restaurant turns out riffs on the traditional pie, but there are a few specialists:

Blue Heaven 729 Thomas St ☎305 296 8666, ⊛blueheavenkw.com. Old Key Westers swear by meringue (instead of whipped cream) as the most authentic crown for Key lime pie. *Blue Heaven's* rendition has this in spades – dense, piquant filling is anchored by a thick cookie-like crust and topped with a colossal cloud of meringue. Slices are a hefty $9.50. Daily 8am–10.30pm.

Kermit's Key West Key Lime Shoppe 200 Elizabeth St ☎305 296 0806, ⊛keylimeshop.com. Serves a pie with a consistency somewhere between gelatine and cake, and a perfect blend of sugary and tart. Slices are $4.50, whole pies $18.95. Daily 9am–9.30pm.

★**Key Lime and Coconut Factory** 412 and 414 Greene St ☎305 296 9515, ⊛theoriginalkeylimepie .com. Easily spotted by its lime-coloured exterior, this little cottage carries a comprehensive selection of citrus products, including ice cream, lime juice and chocolate-dipped popsicles. But it's the eponymous pie that demands your attention – tart, bold and outstanding, with a thin graham-cracker crust and airy whipped-cream topping. Slices are $4.95, whole pies $22. Daily 10am–11pm.

★**Rooftop Café** 308 Front St ☎305 294 2042, ⊛rooftopcafekeywest.com. The insider's choice. The secret of this addictive recipe is twofold: a top layer of fluffy meringue and the gooey graham-cracker crust which oozes with a tangy syrup made with lime juice and traces of melted butter. Slices are $7. Daily 11am–10pm.

room rather than the anodyne modern extension out back. Once you've settled in, pick from a menu of northern Italian specials like spinach and ricotta dumplings, linguine with clams, or duck leg confit. Mains $22–34. Daily 6–11pm.

★**Azur Restaurant** 425 Grinnell St ☎305 292 2987, ⊛azurkeywest.com. Arguably the best restaurant in town, and certainly the best service; the superb Mediterranean-influenced food (think braised lamb ribs with Moroccan chick peas or daily fish carpaccio) is served up in a cool blue dining room with a little waterfall. If nothing else, come for the Key lime pie-stuffed French toast for breakfast ($10.75). Dinner mains average $25. Mon–Fri 8am–10pm, Sat & Sun 9am–10pm.

Better than Sex 926 Simonton St ☎305 296 8102, ⊛betterthansexkeywest.com. Exceptional desserterie with candlelit, bordello-style decor. The menu's over-the-top innuendos are a bit corny (cocktails have names like "adult apple" and "the gyration"), but still, if you answer to a higher power named "Dessert" this place is a must – you'll crave the "peanut butter perversion" (peanut butter pie on a chocolate cookie crust; $12.69) and red velvet cheesecake ($12.69) long after you've left the island. Reservations recommended. Wed–Sun 6pm–midnight.

★**Blue Heaven** 729 Thomas St, at Petronia St ☎305 296 8666, ⊛blueheavenkw.com. Sit in this dirt yard in Bahama Village where Hemingway once refereed boxing matches and enjoy the superb food while chickens wander aimlessly and cats lounge at your feet. For breakfast, try the mouthwatering banana bread or the lobster Benedict; for dinner, the pork tenderloin with sweet potato is a standout. Dinner mains start at $20. Daily 8am–10.30pm.

BO's Fish Wagon 801 Caroline St ☎305 294 9272, ⊛bosfishwagon.com. Quirky local institution that looks like a cross between a junk yard and a seafood shack – napkins are a self-serve roll of paper towel, and most of the interior has been salvaged from dumpsters (the showstopper's an entire wrecked truck). The simple menu is excellent: best bets are the fried fish sandwich of the day for $10.50 (add $1 for grilled) or the soft-shell crab sandwich for $11.75. Beers are just $4.50 and every Friday evening there's an impromptu gathering of jamming local musicians. Located by the Seaport, it's a useful stop before heading out on a boat tour. Daily 11am–9.30pm.

The Café 509 Southard St ☎305 296 5515. Excellent vegetarian and vegan spot patronized by even the pickiest carnivores. The menu travels from *kung pao* tofu to veggie burgers to fig and gorgonzola pizza, and there is toothsome carrot cake and Key lime pie. Mon–Sat 11am–10pm, Sun 10am–3pm & 5–10pm.

Café Marquesa 600 Fleming St ☎305 292 1244, ⊛marquesa.com. Chichi, hushed café inside the *Marquesa Hotel* that's the best fine-dining spot in the city. It offers an imaginative New American menu – expect great seafood like sesame-crusted Atlantic salmon ($33) and Key West blue crab cakes with radicchio ($16). Reservations strongly recommended. Daily 6–10pm.

El Siboney 900 Catherine St ☎305 296 4184, ⊛elsiboneyrestaurant.com. A little out of the way, but well worth the effort for some of the best – and best-value – Cuban food on the island. Sit at canteen-style tables with red-and-white-chequered tablecloths and ask the wait staff for recommendations; specials might include red snapper and mahi-mahi ($13.95), cubano sandwiches

($7.25) and punchy home-made *sangría*. Daily 11am–9.30pm.

★**Garbo's Grill** 129 Simonton St ☎305 304 3004, ⓦgarbosgrillkw.com. Mind-blowingly delicious little cart with imaginative Mexican food hybrids like mango and Brie *quesadillas* ($7) and Korean beef BBQ burritos (short ribs, Napa cabbage, daikon and citrus soy dressing in a tortilla; $8.75). Regulars practically need an intervention from the mahi-mahi tacos ($7.75). Tues–Sat 11.30am–5pm.

★**Hogfish Bar and Grill** 6810 Front St, Stock Island (5 miles north of Old Town) ☎305 293 4041, ⓦhogfishbar.com. Follow a meandering route north out of the city – essentially till you can see Stock Island's harbour – and you'll arrive at this dockside favourite. *Hogfish* has a fun, laidback atmosphere, but it's serious about seafood: you could happily while away the day on its pier, swilling beers and sharing smoked fish dip ($10.95), conch salad ($10.95) and hogfish sandwiches on Cuban bread ($14.95). Daily 11am–11pm (bar open till 3am).

★**Paseo's** 1000 Eaton St ☎305 517 6740. Affordable, delicious Caribbean food – juicy pork sandwiches, rice and beans and fish curry – ordered from a counter and messily eaten at a handful of outdoor tables. Be sure to order the fire-roasted corn, slathered with a heavenly blend of Parmesan cheese and coriander (cilantro). Wed–Sun 11am–7pm.

★**Sarabeth's** 530 Simonton St ☎305 293 8181, ⓦsarabethskeywest.com. Outpost of the New York restaurant, stashed in an old wooden clapboard house with whirring ceiling fans and a soothing jazz soundtrack, all of which give the place a welcoming vibe. The food's equally homestyle, from the herby, moist roast chicken served with crisp green beans ($18.50) to a turkey club with maple mustard mayo ($14.75). It's especially buzzy during brunch – try the almond-crusted cinnamon French toast ($10.50). Wed–Sun 8am–3pm & 6–9.30pm.

Seven Fish 632 Olivia St ☎305 296 2777, ⓦ7fish.com. This little-known bistro, easy to miss in its tiny white corner building, serves some of the tastiest food in Key West – there are just over a dozen tables, so it's worth making a reservation. The food is simple and delicious – shrimp scampi for $20 and meatloaf for $18. Save room for the sweet potato pie ($8.50). Mon & Wed–Sun 6–10pm.

DRINKING AND NIGHTLIFE

The carefully cultivated "anything goes" nature of Key West is exemplified by the **bars** that make up the bulk of the island's **nightlife**. These gregarious, rough-and-ready affairs are often open until 4am and offer a cocktail of yarn-spinning locals, revved-up tourists, and (often) live blues, funk, country, folk or rock music. The mainstream bars are grouped around the northern end of Duval Street, no more than a few minutes' stagger apart. Much of Key West's best nightlife, though, revolves around its **restaurants**, and the best are far from Mallory Square's well-beaten path.

BARS, CLUBS AND LIVE MUSIC VENUES

★**Captain Tony's Saloon** 428 Greene St ☎305 294 1838, ⓦcapttonyssaloon.com. This rustic saloon was the original *Sloppy Joe's* between 1933 and 1937 until its owner, rumrunner Joe Russell, decamped to the current location in protest at a $1 rise in rent. It's renowned as a hangout of Ernest Hemingway – he met his third wife, Martha Gellhorn, here. One of the better choices for live music as well as a busy pool table, and a must-stop for Hemingway fans. Daily 10am–1am.

SHOPPING IN KEY WEST

Don't be discouraged by the tacky T-shirt shops clogging Duval Street – when you head off this beaten track, you'll find excellent wares to browse. Best-known are Key West's fragrant cigar purveyors – the island used to be a major producer of cigars, and now the traditional industry survives in a few workshops. There are some diverting bookstores as well, fitting for a city of literary giants.

★**Bésame Mucho** 315 Petronia St ☎305 294 1928, ⓦbesamemucho.net. Hands down, the nicest local shopping venue is this mint-green Conch house near *Blue Heaven* restaurant (see p.146). Bésame is artfully arrayed with home goods, rum aftershave, hand cream, letter-pressed stationery, jewellery and treasures such as small, silver Mexican *milagros* (Spanish for "miracles"), traditionally used in prayer. Mon–Sat 10am–6pm, Sun 10am–4pm.

Cuban Leaf Cigar Factory 310 Duval St ☎305 295 9283, ⓦcigars-tobacco-shopping.com. The best shops to pick up cigar souvenirs are where stogies are hand-rolled on-site – this place is one of the last of Key West's workshops. Daily 11am–10.30pm.

Key West Island Bookstore 513½ Fleming St ☎305 294 2904, ⓦkeywestislandbooks.com. The best local outlet for books, packed with the works of Key West authors and Keys-related literature. There's also a first-rate selection of rare and secondhand books. Mon–Sat 10am–9pm, Sun 10am–6pm.

2

GAY AND LESBIAN KEY WEST

Gay life in Key West is always vibrant and attracts frolicking hordes from North America and Europe. The party atmosphere is laidback, sometimes outrageous, and there's an exceptional level of integration between the straight and gay communities.

The tragedy of AIDS has hit Key West hard since the mid-1980s. A sombre but important trip to the ocean at the end of White Street reveals a striking **AIDS memorial** (W keywestaids.org), where blocks of black granite embedded in the walkway are engraved with a roll call of the more than 1000 people in Key West, including mayor Richard Herman, who died of the disease.

Stop in at the gay and lesbian chamber of commerce, the **Key West Business Guild**, 513 Truman Ave (Mon–Sat 9am–5pm; 305 294 4603 or 800 535 7797, W gaykeywestfl.com); the team here is chatty and so informed that it's a better information source for any traveller than the mainstream Chamber office. The Guild runs a terrific gay-themed, ninety-minute historic trolley tour, which leaves at 4pm every Saturday (Nov–April) from the depot at the corner of Duval and Angela streets ($25, cash only). There is also a smart little exhibit on playwright Tennessee Williams (305 842 1666, W twkw.org), a long-time resident of Key West (see p.139).

The unofficial gay beach is **Higgs Beach**, at the southern end of Reynolds Street; to cruise on water rather than land, take one of the day or evening **boat trips** departing from the old port – one of the best is Blu Q (305 923 7245, W bluqkeywest.com). You can head on regular gay or lesbian two-hour sunset trips ($49 per person including drinks) or opt for daytime sailing and snorkelling jaunts ($99 including lunch). For information on what's happening pick up a copy of the free Q Magazine monthly guide (W keywestgayrag.com) from hotels and restaurants, or check the Business Guild website.

BARS AND CLUBS

801 Bourbon Bar 801 Duval St 305 294 4737, W 801bourbon.com. Drag shows upstairs every night at 9pm and 11pm ($10 each, but if they stamp your hand at the 9pm show, they'll let you back in at 11pm for free), while downstairs you'll find a nondescript bar with a mixed, slightly older crowd that opens onto Duval St, so you can watch passers-by. Daily 9am–4am.

Aqua 711 Duval St 305 294 0555, W aquakeywest .com. Large, pumping club with a massive dancefloor; the music's usually Top 40 hits, and there is also karaoke Monday to Thursday (from 11pm). Drag shows nightly ($15) at 9pm (Fri & Sat additional show at 11pm); the dancing gets going after the shows wrap up. Reservations taken – and recommended – for the 9pm show. Daily 3pm–2am.

Bobby's Monkey Bar 900 Simonton St 305 294 2655. A great place for a quiet drink, this mixed gay/straight bar is a welcoming pub-style joint. Pool tables,

frequent Wii-playing on the tube, and karaoke four nights a week at 9.30pm (Mon, Thurs, Fri & Sun). Cash only. Daily noon–4am.

★**Bourbon Street Pub** 724 Duval St 305 294 9354, W bourbonstpub.com. A huge pub complex with five bars, numerous TV screens and a pleasant garden, lit by tiki torches out back and complete with large hot tub. There are go-go boys every night, underwear-clad bartenders, and $5 drink specials. The youngish crowd is a diverse blend of locals and tourists. Daily 10am–4am.

La-Te-Da 1125 Duval St 305 296 6706 or 877 528 3320, W lateda.com. The various bars and discos of this hotel complex have long been a favourite haunt of locals and visitors. The pool bar hosts a popular tea dance every Sunday from 4pm, while the upstairs Crystal Room is one of the best-known showcases for drag divas in town – in season (usually Dec–April) there are usually shows Wed–Sat at 8pm or 9pm ($26); call for schedule rest of year.

Green Parrot 601 Whitehead St 305 294 6133, W greenparrot.com. Grubby old-time pub that's been a landmark for more than 120 years. Drinks are cheap, the place is full of locals, and there are antique bar games alongside the pool tables. Often hosts live music at weekends on its small stage. Daily 10am–4am.

Hog's Breath Saloon 400 Front St 305 296 4222, W hogsbreath.com. Despite its central location, and the boozed-up patrons staggering out of the front door whatever the time of day, this bar's one of the best spots in

town to catch live music, generally for free. Lots of bottled beers and cocktails, and Sam Adams and Yuengling on draft. Also does juicy burgers for $9.49. Daily 10am–2am.

Margaritaville 500 Duval St 305 292 1435, W margaritaville.com. Owner Jimmy Buffett – a Florida legend for his rock ballads extolling a laidback life in the sun – occasionally pops in to join the live country bands that play here nightly. Enjoy the music, but skip the below-average bar food. Now a national chain. Daily 10am–11pm.

★**The Porch** 429 Caroline St ☎ 305 517 6358, ⓦ theporchkw.com. A two-storey house painted absinthe green and fronted by wide verandas, *The Porch* is classier than many Key West bars, but certainly not stuffy – a laidback mix of regulars unwinds here with high-quality beer and wine. Mon–Sat 10am–2am, Sun noon–2am.

★**Rum Bar** 1117 Duval St, in the Speakeasy Inn ☎ 305 296 2680, ⓦ speakeasyinn.com. Located in the lobby of the *Speakeasy Inn* (see p.143), this small, boisterous bar has excellent bartenders: cocktails are made with freshly grated nutmeg, squeezed fruits and home-made infusions. Try the "painkiller", the house's signature blend of coconut milk, oranges, rum and spice. Daily 11am–midnight.

Schooner Wharf 202 William St ☎ 305 292 3302, ⓦ schoonerwharf.com. Right on the water in the Seaport, this rustic, wooden, alfresco bar with a sandy floor and plenty of nautical knick-knacks is a local favourite for great live tunes and beer-drinking under the stars. Daily 7am–3am.

Sloppy Joe's 201 Duval St ☎ 305 294 5717. Despite the memorabilia on the walls, this bar – with live rock or blues daily beginning at noon – is not the one made famous by Ernest Hemingway's patronage (that's *Captain Tony's Saloon* round the corner). The constant stream of cruise-ship passengers and karaoke-sounding rock acts can be offputting, but brave the hordes for one of the frozen drinks, slopped in a plastic cup and dressed with a cherry: for $7.50, the *piña coladas* are some of the stiffest, tastiest cocktails around. Daily 10am–4am.

Virgilio's On Appelrouth Lane, adjoining La Trattoria at 524 Duval St ☎ 305 296 1075, ⓦ virgilioskeywest.com. This glitterball-crowned martini bar has an outdoor patio, as well as small indoor bar and stage, for live music nightly from 10.30pm until 1am (expect loud, zesty Cuban bands). Drinks are served with a flourish, as each cocktail's overflow is presented alongside your glass in a mini-carafe on ice (martinis are $5 on Mon). Daily 7pm–2am.

KEY WEST FESTIVALS

Key West celebrates everything from Hemingway's birthday to the "independence" of the Conch Republic through a line-up of famously boisterous festivals throughout the year. Get precise dates on all of these from the Chamber of Commerce (see p.142) or check online at the sites listed below.

JANUARY
Key West Literary Seminar ☎ 888 293 9291, ⓦ kwls.org. Four-day celebration of the island's famous four – Tennessee Williams, Ernest Hemingway, Robert Frost and Thornton Wilder. Includes seminars, discussions and readings with well-known living authors as well as special tours, headquartered in and around the San Carlos Institute.

MARCH
Conch Shell Blowing Contest ☎ 305 294 9501, ⓦ oirf.org. Also called the "Conch Honk", this is usually held at the Oldest House Museum (see p.132). Anyone can enter (free), and you can buy a conch shell on-site if you don't have your own. Participants are judged according to the strength and originality of their melody.

APRIL
Conch Republic Independence Celebration ☎ 305 292 3302, ⓦ conchrepublic.com. A week of raucous celebrations starting with a symbolic raising of the Conch Republic flag at Fort Taylor, and including a drag race, parades, mock battles and lots of serious partying. Commemorates the declaration of the Keys' independence from the US in 1982 (see box, p.130).

JUNE
Key West Pride ☎ 305 294 4603, ⓦ keywestpride.org. This jubilant city does Pride proud with massive parades, street fairs, drag shows and pageants.

JULY
Hemingway Days ☎ 305 294 5717, ⓦ sloppyjoes.com. Literary seminars, writers' workshops, daft trivia competitions, a wacky "Running of the Bulls", and look-alike contests commemorate Ernest Hemingway, Key West's best-known writer. Held around his birthday on July 21.

OCTOBER
Fantasy Fest ☎ 305 296 1817, ⓦ fantasyfest.com. A gay-dominated version of Mardi Gras that elects its own King & Queen in a sequin-spangled parody of a high school prom. There are outrageous costumes paraded throughout Duval Street and for ten days it's a raunchy, adults-only good time. If you want a room for this celebration you'll need to book well in advance and expect significant rate hikes.

Goombay Festival ⓦ bahamavillagegoombay.com. Popular Caribbean street party in Bahama Village that's held during Fantasy Fest.

DECEMBER
Lighted Boat Parade ☎ 305 292 3302, ⓦ schoonerwharf.com. Twinkling lighted boats, decked out with garlands and festive palm trees, sail in and around Key West Harbor.

New Year's Eve ☎ 305 294 2587. Key West's party town reputation serves it well for this huge, boisterous night along Duval St with its twin markers of midnight: a conch that drops on the roof of *Sloppy Joe's* and a giant falling slipper (complete with drag queen) outside the *Bourbon Street Pub*. There's also much Mardi Gras bead-throwing.

DIRECTORY

Hospitals 24hr emergency room at Lower Keys Medical Center, 5900 College Rd, Stock Island (☎305 294 5531, ⊛lkmc.com).

Internet There are free terminals at Monroe County Library, 700 Fleming St (Mon, Tues, Thurs & Fri 9.30am–6pm, Wed 9.30am–8pm, Sat 10am–6pm; ☎305 292 3595, ⊛keyslibraries.org; internet use ends 30min before library closure).

Laundry Try Old Town Laundry, 517 Truman Ave (daily 8am–10pm; ☎305 295 9022; $2.50 per load, or $10 to leave it).

Police Emergency ☎911, non-emergency ☎305 809 1111.

Post office 400 Whitehead St (Mon–Fri 8.30am–5pm, Sat 9.30am–noon; ☎305 294 9539 or ☎800 275 8777, ⊛usps.gov).

Dry Tortugas National Park

Open 24hr • $5, valid for seven days • ☎305 242 7700, ⊛nps.gov/drto

Though getting to **Dry Tortugas National Park**, nearly seventy miles from Key West, takes some time and a fair amount of cash, it's worth the effort; approaching the weathered stone walls of Fort Jefferson – which rise mirage-like in the distance as you draw near – is a breathtaking experience. Set deep in the Gulf of Mexico, this fortified rock has a curious military history, pristine, fish-filled waters, and a real sense of isolation and tranquillity. It's also a paradise for bird lovers: the Dry Tortugas are home to significant colonies of sooty terns, frigate birds and brown noddies.

Spanish conquistador Juan Ponce de León named the islands after the large numbers of turtles (*tortugas* in Spanish) he found here in 1513 – the "dry" was added later to warn mariners of the islands' lack of fresh water. Comprising Garden Key and seven neighbouring reef islands, the park was created primarily to protect the nesting grounds of the **sooty tern** – a black-bodied, white-hooded bird unusual among terns for choosing to lay its eggs in scrubby vegetation and bushes. From early January, these and a number of other winged rarities show up on Bush Key, and are easily spied with binoculars from Fort Jefferson on Garden Key.

Garden Key and Fort Jefferson

Garden Key might be the last place you'd expect to find the US's largest nineteenth-century coastal fortification, but **Fort Jefferson** is exactly that. Started in 1846 and intended to protect US interests on the Gulf, the fort was never completed, despite thirty years of construction. Instead it served as a prison, until intense heat, lack of fresh water, outbreaks of disease, and savage weather made the fort as unpopular with its guards as its inmates. The most famous of the latter was Dr Samuel Mudd, who, beginning in 1865, served four years of a life sentence here before being pardoned by President Andrew Johnson for his alleged involvement in the assassination of Abraham Lincoln. In 1874, after a hurricane and the latest yellow fever outbreak, the fort was abandoned. Look for changes in brick colour: shifts mark the outbreak of the Civil War, when the Union-loyal fort was no longer able to buy supplies from Key West. Bricks shipped down from the north – at the top of the walls – have weathered the hot, humid climate less successfully than local materials at the base. Ferry trips include a 45-minute tour of the fort; alternatively, following the signposted **walk** and viewing the odds and ends in the small **visitor centre** at the entrance won't take more than an hour.

Boat trips include another couple of hours to explore the enticing beaches and water ringing the fort. Visibility is excellent in summer and you'll see plenty of fish (and occasionally turtles) lazing in the moat and off the beach and pier; note, though, there isn't much coral close to Garden Key itself. Barracuda are common, as are multicoloured clown parrotfish, and you'll spy great flocks of frigate birds on nearby Long Key and sooty terns (Feb–Sept) on Bush Key.

ARRIVAL AND DEPARTURE

By plane You can get to Garden Key by air in 40min with Key West Seaplane Adventures from the Key West airport ($295 half-day, $515 full day; ☎305 293 9300, ⓦ keywestseaplanecharters.com) – a beautiful if pricey trip that takes you low over the turquoise water.

By boat Less expensive and more relaxed is the high-speed ferry from the Historic Seaport (2hr 15min; boat

DRY TORTUGAS NATIONAL PARK

leaves Key West daily at 8am): *Yankee Freedom III* (100 Grinnell St; $170; ☎305 294 7009 or ☎800 634 0939, ⓦ drytortugas.com). The price includes breakfast, lunch, guided tour and snorkel gear. After a few leisurely hours at the fort, the ferry leaves Garden Key at 3pm, returning to the mainland by 5.30pm.

2

ACCOMMODATION

Fort Jefferson campsites Avid birdwatchers can camp at Fort Jefferson for up to fourteen days, though given its lack of amenities you have to come well prepared with your own supplies of water and food (and be ready to carry out your rubbish); only in an emergency can you count on help from the park rangers. A brilliant starscape and a very active bird community will be your constant companions, however. $\overline{\underline{S}3}$ per person

The Everglades

EVERGLADES SUNSET

The Everglades

One of the country's most celebrated natural areas, the Everglades is the largest subtropical wilderness in the United States, a vast watery expanse with a raw but subtle appeal that makes a stark contrast to America's more mountainous national parks. The most dramatic sights are small pockets of trees poking above a completely flat sawgrass plain, yet these wide-open spaces resonate with life, forming part of an ever-changing ecosystem, evolved through a unique combination of climate, vegetation and wildlife. Traditionally encompassing everything south of Lake Okeechobee, only a comparatively small section around Florida's southern tip is under the federal protection of Everglades National Park.

Established in 1947, the park was created not simply because of the region's sheer beauty, but rather to protect the mind-boggling web of life that calls it home – comprising an astonishing nine natural habitats, it supports more than 350 species of bird alone, as well as fifty reptile varieties (including the American alligator, the park's unofficial mascot). Hot, buggy and majestic, its humid hammocks and density of flora provide a welcome contrast to theme parks and nightclubs, and visitors here are spoilt for mesmerizing hiking, kayaking and wildlife-spotting opportunities.

EVERGLADES ESSENTIALS

ARRIVAL AND INFORMATION

By car Everglades National Park has three main entrances. The popular southern section of the park can be reached by taking the Florida's Turnpike Extension to Homestead, where it drops you on US-1 South. Turn right at the first traffic light (onto West Palm Drive, or 344th St) and follow the signs for the park entrance. Centrally located Shark Valley can only be accessed from two-lane US-41 (the Tamiami Trail), 25 miles from Florida's Turnpike. US-41 runs along the northern edge of the park between Miami and Naples, and also provides the only land access to the park entrance at Everglades City, the Big Cypress National Preserve and the Miccosukee Indian Village. There is no direct road between Flamingo and Everglades City, although you could connect the dots by canoe via the Wilderness Waterway (see box, p.159).

By tour There is no public transport along US-41, nor to any of the park entrances, though day-trips are organized by almost every tour operator in Miami and Naples (see p.255) as well as by the *Everglades International Hostel* in Florida City (see p.169).

Park entry fees Park entry is free at Everglades City, although from here you can travel only by boat or canoe. At the other entrances it's $10 per car and $5 for pedestrians and cyclists. Entry tickets are valid for seven days and can be used at any entrance.

Tourist information Contact park headquarters at ☎ 305 242 7700, ⬀ nps.gov/ever.

ACCOMMODATION

In the park Apart from two drive-in campsites (see p.160 & p.165), accommodation within the park is limited to forty-plus backcountry campgrounds. In most cases these are raised wooden platforms with a roof and chemical toilet, accessible by boat or canoe. To stay, you need to pick up a backcountry permit ($10 plus $2 per person, free May–Nov), from the closest visitor centre, no more than 24hr beforehand. One backcountry site at Flamingo, Pearl Bay, is accessible to disabled visitors, with lower ground access to huts and other facilities.

EVERGLADES ALLIGATOR

Highlights

❶ The Anhinga Trail In season, this popular hiking path is teeming with herons, egrets and plenty of alligators. **See p.158**

❷ Shark Valley Cycle or join the entertaining – and educational – tram tour into the heart of the "River of Grass", where you're bound to see plenty of wildlife such as otters and gators. See p.160

❸ Big Cypress Seminole Reservation Soak up Seminole culture and walk a fascinating boardwalk trail through cypress swamp at the Ah-Tah-Thi-Ki Museum. **See p.163**

❹ Fakahatchee Strand Roam through this alluring swamp of dwarf cypress trees and royal palms, domain of the rare Florida panther. See p.163

❺ Everglades City Take a kayaking tour, crack into buttery crab claws or just catch the breeze coming off the bay in this charming backwater. See p.165

❻ Ten Thousand Islands Ply the waters of this archipelago of dense mangrove cays, home to pelicans, dolphins and sea turtles, by boat or by canoe. **See p.165**

HIGHLIGHTS ARE MARKED ON THE MAP ON P.156

Outside the park Convenient bases outside the park include Florida City (see p.168), Everglades City (see p.165), Naples (see p.251) and Homestead (see p.168).

WHEN TO VISIT

Winter The park is open year-round, but the most favourable time to visit is winter (Dec–April). In this cooler season, receding floodwaters cause wildlife to congregate around gator holes, ranger-led activities are frequent, the humidity tamps down, and mosquitoes are bearable.

Summer In summer (May–Sept), afternoon storms flood the prairies, park activities are substantially reduced, and mosquitoes are a severe annoyance.

Shoulder seasons Visiting between seasons is also a good idea (April to early May and mid-Oct to Nov). The park is less crowded at this time, and has mild weather, although ranger activities are curtailed.

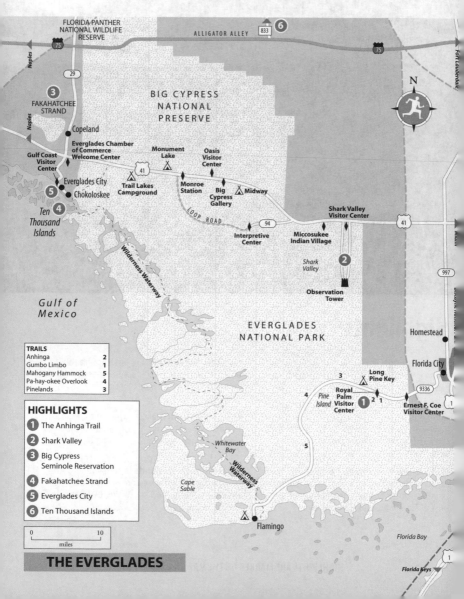

TRAILS

Anhinga	2
Gumbo Limbo	1
Mahogany Hammock	5
Pa-hay-okee Overlook	4
Pinelands	3

HIGHLIGHTS

1. The Anhinga Trail
2. Shark Valley
3. Big Cypress Seminole Reservation
4. Fakahatchee Strand
5. Everglades City
6. Ten Thousand Islands

0 — 10 miles

THE EVERGLADES

Southern section

The **southern section** of the park – containing the Pine Island area and Flamingo – holds virtually everything that makes the Everglades tick. Spend a well-planned day or two here for an introduction to the park's complex ecology, starting at its largest information hub, the **Ernest Coe Visitor Center** (see p.159). From here the road passes through the **park entrance**, and continues for 38 miles to the tiny coastal settlement of Flamingo, a one-time pioneer fishing colony now comprising a marina and campground. The short **walking trails** (none longer than half a mile) along the route will keep you engaged for hours; devote at least one day to walking and another to the **canoe trails** close to Flamingo.

EVERGLADES ECOLOGY

Appearing as flat as a tabletop, the limestone on which the Everglades stands (once part of the sea bed) actually tilts very slightly – a few inches over seventy miles – toward the southwest. For thousands of years, water flowed as a sixty-mile-wide sheet through the Everglades, from Lake Okeechobee to the coast. This sheet flow replenishes the **sawgrass**, which grows on a thin layer of soil – or "marl" – formed by decaying vegetation on the limestone base, and gives birth to the algae at the foot of a complex food chain that sustains much larger creatures, most notably alligators.

ALLIGATORS

Alligators earn their "keepers of the Everglades" nickname during the dry winter season. After the summer floodwaters have reached the sea, drained through the bedrock, or simply evaporated, the Everglades is barren except for the water accumulated in ponds or "gator holes" – created when an alligator senses water and clears the soil covering it with its tail. Besides nourishing the alligator, the pond provides a home for other wildlife until the summer rains return.

HAMMOCKS, BAYHEADS AND PINEWOODS

Sawgrass covers much of the Everglades, but where natural indentations in the limestone fill with marl, tree islands – or **hammocks** – appear, just high enough to stand above the flood waters and fertile enough to support a variety of trees and plants. Close to hammocks, often surrounding gator holes, you'll find wispy, green-leafed willows. Smaller patches of vegetation, like small green humps, are called "**bayheads**" Pinewoods grow in the few places where the elevation exceeds 7ft and, in the deep depressions that hold water the longest, dwarf cypress trees flourish, their treetops forming a distinctive "cypress dome" when large numbers cover an extensive area.

THREATS AND PRESERVATION

Everglades National Park is as fragile as it is fascinating. Florida experienced major population growth in the twentieth century, and the subsequent damage caused by uncontrolled hunting, road building and draining the Everglades for farmland gave rise to a significant **conservation lobby**. In 1947, a section of the Everglades was declared a national park, but unrestrained commercial use of nearby areas continued to upset the Everglades' natural cycle. The 1200 miles of canals built to divert the flow of water away from the Everglades toward the state's expanding cities, the poisoning caused by agricultural chemicals from the farmlands around Lake Okeechobee, and the broader changes wrought by global warming and invasion by non-native species, threaten to turn Florida's greatest natural asset into a wasteland.

In an attempt to increase the natural sheet flow in the Everglades, Congress authorized a thirty-year, $7.8 billion plan in 2000 to dismantle miles of levees and canals, and divert and store part of the 1.7 billion gallons of water lost each day (in the flow from Lake Okeechobee to the ocean) for later use. A potentially major step forward was made in 2008 when the government purchased **sugar-cane plantations** to the south of Lake Okeechobee for $1.34 billion, though it remains to be seen how much of this land will actually be set aside for restoration. Given the complexity of the project, it will be some time before it's clear whether the plan will produce any of the desired results.

3

Pine Island

Hwy-9336 • Trails open 24hr

The first section of this part of the park is known as **Pine Island**, containing some of the most rewarding hiking trails in the Everglades. Pop into the barebones **Royal Palm Visitor Center**, four miles from the main park entrance, which usually hosts ranger activities but has little in the way of information, though there is a small gift and book store (daily: April–Dec 9am–4.15pm; Jan–March 8am–4.15pm).

Anhinga Trail

Park visitors eager to spot an **alligator** tend to be satisfied by walking the **Anhinga Trail** here; the reptiles are easily seen during the winter, often splayed near the trail, looking like plastic props. They're notoriously lazy, but give them a wide berth, as they can be extremely swift if provoked. Turtles, herons and the odd garfish are also likely to turn up on the route, and keep an eye out for the bizarre **anhinga**, a black-bodied bird resembling an elongated cormorant, which, after diving for fish, spends ages drying itself on rocks and tree branches with its white-tipped wings fully spread. Get an early start on the trail to beat the crowds.

Gumbo Limbo Trail

Next to the Anhinga Trail, but very different, the **Gumbo Limbo Trail** is a hardwood jungle hammock packed with exotic subtropical growths: strangler fig, red-barked gumbo limbo, royal palm, wild coffee and resurrection ferns. The latter appear dead during the dry season, but "resurrect" themselves in the summer rains to form a lush collar of green.

Pinelands Trail

In comparison to the Gumbo Limbo Trail, the **Pinelands Trail**, three miles further on, offers an undramatic half-mile ramble through a forest of slash pine, though the solitude comes as a welcome relief after the busier walks. Green-fingered visitors take note: plant diversity on this trail rivals that of sea life in a coral reef. The hammering of woodpeckers is often the loudest sound you'll hear.

Pa-hay-okee Overlook Trail

A variety of birdlife – including egrets, red-shouldered hawks and circling vultures – is viewable six miles beyond the Pinelands Trail from the **Pa-hay-okee Overlook Trail**, which emerges from a stretch of dwarf cypress to face a sweeping expanse of sawgrass. *Pa-hay-okee* is a Seminole word meaning "grassy waters", an apt description that exemplifies how people struggle to define this region that is not quite water, not quite land.

Mahogany Hammock Trail

The mahogany trees of the **Mahogany Hammock Trail**, seven miles from the Overlook Trail, are surprisingly small despite being the largest of the type in the country. A greater draw are the colourful snails and golden orb spiders lurking among their branches. You'll also spy the wonderfully named gumbo limbo, known colloquially as the "sunburn tree" or "tourist tree", owing to its peeling red bark.

Flamingo and around

A century ago, the only way to reach **FLAMINGO** was by boat, a fact that failed to deter a small group of settlers who came here to fish, hunt, smuggle, and get paralytic on moonshine whiskey. It didn't even have a name until the opening of a post office made one necessary: "Flamingo" was eventually chosen due to the flocks of lanky pink-plumed birds that seasonally inhabited the area. While it's hard to spot flamingos nowadays, you will find an abundance of another bright bird – the roseate spoonbill – often mistaken for its peach-coloured friend.

The completion of the road to Homestead in 1922 was expected to bring boom times to Flamingo, but as it turned out, most people seized on it as a chance to leave. None of the old buildings remain, and the main trade of present-day Flamingo is servicing the needs of sport-fishing fanatics. The **marina store** (Mon–Fri 7am–5.30pm, Sat & Sun 6am–5.30pm; ☎239 695 3101) is the go-to place for buying supplies and snacks. The nearby **visitor center** (see below) has a great viewing deck overlooking the bay, maps on local walks, and a small exhibition on regional fauna and flora.

Canoe trails

Tandem canoes $22/half-day, $32/day, $40/24hr, kayaks $35/half-day, $45/day, $55/24hr • ☎ 239 695 3101, Ⓦ evergladesnationalparkboattoursflamingo.com

You'll find several walking trails within reach of Flamingo, but more promising are the numerous **canoe trails**. Rent a tandem canoe or kayak from the marina store (see above), and get maps and advice from the visitor centre (see below). An easy-going option – if you've no experience whatsoever, it's best to hop on a guided tour via the visitor centre – is the two-mile **Noble Hammock Trail**, passing through sawgrass and around dense mangroves. Segments of the trail are very narrow, though, and do require some agility. An alternative, the **Mud Lake Loop** (6.8 miles), links the Buttonwood Canal, Coot's Bay, Mud Lake and the Bear Lake Canoe Trail, with plenty of opportunities for prime birdwatching.

Backcountry Boat Cruise

Multiple tours daily, check website as times vary according to season; 1hr 45min • $32.25 • In season, reserve at least 36hr in advance on ☎ 239 695 3101, Ⓦ evergladesnationalparkboattoursflamingo.com

If you lack faith in your own abilities, take a **guided boat trip** from the marina. The **Backcountry Boat Cruise** makes a tranquil foray around the mangrove-enshrouded Coot and Whitewater bays, from where you'll see plenty of waterbirds and a cantankerous gator or two.

ARRIVAL AND INFORMATION   SOUTHERN SECTION

By car Pine Island is an hour's drive from downtown Miami. You will be reliant on your vehicle – there is no public transport in the park.

By tour bus Island Queen Cruises runs 6hr tours from Miami to the southern section of the Everglades ($55; ☎305 379 5119, Ⓦ islandqueencruises.com); the cost includes an airboat ride at Everglades Safari Park (see box, p.164).

Ernest Coe Visitor Center The park's largest source of information is located at the southern entrance at 4001 Hwy-9336, Homestead (daily: mid-April to mid-Dec 9am–5pm; mid-Dec to mid-April 8am–5pm; ☎305 242 7700, Ⓦ nps.gov/ever).

Flamingo Visitor Center On Hwy-9336, 38 miles southwest of the Ernest Coe Visitor Center (Jan–April daily 8am–4.30pm; May–Dec staffed intermittently; ☎239 695 2945, Ⓦ nps.gov/ever).

WILDERNESS WATERWAY

Anybody adequately skilled with the paddle, equipped with rough camping gear, and with a week to spare should have a crack at the 99-mile **Wilderness Waterway**, a marked kayak trail between Flamingo and Everglades City, with numerous backcountry campgrounds en route. Take a compass, maps and ample **provisions**, including at least a gallon of water per person per day. Carry supplies in hard containers, as raccoons can chew through soft ones. Be sure to leave a detailed plan of your journey and its expected duration with a park ranger. Finally, pay heed to the latest weather forecast and note the tidal patterns if you're canoeing in a coastal area. If you need help with **planning the trip**, kayak rentals or lifts to the waterway, contact the Flamingo marina (see above) or *Everglades International Hostel* (p.169). Also quite useful is the National Park Service's printable wilderness trip planner, which includes a gear checklist and campsite descriptions (Ⓦ nps.gov/ever).

ACCOMMODATION AND EATING

It's a good idea to stop for a **snack or drink** before entering the southern section of the park – otherwise you'll have to wait until Flamingo, 38 miles on, where there is just one in-season **restaurant**, and the **marina store,** which sells basic snacks and food. Your last chance for refreshments is the enticing *Gator Grill* (see p.169).

Alternative D The park's lone motel at Flamingo sustained major damage during hurricanes Katrina and Wilma in 2005, and the ambitious ecofriendly replacement – dubbed "Alternative D" – is not expected to open until 2030 or later. Check ⓦnps.gov/ever for updates.

★**Flamingo Campground** 38 miles south of Ernest Coe Visitor Center, Flamingo ☏877 444 6777, ⓦrecreation.gov. Well-equipped campground at the end of Hwy-9336, with 234 drive-in sites (55 with a view of the water), hot showers, picnic tables, grills and 41 sites with electric hook-ups for RVs. The price below is for high season; tent sites are free May–Sept. You can make

reservations up to six months in advance. Note that there is just one restaurant in Flamingo (the *Buttonwood Café*), and it's only open Nov–April. Camping $\overline{\$16}$, RV sites $\overline{\$30}$

Long Pine Key Campground Off Hwy-9336, 6 miles west of Ernest Coe Visitor Center on Hwy-9336 ☏305 242 7873, ⓦnps.gov/ever. Attractive campground with 108 sites for tents and RVs, restrooms and water, but no hook-ups or showers – the hostel in Florida City (see p.169) offers showers for $5. No reservations – check the instructions on the bulletin board just inside the park entrance. Closed June–Oct. $\overline{\$16}$

Shark Valley

Park Trails open 24hr; parking area open 8.30am–6pm • **Tram tour** Dec–April 9am–4pm, hourly; May–Nov daily at 9.30am, 11am, 2pm & 4pm; reservations recommended Dec–April • $22, children 3–12 $12.75 • ☏305 221 8455, ⓦsharkvalleytramtours.com

In no other section of the park does the Everglades' "River of Grass" tag seem as appropriate as it does at **Shark Valley**. From here the sawgrass plain stretches as far as the eye can see, dotted by hardwood hammocks and the smaller bayheads. This area is quite popular with hikers on full-moon nights; the parking area is closed after 6pm, so leave your vehicle along the road near the entrance. You won't see any sharks here: the "valley" is actually part of the Shark River Slough, which ends up emptying into Florida Bay (where you will find sharks).

Aside from a few simple walking trails close to the **visitor centre** (see below), you can see Shark Valley only from a fifteen-mile loop road. At the far point of the loop (7 miles), a 45ft **observation tower** offers a panoramic overview of the plains.

Too lengthy and lacking in shade to walk comfortably, and off limits to cars, the loop is ideally explored by **bike**. Alternatively, a highly informative two-hour **tram tour** stops frequently to view wildlife. If touring by bike, set out as early as possible (the wildlife is most active in the cool of the morning), ride slowly and stay alert: otters, turtles and snakes are plentiful but not always easy to spot, and the abundant alligators often keep uncannily still. During September and October you'll come across female alligators tending their young; watch them from a safe distance. You can see more of the same creatures – and a good selection of birdlife – from the observation tower.

ARRIVAL, GETTING AROUND AND INFORMATION   SHARK VALLEY

By bike Bike rental is available at the visitor center (daily 8.30am–4pm; $8.50/hr; return by 5pm).
By car Shark Valley is just off US-41. It's about a 50min drive to get here from downtown Miami.

Shark Valley Visitor Center US-41 (Tamiami Trail), 25 miles west of Florida's Turnpike (daily 9.15am–5.15pm; ☏305 221 8776, ⓦnps.gov/ever).

ACCOMMODATION

Gator Park 24050 SW 8th St (US-41) ☏305 559 2255, ⓦgatorpark.com. Camping and RV hook-ups are available

at this popular airboat and alligator park, 12 miles west of Florida's Turnpike and 13 miles east of Shark Valley. $\overline{\$30}$

Miccosukee Indian Village

Mile Marker 70, US-41 (Tamiami Trail) • Daily 9am–5pm • $10, children 6–12 $6 • ☎ 305 552 8365, ⓦ miccosukee.com

A mile west of Shark Valley, the **Miccosukee Indian Village** symbolizes the tribe's uneasy compromise with modern America. In the souvenir shop, good-quality traditional crafts and clothes stand side by side with blatant tat, and in the "village" men turn logs into canoes, women cook over open fires, and alligator-wrestling shows are de rigueur. Despite the authentic roots, it's such a contrived affair that anyone with an ounce of sensitivity can't help but feel uneasy. Since it's one of the few introductions to Native American life in the Everglades, it's hard to resist taking a look, though a trip to the Ah-Tah-Thi-Ki Museum (see p.168) in the Big Cypress Seminole Reservation would be much more rewarding. If you're visiting at the end of December, check out the **Indian Arts Festival** held at the village, when Native American artisans from all over the country gather to display their work.

Airboat tours

Daily 9am–4.30pm • $16 per person • ☎ 305 480 1924

Across the road from the Miccosukee Indian Village, the tribe runs thirty-minute **airboat tours**. These take in a traditional Miccosukee hammock camp, where you can learn a little more about the local wildlife and the history and culture of the tribe. The thirty-minute tours can be hit-or-miss, as the enthusiasm of the guides tends to vary.

FLORIDA'S SEMINOLE AND MICCOSUKEE TRIBES

Against all the odds, Florida's **Seminole** and **Miccosukee** Indians have created a thriving community in the same swamps and sawgrass plains where their ancestors – less than two hundred survivors of the last Seminole War in 1858 – held out against the US Army. They never surrendered to the US government, and there is much pride in the epithet "unconquered people". Many more Seminoles live in the Midwest, where they were moved in the nineteenth century.

BRIEF HISTORY

Florida's original native inhabitants – tribes like the Calusa and the Tequesta – died out in the eighteenth century and by the 1760s bands of Creeks from Georgia and Alabama had moved into the state – Seminole was a transliteration of the Spanish word "cimarrónes" meaning wild or free people, and came into use around this time. Pushed further into the Everglades in the nineteenth century, the Seminoles lived on hammocks in open-sided *chickee* huts built from cypress and cabbage palm, and traded, hunted and fished across the wetlands by canoe. Development and drainage of the Everglades in the 1920s ended this way of life, and the tribe turned to tourism and farming (mainly cattle-ranching) to make a living. The division between the Miccosukee and Seminole occurred in the 1950s and is somewhat controversial. The Miccosukee are descendants of what were once known as Trail Seminoles, who lived along the Tamiami Trail; when the Seminole tribe reorganized in 1957, this group opted to remain independent. Despite recent attempts on both sides to emphasize differences, both tribes speak the same Mikisúkî language.

THE TRIBES TODAY

In 1979 the Seminoles were the first Native American tribe to develop **gaming** as a form of income (see p.186), and today their million-dollar revenues pay for universal health care, financial support for education, full senior care and modern community centres. The six Seminole reservations at Hollywood (the headquarters), Big Cypress, Brighton, Fort Pierce, Immokalee and Tampa (with a total population of around 3300) exercise their own sovereignty and have plenty of spare cash; the tribe purchased the **Hard Rock Cafe** franchise in 2006.

Big Cypress National Preserve and around

The logging era (1943–57) led to the destruction of thousands of towering **bald cypress trees** – whose durable wood is highly marketable – that lined roadside sloughs along US-41 (built in 1928). By the 1970s, attempts to drain these acres and turn them into residential plots posed a threat to nearby Everglades National Park, and the government created the **Big Cypress National Preserve** in 1974 – a vast expanse of protected land mostly on the northern side of US-41. Today one third of the preserve is covered in cypress trees (mostly the dwarf pond variety), though the giant cypress has largely vanished.

Florida National Scenic Trail

US-41

The only way to traverse the whole of the Big Cypress National Preserve is via a rugged 37-mile (one-way) hiking trail, part of the **Florida National Scenic Trail**. The **Oasis Visitor Center** (see p.164) on US-41 divides the trail into a thirty-mile section north of US-41 and a seven-mile section south of the highway. Visitors are required to pick up a free backcountry permit, for either day or overnight access.

Fire Prairie Trail

Turner River Rd, 14 miles north of US-41

More manageable hiking routes than the Florida National Scenic Trail include the five-mile (round-trip) **Fire Prairie Trail**; its slight elevation means it tends to be on the dry side, giving colourful prairie flowers a chance to bloom in the spring.

Big Cypress Gallery

52388 Tamiami Trail (US-41) • Daily 10am–5pm • Oct–March swamp walks every Mon, Thurs & Sat; 1hr 30min; reservations required • Swamp walks $50 • ☎ 239 695 2428, ⓦ clydebutcher.com

Half a mile east of the Oasis Visitor Center sits the **Big Cypress Gallery**, which exhibits the amazing work of Everglades photographer Clyde Butcher, capturing all the beauty and magic of the area. Framed photographs are on the expensive side ($500 and up), but they also come as smaller cards that make perfect souvenirs (boxes from $16.50). Additionally, in season, the gallery leads **swamp walks** (1hr 30min) – delightful trudges through waist-high water and a canopied cypress dome. Fans of the area (or the art) can also rent Clyde's swamp cottage or bungalow (see p.165), located behind the gallery.

Loop Road

For a bone-shaking but wildlife-packed off-road excursion, turn left off US-41 at Monroe Station, four miles west of the Oasis Ranger Station, onto the 24-mile **Loop Road**, a gravel track that's potholed in parts and prone to sudden flooding as it winds its way through cypress strands and pinewoods. Once you reach Pinecrest, things get easier: the road becomes paved and, after another twenty minutes or so, rejoins US-41 at Forty Mile Bend, just west of the Miccosukee Indian Village. Alligators are as common as lizards on the road (sometimes blocking it), and you'll see plenty of white ibis and sometimes snakes; if you're very lucky, you might spot a black bear or panther.

Fakahatchee Strand Preserve State Park

Hwy-29 • Ranger-guided walks ☎ 239 695 4593, ⓦ floridastateparks.org

After a trip to the Big Cypress National Preserve be sure to visit the nearby **Fakahatchee Strand Preserve State Park**, directly north of Everglades City. This water-holding slough

3

AIRBOAT TOURS

Airboat tours are synonymous with the Everglades, although their use is contentious. Environmentalists argue that the noisy craft frighten wildlife and impact the area's tranquil soundscape. Even worse, it's feared they disrupt the fragile web of algae and flora found just beneath the water's surface. On the other hand, the rides bring an additional 300,000 visitors – and their dollars – to the park each year. Proponents would also argue that airboat tours are an exhilarating and unique way to experience parts of the Everglades that you wouldn't otherwise see. In any case, since Everglades National Park was declared a wilderness area under the 1978 Wilderness Act, airboating in the majority of the park is being phased out. The three tour operators listed below are located on the south side of US-41, and were grandfathered in under another legislation – the Everglades Expansion Act of 1989 – which brought them into park boundaries.

Coopertown 22700 SW 8th St (US-41), Miami, 11 miles west of Florida's Turnpike ☎ 305 226 6048, ⓦ coopertownairboats.com. Operating since 1945, Coopertown is the oldest airboat tour company in the area and offers an informative 45min tour ($23, children 6–11 $11) through 9 miles of sawgrass. Daily 9am–5.30pm.

Everglades Safari Park 26700 SW 8th St (US-41), Miami, 15 miles west of Florida's Turnpike ☎ 305 226 6923, ⓦ evergladessafaripark.com. The shortest tour, at 30–40min ($23, children 5–11, $12), and also

offers the obligatory wildlife shows. Daily 9am–5pm.

Gator Park 24050 SW 8th St, Miami, 12 miles west of Florida's Turnpike ☎ 305 559 2255 or ☎ 800 559 2205, ⓦ gatorpark.com. Offers a somewhat slicker tour than Coopertown, lasting 35–40min ($22.99, children 6–11, $11.99; cheaper online), though it doesn't cover as large an area inside the park. After the tour, you'll be subjected to the slightly disturbing "alligator wrestling" and wildlife show. Daily 9am–5pm.

sustains dwarf cypress trees (grey and spindly during the winter, draped with green needles in summer), a stately batch of royal palms, spiky-leafed air plants, and masses of orchids, including the elusive ghost orchid, famously depicted in the film *Adaptation*. You should see plenty of wildlife from the Big Cypress Bend Boardwalk just off US-41, or along the eleven-mile Jane's Scenic Drive off Hwy-29. If possible, see them on a **ranger-guided walk**.

Florida Panther National Wildlife Reserve

Hwy-29, just north of I-75 • ☎ 239 353 8442, ⓦ fws.gov/floridapanther

North of the Fakahatchee Strand along Hwy-29, the **Florida Panther National Wildlife Reserve** protects the remaining 100 to 160 panthers that inhabit the Everglades, endangered after years of over-hunting. You can walk the 1.3-mile loop trail into the reserve, though realistically you're as likely to see a panther as you are to win the Florida lottery.

ARRIVAL AND INFORMATION   BIG CYPRESS NATIONAL PRESERVE

By car Big Cypress is a 1hr 30min drive from Miami via US-41, and 45min from Naples via I-75 and Hwy-29. There is no public transport in or around the preserve.

Oasis Visitor Center 52105 Tamiami Trail (US-41); daily 9am–4.30pm; ☎ 239 695 1201, ⓦ nps.gov/bicy). Staffed by helpful rangers and stocked with plenty of maps and

brochures. In season (Nov to mid-April), the centre offers free 2hr, guided swamp walks and full-day canoe trips (call for times and reservations). If you'd like to spot a gator, the boardwalk in front of the centre is a magnet for the crotchety reptiles.

TOURS

Capt. Steve's Swamp Buggy Adventures ☎ 877 871 5386, ⓦ captainsteveswampbuggyadventures.com. Flush a gator from his cave, track panther paw marks and ogle air plants under the auspices of the characterful Captain Steve and his off-roading "swamp buggy." A signature Big Cypress experience. 4hr; $450 for six adults.

Everglades Adventure Tours ☎ 800 504 6554, ⓦ evergladesadventuretours.com. Kayaking trips (2hr; $89), swamp hikes (3hr; $89) and pole boat tours (1–3hr; $69–199), these last propelled by naturalist skiffers. The same folks run the *Trail Lakes Campground* (see p.165).

ACCOMMODATION

Clyde & Niki Butcher's Swamp Cottage and Bungalow 52388 Tamiami Trail (US-41), Ochopee ☎ 239 695 2428, ⓦ clydebutcher.com. Get cosy in the swamp cottage where the Butchers lived for sixteen years, or the nearby bungalow, both just behind the photography gallery (see p.163). The second-floor cottage has two bedrooms, two baths, a kitchen, satellite TV, laundry and a sunroom overlooking a pristine pond; the ground-level bungalow has two bedrooms, one bath, a small kitchen, local TV, wi-fi, and views of swampland cypress trees. There is fabulous art in both. Cottage $\overline{\$275}$, bungalow $\overline{\$225}$

Midway Campground US-41 ☎ 239 695 1201, ⓦ nps .gov/bicy. Snugly set amid lush vegetation, this is the best-equipped of the two designated campgrounds in the preserve, 2 miles from the Oasis Visitor Center and complete with flush toilets, grills, drinking water, 26 RV sites with

hook-ups and ten tent sites. Reserve online at ⓦ recreation .gov. Camping $\overline{\$24}$, RV sites $\overline{\$30}$

Monument Lake Campground US-41, near Monroe Station ☎ 239 695 1201, ⓦ nps.gov/bicy. Located next to a small lake 5 miles west of the Oasis Visitor Center, the other official preserve campsite offers restrooms, fire circles and drinking water. RV sites are without hook-ups here. Open mid-Aug to mid-April. Reserve online at ⓦ recreation .gov. Camping $\overline{\$24}$, RV sites $\overline{\$28}$

Trail Lakes Campground 40904 Tamiami Trail (US-41), Ochopee ☎ 239 695 2275, ⓦ evergladescamping .net. Privately owned campground around 17 miles west of the Oasis Visitor Center on US-41, sharing a site with the eccentric but oddly intriguing Skunk Ape Research Headquarters. There are hot showers, a bathhouse and wi-fi. Also runs great ecotours (via Everglades Adventure Tours; see p.165). Camping $\overline{\$25}$, RV sites $\overline{\$35}$

EATING

★**Joanie's Blue Crab Café** 39395 US-41 in Ochopee ☎ 239 695 2682, ⓦ joaniesbluecrabcafe.com. In this colourful shack crammed with knick-knacks, you can grab a beer from the cooler and dine on a meal of crab cakes, gator pieces and Indian fry bread, or choose from a selection of huge

burgers and fish dishes (main courses $9–17). Opposite, make a stop at the world's smallest post office, squashed into a 7ft-by-8ft hut that was originally an irrigation pipe shed built in 1953. Frequent live music. 11am–5pm; closed Wed year-round, also Tues in summer.

Everglades City and around

Created by advertising tycoon Barron Collier in the 1920s, sleepy **EVERGLADES CITY** serves as a good base from which to explore the **Ten Thousand Islands** section of the Everglades, but also warrants a visit in its own right.

Smitten with southwest Florida, Collier began pouring money into the area in the early 1920s, and after the state named Collier County in his honour in 1923, he established Everglades City as the county seat. Despite the completion of the Tamiami Trail in 1928, the "city" never really took off, and after Hurricane Donna levelled the place in 1960, the county government and most businesses relocated to Naples. Everglades City has been a pleasant backwater ever since, existing largely to serve the tourist trade.

Museum of the Everglades

105 W Broadway • Mon–Sat 9am–4pm • Suggested $2 donation • ☎ 239 695 0008, ⓦ evergladesmuseum.org

Some of the properties left standing in the wake of Hurricane Donna have been restored, offering a glimpse into life before the destruction. One such building is the **Museum of the Everglades**, housed downtown in what used to be the old laundry when it was built in 1927. It now displays a small exhibition documenting the last two thousand years in the southwest Everglades, enhanced by a selection of artefacts and old photographs.

Ten Thousand Islands

The main attraction here lies offshore, in the numerous mangrove islands scattered like jigsaw-puzzle pieces along the coastline – aptly named **Ten Thousand Islands** and

TEN THOUSAND ISLANDS ACTIVITIES AND TOURS

The only way to really experience the Ten Thousand Islands is to get onto the water. Ignore the ecologically dubious tours advertised along the roadside and take one of the park-sanctioned boat trips run by **Everglades National Park Boat Tours** (underneath the dockside visitor centre; daily 9am–5pm; every 30min mid-Dec to mid-April, hourly rest of year; from $31.80 for a 1hr 30min tour; ☎ 239 695 2591 or ☎ 866 628 7275). Expect to see plenty of birds year-round (herons, ospreys and fish-feeding pelicans), as well as dolphins and turtles; manatees are less easy to spot. You can also **rent canoes and kayaks** here (canoe rental $24/day; double kayak rental $55/day).

Everglades Rentals and Eco Adventures, located at the *Ivey House* (see below), offers a range of activities from November to April (some tours are operated year-round), from a "kayak into a new day" paddle to a twilight trip that's concluded by headlamp (guided kayak tours $99 guests, $124 non-guests; ☎ 239 695 3299, ⓦ evergladesadventures.com). Canoe, kayak and equipment rentals are also available (canoe rentals $35/day), as well as shuttle services.

3

forming part of the largest mangrove forest in North America. For an introduction, visit the dockside **Gulf Coast Visitor Center** (daily: Nov–April 8am–4.30pm; May–Oct 9am–4.30pm; ☎ 239 695 3311, ⓦ nps.gov/ever), half a mile south of the town centre, which has a small array of displays highlighting local flora and fauna (including a lead-like manatee rib), and DVDs played on demand.

Chokoloskee Island

Beyond the visitor centre the road continues for another four miles across the causeway to **Chokoloskee Island**, connected to the mainland in 1956. Archeologists believe the whole island started life as a vast shell midden created by the lost **Calusa** civilization.

Smallwood Store

360 Mamie St • Daily: Dec–April 10am–5pm; May–Nov 11am–5pm • $5 • ☎ 239 695 2989, ⓦ smallwoodstore.com

Nothing remains from the period of the Calusa, and the main reason to visit this sleepy boating community – aside from its excellent Cuban restaurant (see opposite) – is for the old Indian trading post of **Smallwood Store**. Pioneer Ted Smallwood built this stilt house out of rock-hard Dade County pine in 1917, and it remains crammed with all sorts of bric-a-brac and curios, old medicinal bottles and machinery. The solid wood counter, rickety roof and creaky veranda cooled by bay breezes are evocative of the days when Ted traded vegetables, tools and salt pork with the Seminoles. You'll also learn about the notorious vigilante killing of local strongman Edgar Watson near here in 1910, dramatized in Peter Matthiessen's novel *Killing Mister Watson*.

ARRIVAL AND INFORMATION

EVERGLADES CITY AND AROUND

By car Everglades City is a 45min drive from Naples and a 1hr 35min trip from Miami. There are no buses or trains to Everglades City.

Everglades Area Chamber of Commerce Welcome

Center At the junction of Hwy-29 and US-41 (daily 9am–4pm; ☎ 239 695 3941, ⓦ evergladeschamber.com). Stop at this wooden, triangular building 4 miles north of the town centre for local information.

ACCOMMODATION

Everglades City Motel 310 Collier Ave, Everglades City ☎ 239 695 4224, ⓦ evergladescitymotel.com. Freshly renovated motel with contemporary bathrooms, fridges, flat-screen TVs with cable, and exceptionally plush beds. Also offers one efficiency equipped with hot plate, toaster

and cutlery. Free bike use and barbecue setup. Doubles **$149**, efficiency **$189**

★**Ivey House** 107 Camellia St, Everglades City ☎ 239 695 3299, ⓦ iveyhouse.com. Offers accommodation with shared bathrooms in a historic 1928 lodge (closed

May–Oct) or in a more upscale inn, where you get TV, phone and private bathroom. Our favourite feature, however, is the indoor pool, lined with potted plants, a little waterfall and a screened-in ceiling that enables you to gaze at the sky while you swim. The inn also offers kayaking tours (see box opposite) and equipment rental. Great complimentary breakfast (eggs, toast, yogurt, oatmeal and fruit), to jump-start the day. Lodge $99, inn $169

Parkway Motel & Marina 1180 Chokoloskee Drive, Chokoloskee ☎ 239 695 3261, ⓦ evergladesparkway motelandmarina.com. Immaculate and cosy motel rooms complete with fridge, bathroom, coffeemaker and a/c. The

knowledgeable owners can sort out boat rentals and guides. $139

Rod & Gun Lodge 200 Riverside Drive, Everglades City ☎ 239 695 2101, ⓦ evergladesrodandgun.com. It used to be an exclusive club whose members included presidents, but now anyone can stay in this 1864 hunting-lodge-style hotel, with pool, spacious veranda and antique cocktail lounge thrown in. The cottages are showing their age, but come with private bath and plenty of character. If you don't stay here, pop by for a drink or just to gape at the historic lobby lined with rifles, alligator skins and animal heads. $110

EATING

In Everglades City, **seafood restaurants** dominate the area, which has provided 95 percent of the world's supply of **stone crab** since the 1940s. Crab season runs from mid-October to mid-May.

Camellia Street Grill 202 Camellia St, Everglades City ☎ 239 695 2003. Pass a multicoloured VW bug, an oversized teapot, bowling balls and bird houses and you'll arrive at this screened-in favourite serving Southern-inflected fare like BBQ pork sandwiches ($8.95) and garlic blue crabs ($19.95). Dockside live music at weekends. Oct–April daily noon–9pm; call for summer hours.

City Seafood 702 Begonia St, Everglades City ☎ 239 695 4700, ⓦ cityseafood1.com. Sublime two-storey restaurant whose riverfront deck takes in boats, palm trees and bobbing birds. All the fish is ultra-fresh (the restaurant doubles as a seafood market), and if you're here during

stone crab season, you'd be a fool not to order a pound of the state's best claws (market price). Otherwise, the enormous grouper sandwich ($10.95) or fried mullet plate ($10.95) is sure to please. Daily 6am–6pm.

Havana Café 191 Smallwood Drive, Chokoloskee ☎ 239 695 2214, ⓦ myhavanacafe.com. Pink, adobe-like house churning out addictive Cuban fare like *huevos rancheros* ($6.95) and pressed *media noche* sandwiches (pork, ham, mustard, and Swiss cheese and pickles on sweet bread; $7.95). Oct–April Mon–Thurs & Sun 7am–3pm, Fri & Sat 7am–8pm.

Big Cypress Seminole Reservation

Just a few miles north of the Big Cypress National Preserve, but only accessible from Hwy-833 off I-75, the **Big Cypress Seminole Reservation** features a couple of attractions that will easily hold your interest for an hour or two; as the largest Seminole reservation in Florida, it's also the best place to meet the locals and get some sense of how the modern tribe lives.

The main settlement begins seventeen miles north of I-75, amid an impressive array of schools, sports facilities, civic buildings and a rodeo arena.

> ## MANATEE TOURS
>
> One of Florida's most endearing inhabitants is the endangered, hippo-like **manatee** (see box, p.383), of which there are an estimated 5000 in the state. Though you might see them anywhere along the coast, their limited population and the difficulty in spotting them means that in practice this is unlikely. If you really want to see a manatee, look for specialist operators such as **Captains Barry and Carol Berger** at the *Port of the Islands Resort* marina, just off US-41 eleven miles west of Hwy-29 (☎ 239 642 8818, ⓦ see-manatees.com; $58), who guarantee sightings (on 1hr 30min trips), or your money back; advance bookings are essential. In the resort's lobby, **Double R's Manatee Eco Tours** (☎ 239 642 9779, ⓦ doublersfishingandtours .com) run similarly focused 2hr 30min and abbreviated 1hr tours ($55 and $25, respectively) around the Ten Thousand Islands.

Ah-Tah-Thi-Ki Museum

34725 W Boundary Rd, Clewiston (exit 49 off I-75) • Daily 9am–5pm • $10 • ☎ 877 902 1113, ⊕ ahtahthiki.com

On the northern side of town lies the principal attraction, the fascinating **Ah-Tah-Thi-Ki Museum**, where a seventeen-minute audiovisual presentation, displays, and a rare collection of clothing and artefacts highlight Seminole history and cultural traditions. The 1.5-mile boardwalk at the back cuts through a tranquil swamp, to a reproduction of an early twentieth-century tourist camp. Panels along the way explain how local plants were used by the Seminole for medicinal purposes.

Homestead and around

Just outside the eastern entrance of Everglades National Park, **southern Miami** has yielded to agriculture along US-1, where broad, fertile fields grow fruit and vegetables for the nation's northern states. Aside from offering as good a taste of Florida farm life – the region produces the bulk of America's winter tomatoes – as you're likely to find so close to its major city, the district can be a money-saving base when visiting the southern section of the Park, or as a stop en route to the Florida Keys.

HOMESTEAD is the agricultural area's main town, and one of Miami's least enticing enclaves. Krome Avenue, just west of US-1, slices through the centre, but besides a number of good restaurants and a few restored 1910s–1930s buildings, time is better spent around Homestead than actually in it. Neighbouring **Florida City** also offers a number of good places to stay.

Coral Castle

28655 S Dixie Hwy • Mon–Thurs & Sun 8am–6pm, Fri & Sat 8am–8pm • $15, children 7–12 $7 • ☎ 305 248 6345, ⊕ coralcastle.com

The one essential stop in these parts is the **Coral Castle**, whose bulky coral-rock sculptures can be found about six miles northeast of Homestead, beside US-1, at the junction with SW 157 Avenue. Remarkably, these fantastic creations, whose delicate finish belies their imposing size, are the work of just one man – the enigmatic **Edward Leedskalnin**. Jilted in 1913 by his 16-year-old fiancée in Latvia, Leedskalnin spent seven years working his way across Europe, Canada and the US before buying an acre of land just south of Homestead. Using a profound – and self-taught – knowledge of weights and balances, he raised enormous hunks of coral rock from the ground, then used handmade tools fashioned from scrap to refine the blocks into chairs, tables and beds. It is thought that the castle was intended as a love nest to woo back his errant sweetheart. Leedskalnin died here in 1951.

You can wander around the slabs (listening to the 30min audio tour), sit on the hard but surprisingly comfortable chairs, swivel a nine-tonne gate with your pinkie, and admire the numerous coral representations of the moon and planets that reflect Leedskalnin's interest in astronomy and astrology; also on display is his 20ft-high telescope. But you won't be able to explain how the sculptures were made. No one ever saw the secretive Leedskalnin at work, or knows how, alone, he could have loaded 1100 tonnes of rock onto the rail-mounted truck that brought the pieces here in 1936.

Biscayne National Park

At the end of Canal Drive (328th St), east of US-1 in Homestead • Water section open 24hr • ☎ 305 230 7275, ⊕ nps.gov/bisc

While most people think of Key Largo as the entrance to the Florida Keys, the region actually begins offshore here at **Biscayne National Park**. The bulk of the park lies beneath the clear ocean waters, where stunning formations of living coral provide a habitat for shoals of brightly coloured fish and numerous other creatures too delicate to survive on their own (see p.112). If you're interested in watersports, summer

(May–Oct) is the **best time to visit** the park, when the water is warm and the reef at its most active. Conversely, if you're looking to visit the park's barrier islands, rangers recommend a winter trip (Nov–April), when the weather is cool and dry and the mosquitoes more manageable.

ARRIVAL AND INFORMATION

By bus From Miami, local buses #34, #35, #38, #70 and #344 head to Homestead ($2.25; ☎ 305 891 3131, ⓦ miamidade.gov/transit).
By car Homestead is about a 50min drive from downtown Miami.

HOMESTEAD AND AROUND

Biscayne National Park Visitor Center Convoy Point, 9700 SW 328th St (daily 9am–5pm; ☎ 305 230 7275, ⓦ nps.gov/bisc). The visitor centre lies at the end of a featureless road, Canal Drive (or 328th St), 9 miles from the US-1 turn-off.

ACCOMMODATION

Everglades International Hostel 20 SW 2nd Ave, Florida City ☎ 305 248 1122, ⓦ evergladeshostel.com. Ten miles east of the park you'll find this lush, inviting hostel, set on an acre of reclaimed natural hammock alive with mango and avocado trees. The friendly staff are dedicated to getting people into the Everglades, whether that means hooking canoes to your car (rentals $30/day) or securing spots on their ecotours, which range from kayaking trips to "wet walks" through the heart of the park (from $65). A swimmable waterfall, a tree house and pancake breakfasts sweeten the stay. Camping $18, dorms $28, doubles $75

Florida City Travelodge 409 SE 1st Ave, Florida City ☎ 305 248 9777, ⓦ tlflcity.com. Usefully located between the Keys, Miami and the Everglades, this mid-level hotel is one of the most comfortable places to stay in Florida City. Decent free breakfast, and a heated outdoor pool with tiki bar. $80
Hampton Inn 2855 NE 9th St, Homestead ☎ 305 257 7000, ⓦ homesteadhamptoninn.com. Plush, renovated hotel with all the trimmings: high thread-count linens, complimentary internet access, flat-screen TVs with cable, a large outdoor pool and a free hot breakfast. $120

EATING AND DRINKING

Black Point Ocean Grill 24775 SW 87th Ave, at SW 248th St, Homestead ☎ 305 258 3918, ⓦ blackpointoceangrill.com. Wear your flip-flops and order a bucket of "voodoo juice" at this lively marina-side restaurant. The food is good (try the smoked fish dip or the burger special, both around $9) but it's more about the casual Keys-y ambience and frequent live music. Mon–Thurs & Sun 11am–10pm, Fri & Sat 11am–1am.
Gator Grill 36650 SW 192nd Ave, Homestead ☎ 786 243 0620. Just around the bend from *Robert is Here* (see below), this pint-sized diner is a great place to sample Everglades treats like frogs' legs in butter sauce ($12.95) and terrific grilled gator ($9.95). It's the last restaurant you hit before entering the park, but even if it weren't, you should still make a point of stopping in. Daily 9am–6pm.
★**Robert is Here** 19200 SW 344th St, Homestead ☎ 305 246 1592, ⓦ robertishere.com. Legendary local fruit stand, serving creamy smoothies blended with whatever fruits are in season, though it's hard to beat the Key Lime milkshakes. Close to the eastern entrance of Everglades National Park. Daily 8am–7pm; closed Sept & Oct.

Rosita's Restaurante 199 W Palm Drive, Florida City ☎ 305 246 3114, ⓦ rositasmexican.com. Delicious Mexican dishes, each accompanied by creamy refried beans and tongue-lashing salsa. The decor's nothing fancy, but the real atmosphere comes from the radio blaring Spanish-language news and music. It's across the street from the hostel (see above). Daily 8.30am–9pm.
Royal Palm Grill 806 N Krome Ave, Homestead ☎ 305 246 5701, ⓦ royalpalmgrillfl.com. Located inside a pharmacy, this nostalgic diner dishes up home-cooked meals amid shelves of bandages and aspirin. A local favourite, it's very well priced – a stack of pancakes is only $3.25, and sandwiches and salads are $4–7. There's a new, expanded location with longer hours at 436 N Krome Ave. Mon–Fri 7am–4pm, Sat & Sun 7am–3pm.
Shiver's BBQ 28001 S Dixie Hwy, Homestead ☎ 305 248 2272, ⓦ shiversbbq.com. Crave-worthy barbecue joint that's been cranking out Florida's best pulled pork ($7.99), ribs ($12.99) and collard greens ($2) for over fifty years. You'll dream about its secret sauce. Mon–Thurs & Sun 11am–9pm, Fri & Sat 11am–10pm.

3

The
southeast

FORT LAUDERDALE BEACH

The southeast

Stretching from the fringes of northern Miami along nearly half of Florida's Atlantic shoreline, the southeast is the sun-soaked, subtropical Florida of popular imagination, with bodies bronzing on palm-dotted beaches as warm ocean waves lap idly against silky sands. With the exception of tranquil Lake Okeechobee, a prime fishing spot an hour inland and quite literally a world apart from the coastal settlements, the main attractions hug the ocean strip. The Gold Coast, the first fifty-odd miles of the southeast coast up to Palm Beach, lies deep within the sway of Miami and comprises back-to-back cities with little to tell them apart – although the largest, Fort Lauderdale, is certainly distinctive.

Its reputation for rowdy beach parties – stemming from years as a student Spring Break destination – is a thing of the past; the city has cultivated a cleaner-cut, sophisticated image, aided by an excellent art museum, an ambitious downtown improvement project and a wave of luxury oceanfront hotels. Further north, diminutive **Boca Raton** is renowned for its 1920s Mediterranean Revival buildings, as designed by the unconventional architect Addison Mizner. Ultimately, though, Mizner is best remembered for his work in **Palm Beach**, a city with a reputation as the bastion of multimillionaires, but which remains accessible to visitors on all budgets.

North of Palm Beach, the population thins, and nature asserts itself forcefully throughout the **Treasure Coast**. Here, rarely crowded beaches flank long, pine-coated barrier islands such as Jupiter and Hutchinson, which boast miles of untainted, rugged shoreline peaceful enough for sea turtles to use as nesting grounds.

GETTING AROUND FLORIDA'S SOUTHEAST

By car The scenic route along the southeast coast is Hwy-A1A, which sticks wherever possible to the oceanside of the Intracoastal Waterway. Beloved of Florida's boat owners, this stretch was formed when the rivers dividing the mainland from the barrier islands were joined and deepened during World War II to reduce the threat of submarine attack. When necessary, Hwy-A1A turns inland and links with the less picturesque US-1. The speediest road in the region, I-95, runs parallel to and about ten miles west of the coastline, and is a worthwhile route if you're in a hurry, although traffic can get quite heavy the closer you get to Miami.

By bus Frequent Greyhound connections link the bigger towns, and a few daily services run to the smaller communities. Local buses, plentiful from the edge of Miami to West Palm Beach, are nonexistent in the more rural Treasure Coast.

By train Along the Gold Coast, there's the option of the dirt-cheap Tri-Rail service, and Amtrak has two daily trains that run along the coast to West Palm Beach, inland to Okeechobee and Orlando and back to the coast at Jacksonville.

4

SPRING TRAINING AT PORT ST LUCIE

Highlights

❶ Fort Lauderdale The city's reputation as a haven for teens and retirees has all but disappeared, replaced by an upmarket image that, along with some lovely buildings and a fine museum, makes it an inviting destination. **See p.177**

❷ Boca Raton Resort and Club Be sure to tour this resort, one of the most intriguing designs by quirky architect Addison Mizner. **See p.189**

❸ Morikami Museum and Japanese Gardens You'll feel like you've been transported to Japan after stepping into an intricate tea ceremony here. **See p.193**

❹ Spring training If you're here in early spring, take in an exhibition baseball game at Jupiter, Fort Lauderdale or Port St Lucie. **See p.204**

❺ Hobe Sound National Wildlife Refuge This refuge on Jupiter Island, north of West Palm Beach, is an extraordinary sea-turtle nesting ground during the summer. **See p.205**

❻ Sebastian Inlet State Recreation Area Sixteen miles north of Vero Beach, this inlet challenges surfers with its roaring ocean breakers. **See p.212**

HIGHLIGHTS ARE MARKED ON THE MAP ON P.174

The Gold Coast

The widely admired beaches and towns occupying the fifty-mile commuter corridor north of Miami make the **GOLD COAST** one of the most heavily populated and touristy parts of the state. The sands sparkle, the nightlife rocks, and many of the communities have an assertively individualistic flavour.

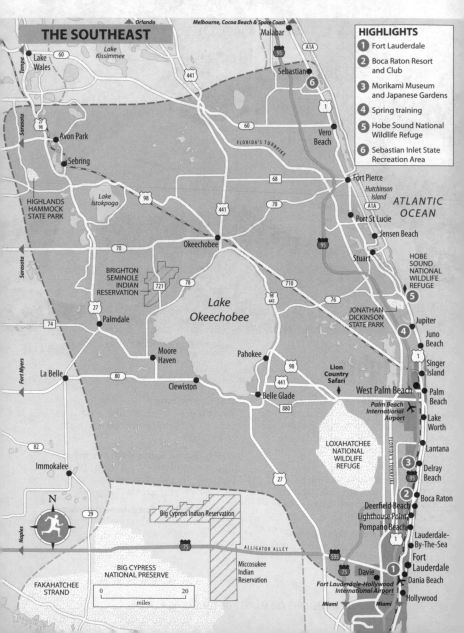

Hollywood

From Miami Beach, Hwy-A1A runs through undistinguished Hallandale Beach before reaching **HOLLYWOOD** – founded and named by a Californian in 1924 – a surprisingly diverse city with a wider beach and more laidback persona than the better-known and much larger Fort Lauderdale, ten miles north.

Hollywood Beach

2 miles east of downtown • Metered parking is available on the side streets off N Ocean Drive, or in two parking garages on Connecticut and Johnson sts, either location for $1.50/hr Mon–Thurs, $2/hr Fri–Sun

Hollywood Beach is by far the town's premier attraction (the beach area is also a wi-fi hotspot). If the sand and surf don't tempt you, allocate an hour to the 2.5-mile-long, pedestrian-only **Broadwalk**, parallel to Hwy-A1A (called Ocean Drive here), a brick-lined promenade where restaurants and cyclists enliven a casual amble. The best bars and restaurants face the beach north of the *Ramada Resort*.

Art and Culture Center of Hollywood

1650 Harrison St, just east of Young Circle • Tues–Fri 10am–5pm, Sat & Sun noon–4pm • $7 • ☎ 954 921 3274, ⊕ artandculturecenter.org

Downtown Hollywood, linked to the beach by Hollywood Boulevard (Hwy-820), offers plenty of bars and restaurants but little in the way of sights, though the temporary art exhibitions at the **Art and Culture Center of Hollywood** are worth a look – the centre also hosts dance performances, theatre and concerts.

ArtsPark

In the middle of Young Circle • ⊕ hollywoodfl.org

The ten-acre **ArtsPark** near downtown is really just a pleasant green space, and not reason enough to leave the beach unless it hosts a concert or event, such as a movie night or food truck festival; see the website for details.

ARRIVAL AND GETTING AROUND   HOLLYWOOD

By car The fastest way to get to and around Hollywood is I 95, which runs north–south about 10 miles west of the coast. If you've got time, take the scenic route, Hwy-A1A, which hugs the coast whenever possible.

By bus The closest Greyhound station is in Fort Lauderdale (see p.182). Local buses are run by Broward County Transit (☎ 954 357 8400, ⊕ broward.org/bct). Route #4 runs up and down Ocean Drive and through Young Circle; timetables are available from the Governmental Center (115 S Andrews Ave, at SW 2nd St), the Broward Central Bus Terminal at W Broward Ave and NW 1st St, and online. A bus pass ($4/day) allows unlimited travel on the buses throughout the county – otherwise it's $1.75 per journey, with no transfers.

By tram (trolley) The Hollywood Trolley (☎ 954 921 3551, ⊕ visithollywoodfl.org/trolley) runs both a beach

line and a downtown line around ArtsPark. Trams depart approximately every half-hour from over a dozen stops ($1 per ride; Wed, Thurs & Sun 10am–10pm, Fri & Sat 10am–11pm).

By train The Amtrak station (3001 Hollywood Blvd) is well linked to the rest of the east coast. To get to the beach from the Amtrak station take the Broward County bus #7 (☎ 954 357 8400, ⊕ broward.org/bct) down Hollywood Blvd to N Federal Hwy and switch to the #4. Fares are $1.75; an all-day pass is $4 and a weekly pass is $16.

The Tri-Rail runs from West Palm Beach to Miami International Airport. Fares are calculated using zones, and range from $6.90 ($5 Sat & Sun) for the full distance, to $2.50 between stations ($5 Sat & Sun).

Destinations Boca Raton (45min); Delray Beach (49min); Fort Lauderdale (17min); West Palm Beach (1hr 15min).

INFORMATION

Tourist information Pick up information from either the Hollywood Office of Tourism, 330 N Federal Hwy (Mon–Fri 8am–5pm; ☎ 954 924 2980), or the office on the beach at

300 Connecticut St (daily 9am–6pm; ☎ 954 924 2936, ⊕ visithollywoodfl.org).

ACCOMMODATION

Reasonably priced motels line Hollywood's oceanside streets, but you'll save a few dollars by staying further inland; try the hotels along US-1, known here as Federal Highway.

Atlantic Sands 310–318 Hayes St ☎954 921 4123, ⓦatlanticsandsfl.com. One block from the Broadwalk, this charming, family-owned motel has comfortable one-bedroom suites with full kitchens. There's also free wi-fi, a group BBQ area and free use of beach chairs, umbrellas and beach toys for the kids. $145

★**Manta Ray Inn** 1715 S Surf Rd ☎954 921 9666, ⓦmantarayinn.com. The one- or two-bedroom suites here are great value, with the hotel right on the beach and all rooms equipped with kitchens and bright rattan furniture. Free parking. $149

Ocean Inn 3405 N Ocean Drive ☎954 923 0313, ⓦoceaninnhollywood.com. Leafy, relaxing B&B just a few minutes from the Broadwalk. The twelve bright rooms range from efficiencies to studios with full kitchenettes. $99

Riptide Hotel 2300 N Surf Rd ☎954 921 7667, ⓦriptidehotel.com. This laidback motel right on the Broadwalk has comfortable rooms with full efficiency kitchens, free parking and wi-fi, and a hopping tiki bar. From $179

EATING AND DRINKING

What it lacks in terms of sights, downtown Hollywood more than makes up for with its restaurants and nightlife, especially around Harrison Street and Hollywood Boulevard, west of US-1 and Young Circle. You'll also find plenty of action along the Broadwalk at the beach.

★**The LeTub Saloon** 1100 N Ocean Drive ☎954 921 9425, ⓦtheletub.com. This local favourite in an old petrol station sits on the Intracoastal Waterway – perfect for sunset dining. The burgers here are outstanding, as is the Key lime pie. Sandwiches from $9. Mon–Thurs & Sun 11am–1am, Fri & Sat noon–2am.

Lola's on Harrison 2032 Harrison St ☎954 927 9851, ⓦlolasonharrison.com. Offers creative main dishes like Coca-Cola BBQ beef ribs and a smoked pork chop with *chimichurri*. Mains from $16. Tues–Thurs 5–9pm, Fri & Sat 5–10pm.

Mama Mia Italian Ristorante 1818 S Young Circle ☎954 923 0555, ⓦmiagrill.com. Specializing in some of the best Italian food in the area: the antipasti plates are

generous and the chicken *cacciatore* delicious. Mains from $15. Daily 11.30am–midnight.

Sardelli Italian Steakhouse 331 Van Buren St ☎954 921 8331. This elegant steakhouse is Hollywood's go-to spot for a special evening. Steaks aren't cheap – the bone-in New York strip is $48 – but they're melt-in-your-mouth tender. The menu also features a variety of delicious pastas from $14 for a half-portion. Mon–Sat 5–11pm.

Taco Beach Shack 334 Arizona St ☎954 920 6523. This popular spot right on Hollywood Beach serves creative cuisine, as well as the Mexican classics. Try the Korean short rib & *kimchi* slaw taco, or the cheesy grilled chicken enchilada for something more traditional. Tacos from $3.75. Daily 11.30am–2am.

Dania Beach

Named for the Danish settlers who arrived in the area in the late nineteenth century, there's not much of note to keep you in the town of **Dania Beach** save for a few pseudo-English antique shops on US-1. The beach is lovely, however, and there's a long fishing pier from which to watch the sunrise.

John U. Lloyd Beach State Park

6503 N Ocean Drive • Daily 8am–sunset; turtle awareness programme June & July Wed & Fri evenings • Cars $4 for one person, $6 for two or more, pedestrians and cyclists $2 • ☎954 923 2833

The sands and coastal vegetation of the **John U. Lloyd Beach State Park** are by far Dania's prime asset. Sitting on a peninsula jutting out into the entrance to the shipping terminal of Port Everglades, the 251-acre park offers three nature trails, one of them weaving through its mangrove, sea grape and guava trees. The main attraction is the 2.5-mile **beach** – it has a wilder, unspoiled feel here, rare on the Gold Coast (though marred somewhat by the constant roar of jets from the nearby airport). In June and July the park runs a **sea turtle awareness programme**, when every Wednesday and Friday evening rangers host campfire talks and a twenty-minute slide show on turtles – if a nesting Loggerhead is spotted nearby, you'll be able to get a look at the real thing (from a distance). Reservations are essential, so call the park for details.

Dania Jai-Alai
301 E Dania Beach Blvd, Hwy-A1A • Live games Tues & Sat noon, 3.30pm & 7pm, Mon & Wed–Fri 7pm • Free • ☎ 954 920 1511, ⓦ betdania.com

Downtown Dania is best known for its jai-alai court, or fronton, the second oldest in the US (after Miami's). At **Dania Jai-Alai**, spectators can bet on or just watch the ancient Basque sport in all its fast-paced glory from a comfortable indoor showplace.

IGFA Fishing Hall of Fame & Museum
300 Gulf Stream Way • Mon–Sat 10am–6pm, Sun noon–6pm • $10 • ☎ 954 922 4212, ⓦ igfa.org

Gawk at live fish in Outdoor World's massive aquarium or, right next door, at the **IGFA Fishing Hall of Fame & Museum**'s world-record-setting catches, where you can also test your skills with virtual-reality fishing exhibits.

ARRIVAL AND DEPARTURE   DANIA BEACH

By car There are no long-distance buses or trains in Dania Beach; by car, it's accessible along the usual routes: I-95 if you're in a hurry or Hwy-A1A for the beach-bound.

EATING

Grampa's Bakery & Restaurant 17 SW 1st St ☎ 954 923 2163. The best breakfast spot in town, this long-time Dania fixture serves fantastic biscuits and gravy alongside all sorts of delectable pastries. Serves lunch and dinner as well. Breakfast mains from $8. Mon 6.30am–3pm, Tues–Sat 6.30am–9pm, Sun 8am–4pm.

Islamorada Fish Company 220 Gulf Stream Way, just off I-95 on Hwy-818 ☎ 954 927 7737, ⓦ restaurants .basspro.com/fishcompany. If you're in need of sustenance, head to large, bustling *Islamorada Fish Company*, adjacent to the Bass Pro Shops Outdoor World, with some of the freshest (and biggest) sushi imaginable alongside the usual seafood dishes. Main dishes from $15. Daily 11am–10pm.

Fort Lauderdale

A thinly populated riverside trading camp at the start of the twentieth century, **FORT LAUDERDALE** came to be known as "the Venice of America" when its mangrove swamps were fashioned into slender canals during the 1920s.

Beginning in the 1930s, intercollegiate swimming contests drew the nation's youth here, a fact seized on by the 1960 teen flick *Where the Boys Are*, which instantly made Fort Lauderdale the country's premier Spring Break destination. Hundreds of thousands of students – around 350,000 in 1985 alone – congregated around the seven miles of sand for a ten-week frenzy of underage drinking and lascivious excess. The students also brought ten weeks of traffic chaos, and ultimately proved a deterrent to regular tourists, so in 1986 the local authorities enacted strict laws to restrict boozing and wild behaviour. Fortunately, it worked and the city began to forge a new identity.

Fort Lauderdale has since emerged as an affluent business and cultural centre dominated by a mix of wealthy retirees and affluent yuppies keen to play up the city's status as a hub for international yachting, and is increasingly popular among upmarket travellers. You'll spend most of your time in the **Riverwalk Arts & Entertainment District**, along **Las Olas Boulevard** or on the **beach**.

Downtown Fort Lauderdale
Downtown Fort Lauderdale boasts an outstanding modern art museum and the ambitious **Riverwalk Arts & Entertainment District**, bringing together art centres and a number of restored older buildings. The area is anchored by the one-and-a-half-mile **Riverwalk** along the north bank of the New River, which starts near **Stranahan House**, skirts the Las Olas Riverfront entertainment complex and ends at the Broward Center for the Performing Arts (see p.185).

FORT LAUDERDALE

▮ ACCOMMODATION

Alhambra Beach Resort	8
The Atlantic Resort & Spa	6
Birch Patio Motel	4
By-Eddy Motel & Apartments	1
Cocobelle Resort	3
La Casa Del Mar	7
Lago Mar Resort and Club	11
The Pillars Hotel	10
Riverside Hotel	12
Royal Palms Resort	5
snooze	9
Victoria Park	2

▮ BARS & CLUBS

America's Backyard	10
American Social	12
Elbo Room	7
Fish Tales on 33rd	1
The Poorhouse	11
Riverside Market	8
Stache 1920s Drinking Den	9

▮ GAY BARS & CLUBS

Alibi	4
Bill's Filling Station	5
Cubby Hole	6
Hunters Nightclub	3
Village Pub	2

● CAFÉS & RESTAURANTS

Bimini Boatyard	11	Rustic Inn	12
Canyon Southwest Café	3	Southport Raw Bar	10
Casablanca Café	5	Steak 954	4
Coconuts	8	Sublime	1
Johnny V Restaurant	14	Sushi Rock	7
Red Cow Restaurant	2	Tap 42	9
Rocco's Tacos	6	Tarpon Bend	13

Stranahan House

335 SE 6th Ave • Entry by tour only, daily at 1pm, 2pm & 3pm; 45min–1hr • $12 • ☎ 954 524 4726, ⓦ stranahanhouse.org

For a reminder of early Fort Lauderdale life, start at the carefully restored **Stranahan House**, just south of the *Cheesecake Factory* on Las Olas Boulevard. Erected in 1901, with high ceilings, narrow windows and wide verandas, the city's oldest surviving structure is a fine example of Florida frontier style, and served as the home and trading post of the turn-of-the-twentieth-century settler Frank Stranahan, hailed as the father of Fort Lauderdale. Stranahan, who established his first trading post on the New River in 1893, was a prosperous dealer in otter pelts, egret plumes and alligator hides, which he purchased from the Seminoles who traded along the river. Financially devastated by the late-1920s Florida property crash, Stranahan drowned himself in the same waterway.

Nova Southeastern University Museum of Art

1 E Las Olas Blvd • Tues, Wed, Fri & Sat 11am–5pm, Thurs 11am–8pm, Sun noon–5pm • $10; special exhibitions extra • ☎ 954 525 5500, ⓦ moafl.org • A short stroll from Stranahan House along the Riverwalk; cut across Huizenga Plaza before you reach Andrews Ave

In a postmodern structure shaped like a slice of pie, the **NSU Museum of Art** provides ample space and light for the best art collection in the state, with an emphasis on modern painting and sculpture.

The museum features frequent large-scale, high-profile exhibitions; highlights of the 6000-piece permanent collection are drawn from the museum's hoard of works from the avant-garde **CoBrA** movement, which began in 1948 with a group of artists from Copenhagen, Brussels and Amsterdam (hence the acronym). CoBrA's art is typified by bright, expressionistic canvases combining playful innocence with deep emotional power. Important names to look for include Asger Jorn, Carl-Henning Pedersen and Karel Appel. The museum also houses the largest collection in the US of works by early twentieth-century American Impressionists. The Glackens wing also includes a period-outfitted drawing room.

Riverwalk Arts & Entertainment District

The most enticing part of downtown begins one block west of the Museum of Art, an area collectively dubbed the **Riverwalk Arts & Entertainment District**, with plentiful places to eat (see p.183). **Las Olas Riverfront** dominates the first section, a mall and entertainment complex in faux Spanish Colonial style, which has never really taken off – it's nevertheless a good place to pick up a water taxi or boat cruise (see box, p.180).

Museum of History

231 SW 2nd Ave • Tues–Sun noon–4pm • $10, includes tour of King-Cromartie House • ☎ 954 463 4431, ⓦ oldfortlauderdale.org

For a glimpse into the city's past, keep walking west along the river to the **Old Fort Lauderdale Village** historic district, at the centre of which is the **Museum of History** on the Riverwalk. The museum occupies the former **New River Inn**, completed in 1905 and the first hotel built in the area to serve Flagler's railway. Exhibits inside tackle the early history of the region – including displays on the Seminole Wars and the modern history of the city from the 1890s to the 1960s.

King-Cromartie House and Philemon Bryan House

King-Cromartie House 229 SW 2nd Ave • Tours Tues–Sun 1pm, 2pm & 3pm • Entry with Museum of History ticket (see above)
Philemon Bryan House 227 SW 2nd Ave

Entry to the Museum of History (see above) includes a tour of the next-door **King-Cromartie House**, built in 1907, where you'll find such futuristic-at-the-time fixtures as the first indoor bathroom in Fort Lauderdale.

Beyond here, the 1905 **Philemon Bryan House** was once the home of the Bryan family, who constructed many buildings in this area, and is now the home of the Historical Society's administrative offices.

WATER TAXIS AND BOAT TOURS OF FORT LAUDERDALE

Though the nickname "**Venice of America**" is a little misleading, you haven't really seen Fort Lauderdale unless you explore its miles of waterways lined with opulent mansions and million-dollar yachts.

WATER TAXIS

Try **Water Taxi** (boats run daily 10am–midnight; ☏954 467 6677, ⓦwatertaxi.com), which operates small covered boats that will pick up and deliver you almost anywhere along the water, from the restaurants near East Oakland Park Boulevard down to the 17th Street Causeway and west to the Las Olas Riverfront and Riverwalk area. These taxis are the best way to see the city, especially because the friendly captains often give unofficial tours, dishing the gossip behind the multimillion-dollar homes and yachts along the way. An **all-day pass** with unlimited usage costs $22; if you're using the taxi after 5pm only, the fare is $15. Water Taxi also runs to Hollywood Beach as far south as the *Crowne Plaza Hollywood Beach Hotel*.

TOURS AND CRUISES

If you'd prefer a more structured **water tour** of the city and its Millionaire's Row, try **Riverfront Cruises**, Las Olas Riverfront at 300 SW 1st Ave (☏954 463 3220, ⓦanticipation.com; $23), which offers enlightening daily 1hr 30min tours departing at 11am, 1pm, 3pm and 5pm; alcoholic drinks are included. For a bit of kitschy fun try the **Jungle Queen Riverboat**, 801 Seabreeze Blvd at Hwy-A1A (☏954 462 5596, ⓦjunglequeen.com), an old-style steamboat that makes daily cruises at 10am and 1.45pm ($21.50 for 1hr 30min cruise; $23.95 for 3hr cruise).

4

ABOVE WATER TAXI, FORT LAUDERDALE

Hoch Heritage Center

219 SW 2nd Ave • Mon–Fri 10am–4pm • Free

Close to SW Second Street, also known as Himmarshee Street, the **Hoch Heritage Center** rounds off the stock of historic buildings in the area, though it serves primarily as a research centre and there's little to see inside for the casual visitor.

Museum of Discovery & Science

401 SW 2nd St • Mon–Sat 10am–5pm, Sun noon–6pm • Museum $14, kids 2–12 $12; museum & film $19, kids $15; film only $9, kids $7 • ☎ 954 467 6637, ⓦ mods.org

Two blocks west of the historic district, the **Museum of Discovery & Science** is among the best of Florida's many child-oriented science museums, where exhibits present the basics of science in numerous ingenious and entertaining ways. The new EcoDiscovery Center has doubled the museum's space, and offers five new exhibit areas, including the Everglades Boat Adventure and Prehistoric Florida. The museum also contains a towering 3-D IMAX **film theatre** that screens daily (check admissions booth for times).

Las Olas Boulevard

Downtown Fort Lauderdale is linked to the beach by **Las Olas Boulevard** – the city's upmarket shopping strip, with no shortage of fashion, art and dining options – and by the canal-side Las Olas Isles, where residents park their cars on one side of their mega-buck properties and moor their luxury yachts on the other. Once across the arching Intracoastal Waterway Bridge, about two miles on, you're within sight of the ocean and the mood changes appreciably. Where Las Olas Boulevard ends, **beachside Fort Lauderdale** begins – T-shirt and swimwear shops suddenly spill out between clusters of restaurants and hotels, punctuating over 23 miles of "Blue Wave" beaches (certified as clean, safe and environmentally friendly).

Fort Lauderdale beach

Along the seafront, **Fort Lauderdale Beach Boulevard** (also known as Atlantic Boulevard), which once bore the brunt of heavy Spring Break partying, underwent a multimillion-dollar facelift in 2005. Only a few beachfront bars bear any trace of the carousing of the past, though the sands, flanked by graciously ageing coconut palms and an attractive promenade, are by no means deserted or dull: joggers, rollerbladers and cyclists create a buzzing beach scene, and a small number of whooping students still turn up each spring.

International Swimming Hall of Fame

1 Hall of Fame Drive • Mon–Fri 9am–5pm, Sat & Sun 9am–2pm • $8 • ☎ 954 462 6536, ⓦ ishof.org

A short way south of the Las Olas Boulevard junction, the **International Swimming Hall of Fame** salutes aquatic sports with a collection that even non-swimmers will enjoy. The two floors are stuffed with medals, trophies and press cuttings pertaining to the heroes and heroines of swimming, diving and many other, more obscure watery activities.

Bonnet House Museum & Gardens

900 N Birch Rd • Tues–Sun 9am–4pm; last tour 3.30pm • $20, or $10 grounds only, tram tour $2 • ☎ 954 563 5393, ⓦ bonnethouse.org

Amid the high-rise hotels dominating the beachside area, Fort Lauderdale's pre-condo landscape can be viewed in the jungle-like 35-acre grounds of **Bonnet House Museum & Gardens**, a few minutes' walk off Fort Lauderdale Beach Boulevard. The house and its tranquil surroundings – including a swan-filled pond and resident monkeys – were designed and built by Chicago muralist Frederic Clay Bartlett in 1920. The tours of the plantation-style abode highlight Bartlett's eccentric passion for art and architecture – and for collecting ornamental animals, dozens of which fill nearly all of the thirty rooms.

Hugh Taylor Birch State Park

3109 E Sunrise Blvd • Daily 8am–sunset; Segway tours daily 10am, noon, 2pm & 4pm • Cars $4 for one person, $6 for two or more, pedestrians and cyclists $2 • ☎ 954 564 4521 • Canoe rentals $5.30/hr, kayaks $10/hr in the lagoon, $20/hr in the ocean; bike rental $12.50/hr, $25/half-day, $35/day; paddleboards $30/hr, $60/4hr; Segway tours $50–100; beach chairs $10/day, beach umbrellas $15/day, ☎ 954 235 5082, ⓦ mcruzrentals.com

The native forest of the **Hugh Taylor Birch State Park** forms a shady backdrop for canoeing on the park's mile-long freshwater lagoon. You can **rent bikes** and take guided **Segway** tours from the park concession, M. Cruz Rentals, at the beach entrance at A1A.

ARRIVAL AND DEPARTURE FORT LAUDERDALE

By plane Fort Lauderdale International Airport (☎ 866 435 9355, ⓦ broward.org/airport) is around 5 miles south of downtown. If you're renting a car, grab a free shuttle bus to the airport's Rental Car Center, an indoor, four-level complex that's home to nearly all of the major rental companies. Alternatively, you can take a taxi or bus #1 ($1.75) into the city.

By car Known as Federal Highway, US-1 runs through the centre of downtown Fort Lauderdale, 3 miles inland from the coast. Just south of downtown, Hwy-A1A veers east off US-1 along SE 17th Street Causeway and runs through ocean-side Fort Lauderdale as Seabreeze Blvd/Beach Blvd. You'll find metered parking everywhere ($1.25/hr), although there's now the option of pay-by-phone parking

on ☎ 888 680 7275. The Government Center Parking Garage on SW 2nd St, near the historic district, charges $2 for the first hour, $1/hr thereafter.

By bus The Greyhound bus station is at 515 NE 3rd St (☎ 954 764 6551).

Destinations Daytona Beach (3 daily; 6hr 25min–11hr 20min); Delray Beach (2 daily; 50min); Fort Pierce (4 daily; 2hr 15min–2hr 45min); Miami (12 daily; 45–55min); Orlando (9 daily; 3hr 30 min–9hr 15min); West Palm Beach (5 daily; 55min–1hr 25min).

By train The Amtrak and Tri-Rail station is 2 miles west of the bus station at 200 SW 21st Terrace, linked to the centre by regular buses #9, #22 and #81 ($1.75).

GETTING AROUND AND INFORMATION

By boat Water taxis and boat tours are a fun way of seeing the city (see box, p.180).

By bus Broward County Transit (☎ 954 357 8400, ⓦ broward.org/bct), the local bus service, runs a handy route (#11; every 30min) along Las Olas Blvd between downtown Fort Lauderdale and the beach; timetables are available from Governmental Center (115 S Andrews Ave, at SW 2nd St), the Broward Central Bus Terminal at W Broward Ave and NW 1st St, and online. A bus pass ($4/day) allows unlimited travel on the buses throughout the county – otherwise it's $1.75 per journey, with no transfers.

By Sun Trolley A great way to get around town is the Sun Trolley (☎ 954 761 3543, ⓦ suntrolley.com), which runs a loop downtown (Mon–Fri 7.30am–6pm; every 15–20min; free), between downtown and the beaches (daily 9.30am–6.30pm), and along Las Olas Blvd (Fri–Mon 9.30am–6.30pm; both routes every 15–20min; $1, or $3 all-day pass). You can hail it anywhere along the route.

Tourist information The centrally located Greater Fort Lauderdale Convention & Visitors Bureau sits at 101 NE 3rd Ave, Suite 100 (Mon–Fri 8.30am–5pm; ☎ 954 765 4466, ⓦ sunny.org).

ACCOMMODATION

Options for staying in downtown Fort Lauderdale are relatively limited, but the scores of motels clustered between the Intracoastal Waterway and the ocean can be good value. The beachfront has the pick of the luxury resorts, with the *Ritz Carlton Ft. Lauderdale* leading the way on style; rates begin around $519 in peak season, so come during off-season for the best bargains.

★**Alhambra Beach Resort** 3021 Alhambra St ☎ 954 525 7601, ⓦ alhambrabeachresort.com. Tucked onto a side street just steps from the sand, this cheery resort offers a variety of rooms, from small but immaculate hotel rooms to a two-bedroom apartment with a full kitchen. There's a small pool, as well as free internet and continental breakfast. Doubles **$119**, apartment **$199**

The Atlantic Resort & Spa 601 N Fort Lauderdale Beach Blvd ☎ 954 567 8020, ⓦ atlantichotelfl.com. This

chic boutique hotel facing the ocean features elegant, spacious rooms and suites, all with an ocean or Intracoastal Waterway view. There's also a luxurious spa, an oceanfront pool and a superb restaurant, *Beauty & the Feast*. **$260**

Birch Patio Motel 617 N Birch Rd ☎ 954 563 9540, ⓦ birchpatio.com. Superb value, a short walk from the beach. Standard doubles are comfy and clean, efficiencies have kitchens and a lot more space. Extras include a small swimming pool, free parking, coin-operated washer and dryer, and internet. $\underline{\$65}$

By-Eddy Motel and Apartments 1021 NE 13th Ave ☎954 764 7555, ⓦbyeddymotel.com. This reasonably priced hotel sits about halfway between Las Olas Blvd and the beach. There's a heated pool, free wi-fi, and all sixteen rooms feature kitchens. $\underline{\$84}$

Cocobelle Resort 2831 Vistamar St ☎954 565 5790, ⓦcocobelleresort.com. Two blocks from the beach, this hotel is a real bargain, with leafy tropical gardens, a tranquil pool and bright, beautifully decorated rooms with tiled floors, free wi-fi and microwave. $\underline{\$129}$

La Casa Del Mar 3003 Granada St ☎954 467 2037, ⓦlacasadelmar.com. This charming gay-friendly hotel was completely redone a few years ago; rooms feature plush beds with crisp linens, flat-screen TVs and kitchenettes. There's also free wi-fi and parking. $\underline{\$119}$

Lago Mar Resort and Club 1700 S Ocean Lane ☎855 209 5677, ⓦlagomar.com. A luxury resort located a little away from the action, with two pools, several restaurants and bars, a full-service spa, and its own private patch of sand. $\underline{\$325}$

★**The Pillars Hotel** 111 N Birch Rd ☎954 467 9639, ⓦpillarshotel.com. Quiet, intimate British-colonial-style hotel with plush rooms, antique furniture, lush gardens and a pool, sitting just a block from the ocean on the Intracoastal. $\underline{\$325}$

Riverside Hotel 620 E Las Olas Blvd ☎954 467 0671, ⓦriversidehotel.com. Built in 1936, the rooms at this comfortable option could use some updating, but the location in the heart of the action downtown on Las Olas can't be beat. If you'd like a quieter room, request one at the back. $\underline{\$249}$

Royal Palms Resort 717 Breakers Ave ☎954 564 6444, ⓦroyalpalms.com. This chic hotel was until recently a clothing-optional enclave for gay men, but has started welcoming women (and guests who prefer to remain clothed.) There's a heated pool, with a poolside bar and spa. Rooms come with Frette linens, wi-fi, flat-screen TVs, iPod docking stations and rain showers in the bathroom. $\underline{\$139}$

★**snooze** 205 N Ft. Lauderdale Beach Blvd ☎954 761 9933, ⓦtakeasnooze.com. There aren't a lot of frills at this oceanfront property – no pool and no phones in the immaculate, spartan rooms, but there is free parking, free wi-fi and use of beach chairs and umbrellas. There's also a budget room with bunk beds. Doubles $\underline{\$74.50}$, bunk room $\underline{\$44.50}$

Victoria Park 855 NE 20th Ave ☎800 926 2285, ⓦthevictoriaparkhotel.com. Within the charming, bungalow-filled Victoria Park neighbourhood is this boutique hotel near the Intracoastal Waterway. The 31 modern rooms are tastefully decorated, and there's also a heated pool in the lush courtyard and free wi-fi. $\underline{\$164}$

EATING

Fort Lauderdale has many affordable, enjoyable **restaurants** featuring everything from Asian creations to home-made conch chowder. The best and most convenient places tend to be grouped on Las Olas Boulevard and along the beachfront.

LAS OLAS BOULEVARD AND AROUND

Johnny V Restaurant 625 E Las Olas Blvd ☎954 761 7920, ⓦjohnnyvlasolas.com. Trendy, upmarket creative American restaurant serving excellent wine and food from local celebrity chef Johnny Vinczencz, such as Lobster, Lobster, Lobster (sherried lobster bisque, baby chilled lobster roll, lobster-crab cake; $18). Mon–Thurs & Sun 11.30am–3pm & 5–11pm, Fri & Sat 11.30am–3pm & 5pm–midnight.

Red Cow Restaurant 1025 N Federal Hwy ☎954 652 1524, ⓦredcowftl.com. Carnivores will not be disappointed at this meat-centric spot, winner of multiple "best barbecue" awards, with the likes of Carolina pulled-pork sandwich ($11) and Texas-style smoked brisket sandwich ($12). Most mains from $15. Mon–Sat 11.30am–10pm, Sun 9.30am–9.30pm.

★**Rocco's Tacos** 1313 E Las Olas Blvd ☎954 524 9550, ⓦroccostacos.com. The crowd noise at this see-and-be-seen Tex-Mex spot on Las Olas can be deafening, but only adds to the party atmosphere. There are eleven different margaritas on offer and the house speciality guacamole (prepared tableside) is to die for. Mains from $13.50. Mon–Thurs & Sun 11am–2am, Fri 11.30am–3am, Sat 11am–3am.

Sushi Rock 1515 E Las Olas Blvd ☎954 462 5541. Don't be put off by the neon lights and dark interior: this is a cool, rock'n'roll-inspired café with good sushi and other Japanese food on the funky menu. Mains around $12. Mon–Thurs & Sun 11.30am–10.30pm, Fri & Sat 11.30am–11.30pm.

Tarpon Bend 200 SW 2nd St ☎954 523 3233, ⓦtarponbend.com. Popular lunch spot, serving good burgers and other standard American grill-type food – best known for its happy-hour cocktails (from 4pm), and handy location near the museum. Sandwiches and burgers from $10.50. Mon & Tues 11.30am–midnight, Wed–Sat 11.30am–3am, Sun 11.30am–11pm.

THE BEACH AND INTRACOASTAL WATERWAY

★**Canyon Southwest Café** 1818 E Sunrise Blvd ☎954 765 1950, ⓦcanyonfl.com. This extremely hip restaurant offers a sophisticated, modern take on Southwestern, Mexican and Asian cuisines; expect dishes like Masala-dusted venison medallions and beef tenderloin burritos (mains from $27). Daily 5–10.30pm.

4

Casablanca Café 3049 Alhambra St ☎954 764 3500, ⓦcasablancacafeonline.com. Great atmosphere and excellent beachfront location, with an enticing menu of Mediterranean-influenced American food like lime-coriander (cilantro) fish tacos and Moroccan kebabs. There's also live music every night. Main dishes from $20. Daily 11.30am–11pm.

Coconuts 429 Seabreeze Blvd ☎954 525 2421, ⓦcoconutsfortlauderdale.com. Just steps from the beach, this long-time favourite serves up delicious seafood dishes such as lobster rolls and conch fritters; the lemon pan-seared chicken is a good alternative for non-fish fans. Mains from $17. Mon–Sat 11.30am–10pm, Sun 10am–10pm.

Steak 954 401 N Fort Lauderdale Beach Blvd (inside the W hotel) ☎954 615 1431, ⓦsteak954.com. Hands down the best steak in Fort Lauderdale, served in a chic, modern dining room – but it doesn't come cheap. An 8oz fillet will set you back $39, a dry-aged New York Strip $47. They also serve breakfast and a tasty brunch (try the short rib Benedict) for considerably less cash. Mon–Thurs 7–11am, 11.30am–2.30pm & 5.30–10pm, Fri 7–11am, 11.30am–2.30pm & 5.30–11pm, Sat 7am–3pm & 5.30–11pm, Sun 7am–3pm & 5.30–10pm.

Sublime 1431 N Federal Hwy ☎954 414 8333, ⓦsublimerestaurant.com. This 100-percent vegan restaurant may not serve meat, but it's not short on flavour. Try the mushroom ravioli with cashew cream and the decadent chocolate cake. Main courses from $15. Tues–Sun 5.30–10pm.

SOUTH FORT LAUDERDALE

★**Bimini Boatyard** 1555 SE 17th St ☎954 525 7400, ⓦbiminiboatyard.com. Well-prepared and -presented salads and seafood, served in a great waterfront location with a patio. Burgers and sandwiches from $11, and dinner mains from $15. Mon–Thurs 11.30am–10pm, Fri & Sat 11.30am–10.30pm, Sun 11am–10pm.

Rustic Inn 4331 Ravenswood Rd ☎954 584 1637, ⓦrusticinn.com. At this ultra-casual crabhouse, on a waterway near the airport, crack open mountains of delicious, steamed soft-shell crabs onto newspaper-covered tables (crab sampler $48). Mon–Sat 11.30am–10.45pm, Sun noon–9pm.

Southport Raw Bar 1536 Cordova Rd ☎954 525 2526, ⓦsouthportrawbar.com. Boisterous local bar offering succulent crustaceans and well-prepared fish dishes at inexpensive prices (shellfish baskets from $6, fresh fish from $9.70). There's an open deck on the water too. Mon–Thurs & Sun 11am–2am, Fri & Sat 11am–3am.

★**Tap 42** 1411 S Andrews Ave ☎954 463 4900, ⓦtap42.com. This hopping gastropub is popular for its bottomless brunch, where you can drink as many Bloody Marys or mimosas as you can hold for $15, but don't overlook the fantastic dinner menu either, filled with thoughtful craft burgers and favourites such as shrimp mac and cheese. There's also a stellar craft beer list. Burgers from $12.50. Mon–Thurs 11.30am–11pm, Fri 11.30am–midnight, Sat 11am–midnight, Sun 11am–11.30pm.

DRINKING AND NIGHTLIFE

In addition to the **bars** listed below, some of the restaurants, particularly *Tap42* and *Tarpon Bend*, are also notable drinking spots. You should also check out **SunTrust Sunday Jazz Brunch** at Riverwalk Park on the first Sunday of each month, when crowds gather for cocktails and snacks sold at food stalls, serenaded by live music (11am–2pm). In general, you'll find more locals partying along Himmarshee Street in the historic district, while tourists tend to stick to the beach.

BARS AND CLUBS

America's Backyard 100 SW 3rd Ave ☎954 449 1025, ⓦmyamericasbackyard.com. This outdoor bar in the Himmarshee St district attracts a young, vibrant crowd. There's often live music and great drink specials most nights. Thurs 10pm–4am, Fri 5pm–4am, Sat 8pm–4am.

American Social 721 E Las Olas Blvd ☎954 764 7005, ⓦamericansocialbar.com. The hottest new bar on Las Olas features comfortable seating, pour-it-yourself craft beers on tap and tasty cocktails. There's also a menu of flatbreads and appetizers should you get peckish from all the beer. Mon–Wed 11.30am–1am, Thurs & Fri 11.30am–2am, Sat 11am–3am, Sun 11am–midnight.

Elbo Room 241 S Fort Lauderdale Beach Blvd ☎954 463 4615, ⓦelboroom.com. This former Spring Break favourite, made famous by the film *Where the Boys Are*, is now a friendly, no-frills beach bar with live bands and a good happy hour. Mon 5pm–2am, Tues–Thurs & Sun 11am–1am, Fri & Sat 11am–2am.

Fish Tales on 33rd 3355 NE 33rd St ☎954 689 2344,

EVENT LISTINGS IN FORT LAUDERDALE

Many bars double as live venues for rock, jazz and blues bands; to find out who's playing where, check the events calendar at ⓦbroward.org/arts, pick up the free *New Times* (ⓦbrowardpalmbeach.com) from newsstands (or just check the highly informative website), or consult the "Showtime" segment of the Friday edition of the local *Sun Sentinel* newspaper.

GAY AND LESBIAN FORT LAUDERDALE

Fort Lauderdale has been one of gay America's favourite holiday haunts for years and has been called San Francisco by the Sea. Like the rest of Fort Lauderdale, the scene has quietened down considerably over the years, but there's still plenty going on. For more **information**, contact the Pride Center at Equality Park at 2040 Dixie Hwy (Mon–Fri 10am–10pm, Sat & Sun noon–5pm; ☎954 463 9005, ⓦpridecenterflorida.org); pick up a copy of *HOTspots! Magazine* (ⓦhotspotsmagazine.com) around town, or a *Rainbow Vacation Planner* from the Convention and Visitors Bureau. For gay-friendly **accommodation**, *La Casa del Mar* (see p.183) and *Royal Palms Resort* (see p.183) are your best bet.

ⓦfishtaleson33rd.com. This local favourite restaurant and bar in North Fort Lauderdale offers an outdoor patio, nightly live entertainment and well-made cocktails. Mon–Fri 11am–2am, Sat 11am–3am, Sun noon–2am.

The Poorhouse 110 SW 3rd Ave ☎954 522 5145, ⓦpoorhousebar.com. This divey joint in the Himmarshee area offers a great beer selection and live music (Thurs–Sun). Daily 8pm–4am.

Riverside Market 608 SW 12th Ave ☎954 358 8333, ⓦtheriversidemarket.com. This neighbourhood joint offers over 550 craft beers, as well as a selection of unique wines and soft drinks. There are couches inside and comfy, dog-friendly outdoor seating as well. Daily 8am–midnight.

Stache 1920s Drinking Den 109 SW 2nd Ave ☎954 449 1044, ⓦstacheftl.com. In the heart of Himmarshee, this 1920s-themed speakeasy features a sign above the door that says "Himmie Health", but you're in the right place. Unique, hand-crafted cocktails are king here: drinks like the acai bramble feature no fewer than five ingredients. Wed & Thurs 8pm–4am, Fri 6pm–4am, Sat 8pm–4am.

GAY BARS AND CLUBS

Gay bars and clubs in Fort Lauderdale fall in and out of fashion; check the listings magazines listed above or ⓦgayftlauderdale.com for the latest hotspots, many of which are located in nearby Wilton Manors.

Alibi 2266 Wilton Drive ☎954 565 2526, ⓦalibiwiltonmanors.com. Formerly *Georgie's Alibi*, this casual sports bar, with a decent menu of hot sandwiches and burgers, offers plenty of special events from football

nights to comedy to drag shows. Mon–Thurs & Sun 11am–2am, Fri & Sat 11am–3am.

Bill's Filling Station 2209 Wilton Drive ☎954 567 5978, ⓦbillsfillingstation.com. This popular spot offers theme nights each week, such as karaoke, drag shows and wine tastings. There are also great drink specials. Mon–Thurs 4pm–2am, Fri 4pm–3am, Sat noon–3am, Sun noon–2am.

Cubby Hole 823 N Federal Hwy ☎954 728 9001, ⓦthecubbyhole.com. This spot is known for attracting Bears, as well as for its excellent burgers and cruising scene. Pool tables and video games add to the fun. Mon–Thurs 11am–2am, Fri & Sat 11am–3am, Sun noon–2am.

Hunters Nightclub 2232 Wilton Drive ☎954 630 3556, ⓦhuntersftlauderdale.com. This new nightclub offers a hopping dancefloor with live DJs Thursday to Saturday nights, as well as karaoke, country dancing and a cabaret show other nights of the week. Mon–Thurs 4pm–2am, Fri 4pm–3am, Sat 2pm–3am, Sun noon–2am.

Village Pub 2283 Wilton Drive ☎754 200 5244, ⓦvillagepubwm.com. This friendly spot offers a crowded outdoor patio, as well as ubiquitous drink specials. Mon–Thurs & Sun 11am–2am, Fri & Sat 11am–3am.

THEATRE

Broward Center for the Performing Arts 201 SW 5th Ave ☎954 522 5334, ⓦbrowardcenter.org. A wide variety of theatre performances, touring musicians and Broadway musicals stop at this venue.

Around Fort Lauderdale

North of Fort Lauderdale, Hwy-A1A passes through a succession of sleepy towns inhabited by a mixture of retirees, snowbirds from the Northeast and the super-rich, and though the beaches remain enticing, there's little in the way of conventional sights. A diversion inland can prove slightly more rewarding: the otherwise nondescript suburbs are brightened by the eccentric town of Davie, and the Hollywood Seminole Reservation.

Davie

An exception to the prevailing factories, housing estates and freeway interchanges surrounding Fort Lauderdale, **DAVIE** lies twenty miles from the coast on Griffin Road,

> ## PROFESSIONAL SPORTS VENUES
>
> Mid-July to August sees the training camp of football's **Miami Dolphins** (☎ 305 943 8000, ⓦ miamidolphins.com) in nearby Davie at the Nova Southeastern University campus, 7500 SW 30th St. Practices are free to attend, but you must request tickets in advance. The BB&T Center at 2555 NW 136th Ave, just west of Fort Lauderdale in Sunrise, is home to the **Florida Panthers** hockey team (☎ 954 835 7000, ⓦ panthers.nhl.com). It's also not far to Miami's major league sports venues (see p.31).

circled by citrus groves, sugar cane and dairy pastures. Davie's roughly 80,000 inhabitants are besotted with the Old West: jeans, plaid shirts and Stetsons are the order of the day.

Bob Roth's New River Groves

5660 Griffin Rd • Daily 8am–5pm • ☎ 954 581 8630, ⓦ newrivergroves.com

Any visit to Davie would be incomplete without a stop at **Bob Roth's New River Groves** indoor/outdoor market, which sells local oranges, grapefruits and other produce, as well as a variety of healthy fruit smoothies. Don't leave without tasting one of the farm stand's famous Key lime pies – they've won multiple state and national awards.

Old Davie School Historical Museum

6650 Griffin Rd • Tues–Sat 10am–4pm • $7 for museum alone, $10 for museum and historic houses • ☎ 954 797 1044, ⓦ olddavieschool.org

Davie's cowboy origins hail from settlers who came here in the 1910s to herd cattle and work the fertile black soil, an agricultural history embodied by the restored **Old Davie School Historical Museum**, which occupies the old Davie school. The museum holds implements of early farm life, as well as plenty of historical photographs and a display on the local wildlife. Behind the museum are the restored Viele House, the oldest in Davie, and the Walsh-Osterhoudt House, both open to visitors.

Bergeron Rodeo Grounds

4271 Davie Rd • **Davie Pro Rodeo** Four times per year in Feb, June, Sept & Nov • $20, children 3–12 $10, or $18/$8 in advance • ☎ 954 680 8005, ⓦ davieprorodeo.com • **Jackpot Rodeo** Wed at 7pm • $4 • ☎ 954 475 9787

The Davie Pro Rodeo is held at the Davie Arena, on the **Bergeron Rodeo Grounds** – look for the rearing white horse sign. You can also check out the cheaper Jackpot Rodeos (with local riders) here on Wednesdays.

Hollywood Seminole Reservation

State Rd 7/US-441 • ⓦ seminoletribe.com

Fifteen minutes southwest from downtown Fort Lauderdale is the **Hollywood Seminole Reservation**, the headquarters of the Seminole tribe and their biggest source of income (see box, p.162). Here you'll find the reservation's main tourist attraction within the fashionable Seminole Paradise complex, the **Seminole Hard Rock Hotel & Casino** (☎ 866 502 7529, ⓦ seminolehardrockhollywood.com). It's the casino that draws most visitors; laws against gaming don't apply to Indian reservations, so you can play slot machines, high-stakes bingo and poker, as well as stock up on tax-free cigarettes. Also inside, *Hard Rock Live* showcases popular performance and sporting events; call ☎ 954 327 5531 or visit the website for its upcoming schedule.

Lauderdale-By-The-Sea

The seventeen miles between Fort Lauderdale and Boca Raton are marked by several sedate beachside communities; Hwy-A1A (much preferable to US-1) is rarely busy, but note that hotels and condos largely block the sea views once you leave north Fort Lauderdale. The most worthy stop is **Lauderdale-By-The-Sea**, around four miles up the coast and one of the best places to don **scuba-diving** gear and explore the reefs, many of which are within one hundred yards of the beach.

Hillsboro Beach

Three miles north of Lauderdale-By-The-Sea, Hwy-A1A crosses the Hillsboro Inlet, which lends its name to the posh canal-side community of **Hillsboro Beach**. There's nothing to detain you here except the offshore restaurant *Cap's Place* (see below).

ARRIVAL AND DEPARTURE

By car All the main car-rental operators are represented at the airport (see p.182). To get to Davie, you'll head west on I-595S. If you're heading north, take either the Florida's

AROUND FORT LAUDERDALE

Turnpike (which charges tolls) or I-595N. To stick closer to the coast, use Hwy-1.

INFORMATION AND ACTIVITIES

Tourist information Lauderdale-By-The-Sea's little Chamber of Commerce is at 4201 Ocean Drive (daily 9am–5pm; ☎ 954 776 1000, ☯ lbts.com).

Diving Try Deep Blue Divers (☎ 954 772 7966, ☯ deepbluedivers.net) at 4348 Ocean Drive, Lauderdale-By-The-Sea, or enquire at the Chamber of Commerce.

ACCOMMODATION

Cheap **motels** abound along the stretch of Hwy-A1A coming into Lauderdale-By-The-Sea, but you'll also find many pleasant **B&Bs**, most along beachfront El Mar Drive, one block east of Hwy-A1A (or Ocean Drive, as it's also known here).

LAUDERDALE-BY-THE-SEA
★**Beachside Village Resort** 4564 N Ocean Drive ☎ 954 652 1216, ☯ thebeachsidevillageresort.com. This immaculate motel features stylishly decorated beach-chic accommodation ranging from hotel rooms to two-bedroom suites with full kitchens. Other amenities include a rooftop deck, tennis court and free use of bikes, snorkelling gear, beach chairs and ocean kayaks. **$129**
Blue Seas Courtyard 4525 El Mar Drive ☎ 954 772 3336, ☯ blueseascourtyard.com. This hacienda-style hotel is one of the most distinctive in town, with rooms decked out in an ebullient Mexican style, replete with

terracotta tiles and arts and crafts from south of the border. **$129**
Sea Spray Inn 4245 El Mar Drive ☎ 954 776 1311, ☯ seasprayinn.com. The immaculate, tropical rooms have lots of wicker and light wood, as well as full kitchens, and ocean views from most balconies. **$125**
Tides Inn Resort 4312 El Mar Drive ☎ 954 772 2933, ☯ tidesinnhotel.com. This 1950s motor lodge recently underwent a full renovation to become one of the area's most stylish hotels. Rooms feature sleek, mid-century furniture and hardwood floors, and there's also a large oceanfront pool and BBQ area. **$200**

EATING AND DRINKING

LAUDERDALE-BY-THE-SEA
Aruba Beach Café 1 Commercial Blvd ☎ 954 776 0001, ☯ arubabeachcafe.com. This place serves up Caribbean-inspired American food, as well as nightly live music in three tropical bars. Mon & Tues 11am–1am, Wed–Sat 11am–2am, Sun 9am–1am.
The Village Grille and Village Pump 4404 El Mar Drive ☎ 954 776 5092, ☯ villagegrille.com. Decades old, this is a good place for seafood, sushi, steaks and cocktails on the beach. Daily: restaurant 8am–11pm; bar 9am–2am.

HILLSBORO BEACH
Cap's Place Offshore in the Intracoastal Waterway ☎ 954 941 0418, ☯ capsplace.com. The food – lots of fresh seafood, with main courses ranging $16–36 – is the main attraction here, but the fact the restaurant doubled as an illegal gambling den during Prohibition adds appeal. Dinner only; booking recommended. Only reachable by ferry (call for directions to the dock). Tues–Sun 5.30–10.30pm.

Boca Raton and around

Palm Beach County's southernmost town, **BOCA RATON** is well known for its affluence. Smartly dressed valets park your car at supermarkets; golf-mad retirees and executives from numerous high-tech industries live here year-round; and Northeasterners fleeing the winter chill make up sixty percent of the population.

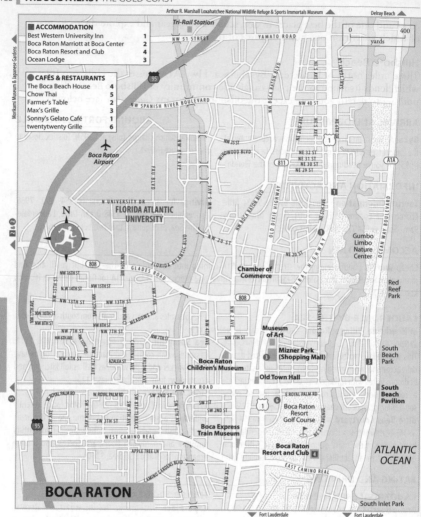

Boca Raton also boasts an abundance of Mediterranean Revival **architecture**, a style prevalent here since the 1920s and preserved by strict building codes. The town's other attractions include some fine beaches and parks.

Downtown Boca Raton

Boca Raton lacks a definitive central area, marked by the landscaped palm trees and upmarket shops of most other South Florida cities. Instead, **downtown** is more spread out, and generally focuses on the area around Palmetto Park Road, Federal Highway and their junction, including the Mizner Park shopping and entertainment complex. Throughout, you'll see signs of Boca Raton's Mediterranean-flavoured architecture, the influence of **Addison Mizner** (see box, p.194), who furnished the fantasies of Palm Beach's fabulously wealthy during the 1920s. Mizner swept into Boca Raton on the tide of the Florida property boom after World War I, bought 1600 acres of land, and began selling plots of a future community, advertised as "beyond realness in its ideality". Envisaging gondola-filled canals, a luxury hotel and a great cathedral dedicated to his mother, Mizner had big plans that were ultimately nipped in the bud by the economic crash of 1926; shortly thereafter, he returned to Palm Beach.

Boca Raton Resort and Club

501 E Camino Real • Guided walking tour first and third Tues of the month Dec–April, second and fourth Tues of the month Jan–May • Tour $15, plus $20 valet ticket • ☎ 561 447 3000, ⓦ bocaresort.com; tours ☎ 561 395 6766, ⓦ bocahistory.org

The buildings Mizner completed left an indelible mark on Boca Raton. His million-dollar *Cloister Inn* grew into the present **Boca Raton Resort and Club**. A pink palace of marble columns, sculptured fountains, and carefully aged wood (the centuries-old effect was accomplished by the hobnailed boots of Mizner's workmen), its tall towers are visible for miles around. Unless you're staying here, you'll have to be satisfied with a drive-by; join the **guided walking tour** run by the Boca Raton Historical Society to get a better look.

Old Town Hall

71 N Federal Hwy; once you're inside, turn left along the corridor from the building's rear entrance • Mon–Fri 10am–4pm • $5 • ☎ 561 395 6766, ⓦ bocahistory.org

The Boca Raton Historical Society and History Museum resides in the historic **Old Town Hall**, completed in 1927. For a glimpse into Boca's formative years, history buffs should check out the society's library, which features historic maps, photos and documents. Guided forty-minute tours offer a peek inside old vaults used for tax collection.

Museum of Art

501 Plaza Real, north end of Mizner Park • Tues–Fri 10am–5pm, Sat & Sun noon–5pm • $8 • ☎ 561 392 2500, ⓦ bocamuseum.org

Mizner Park contains the airy **Museum of Art**, which has benefited from generous patrons and inspired curatorship to become one of Florida's finest small art museums. Besides temporary exhibitions by both international and Florida artists, the museum has a permanent collection featuring an outdoor **sculpture garden**, the **Mayers Collection of Modern Masters** – 53 works including drawings by Degas, Matisse, Picasso and Seurat – and a formidable trove of **West African art**, among other displays. There's also the nearby, open-air **Mizner Park amphitheatre** for concerts (ⓦ myboca.us /pages/mizneramphi/).

Boca Raton Children's Museum

498 Crawford Blvd • Mon–Sat 10am–5pm • $5 • ☎ 561 368 6875, ⓦ cmboca.org

For a change of pace, turn to the **Boca Raton Children's Museum**. Housed in a 1912 driftwood "cracker" cottage – the simple abode of early Florida farmers – the museum stocks entertaining remnants from the pioneer days, alongside kid-friendly exhibitions.

Boca Express Train Museum

Junction of Dixie Hwy and SE 8th St • Jan–April first and third Fri 1 & 2pm • $10 • ☎ 561 395 6766, ⓦ bocahistory.org

Near the Old Town Hall (see above) is the Historical Society-owned **Boca Express Train Museum**, a historic site comprising the old 1930 railroad depot and two restored 1947 streamliner rail cars. Admission includes a guided tour of the museum and rail cars, courtesy of the society.

Sports Immortals Museum and Memorabilia Mart

6830 N Federal Hwy • Mon–Fri 10am–6pm, Sat 11am–5pm • $10, children under 12 $7 • ☎ 561 997 2575

Sports fans will revel in the **Sports Immortals Museum and Memorabilia Mart**, about four miles north of downtown Boca Raton. The museum houses an overwhelming assortment of sporting mementos, from Muhammad Ali's championship belt to the baseball that killed the ballplayer Ray Chapman in 1920. The main focus, however, is the **memorabilia store**, one of the largest in the US, where you can buy balls, plaques, helmets and autographs from every major sport.

Boca Raton's beaches

All four of Boca Raton's fine **beaches** are open to the public, but they are walled in by tall rows of palm trees, sea grape and Australian pine, so it's unlikely you'll stumble across them as you drive along Hwy-A1A, also known as Ocean Boulevard here. The three that are also city-owned parks come with hefty daily **parking fees** ($15–18), so they tend to be the preserve of select Floridians who can purchase permits. To avoid the steep costs, your best bet is to park elsewhere and walk, or head north to Delray Beach, which is much cheaper (see p.192).

South Inlet Park

1100 S Ocean Blvd • Parking $2/hr Mon–Fri, $3/hr Sat, Sun & holidays • Look for the entrance on the right off Hwy-A1A, just before the Boca Raton Inlet

The southernmost patch, **South Inlet Park**, is the smallest and quietest of the quartet of beaches, often deserted in midweek save for a few people fishing along its short jetty. There are also picnic tables and a playground here.

South Beach Park

400 N State Rd/Hwy-A1A • Parking $15 Mon–Fri, $17 Sat & Sun

South Beach Park, about a mile north of South Inlet Park, is a surfers' favourite, though the actual beach is a fairly tiny area of coarse sand. The park's entrance is about a quarter of a mile north of the attractive **South Beach Pavilion**, where a small car park offers cheaper parking.

Gumbo Limbo Nature Center

1801 N Ocean Blvd • Mon–Sat 9am–4pm, Sun noon–4pm; sea turtle walks May to early July weekdays at 8.45pm (call for specific days) • $5 donation suggested; walks $17 non-members, $12 members but prices subject to change • ☎ 561 544 8605, ⓦ gumbolimbo.org

Red Reef Park, a mile further on from South Beach Park, is far better for sunbathing, swimming and snorkelling – activities that should be combined with a walk around the twenty-acre **Gumbo Limbo Nature Center**, directly across Hwy-A1A. The centre's wide boardwalks take you through a tropical hardwood hammock and a mangrove forest between the Intracoastal Waterway and the Atlantic Ocean; watch for osprey, brown pelican and the occasional manatee lurking in the warm waters. Between the end of May and early July, you can join the centre's scheduled walks to observe **sea turtles**. These are extremely popular, so be sure to make a reservation well in advance online.

Spanish River Park

A mile north of Red Reef Park on Hwy-A1A; entrance on the left • Parking $16 Mon–Fri, $18 Sat & Sun • Get here early to find free parking kerbside spaces at the end of Spanish River Blvd, a short walk from the entrance

Boca Raton's most explorable beachside area is **Spanish River Park**. Here, sandwiched between the Intracoastal Waterway and the ocean, you'll find fifty acres of lush vegetation, most of which is only penetrable on secluded trails through shady thickets. Aim for the 40ft observation tower for a view across the park and much of Boca Raton. The adjacent beach is a slender but serviceable strip, linked to the park by several tunnels beneath the highway.

Arthur R. Marshall Loxahatchee National Wildlife Refuge

10216 Lee Rd • Daily sunrise–sunset, visitor's centre 9am–4pm daily, tram tours weekly; call ahead for schedule and reservations • Cars $5 or annual car pass for $12, pedestrians and cyclists $1 • Canoe rentals $32/day; kayak rentals $25/day for solo, $35/day for double • ☎ 561 732 3684, visitor's centre and gift shop ☎ 561 734 8303; ⓦ loxahatcheefriends.com

Boca Raton makes a good base from which to visit the excellent **Arthur R. Marshall Loxahatchee National Wildlife Refuge**, about twenty miles northwest of the city just off

US-441. The 220-odd square miles of sawgrass marshes – the northerly extension of the Everglades (see p.154) – are penetrable on two easy **walking trails** from the visitor centre. One trail is a half-mile boardwalk that meanders above a cypress swamp, while the grassy Marsh Trail (0.8 miles) loops around one area of wetlands to an observation tower, with the option to walk further around additional marshes. You're likely to see quite a bit of the local wildlife – alligators, snakes, turtles and a wide variety of local birds, including the endangered snail kite. There's also a 5.5-mile **canoe trail**, should you wish to take to the water.

Loxahatchee Everglades Tours
15490 Loxahatchee Rd • Tours hourly 9am–4pm; 50min, 70min or 90min tours • $45/$65/$90 • ☎ 561 482 6107 or ☎ 561 271 1880, ⓦ evergladesairboattours.com

It's possible to explore the refuge by **airboat**, which you can arrange at **Loxahatchee Everglades Tours**, off State Road 7/US-441, fifteen miles due west of downtown Boca Raton. Tours typically encounter alligators, turtles and a wide variety of birds.

ARRIVAL AND DEPARTURE   BOCA RATON

By bus The nearest Greyhound bus terminal is in Delray Beach, 1587 SW 4th Ave (☎561 272 6447). To get to downtown Boca Raton from here, you must first walk (or cab) half a mile west to Delray Plaza, where you can catch Palm Beach County bus #1 south ($2 or $5 all day;

☎ 561 841 4200, ⓦ pbcgov.com/palmtran).
By train The Tri-Rail station is off I-95, at 680 Yamato Rd (☎ 800 874 7245); shuttle buses connect with the town centre.

GETTING AROUND AND INFORMATION

By car Boca Raton covers a large area, and it's much easier to get around if you have your own car. Roads are rarely busy, but with the exception of Mizner Park (where the parking garage is free), parking can be expensive, especially at the beaches.
By bus Palm Tran bus #91 ($2 each way, $5 all-day pass; ☎ 561 841 4200, ⓦ pbcgov.com) operates daily one to two

times an hour between Mizner Park through downtown west via Glades Road to the Sandalfoot Square shopping centre.
Tourist information The Chamber of Commerce is at 1800 N Dixie Hwy (Mon 9.30am–5pm, Tues–Fri 8.30am–5pm; ☎561 395 4433, ⓦ bocaratonchamber .com).

ACCOMMODATION

Best Western University Inn 2700 N Federal Hwy ☎561 395 5225, ⓦ bestwestern.com. West of the Intracoastal Waterway, North Federal Hwy has its fair share of hotels, some made more affordable by the inland location; try the *Best Western*, which has a pool and fitness centre, and offers a free shuttle to the beach and a complimentary hot breakfast. $169
Boca Raton Marriott at Boca Center 5150 Town Center Circle ☎561 392 4600, ⓦ marriot.com. Contemporary, stylish rooms feature luxurious beds, and

bathrooms have rainfall showers. There's a large gym, a jogging trail and pool area as well. $149
Boca Raton Resort and Club 501 E Camino Real ☎561 447 3000, ⓦ bocaresort.com. If you want to stay in luxury, this is the place (see p.189). $289
★**Ocean Lodge** 531 N Ocean Blvd ☎561 395 7772, ⓦ oceanlodgeflorida.com. This eighteen-room gem near the beaches features suites with kitchenettes, flat-screen TVs, free wi-fi and complimentary continental breakfast. There's also a heated pool. $209

EATING AND DRINKING

The Boca Beach House 887 E Palmetto Park Rd ☎ 561 826 8850. The owners source some of their ingredients from their own garden at this popular breakfast and lunch spot. Pesto-infused chicken salad and the horseradish-crusted fish are sandwich standouts. Sandwiches $10.40–15. Mon–Fri 8am–3pm, Sat & Sun 8am–4pm.
Chow Thai 23034 Sandalfoot Plaza Drive ☎561 487 8414, ⓦ chowthai.info. Excellent Thai food awaits in this unassuming strip-mall location. Start with the spicy papaya

salad and move on to the *pad kee mao*, wild rice noodles sautéed with chilli paste. Main courses average $10–15. Mon–Fri 11am–3pm & 4.30–10pm, Sat 4.30–10pm, Sun 4.30–9pm.
★**Farmer's Table** 1901 N Military Trail ☎561 417 5836, ⓦ farmerstableboca.com. This earthy, warm restaurant takes its mission of serving healthy, local food seriously. Menu standouts include cauliflower and Brie flatbread and *zahtar*-spiced salmon. Mains $16–23.

4

Mon–Thurs & Sun 8am–10pm, Fri & Sat 8am–11pm.
Max's Grille 404 Plaza Real ☎561 368 0080, ⓦmaxsgrille.com. One of the best options at Mizner Park, featuring upmarket American dishes with Asian influences; try the Thai steak salad or chilli-roasted fish tacos for lunch. Most main courses $19–29. Mon–Thurs 11.30am–10pm, Fri 11.30am–11pm, Sat 11am–11pm, Sun 11am–10pm.
Sonny's Gelato Café 2151 N Federal Hwy ☎561 362 0447, ⓦrealgelato.com. Some of the tastiest gelato in south Florida; choose from a range of flavours including

Nutella and cannoli, as well as a robust menu of panini, pastas and subs. Sandwiches start at $8. Mon–Fri 7am–11pm, Sat 9am–11.30pm, Sun 1–10.30pm.
★**twentytwenty Grille** 141 Via Naranjas #45 ☎561 990 7969, ⓦtwentytwentygrille.com. The contemporary American menu at this trendy yet welcoming spot focuses on the freshest ingredients available. Start with the "smooth" corn chowder and move on to the salted, cinnamon-rubbed duck breast. Main dishes $24–33. Daily 5–10pm.

North towards Palm Beach

Heading north from Boca Raton along Hwy-A1A it's 26 miles to Palm Beach, a generally stress-free route through shoulder-to-shoulder towns with pleasant beaches and parks; Delray Beach makes the most worthwhile stop.

Delray Beach

Five miles north of Boca Raton, **Delray Beach** warrants a lengthy stop – you'll need at least half a day to do it justice – with the **Morikami Museum** a worthy detour inland.

The powdery-sanded **municipal beach**, at the foot of Atlantic Avenue, is rightly popular and is one of the few in Florida where you can sometimes see the Gulf Stream current – a cobalt-blue streak about five miles offshore. Metered parking is available along the seafront ($1.50/hr).

Sandoway House Nature Center

142 S Ocean Blvd • Tues–Sat 10am–4pm, Sun noon–4pm; shark feedings Tues–Sat at 10.30am, Sun at 1.30pm • $4 • ☎561 274 7263, ⓦsandowayhouse.org

For a greater understanding of south Florida's fragile marine and freshwater environments, visit the **Sandoway House Nature Center**, located within a 1936 beachfront house, just south of Atlantic Avenue. Exhibits include a shell gallery and a coral reef ecosystem display, home to reef fish and nurse sharks.

Cornell Museum

51 N Swinton Ave • Tues–Sun 10am–4.30pm • $5 • ☎561 243 7922, ⓦdelraycenterforthearts.org

A mile inland along Atlantic Avenue, an imposing schoolhouse dating from 1913 is now the **Cornell Museum**, part of **Old School Square**, a group of buildings restored and converted into the Delray Beach Center for the Arts. The spacious two-storey museum hosts rotating American art and craft exhibitions in its six gallery spaces; featured artists are usually south Florida-based, and the standard of work is generally high.

Cason Cottage Museum

5 NE 1st St • Nov–April Wed–Fri guided tours on the hour 11am–3pm • $4 • ☎561 274 9578

Near the Cornell Museum, the **Delray Beach Historical Society** runs the **Cason Cottage Museum**, a house erected circa 1924 for Rev John R. Cason, member of an illustrious local family. The tours seek to tell the history of Delray Beach through the Cason family, and the cottage warrants a look for its simple woodframe design based on pioneer-era Florida architecture as well.

Ethel Sterling Williams History Learning Center

111 N Swinton Ave • Wed–Fri 11am–3pm • Admission included with Cason House ticket • ☎561 274 9578

The Delray Beach Historical Society's **History Learning Center**, at the restored 1908 Hunt House around the corner from the Cason Cottage Museum, is open three days a week for history research, and also plays host to rotating local history exhibits.

The Morikami Museum and Japanese Gardens

4000 Morikami Park Rd • Tues–Sun 10am–5pm; teahouse Oct–June one Sat of the month (check the website as it varies) • Adults $15, children $9; tea ceremony $5 • ☎ 561 495 0233, ⓦ morikami.org

The suburbs west of Delray Beach might be the last place you'd expect to find a formal Japanese garden, Shinto shrine, teahouse, and a museum recording the history of a Japanese agricultural colony, but at the **Morikami Museum and Japanese Gardens** you'll find all four. These are reminders of a group of Japanese farmers who came here in the early twentieth century at the behest of the Florida East Coast Railway to grow tea and rice and to farm silkworms in a colony called Yamato, but ended up selling pineapples until a blight killed off the crop in 1908. Most of the settlers departed by the 1920s.

A permanent exhibit of artefacts and photographs commemorate the colony in the site's original building, the Yamato-kan, which also serves as a model of a traditional Japanese residence. Across the beautifully landscaped grounds, additional galleries in the principal museum stage themed exhibitions drawn from their 7000-piece archive of Japanese art objects and artefacts. A traditional **teahouse**, assembled here by a Florida-based Japanese craftsman, is used one Saturday of the month (Oct–June) for tea ceremonies. Check the website for specific dates.

Lantana

One of the first towns established on the Gold Coast, **LANTANA** retains a few original wood buildings on its main street, Ocean Avenue, but the real highlight here is the **Old Key Lime House** restaurant (see p.194). One of the oldest structures in south Florida, the creaky pinewood house was built in 1889 by pioneer Morris Lyman, but the most enticing section today is the outdoor deck (protected by a Seminole palm-thatched *chickee* roof) looking out over Lake Worth, replete with resident pelicans and a new manatee viewing deck.

Lake Worth

Hwy-A1A charts a picturesque course from Lantana along ten-odd miles of slender barrier islands, with ocean views on one side and the Intracoastal Waterway – plied by luxury yachts and lined with opulent homes – on the other. Three miles north of Lantana, **Lake Worth**'s distinct downtown district, east of I-95 along the parallel Lake and Lucerne avenues, can get lively on weekend nights, with a handful of outdoor bars and cafés.

From Lake Worth, Palm Beach (via Hwy-A1A) and West Palm Beach (via US-1) are just a few miles north.

ARRIVAL AND TOURS

By bus The local Palm Tran bus #1 ($2, or $5 all day; ☎ 561 841 4287) runs every 20–30min (hourly on Sun) through towns between Boca Raton and West Palm Beach.

By tram (trolley) The Spady Cultural Heritage Museum

NORTH TOWARDS PALM BEACH

organizes edifying historic tram (trolley) tours on the second Saturday of the month (Sept–May; $20; ⓦ spadymuseum.com), taking in Delray Beach's five historic districts with an expert guide.

ACCOMMODATION

DELRAY BEACH

Colony Hotel & Cabana Club 525 E Atlantic Ave ☎ 561 276 4123, ⓦ thecolonyflorida.com. This resort-style hotel, with its garnet-and-pale-yellow awning, has been a fixture since 1926; rooms come with many of the original mahogany furnishings. There's a free breakfast buffet and wi-fi, and an on-site saltwater pool; its private beach is located 2 miles away, reachable by complimentary shuttle. **$195**

★Crane's BeachHouse 82 Gleason St ☎ 561 278 1700, ⓦ cranesbeachhouse.com. This gracefully laidback resort features tropical-themed rooms, a popular bamboo tiki bar, which hosts frequent live music, and miniature

waterfalls. One block from the beach. **$259**

Sundy House 106 S Swinton Ave ☎ 561 272 5678, ⓦ sundyhouse.com. This cute twelve-room boutique hotel is tucked into an acre of lush tropical gardens downtown. Each of the rooms has a unique theme, and there's a gorgeous natural swimming pool on-site. **$339**

Wright by the Sea 1901 S Ocean Blvd ☎ 561 278 3355, ⓦ wbtsea.com. Friendly oceanside hotel, with helpful staff, spacious rooms with well-equipped kitchens, and a fabulous location close to all the action. Thoughtful extras include free daily newspapers, cabanas on the beach and wi-fi. Rates halve in the summer. **$129**

EATING AND DRINKING

DELRAY BEACH

Caffè Luna Rosa 34 S Ocean Blvd ☎561 274 9404, ⓦ caffelunarosa.com. Serves casual Italian food in an attractive exposed-brick space hung with unusual artwork, and features occasional live music – you can also sit outside. Lunchtime pastas $9–18, pizzas from $11 – add around $6 for dinner, when there's also a bigger choice of Italian seafood dishes from £24. Daily 7am–3.15pm & 4–10pm.

Joseph's Wine Bar 200 NE 2nd Ave ☎561 272 6100, ⓦ www.josephswinebar.com. This relaxed but elegant wine bar serves Mediterranean-influenced lunch and dinner, as well as killer breakfast frittatas. There's a wine selection of over 2000 bottles as well. Main courses $21–36. Daily 11am–10pm.

Max's Harvest 169 NE 2nd St ☎561 381 9970. The farm-to-fork craze has come to Delray in the delicious form of this homely spot, which serves local meat and produce. Try the truffled, devilled eggs followed by pork schnitzel. Main courses $21–34. Mon–Thurs 6–10pm, Fri 5–10.30pm, Sat 10am–2.30pm & 5–10.30pm, Sun 10am–2.30pm & 5–9pm.

Sandwiches by the Sea 1214 E Atlantic Ave ☎561 272 2212. This tiny but excellent lunch spot has good salads, sandwiches (from $4.50–7.50) and amazing frozen yogurt shakes ($3.50). There's patio seating behind the restaurant, or you can take your subs to the beach. Daily 9am–5pm.

LANTANA

★Old Key Lime House 300 E Ocean Ave, just off US-1 on the way to the beach ☎561 582 1889, ⓦ oldkeylimehouse.com. The seafood at this historic restaurant (see p.193) is excellent – standouts are the crab cakes ($25) and fish dip ($10) – but you must try the Key lime pie ($7.50 per slice), a wedge of creamy lime heaven. Mon–Thurs & Sun 11am–10pm, Fri & Sat 11am–11pm.

LAKE WORTH

Benny's On The Beach 10 Ocean Blvd ☎561 582 9001, ⓦ bennysonthebeach.com. Located on the Lake Worth Pier, this waterfront watering hole serves up great breakfasts, fresh seafood and killer views. The lobster Benedict ($19) is a breakfast speciality; try the Baja fish tacos for dinner ($15). Daily 6am–10pm.

★Chris' Taverna 6338 Lantana Rd ☎561 964 4233, ⓦ christaverna.com. This lively spot offers great service and authentic Greek specialities like *pastitsio*, *spanakopita* and mouthwatering *gyros*. Main dishes $15–25. Mon–Thurs 11am–9pm, Fri & Sat 11am–10pm, Sun 11.30am–9pm.

Safire 817 Lake Ave ☎561 588 7768, ⓦ safirelakeworth .com. This Asian-fusion restaurant successfully combines Thai and Japanese flavours in imaginative dishes like seafood *pad thai* and salmon teriyaki. Tues–Fri 11.30am–3pm & 5–10pm, Sat & Sun 5–10pm.

Palm Beach

A small island town of extraordinary architecture, glorious gardens, and streets so clean you could eat your dinner off them, for over a century **PALM BEACH** has been

PALM BEACH'S ARCHITECT: ADDISON MIZNER

A former gold miner and prizefighter, **Addison Mizner** was an unemployed architect when he arrived in Palm Beach in 1918 from California to recuperate from the recurrence of a childhood leg injury. Inspired by the medieval buildings he'd seen around the Mediterranean, Mizner, financed by an heir to the Singer sewing machine fortune, built the **Everglades Club** at 356 Worth Ave, which is now off-limits to the public. Described by Mizner as "a little bit of Seville and the Alhambra, a dash of Madeira and Algiers", the Everglades Club was the first public building in Florida erected in the Mediterranean Revival style, and fast became the island's most prestigious social club.

The success of the club, and the house he subsequently built for society bigwig Eva Stotesbury, won Mizner commissions all over Palm Beach as the wintering wealthy decided to swap their suites at one of Henry Flagler's hotels for a "million-dollar cottage" of their own.

Brilliant and unorthodox, Mizner's loggias and U-shaped interiors made the most of Florida's pleasant winter temperatures, while his twisting staircases to nowhere became legendary. Pursuing a medieval look, Mizner used untrained workmen to lay roof tiles crookedly, sprayed condensed milk onto walls to create an impression of centuries-old grime, and fired shotgun pellets into wood to imitate worm holes. By the mid-1920s, Mizner had created the **Palm Beach Style** – which Florida architecture buff Hap Hattan called "the Old World for the new rich" – and would go on to fashion much of Boca Raton (see p.190).

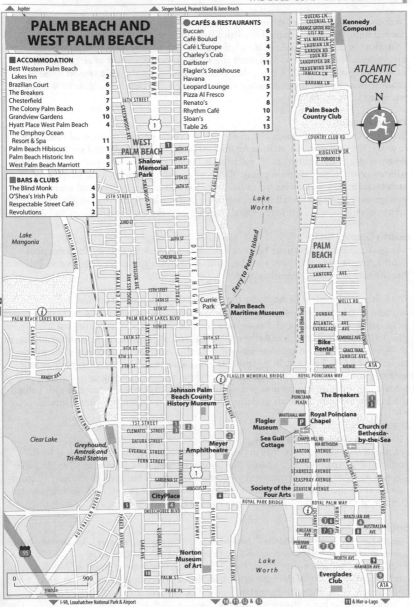

PALM BEACH AND WEST PALM BEACH

ACCOMMODATION

Best Western Palm Beach Lakes Inn	2
Brazilian Court	6
The Breakers	3
Chesterfield	7
The Colony Palm Beach	9
Grandview Gardens	10
Hyatt Place West Palm Beach	4
The Omphoy Ocean Resort & Spa	11
Palm Beach Hibiscus	1
Palm Beach Historic Inn	8
West Palm Beach Marriott	5

BARS & CLUBS

The Blind Monk	4
O'Shea's Irish Pub	3
Respectable Street Café	1
Revolutions	2

CAFÉS & RESTAURANTS

Buccan	6
Café Boulud	3
Café L'Europe	4
Charley's Crab	9
Darbster	11
Flagler's Steakhouse	1
Havana	12
Leopard Lounge	5
Pizza Al Fresco	7
Renato's	8
Rhythm Café	10
Sloan's	2
Table 26	13

synonymous with the kind of lifestyle only fabulous wealth can buy. The nation's upper crust began wintering here in the 1890s, after **Henry Flagler** brought his railway south and built two luxury hotels on this then-secluded, palm-filled island; only *The Breakers* is still open (see p.196). Throughout the 1920s, **Addison Mizner** (see box opposite) sparked a vogue for Mediterranean-style architecture, blanketing the place in arcades, courtyards and plazas – and the first million-dollar homes. Since then, corporate tycoons, sports heroes, jet-setting aristocrats, rock stars and CIA directors have all flocked here, eager for a taste of the Palm Beach magic.

Summer is very quiet and the most affordable time to stay here. The pace heats up between November and May, with the winter months a whirl of elegant balls, fund-raising dinners and charity galas. Winter also brings the **polo season** – the promise of a chukka or two is guaranteed to bring Palm Beach residents to Wellington, where matches are held.

Worth Avenue

Walking is the best way to see the moneyed isle; you'll get the measure of Palm Beach in a day, starting with the main residential section of the city. **Worth Avenue**, filled with designer stores and upmarket art galleries, is a good place to start your stroll, if only to window-shop. Other than shopping, the most appealing aspect of the street is its **architecture**: look out for stucco walls, crafted Romanesque facades and narrow passageways leading to small, charming courtyards called "vias" that might be adorned with miniature bridges, spiral staircases, quirky statues or fountains.

South County Road

The government and business heart of Palm Beach lies along **County Road** north of Worth Avenue, where Mizner's Mediterranean Revival themes are displayed in Palm Beach's tidy local administration offices.

The Episcopal Church of Bethesda-by-the-Sea and Cluett Memorial Garden

141 S County Rd • **Cluett Memorial Garden** Mon–Fri 8am–5pm, Sat & Sun 8am–4pm; free guided tours Jan–May & Sept–Nov second and fourth Sun of the month at 12.15pm; June–Aug every fourth Sun of the month at 11.15am • Free • ☎ 561 655 4554

The 1926 **Episcopal Church of Bethesda-by-the-Sea**, a fifteen-minute walk further north of Worth Avenue, is a handsome imitation-Gothic structure replacing the island's first church, which had been built in 1889. The hushed interior features a timber ceiling, wooden pews and a series of large stained-glass windows depicting saints and Biblical scenes, but the hidden gem here is the **Cluett Memorial Garden**, a peaceful spot behind the hushed cloisters in which to claim a stone pew and tuck into a picnic lunch.

The Breakers

1 S County Rd • ☎ 888 273 2537, 🖳 thebreakers.com

A little over a mile north of Worth Avenue, South County Road is straddled by the golf course of **The Breakers**, a castle-like hotel established by Flagler in 1896, and the greatest of Palm Beach's ultra-swanky resorts (the current building dates from 1926, modelled on the Villa Medici in Rome). If the room rates put you off, you can catch a glimpse of the ornate lobby on a visit to the hotel's high-end shops or restaurants.

Society of the Four Arts

2 Four Arts Plaza • Galleries open Sept & Oct Mon–Fri 10am–3pm, Nov–April Mon–Sat 10am–5pm & Sun 1–5pm; library open Mon–Fri 10am–5pm, Sat also 10am–1pm from Nov–April • Galleries $5; library free • ☎ 561 655 7226, 🖳 fourarts.org

Four blocks west of County Road, Royal Palm Way leads to the stuccoed buildings and gardens of the **Society of the Four Arts**. Aside from presenting art shows, concerts, films and lectures of an impressive standard between early December and mid-April, the organization also has a library worth browsing.

Flagler Museum

1 Whitehall Way • Tues–Sat 10am–5pm, Sun noon–5pm; tours Tues–Sat 11am & 2pm, Sun 12.30pm & 2.30pm • $18; tours free • ☎ 561 655 2833, 🖳 flaglermuseum.us

Just west of The Breakers along Cocoanut Row you'll see the white Doric columns fronting Whitehall, also known as the **Henry Morrison Flagler Museum**. Whitehall was a

$4-million wedding present from Flagler to his third wife, Mary Lily Kenan, whom he married (after controversially persuading the Florida legislature to amend its divorce laws) in 1901. Like many of Florida's first luxury homes, Whitehall's interior design was modelled after the great buildings of Europe. Among the more than 75 rooms are an Italian Renaissance library, a French Louis XIV music room, a billiard room with a Swiss-style mantel, a hallway modelled on the Vatican's St Peter's Basilica, and a Louis XV grand ballroom. Each is richly stuffed with ornamentation and has its own distinct style, often emulating well-known historical architecture.

Flagler was in his 70s when Whitehall was built, 37 years older than his bride and not enamoured of the banquets and balls she continually hosted, and may have stolen up to bed using a concealed stairway, designed to allow the house staff to move throughout the structure unobtrusively. From the portico's 110ft hallway, informative hour-long free docent-led **guided tours** depart twice daily, and will leave you giddy with the tales and sights of the earliest Palm Beach excesses. Don't miss the spectacular views of West Palm Beach from Flagler's enormous backyard, where the Flagler Kenan Pavilion holds Flagler's private railcar, No. 91, which was part of the first train to arrive in Key West following the completion of the Over-Sea Railroad in January of 1912.

Royal Poinciana Chapel

60 Cocoanut Row • Services Sun at 10.30am • Free • ☎ 561 655 4212

Next door to the Flagler Museum, you'll notice the square bell tower of the **Royal Poinciana Chapel**, which dates from 1898. Flagler had built the original structure on the grounds of his *Royal Poinciana Hotel*, but the shingled church was moved to its current locale and reconstructed in 1973. It still has interdenominational services every Sunday morning, but is otherwise usually closed to visitors.

Sea Gull Cottage

60 Cocoanut Row, next to the Royal Poinciana Chapel • To arrange a tour call ☎ 561 655 4212, ⓦ royalpoincianachapel.org

Look out for **Sea Gull Cottage** at the back of the Royal Poinciana Chapel, Flagler's first home in Palm Beach and the town's oldest remaining house, built in 1886 and purchased by Flagler in 1893. It was originally located on the Intracoastal Waterway, and moved here in 1984. Now owned and used by the church, for the Sunday school and as a youth centre, you can arrange a small group tour by calling the chapel.

The Lake Trail

The points of interest beyond Royal Poinciana Way are best viewed from the three-mile **Lake Trail**, a bicycle and pedestrian path skirting the edge of Lake Worth, almost to the northern limit of the island. A bike is the ideal mode of transport here; rent one from **Palm Beach Bicycle Trail Shop** (see opposite).

Peanut Island

Just off the north coast of Palm Beach Island, in the middle of Lake Worth, **Peanut Island** makes for an off-beat day-trip, though it can get crowded at the weekends; camping is available (see p.200). Home to the JFK bunker, most of the island is now a county park; it's relatively unspoiled and thickly forested, surrounded by clear, calm water and can only be reached by boat, making it blissfully free of car traffic.

The island was created in 1918 from landfill excavated from Lake Worth, and though it covers eighty acres, only the outer sections are open to the public – you can walk the entire perimeter along a 1.25-mile path. Other than taking in the fresh air and lake views, you can swim at the **beach** or spot tropical fish and occasional manatees in the **snorkelling lagoon**, which has a shallow-water reef.

GETTING TO PEANUT ISLAND

Palm Beach Water Taxi (☎ 561 683 8294, ⓦ sailfishmarina.com) runs a shuttle service to the island ($12), and also organizes shuttles around the area and guided tours from Sailfish Marina, 98 Lake Drive, in Palm Beach Shores on Singer Island. You could also try **Captain Joe's Peanut Island Ferry** (☎ 561 339 2504) from Riviera Beach Marina ($10), at the end of E 13th St in Riviera Beach, opposite the island and just north of West Palm Beach on US-1. You can rent a **kayak** ($30/2 hr, $45/4hr, $60/day) or stand-up paddleboards ($30/2hr, $40/4hr, $60/day) from Paddle Boarding Palm Beach (☎ 561 313 6011), or a **jet ski** ($85/hr) or **powerboat** (from $180/2hr) from Blue Water Powerboat Rentals nearby (☎ 561 840 7470, ⓦ bluewaterboatrental .com). You can also take a ferry from the Palm Beach Maritime Museum's centre in Currie Park (☎ 561 848 2960), West Palm Beach – ferries depart Thursday to Sunday to coincide with tours of the JFK bunker; call to make a reservation.

Palm Beach Maritime Museum

Thurs–Sun 11am–4pm • Entry by guided tour only • $14 • ☎ 561 849 2960, ⓦ pbmm.org

If the sun gets too much, check out the **Palm Beach Maritime Museum** on the south side of Peanut Island, comprising a former US Coast Guard Station and **President Kennedy's command post and bomb shelter**, a barebones but atmospheric bunker constructed during the Cuban Missile Crisis in the early 1960s (the Kennedys had a home in Palm Beach at the time). There's a small snack bar on-site selling sodas, ice cream and frozen wraps.

ARRIVAL AND DEPARTURE   PALM BEACH   4

By plane Palm Beach International Airport is a few miles southwest of downtown West Palm Beach (see p.202). Palm Tran bus ($2, $5 all-day pass; ☎ 561 841 4200, ⓦ pbcgov.com/palmtran) has a stop at the airport for transport into Palm Beach; catch bus #44 for locations downtown and to transfer to the Tri-Rail. Most of the major car rental companies also have outlets at the airport.

By car If you're arriving by car from US-1 or I-95, take Okeechobee Blvd east into Palm Beach; otherwise,

Hwy-A1A is the most direct route. Metered parking is available on the seafront ($5/hr), but you can usually park for free (2hr max) on most streets.

By bus Public transport to Palm Beach is limited, and all long-distance terminals are located in West Palm Beach (see p.202). To get to Palm Beach from West Palm Beach, take any Palm Tran bus to the West Palm Beach Intermodal Transit Center at 150 Clearwater Drive, then transfer to the #41 (no Sun service).

GETTING AROUND AND INFORMATION

By bike You can rent a bike from Palm Beach Bicycle Trail Shop, 223 Sunrise Ave (Mon–Sat 9am–5.30pm, Sun 10am–5pm; ☎ 561 659 4583, ⓦ palmbeachbicycle.com), a few blocks north of Royal Poinciana Way, for $15/hr, $29/4hr, $39/24hr.

By boat There are water taxis and ferries to Peanut Island

(see box above).

Tourist information The Palm Beach Chamber of Commerce, 400 Royal Palm Way, Suite 106 (Mon–Fri 9am–6pm; ☎ 561 655 3282, ⓦ palmbeachchamber.com), provides all the usual free maps, brochures and information.

ACCOMMODATION

Comfort and elegance are the key words in Palm Beach, and prices vary greatly depending on the time of year. Visit between mid-April and mid-November to save money, as that's when many hotels offer deals. It's always cheaper to stay outside Palm Beach and visit by day, something easily done from West Palm Beach even without a car (see p.202).

★**Brazilian Court** 301 Australian Ave ☎ 561 655 7740, ⓦ thebraziliancourt.com. An elegant and intimate hotel, comprising Spanish-style villas surrounding a fountained courtyard. It's also the home of internationally acclaimed chef Daniel Boulud's French-American *Café Boulud*, as well as the swanky Frederic Fekkai Salon & Spa. $339

The Breakers 1 South County Rd ☎ 888 273 2537, ⓦ thebreakers.com. The beachy but chic rooms here are as posh as you'd expect, and a 2011 renovation made them even more elegant. There are four pools, a long, private beach and a fantastic on-site spa that even offers treatments for the kids. See p.196. $550

Chesterfield 363 Cocoanut Row ☎ 561 659 5800,

Ⓦ chesterfieldpb.com. Opulent boutique hotel, with antique-filled rooms and a popular nightclub, the *Leopard Lounge*. Serves a traditional English tea every afternoon in the wood-panelled library. **$325**

The Colony Palm Beach 155 Hammon Ave Ⓣ 561 655 5430, Ⓦ thecolonypalmbeach.com. Steps away from chic Worth Avenue, the lovely and convenient *Colony* has hosted former presidents, sheiks and Hollywood royalty. Rooms feature luxuriant sheets, pillow-top mattresses and wi-fi. Rates include a full English breakfast. **$440**

★**The Omphoy Ocean Resort & Spa** 2842 S Ocean Blvd, Ⓣ 561 540 6440, Ⓦ omphoy.com. The first new oceanfront hotel in Palm Beach for almost twenty years, the *Omphoy* keeps the bar for luxury high. The lobby and guest rooms are chic and stylish, and there's a gorgeous infinity pool and spa as well. **$269**

Palm Beach Historic Inn 365 S County Rd Ⓣ 561 832 4009, Ⓦ palmbeachhistoricinn.com. A friendly, centrally located B&B, offering continental breakfast, free parking and some of the best rates in town in the off-season. **$159**

Peanut Island campground Ⓣ 561 845 4445. If you want to stay the night on Peanut Island, there's a campground with restrooms and indoor showers, which can be reserved three months in advance. **$31**

EATING

Buccan 350 S County Rd Ⓣ 561 833 3450, Ⓦ buccanpalmbeach.com. This bright, stylish spot specializes in small plates made with local, fresh ingredients. Inventive dishes range from squid-ink *orecchiette* pasta to a hot-dog panini. Dishes start at $5.50. Mon–Sat 5pm–midnight, Sun 5–11pm.

★**Café Boulud** 301 Australian Ave Ⓣ 561 655 6060, Ⓦ cafeboulud.com/palmbeach. This classy French-American café in the *Brazilian Court* hotel is worth a visit even if you're staying elsewhere. The sunburst trout and roasted beet salad are standouts, as is the three-course fixed-price brunch on Saturday and Sunday ($32). Breakfast daily 7–11am; brunch Sat & Sun 11am–2.30pm; lunch Mon–Fri noon–2.30pm; dinner daily 5.30–10pm.

Café L'Europe 331 S County Rd Ⓣ 561 655 4020, Ⓦ cafeleurope.com. If money's no object (plan to spend at least $70 a head) and you're dressed to kill, make for this super-elegant French restaurant, where the menu includes an award-winning wine list, a variety of caviar ($45–140), and dishes like Maine lobster risotto and roasted crispy Long Island half-duckling. Dinner mains start at $34. Wed–Sun 6–9.30pm.

Charley's Crab 456 S Ocean Blvd Ⓣ 561 659 1500, Ⓦ muer.com. Serves up a mean shrimp cocktail among other scrumptious seafood offerings (and a killer Sunday brunch) in a lovely location overlooking the dunes. Main courses start at $24. Mon–Sat 11.30am–10pm, Sun 11am–10pm.

Flagler Steakhouse 1 S County Rd Ⓣ 561 659 8488, Ⓦ thebreakers.com. Steaks aren't cheap at this elegant steakhouse in *The Breakers* – averaging around $60 – but they are delicious and perfectly prepared. The recently redesigned dining room evokes a luxurious gentleman's club, so dress smartly for dinner. If you're on a budget, try the steakhouse burger for $23, or a great variety of fish dishes for around $40. Daily 11.30am–9pm.

Leopard Lounge 363 Cocoanut Row Ⓣ 561 659 5800, Ⓦ chesterfieldpb.com. Another hotel restaurant, this one at the *Chesterfield*, the *Leopard Lounge* dining room features plenty of eponymous decorative accents. Sandwiches are under $20, mains start from $28. Daily 7am–11pm.

Pizza Al Fresco 14 Via Mizner Ⓣ 561 832 0032, Ⓦ pizzaalfresco.com. This attractive, European-style restaurant with courtyard seating is a great alternative to pricier Worth Ave restaurants, serving tasty brick-oven pies for $15–25, sandwiches from $12.50, and baked pastas starting at $14.50. Daily 9am–10pm.

Renato's 87 Via Mizner Ⓣ 561 655 9752, Ⓦ renatospalmbeach.com. This upscale Italian restaurant features romantic alfresco dining and serves fantastic home-made pastas and gnocchi, as well as impressive mains such as osso buco and veal scallopine. Pastas from $22; main dishes from $27. Mon–Sat 11.30am–3pm & 6–10pm, Sun 6–10pm.

THRIFT SHOPPING IN PALM BEACH

Amazingly high-class threads, some of them discarded after only a single use, turn up in Palm Beach's **thrift and consignment stores**, though you'll usually pay above normal thrift-store prices. Worth perusing are The Church Mouse, 378 S County Rd (Oct–May Mon–Sat 10am–5pm; Ⓣ 561 659 2154); Goodwill Embassy Boutique, 210 Sunset Ave (Mon–Sat 9am–5pm, Sun 10am–5pm; Ⓣ 561 832 8199); and World Thrift, 2425 N Dixie Hwy in Lake Worth (Mon–Sat 9am–6pm).

DIVING IN PALM BEACH COUNTY

The waters around Palm Beach County – including Boynton Beach, Delray Beach, Boca Raton, Palm Beach and Jupiter – are near the **Gulf Stream**, allowing for warm temperatures (especially in summer), outstanding visibility (especially in winter), and ideal drift diving conditions. Large game fish, spiny lobster, stingray, moray eel, angelfish, parrotfish, sea turtle and nurse shark are among the wide variety of **marine life** you can spot in the reefs, wrecks, tunnels and crevices. There's also a large seasonal aggregation of spawning goliath grouper – some upwards of 300lb – from August to October. **Blue Heron Bridge** (20ft) in West Palm is one of the area's most popular sites, though you'll have to time your dive with the tides. Most outfitters offer reef dives (45–65ft), wreck dives (85–95ft) and night dives; prices vary depending on what, if any, of your own equipment you might have. Generally, you can expect to pay about $75 for a two-tank day-dive, plus $20–60 for tanks and other equipment. Reputable outfitters include the following:

Jupiter Dive Center 1001 N Hwy-A1A Alternate, Jupiter ☎ 561 745 7807, ⓦ jupiterdivecenter.com. Daily 8am–6pm.
Pura Vida Divers 2513 Beach Court, Singer Island ☎ 561 840 8750 or ☎ 888 348 3972,

ⓦ puravidadivers.com. Mon 9am–3pm, Tues–Fri 9am–6pm, Sat & Sun 9am–5pm.
The Scuba Club 4708 N Flagler Drive, West Palm Beach ☎ 561 844 2466, ⓦ thescubaclub.com. No Monday dives. Tues–Sun 8.30am–5pm.

West Palm Beach and around

Founded to house the workforce of Flagler's Palm Beach resorts, **WEST PALM BEACH** has long been in the shadow of its glamorous neighbour across the lake. The last few decades have seen the town come into its own, with smart new office buildings, a scenic lakeside footpath, and tasty restaurants and inviting shops opening along Clematis Street. Above all, West Palm Beach holds the promise of **accommodation and food** at more reasonable prices than in Palm Beach, and it's the closest you'll get to the island using public transport – Palm Tran buses from Boca Raton and Greyhound services stop here, leaving a short walk to Palm Beach over one of the Lake Worth bridges.

Downtown West Palm Beach

In the late 1950s, the boom of shopping malls in Palm Beach practically shut down the street life in **downtown West Palm Beach**. Today, the area has undergone something of a renaissance, with a few areas worth checking out.

Clematis Street and around

The best place to hang out is **Clematis Street**, home to a diverse mix of restaurants, shops and galleries, and a busy schedule of cultural activities like daytime lunch concerts. Colourfully landscaped, the street stretches from the heart of downtown (where the 500 block contains some of its original 1920s buildings), to the Intracoastal Waterway, culminating with an attractive **fountain** in Centennial Square. Here you can enjoy the popular and free "Clematis by Night" concerts every Thursday evening (6–9pm; ⓦ clematisbynight.net). The Clematis Street downtown district also includes the spacious outdoor **Meyer Amphitheatre** on S Flagler Drive, where the concert series "Sunday on the Waterfront" is held on the third Sunday of every month. Nearby a farmers' market turns everything green on Saturday mornings (mid-Oct to May 9am–1pm).

The faux-European plazas of **CityPlace** (☎ 561 366 1000, ⓦ cityplace.com), a huge and airy shopping, dining and entertainment complex at Okeechobee Boulevard and S Rosemary Avenue, is conveniently connected to Clematis Street by a free daily tram (trolley; every 20–30min; yellow line Mon–Wed & Sun 11am–9pm, Thurs–Sat 11am–11pm; green line Mon–Fri 7am–6pm, Sat 9am–6pm, Sun 11am–6pm).

Norton Museum of Art

1451 S Olive Ave • Tues, Wed, Fri & Sat 10am–5pm, Thurs 10am–9pm, Sun 11am–5pm; free tours Fri–Sun 2pm • $12, free for children 12 and younger • ☎ 561 832 5196, ⓦ norton.org

Other than shopping and eating, one reason to linger in downtown is the **Norton Museum of Art**, a mile south of the downtown area. Together with some distinctive European paintings and drawings by Braque, de Chirico, Matisse, Picasso and others, the museum boasts a solid grouping of twentieth-century American works: Duane Hanson's eerily lifelike sculpture *Young Worker* and Roger Brown's dark *Guilty Without Trial: Protected by the Bill of Rights* are among the most impressive.

Richard and Pat Johnson Palm Beach County History Museum

300 N Dixie Hwy • Tues–Sat 10am–5pm • Free • ☎ 561 832 4164, ⓦ historicalsocietypbc.org

Inside the restored 1916 courthouse is the entertaining **Richard and Pat Johnson Palm Beach County History Museum**, where you'll find an absorbing interpretation of Palm Beach history, utilizing touch-screen maps on a fifty-inch screen (highlighting the most dramatic events). Special exhibitions on city notables such as Addison Mizner are organized too.

Lion Country Safari

2003 Lion Country Safari Rd, off Hwy-80/Southern Blvd • Mon–Fri 10am–5pm, Sat & Sun 9.30am–5.30pm; last vehicles admitted 4 or 4.30pm • $29.95, children 3–9 $21.95; parking $6 • ☎ 561 793 1084, ⓦ lioncountrysafari.com

West Palm Beach makes a good base for a day-trip to the **Lion Country Safari**, twenty miles inland from West Palm Beach, where African and Asian wildlife is the star attraction. Lions, elephants, giraffes, chimpanzees, zebras and ostriches are among the creatures roaming a 500-acre preserve in which human visitors are confined to their cars. There's also a walk-through park with a petting zoo.

ARRIVAL AND DEPARTURE   WEST PALM BEACH

By plane Palm Beach International Airport, 1000 James L. Turnage Blvd (☎ 561 471 7400, ⓦ pbia.org), is just off I-95 (special exit between exits 68 and 69), a few miles southwest of downtown West Palm Beach. You can take Palm Tran bus #2 ($2) or a taxi into the city – free shuttles connect with the Tri-Rail station. All the major car rental companies have counters at the airport.

By car West Palm Beach is easy to navigate by car. I-95 is the main north–south thoroughfare, and Hwy 1 – here called the Dixie Highway – runs right through the middle of town.

By bus The Greyhound station (☎ 561 833 8534) is located at 205 S Tamarind Ave, and linked by regular shuttle buses to the downtown area. Most local Palm Tran (☎ 561 841 4287) bus routes converge at the West Palm Beach Intermodal Transit Center.

Destinations Daytona Beach (2 daily; 5hr 25min–6hr 30min); Fort Pierce (4 daily; 1hr); Miami (4 daily; 1hr 55min–2hr 20min); Tampa (4 daily; 6hr 15min–8hr 15min).

By train The Tri-Rail and West Palm Beach Amtrak stations are located at nos. 203 and 209 S Tamarind Ave respectively, and linked by regular shuttle buses to the downtown area.

INFORMATION

Tourist information The Chamber of Commerce, 401 N Flagler Drive, at 4th St (Mon–Fri 8.30am–5pm; ☎ 561 833 3711, ⓦ palmbeaches.org), has stacks of free leaflets and can answer questions on the Palm Beach County area. Coming from I-95, stop at the Palm Beach County

Convention and Visitors Bureau (Discover Palm Beach County), 1555 Palm Beach Lakes Blvd, Suite 800 (Mon–Fri 8.30am–5.30pm; ☎ 561 233 3000, ⓦ palmbeachfl.com), which also provides free maps, brochures and information on the whole region.

ACCOMMODATION

Best Western Palm Beach Lakes Inn 1800 Palm Beach Lakes Blvd ☎ 561 683 8810, ⓦ bestwestern westpalm.com. You can often find good bargains at this motel, which has recently been renovated, sparkling clean rooms, a small tropical pool and free continental breakfast; it's across from the Palm Beach Mall, about 15min from

downtown. $109

Grandview Gardens 1608 Lake Ave ☎ 561 833 9023, ⓦ grandview-gardens.com. Each of the rooms at this gem of a B&B is individually decorated in a Spanish Mediterranean style and has a private terrace overlooking the pool. $149

Hyatt Place West Palm Beach 295 Lakeview Ave ☎561 655 1454, ⊚westpalmbeach.place.hyatt.com. One of the nicer area chains, this smart hotel offers everything you'd expect – comfortable beds, complimentary wi-fi, 42" flat screens and a great location. **$179**

★**Palm Beach Hibiscus** 213 S Rosemary Ave ☎561 833 8171, ⊚palmbeachhibiscus.com. This lovely B&B consists of two houses built in 1917, lovingly restored, and

sitting nestled in a lush tropical courtyard. There are eight comfortable rooms, many with four-poster beds. The outdoor dining space, *Our Backyard Bar*, serves dinner to the public. **$179**

West Palm Beach Marriott 1001 Okeechobee Blvd ☎561 833 1234, ⊚marriott.com. Centrally located, reliable business hotel, very close to the shops and restaurants of CityPlace. Rooms have all the usual amenities, including wi-fi. **$161**

EATING

★**Darbster** 8020 S Dixie Hwy ☎561 586 2622, ⊚darbster.com. Named for the owners' poodle, Darby, this all-vegan restaurant won't leave carnivores feeling deprived. The tempeh Reuben sandwich and grilled cauliflower main are standouts. Sandwiches from $9, main courses from $13. Tues–Fri 5–10pm, Sat 10.30am–3pm & 5pm–10pm, Sun 10.30am–3pm & 5–9pm.

Havana 6801 S Dixie Hwy ☎561 547 9799, ⊚havanacubanfood.com. This family-owned Cuban restaurant has been a WPB fixture since 1993. You can't go wrong with a classic Cuban sandwich with a side of *tostones* and black beans. Sandwiches from $6.29. Mon–Thurs & Sun 11am–10pm, Fri & Sat 11am–11pm.

Rhythm Café 3800A S Dixie Hwy ☎561 833 3406, ⊚rhythmcafe.cc. Be sure to make reservations for a seat at one of the twelve tables in this tiny, eclectic restaurant.

The scallops are justly popular, and the goat's cheese pie is as decadent as it sounds. Main courses from $20. Tues–Sat 5.30–10pm, Sun 5.30–9pm.

Sloan's 112 Clematis St ☎561 833 3335, ⊚sloansonline .com. Great downtown spot for baked goods and ice cream in creative flavours such as cotton candy (candyfloss) and tiramisu with fanciful old-time candy store decor. There's another outpost at CityPlace. Scoops from $5. Mon–Wed & Sun noon–10pm, Thurs–Sat noon–11pm.

Table 26° 1700 S Dixie Hwy ☎561 855 2660, ⊚table26palmbeach.com. This casual yet classy spot serves "global comfort food", such as waygu meatloaf and buttermilk fried chicken, as well as a fantastic brunch – try the cinnamon doughnut holes or Dixie biscuits and gravy. Main dishes from $19. Mon–Thurs 5–10pm, Fri & Sat 5–11pm, Sun 10.30am–2pm & 5–10pm.

DRINKING AND NIGHTLIFE

There are plenty of clubs and bars in West Palm, but do note that turnover is relatively high, so make sure to call ahead before you head out.

The Blind Monk 410 Evernia St #107 ☎561 833 3605, ⊚theblindmonk.com. This swanky wine bar has an elegant atmosphere, and serves wines by the glass and bottle, as well as a good selection of craft beers and tasty small bites. Mon–Thurs & Sun 4pm–midnight, Fri & Sat 4pm–2am.

O'Shea's Irish Pub 531 Clematis St ☎561 833 3865, ⊚osheaspub.com. This fun bar does a fine job of reproducing all the usual Irish pub classics: gut-busting breakfast plates, Guinness and Murphy's stout on draft, and live music at the weekends. There's also a yappy hour on Mondays, when dog owners can bring Fido and get a free drink on the patio. Mon–Thurs & Sun 11am–3am, Fri & Sat 11am–4am.

Respectable Street Café 518 Clematis St ☎561 832 9999, ⊚sub-culture.org/respectable-street. Check out this long-standing loud, dark dance club with DJs, live local and national acts (cover usually $10–20), and frequent drink specials. Thurs–Sat 10pm–4am.

Revolutions 700 S Rosemary Ave ☎561 203 6188, ⊚revolutionsbowl.com. The retro fascination with bowling alleys is well realized at this fun spot in CityPlace. There are twenty lanes and a hopping bar scene with either a DJ or live music on Friday and Saturday nights. There's a good menu as well, featuring pizzas, burgers and sandwiches. Mon–Thurs & Sun 11am–midnight, Fri & Sat 11am–2am.

The Treasure Coast

West Palm Beach marks the end of the southeast coast's heavily populated (and affluent) sections. The next eighty miles – dubbed the **TREASURE COAST** for the booty of a Spanish galleon that sank here in 1715 – has seen a much slower rate of expansion than its neighbours to the south, leaving wide-open spaces, ruggedly beautiful barrier islands, and magnificent swathes of quiet beach that attract Florida's nature lovers, as well as a small band of well-informed sun-seekers.

Singer Island

North of West Palm Beach, Hwy-A1A swings back to the coast at **SINGER ISLAND**, which gets its name from the sewing-machine heir Paris Singer, a prominent property developer in the area.

John D. MacArthur Beach State Park

Daily 8am–sunset; nature centre daily 9am–5pm • Cars $5, pedestrians and cyclists $2; kayak rentals $12/hr for a single, $18/hr for a double; kayak tours $25 single, $40 double • ☎ 561 624 6950, ⊛ floridastateparks.org

On the northern end of the island you'll find the **John D. MacArthur Beach State Park**. A twenty-minute nature walk winds through a mixed maritime hammock; elsewhere, a 1600ft boardwalk crosses a mangrove-fringed estuary – popular among manatees, wading birds (at low tide), and a wide variety of fish – to a picturesque beach bordered by sea grape trees. From the boardwalk's end, some worthwhile dirt trails lead off behind the barrier beach's dunes; the park also offers kayak rentals, ranger-led kayak tours, free evening concerts in its covered amphitheatre and summertime turtle walks.

Juno Beach

There's a large, free car park at Juno Beach Park

The few miles north of Singer Island are mostly golf courses and planned retirement communities, but one good stop is **JUNO BEACH**, where Hwy-A1A follows a high coastal bluff from which it's relatively easy to find paths down over the protected dunes to the uncrowded sands below – leave your car at **Juno Beach Park**, where you'll find a beach with a snack bar, lifeguards on duty, restrooms and a fishing pier.

Loggerhead Marinelife Center

14200 Hwy-1 • Mon–Sat 10am–5pm, Sun 11am–5pm; turtle expeditions Wed & Sat evenings, June & July; reservations taken from May • Free admission to centre; expeditions $17 • ☎ 561 627 8280, ⊛ marinelife.org

The **Loggerhead Marinelife Center** is intended for kids, but is also of interest to adults keen to brush up on their knowledge of marine life, and **sea turtles** in particular. There's a turtle hospital and informative displays on their life cycles here, and it's one of a few places along the Treasure Coast where you can go on expeditions to watch the turtles as they steal ashore to lay eggs under cover of darkness (June and July only). Reservations for this are essential; the centre can provide you with further details.

Jupiter and Jupiter Island

Splitting into several colourless districts around the wide mouth of the Tequesta River, **JUPITER**, about six miles north of Juno Beach, was a rumrunners' haven during the Prohibition era; these days it's better known as the home town of actor Burt Reynolds. Just north of Jupiter itself is **Jupiter Island**, an affluent barrier island primarily worth visiting for its preserves and parks.

BASEBALL ON THE TREASURE COAST

Baseball enthusiasts will be pleased to note sleepy Jupiter plays host to two major league teams for spring training: the **Miami Marlins** (⊛ marlins.mlb.com) and **St Louis Cardinals** (⊛ cardinals.mlb.com), the 2011 World Series champions. Both play at the Roger Dean Stadium, 4751 Main St (☎ 561 775 1818, ⊛ rogerdeanstadium.com), between late February and late March – check the websites for schedules and tickets. A bit further north, at Port St Lucie, the **New York Mets** (⊛ mets.mlb.com) hold court at Tradition Field, 525 NW Peacock Blvd (☎ 772 871 2115, ⊛ traditionfield.com).

Hibel Museum of Art

On the Florida Atlantic University campus at the corner of University Blvd and Main St • Tues–Fri 11am–4pm • Free • ☎ 561 622 5560, ⓦ hibelartmuseum.org

Forget Warhol and Rothko; the most commercially successful artist in the US is Edna Hibel, a nonagenarian resident of Singer Island and the only female artist ever to paint for ten decades straight. Hibel turns 98 in 2015, and poor eyesight means she's less prolific in creating new canvases of serene Asian and Mexican women or mothers and children. Pay a visit, though, to the **Hibel Museum of Art**, if only to admire the unflappable devotion of the guides, and to figure out why Hibel originals change hands for $75,000 at the gallery shop.

River Center

805 N US-1 in Burt Reynolds Park • Tues–Sat 9am–4pm • Free • ☎ 561 743 7123, ⓦ loxahatcheeriver.org

For a well-presented introduction to the ecology of the Loxahatchee River, visit the **River Center** in **Burt Reynolds Park**, centrally located and named after Jupiter's favourite son. A combination of static displays, interactive exhibits and live tanks trace the river system, from freshwater cypress swamp to seagrass-dominated estuary to marine ecosystems.

Jupiter Inlet Lighthouse & Museum

500 Captain Armour's Way; you'll see the lighthouse from US-1, off Beach Rd (Rte-707) • Jan–April daily 10am–5pm; May–Dec Tues–Sun 10am–5pm; last tour 4pm • $9 • ☎ 561 747 8380, ⓦ jupiterlighthouse.org

Worth a stop – and a climb – is the red-brick **Jupiter Inlet Lighthouse & Museum** on the north bank of Jupiter Inlet; it was completed in 1860 – making it the oldest building in Palm Beach County – and houses an absorbing museum detailing the history of the region. You can keep following Beach Road (Rte-707) for Jupiter Island.

Blowing Rocks Preserve

Jupiter Island • Daily 9am–4.30pm • $2 • ☎ 561 744 6668

Two miles into **Jupiter Island** on Beach Road (which starts back in Jupiter Town on US-1, at the lighthouse), pull up at the **Blowing Rocks Preserve**. Here a limestone outcrop covers much of the beach and powerful incoming tides are known to drive through the rocks' hollows, emerging as gusts of spray further on. At low tide, it's sometimes possible to walk around the outcrop and peer into the rock's sea-drilled cavities. Visit the **Hawley Education Center** (same hours; free) across the road from the car park, which has displays on Jupiter Island habitats and one called Tides of Life, exploring Nature Conservancy work in Florida as well as globally. There's also a **trail** into the thick mangroves on Indian River Lagoon.

Hobe Sound Beach Park

Free parking

Beyond Blowing Rocks Preserve, Beach Road continues for another 6.5 miles through the exclusive residences of Jupiter Inlet Colony and Jupiter Island, before reaching **Hobe Sound Beach Park** – frustratingly, you'll hardly glimpse the sea the whole way. The 300ft stretch of pretty, shell-strewn beach here is just begging for a towel and umbrella.

Hobe Sound National Wildlife Refuge

Daily sunrise–sunset; turtle walks late May to July Tues & Thurs evenings, reservations accepted from April 1; nature centre Mon–Sat 9am–3pm • Turtle walks $5; nature centre free • Wildlife refuge ☎ 772 546 6141; turtle hikes and nature centre ☎ 772 546 2067, ⓦ hobesoundnaturecenter.com

The beach at Hobe Sound Beach Park is pleasant enough, but you're better off heading two miles north on North Beach Road to the 1000-plus acres of **Hobe Sound National Wildlife Refuge**. Having achieved spectacular success as a nesting ground for sea turtles during the summer, the refuge is also rich in birdsong, with the rare scrub jay among its tuneful inhabitants. To learn more about the refuge's flora and fauna, retrace your steps to Hobe Beach and head inland on County Road 708, turning south when you hit US-1; a short drive from here lies the refuge's **nature centre**, which has exhibits on native habitats, endangered species and tanks with baby alligators, as well as two short **nature trails**, one of which leads down to the pretty shores of the Indian River Lagoon.

St Lucie Inlet Preserve State Park

Daily 8am–sunset • Entry: boats $3, kayaks and canoes $2 • ☎ 772 219 1880, ⓦ floridastateparks.org/stlucieinlet

The car park of Hobe Sound National Wildlife Refuge is the furthest point north your vehicle can travel on Jupiter Island, but there's still more to see. The more than 900 acres of **St Lucie Inlet Preserve State Park** include mangrove-lined creeks and over two miles of beach, accessible only by water or by walking the nearly five miles of beach from the Hobe refuge. The park's remoteness makes it a special place to visit, and also a very difficult one to get to. There is a kayak launch site directly across the **Intracoastal Waterway** in Stuart (at the eastern end of Cove Rd), and a kayak rental outfitter five miles from there (South River Outfitters, 7647 Lost River Rd; Wed–Fri 9am–4pm, Sat & Sun 9am–5pm; single kayak $26/half-day, double kayak $36/half-day, canoe $36/half-day; ☎772 223 1500, ⓦsouthriveroutfitters.com), but you have to find your own way of getting the kayak to the water.

Jonathan Dickinson State Park

Daily 8am–sunset • Cars $6, pedestrians and cyclists $2 • ☎ 772 546 2771, ⓦ floridastateparks.org/jonathandickinson

Two miles south of the Hobe Sound nature centre on US-1, the **Jonathan Dickinson State Park**, named for a Quaker who washed ashore here in 1696, preserves a natural landscape quite different from what you'll see at the coast. Climb up the observation tower atop **Hobe Mountain**, one mile from the entrance, an ancient 86ft-high sand dune, for sweeping views of the ocean, the Intracoastal and the entire park, including the sand pine scrub and palmetto (a stumpy, tropical palm fan) flatlands.

The Trapper Nelson Interpretive Center and Kimbell Center

The more adventurous can drive four miles to the end of the park road, **rent a canoe or kayak** ($16/2hr, $5 for each additional hour for canoes; $15/2hr for a single kayak, $20/2hr for a double kayak, $6 for each additional hour) from the concession store (daily 9am–5pm; ☎561 746 1466), and explore the mangrove-lined **Loxahatchee River**, Florida's first river to be federally designated as "wild and scenic". Don't be put off by the preponderance of alligators; continue paddling to the **Trapper Nelson Interpretive Center** (Mon & Thurs–Sun 9.30am–4.30pm; by river only), where rangers give guided tours of the former homestead of a "wild man" pioneer from the 1930s who, in his 38 years here, built log cabins, tropical gardens and a wildlife zoo. Allow three to four hours for a round trip. A less strenuous way to reach it is to take a two-hour guided **boat tour** (4 daily at 9am, 11am, 1pm & 3pm; $19, children 6–12 $12); call the concession to make reservations. Also near the concession, the **Kimbell Center** (daily 9am–5pm; free; ☎561 745 5551) highlights the cultural and natural resources of the park with interactive displays.

Hiking trails

The park also offers a network of **hiking trails**, including the leisurely, one-hour **Kitching Creek trail** and the nine-mile **East Loop trail**, which starts and ends at the entrance and passes through two primitive campgrounds (obtain maps at the entrance office). Keep your eyes open for snakes, birds, alligators, deer, bobcats, and some of the park's 140 species of bird.

ARRIVAL AND DEPARTURE   JUPITER AND JUPITER ISLAND

By car Jupiter and Jupiter Island are reachable via I-95 and/or Hwy-1.

By bus Public transport to Jupiter is extremely limited, but you can take Palm Tran bus #10 ($1.50) from Gardens Mall in Palm Beach Gardens to central Jupiter (no Sun service).

ACCOMMODATION AND EATING

Jonathan Dickinson State Park ☎ 800 326 3521, ⓦ reserveamerica.com. There are campgrounds with water and electricity at Jonathan Dickinson State Park, but space must be booked in advance. In addition to RV and tent sites, rustic cabins are available. Camp sites $26, cabins $80

★**Little Moir's Food Shack** 103 S Hwy-1

☎ 561 741 3626, ⓦ littlemoirs.com/food-shack.com. Festively decorated with bamboo, surfboards and tropical paintings, this place serves up some of the area's best seafood in creative, Caribbean- and Asian-inspired ways, with an extensive beer list. It's tucked into a Publix strip mall off the highway. Mon–Wed 11am–9.30pm, Thurs–Sat 11am–10pm.

Stuart and Hutchinson Island

HUTCHINSON ISLAND, another long barrier island, lies immediately north of Jupiter Island. To reach it (with either US-1 or Hwy-A1A), you'll first pass through the surprisingly congested and downtrodden strip malls of **STUART**, which nevertheless has a small but attractive downtown district on the south bank of the St Lucie River. Along the river you'll find an attractive riverside walk with speciality stores and restaurants.

Stuart Heritage Museum

161 SW Flagler Ave • Daily 10am–3pm • Free • ☎ 772 220 4600, ⓦ stuartheritagemuseum.com

Among the century-old wooden buildings proudly preserved on and around Flagler Avenue is the 1901 general store that now houses the **Stuart Heritage Museum**. Staffed by enthusiastic volunteers, it's built of rock-hard Dade County pine and filled with memorabilia and artefacts from the town's early years, with displays on such diverse topics as the local Seminole tribes, the pineapple industry and the great Flagler himself.

Hutchinson Island

Largely hidden behind thick vegetation, several beautiful beaches line twenty-mile-long **Hutchinson Island**, located to the east of Stuart along Hwy-A1A, which is also known as Ocean Boulevard once it traverses the Indian River.

Gilbert's Bar House of Refuge

301 SE MacArthur Blvd • Mon–Sat 10am–4pm, Sun 1–4pm • $8, children $3 • ☎ 772 225 1875, ⓦ houseofrefugefl.org

Once you're on the island, a right turn onto MacArthur Boulevard brings you past the *Marriott* and a mile of condos to **Gilbert's Bar House of Refuge**, a convincingly restored refuge for shipwrecked sailors that was one of ten erected along Florida's east coast in 1876, and is the only one still standing.

Bathtub Reef Park

1585 SE MacArthur Blvd • 24hr • Free parking

A mile south of the House of Refuge, **Bathtub Reef Park** lives up to its name; at low tide, a series of exposed reefs just offshore creates a protected, bath-like swimming area ideal for snorkellers and just about anybody else looking to loll about in calm, warm waters.

Elliott Museum

825 NE Ocean Blvd • Daily 10am–5pm • $14, children 6–12 $6 • ☎ 772 225 1961, ⓦ elliottmuseumfl.org

Back on Hwy-A1A and next to **Stuart Beach**, a wide and low-key stretch of sand where locals generally outnumber tourists, you'll find the **Elliott Museum**. Initially established to commemorate inventor Sterling Elliott, the newly rebuilt museum houses an impressive collection of vintage automobiles and boats, as well as a re-creation of a Stuart Main Street at the turn of the twentieth century. Rotating exhibits feature science, technology and design themes.

Florida Oceanographic Coastal Center

890 NE Ocean Blvd • Mon–Sat 10am–5pm, Sun noon–4pm; nature walks Mon–Sat at 10.15am, 11.45am & 2.45pm, Sun at 2.15pm • $12, children $6 • ☎ 772 225 0505, ⊛ floridaocean.org

Across the street from the Elliott Museum, the **Florida Oceanographic Coastal Center** offers hands-on opportunities for learning about Florida's marine life, including a stingray touch tank, a large game-fish lagoon, and looping mile-long nature trail. If you want to know what you're looking at, take one of the guided nature walks. You can also participate in the daily feeding of game fish and stingrays (check the website for times).

Jensen Beach

North of the Elliott Museum, **Jensen Beach** straddles the Indian River and has a small, pleasant beach on its oceanside. To reach the northern half of the island, known as North Hutchinson Island (see p.211), you'll need to pass through Fort Pierce, another eighteen tranquil miles on Hwy-A1A, though there's little point in stopping along the way.

ARRIVAL AND INFORMATION   STUART AND HUTCHINSON ISLAND

By car Stuart and Hutchinson Island are reachable via I-95 and/or Hwy-1.

By bus Public transport is extremely limited, but Martin County Transit does run one north/south route through Stuart as well as one on the Treasure Coast. The fare is

$1.50; check ⊛ transit.martin.fl.us/ for route details.
Tourist information You can pick up maps and the like from the Chamber of Commerce at 1650 S Kanner Hwy, half a mile west of US-1 (Mon–Thurs 8.30am–4pm, Fri 8.30am–1pm; ☎ 772 287 1088, ⊛ stuartmartinchamber.org).

ACCOMMODATION AND EATING

Bluewater Beach Grill 2025 Seaway Drive ☎ 772 466 0023, ⊛ bluewaterbeachgrill.com; map opposite. This waterfront spot on south Hutchinson Island is popular with surfers and serves up great tacos, wings, salads and burgers. Average main $10. Daily 11am–10pm.

District Table & Bar 900 SE Indian St ☎ 772 324 8357; map opposite. The Southern-inspired fare at this welcoming spot is seasonally driven and so menus change frequently. Menu standouts are the house charcuterie plate and the chicken-liver mousse with a cornmeal waffle. Mains from $18. Tues–Thurs & Sun 5–10pm, Fri & Sat 5–11pm.

Four Fish Inn & Marina Near the banks of the Indian River at 2225 NE Indian River Drive, Jensen Beach ☎ 772 334 0936, ⊛ aamarina.com. Avoid Hutchinson Island's often-pricey accommodation rates by staying at this tropical-themed place with colourful and fully equipped studio apartments in Jensen Beach, just northeast of downtown Stuart. $75

The Gafford 47 SW Flagler Ave, Stuart ☎ 772 221 9517, ⊛ thegafford.com. Named for a gigantic 18oz bone-in ribeye steak called the Gafford, this classy establishment serves up lots of well-prepared meat and fish. The BBQ grilled salmon and fried chicken are other menu standouts. Mains from $15. Tues–Thurs & Sun 4–9pm, Fri & Sat 4–10pm.

Inn Shephard's Park Bed & Breakfast 601 SW Ocean Blvd ☎ 772 781 4244; map opposite. This charming four-room B&B is within walking distance of downtown Stuart. You'll get a tasty continental breakfast as well as complimentary beach chairs, bicycles and coolers for your visit to nearby Hutchinson Beach. $150

Riverwalk Café 201 SW St Lucie Ave, Stuart ☎ 772 221 1511, ⊛ riverwalkcafeandoysterbar.net. For a bite to eat in downtown Stuart, try this cosy café, located at the start of the Riverwalk. Mon–Thurs 11.30am–9pm, Fri 11.30am–10pm, Sat 5–10pm.

Fort Pierce

The bulk of workaday **FORT PIERCE** (looped through by Hwy-A1A) lies two miles inland, across the Intracoastal Waterway, where tourism plays second fiddle to processing and transporting the produce of Florida's citrus farms. If you're driving north along Hwy-A1A, you'll hit the scrappy beach side of town first, with a motley assembly of motels, bars and restaurants.

Marine Center

420 Seaway Drive • Tues–Sat 10am–4pm, Sun noon–4pm, Mon 10am–4pm from Jan to March • $4; free first Tues of month • ☎ 772 462 3474

En route to downtown Fort Pierce, and beside the South Bridge to the mainland, the **Marine Center** houses the **Smithsonian Marine Ecosystems Exhibit**, a thoughtful

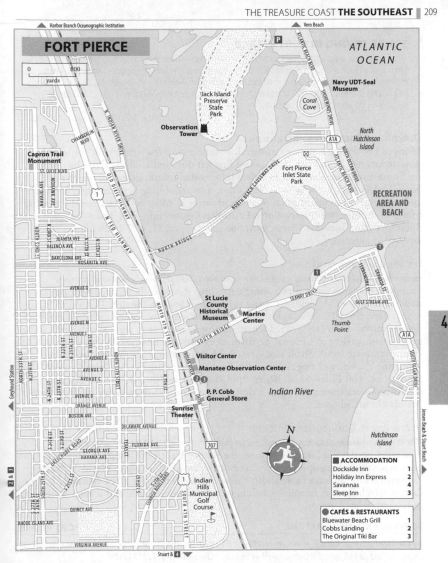

introduction to the marine life within Indian River Lagoon, through aquariums, touch tanks and displays.

St Lucie County Regional History Center

414 Seaway Drive • Wed–Sat 10am–4pm, Sun 1–4pm • $4 • ☎ 772 462 1795

Near the Marine Center, the **St Lucie County Regional History Center** houses a full-sized Seminole *chickee* (a palm-thatched hut), a solid account told in words and pictures of the Seminole Wars, the 1838 fort from which Fort Pierce took its name, and a re-creation of P.P. Cobb's general store, the hub of the early twentieth-century town. Outside the museum at the **Gardner House**, a 1907 "cracker" cottage, note the tall ceilings and many windows that allowed the muggy Florida air to circulate in the days before air conditioning.

SCUBA DIVING IN FORT PIERCE

The Fort Pierce area, with several offshore shipwrecks – some dating back to the time of the Spanish galleons – and an abundance of Florida lobsters, is known for good **scuba diving**, especially in the summer months when the waters are warmer and calmer. Try Dive Odyssea, 621 N 2nd St (☎772 460 1771, ⓦdiveodyssea.com), for local diving trips in the $100 range (including equipment and a wetsuit).

Downtown Fort Pierce and around

Much of Fort Pierce is starkly industrial, but there are a few worthwhile stops in the **downtown area**. From Hwy-A1A, take a first left onto Indian River Drive just beyond the South Bridge for Fort Pierce's **visitor information centre**, located in the historic Seven Gables House (see below). Next door, if you're visiting between mid-November and early April, you might catch sight of manatees in Moore's Creek from the viewing bridge of the **Manatee Observation & Education Center** (July–Sept Thurs–Sat 10am–5pm; Oct–June Tues–Sat 10am–5pm, Sun noon–4pm; $1; ☎772 429 6266, ⓦmanateecenter.com).

Historic downtown district

You can park on most of the streets downtown for free (2hr max) and there's a free public garage between A and Orange aves

From the Manatee Center it's a short drive into the expertly restored **historic downtown district**. A highlight is the refurbished **Sunrise Theatre**, 117 S 2nd St, which dates from 1923, was closed in 1983 and reopened following a $12-million-dollar renovation in late 2005. Identifiable by its retro neon sign, the theatre hosts a wide variety of national performances and concerts (☎772 461 4775, ⓦsunrisetheatre.com). Stroll along nearby Avenue A towards the harbour to see some fine examples of original wooden houses, including the **P.P. Cobb General Store** at no. 100 (Tues–Sat 8.30am–9pm, Sun 10am–4pm; ☎772 465 7010, ⓦppcobbgeneralstore.com), now a deli serving sandwiches and over five hundred brands of bottled beer.

Harbor Branch Oceanographic Institute

5600 N US-1 • Ocean Discovery Center Mon–Fri 10am–5pm, Sat 10am–2pm • Free • ☎772 242 2293, ⓦfau.edu/hboi

Five miles north of St Lucie Boulevard, the **Harbor Branch Oceanographic Institute** is a phenomenally well-equipped deep-sea research centre belonging to Florida Atlantic University. You can learn more about the work conducted here at the **Ocean Discovery Center**, which features interactive exhibits, tanks of tropical fish, and regular screenings of research-related videos.

ARRIVAL AND INFORMATION · FORT PIERCE

By car Hwy-1 cuts right through downtown Fort Pierce; if you're travelling via I-95, get off at Orange Ave/Hwy 68 and head east for about 4 miles.

By bus The Greyhound bus station (☎772 461 3299) is 6 miles from downtown at 7150 Okeechobee Rd, near the junction of Hwy-70 and Florida's Turnpike. A taxi from here to the beach will cost around $20, and downtown $27; try Checker Cab (☎772 878 1234).

Tourist information The visitor information centre is in Seven Gables House at 482 Indian River Drive (Tues–Fri 10am–5pm, Sat 10am–4pm; ☎772 468 9152).

ACCOMMODATION

Dockside Inn 1160 Seaway Drive ☎772 468 3555, ⓦdocksideinn.com. You can join fishing locals at this comfortable inn, which has five fishing piers, numerous boat slips, and waterfront BBQ grills for cooking up your catch, in addition to a pool and a variety of rooms and apartments. **$79**

Holiday Inn Express 7151 Okeechobee Rd ☎772 464 5000, ⓦhiexpress.com. One of the smarter motels in the area, with spacious rooms and all the usual amenities, including laundry, a small pool, a filling complimentary breakfast and free wi-fi. **$82**

Savannas 1400 Midway Rd ☏772 464 7855. For camping, head inland and 7 miles south of downtown Fort Pierce along Rte-707 to this sizeable square of reclaimed marshland beside the Indian River. You can explore the surrounding unspoiled landscape on one of the site's nature trails, or rent a kayak ($5/hr). Camping $10–15.25 for tent

sites, $25.25 for sites with electricity
Sleep Inn 2715 Cross Road Parkway ☏772 595 6080, ⓦsleepinn.com. A worthy alternative to the *Holiday Inn*, this chain motel features neat, comfy rooms, a small pool, free wi-fi and a continental breakfast.$70

EATING AND DRINKING

Cobb's Landing 200 N Indian River Drive ☏772 460 9014, ⓦcobbs-landing.com. Sit on the patio overlooking the marina at this casual, friendly fish house in downtown Fort Pierce. Try the fresh catch of the day or the flavourful coconut shrimp bowl ($18). Mon–Thurs & Sun 11am–10pm, Fri & Sat 11am–11 pm.
The Original Tiki Bar 2nd Ave A at the Fort Pierce

Marina ☏772 461 0880, ⓦoriginaltikibar.com. Everything about this waterfront bar and restaurant, from the thatched roof to the candy-coloured walls and tribal masks adorning the walls, screams tiki kitsch – in a good way. There's a great raw bar, soups and sandwiches, and mains for around $17. Daily 11am–10pm.

North Hutchinson Island

Lots of high-rise condos and time-shares make for somewhat less than inspiring views on this stretch of barrier island; nevertheless, there are some lovely beaches and great state parks worthy of a stop.

Fort Pierce Inlet State Park
Entrance just off Hwy-A1A • Daily 8am–sunset • Cars $6, pedestrians and cyclists $2 • ☏772 468 3985

Covering 340 acres at the southern tip of North Hutchinson Island, **Fort Pierce Inlet State Park** overlooks the Fort Pierce Inlet and the community's beach. It's a scenic setting for a picnic, as well as a launch site for local surfers.

Navy UDT-SEAL Museum
3300 N Hwy-A1A • Tues Sat 10am–4pm, Sun noon–4pm • $8 • ☏772 595 5845, ⓦnavysealmuseum.com

Located between North Hutchinson Island's two state parks, the **Navy UDT-SEAL Museum** is dedicated to the US Navy's Frogman demolition teams. During World War II, the UDTs (Underwater Demolition Teams) trained on Hutchinson Island, which, like most of Florida's barrier islands, was off-limits to civilians at the time. The more elite SEALs (Sea Air Land) came into being later during the 1960s. The museum's outdoor exhibits include a Vietnam-era Huey helicopter, Apollo training crafts, and several beach obstacles used for training that have been recovered from the ocean.

KAYAKING THE INDIAN RIVER LAGOON

Boating opportunities abound in southern Florida, but some of the best flat-water **kayaking** in the world can be found on the **Indian River Lagoon**, home to a wide array of wildlife including pelican, osprey, dolphin, manatee, stingray and sea turtle. The lagoon is actually a saltwater estuary, stretching 156 miles from the Space Coast to Jupiter, with a width that varies between a half-mile and five miles.

A couple of outfitters in the area offer guided excursions to various parts of the lagoon – a great idea if you're new to the area. Call ahead to check schedules or make a reservation.

A Day Away Kayak Tours ☏321 268 2655, ⓦadayawaykayaktours.com. Tours (1hr 30min–2hr) launch most days from Haulover Canal — be sure to check website for directions. $30 including kayak rental.

Adventure Kayaking Tours Vero Beach ☏772 567 0522, ⓦpaddleflorida.com. Daily 3hr tours from $45; children 12 years and under $25. Longer camping trips are offered Nov–May.

Vero Beach and around

A preponderance of private communities block Hwy-A1A's ocean view for much of the drive north, until North Hutchinson Island imperceptibly becomes Orchid Island and you reach **VERO BEACH**, the area's sole community of substance and one with a pronounced upmarket image. It makes an enjoyable hideaway, however, with a fine group of beaches around Ocean Drive, parallel to Hwy-A1A.

Sebastian Inlet State Park

9700 S Hwy-A1A • 24hr • Cars $4 for one person, $8 for two or more, pedestrians and cyclists $2 • ☎ 321 984 4852, ⓦ floridastateparks.org

Tiny beachside communities dot the rest of Orchid Island but you'll find most activity near the **Sebastian Inlet State Park**, sixteen miles north of Vero Beach. Roaring ocean breakers lure surfers here, particularly during the bimonthly surfing contest, and anglers cram the jetties for the finest saltwater fishing on Florida's east coast.

McLarty Treasure Museum

Sebastian Inlet State Park • Daily 10am–4pm • $2 • ☎ 772 589 2147

The **McLarty Treasure Museum** tells the story of the 1715 Spanish Fleet that ran aground just offshore (and gave its name to this stretch of coast), through artefacts, displays and video presentations.

Sebastian Fishing Museum

Sebastian Inlet State Park • Daily 10am–4pm • Free, though park admission is required

You can explore local fishing history at the **Sebastian Fishing Museum**, which contains a replica of an original fish house, a home-made fishing boat, nets, fishing gear and old photos of the Indian River Lagoon. There's also a twenty-minute video on commercial fishing in Sebastian.

ARRIVAL AND ACTIVITIES

By car The area is accessible by I-95 or Hwy-1.

Boat and kayak rental You can rent powerboats (from $200/day) and kayaks ($45/day for a single) at the Sebastian Inlet Marina, 9502 S Hwy-A1A (☎ 321 724 5424, ⓦ sebastianinlet.com).

VERO BEACH AND AROUND

Manatee and dolphin watching Contact River Queen Cruises at Mulligan's Docks, 806 Indian River Drive (☎ 772 589 6161 or ☎ 888 755 6161, ⓦ sebastianriverqueencruises .com), which runs daily cruises on Indian River Lagoon for $28–232 (1hr 30min–3hr).

ACCOMMODATION AND EATING

The Driftwood Resort 3150 Ocean Drive, Vero Beach ☎ 772 231 0550, ⓦ verobeachdriftwood.com. There's little to tempt you from the sands but it's worth checking out this 1930s hotel, now home to fully equipped studios and apartments, erected from a jumble of driftwood, bells, religious statuary, mosaics, flea-market finds and pieces of demolished Palm Beach mansions. $125

Scampi Grill 2054 11th Ave, Vero Beach ☎ 772 563 9766. This romantic Italian bistro serves up lots of traditional dishes and home-made pasta. Try the penne and shrimp à la vodka or the veal piccata. Mains from $18. Mon–Sat 5–10pm.

Sebastian Inlet State Park campsite ⓦ reserve america.com. There is some great camping in the park; all 43 pitches have water and electrical hook-ups, a fire ring with grill and a picnic table. $28

Waldo's At the Driftwood Resort, 3150 Ocean Drive, Vero Beach ☎ 772 231 7091, ⓦ waldosvero.com. The ocean- and poolside restaurant bar of *the Driftwood Resort* (see above) serves items like beer-battered mahi-mahi fingers, salads and Cajun fish sandwiches (around $10 for lunch), as well as more substantial dinner selections. Mon–Thurs 11am–10pm, Fri & Sat 11am–11pm, Sun 11am–9pm.

South central Florida

Sandwiched in the triangle between the affluent beaches of Palm Beach and Tampa Bay, and the vacation haunts of Orlando, **SOUTH CENTRAL FLORIDA** seems a world away. The area is worth a brief stop primarily for a taste of rural Florida, which has seen little of the wealth or tourism from the coast. Farming rules here: orange groves, cattle herds and sugar-cane plantations laced with small towns dot the landscape.

Traditional tourism, such as it is, focuses on the region's numerous **lakes**, though unless you enjoy **fishing** (which is, to be fair, top-notch), these tend to be fairly dull. Several of the region's small towns were big towns around the turn of the twentieth century and are keen to flaunt their glory days. Nearby you'll find some refreshingly under-hyped attractions, which were bringing tourists into the state back when Walt Disney was just a schoolboy.

Lake Okeechobee and around

Completely encircled by a massive dyke and invisible from nearby roads, it can be frustratingly difficult to get your first glimpse of **Lake Okeechobee**. Drive up to the top of the dyke and you're in for a bit of a shock: this vast expanse of water can seem like a mini sea, with the far shore too distant to make out. After that first look, though, it's hard to get excited about Lake Okeechobee; utterly featureless, it's surrounded by pancake-flat farmland. The main draw is some of the best **freshwater fishing** in the US, with large-mouthed bass, speckled perch and blue gill the most prized targets. Bird-lovers will also enjoy the lake, as over 120 varieties have been spotted, including the endangered snail kite. Other inhabitants include bobcats, alligators, turtles, otters, snakes and, occasionally, manatees, and you'll definitely see great flocks of white egrets.

Brief history

For centuries, the lake was home exclusively to Native Americans (who named the lake Ok Ichobi or "Big Water" in their Seminole language). The area's first farming settlers began arriving in 1910, encouraged by the work carried out by wealthy Philadelphian Hamilton Disston, who, in the nineteenth century, started dredging canals and draining the surrounding land for agriculture. Next came the railroads, extending around three-quarters of the lake by the late 1920s and providing easy access to the rest of the state.

The lake has always played an important role not only in the lives of communities close to its shores, but also in the life cycle of the **Everglades**. After a devastating hurricane in 1928, a retaining wall, the 35ft-high Herbert Hoover Dike, was built to ring the lake, and the lake has since served as both a flood-control safety valve during hurricane season and a freshwater storage reservoir. Traditionally, Okeechobee has drained slowly south to nourish the Everglades after the summer rains, but ever-increasing demands on its fresh water for the agriculture industry and human consumption continue to strain the Everglades' delicate ecosystem (see p.157).

The lake

Covering 750 square miles and ranging from ten to fourteen feet in depth, **Lake Okeechobee** is fed by the several rivers, creeks and canals that make up the state-traversing Okeechobee Waterway. Although tourist brochures herald the lake as an unspoiled natural landscape, its condition has been a hot environmental issue in Florida for years. Specifically, environmentalists and fishermen have long contested the pumping of billions of gallons of polluted farm runoff into the lake, via the massive pumps along its southern edge; a long-promised clean-up has yet to occur, although a recent court ruling banning "backpumping" may mean a clean-up is finally in store. **Boat tours** are the only way to get onto the water, but fishing fans will get the most out of the lake.

4

Lake Okeechobee Scenic Trail

🕿 352 378 8823, 🌐 floridatrail.org

Perfect if you fancy a challenge, the 110-mile **Lake Okeechobee Scenic Trail** circles the entire lake (most of it along the dyke), with several campgrounds along the way, though hiking the whole thing gets extremely monotonous – **cycling** at least some of it is more fun. For more information, call the Florida Trail Association on the number above.

Okeechobee town

The lakeside community of **OKEECHOBEE**, with plenty of accommodation, food and entertainment, is a prime base from which to explore the area, though its main highways roar with traffic and are lined with miles of grim strip-malls. Most people come here for the superb **fishing** (see opposite).

The town was originally designed by the ubiquitous Henry Flagler (see p.453), whose grandiose plan demanded wide streets and wood-framed buildings, some of which remain in the historic downtown area. The best examples are the **Historical Society Museum & Schoolhouse**, 1850 Hwy-98 N (by appointment only; free; 🕿 863 763 4344), and the 1926 **County Court House** at 304 NW 2nd St (private offices), a pretty example of Mediterranean Revival architecture, a style much favoured by Flagler.

Brighton Seminole Indian Reservation

Leaving Okeechobee via Hwy-441, follow Rte-78, which charts a 34-mile course along the west side of the lake, crossing over the Kissimmee River and continuing into the treeless expanse of Indian Prairie, part of the 35,000-acre **Brighton Seminole Indian Reservation**. To drive into the heart of the reservation, head up Rte-721 (21 miles from Okeechobee).

The Seminoles migrated here in the eighteenth century from Georgia and Alabama (see box, p.162); about 450 remain, as successful cattle farmers. The current residents maintain many aspects of their ancient culture (such as consulting medicine men and speaking their native language), and while handicrafts may be offered from the roadside, you won't find any of the tacky souvenir shops common to reservations in more populous areas.

Seminole Casino

Brighton Seminole Indian Reservation · Daily from 10am · 🕿 866 222 7466 or 🕿 863 467 9998, 🌐 seminolebrightoncasino.com

The tribe runs the **Seminole Casino**, which is open 24/7 and features video gaming, poker, and "high stakes" bingo (call or check website for schedule). The casino acts as a sort of social club for the entire area (mostly non-Seminole), and you've a better chance of meeting Seminole locals in nearby *Alice's Restaurant* (see p.216).

Clewiston

From the Seminole reservation you can continue around the lake for around 27 miles to **CLEWISTON**, which is dominated by the US Sugar Corporation and the company's multimillion-dollar profits. On the way you'll pass miles of **sugar cane** – evidence of Florida being the top sugar producer in the country. First impressions aside – the town is a dreary looking place, lined with fast-food outlets and cheap motels – Clewiston is one of the more rewarding stops around the lake, with relatively plentiful accommodation, though squarely aimed at fishermen. The **Clewiston Museum** at 109 Central Ave, just off US-27 (Mon–Fri 9am–4pm; $4; 🕿 863 983 2870, 🌐 clewistonmuseum.org), provides an interesting rundown of the agricultural and cultural history of the area.

To get out onto Lake Okeechobee itself (Clewiston is lauded for its **largemouth bass fishing**), contact Big "O" Airboat Tours (see opposite).

ARRIVAL AND DEPARTURE

By car South central Florida isn't well served by interstates or public transport; your best bet for getting around is by car. The Lake Okeechobee area is served by three highways, which join to encircle the lake and allow access to the

LAKE OKEECHOBEE AND AROUND

towns dotted around its shores.
By train Although Okeechobee town is relatively easy to get to – Amtrak has a depot at 801 N Parrott Ave – there is no local public transport system.

INFORMATION AND ACTIVITIES

OKEECHOBEE TOWN AND LAKE

Tourist information The Chamber of Commerce of Okeechobee County is at 55 S Parrott Ave (Mon–Fri 9am–noon & 1–4pm; ☎863 467 6246, ⓦokeechobeebusiness.com).
Fishing Contact Garrard's Tackle Shop, 4259 US-441 S (☎863 763 3416, ⓦokeechobeebassguides.com), for all the gear and a guide to help ensure you catch something (full-day guide service $350). The Okeechobee Fishing Headquarters (☎863 763 2248, ⓦfishokeechobee.com) provides a similar service and prices.
Walking The Florida Trail Association can be contacted on ☎352 378 8823, or see ⓦfloridatrail.org.

CLEWISTON

Tourist information The Clewiston Chamber of Commerce is at 109 Central Ave, just off US-27 (Mon–Fri 9am–4pm; ☎863 983 7979, ⓦclewiston.org).
Boat rental You can rent powerboats from Big "O" Airboat Tours (see p.213) from $79/day.
Bus tours The Chamber of Commerce runs the engaging Sugarland Tour from the tourist office, a half-day bus tour (Mon–Fri Oct–March 9.30am–1pm; $38, Clewiston Museum admission) that takes in a sugar-cane farm, a sugar refinery and a look at the lake. Reservations are essential.
Fishing Big "O" Guide Service (☎888 769 3474, ⓦbigofishing.com), at Roland & Mary Ann Martin's Marina, 920 E Del Monte Ave, organize bass-fishing expeditions.

ACCOMMODATION

OKEECHOBEE TOWN

Best Western Lake Okeechobee 3975 US-441 S ☎863 357 71000, ⓦbestwestern.com. The spacious, clean rooms at this chain motel feature microwaves, refrigerators and free wi-fi. $169
Hampton Inn 1200 State Rd 70 E ☎863 824 0003, ⓦhamptoninn1.hilton.com. This comfortable chain motel sits in the middle of town, and offers free wi-fi, a fitness room, pool and complimentary hot breakfast. $135
Holiday Inn Express 3101 US-441 S ☎863 357 3529, ⓦhiexpress.com. Another good standby chain motel, this outpost offers comfortable rooms with mini-fridges and microwaves, and includes a free breakfast buffet. $172
Okeechobee KOA 4276 US-441 S ☎863 763 0231, ⓦkoa.com. Just outside town as you're heading towards the lake on US-441, you'll find the largest KOA campground in North America. There's a nine-hole golf course on the premises, as well as miniature golf, tennis courts, three pools (one for adults only) and a lounge. Camping $36.25, RV sites $74.25, one-room cabins (sleeping up to four) $64

BRIGHTON SEMINOLE INDIAN RESERVATION

Brighton Seminole Trading Post and Campground 14685 Reservation Rd ☎863 357 6644. A mile beyond the entrance to the reserve, heading north, this campground (full hook-ups) is also a basic convenience store selling some simple arts and crafts. $40

CLEWISTON

Clewiston Inn 108 Royal Palm Ave ☎863 983 8151 ⓦclewistoninn.com. If you're looking for a bit of Old Florida charm, the historic *Clewiston Inn*, notable for its Southern-style hospitality, offers simple yet comfortable rooms, free wi-fi and a 360-degree mural of local wildlife in its "Everglades" cocktail lounge. $119
Roland & Mary Ann Martin's Resort 920 E Del Monte Ave ☎863 983 3151, ⓦrolandmartinmarina .com. A variety of room options as well as RV hook-ups, tent sites and an outfitter shop, plus the *Galley* restaurant and *Tiki Bar*. Tent sites $15, RV hook-ups $35, doubles $78

EATING AND DRINKING

OKEECHOBEE TOWN

Cowboys BBQ and Steak Company 20 NE 7th Ave ☎863 467 1104, ⓦcowboysbarbqueandsteakco .com. Lots of barbecue dishes, good burgers and steaks abound at this down-home locals' joint. Steaks from $20. Mon–Wed & Sun 11am–10.30pm, Thurs–Sat 11am–midnight.

Lightsey's 10430 Hwy-78 W ☎863 763 4276. Heading further south on Hwy-78, a few miles out of town, this place serves a selection of fresh fish and home-style food at reasonable prices, along the banks of the Kissimmee River. Main dishes from $15. Mon–Thurs & Sun 11am–9pm, Fri & Sat 11am–10pm.

4

PICK-YOUR-OWN FLORIDA FRUITS

South central Florida is littered with **tropical fruit farms**, many offering seasonal pick-your-own rates. Below are some of the best.

Erickson Farm 13646 Hwy-441, at Canal Point on the eastern shore of Lake Okeechobee ☎561 924 7714, ⦿ericksonfarm.com. There's no pick-your-own option here, but the farm does sell fresh mangoes, sweet white onions and avocados in season at a small farm stand, open each July and August. Mon–Fri & Sun 10am–6pm.

Henscratch Farms 980 Henscratch Rd, Lake Placid ☎863 699 2060, ⦿henscratchfarms.com. Sells strawberries, blueberries, grapes and free-range eggs

– you can pick your own fruit in season. June & July Tues–Fri 10am–2pm, Sat 10am–4pm, Sun noon–4pm; Aug–Nov Tues–Sat 10am–4pm, Sun noon–4pm; Dec–May Tues–Sat 10am–5pm, Sun noon–4pm.

Jack Green Farms 1250 Broadus Williams Rd, Zolfo Springs ☎863 860 8354. This commercial blueberry farm opens up to u-pick guests for seven weeks from early May to June, but call ahead to check availability. Daily 8am–sunset.

BRIGHTON SEMINOLE INDIAN RESERVATION

Alice's Restaurant 17410 Reservation Rd ☎863 467 2226. Locals hang out at this tiny diner on the main road – try the great Indian tacos. Dinner mains from $8. Mon–Fri 7am–9pm, Sat 8am–4pm.

CLEWISTON

Galley At Roland & Mary Ann Martin's Resort, 920 E Del Monte Ave ☎863 983 3151 or ☎800 473 6766. A popular restaurant with great burgers from $5.50. The *Tiki Bar* is also on-site. Daily 6am–9pm.

North of Lake Okeechobee

The section of US-27 that runs **north from Lake Okeechobee** is among Florida's least eventful roads: a four-lane snake through a landscape of gentle hills, lakes, citrus groves and sleepy communities dominated by retirees. Busy with farm trucks, the highway itself is far from peaceful, but provides an interesting course off the beaten track if you're making for either coast.

Sebring

From Okeechobee town it's 48 miles via US-27 or US-98 to **SEBRING**. Other than a few old wooden buildings, and a handful of stores and restaurants, the main feature of the town is pretty but unspectacular Lake Jackson, lined with motels on its south side (along US-27).

Sebring's tranquillity is shattered each March when thousands of motor-racing fans arrive for the gruelling **12 Hours of Sebring race** (☎800 626 7223, ⦿sebringraceway .com), held at Sebring International Raceway about ten miles east of town; if you're passing through around this time, plan accordingly.

Highlands Hammock State Park

5931 Hammock Rd • Daily 8am–sunset; tram tour Nov–April Tues–Sun at 1pm, May–Oct Thurs–Sat 1.30pm • Cars $4 for one person, $6 for two or more, pedestrians and cyclists $2; tram tour $5 • ☎863 386 6094

The orange groves and cypress swamp trails inside **Highlands Hammock State Park**, four miles west of Sebring, make a worthy diversion. Watch out for white-tailed deer and time your visit to coincide with the popular and informative ranger-guided **tram tour**.

Avon Park

Twelve miles north of Sebring on Rte-17 is **AVON PARK**. Rte-17 becomes Main Street in **downtown**, a sleepy area of older buildings and a few antique stores. The **Avon Park Depot Museum** at 3 N Museum Ave (Wed–Fri 10am–3pm, free; ☎863 453 3525) contains a simple display of local history.

ARRIVAL AND DEPARTURE

By car This part of south central Florida isn't well served by interstates or public transport; your best bet for getting

NORTH OF LAKE OKEECHOBEE

around is by car. The main road through Sebring is Hwy-17.

ACCOMMODATION AND EATING

SEBRING

Kenilworth Lodge 1610 Lakeview Drive ☎ 863 385 011 ⓦ kenilworthlodge.com. The historic *Kenilworth Lodge* is a mammoth Spanish-style hotel restored to some of its former grandeur, with lake views. Continental breakfast included. $99

Sebring Diner 4040 US-27 S ☎ 863 385 3434. For authentic American and local specialities, like home-made burgers and Salisbury steak, try the Art Deco *Sebring Diner*. 6am–3pm; closed Tues.

HIGHLANDS HAMMOCK STATE PARK

Highlands Hammock State Park campsites ⓦ reserveamerica.com. There are 143 campsites in the

park, most with electrical and water hook-ups. Camping $22

AVON PARK

The Depot 21 W Main St ☎ 863 453 5600. Grab a Southern-style breakfast of cheese grits or biscuits and gravy or a simple lunch of cold subs, salad and home-made soup. Mon–Fri 6am–2pm, Sat 6–11am.

Hotel Jacaranda 19 E Main St ☎ 863 453 2211, ⓦ hoteljac.com. Built in 1926, this hotel has been beautifully restored by its current owners, the South Florida Community College. Its restaurant specializes in Southern-style lunch buffets for $8.59 (Nov–May) and dinner buffets for $11.50 (Jan–March). $60

4

Sarasota and the southwest

CORKSCREW SWAMP SANCTUARY

5

Sarasota and the southwest

A string of barrier-island beaches runs the length of the Gulf in Florida's southwest, and although these tend to draw the biggest crowds, the towns have plenty in their favour too. The main attraction is Sarasota, custodian of an arts legacy passed down at the turn of the twentieth century by John Ringling, the circus entrepreneur. The fruits of this legacy are to be seen all over this inviting city, with a handful of great museums and a vibrant theatre and arts district. Closer to the shore, you'll find an active yacht culture and plenty of opportunities to get out on the water, or just enjoy a perfect waterfront sunset with cocktail in hand.

Further south, Thomas Edison was one of a number of scientific pioneers who took a fancy to palm-studded **Fort Myers**, a small and attractive city that feels like a metropolis next to its intimate island neighbours, **Sanibel** and **Captiva**, which boast a mix of lovely beaches, quiet nature and charming restaurants. Further down the coast, **Naples** offers a plethora of shopping, dining and beach-going options. However, there's more to Florida's southwest coast than sun, sand and sea. A healthy mixture of history, culture and wildlife awaits discovery for those prepared to venture off the tourist trail.

Sarasota and around

Rising on a gentle hillside beside the blue waters of Sarasota Bay, **SARASOTA** is affluent and welcoming, cosmopolitan and laidback. This is the city where **golf** was first introduced to Florida from Scotland and it remains a popular sport, with more than thirty courses within minutes of the downtown area. Sarasota is also one of the state's leading cultural centres, home to galleries, museums, artists and respected performing arts companies. Opera- and theatre-goers in formal attire join hip students in cafés and wine bars, and the tone of the town is intelligently upbeat. Sarasota is also recognized for its strong circus ties; a few miles north up the Tamiami Trail (US-41), the **Ringling Museum Complex** – home of the late art-loving circus magnate – makes for an enlightening diversion. And the sugary barrier-island **beaches**, a couple of miles away across the bay, are a lounger's paradise.

Downtown Sarasota

Restored architectural oddities, an excellent theatre and some of the best bookstores in Florida make **downtown Sarasota** a worthy break from the beaches. Start at the **Sarasota County Visitor Information Center** on Lemon Avenue for lots of free brochures and a helpful staff.

THE RINGLING MUSEUM

Highlights

❶ Ca' d'Zan and the Ringling Museum
Experience the source of Sarasota's circus legacy: an imposing home, a circus museum and a breathtaking art museum rolled into one. **See p.223**

❷ Myakka River State Park Fifty-seven square miles of wetland, prairie and woodland make this a great spot to take a hike; or paddle the fourteen winding miles of the Myakka River and take in the flora and fauna, such as alligators, egrets and blue heron. **See p.231**

❸ Edison and Ford Winter Estates Visit the historic off-season homes of two men who changed the world. **See p.238**

❹ Sanibel and Captiva islands The antitheses and yet the penultimate of Florida beach towns, these quiet beauties offer miles of gorgeous beaches and a chance to see Florida as it once was. **See p.244**

❺ Corkscrew Swamp Sanctuary Best seen from its impressive boardwalk, which meanders several miles through wet prairie, pine flatland and a bald cypress forest. **See p.250**

❻ Naples This pampered and surprisingly friendly town is all about relaxation, with a fine stretch of beach, fashionable shops and jaw-dropping sunsets. **See p.251**

HIGHLIGHTS ARE MARKED ON THE MAP ON P.222

5

Van Wezel Performing Arts Hall

777 N Tamiami Trail • Tours first Tues of the month Oct–May 10am • Tours $5 • ☎ 941 953 3368 or ☎ 800 826 9303; tours ☎ 941 953 3368, Ⓦ vanwezel.org

The enormous purple form of the **Van Wezel Performing Arts Hall** was designed by the Frank Lloyd Wright Foundation in 1968 to resemble a seashell. The programme includes musicals, dance, comedy and plays (see p.231). Take a backstage **tour** to explore behind the scenes and see the collection of the local Fine Arts Society.

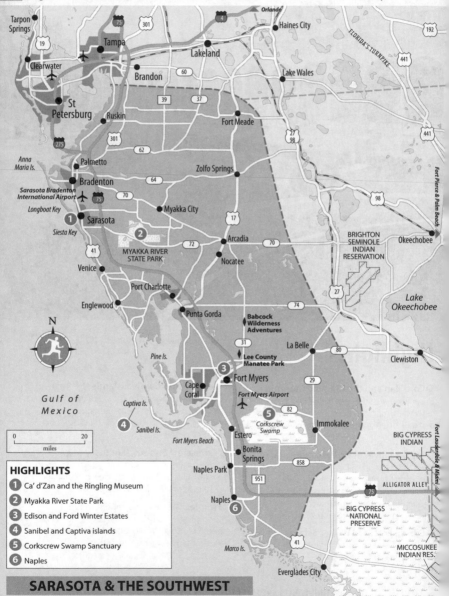

HIGHLIGHTS

1. Ca' d'Zan and the Ringling Museum
2. Myakka River State Park
3. Edison and Ford Winter Estates
4. Sanibel and Captiva islands
5. Corkscrew Swamp Sanctuary
6. Naples

SARASOTA & THE SOUTHWEST

SARASOTA BOOKSTORES

Anyone bemoaning the lack of decent **bookstores** in Florida should take heart that a few remain in Sarasota. Bookstore1Sarasota, at 1359 Main St, has incredibly knowledgeable staff and hosts lots of literary events (Mon–Sat 10am–7pm, Sun 10am–2pm; ☎ 941 365 7900, ⓦ bookstore1sarasota.com), while at 1488 Main St you'll find both Book Bazaar, which stocks used and out-of-print titles, and rare book dealer A. Parker's (both Mon–Sat 10am–5pm, Sun noon–4pm; ☎ 941 366 2898, ⓦ aparkers.com).

Selby Public Library

1331 1st St • Mon–Thurs 10am–8pm, Fri & Sat 10am–5pm • ☎ 941 861 1100

Heading into the heart of downtown, don't miss the **Selby Public Library**, with an exterior that could have been lifted out of a grandiose Hollywood epic. Inside, you'll find a well-stocked library, with a fish tank and lots of computers with free internet access (it also has free wi-fi).

Sarasota Opera House

61 N Pineapple Ave • Box office daily 10am–4pm • Tickets $19–120 • ☎ 941 328 1300, ⓦ sarasotaopera.org

Opposite the library on the corner of First Street and Pineapple Avenue sits the **Sarasota Opera House**. Opened in 1926 and renovated in 2008, this Mediterranean Revival building hosted the Ziegfeld Follies and a young Elvis Presley. The best time to catch a performance is during the **Winter Opera Festival** every February and March, when Opera Lovers' Weekends feature four operas in three days, starting at around $19 per show.

Burns Court

South of Main Street, a few blocks past the pretty Methodist Church on Pineapple Avenue, lies **Burns Court**, a hidden lane of 1920s bungalows with Moorish details. Almost all the Spanish/Mediterranean buildings in town were built just before the Depression, when the style was most in vogue. At the end of this lane stands the startlingly pink **Burns Court Cinema**, a great alternative film-house run by the Sarasota Film Society (see p.231).

Towles Court Arts District

Between Osprey Ave and US-301/Washington Blvd • In high season galleries open Tues–Sat 11am–4pm, also 6–10pm on third Fri of each month • Free • ⓦ towlescourt.com • Parking on nearby Adams Lane

Walk a few blocks east to reach the **Towles Court Arts District**, a cluster of wooden bungalows and cottages taking up a two-block stretch of Morrill Street and Adams Lane. You can browse the galleries here, which are usually open to the public. The district is adjacent to the **Laurel Park Historic District**, packed with graceful wooden homes.

The Ringling Museum Complex

Beside US-41 at 5401 Bay Shore Rd • Daily 10am–5pm, Museum of Art and Circus Museum open until 8pm Thurs, Bayfront Gardens open daily 9.30am–6pm • $25, children 6–17 $5, children under 6 free; Thurs 5–8pm limited admission $10, children $5 • ☎ 941 359 5700, recorded information ☎ 941 351 1660, ⓦ ringling.org • The museum ranges over 66 acres, with buildings linked by clearly signposted pathways; trams connect the main areas as well. To get here from downtown Sarasota, take bus #99

Two miles north of downtown Sarasota is the **Ringling Museum Complex**, whose star attraction, the **Ringling Museum of Art**, contains the house and art collections of multimillionaire John Ringling. When he moved to Sarasota in 1911, Ringling not only poured money into the fledgling community, but also gave it a taste for fine arts it has never lost.

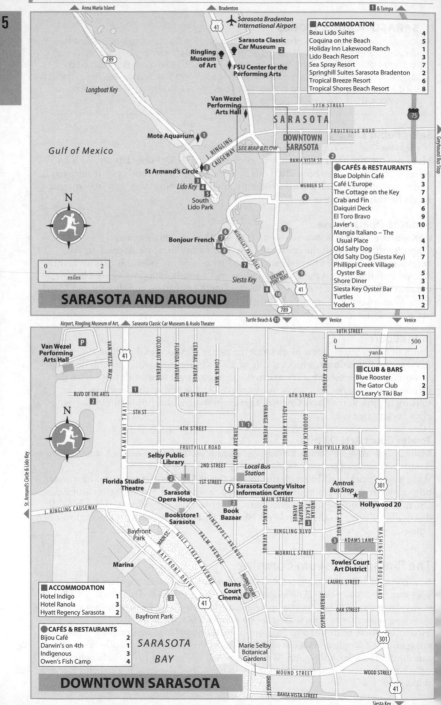

△ Anna Maria Island   ▲ Bradenton   **1** & Tampa △

✈ Sarasota Bradenton International Airport

ACCOMMODATION

Beau Lido Suites	4
Coquina on the Beach	5
Holiday Inn Lakewood Ranch	1
Lido Beach Resort	3
Sea Spray Resort	7
Springhill Suites Sarasota Bradenton	2
Tropical Breeze Resort	6
Tropical Shores Beach Resort	8

Longboat Key

Gulf of Mexico

Ringling Museum of Art

Sarasota Classic Car Museum

FSU Center for the Performing Arts

Van Wezel Performing Arts Hall

SARASOTA

17TH STREET

FRUITVILLE ROAD

Mote Aquarium

DOWNTOWN SARASOTA

SEE MAP BELOW

BAHIA VISTA ST

St Armand's Circle

Lido Key

South Lido Park

WEBBER ST

CAFÉS & RESTAURANTS

Blue Dolphin Café	3
Café L'Europe	3
The Cottage on the Key	7
Crab and Fin	3
Daiquiri Deck	6
El Toro Bravo	9
Javier's	10
Mangia Italiano – The Usual Place	4
Old Salty Dog	1
Old Salty Dog (Siesta Key)	7
Phillippi Creek Village Oyster Bar	5
Shore Diner	3
Siesta Key Oyster Bar	8
Turtles	11
Yoder's	2

Bonjour French

Siesta Key

N

0   2
miles

SARASOTA AND AROUND

Airport, Ringling Museum of Art, ▲ Sarasota Classic Car Museum & Asolo Theater   Turtle Beach & **11** ▽   ▽ Venice   ▽ Venice

Van Wezel Performing Arts Hall

10TH STREET

0   500
yards

CLUB & BARS

Blue Rooster	1
The Gator Club	2
O'Leary's Tiki Bar	3

BLVD OF THE ARTS

6TH STREET

6TH STREET

N

5TH ST

4TH STREET

4TH STREET

FRUITVILLE ROAD

FRUITVILLE ROAD

Selby Public Library

2ND STREET

1ST STREET

Local Bus Station

Florida Studio Theatre

Sarasota Opera House

Sarasota County Visitor Information Center

Amtrak Bus Stop

Hollywood 20

MAIN STREET

Bookstore1 Sarasota

Book Bazaar

RINGLING BLVD

Bayfront Park

ADAMS LANE

Marina

MORRILL STREET

Towles Court Art District

LAUREL STREET

Burns Court Cinema

OAK STREET

Bayfront Park

SARASOTA BAY

Marie Selby Botanical Gardens

ACCOMMODATION

Hotel Indigo	1
Hotel Ranola	3
Hyatt Regency Sarasota	2

CAFÉS & RESTAURANTS

Bijou Café	2
Darwin's on 4th	1
Indigenous	3
Owen's Fish Camp	4

MOUND STREET

WOOD STREET

BAHIA VISTA STREET

DOWNTOWN SARASOTA

Siesta Key ▽

Ringling made his money as part owner of the fantastically successful Ringling Brothers Circus (which began touring the US during the 1880s and acquired the Barnum & Bailey show in 1907), and ploughed the business's profits into railways, oil and land. By the 1920s, he had acquired a fortune estimated at $200 million. Charmed by Sarasota and recognizing its investment potential, Ringling built the first causeway to the barrier islands and made the town his circus's winter base, saving a fortune in northern heating bills and generating tremendous publicity for the town in the process. His greatest gift to Sarasota, however, was a Venetian Gothic mansion – a combination of European elegance and American-millionaire extravagance – and an incredible collection of European Baroque paintings, displayed in a museum built for the purpose beside the house. Grief-stricken following the death of his wife Mable in 1929, Ringling was unprepared for the stock market crash of the same year, and lost much of his wealth. He died in 1936, reportedly with just $300 to his name – though still in possession of the art collection now on display.

The Ringling House: Ca' d'Zan
Tours 11am–4pm on the hour • $5; "Private Places" tours $20

Begin your exploration of the Ringling estate by walking through the gardens to the former Ringling residence, the 56-room **Ca' d'Zan** ("House of John" in Venetian dialect). A lavish but not tasteless piece of work situated serenely beside Sarasota Bay, it was the dilapidated setting for the 1998 film adaptation of *Great Expectations*. Completed in 1926, at a cost of approximately $1.5 million, the house was planned around an airy, two-storey living room marked on one side by a fireplace of carved Italian marble and on the other by a $50,000 Aeolian self-playing pipe organ. The other rooms are similarly decorated with expensive items, but unlike their mansion-building contemporaries elsewhere in Florida, the Ringlings knew the value of restraint. Their spending power never exceeded their sense of style, and the house remains a triumph of taste and proportion. You can tour the first floor, but to see the bedrooms on the second floor (husband and wife had separate suites), you must join a regular volunteer-led tour; to see it all, take the 45-minute **"Private Places" tour**, which explores the upper floors, guest rooms, game room and, weather permitting, visits the Belvedere tower at the top of the 81ft-high mansion.

Ringling Museum of Art
Docent-led tours free

On trips to Europe to scout for new circus talent, Ringling became obsessed with **Baroque art** – then wildly unfashionable – and over seven years, led largely by his own sensibilities, he acquired an impressive collection of Old Masters, now totalling around 750 and regarded as one of the finest of its kind in the US. To display the paintings, Ringling selected a patch of Ca' d'Zan's grounds and erected a spacious **museum** around a mock fifteenth-century Italian *palazzo*, decorated with his stockpile of high-quality replica Greek and Roman statuary. As with Ca' d'Zan, the very concept initially seems absurdly pretentious but, like the house, the idea works, and the architecture matches the art with great aplomb. Take **the free, guided tour**, departing regularly from the entrance, before wandering around at your leisure. Five enormous paintings by **Rubens**, commissioned in 1625 by a Habsburg archduchess, and the painter's subsequent *Portrait of Archduke Ferdinand*, are the undisputed highlights of the collection, but they shouldn't detract from the excellent canvases in succeeding rooms: a wealth of talent from Europe's leading schools of the mid-sixteenth to mid-eighteenth centuries. Watch out, in particular, for the finely composed and detailed *The Rest on the Flight to Egypt* by Paolo Veronese, and the entertaining *Building of a Palace* from Piero di Cosimo.

5

Ringling Circus Museum and Tibbals Learning Center

The Ringling fortune had its origins in the big top, and the **Ringling Circus Museum** is worth a visit for a glimpse into the family business. The museum also includes the next-door **Tibbals Learning Center**, featuring vintage circus posters and comprehensive displays on the history of the American circus. Its star attraction, however, is the largest **miniature circus** in the world – the astonishingly meticulous Howard Bros Circus, a 3800-square-foot, three-quarter-inch-to-one-foot replica of the Ringling Bros and Barnum & Bailey Circus, built by Howard Tibbals, a master model-builder and circus fan. It was a forty-year labour of love for Tibbals; he grew up fascinated by the travelling circus and its many detailed components, all of which he painstakingly re-created in his exhibit: 41,000 pieces, including eight tents, 55 railroad cars, 152 wagons, 7000 folding chairs, hundreds of animals, and thousands of performers and circus workers.

The rest of the Circus Museum contains tiger cages and wagons once used to transport animals and equipment; a spotlight on Cecil B. DeMille's film, *The Greatest Show on Earth* (some of which was filmed in Sarasota); memorabilia of famous dwarfs and performers; and a tribute to Gunther Gebel-Williams, the legendary animal trainer who never missed a day of work in over 12,000 performances, before passing away in 2001. Nearby, a banyan tree shades the circular *Banyan Café*, where you can grab lunch or a snack.

The Visitors Pavilion and Historic Asolo Theater

In the 1950s, the museum transported and reassembled an eighteenth-century, Italian-court playhouse from the castle of Asolo to the grounds of the estate. The fully restored **Historic Asolo Theater** is the centrepiece of the **Visitors Pavilion**, which also includes the elegant *Treviso* restaurant and a gift shop. The buzz, though, mostly surrounds the theatre, which is open for performances, lectures, films and concerts (☎941 360 7399, ⓦ ringling.org).

Asolo Repertory Theatre

5555 N Tamiami Trail (located in the FSU Center for the Performing Arts adjacent to the Ringling Museum of Art, with shared parking) • Free tours available; call ☎ 941 351 9010 ext. 3000 to schedule • Tickets $15–80 • ☎ 941 351 8000 or ☎ 800 361 8388, ⓦ asolorep.org

Just outside the main entrance to the museum you'll see the **Florida State University Ringling Center for the Performing Arts**, home to the **Asolo Repertory Theatre company** (see p.231), which stages up to ten productions every season spanning both contemporary and classical works. In addition to the modern Cook Theatre, shows are held in the elegant, gilded interior of the Mertz Theatre, originally built in 1903 as an opera house and brought over from Dunfermline, Scotland, as well as the Historic Asolo Theater, inside the Ringling Museum.

Sarasota Classic Car Museum

5500 N Tamiami Trail • Daily 9am–6pm • $9.85, children $6.50 • ☎ 941 355 6228, ⓦ sarasotacarmuseum.org

Vintage car enthusiasts will love the **Sarasota Classic Car Museum**, across US-41 from the entrance to the Ringling Museum Complex. The museum features an ever-changing collection of over 100 years of automotive history, from pristine vintage autos to raucous muscle cars. Nearly 75 aged vehicles – including John Lennon's Mercedes Roadster and a dragster driven by Don Garlits are gathered together with hurdy-gurdies, cylinder discs, an enormous Belgian pipe organ, and nickelodeons.

The Sarasota beaches

Although the powdery white sands of the **Sarasota beaches** – fringing several barrier islands, which continue the chain beginning off Bradenton – haven't exactly been spared the attentions of property developers, they're worth a day of anybody's time, either to lie back and soak up the rays, or to seek out the few remaining isolated stretches. The sunsets alone make this area worth a visit, but one of the islands, **Siesta Key**, is also renowned for its powdery-fine, quartz-like sand. Siesta Key and **Lido Key** are both accessible by car or bus from the mainland, but there's no direct link between the two. If you're travelling by car, be forewarned: the beach roads are very busy in high season, and the tailbacks heading away from the beach near the day's end might ruin any relaxation you gained on the sands.

Lido Key

Bus #4 or #18; free parking for 3hr at St Armands Circle

The Ringling Causeway crosses yacht-filled Sarasota Bay from the foot of Main Street to **Lido Key** and flows into **St Armands Circle**, a traffic circle packed with mostly upmarket shops and restaurants two miles from downtown. At its centre is the **Circus Ring of Fame**, a series of plaques commemorating famous circus performers, which encircles a small park dotted with some of Ringling's replica classical statuary. Once you've browsed the park and shops, continue west on Ringling Boulevard to **Lido Key Beach**, which is relatively condo-free at its northern end (though the main car park is further south).

South Lido Nature Park

Daily 6am–11pm • Free

Heading south for around two miles, Benjamin Franklin Drive passes more accessible beaches until you come to the first of two entrances to the attractive **South Lido Nature Park**, also called **Ted Sperling Park**; this one leads to a kayak trail through the mangroves (see p.228) and a refreshing 45-minute hiking trail along the coast. The second entrance lies at the end of Benjamin Franklin Drive, where a belt of dazzlingly bright sand faces the ocean beyond a large grassy park, although with no lifeguards and exceptionally strong currents, swimming is not advised; you can swim or just loll on the smaller patch of sand facing the calmer waters of Sarasota Bay near the car park, shaded by Australian pines.

Mote Aquarium

1600 Ken Thompson Parkway • Daily 10am–5pm • $19.75, children 4–12 $14.75 • ☎ 941 388 4441, ⓦ mote.org

Away from the beaches, the only place of consequence on Lido Key is the **Mote Aquarium**, a mile north of St Armands Circle on City Island. The aquarium is the public offshoot of a marine laboratory that studies the ecological problems threatening Florida's sea life, such as the red tide, a mysterious algae that blooms every few years, devastating the ecosystem. You'll see plenty of live sea creatures, including sea horses, and also manatees, sea turtles, dolphins and sharks at the Marine Mammal Center, which houses its rehabilitation programme. Guests can also safely pet sea urchins, crabs and stingrays.

SARASOTA'S CIRCUSES

The circus spirit is alive and well in Sarasota, and it's well worth catching a performance if you're here during the season of one of the following Sarasota-based circus companies, both under the umbrella of the Circus Arts Conservatory (CAC; call or check websites for schedule information).

Circus Sarasota ☎ 941 355 9805, ⓦ circusarts.org. The professional arm of the CAC offers stellar performances every February at its Big Top adjacent to the Ed Smith Stadium at the corner of 12th St and Tuttle Ave, 5 miles west of I-75 (Exit 210).

Sailor Circus ☎ 941 355 9805, ⓦ circusarts.org. You can catch the community's youth performers, from 10- to 17-years-old, in this professional-calibre circus, perhaps the most unique show in town, which runs holiday (Dec) and spring (March/April) performances in its arena at 2075 Bahia Vista St, south of downtown.

5

Siesta Key

Reached via Siesta Drive off US-41, about 5 miles south of downtown Sarasota • Bus #10 or #11; parking free throughout the island, though spaces go fast in peak season

Far more refreshing and laidback than Lido Key, **Siesta Key** attracts a younger crowd. Clusters of shops, restaurants and bars form **Siesta Key Village**, along Ocean Boulevard, but beach-lovers should head straight to **Siesta Key Beach**, beside Beach Road, where the sand has an uncommon sugary texture due to its origins as quartz (not the more usual pulverized coral). It's a wide, white strand that can – and often does – accommodate thousands of sun-worshippers. To escape the crowds, continue south on Beach Road (which becomes Midnight Pass Rd when it meets Stickney Point Rd from the mainland) for six miles to **Turtle Beach**, a small, secluded stretch of sand not as soft or floury as what you'll find further north, but much quieter. **Bike and kayak rentals**, as well as motor scooters and beach equipment, are available at Siesta Sports Rentals (see below).

ARRIVAL AND DEPARTURE

SARASOTA

By plane Sarasota Bradenton International Airport (☎ 941 359 2770, ⓦ srq-airport.com) is around 4 miles north of downtown, just off US-41; bus #2 runs into downtown Sarasota every hour (Mon–Sat), and taxis meet most flights. All the major car rental companies have branches at the airport.

By car Whether you're arriving from the north or south, US-41 (usually referred to here as the Tamiami Trail) zips through Sarasota, passing the main causeway to the islands just west of downtown and skirting the Ringling Complex to the north. Parallel to the Tamiami, I-75 is the

quickest way to travel longer distances into and out of town. Park for up to two hours for free along some downtown streets, though meters are starting to appear.

By bus Arriving by Greyhound bus, you'll wind up far east of downtown in Fruitville at the terminal at 19 East Rd (☎ 941 377 5658); take SCAT #1 to get downtown for further transfers.

Destinations Daytona Beach (1 daily; 5hr 50min); Fort Lauderdale (2 daily; 5–6hr); Miami (2 daily; 6–7hr 45min); Naples (1 daily; 3hr); Orlando (2 daily; 3hr 45min–5hr); St Petersburg (2 daily; 45min); Tampa (2 daily; 1hr 25min); West Palm Beach (2 daily; 4hr 45min–6hr 40min).

GETTING AROUND

By bus Local bus routes run by Sarasota County Area Transit, or SCAT (Mon–Sat 4.30am–8.30pm; limited routes on Sun; ☎ 941 861 1234, ⓦ scgov.net/scat), radiate out from the downtown Sarasota terminal on Lemon Ave, between 1st and 2nd sts. Useful routes are #99 to the Ringling Complex; #4 to Lido Key; #18 to Longboat Key; #11 to Siesta Key; and #17 to Venice Beach. Fares are $1.25 per journey; day-passes are $4. The Amtrak bus from Tampa pulls in a few blocks east, at the Hollywood 20 cinema, 1993 Main St (see p.231).

By bike and scooter If you're around for a week or more,

a good way to explore the town and the islands is by renting a bike ($15/day, $40/week) from Sarasota Bicycle Center, 4084 Bee Ridge Rd (☎ 941 377 4505). For rentals on Siesta Key, head to Siesta Sports Rentals, 6551 Midnight Pass Rd (☎ 941 346 1797, ⓦ siestasportsrentals.com), who rent out bikes ($5/hr, $15/day; $12/day for a beach cruiser), kayaks ($30/4hr, $45/day) and motor scooters ($65/day).

By taxi Try Diplomat Airport Transportation (☎ 941 365 8294 or ☎ 877 859 8933) or Yellow Cab of Sarasota (☎ 941 955 3341).

INFORMATION AND TOURS

Tourist information The Sarasota County Visitor Information Center is at 14 Lemon Ave (Mon–Sat 10am–6pm; ☎ 941 706 1253, ⓦ sarasotafl.org). In Siesta Key, the small and friendly Chamber of Commerce is at 5118 Ocean Blvd (Mon–Fri 9am–5pm; ☎ 941 349 3800, ⓦ siestakeychamber.com).

Event listings Look out for the free magazines *Sunny Day* (ⓦ sunnydayguide.com) and *See* (ⓦ see-florida.com /sarasota-bradenton), and the Thursday edition of the *Sarasota Herald Tribune* (ⓦ heraldtribune.com), which has a pull-out section, "Ticket", with entertainment listings.

ACCOMMODATION

On the mainland, you're most likely to end up in the corridor of chain hotels and motels running the length of US-41 between the Ringling Complex and south of downtown Sarasota. Prices are generally higher at the beach resorts, but there are a few budget options close to the sand.

DOWNTOWN

Holiday Inn Lakewood Ranch 6231 Lake Osprey Drive ☎ 941 782 4400, ⓦ hilr.com. Flashy contemporary design

characterizes this standby, about 15min northeast of downtown near I-75, with LCD TVs, microwaves, fridges, a nice pool, fitness centre and nearby nature trails. **$130**

★**Hotel Indigo** 1223 Blvd of the Arts ☏ 941 487 3800, ⓦsrqhotel.com. Fabulous boutique hotel, with bright, bold colours and tropical art splashed across the walls, wooden floors and spotlessly clean rooms, all with CD players and some with fridges. **$184**

Hotel Ranola 118 Indian Place #6 ☏ 941 951 0111, ⓦhotelranola.com. Small, hip boutique hotel, with just nine rooms and excellent service; crisp, stylish rooms come with plasma TVs, hardwood floors, iPod docks, full kitchens and free wi-fi, and it's an easy walk to Main St. **$169**

Hyatt Regency Sarasota 1000 Blvd of the Arts ☏ 941 953 1234, ⓦsarasota.hyatt.com. This centrally located hotel near the Ringling Causeway underwent a complete renovation in 2011. The funky, stylish rooms boast brand-new bathrooms, Hyatt's unusually comfortable beds, iPod docks, LCD TVs and soothing views of Sarasota Bay (request one of the upper floors). You also get a lagoon-style pool and fitness centre – but wi-fi is $9.95 a day. **$249**

Springhill Suites Sarasota Bradenton 1020 University Parkway ☏ 941 358 3385, ⓦmarriott.com. You'll find all the usual amenities, including wi-fi and mini kitchens, in the tidy rooms at this *Marriott* by the airport, not far from the Ringling Museum. **$125**

THE BEACHES

Beau Lido Suites 149 Tyler Drive, Lido Key ☏ 941 726 5098, ⓦbeaulido.com. Steps from the beach and offering a variety of basic rooms, houses and an apartment; most have kitchenettes with stove, refrigerator and microwave. **$85**

Coquina on the Beach, 1008 Ben Franklin Drive, Lido Key ☏ 941 388 2141 ⓦcoquinaonthebeach.com. This homely, charming hotel right on the beach offers spacious studios and suites with fully equipped kitchens in a central spot near St Armands Circle. **$139**

Lido Beach Resort 700 Ben Franklin Drive, Lido Key ☏ 941 388 2161, ⓦlidobeachresort.com. Modern, elegant rooms in a variety of sizes, most with kitchenettes or microwaves. Rooms in the south tower offer views over the sand or the city skyline. **$189**

★**Sea Spray Resort** 574 Canal Rd, Siesta Key ☏ 941 822 0520, ⓦtheseasprayresort.com. Sixteen immaculate, tropically decorated suites feature full, modern kitchens (some kitchenettes) and plenty of space. It's across the street from a quieter section of beach and about a 10min stroll into Siesta Key Village. **$235**

Tropical Breeze Resort 140 Columbus Blvd, Siesta Key ☏ 941 349 1125, ⓦtropicalbreezeinn.com. Rooms range from standard doubles to a four-bedroom pool house at this laidback, centrally located resort. Most rooms have modern kitchens with granite worktops and new appliances; there are three pools and fifteen grills for barbecuing, and it's walking distance to the beach and Siesta Key Village. **$205**

Tropical Shores Beach Resort 6717 Sara Sea Circle, Siesta Key ☏ 941 349 3330, ⓦtropicalbeachresorts .com. One of three great, adjacent resorts with a variety of rooms, all with modern decor, kitchens and free wi-fi. The hotel faces a lovely stretch of beach, and there are plenty of activities to keep the kids amused. **$149**

EATING

Sarasota's restaurant and café culture is particularly vibrant, and while exquisite restaurants (with prices to match) are everywhere, you'll still find plenty of budget options. The Downtown Farmers' Market (Sat 7am–noon; ⓦsarasotafarmersmarket.org), at the corner of Main Street and Lemon Avenue, is also worth checking out for its freshly baked pastries and coffee.

DOWNTOWN

Bijou Café 1287 1st St ☏ 941 366 8111, ⓦbijoucafe .net. Popular fine-dining restaurant in the theatre and arts district, with French-influenced seafood and meat served in understated surroundings. Main courses $20–40. Mon–Fri 11.30am–2pm & 5–9pm, Sat 5–9pm.

Darwin's on 4th 1525 4th St ☏ 941 343 2165, ⓦdarwinson4th.com. This Peruvian Gastro Brewpub – as unlikely as that sounds – really works. The menu features street food with a Peruvian twist, such as ceviche, pork tacos, and chicken wings with lime and soy sauce. The on-site artisan brewery features tasty, creative craft beers. Mains from $14. Mon–Thurs 5–10pm, Fri & Sat 5pm–midnight.

El Toro Bravo 2720 Stickney Point Rd ☏ 941 924 0006, ⓦeltorobravosarasota.com. Tucked into a strip mall, this fantastic Mexican restaurant offers up favourites such as *fajitas*, *chimichangas* and burritos, as well as great weekly food and drink specials — tacos are only $1.50 on Tuesdays. Main courses $10–15. Mon–Fri 11am–2pm & 5–9pm, Sat 5–9pm.

★**Indigenous** 239 S Links Ave ☏ 941 706 4740, ⓦindigenoussarasota.com. The menu at this meticulously restored Towles Court Bungalow changes throughout the year according to seasonal availability. Food is mostly local and all is conscientiously sourced. Begin with the wild mushroom bisque and then move on to the *cobia crudo*. Tues–Sat 5.30–8.45pm.

Mangia Italiano – The Usual Place 2157 Siesta Drive ☏ 941 952 9106, ⓦtheusualplacerestaurant .com. Authentic Italian food served up in a welcoming atmosphere. Try the antipasto plate if you come with a crowd; pastas and pizza are made from scratch. Most mains from $16. Mon–Sat noon–2.30pm and 4–10pm.

Owen's Fish Camp 516 Burns Lane ☎941 951 6936, ⓦowensfishcamp.com. Right next door to the Burns Cinema, this charming spot is an upscale, landlocked paean to all things piscine. The driftwood walls are covered in nautical knick-knacks, and the wait for a table is well worth it for standouts like the Bloody Mary oyster shooters, the fried green tomato salad, and the naked fish of the day. Main dishes from $14. Mon–Thurs & Sun 4–9.30pm, Fri & Sat 4–10.30pm.

Phillippi Creek Village Oyster Bar 5353 S Tamiami Trail ☎941 925 4444, ⓦcreekseafood.com. Picnic tables and paper towels add to the casual atmosphere at this excellent waterfront seafood spot. Reasonable prices and great food – try one of the Creek Combo pots with oysters, shrimp and corn on the cob – ensure a big crowd, so get there early for your spot at the table. Mon–Thurs & Sun 11am–10pm, Fri & Sat 11am–10.30pm.

Yoder's 3434 Bahia Vista St ☎941 955 7771, ⓦyodersrestaurant.com. Sarasota has thriving Mennonite and Amish communities, and this local favourite has won awards for the home-made goodness of its old-fashioned Amish cuisine, especially its breakfasts and massive peanut butter cream pies ($4.50 a slice). Mon–Thurs 6am–8pm, Fri & Sat 6am–9pm.

ST ARMANDS CIRCLE AND LIDO KEY

Blue Dolphin Café 470 John Ringling Blvd ☎941 388 3566, ⓦbluedolphincafe.com. Come to this convivial, informal diner just off St Armands Circle for hearty breakfasts ($6–9) guaranteed to fill you up. There's another location on Longboat Key. Daily 7am–2pm.

Café L'Europe 431 St Armands Circle ☎941 388 4415, ⓦcafeleurope.net. Innovative and award-winning – if a bit pricey – restaurant with French, Italian and Spanish influences, popular with locals for an upscale date night. Main courses average around $35. Mon & Sun 11.30am–3pm, Tues–Thurs 11.30am–3pm & 5–9pm, Fri & Sat 11.30am–3pm & 5–10pm.

Crab and Fin 420 St Armands Circle ☎941 388 3964. This long-standing St Armands' favourite specializes in seafood. There's an extensive raw oyster bar menu; other standouts include the Florida alligator and seafood gumbo.

Mains from around $20. Mon–Thurs & Sun 11.30am–10pm, Fri & Sat 11.30am–10.30pm.

Old Salty Dog 1601 Ken Thompson Pkwy (on City Island) ☎941 388 4311, ⓦtheoldsaltydog .com. Near the bridge to Longboat Key (opposite Mote Aquarium), you'll find this ultra-casual beach shack serving an infamous quarter-pound deep-fried hot dog and more – its laidback vibe and location are the main reasons for a visit, with grand views across the bay. Mon–Thurs & Sun 11am–9.30pm, Fri & Sat 11am–10pm.

★**Shore Diner** 465 John Ringling Blvd ☎941 296 0301, ⓦshorebrand.com/pages/shore-diner. This chic spot is inspired by mid-century California beach culture, and the light, refreshing menu offers salads such as a local kale Caesar and mains such as a roasted cauliflower "steak". Mains from $14. Mon–Thurs 11am–10pm, Fri & Sat 11am–11pm, Sun 10am–10pm.

SIESTA KEY

Bonjour Frenchcafe 5214 Ocean Blvd ☎941 346 0600, ⓦbonjourfrenchcafe.com. This sunny French-themed spot offers all the classics, from croissants and crêpes (try the *crêpe tatin*) for breakfast to *croque monsieur* and *coqauvin*. Breakfast mains for less than $10; lunch mains $15–19. Daily 7am–4pm.

The Cottage On The Key 153 Avenida Messina, Siesta Key Village ☎941 312 9300, ⓦcottagesiestakey.com. There's excellent people-watching on the front deck of *The Cottage*, but it's the food that's the real draw. The tapas-style menu is perfect for sharing; try the tuna tartare tacos and crab sliders. There's also a variety of sandwiches and surf-and-turf options if you don't feel like sharing. Main courses from $27. Mon–Thurs & Sun 11am–10pm, Fri & Sat 11am–midnight.

Javier's 6621 Midnight Pass Rd ☎941 349 1792, ⓦjaviersrestaurant.com. Come here for a taste of Peru and an extensive menu of seafood, steaks, ribs, pasta and decadent desserts. Main courses are $17–25. Tues–Sat 5–9pm.

Turtles 8875 Midnight Pass Rd, Turtle Beach ☎941 346 2207, ⓦturtlesrestaurant.com. Well-priced seafood dinners ($10–15) served at tables overlooking Little Sarasota Bay, at the southern tip of Siesta Key. Daily 11.30am–9pm.

DRINKING AND NIGHTLIFE

On weekends, nightlife along Sarasota's Main Street attracts students looking to chill, as well as a more rough-and-ready, good-old-boys crowd. Siesta Key Village on Siesta Key also offers a hot bar-hopping scene.

Blue Rooster 1525 4th St ☎941 388 7539, ⓦblueroostersrq.com. This *soi-disant* juke joint offers one of Sarasota's best live-music venues, focusing mostly on jazz, blues and gospel. There's also a tasty menu featuring

Southern standbys such as shrimp and grits and chicken and waffles. Wed 5–11pm, Thurs 5pm–midnight, Fri & Sat 5pm–1am, Sun 5–10pm.

Daiquiri Deck 5250 Ocean Blvd, Siesta Key Village

📞941 349 8697, 🌐daiquirideckssiestakey.com. Cool down with frozen daiquiris at this hugely popular – if a bit of a meat market – after-beach venue. They also have a raw bar, great snacks and burgers (from $10). There are other locations in St Armands Circle and Venice. Daily 11am–2am.

The Gator Club 1490 Main St, downtown 📞941 366 5969, 🌐thegatorclub.com. *The Gator* continually wins the prize for loudest bar. Set in a huge warehouse, it features live dance music every night at 9.30pm, and a Scotch bar and pool tables upstairs. Mon–Sat noon–2am, Sun 8pm–1am.

Old Salty Dog 5023 Ocean Blvd, Siesta Key Village 📞941 349 0158, 🌐theoldsaltydog.com. One of the more popular bars on Siesta Key, this English-themed sister bar to the *Salty Dog* restaurant on City Island (see p.230) offers tasty pub fare and a wide, dog-friendly (naturally)

deck. Mon–Thurs & Sun 11am–9.30pm, Fri & Sat 11am–10pm; bar open till midnight daily.

O'Leary's Tiki Bar 5 Bayfront Drive, downtown 📞941 953 7505, 🌐olearystikibar.com. This casual outdoor bar is the go-to happy hour spot for locals. Right on Sarasota Bay, there's a full menu of munchies like fried alligator bites and nachos, as well as live music almost every night. Daily 8am–10pm.

★ **Siesta Key Oyster Bar** 5238 Ocean Blvd, Siesta Key 📞941 346 5443, 🌐skob.com. Come for the oyster happy hour (a dozen for $7), stay for the great live music and hopping scene late into the night. The deck plays host to live bands and a bustling crowd, while the walls inside are papered with the signed dollar bills of visitors past. Mon–Thurs 11am–midnight, Fri & Sat 11am–2am, Sun 9am–midnight.

ENTERTAINMENT

The Sarasota area lives up to its billing as "Florida's Cultural Coast". For full details of arts events, pop into the Sarasota Visitors Center (see p.228) or check 🌐sarasotafl.org for a full calendar of events. Drama devotees are well catered for, as some of the state's top small theatre groups are based in Sarasota.

Asolo Repertory Theatre 5555 N Tamiami Trail 📞941 351 8000 or 📞800 361 8388, 🌐asolorep.org. The centre's major repertory, the Asolo Theatre Company, stages classic and contemporary plays as well as commissioned new work and musical theatre (tickets $15–80).

Burns Court Cinema 506 Burns Lane 📞941 955 3456, 🌐filmsociety.org. The cinema that hosts Sarasota's Cine-World film festival in November, showing over fifty of the best international films of the year on its three screens. For tickets ($8) and schedules, call the box office.

Florida Studio Theatre 1241 N Palm Ave 📞941 366 9000, 🌐floridastudiotheatre.org. Hosts Sarasota's most contemporary theatrical events in three downtown venues:

the Keating Theatre and Gompertz Theatres, the Goldstein and John C. Court Cabaret, and Bowne's Lab Theatre (tickets from $12 for improv, $29 for plays).

Hollywood 20 1993 Main St 📞941 365 2000 or 📞941 954 5768 for recorded information, 🌐regmovies.com. All mainstream films are shown at this distinctive (and popular) Art Deco theatre. Inside, a neon-lilac glow bathes the popcorn-devouring crowds.

Van Wezel Performing Arts Hall 777 N Tamiami Trail 📞941 953 3368 or 📞800 826 9303, 🌐vanwezel.org. Affectionately called "the Purple Cow" or "the Purple Palace" – depending on who you ask – this hall has a varied programme of musicals and dance performances.

Myakka River State Park

13207 SR-72 • Daily 8am–sunset; $6 per vehicle; $4 single-occupant vehicle; 🌐floridastateparks.org/myakkariver • 3–4 boat tours daily, 2 tram tours daily except June–early Dec; tram and airboat tours $12, children 6–12 $6 • 📞941 365 0100, 🌐myakkawildlife.com • Canoes and kayaks $20 first hr, then $5/hr; 📞941 923 1120, 🌐myakkaoutpost.com • Take SR-72 for about 14 miles east of Sarasota

If all you've seen thus far are beaches and theme parks, broaden your horizons by travelling nine miles east of Sarasota on SR-72 (as the local state road is known), where you'll find the marshes, pinewoods and prairies of **Myakka River State Park**, a great tract of rural Florida barely touched by humans. On arrival, drop into the **visitor centre** for insight into this fragile (and threatened) ecosystem, and then explore the park on its numerous walking paths, enjoy the seven-mile scenic drive, or rent a canoe or kayak and glide the calm expanse of the **Upper Myakka Lake**. Myakka Wildlife Tours offer narrated one-hour **tram and airboat tours** through the wildlife habitats, explaining the ecology of the area and pointing out animals. If you're equipped for hiking, following the 39 miles of trails through the park's wilderness preserve is a better way to get close to the cotton-tailed rabbits, deer, turkey, bobcats and alligators living in the park; stop at the entrance office first to register, pick up

5

maps and check weather conditions – be prepared for hot, wet conditions during the summer months.

Big Flats and Old Prairie ☎941 361 6511, ⓦreserveamerica.com. Other than the six primitive campgrounds on the hiking trails ($5 per person per night), park accommodation comprises two well-equipped campgrounds, *Big Flats* and *Old Prairie*, and five log cabins ($70 a night; ☎800 326 3521) that can sleep up to six people. These are very popular, so it's a good idea to book well in advance. Camping $26

Bradenton and around

A major producer of tomatoes and orange juice, **BRADENTON** is a hard-working town across from Palmetto on the south side of the broad Manatee River, with a centre comprising several unsightly miles of strip mall and office buildings. While mainland Bradenton is far from exciting, **Anna Maria Island** (the northernmost point of a chain of barrier islands running from here to Fort Myers) and the **Bradenton beaches** eight miles west of downtown make up for Bradenton proper's lack of charm. Rather than travel inland, take Hwy-789 for a more picturesque (if slightly longer) route to and from Sarasota.

South Florida Museum

201 10th St W • Tues–Sat 10am–5pm, Sun noon–5pm; Jan–April & July also Mon 10am–5pm • $18, children $14, including admission to Bishop Planetarium • ☎941 746 4131, ⓦsouthfloridamuseum.org

The **South Florida Museum** takes a wide-ranging look at the region's past through artefacts and exhibits related to its early settlers and natural history. The most popular attraction is the **aquarium**, home to Snooty the manatee. Born in 1948, Snooty is the oldest manatee born in captivity, and the community celebrates his birthday every July (thousands turned up for his 65th birthday party in 2013). If aquariums are your thing, you'll find that this one is intelligently laid out to provide varying views of Snooty and his poolmates, but ten minutes of watching them glide about is generally enough. Admission also includes entry to the **Bishop Planetarium** where three different shows are presented on a regular basis, as well as special screenings from time to time; live star talks are presented at weekends.

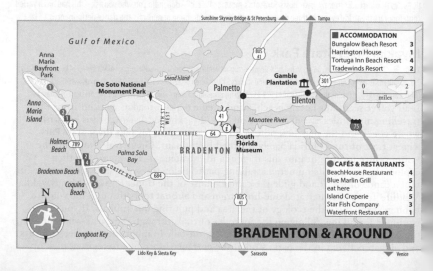

De Soto National Memorial

Northern end of 75th St W • Daily 9am–5pm • Free • ☎ 941 792 0458, ⓦ nps.gov/deso

Five miles west of central Bradenton, Manatee Avenue (the main route to the beaches) crosses 75th Street West, where you'll find the pretty **De Soto National Memorial**, its waterfront lawn dotted by twisted gumbo limbo trees. This is believed to be near the spot Spanish conquistador **Hernando de Soto** came ashore in 1539. The four-year De Soto expedition (see p.446), hacking through Florida's dense subtropical terrain and wading through its swamps, led to the European discovery of the Mississippi River – and numerous pitched battles with Native Americans. The park's **visitor centre** contains artefacts and exhibits explaining the expedition's effect on Native Americans, and an engrossing twenty-minute film depicting the expedition is shown on demand. The interpretive **De Soto Expedition Trail** (0.75 miles) invites visitors to experience a coastal landscape similar to that encountered by De Soto and his men centuries ago; 45-minute guided trail walks are offered based on ranger availability. You can also poke around a replica of Camp Uzita, the first Spanish base, near the car park. From mid-December to mid-April, park rangers dressed as sixteenth-century Spaniards offer informative titbits on the lifestyles of Florida's first adventurers (including weapons demonstrations and kid-friendly hands-on exhibits).

Anna Maria Island and the Bradenton beaches

The beachside bars on **Anna Maria Island** ten miles away from central Bradenton are bright and convivial. From the end of Manatee Avenue, turn left and head two miles along Gulf Drive for **Bradenton Beach**, with its small but attractive historic district centred on **Bridge Street**. Keep driving to the end of the island and **Coquina Beach**, where the swimming is excellent. If you're after tranquillity, take a right at the end of Manatee Avenue instead for **Anna Maria Bayfront Park**, at the eastern end of Pine Avenue at the island's northern tip, which has stellar views across the bay to the Sunshine Skyway Bridge; you can watch pelicans feed from the nearby pier, and sometimes dolphins, though the beach itself is nothing special. Further down the road, you can **rent bikes** from Beach Bums (see p.234).

The Gamble Plantation

3708 Patten Ave • Visitor centre Mon & Thurs–Sun 9am–11.45pm & 12.45–5pm; park grounds close at sunset; six tours daily from 9.30am • Plantation free; tours $6, children 6–12 $4 • ☎ 941 723 4536, ⓦ floridastateparks.org/gambleplantation

If you have time, head across the Manatee River from downtown Bradenton and along Tenth Street (US-301) to riverside **ELLENTON**, where the 1840s **Gamble Plantation Historic State Park** contains one of the oldest homes on Florida's west coast and the only slave-era plantation this far south. Composed of thick, tabby walls (a mixture of crushed shell and molasses) and girded on three sides by sturdy columns, the house belonged to Confederate major Robert Gamble, a failed Tallahassee cotton planter who ran a sugar plantation here before financial uncertainty caused by the impending Civil War forced him to leave. In 1925, the mansion was designated the **Judah P. Benjamin Confederate Memorial** in remembrance of Confederate Secretary of State Benjamin, who reportedly took refuge here in 1865 after the fall of the Confederacy. With Union troops in hot pursuit, he is believed to have hidden here until friends found him a boat in which he sailed from Sarasota Bay to England, where he began practising law. A showcase of wealthy (and white) Old South living, the house – stuffed to the rafters with period fittings – is open Thursday to Monday, and admission is by **guided tour**.

ARRIVAL AND DEPARTURE	**BRADENTON AND AROUND**

By plane Sarasota Bradenton International Airport (☎ 941 359 2770, ⓦ srq-airport.com) is around 9 miles south of downtown Bradenton, just off US-41; MCAT bus #99 runs north to downtown Bradenton and south to

5

downtown Sarasota every 30min (Mon–Sat), and taxis meet most flights. All the major car rental companies have branches at the airport.

By car Whether you're arriving from the north or south, US-41 (usually referred to here as the Tamiami Trail) zips through Bradenton on the way to Tampa in the north and Sarasota directly to the south. Parallel to the Tamiami, I-75 is the quickest way to travel longer distances into and out of town.

GETTING AROUND AND INFORMATION

By bike You can rent bikes on Anna Maria Island from Beach Bums, 427 Pine Ave (daily 9am–5pm; $5/hr, $14/day; ☎ 941 778 3316).

By bus The most useful stops for travellers using the MCAT buses (☎ 941 749 7116, ⓦ mymanatee.org) are the DeSoto Station, 820 301 Blvd W, and the Downtown Station, 13th St W, which both provide transfers to the beach. Most routes operate from 5.30am to 8pm (Mon–Sat). Fares are $1.25 each way, with a $0.25 transfer fee. There are also trolleys operating on Anna Maria Island (daily 6am–10.30pm; free) and Longboat Key (daily 5.30am–8pm, $1.25 each way).

Tourist information In central Bradenton, the Manatee Chamber of Commerce is at 222 10th St W (Mon–Fri 9am–5pm; ☎ 941 748 3411, ⓦ manateechamber.com), while the Anna Maria Island Chamber of Commerce is at 5313 Gulf Drive N (Mon–Fri 9am–5pm; ☎ 941 778 1541, ⓦ annamariaislandchamber.org).

ACCOMMODATION

Accommodation is plentiful on the beaches, ranging from homely B&Bs to inns. For those on a budget, suitable places tend to be a long way from the sands, and Bradenton can be rather dreary away from the water. Rates always increase at weekends.

Bungalow Beach Resort 2000 Gulf Drive N, Bradenton Beach ☎ 941 778 3600, ⓦ bungalowbeach .com. A variety of cheery bungalows and rooms, from studios to three-bedrooms with hardwood floors and bright white linens, as well as friendly hosts, make this spot a great find. Some rooms have cathedral ceilings and private porches. Efficiencies $189, bungalows $339

Harrington House 5626 Gulf Drive, Holmes Beach ☎ 941 778 5444, ⓦ harringtonhouse.com. This cosy B&B is a restored 1925 country-style inn that's right on the Gulf, with a variety of rooms and three other beachside properties to choose from. Book ahead. $189

★**Tortuga Inn Beach Resort** 1325 Gulf Drive N,

Bradenton Beach ☎ 941 778 6611, ⓦ tortugainn .com. This sunny, friendly spot is a gem – rooms range from standard hotel rooms to two-bedroom apartments, all with at least a mini-kitchen. There's a great pool, and it's right across from the beach – grab the complimentary beach chaises, umbrellas and towels on your way over. $150

Tradewinds Resort 1603 Gulf Drive N, Bradenton Beach ☎ 941 779 0010, ⓦ tradewinds-resort.com. This charming Key West-style resort features a variety of one-bedroom pastel cottages and villas with an enviable location right on a private stretch of beach, shared with *Tortuga Inn Beach Resort*. $145

EATING

You'll find a number of pleasant restaurants near or on the beaches. Seafood is of course a speciality on most menus; look out for the local stone crabs, which feature on most menus from October to May.

★**BeachHouse Restaurant** 200 Gulf Drive N, Bradenton Beach ☎ 941 779 2222, ⓦ beachhouse .groupersandwich.com. Eat in the airy dining room or alfresco on the waterfront deck at this Anna Maria Island favourite. There's often live music and always a killer happy hour, with great food specials. Seafood mains (mostly $15–25) are the speciality of the house. Mon–Thurs & Sun 11.30am–9pm, Fri & Sat 11.30am–10pm.

Blue Marlin Grill 121 Bridge St, Bradenton Beach ☎ 941 896 9737, ⓦ bluemarlinami.com. This tasty seafood spot is located in a vibrant blue, nautically themed 1920s cottage. Standouts on the menu include locally caught fish prepared a number of ways (try the Thai chilli citrus glaze), and there's live entertainment in the courtyard every Friday and

Saturday night. Mon–Sat 5–10pm, Sun 5–9pm.

★**eat here** 5315 Gulf Drive, Holmes Beach, ☎ 941 778 0411, ⓦ eathereflorida.com. This casual, friendly spot has one of the area's most progressive menus, with tasty, healthy items like the keenwa (quinoa) vegan salad and tempura beets; or go all out and order the poutine, heart-attack hot dog or outstanding pot roast. Daily 5–10pm.

Island Creperie 127 Bridge St, Bradenton Beach ☎ 941 778 1011, ⓦ bistrotfl.com. Delicate crêpes stuffed with strawberry jam as well as savoury buckwheat crêpes ($7–10) will compete for your attention at this cute spot. Daily 8.30am–2pm & 5.30–9pm.

Star Fish Company 12306 46th Ave W, Cortez ☎ 941 794 1243, ⓦ starfishcompany.com. Heading back to the

mainland on Hwy-684 (Cortez Rd), it's worth stopping at the fishing shacks of Cortez, where you'll find this friendly place serving huge fresh shellfish platters for under $15. Cash only. Mon & Sun 11.30am–3pm, Tues–Sat 11.30am–8pm.
Waterfront Restaurant 111 S Bay Blvd S, near the end of Pine Ave, Anna Maria ☎941 778 1515, ⓦthewater

frontrestaurant.net. Come here for more upmarket seafood dishes, enhanced by soothing views of the pier and Gulf. Highlights include the shrimp and grits ($23) and choice of local fish including snapper, but they also do plenty of grilled meats. Dinner main courses $20–32. Mon–Thurs & Sun 11.30am–9pm, Fri & Sat 11.30am–10pm.

Venice and around

In 1960, the Ringling Circus moved its winter base twenty miles south from Sarasota to **Venice**, a small, laidback town best visited for its gorgeous **beaches**, which draw everyone from watersports enthusiasts to sunbathing pensioners.

The **downtown area** is centred on palm-lined Venice Avenue (which runs one mile from the Tamiami Trail, US-41, to the beach), with plenty of small shops and cafés along the way; though traces of Italianate architecture remain, you'll need a vivid imagination to see any connection to its European namesake.

You can always entertain yourself by searching for the **sharks' teeth** commonly washed ashore here – Venice does, after all, bill itself as the "Shark's Tooth Capital of the World". The **fishing pier**, two miles south of downtown off Harbor Drive, is a beautiful spot from which to watch the sun dip below the horizon, and offers a good perspective on the town's extensive beaches and (thankfully) not-so-developed seafront.

ARRIVAL AND DEPARTURE   VENICE

By car Getting to Venice really requires your own transport; you can take the scenic route — Tamiami Trail (US-41)

from Sarasota — or opt for I-75 and exit at Jacaranda Ave for Venice Ave, which takes you right downtown.

GETTING AROUND AND INFORMATION

By bus Local bus #13 (☎941 316 1234; $1.25) runs up and down Venice Ave to the beach.
By car Parking at the beachfront is limited to a couple of small car parks, but you can also leave your car along Venice

Ave (both free of charge).
Tourist information The Chamber of Commerce is at 597 Tamiami Trail S (Mon–Fri 8.30am–5pm; ☎941 488 2236, ⓦvenicechamber.com).

ACCOMMODATION

The Inn at the Beach Resort 725 W Venice Ave ☎941 484 8471, ⓦinnatthebeach.com. Aims for a resort-like feel, with personalized service, free continental breakfast and newspapers, and a heated palm-fringed pool. **$170**
Venice Beach Villas Two locations near the beach: 501 W Venice Ave and 505 Menendez St ☎941 488 1580, ⓦvenicebeachvillas.com. It's a short walk to the beach

but worth it for the immaculate, spacious rooms and good amenities like complimentary bicycles, free wi-fi and fully equipped kitchens in most rooms. **$130**
Venice Campground Near I-75 at 4085 E Venice Ave ☎941 488 0850, ⓦcampvenice.com. Offers both primitive and equipped tent sites as well as simple cabins (reserve well in advance) in an old-growth oak hammock by the Myakka River. Camping **$43**, cabins **$75**

EATING AND DRINKING

Blu' Island Bistro 625 S Tamiami Trail ☎941 485 8200, ⓦbluislandbistro.com. This beach-chic spot puts a gourmet twist on everyday favourites such as kobe beef sliders and pork chops with white balsamic fig glaze. Breakfast is also tasty, with standouts like the oven-roasted seasonal veggie omelette. Most mains under $25. Daily 7.30am–3pm & 5–8.30pm.
Robbi's Reef 775 US-41 Bypass S ☎941 485 9196, ⓦrobbisreef.com. Great fresh seafood prepared simply in a casual atmosphere, complete with two large saltwater fish tanks. The Gulf Coast shrimp is a standout; most mains

under $15. Tues–Sat 11am–2pm & 4–9pm.
Sharky's 1600 Harbor Drive S ☎941 488 1456, ⓦsharkysonthepier.com. At the base of the pier, this is *the* spot to enjoy the sunset while munching on seafood, pastas and steak. Mon–Thurs & Sun 11.30am–10pm, Fri & Sat 11.30am–midnight.
The Soda Fountain 349 W Venice Ave ☎941 488 7600. A charmingly old-fashioned diner, great for delicious milkshakes, ice creams and sandwiches. Mon–Sat 11am–9pm, Sun noon–4pm.

5

Punta Gorda

About thirty miles south of Venice, **PUNTA GORDA** could be dismissed as another west-coast retirement community, but it does warrant exploring. While you won't find impressive beaches, you will encounter large, Southern-style houses on the riverfront and an unhurried pace of life that contrasts sharply with the frantic US-41 running through town.

Get maps at the Chamber of Commerce (see below) for the monuments and grand mansions scattered around the well-preserved **downtown district**, which spans several blocks south of the river, as well as for the fourteen historic **murals** painted along the walls of its main streets. There are also free tours of the **Chamber Building** (Tues, Thurs & Fri 11am–3pm), housed in the gracious 1903 A.C. Freeman House. Further along the banks of the river on West Retta Esplanade lies **Fishermen's Village**, a quaint collection of unusual shops and restaurants with a working marina housed in the old city docks – an appropriate extension to a town that got its name from Cuban fishermen in the early nineteenth century.

ARRIVAL AND DEPARTURE
PUNTA GORDA

By car Continuing south from Venice, you may arrive in Punta Gorda via Hwy-41, which goes through downtown, or on I-75. Exit at US-17.

INFORMATION AND TOURS

Tourist information After crossing the Peace River on US-41, take the first right for the Charlotte County Chamber of Commerce, 311 W Retta Esplanade (Mon–Thurs 8am–5pm, Fri 8am–4.30pm; ☎941 639 2222, ⓦ charlottecountychamber.org).

Tours A collection of boat-tour operators line the pier, offering trips around the harbour and further afield to Cayo Costa Island and Cabbage Key (see p.248); King Fisher Fleet (☎941 639 0969, ⓦ kingfisherfleet.com) runs full- and half-day cruises and shorter nature and sunset boat trips, starting at $17.95 for 1hr 30min, as well as deep-sea and back-bay fishing excursions.

ACCOMMODATION

You've got two choices in Punta Gorda: the string of motels on US-41, which are usually cheaper, or if you're charmed enough to stay, try one of the waterfront accommodation options in the town itself.

Banana Bay Motel 23285 Bayshore Rd ☎941 743 4441, ⓦ bananabaymotel.com. This homely motel nestled into a secluded waterfront setting on Charlotte Harbor, across the bridge from Fishermen's Village Marina. Rooms are a bit dated, but comfortable, and range from standard motel-style doubles to efficiencies. If there's a good crowd, the on-site tiki bar makes for a fun night as well. **$69**

INTO THE WILD

For a glimpse of untamed Florida – without having to traipse through the wild for days – try **Babcock Wilderness Adventures**, 8000 State Rd 31 (☎800 500 5583, ⓦ babcockwilderness .com). Forty miles northeast of Fort Myers (take Exit 143 on I-75) and about 25 miles east of Punta Gorda (Exit 164 on I-75, or east on Hwy-74), this ecotourism outfit offers ninety-minute swamp-buggy tours through the state-owned Crescent B Ranch and **Telegraph Cypress Swamp** (Nov–April morning and afternoon tours, $24 adults/$16 children; May–Oct mornings only $22/$12; reservations essential). From open fields with wild pigs and cracker cattle to swamp areas where alligators carpet the pathway, the tours will take you through ever-changing terrain. Highlights include the **bald cypress swamp**, a primeval scene of stunning trees and blood-red bromeliads reflected in still, tea-coloured water, and **a gold Florida panther**, although it's not purebred (only around fifty of those are left). In the movie-set-turned-museum, where Warner Bros shot the 1995 film *Just Cause* with Sean Connery, you can take a break from the wilderness and learn more about the ranch's history, and that of the surrounding area. For food, bring a picnic lunch, or snack on fried gator bites, hot dogs and burgers at the ranch's seasonal restaurant, *Gator Shack*.

5

Fishermen's Village 1200 W Retta Esplanade ☎941 639 8721, ⓦfishville.com. You can rent two-bedroom villas here; amenities include a beach area, tennis courts, free use of bikes and a heated pool. **$140**

Four Points by Sheraton Punta Gorda Harborside 33 Tamiami Trail ☎941 637 6770, ⓦstarwoodhotels .com. By far the nicest of the area's chain motels, this place sits on the edge of Charlotte Harbor near downtown. Brightly painted rooms feature plush, comfortable beds, flat-screen TVs and free wi-fi. **$108**

EATING AND DRINKING

Harpoon Harry's At the end of the pier in Fishermen's Village Marina ☎941 637 1177, ⓦharpoonharrys.com. Enjoy raw oysters, clams and hearty sports-pub food to the accompaniment of live music at weekends. Mon–Thurs & Sun 11am–10pm, Fri & Sat 11am–2am.

Nav-a-Gator Grill 9700 SW Riverview Circle in Lake Suzy, further up the Peace River ☎941 627 3474, ⓦnav -a-gator.com. This grill serves up gator bites, shrimp, burgers, conch, and even peanut butter sandwiches, with live bands covering Jimmy Buffett and the like most weekends. They also offer narrated, eco boat tours of the river (1hr 30min; $24.95) and airboat rides (1hr; $44.95). You can drive here, but if you've got the means, arrive by boat or seaplane – there's a seaplane dock and a helicopter landing pad. Restaurant daily 11am–8pm; boat tours Mon–Fri 10am–3pm, Sat & Sun 10am–5pm.

Fort Myers and around

Though lacking the sophistication of Sarasota (50 miles north) and the exclusivity of Naples (20 miles south), **FORT MYERS** nonetheless holds some appeal, primarily as the jumping-off point for the charming islands of Sanibel and Captiva, fifteen miles south and west (see p.244). The town took its name from Abraham Myers, who helped re-establish a fort here in 1850 during the Seminole Indian Wars. Fortunately, most of the town's late-twentieth-century growth occurred in North Fort Myers, across the wide Caloosahatchee River, and so the traditional centre has been left relatively unspoiled. The workplace of inventor **Thomas Edison**, who passed more than forty winters in Fort Myers, provides the strongest cultural interest, while balmy sands await at **Fort Myers Beach**.

Downtown Fort Myers

Crossing the Caloosahatchee River, US-41 hits **downtown Fort Myers**, which nestles by the river's edge. Modern office buildings dominate, but the historic riverfront area, dubbed the **Fort Myers River District**, has far more appeal. Ambitious and largely successful renovations have transformed this area, particularly along Main and First streets between Broadway and Jackson Street.

Highlights include the colourful **Arcade Theatre**, 2267 First St (☎239 332 4488 or ☎877 787 8053, ⓦfloridarep.org), home to the top-notch Florida Repertory Theatre. The Sidney & Berne Davis Art Center, 2301 First St (☎239 333 1933, ⓦfl-arts.org), housed in the wonderfully restored 1933 Federal Building, hosts concerts and art shows.

Southwest Florida Museum of History

2031 Jackson St • Tues–Sat 10am–5pm • $9.50 • ☎239 321 7430, ⓦswflmuseumofhistory.com

For a thorough insight into the town's past, stop by the **Southwest Florida Museum of History**, where exhibits include a full-sized "cracker" house and the rusty 84ft-long *Esperanza*, one of the longest private Pullman rail cars built in the United States. Not aiming to compete, it leaves details of the most recent star of Fort Myers' history – Thomas Edison – to the museum estates on McGregor Boulevard.

The Edison and Ford Winter Estates

2350 McGregor Blvd • Daily 9am–5.30pm; Inside the Lab tours Tues & Fri at 10.30am, gardens and estate tour Wed at 10.30, behind the scenes tour Thurs at 10.30am; historian-guided tours on the hour 10am–4pm daily • Self-guided homes and gardens tour $20; botanical tour $30; historian-guided tour $25 • ☎239 334 7419, ⓦedisonfordwinterestates.org

In 1885, six years after inventing the improved incandescent light bulb, **Thomas Edison**

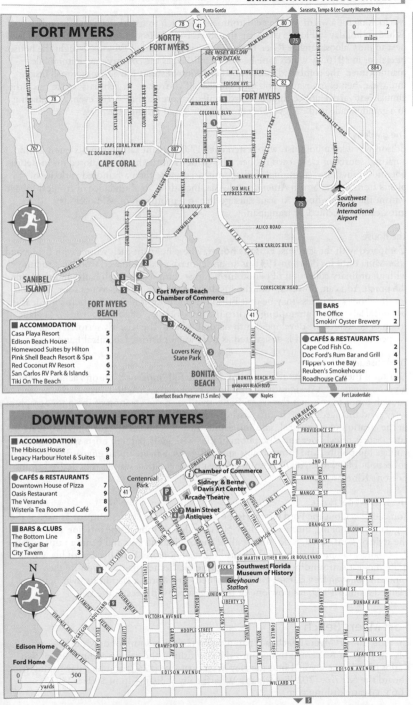

FORT MYERS

Punta Gorda • Sarasota, Tampa & Lee County Manatee Park

NORTH FORT MYERS

SEE INSET BELOW FOR DETAIL

M. L. KING BLVD
EDISON AVE

FORT MYERS

WINKLER AVE
COLONIAL BLVD

CAPE CORAL

CAPE CORAL PKWY
EL DORADO PKWY
COLLEGE PKWY

DANIELS PKWY

SIX MILE CYPRESS PKWY

GLADIOLUS DR

Southwest Florida International Airport

ALICO ROAD
SAN CARLOS BLVD

SANIBEL ISLAND

CORKSCREW ROAD

FORT MYERS BEACH

Fort Myers Beach
Chamber of Commerce

Lovers Key
State Park

BONITA BEACH

BONITA BEACH RD
BAREFOOT BEACH BLVD

Barefoot Beach Preserve (1.5 miles) • Naples • Fort Lauderdale

■ BARS
The Office	1
Smokin' Oyster Brewery	2

● CAFÉS & RESTAURANTS
Cape Cod Fish Co.	2
Doc Ford's Rum Bar and Grill	4
Flipper's on the Bay	5
Reuben's Smokehouse	1
Roadhouse Café	3

■ ACCOMMODATION
Casa Playa Resort	5
Edison Beach House	4
Homewood Suites by Hilton	1
Pink Shell Beach Resort & Spa	3
Red Coconut RV Resort	6
San Carlos RV Park & Islands	7
Tiki On The Beach	2

DOWNTOWN FORT MYERS

■ ACCOMMODATION
The Hibiscus House	9
Legacy Harbour Hotel & Suites	8

● CAFÉS & RESTAURANTS
Downtown House of Pizza	7
Oasis Restaurant	9
The Veranda	8
Wisteria Tea Room and Café	6

■ BARS & CLUBS
The Bottom Line	5
The Cigar Bar	4
City Tavern	3

Centennial Park

Chamber of Commerce
Sidney & Berne Davis Art Center
Arcade Theatre
Main Street Antiques

DR MARTIN LUTHER KING JR BOULEVARD

Southwest Florida
Museum of History
Greyhound
Station

Edison Home

Ford Home

was looking for a warm working environment in which to spend the winter months. While on holiday in Florida that year, the 38-year-old Edison purchased 13.5 acres of land next to the Caloosahatchee River. **Henry Ford**, a close friend of Edison's, bought the house next door in 1916, by which time he was established as the country's top automobile manufacturer. The combined **Edison and Ford Winter Estates** provide some small insight into these men of innovation and their families. If you're here in February, try to catch the annual **Festival of Light** celebration (W edisonfestival.org), a three-week event culminating in a grand parade held each year in commemoration of Edison's birthday.

The gardens

Edison was a keen botanist, who tested over 17,000 plant samples in his quest to find a natural source of US-grown rubber. The **gardens** of the house (explored on in-depth botanical tours) are sensational. Edison nurtured more than a hundred varieties of plants from Africa, South America and Asia, including an abundance of tropical foliage – from the extraordinary African sausage tree to a profusion of wild orchids, intoxicatingly scented by frangipani.

The house

Compared with the gardens, Edison's **house**, where he spent each winter with his second wife Mina until his death in 1931, is an anticlimax: a palm-cloaked wooden structure with an ordinary collection of period furnishings glimpsed through half-windows from the porch. You can, however, tour the inside with the behind-the-scenes tour. A reason for the abode's plainness may be that Edison spent most of his waking hours inside the **botanical laboratory**, attempting to turn the latex-rich sap of *Solidago edisonii* (a giant strain of goldenrod he developed) into natural rubber. The recently restored laboratory is open to the public and is designated as a National Historic Chemical Landmark.

The museum

Not until the tour reaches the **museum** does the full impact of Edison's achievements become apparent. A design for an improved stock-ticker machine provided him with enough funds to conduct the experiments that led to the creation of the phonograph in 1877, and financed research into passing electricity through a vacuum, which resulted in the creation of a practical, safe and economical incandescent light bulb two years later. Scores of cylinder and disc phonographs with gaily painted horn-speakers, bulky vintage light bulbs, and innumerable spin-off gadgets make up an engrossing collection. Here, too, you'll see some of the ungainly cinema projectors derived from Edison's Kinetoscope.

The Ford Winter Home

You can check out the **Ford Winter Home** on a behind-the-scenes tour (or as part of the regular tour, looking through the half-glass windows), though the interior, restored to the style of Ford's time, lacks almost all of the original fittings and bears an unassuming appearance. Despite becoming the world's first billionaire, Ford lived with his wife in quite modest surroundings. Before leaving the old homes, pause to admire the sprawling **banyan tree** outside the ticket office – it's worth a visit in its own right. Planted around 1927, it's now one of the largest banyan trees in the US.

Fort Myers Beach

En route to **Fort Myers Beach**, a separate town ten miles south of downtown Fort Myers, you'll cross a small bridge into the tiny fishing and sailing community of **San Carlos Island**, where you'll find the Key West boat (see p.242) and half-day fishing trips aboard the *Sea Trek* (702 Fisherman's Wharf; daily 9.30am–4pm; $60; T 239 765 7665, W seatrekfishing.com).

5

BASEBALL IN FORT MYERS

The 2007 World Series champions **Boston Red Sox** come to Fort Myers every year for spring training, basing themselves at City of Palms Park, 2201 Edison Ave – check ⓦ boston.redsox .mlb.com for tickets and schedules. The **Minnesota Twins** play at Hammond Stadium, 14100 Six Mile Cypress Parkway (ⓦ minnesota.twins.mlb.com).

The longer causeway from San Carlos Island brings you to seven-mile **Estero Island** and Fort Myers Beach, a cheerfully commercialized town a bit less refined than the southwest's other popular beach strips – think T-shirt, swimsuit and ice-cream shops, and plenty of busy beach bars. Most of the action happens where the bridge ends, near the short fishing pier or at the **Lynn Hall Memorial Park**. The pedestrian-only area called Times Square, identified by the great clock in its middle, often draws crowds checking out the street performers. If that's not your scene, you might want to head for the quieter stretches of beach further south. You'll find over thirty beach access points with free parking (clearly marked from Estero Blvd) and lots of accommodation along the road, which runs the length of the island.

Lovers Key State Park

Daily 8am to sunset; tram daily 9am–4pm; shop daily 9am–5pm • Canoes $58/day, $48/half-day; one-person kayaks $58/day, $38/half-day; two-person kayaks $68/day, $58/half-day; bikes $20/half-day; standup paddleboards $38/2hr; cars $4 for one person, $8 for two or more, pedestrians and cyclists $2; beach chairs $7/day, umbrellas $13/day • ☎ 239 463 4588, shop ☎ 239 765 7788 • Free tram runs regularly between the beach and the main concession shop, near the car park

Fort Myers Beach becomes quieter and increasingly residential as you press south. Estero Boulevard eventually swings over a slender causeway to **Lovers Key State Park**, actually a series of interconnecting mangrove islands forming a chain to **Bonita Beach** six miles further south. The main park entrance is around a mile from the causeway, and you can reach the beaches – among the quietest and prettiest in the region – via a short footpath over a couple of mangrove-fringed islands and several mullet-filled, man-made canals. If you don't fancy the walk, or are lugging beach chairs, a free tram runs regularly between the beach and the main shop. If you crave some outdoor action, hike the worthwhile **Black Island Trail** (2.5 miles, but shortcuts are built in), or go exploring by canoe, kayak or bicycle, all of which can be rented at the shop.

Lee County Manatee Park

10901 Hwy-80 • Daily 8am–sunset; visitor centre Nov–March 9am–4pm, closed April–Oct • ☎ 239 690 5030 • Exit 141 off I-75; parking May–Nov $1/hr or $5/day, Dec–April $2/hr or $5/day

As might be guessed, manatees are the centre of attention at the **Lee County Manatee Park**, northeast of downtown Fort Myers. Here, along the banks of the Orange River, information boards explain how manatees are identified by their scar patterns, which are caused by collisions with boat propellers. Those most often sighted – usually the most scarred – are given names. Due to its proximity to the interstate and the Florida Power & Light plant, the park isn't too aesthetically pleasing. Still, you're likely to see a number of manatees, which enjoy the warm water generated by the plant, mostly from November to March. The best time to spot them is early in the morning, in the first inlet, where they tend to congregate because it's calm and shallow. From November to March there are also free naturalist-led interpretive talks covering not only manatees but also the area's butterflies and plants.

ARRIVAL AND DEPARTURE

FORT MYERS AND AROUND

By plane Around 9 miles southeast of downtown, Southwest Florida International Airport (☎ 239 590 4800, ⓦ flylcpa.com) is accessible from I-75 via Daniels Parkway.

LeeTran bus #50 (daily 7.30am–8pm; $1.25) links the airport with Daniels Parkway and US-41, but you'll need to change at least once to get to the beach or downtown. Taxi

5

rates from the airport are charged according to a zone system: the historic downtown area is $30, Fort Myers Beach $50, and Sanibel and Captiva islands $56–75. The major car rental companies are all represented at the airport.

By boat If you're heading to Key West from Fort Myers, opt for the high-speed catamaran, a trip that takes about 3hr 30min each way. Key West Express (☏ 239 463 5733 or ☏ 888 539 2628, ☼ seakeywestexpress.com) has boats

leaving from 1200 Main St, in Fort Myers Beach. Trips cost approximately $89 one way or $119–149 return, with flexible dates.

By bus The Greyhound station is in downtown Fort Myers at 2250 Widman Way (☏ 239 334 1011).

Destinations Fort Lauderdale (3 daily; 3hr); Miami (3 daily; 4–5hr); Naples (2 daily; 1hr); Orlando (2 daily; 6hr–7hr 30min); Tampa (3 daily; 3hr 45min).

GETTING AROUND

By car US-41 is known here as Cleveland Ave; Hwy-80 runs through downtown Fort Myers and curves into McGregor Blvd (also called 867) to the west, where you'll find the Edison home (see p.238). If you're arriving from US-41, the exit for McGregor Blvd is clearly marked. Parking is usually easy downtown, with plenty of free 2hr kerbside spots. A car park near the river, offers metered spaces for $1/hr.

By bus Although the local buses don't travel the length of

McGregor, #20 (Mon–Sat; $1.25; ☏ 239 533 8726, ☼ rideleetran.com) will get you closest to the Edison home. To get from downtown Fort Myers to the beaches, take bus #140 south to Bell Tower and change to bus #50 to Summerlin Square, where you can catch the Beach Trolley (50¢) to Fort Myers Beach; this continuously (daily from approximately 6.30am to 9.30pm) runs the full length of Fort Myers Beach to Lovers Key and Bonita Springs along Estero Blvd.

INFORMATION

Fort Myers The Chamber of Commerce is at 2310 Edwards Drive (Mon–Fri 8.30am–4.30pm; ☏ 239 332 3624 or ☏ 800 366 3622, ☼ fortmyers.org), and the Visitor and Convention Bureau is at 2201 2nd St, Suite 600 (Mon–Fri

8am–5pm; ☏ 239 338 3500 or ☏ 800 237 6444, ☼ fortmyers-sanibel.com).

Fort Myers Beach 1661 Estero Blvd, Suite 8 (Mon–Fri 9–5pm; ☏ 239 454 7500, ☼ fortmyersbeachchamber.org).

ACCOMMODATION

Accommodation costs are low in and around Fort Myers between May and mid-December, when thirty to sixty percent is generally lopped off the standard rates. In high season, however, not only do prices skyrocket, but available rooms are few and far between. The decent selection of chain motels on US-41 north of downtown make an economical option; alternatively, at the beaches, try motel-lined Estero Boulevard and be prepared to spend at least $150 in season (as low as $60–100 otherwise).

FORT MYERS

The Hibiscus House 2135 McGregor Blvd ☏ 239 332 2651, ☼ thehibiscushouse.net. This pretty 1912 B&B is outfitted in Victorian style and is within walking distance of the Edison and Ford Winter Estates, as well as dining and entertainment options, and a 15min drive from Sanibel. $149

Homewood Suites by Hilton 5255 Big Pine Way ☏ 239 275 6000, ☼ homewoodsuitesftmyers.com. For considerable luxury without pomp, and big reductions out of season, try the *Homewood Suites*, which offers a complimentary hot breakfast and evening cocktails, heated pool, fitness centre and business amenities. $189

Legacy Harbour Hotel & Suites 2036 W 1st St ☏ 239 332 2048, ☼ legacyharbourhotel.com. Comfortable one- and two-bedroom suites offer full kitchens and lots of space; there are also studio rooms available. There's a complimentary light breakfast, heated swimming pool and friendly poolside bar. $139

San Carlos RV Park & Islands 18701 San Carlos Blvd

☏ 239 466 3133, ☼ sancarlosrv.com. En route to Fort Myers Beach, you'll pass this campground, which has plenty of bayfront sites. $43

FORT MYERS BEACH

Casa Playa Resort 510 Estero Blvd ☏ 239 765 0510, ☼ casaplayaresort.com. The potted plants painted on the facade give this pink hotel a 1950s feel. Each of the 35 rooms is privately owned and individually decorated, but all have screened balconies and kitchenette facilities. $199

★**Edison Beach House** 830 Estero Blvd ☏ 239 463 1530, ☼ edisonbeachhouse.com. This pretty pink hotel on the beach offers all-suite accommodation with full kitchens and en-suite laundry. There's also a heated freshwater pool. $175

Pink Shell Beach Resort & Spa 275 Estero Blvd ☏ 239 463 6181, ☼ pinkshell.com. A comfortable beachfront resort with a full-service spa, three heated pools, a poolside bar and grill, a fishing pier and Gulf-view rooms, all with full kitchens or kitchenettes. A recently completed beach restoration means even more sandy spots for your towel. $209

Red Coconut RV Resort 3001 Estero Blvd ☎239 463 7200, ⓦredcoconut.com. The only campground right on the beach. RV sites include basic cable, internet and picnic tables. **$66.60**

Tiki On the Beach 4360 Estero Blvd ☎239 463 9547, ⓦtikionthebeach.com; map p.239. This beachfront gem offers both gulf-front and courtyard rooms, all of them spotless and cheery. Some rooms have full kitchens. **$151**

EATING

FORT MYERS

Cape Cod Fish Co. 15501 Old McGregor Blvd ☎239 313 6462. There's lots of fresh, tasty seafood on offer at this homely joint. Start with the New England clam chowder followed by a classic "lobstah" roll. Mains from $14. Tues–Sun noon–8pm.

Downtown House of Pizza 1520 Hendry St ☎239 337 3467, ⓦdowntownhouseofpizza.com. Best pizza pie (from $11) and slices (from $2.50) in town, with $3 draft beers to wash them down. Also does sandwiches from $6. Check the website for coupons. Mon, Tues & Sun 11am–10pm, Wed–Sat 11am–3am.

Oasis Restaurant 2260 Martin Luther King Jr Blvd ☎239 334 1566, ⓦoasisatfortmyers.com. Stop in at this friendly, family-owned, always busy spot for cheap all-day breakfasts and large burgers. Mon & Tues 7am–3pm, Wed–Sat 7am–8pm, Sun 7am–2pm.

★**Reuben's Smokehouse** 11506 S Cleveland Ave ☎239 931 0420 or ☎866 928 2789, ⓦreubens smokehouse.com. This popular BBQ joint smokes its own ribs, brisket, chicken and pork. There's also a fantastic pot roast and chicken and dumplings and you can finish your carnivorous repast with a piece of chocolate caramel bread pudding – this is not the place for those watching their figures. Mains from $9. Tues–Sat 11am–8pm.

Roadhouse Café 15660 San Carlos Blvd ☎239 415 4375, ⓦroadhousecafefl.com. Great food with live jazz music every night, with a separate lounge that's open until 10 or 11pm. The chicken Homard (chicken stuffed with lobster and Swiss cheese) is delicious, and there's a nice variety of steaks, chops, fish and pasta as well. Main

courses from $20. Mon–Thurs & Sun 4.30–9pm, Fri & Sat 4.30–10pm.

The Veranda 2122 2nd St ☎239 332 2065, ⓦverandarestaurant.com. The casual elegance of the Old South lives on in this restaurant, which occupies two 1902 houses and a lush courtyard of mango trees. Tuck into regional specialities like Southern grit cakes and Southern-fried soft shell crab. While dinner can be pricey ($30–45), lunch is very reasonable ($12–18). Reservations recommended. Mon–Fri 11am–4pm & 5.30–10pm, Sat 5.30–10pm.

Wisteria Tea Room and Café 2512 2nd St ☎239 689 4436, ⓦwisteriatearoom.com. This charming downtown tea room opened in 2011, and here you'll find English tea with a Southern touch. Opt for a light lunch of soup and salad or go for a full English tea complete with scones and Devonshire cream. Mon–Sat 11am–3pm.

FORT MYERS BEACH

Doc Ford's Rum Bar and Grill 708 Fisherman's Wharf ☎239 765 9660, ⓦdocfordsfortmyersbeach.com. Festive bayfront bar and restaurant on San Carlos Bay, this convivial joint has a great atmosphere and regular live music (Wed & Fri–Sun). There are good appetizers, sandwiches, a raw bar – and a killer mojito. Daily 11am–10pm.

Flipper's on the Bay 8771 Estero Blvd ☎239 765 1025, ⓦflippersotb.com. Inside *Lover's Key Resort*, this bayfront outdoor restaurant is perfect for sunsets and dolphin-spotting. The coconut shrimp is a standout, as well as the pan-seared sea scallops. Mains from $19. Mon–Thurs & Sun 7.30am–9pm, Fri & Sat 7.30am–10pm.

NIGHTLIFE

Fort Myers' nightlife scene is small but constantly changing and you'll usually find some lively bars on a stroll through downtown or along Estero Boulevard in Fort Myers Beach; alternatively, check ⓦdowntownftmyers.com for more options. There's also a gay and lesbian scene in the city; the best places are indicated in the listings below.

The Bottom Line 3090 Evans Ave ☎239 337 7292, ⓦtblnightclub.com. This long-running gay nightspot is a cavernous bar and club tucked away in a desolate stretch of downtown; nightly events range from drag shows to DJs to karaoke. Daily 2pm–2am.

The Cigar Bar 1502 Hendry St ☎239 337 4662, ⓦworldfamouscigarbar.com. Laidback yet stylish bar, filled with leather chesterfields and the mounted heads of bison, oryx and bear (often sporting cigars themselves). Choose from a huge range of bourbons, single malts and

smokes. Mon–Sat 10am–2am, Sun noon–2am.

City Tavern 2206 Bay St ☎239 226 1133, ⓦmycitytavern.com. Downtown in the River District, this tavern has a great happy hour that runs from 11am to 7pm and a busy scene until the wee hours of the morning, as well as live music (Thurs–Sat nights). There are also plentiful flatbreads and sandwiches (including four types of grilled cheese) should you need to soak up some of the booze. Daily 10am–2am.

The Office 3704 Cleveland Ave ☎239 936 3212,

5

ⓦ officepub.com. This congenial gay pub in the Pizza Hut Plaza has a lively happy hour and various themes, such as "underwear night". Daily noon–2am.

Smokin' Oyster Brewery 340 Old San Carlos Blvd ⓣ 239 463 3474, ⓦ smokinoyster.com. Known by locals as SOB, there's live music every night on the deck outside, as well as a tasty menu, heavy on the bivalves and crustaceans. Mon–Thurs & Sun 11am–10pm, Fri & Sat 11am–10.30pm; bar open 1hr later than restaurant closing time.

Sanibel and Captiva islands and around

Despite being mobbed by tourists in high season, Sanibel and Captiva islands, 25 miles southwest of Fort Myers, have managed to retain much of their old Florida charm; a laidback island aura, natural beauty and shell-strewn beaches. Despite vociferous opposition from locals, **Sanibel Island**, the most southerly of an island grouping around the mouth of the Caloosahatchee River, was linked by road to the mainland in 1963. Thankfully, strict land-use laws have since prevented the island from sinking beneath holiday homes and hotels; there are no high resorts to mar the view, and environmental groups continue to buy up land, thereby blocking future development. North of Sanibel, a road continues to the much smaller, less populated **Captiva Island**, which, with fewer restaurants and people, has even more of a tranquil island vibe.

Sanibel Island

Although **SANIBEL ISLAND** boasts plenty of enticing attractions away from the sands, most people come here for the **beaches**. While these are certainly appealing, public access is limited and they're not as spectacular as the glossy brochures might have you believe. Signs prohibit parking everywhere you look (parking and speeding regulations are strictly enforced), and in winter the car parks tend to get clogged.

Sanibel Lighthouse
Viewable from the outside only • Park at the beach

When you come over on the toll bridge, the first thing you'll see is the 98ft **Sanibel Lighthouse** (erected in 1884), an unattractive iron-framed relic most arrivals feel obliged to inspect before spending time on the presentable beach at its foot, a popular shell-collecting spot.

Sanibel Historical Museum and Village
950 Dunlop Rd • May to mid-Aug Wed–Sat 10am–1pm; Nov–April 10am–4pm • $10 • ⓣ 239 472 4648, ⓦ sanibelmuseum.org

From the beach, follow Periwinkle Way and turn right onto Dunlop Road, passing the island's tiny city hall on your way to the **Sanibel Historical Museum and Village**. The museum is a 1913 "cracker"-style home with furnishings and photos of early Sanibel arrivals – those who weren't seafarers tried agriculture until the soils were ruined by

---

SHELLING ON SANIBEL AND CAPTIVA ISLANDS

Both Sanibel and Captiva are littered with **shells**. Literally tonnes of them are washed ashore with each tide, and the popularity of shell collecting has led to the bent-over condition known as "Sanibel Stoop". The potential ecological upset of too many shells being taken away has led to laws forbidding the removal of any live shells (those with a creature still living inside) on pain of a $500 fine or a prison sentence. Novices and seasoned conchologists alike will find plenty to occupy them on the beaches; to identify your find, consult one of the illustrated shell charts included in most of the giveaway tourist magazines – or check the exhibits at the Bailey-Matthews Shell Museum (see opposite) or at the Sanibel Shell Show in early March. Top three shelling tips: hit the sands after storms, when numerous shells are deposited; search during low tide, when more shells are exposed; and go at dawn for first pickings.

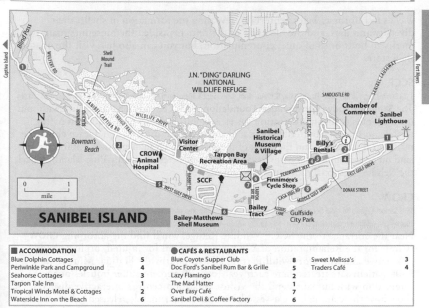

J.N. "DING" DARLING
NATIONAL
WILDLIFE REFUGE

SANIBEL ISLAND

■ ACCOMMODATION		● CAFÉS & RESTAURANTS			
Blue Dolphin Cottages	5	Blue Coyote Supper Club	8	Sweet Melissa's	3
Periwinkle Park and Campground	4	Doc Ford's Sanibel Rum Bar & Grille	5	Traders Café	4
Seahorse Cottages	3	Lazy Flamingo	2		
Tarpon Tale Inn	1	The Mad Hatter	1		
Tropical Winds Motel & Cottages	2	Over Easy Café	7		
Waterside Inn on the Beach	6	Sanibel Deli & Coffee Factory	6		

saltwater blown up by hurricanes – and the village consists of a cluster of restored island buildings, including an old schoolhouse, post office and general store.

Bailey Tract

Tarpon Bay Rd • Daily sunrise–sunset • Free

Continue along Periwinkle Way to Tarpon Bay Road, which cuts north–south across the island; going south, you'll pass the hundred-acre **Bailey Tract**, a freshwater marsh that is part of the Wildlife Refuge (see p.246). Here, five clearly marked, colour-coded hiking and biking trails take you past ponds, canals and a red mangrove island – a habitat of bobcats, alligators, snakes and many freshwater bird species.

Gulfside City Park

Open sunrise–sunset

Resorts line the beaches along West Gulf Drive, but if you head east along Casa Ybel Road, and then all the way down Algiers Lane, you'll find the more promising **Gulfside City Park**, 47 acres of palm forest and wetlands, as well as a slender strip of sandy beach and a nicely secluded picnic area. If you follow the narrow bike path veering off Algiers Road (no parking; cycle or walk from the beach), you'll find two little gems, hidden from the street by thick vegetation: a tiny **cemetery**, where a few wooden markers commemorate those who perished over a century ago, and the 22-acre **Gulfside Park Preserve**, which encircles a pond and has a walking trail through palm groves and sea grape trees.

Bailey-Matthews Shell Museum

3075 Sanibel-Captiva Rd • Daily 10am–5pm • $11, children 5–17 $5; shell store free • ☎ 239 395 2233 or ☎ 888 679 6450, ⓦ shellmuseum.org

Taking the local love of shells to its logical conclusion, the nonprofit **Bailey-Matthews Shell Museum** is devoted entirely to molluscs from all over the world. A cornucopia of shells in all colours, shapes and sizes is spread before you in such a way as to inform as well as entertain, revealing the formation of shells, their diversity and uses, and the life cycle of the critters inside. The museum's main room merits an hour or so of quiet contemplation, but you can also just visit the on-site shell store.

SCCF

3333 Sanibel-Captiva Rd • Mon–Fri: Oct–May 8.30am–4pm; June–Sept 8.30am–3pm • $5, under 17 free • ☎ 239 472 2329, ⓦ sccf.org

The **Sanibel-Captiva Conservation Foundation**, or **SCCF**, runs a nature centre with four miles of trails (with an observation tower), exhibits, a touch tank, aquariums with turtles and snakes, a butterfly house and a native plant nursery. You'll learn about the many nearby habitats and the work of the SCCF, which manages over 1300 acres of land on both islands (and owns an additional 500 acres on nearby Pine Island). Check the website for special tours and programmes.

CROW

3883 Sanibel-Captiva Rd • Mid-Dec to April Mon–Fri 10am–4pm, wildlife presentations at 11am & 2pm; May to mid-Dec Mon–Fri 10am–4pm, wildlife presentations at 11am • $5 • ☎ 239 472 3644, ⓦ crowclinic.org

Near the entrance to the SCCF Wildlife Refuge, you'll find the absorbing **CROW** (Clinic for the Rehabilitation of Wildlife), a hospital for injured, orphaned and sick native and migratory wildlife from all over southwest Florida. More than 3000 patients are treated here each year (over 80 percent suffer injuries due to interaction with humans), and the visitor education centre's interactive displays show how these animals are assessed, treated and ultimately released. Though the clinic itself is off-limits to the public, the visitor education centre includes interactive educational displays and live webcams, which immerse visitors in the patient rehabilitation process.

The J.N. "Ding" Darling National Wildlife Refuge

Just off Sanibel-Captiva Rd • Wildlife drive Mon–Thurs, Sat & Sun 7/7.30am–sunset; information centre daily: Jan–April 9am–5pm; May–Dec 9am–4pm • Cars $5, cyclists and pedestrians $1 • ☎ 239 472 1100, ⓦ fws.gov/dingdarling

In contrast to the fluffy white beaches along the Gulf side of Sanibel Island, the opposite edge comprises shallow bays, creeks and a vibrant wildlife habitat under the protection of the **J.N. "Ding" Darling National Wildlife Refuge**. The main entrance and **information and education centre** are two miles west of Tarpon Bay Road (and about a mile on from the SCCF). The refuge is home to many species, including bobcat, marsh rabbit and gopher tortoise; most commonly spotted are alligators, raccoons and a wide variety of birds including brown pelicans, ospreys, double-breasted cormorants, herons and egrets, red-shouldered hawks and red-bellied woodpeckers. Keep an eye out for bald eagles, distinguishable from ospreys by their pure-white heads, necks and tails, and graceful roseate spoonbills.

SANIBEL WILDLIFE TOURS AND BOAT RENTALS

To see the J.N. "Ding" Darling National Wildlife Refuge from the water, head to the **Tarpon Bay Recreation Area** at the northern end of Tarpon Bay Road, where Tarpon Bay Explorers (daily mid-Feb to Sept 8am–6pm; Oct to mid-Feb 8am–5pm; ☎ 239 472 8900, ⓦ tarponbayexplorers.com) runs a variety of boat and kayak tours, in addition to an interpretive **tram tour** of Wildlife Drive ($13, children 12 and under $8). Popular options include the **kayak tour** ($30, children $20) through the mangrove tunnels of the Commodore Creek Water Trail, and **sealife cruise** ($23 daytime cruise, children $15; $30 breakfast and evening cruises, children $18). You can also **rent kayaks** here ($25/2hr for a single, $33/2hr for a double, $12.50/16.50/hr thereafter).

The trails

The four-mile, one-way **Wildlife Drive** requires slow speeds and plenty of stops if you're to see the well-camouflaged residents by car; for this reason, bikes are really the way to go (see p.248). Additionally, the **Indigo Trail**, a less-travelled, two-mile path for hikers and bikers only, begins just beyond the information centre; look out for alligators in the brackish water canal on the trail's south side. You'll also find a second, much shorter (a quarter of a mile) trail close to the north end of Wildlife Drive – the **Shell Mound Trail**, a twisty boardwalk through a hardwood hammock of mangrove, buttonwood and a few lime trees (which remain from efforts to cultivate the island), all of which have grown atop an ancient Calusa Indian shell mound.

Bowman's Beach

Sanibel's loveliest, and most popular, swathe of crushed-shell sand is wide **Bowman's Beach** on the island's western end, reachable via Bowman's Beach Road off Sanibel-Captiva Road just before Blind Pass. Attracting shell-hunters and sunbathers, it offers restrooms and a shady picnic spot, along with spectacular sunsets, though you won't find much shade on the beach itself.

Captiva Island

Immediately north of Bowman's Beach, Sanibel-Captiva Road becomes Captiva Drive as it crosses Blind Pass by bridge and reaches **CAPTIVA ISLAND**, markedly less developed than Sanibel and inhabited year-round by only a few hundred people. It makes for a pleasant day-trip, especially if you stay to enjoy the sunset: unlike Sanibel, Captiva faces due west on its Gulf side. It lacks the bike paths of Sanibel, and narrow streets make riding risky, so you're best off driving here.

The beach can be accessed at two principal car parks: just beyond the bridge from Sanibel, and at the other end of Captiva Drive, where the public road terminates at the *South Seas Island Resort* (see p.248), where you can catch a **boat trip** to the neighbouring islands. Besides the few attractive restaurants and beaches, the sole site of note on Captiva Island is the tiny Chapel-by-the-Sea.

Captiva Chapel By The Sea

11580 Chapin Lane (down Wiles Drive) • Open most days mid-Nov to mid-April; call ahead before visiting • ☎ 239 472 1646

Often used for weddings, the tiny, interdenominational **Chapel By The Sea**, built in 1903, is open most days mid-November to mid-April. Don't miss the nearby **cemetery**, an unusual and historic spot where many of the island's original settlers are buried.

BOAT AND KAYAK TRIPS FROM CAPTIVA ISLAND

Organized boat trips by **Captiva Cruises** (daily 8am–5pm; ☎ 239 472 5300, ⓦ captivacruises .com) leave from either the docks of the *South Seas Island Resort* (see p.248) or from McCarthy's Marina on the Bayside of Andy Rosse Lane. The trips on offer include **dolphin-spotting**, **sunset serenade**, and **shelling trips** (to North Captiva or Cayo Costa), but the best of them is the **lunch cruise**, departing at 10am and returning at 3pm, allowing two hours ashore on either Cabbage Key (see p.248) or the private Useppa Island, home to the gourmet *Collier Inn* and a more casual, seasonally open bar-restaurant. The $40 price does not include food while ashore – there's no obligation to eat once you land, but taking your own food on the boat isn't allowed. Another option, offered seasonally only, is the six-hour trip to the seaside village of Boca Grande on Gasparilla Island for $50. Whenever you sail, you're likely to see dolphins.

Captiva Kayaks 11401 Andy Rosse Lane ☎ 239 395 2925, ⓦ captivakayaks.com. Rents kayaks ($25/hr or $55/4hr) and organizes tours ($50–60) from McCarthy's Marina. Daily 9am–5pm.

5

Cabbage Key

Of a number of small islands just north of Captiva, **Cabbage Key** is the one to visit. Even if you arrive on the lunch cruise from Captiva (see box, p.247), skip the unexciting food in favour of prowling the footpaths and small marina: there's a special beauty to the isolated setting and the panoramic views across Pine Island Sound. Take a peek into the restaurant and bar of the *Cabbage Key Inn* (see opposite) to see over $30,000 worth of dollar bills, each one signed by the person who pinned it up.

ARRIVAL AND DEPARTURE   SANIBEL AND CAPTIVA ISLANDS AND AROUND

By car The lack of public transport both to and on the islands makes day-trips virtually impossible without a car – though once you're here, all you really need is a bicycle. To reach Sanibel and Captiva from mainland Fort Myers, take College Pkwy west off of US-41, turning almost immediately south onto Summerlin Rd which winds its

way to Sanibel Causeway, a series of three bridges linking to the island. There's a $6 vehicle toll to get onto Sanibel (parking is $2/hr in car parks on both islands, 7am–7pm daily). The further west and north you travel, the more likely you are to find space.

GETTING AROUND AND INFORMATION

By bike The lack of public transport on Sanibel means that without a car, you'll have to rent a bike – a great way to get around regardless because of the island's flat terrain and well-maintained bike paths. Bear in mind bikes are generally not allowed on the beaches. Finnimore's Cycle Shop, 2353 Periwinkle Way (daily 9am–4pm; ☎ 239 472 5577, ⓦ finnimores.com), and Billy's Rentals, 1470 Periwinkle Way (daily 8.30am–5pm; ☎ 239 472 5248, ⓦ billysrentals.com), both offer good selections; single-speed bike rental costs $15/day, mountain bikes $25/day (Finnimore's is $1 cheaper).

By scooter Billy's rents scooters for $70/day.
By Segway Opposite Billy's at 1509 Periwinkle Way is Segway of Sanibel, offering 90min guided tours of the island on Segways (daily 9am, 11.30am & 2pm; $60; ☎ 239 472 3620, ⓦ segwaysanibel.com). Call in advance as each tour can only accommodate five people.
Tourist information The Chamber of Commerce and Visitor Center, 1159 Causeway Rd (daily 9am–5pm; ☎ 239 472 1080, ⓦ sanibel-captiva.org), is packed with essential information and free publications.

ACCOMMODATION

SANIBEL

Blue Dolphin Cottages 4227 W Gulf Drive ☎ 239 472 1600, ⓦ bluedolphincottages.com. This friendly inn features nine rooms, either efficiencies or one-bedroom suites right on the Gulf. All have private decks and fully equipped kitchens – make sure to take advantage of the free continental breakfast though. Efficiencies $144, suites $224
Periwinkle Park and Campground 1119 Periwinkle Way ☎ 239 472 1433, ⓦ sanibelcamping.com. The only campground on either of the two islands, this centrally located site features a popular on-site aviary. $35
Seahorse Cottages 1223 Buttonwood Lane ☎ 239 472 4262, ⓦ seahorsecottages.com. Comfortable, thoughtfully decorated cottages on the island's eastern end offer an intimate, adults-only environment with antique oak furniture, a garden pool and complimentary bikes. $100
★Tarpon Tale Inn 367 Periwinkle Way ☎ 239 472 0939, ⓦ tarpontale.com. Near both the bay and the Gulf on the far eastern end of the island, this bright, airy inn has one-bedroom suites, studios with full kitchens, and efficiencies with mini-fridges, all decorated in white wicker and antique oak. Each room comes with two complimentary bikes, beach chairs, carts and umbrellas. Efficiencies $180,

studios $210, suites $260
Tropical Winds Motel & Cottages 4819 Tradewinds & Jamaica Drive ☎ 239 472 1765, ⓦ sanibeltropicalwinds.com. Right on the Gulf, this charming blue-and-white resort features bright efficiencies close to the beach and one-bedroom cottages set a little further back from the sand. Efficiencies $199, cottages $235
Waterside Inn on the Beach 3033 W Gulf Drive ☎ 239 472 1345, ⓦ watersideinn.net. A colourful, friendly
place right on the beach, with spacious accommodation in rooms, efficiencies and cottages. Doubles $155, efficiencies $179, efficiency, cottages $206

CAPTIVA

Captiva Island Inn 11509 Andy Rosse Lane ☎ 239 395 0882, ⓦ captivaislandinn.com. Near the island's restaurants and shops, and a short walk to the beach, this charming bed and breakfast offers everything from rooms to houses, plus complimentary bikes. $99
South Seas Island Resort 5400 Plantation Rd ☎ 239 472 5111, ⓦ southseas.com. Captiva's tip is covered by the picturesque golf course, multiple pools and tennis courts, restaurants and Polynesian-style villas of the

swanky *South Seas Island Resort.* $239

'Tween Waters Inn 15951 Captiva Rd ☎ 239 472 5161 ⓦ tween-waters.com. Nestled between the Gulf and Pine Island Sound, this historic resort features tennis courts, a marina, pool and day-spa. Enquire about walk-in specials, when rates are discounted. $260

CABBAGE KEY

Cabbage Key Inn ☎ 239 283 2278, ⓦ cabbagekey .com. The inn offers six recently refurbished rooms and seven rustic one- to three-bedroom cottages and a good restaurant (see p.250); reserve at least a month in advance. Rooms $129, cottages from $185

EATING AND DRINKING

The islands' isolation offers a relaxing **eating and drinking** experience, with seafood standing out (naturally) as the islands' speciality. You'll find restaurants all over Sanibel, while Captiva has fewer haunts, and most are clustered near the island's northern end. As for **nightlife**, don't expect to find a wild scene – young locals head to Fort Myers and Fort Myers Beach for that. Note that many restaurants on Sanibel and Captiva close for the entire month of September.

SANIBEL

★**Blue Coyote Supper Club** 1100 Par View Drive ☎ 239 472 9222, ⓦ bluecoyotesupperclub.com. Within the clubhouse of the Sanibel Island Golf Club, this trendy spot features eclectic art on the walls and an impeccably executed, meat-heavy menu. Try the seared sea scallops atop pancetta followed by the prime New York strip steak. Tues–Thurs 11am–3pm & 5–9pm, Fri & Sat 11am–3pm & 5–10pm.

Doc Ford's Sanibel Rum Bar & Grille 975 Rabbit Rd ☎ 239 472 8311, ⓦ docfordssanibel.com. This friendly sports bar sits near the Wildlife Refuge. The rum bar boasts more than forty varieties, and the excellent, tropical-inspired lunch and dinner dishes include "island-style shrimp and grits" and "Campeche" (grilled) fish tacos. There's another outpost on Captiva. Daily 11am–10pm.

Lazy Flamingo 1036 Periwinkle Way ☎ 239 472 6939, and 6520-C Pine Ave ☎ 239 472 5353, ⓦ lazyflamingo .com. Very popular island mainstay, featuring a moderately priced raw bar and seafood grill with a nautical theme, and two Sanibel locations. Daily 11am–midnight.

The Mad Hatter 6467 Sanibel Captiva Rd ☎ 239 472 0033. This cosy, romantic restaurant is a great special occasion spot, and features "New American" cuisine, such as blue crab cakes and black truffle sea scallops. Main dishes $29–45. Tues–Sun 6–9pm; closed Sept.

Over Easy Café 630 Tarpon Bay Rd ☎ 239 472 2625, ⓦ overeasycafesanibel.com. Feast on breakfast – served all day – in this brightly coloured, amiable diner. Try the Egg Reuben sandwich on a bagel ($7.99) or the Gulf shrimp, tomato and cheese omelette ($9.99). Daily 7am–3pm.

Sanibel Deli & Coffee Factory 2330 Palm Ridge Rd ☎ 239 472 2555, ⓦ sanibeldeli.com. Grab a great morning cappuccino, a sandwich or wrap for the beach, or some of the island's best pizza at this popular local deli. Mon 7am–3pm, Tues–Sat 7am–8pm, Sun 8am–7pm.

Sweet Melissa's 1625 Periwinkle Way ☎ 239 472 1956, ⓦ sweetmelissascafe.net. One of the island's most romantic dinner spots also serves some of its most creative cuisine. Try the sautéed sweetbreads ($14) and the fish stew, which features shrimp, scallops, clams, mussels, fish and chorizo ($32). Mon–Fri 11am–2.30pm, Mon–Sat 5–10pm.

★**Traders Café** 1551 Periwinkle Way ☎ 239 472 7242, ⓦ traderssanibel.com. Homely pine walls and crisp white tablecloths add to the atmosphere at this airy café and store, which serves fresh, American-style bistro food. Try the BBQ ribs and potatoes au gratin ($24), or if you feel like seafood, the lump crab and spinach-filled Gulf shrimp can't be beat ($26). There's live entertainment on Tuesday and Thursday evenings as well. Mon–Sat 11am–2.30pm & 5–9pm.

CAPTIVA

★**Key Lime Bistro** Captiva Island Inn, 11509 Andy Rosse Lane ☎ 239 395 4000. Start your meal properly with a delicious Key lime martini at this gregarious spot within *Captiva Island Inn*. The menu favours seafood, but there are also lots of pasta dishes (try the sausage and peppers), some fantastic risottos and – naturally – a killer Key lime pie. There's also nightly live music. Main courses $14–28. Daily 8am–10pm.

Mucky Duck 11546 Andy Rosse Lane ☎ 239 472 3434, ⓦ muckyduck.com. This prime sunset-watching spot serves an affordable lunch ($9–13) but gets pricier at dinner ($20–27). The menu is heavy on seafood, but also features chicken Marsala, pork chops and steak. The English-themed bar serves sixteen beers on draft and pints of margarita ($6). Get there early, as it gets crowded. Daily 11.30am–3pm & 5–9pm.

Old Captiva House 'Tween Waters Inn, 15951 Captiva Drive ☎ 239 472 5161, ⓦ tween-waters.com. Within the *'Tween Waters Inn* is *Old Captiva House*, offering upscale cuisine in a homely, welcoming atmosphere. Try the *escargot en croute* followed by the island snapper wrap for a unique take on surf and turf. Dinner mains $23 and up. Daily 7.30–11am & 5.30–9.30pm.

5

CABBAGE KEY
Cabbage Key Inn ☎ 239 283 2278, ⓦ cabbagekey
.com. The lunchtime menu at this inn features good salads,
seafood and sandwiches; dinner is heavy on fish dishes
like mahi-mahi and marinated sautéed shrimp (mains
$18–30). Daily 11.15am–8.30pm.

South of Fort Myers

While Sanibel and Captiva islands warrant a few days of exploration, there's less to
keep you occupied on the mainland on the seventy-mile journey **south of Fort Myers**
towards Naples. The towns you'll pass through aren't as appealing as the nearby beaches
or the interesting vistas of Florida's interior. Set aside a few hours, however, to examine
one of the stranger footnotes to Florida's history: the oddball religious community of
the Koreshans.

Koreshan State Historic Site

3800 Corkscrew Rd • Daily 8am–sunset; tours Jan–March Sat & Sun 10am; 1hr–1hr 30min • Cars $5, $4 for single occupant vehicle,
pedestrians and cyclists $2; tours $2 • ☎ 239 992 0311, ⓦ floridastateparks.org/koreshan

One of the most bizarre episodes in Florida history began in 1894, when followers of a
new faith, Koreshanity, came from Chicago to establish their "New Jerusalem" 22 miles
from Fort Myers. The Koreshans are long gone, but you can learn more about their
Utopian beliefs by exploring their quixotic former settlement, preserved today as the
tranquil **Koreshan State Historic Site**, just south of Estero beside US-41.

The flamboyant leader of the Koreshans, **Cyrus Teed**, believed that the entire universe
existed within a giant, hollow sphere (he later changed his name to "Koresh", which is
Hebrew for Cyrus and means "the anointed of God"). Among the other tenets of
Koreshanity were celibacy outside marriage, shared ownership of goods, and gender equality.
The aesthetes who came to this desolate outpost, accessible only by boat along the alligator-
infested Estero River, quickly learned new skills in farming and house building, and marked
out 30ft-wide boulevards, which they believed would one day be the arteries of a city
inhabited by ten million enlightened souls. In fact, at its peak in 1907, the community
numbered just two hundred. After Teed's death in 1908, the Koreshans fizzled out, with the
last real member – who arrived in 1940, fleeing Nazi Germany – dying in 1982.

Along the crushed-shell paths of the site, several of the Koreshan buildings have been
restored, including Teed's 1896 home (also known as the **Founder's House**), where
exhibits and a video help put the site into context, and the **Planetary Court** (1904),
meeting place of the seven women – each named for one of the seven known planets
– who governed the community. You can take ranger-led **tours** at 10am or 2pm from
January to March, and at 10am April to December.

ARRIVAL AND DEPARTURE   KORESHAN STATE HISTORIC SITE

By car With no viable public transport nearby, you'll need
a car to get to Koreshan. The site is at the intersection of
Corkscrew Rd and S Tamiami Trail (US-41). If you're
travelling on I-75, take the Corkscrew Rd exit west.

ACCOMMODATION

Estero River campsites ☎ 800 326 3521, ⓦ florida
stateparks.reserveamerica.com. There are 54 campsites
within the pinelands along the Estero River, some close to
the water; twelve are reserved for tents only. Amenities
include BBQ grills, a boat ramp, working toilets and
showers, a picnic area and a playground. **$26**

Corkscrew Swamp Sanctuary

375 Sanctuary Rd W • Daily 7am–5.30pm; last admission 1hr before closing • $12 • ☎ 239 348 9151, ⓦ corkscrew.audubon.org

Fifteen miles inland from the Koreshan State Historic Site on Hwy-846 (branching
from US-41 a few miles south of Bonita Springs), you'll get a real contrast to coastal

Florida at the National Audubon Society's **Corkscrew Swamp Sanctuary**. Here you'll find a well-maintained 2.25-mile **boardwalk trail** through the largest stand of virgin bald cypress trees in North America. The trees loom amid a dark and moody swamp landscape of pine flatwood, wet prairie and sawgrass ponds. Much of the surrounding area – presently safeguarded by the Big Cypress National Preserve (see p.163) – used to look like this; however, uncontrolled logging felled the 500-year-old trees, partly for war efforts, and severely reduced Florida's population of **wood stork**, which nest a hundred feet up in the treetops. The remaining wood stork colony is still the largest in the country, but now faces the threat of falling water levels and never-ending development. Look out also for river otters, white-tailed deer, anhinga birds, herons, alligators, red-shouldered hawks and black bears (in summer).

You'll find one of the park's unique features near the toilets. Here, a remarkably simple "living machine" aids water management in the park by recycling waste from the toilets to produce purified water. Within a visually pleasing, plant-filled greenhouse, the cycle relies on sunlight, bacteria, algae and snails to break down the waste, a process later continued by vegetation, small insects and animals.

Naples

Like the rest of south Florida, it's easy to forget **NAPLES** was a frontier town little more than a hundred years ago. The first trading posts appeared in the 1870s, followed by the first hotel in 1889; millionaire Barron Collier (see p.165) bought most of the town in the 1920s. The area remained a sleepy outpost until the 1950s, when condominium development began in earnest.

Thirty-six miles south of Fort Myers, Naples is still cushioned in wealth. On lazy summer days, the most action in town is from the sprinklers spraying perfectly manicured lawns. While the city has its fair share of wealthy retirees, it's surprisingly accessible and more diverse than you might expect. The **beaches** are magnificent – stretching north from Naples City Pier are eleven miles of gorgeous public sands, though the condo-lined shore means access can be tricky – and away from the Gulf coastline, the town itself has plenty to amuse you.

Downtown Naples

Downtown Naples is split by opulent Fifth Avenue South running east–west, with its high-end clothes shops, boutique hotels and restaurants.

Sugden Community Theater

701 5th Ave S • ☎ 239 263 7990, ⓦ naplesplayers.com

On Fifth Avenue look out for the **Sugden Community Theater**, home of the well-regarded **Naples Players**, tucked away between the glitzy shops; check the website for upcoming shows, which can be anything from musicals and comedies to more serious plays.

Tin City

1200 5th Ave S • Mon–Sat 10am–9pm, Sun noon–5pm, restaurants Mon–Thurs & Sun 11am–10pm, Fri & Sat 11am–11pm • Shop admission free • ⓦ tin-city.com • Leave your car in the Tin City Park-n-Walk Lot on 6th Ave (free)

Near the posh chain stores and boutiques of Fifth Avenue are the somewhat kitschy shops and restaurants of the colourful **Tin City** complex, a former 1920s clam shelling and oyster processing plant. While here, pop in for complimentary tropical-fruit wine tastings at The Naples Winery (☎ 239 732 9463, ⓦ thenapleswinery .com – try the Mama Guava). Fishing tours and bay cruises depart from the river here (see p.254).

5

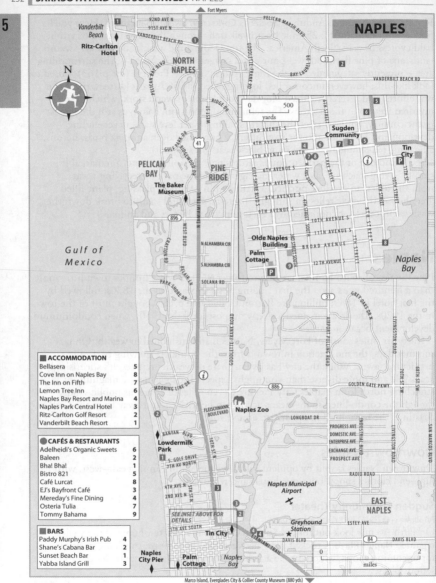

ACCOMMODATION

Bellasera	5
Cove Inn on Naples Bay	8
The Inn on Fifth	7
Lemon Tree Inn	6
Naples Bay Resort and Marina	4
Naples Park Central Hotel	3
Ritz-Carlton Golf Resort	2
Vanderbilt Beach Resort	1

CAFÉS & RESTAURANTS

Adelheidi's Organic Sweets	6
Baleen	2
Bha! Bha!	1
Bistro 821	5
Café Lurcat	8
EJ's Bayfront Café	3
Mereday's Fine Dining	4
Osteria Tulia	7
Tommy Bahama	9

BARS

Paddy Murphy's Irish Pub	4
Shane's Cabana Bar	2
Sunset Beach Bar	1
Yabba Island Grill	3

Olde Naples Building

1148 3rd St, on the corner of Broad Ave

The second main downtown area to explore lies seven blocks south along Third Street South (between Broad and 14th aves), where you'll find yet more shopping and cafés, as well as Gallery Row (a concentration of art galleries along Broad Ave). Look out for the **Olde Naples Building**, which, since its construction in 1922, has been everything to Naples – its first town hall, a courthouse, drugstore, movie theatre, community church, tap dance school and café, though it has stood empty for quite some time.

Palm Cottage

137 12th Ave S • Tues–Sat 1–4pm,• $10 including guided tour • ☎ 239 261 8164, ⓦ napleshistoricalsociety.org

A block away from the Olde Naples Building, the 1895 **Palm Cottage** is the oldest house in town and one of the few houses left in Florida built of tabby mortar (made by burning seashells). Once the home of Walter N. Haldeman, who built the first hotel in Naples, it's now owned by the historical society. To see the beautifully preserved interior, take a **guided tour**.

Naples City Pier

Started in 1888 as a passenger dock, historic **Naples City Pier** has been rebuilt many times; the latest incarnation dates from 1960. Unusually, you can fish here without a licence, but it's also a popular place to watch the sunset and access the beach.

Lowdermilk Park

Off Gulf Shore Blvd N • Park in the visitor section and pay at the machine (25¢/10min)

The liveliest of the local sands, especially at weekends, is **Lowdermilk Park**, about one mile from US-41 and two miles north of the pier; extras include two beach volleyball courts and a handful of resident ducks in the pond opposite.

The Ritz-Carlton

280 Vanderbilt Beach Rd • ☎ 239 598 3300, ⓦ ritzcarlton.com • Valet parking at the hotel $5/day for local day-guests $28/day for overnight parking; there's a Collier County parking garage for the beach next door for $8/day

To ogle the fruits of Naples' wealth, head north up US-41 to Vanderbilt Beach and the **Ritz-Carlton Hotel**. The building looks like a 1930s vision of classical decadence, but it actually appeared in the late 1980s. While you'd need around $2600 for a night in the Presidential Suite, sweeping through the grand entrance for a coffee at the bar is an inexpensive way to appreciate the hotel's towering splendour.

Philharmonic Center for the Arts

5833 Pelican Bay Blvd • ☎ 239 597 1900 or ☎ 800 597 1900, ⓦ artisnaples.org

Enjoy Naples' growing cultural arts scene at the **Philharmonic Center for the Arts**, with an orchestra hall, a black box theatre, and several art galleries; programmes run the gamut from Broadway to Beethoven, and events include film screenings and music lectures.

The Baker Museum

5833 Pelican Bay Blvd • Tues 10am–8pm, Wed–Sat 10–4pm, Sun noon–4pm • $10 • ☎ 239 597 1111, ⓦ artisnaples.org

In the same complex as the Philharmonic Center for the Arts you'll also find **The Baker Museum**, a three-storey museum with rotating national and international exhibits and a permanent collection including American Modernists (Alfred Stieglitz, Stuart Davis) and twentieth-century Mexican masters (Diego Rivera, Rufino Tamayo). Don't miss the Persian ceiling and spectacular chandeliers by glass artist Dale Chihuly. You can eat outside in the *Café Intermezzo*.

Collier County Museum

3331 Tamiami Trail E, east of downtown Naples; the museum is behind the county government centre • Mon–Sat 9am–4pm • Free • ☎ 239 252 8476, ⓦ colliermuseums.com

The sprawling Naples suburbs east of US-41 hold little interest, but the **Collier County Museum** is definitely worth seeking out. The small but well-presented exhibition room covers local events from prehistory to World War II, with particular

5

attention paid to Seminole history, and the arrival of advertising magnate and founding father Barron Gift Collier in 1911. Outside, the tranquil **gardens** contain an eclectic assortment of exhibits, including a Sherman tank, a steam engine and a reproduction of a Seminole village.

ARRIVAL AND DEPARTURE NAPLES

By car Downtown, the beaches and most sights are easily accessible from US-41 (Tamiami Trail), though the fastest route from Miami and the east coast is I-75, which bypasses Naples around 4 miles east of US-41.

By bus The Greyhound terminal is at 2669 Davis Blvd (☎ 239 774 5660) in Naples, but the city is very spread out and best explored by car. To get to downtown Naples, take

the Naples CAT bus #13 or #14 to downtown Naples. Fares are $1.50 each way; transfers are 75¢.

Destinations Fort Lauderdale (2 daily; 2hr); Fort Myers (2 daily; 1hr); Miami (4 daily; 3hr–3hr 40min); Orlando (2 daily; 7hr 15min–8hr 30min); St Petersburg (2 daily; 4hr); Tampa (2 daily; 5hr).

GETTING AROUND AND INFORMATION

By car It's best to get around by car. You can park anywhere along 5th Ave S (free), but get here early to secure a space.

Tourist information The Visitor Information Center, 900 5th Ave S (Mon–Sat 9am–5pm, June–Sept also Sat 10am–2pm; ☎ 239 262 6141, ⊛ napleschamber.org), is one of the best stocked in the state, with information on restaurants and hotels.

Tours You can take bus and walking tours of Naples' sights (see box below). Back-bay fishing tours ($75/half-day), deep-sea fishing tours ($85/half-day) and sightseeing and sunset cruises of the bay ($35/1hr 30min) depart from the river at Tin City (☎ 239 263 4949, ⊛ purenaples.com); dolphin sightings are fairly common. The Visitor Information Center has details on various boat, manatee and Everglades tours (see box opposite).

ACCOMMODATION

Bellasera 221 9th St S ☎ 239 649 7333, ⊛ bellasera naples.com. Centrally located, romantic resort hotel with Italianate architecture, a fitness centre, an attractive pool and courtyard, and a popular Mediterranean restaurant and lounge. **$339**

Cove Inn on Naples Bay 900 Broad Ave S ☎ 239 262 7161, ⊛ coveinnnaples.com. This comfortable inn is a condo-hotel, so each room is decorated a bit differently according to the owner's individual taste – although all feature private balconies and are convenient for walking everywhere in Old Naples. **$89**

The Inn on Fifth 699 5th Ave S ☎ 239 403 8777, ⊛ innonfifth.com. This Mediterranean-style boutique hotel on Naples' main drag fits right in with the subdued wealth and chic stores. The well-appointed rooms all have terraces. **$399**

Lemon Tree Inn 250 9th St S ☎ 239 262 1414,

⊛ lemontreeinn.com. This homely inn – some rooms have teak four-poster beds – offers complimentary continental breakfast and lemonade in the lobby, plus a pool and garden. **$143**

★ **Naples Bay Resort & Marina** 1500 5th Ave S ☎ 239 530 1199, ⊛ naplesbayresort.com. This lovely resort on Naples Bay offers a variety of rooms, from well-appointed kings to luxurious one- and two-bedroom suites. Many rooms overlook the Naples Bay Marina. There's an on-site pool but guests also have access to the resort-like Club at Naples Bay Resort next door to the property, which offers a spa, gym, gigantic pool with a lazy river, as well as a quieter adults-only pool. **$229**

Naples Park Central Hotel 40 9th St N ☎ 239 435 9700, ⊛ naplesparkcentral.com. This boutique hotel offers thirty tasteful rooms with fridges, microwaves and flat-screen TVs. There's free wi-fi, and the hotel is about seven blocks from

---

NAPLES BUS AND WALKING TOURS

If you don't have a car (or just want a break from driving), a good way to explore Naples and its history is to embark on a Naples Trolley Tour. Running daily from 8.30am to 5.30pm (last tour leaves 3.30pm; ☎ 239 262 7300 or ☎ 800 592 0848, ⊛ naplestrolleytours.com), these entertaining and educational tours last nearly two hours, departing from the Experience Naples Visitor Center (daily 8am–4pm) near Tin City at 1010 6th Ave S, but you can hop on/hop off at any of the 21 stops in town with the all-day pass. Fares are $27 (children $13). You can pick up Naples Historical Society-guided **walking tours** of the Historic District around Palm Cottage (every Wed at 9.30am for $16; ☎ 239 261 8164; reservations essential).

5

GETTING TO THE EVERGLADES

There's no public transport to the Everglades (see p.154), so if you don't have a car, a good option is to take a day-trip from Naples or Marco Island (see p.256). Everglades Excursions (☎239 262 1914 or ☎800 592 0848, ⓦeverglades-excursions.com) run full- and half-day tours that include guided safari transport, a jungle cruise and an airboat ride through Everglades National Park, and a tour of Everglades City. Half-day tours cost $89; full-day tours are $129, including lunch. You can usually find discount coupons of up to $5 in the tourist booklets at the Visitor Center (see opposite).

the beach and four from downtown. **$149**

Ritz-Carlton Golf Resort 2600 Tiburon Drive ☎239 593 2000, ⓦritzcarlton.com. Similar to Naples' other *Ritz-Carlton* (see p.253), which is on the beach, but cheaper and a bit more low-key, with lusher grounds and a cordial staff. All the amenities you could possibly think of (for a steep price). Check for off-season specials. **$499**

★**Vanderbilt Beach Resort** 9225 Gulf Shore Drive N

☎239 597 3144 or ☎800 243 9076. The same family has owned this friendly hotel for over fifty years, and their care is evident in both the spotless rooms and warmth to guests. Choose from a variety of accommodation, from studio rooms to deluxe two-bedroom units. All have full-size refrigerators, microwaves and stovetops, as well as free wi-fi. Beach towels, chairs and umbrellas are also included in your stay. **$220**

EATING AND DRINKING

There's a welcome lack of the usual fast-food chains in Naples. Even the food in casual restaurants is done well here, though not surprisingly, it's often more expensive than elsewhere in the state. To dine at the nicer spots without blowing your budget, keep your eyes open for early bird and prix-fixe specials.

RESTAURANTS

Adelheidi's Organic Sweets 505 5th Ave S ☎239 304 9870, ⓦadelheidisorganics.com. The best gelato in town, and it's all organic. Try creative flavours like strawberry-basil or chocolate-lavender or go old school with the delicious vanilla bean. Mon–Fri & Sun 10am–10.30pm, Sat 10am–11.30pm.

Baleen 9891 Gulf Shore Drive ☎239 598 5707, ⓦlaplayaresort.com. One of the few beachfront restaurants in Naples, this charming fine-dining spot is housed in the *LaPlaya* resort. Sit in the more formal dining room or on the casual terrace, and try dishes like Florida Keys snapper or broiled lobster risotto (main courses from $32). Daily 7am–2.30pm & 5.30–10pm.

Bha! Bha! 865 5th Ave S ☎239 594 5557, ⓦbhabhapersianbistro.com. Classical and new Persian cuisine, with most dishes around $22–32 and occasional live music and belly dancing. Try the delicious lamb *bademjune*, in a tomato and lemon sauce, with grilled vegetables, sautéed aubergine (eggplant) and sour grapes. Mon–Thurs & Sun 5–9pm, Fri & Sat 5–10pm.

Bistro 821 821 5th Ave S ☎239 261 5821, ⓦbistro821 .com. Local favourite offering Italian-, French- and Asian-inspired dishes, from seafood risotto ($18.95) to roasted duck ($28.95) to coconut, ginger and lemongrass-encrusted snapper ($31.95). Mon–Thurs & Sun 5–10pm, Fri & Sat 5–10.30pm.

Café Lurcat 494 5th Ave S ☎239 213 3357, ⓦcafelurcat.com. Romantic, two-storey Spanish Revival building, with fine American cuisine (try the well-priced

early bird menu; $22.95 for three courses before 6.30pm) and a lighter downstairs bar menu of small plates like the popular Lurcat burger ($9.50) and warm cinnamon-sugar doughnuts ($8.50). Daily 5–10pm; bar opens at 4pm.

EJ's Bayfront Café 469 Bayfront Place ☎239 353 4444, ⓦejsbayfrontcafe.com. This homely spot serves a tasty breakfast all day, either inside or outside on a pet-friendly patio. Scrambles, skillets and pancakes are all tasty, but you must try the cheesy hash-brown casserole – you may end up ordering two. Breakfast mains from $7–12, lunch $9–11. Daily 7.30am–3pm.

★**Mereday's Fine Dining** 1500 5th Ave S (Naples Bay Resort) ☎239 732 0784, ⓦmeredaysnaples.com. Fine dining without being fussy, this sleek, modern space offers two-, three-or four-course tasting menus, which change frequently and include dessert. Diners can choose from creative dishes such as a roasted heirloom beet salad and stuffed quail with dried cranberry and pancetta. Non-carnivores won't be left out with menu dishes such as the curried vegetable tagine, and the chef will prepare exclusively vegan options if requested. Two courses with dessert from $55; four courses $95. Bar daily from 4pm, dinner 5–9pm.

★**Osteria Tulia** 466 5th Ave S ☎239 213 2073, ⓦtulianaples.com. You'll feel as though you've stumbled into a classic Italian farmhouse kitchen in this homely yet modern spot on 5th Ave. Chef and owner Vincenzo Betulia is usually in the kitchen, preparing such delicious dishes as home-made ricotta, fried veal sweetbreads and home-made pastas such as the melt-in-your-mouth tortelloni

5

with roasted beef shortrib. Main courses $16–32. Daily 11.30am–3pm & 5–10pm.

Tommy Bahama 1220 3rd St S ☎239 643 6889, ⓦtommybahama.com. You'll always find a crowd at this tropical café, which has a large outdoor patio and sits between the Tommy Bahama clothing stores. Enjoy sandwiches, salads and grilled seafood, washed down with a glass of wine or two. Main courses $18–30. Mon–Thurs & Sun 11am–10pm, Fri & Sat 11am–11pm.

BARS

Paddy Murphy's Irish Pub 457 5th Ave S ☎239 649 5140, ⓦpaddymurphys.com. Staff from the local bars and restaurants descend on this pub for a drink when it's quitting time. Listen to live music (usually Irish earlier in the night) or a DJ seven nights a week until 2am (midnight on Sun). Daily 10am–2am.

Shane's Cabana Bar 495 Bayfront Place ☎239 732 6633. This small, *palapa*-covered drinks-only bar sits directly over the water of Naples Bay and attracts a mostly after-work crowd for happy hour, shutting down by 11pm. There are plentiful nightly specials, and the margaritas are excellent. Daily 3–11pm.

★**Sunset Beach Bar** at Naples Beach Hotel & Golf Club, 851 Gulf Shore Blvd N ☎239 261 2222 ext 2938. Casual grill and Gulf-side bar also open to non-guests of the hotel, and the best spot to sip tequila while watching the sunset. Serves lunch and light dinner fare, with daily live music in season. Mon–Thurs & Sun 11am–midnight, Fri & Sat 11am–1am.

Yabba Island Grill 711 5th Ave S ☎239 262 5787, ⓦyabbaislandgrill.com. The tables are moved aside at this great Caribbean grill after 10.30pm on Friday and Saturday nights to make way for a DJ and dancefloor, and the young crowd that works it. Mon–Thurs & Sun 4.30–9pm, Fri & Sat 4.30–10pm.

Marco Island

Home to several ritzy beach resorts and a largely residential community of palm-lined boulevards, **MARCO ISLAND** (about 20 miles south of Naples) makes a pleasant detour if you need a break from the crowds elsewhere.

Marco Island Historical Museum

180 S Heathwood Drive • Tues–Sat 9am–4pm • Free • ☎239 642 1440, ⓦthemihs.org

Long before white settlers arrived here in the 1870s, Marco Island was an important Calusa settlement, and in 1896 archeologists unearthed one of the most sensational caches of wooden artefacts ever found in North America – the most famous being a six-inch wooden panther-like figure, dubbed the **Key Marco Cat** (dating from 500–800 AD), and now housed in the Smithsonian Museum (Washington, DC). You can check out a replica, along with Calusa shells, tools, masks and necklaces at the **Marco Island Historical Museum**. Temporary and travelling exhibits also explore what life was like for pioneer settlements in a fishing village, pineapple plantation and clam cannery up to the beginning of modern development in the 1960s. There's also a small gift shop, selling jewellery, books and Calusa art reproductions.

Tigertail Beach Park

Hernando Drive, accessed from Kendall Drive off Collier Blvd • Daily 8am–sunset • Parking $8/day or $1.50/hr • ☎239 252 4000

The whole western edge of Marco Island is lined with brilliant white crushed-shell beaches, though access can be problematic. The best spot to relax or take in the sunset is **Tigertail Beach Park**, which has a picnic area with grills, restrooms and rental of beach gear.

ARRIVAL AND INFORMATION

MARCO ISLAND

By car From Naples, take US-41 to Hwy-951.

By bus You can take the Naples CAT Marco Express bus #21 or #121 from east of downtown Naples to central Marco Island daily for $2.50. Bus service runs from around 8.15am to 4pm.

By guided tour You can get to the Everglades from Marco Island with Everglades Excursions (see box, p.255).

Tourist information The Chamber of Commerce is at 1102 N Collier Blvd (Mon–Fri 9am–5pm; ☎239 394 7549 or ☎888 330 1422, ⓦmarcoislandchamber.org).

EATING AND DRINKING

The Bar and Bistro at Marek's 1121 Bald Eagle Drive ☎239 642 9948, ⓦmareksmarcoisland.com. The more casual cousin of *Marek's Collier House Restaurant* next door, this top-notch bistro offers perfectly prepared steaks and burgers, as well as a variety of pastas and seafood dishes. There's also an English-themed menu with items such as cottage pie and chicken curry for homesick Brits. Mains $13.50–35. Tues–Sat 5–10pm.

★**Fin Bistro** 317 N Collier Blvd ☎239 970 6064, ⓦfinbistro.com. This simple, popular seafood spot is one of the busiest in town, so make sure to reserve ahead on weekends. Menu standouts include pan-roasted Gulf prawns and Florida spiny lobster. Don't miss the Key lime flan for dessert. Mains $23–27. Mon–Sat 5.30–10pm.

Guy and Lisa's Philly Grille 1000 N Collier Blvd, Heritage Square Shopping Plaza ☎239 394 2222, ⓦphilly-grille.com. Another good bet for lunch or dinner, this local favourite serves fantastic sandwiches and flatbreads. Try the Philly cheese steak, the lobster BLT or the smoked salmon flatbread for something a little lighter. Mon–Sat 11am–2pm & 5–10pm.

Stan's Idle Hour 221 Goodland Drive W ☎239 394 3041, ⓦstansidlehour.net. Located in Goodland, a fishing village at the eastern end of the island (south off San Marco Rd), this ramshackle fish shack – one of many in the area – serves fresh seafood in baskets or sandwiches and features live music most nights, as well as a dance known as the "buzzard lope", invented by the restaurant's wacky owner. Seafood main courses range $16–32. Tues–Sun 11am–10pm; closed Aug & Sept.

Orlando and Disney World

FIREWORKS, DISNEY'S MAGIC KINGDOM

Orlando and Disney World

6

Although it began as a quiet farming town, a little over forty years ago everything changed for Orlando, which now has more visitors than any other place in the state. Though reminders of the old Florida are still easy to find in and immediately north of the city, most people get no closer to Orlando's heart than a string of motels along US-192, just south of Disney World, or International Drive, five miles southwest of downtown Orlando: a boulevard of hotels, shopping malls and chain restaurants. The cause of the transformation is, of course, Walt Disney World, a group of state-of-the-art theme parks that lure millions every year to a forty-square-mile plot of previously featureless scrubland.

It's possible to pass through the Orlando area and not visit Walt Disney World, but there's no way to escape its impact – even the road system was reshaped to accommodate the park, and, whichever way you look, billboards feature the Mouse and friends. Amid a plethora of would-be tourist targets, only **Universal Orlando** and **SeaWorld Orlando** offer serious competition to the most finely realized concept in escapist entertainment anywhere on earth. The theme parks' influence has spread **south of Orlando**, especially in the seemingly perfect, Disney-like town of **Celebration**. Venture a few miles **north of Orlando**, however, and the real world starts to reassert itself, albeit very gently, in the form of a quaint Victorian-era town called **Mount Dora** and the hidden village of **Cassadaga**, populated almost entirely by spiritualists.

GETTING AROUND   **ORLANDO AND DISNEY WORLD**

By car The major cross-Florida roads form a web-like mass of intersections in or around Orlando and Walt Disney World.

Florida's Turnpike Cuts northwest–southeast, avoiding Disney World and downtown Orlando altogether; there is a toll for this road.

Hwy-528 (the Beeline Expressway) Stems from International Drive and heads for the east coast.

I-4 Passes southwest–northeast through Disney and continues through downtown Orlando and north to Daytona Beach where it joins up with I-95 N.

US-192 (the Irlo Bronson Memorial Hwy) Crosses I-4 just south of Disney and charts an east–west course through the towns of Kissimmee and St Cloud.

Orlando

Given the dominance of Walt Disney World and its rival theme parks, it's easy to overlook the fact that Orlando is a vibrant city in its own right. The compact **downtown**, with a small but growing crop of high-rise buildings and smart residential

GRINGOTTS BANK, DIAGON ALLEY

Highlights

❶ Downtown Orlando nightlife Hop from craft cocktail purveyors to wine bars to lively clubs in one of Florida's after-dark hotspots. **See p.262**

❷ Blizzard Beach Demonstrating it can work its magic in all domains, Disney has created this excellent water park to provide a break from trudging around the theme parks. **See p.282**

❸ Wizarding World of Harry Potter and Diagon Alley Undoubtedly the most exciting new attractions to hit the theme parks in years, the Harry Potter section of Islands of Adventure and new Diagon Alley at Universal Studios are pure magic for Muggles. **See p.289**

❹ Gatorland Watch the alligators being fed – or wrestled – at this less-heralded theme park between Orlando and Kissimmee. **See p.296**

❺ Winter Park Small boutiques, charming cafés and a great museum combine to make a stroll along Park Avenue in Winter Park a must-do. **See p.298**

❻ Cassadaga This spiritualists' village deep in the forest is just about as far from the classic Orlando vacation experience as you can get. **See p.303**

❼ Blue Spring State Park The St John's River, which runs through the park, is a prime place to spot manatees. **See p.304**

HIGHLIGHTS ARE MARKED ON THE MAP ON P.262

neighbourhoods, features several good museums and galleries, and the best nightlife in central Florida. This said, most visitors haven't come to Orlando to sample more than an afternoon or two of its unheralded cultural refinement, and will inevitably gravitate southwest of the downtown area before too long to join the fun and frolics at the parks. Here, along the strip of hotels, restaurants, shopping malls and the multitude of other tourist attractions that is **International Drive**, the Orlando you had always expected rears its mouse-eared head, to the delight of kids and kids-at-heart.

Downtown Orlando

Orlando's sprawling geography is redeemed by its vibrant **downtown**, an area still largely overlooked by visitors. Ongoing urban rejuvenation has led to an appealing mix of luxury condos and refurbished bungalows, trendy restaurants and excellent nightlife. Coupled with the fact that everything of consequence can be visited on foot within an hour, downtown has become an enticing area to explore.

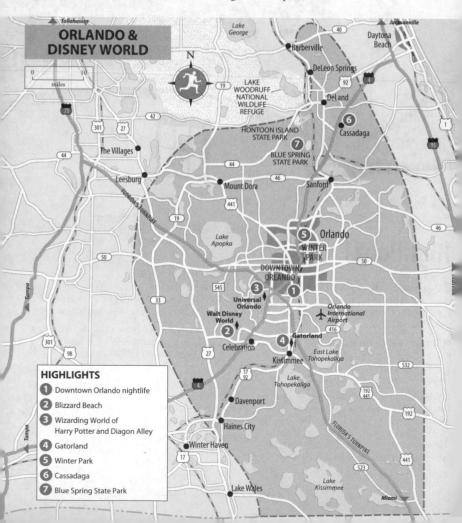

ORLANDO & DISNEY WORLD

0   10
miles

HIGHLIGHTS

1 Downtown Orlando nightlife
2 Blizzard Beach
3 Wizarding World of Harry Potter and Diagon Alley
4 Gatorland
5 Winter Park
6 Cassadaga
7 Blue Spring State Park

Orange Avenue

Begin by dawdling along **Orange Avenue**, home of lunch-seeking office workers by day and bar- and club-hoppers at night. Sightseeing here is limited to one building of architectural interest: the late 1920s **First National Bank** building on the corner of Church Street.

Orange County Regional History Center

65 E Central Blvd • Mon–Sat 10am–5pm, Sun noon–5pm • $12 • ☎ 407 836 8500 or ☎ 800 965 2030, ⓦ thehistorycenter.org

One block east of Orange Avenue, you'll find the informative **Orange County Regional History Center**, housed in the restored 1927 Orange County courthouse. Interactive exhibits trace the history of the area from 10,000 BC to the present day, but the most effective displays are the old photos and re-created hotel lobbies and grocers' stores which give a revealing glimpse of Orlando's pre-Disney days as a quiet agricultural town.

Dr. Philips Center For The Performing Arts

445 S Magnolia Ave • Box office Mon–Fri 10am–4pm • $12 • ☎ 844 513 2014, ⓦ drphillipscenter.org

The gorgeous, brand-new **Dr. Philips Center For The Performing Arts** opened in late 2014 just a block east of Orange Avenue. It plays host to Broadway musicals, the Orlando Ballet, touring rock groups and more. Even if you're not seeing a show, the soaring, nearly all-glass building is worth a visit just to admire the architecture.

Lake Eola and around

A 10min walk east of Orange Ave • Paddleboats $15/30min

Some of the wooden homes built by Orlando's first white settlers in the mid-nineteenth century stand next to fancy high-rise condos around scenic **Lake Eola**. Stroll the one-mile path skirting the lake, or get on the water by renting a paddleboat shaped like a swan. The several streets on the eastern side of the lake comprise **Thornton Park**, a trendy neighbourhood full of hip restaurants, bungalows and bars – a pleasant spot to relax in what feels like a village within the city.

Loch Haven Park

A large lawn wedged between two small lakes, **Loch Haven Park**, three miles north of downtown Orlando, contains the city's concentration of museums and playhouses. Both the **Orlando Shakespeare Theater** (ⓦorlandoshakes.org) and the **Orlando Repertory Theatre** (ⓦorlandorep.com) stage productions of old standards and new hits.

Orlando Museum of Art

2416 N Mills Ave • Tues–Fri 10am–4pm, Sat & Sun noon–4pm • $8 • ☎ 407 896 4231, ⓦ omart.org

Permanent collections of recent and ancient American art and African artefacts back up the **Orlando Museum of Art**'s usually excellent temporary exhibitions of modern paintings, sculptures and the like, culled from some of the finest collections in the world.

Orlando Science Center

777 E Princeton St • Mon–Thurs & Sun 10–5pm, Fri & Sat 10am–9pm • $19, includes one Hollywood movie • ☎ 407 514 2000 or ☎ 888 672 4386, ⓦ osc.org

Children will enjoy roaming around the **Orlando Science Center**, a multi-level complex where plentiful interactive exhibits explain the fundamentals of many branches of science. The main draw for adults is the CineDome, a huge cinema and planetarium, where documentary-style films about various natural phenomena are shown daily.

6

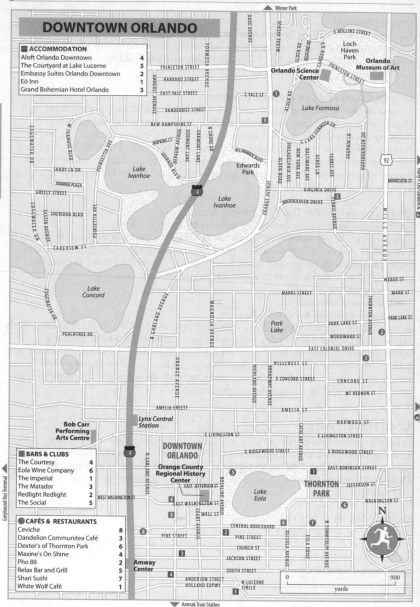

DOWNTOWN ORLANDO

■ ACCOMMODATION

Aloft Orlando Downtown	4
The Courtyard at Lake Lucerne	5
Embassy Suites Orlando Downtown	2
Eö Inn	1
Grand Bohemian Hotel Orlando	3

■ BARS & CLUBS

The Courtesy	4
Eola Wine Company	6
The Imperial	1
The Matador	3
Redlight Redlight	2
The Social	5

● CAFÉS & RESTAURANTS

Ceviche	8
Dandelion Communitea Café	3
Dexter's of Thornton Park	6
Maxine's On Shine	4
Pho 88	2
Relax Bar and Grill	5
Shari Sushi	7
White Wolf Café	1

Harry P. Leu Gardens

1920 N Forest Ave • Gardens: daily 9am–5pm; house: guided tours Aug–June daily 10am–4pm • $10, including tour of Leu House •
☎ 407 246 2620, ⓦ leugardens.org

A green-fingered Orlando businessman purchased the fifty-acre **Harry P. Leu Gardens**, a mile east of Loch Haven Park, in 1936 to show off plants collected from around the world. After seeing the orchids, roses, azaleas and the largest camellia collection outside of California, take a trip around **Leu House**, the late nineteenth-century farmhouse where Leu and his wife lived, now maintained in the simple but elegant style of their time and laced with family mementos.

International Drive and around

Devoid of the traditional charm found in downtown Orlando and adjacent communities, **International Drive (or "I-Drive")**, five miles southwest of downtown, is still worth a short visit for its myriad attractions – some good, others not so good. The strip boasts **Wet 'n' Wild** and **Aquatica**, two water parks to rival those at Disney World, as well as other attractions such as **WonderWorks**, a quirky museum imaginatively housed in an upside-down house. I-Drive is also good for **shopping**, with several malls competing for your business. The best of these is the massive Prime Outlets International, at the northern end of I-Drive at no. 4951 (☎407 352 9600), which has 180 shops offering discounted prices on popular name brands.

Aquatica

5800 Water Play Way, on International Drive across from SeaWorld Orlando • Daily: winter 10am–5pm; summer 9am–8pm • $51 for children and adults • ☎ 888 800 5447, ⓦ aquaticabyseaworld.com

Combining live animal attractions with wave pools, slides and beaches, this water park by SeaWorld Orlando represents an original take on a well-worn idea, although the main attraction is still the water rides. In the new **Ihu's Breakaway Falls** drop waterslide, guests plummet from a platform 80ft high in one of four tubes, three of which feature a trap door. Riders don't know who will "break away" first as they freefall for as much as 40ft before hitting 360-degree spirals. Wear a secure swimsuit.

The Holy Land Experience

4655 Vineland Rd, at Conroy Rd, next to I-4 (Exit 78) • Tues–Sat 10am–6pm • $50, children 6–12 $35, children 3–5 $20 • ☎ 407 872 2272 or ☎ 800 447 7235, ⓦ theholylandexperience.com

The **Holy Land Experience** opened in 2001 with the primary aim to educate rather than wow the crowd – don't expect Noah's Ark flume rides and David vs. Goliath rollercoasters. The Christian message is instead preached through the park's architecture, which features key locations from the Bible. Various religious exhibits, films and shows recount pivotal events during Jesus' lifetime, among them The Passion, a new show that tells the story of Jesus' journey to crucifixion.

Pirate's Cove Adventure Golf

Two locations: 8501 International Drive in Orlando and Crossroads Shopping Center, corner of I-4 and Hwy-535 in Lake Buena Vista • Orlando daily 9am–11.30pm, Lake Buena Vista 9am–11pm • $10.45–14.95, children 3–12 $9.45–13.95, depending on the course • International Drive ☎ 407 352 7378, Lake Buena Vista ☎ 407 827 1242, ⓦ piratescove.net

This is miniature golf at its inventive best. Choose from several challenging, fanciful courses, and putt your way through caves, over footbridges and under waterfalls, with pirates scrutinizing your every stroke.

SkyVenture

6805 Visitors Circle, off International Drive, across from Wet 'n' Wild • Daily 10am–10pm • $59.95 • ☎ 407 903 1150 or ☎ 800 759 3861, ⓦ iflyorlando.com

Fly on a column of air without a parachute in this realistic freefall skydiving simulator. The whole process takes about an hour, although the actual diving, in an indoor wind tunnel, only lasts for a couple of minutes. If you can't get enough of that weightless feeling, return flyers are eligible for discounts.

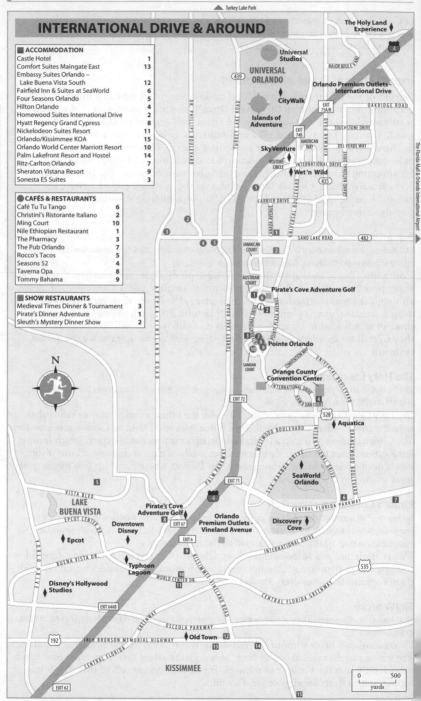

INTERNATIONAL DRIVE & AROUND

ACCOMMODATION

Castle Hotel	1
Comfort Suites Maingate East	13
Embassy Suites Orlando – Lake Buena Vista South	12
Fairfield Inn & Suites at SeaWorld	6
Four Seasons Orlando	5
Hilton Orlando	4
Homewood Suites International Drive	2
Hyatt Regency Grand Cypress	8
Nickelodeon Suites Resort	11
Orlando/Kissimmee KOA	15
Orlando World Center Marriott Resort	10
Palm Lakefront Resort and Hostel	14
Ritz-Carlton Orlando	7
Sheraton Vistana Resort	9
Sonesta ES Suites	3

CAFÉS & RESTAURANTS

Café Tu Tu Tango	6
Christini's Ristorante Italiano	2
Ming Court	10
Nile Ethiopian Restaurant	1
The Pharmacy	3
The Pub Orlando	7
Rocco's Tacos	5
Seasons 52	4
Taverna Opa	8
Tommy Bahama	9

SHOW RESTAURANTS

Medieval Times Dinner & Tournament	3
Pirate's Dinner Adventure	1
Sleuth's Mystery Dinner Show	2

Wet 'n' Wild

6200 International Drive · Daily 9.30am–9pm in summer, shorter hours in winter · $56 at gate or $46 online, children 3–9 $51 or $41 online · ☎ 407 351 1800 or ☎ 800 992 9453, ⓦ wetnwildorlando.com

Orlando's original water park has stood the test of time and continues to offer stiff competition to Disney's water parks and SeaWorld's Aquatica. Unfettered by Disney's predilection for fantastical themes, **Wet 'n' Wild** has put all of its energy into providing the most fun and exciting attractions possible. Thrill rides such as the new **Aqua Drag Racer** begins 65ft above ground, where four riders race each other head first down more than 350ft of track. The park offers slightly less intimidating flume and tube rides too, such as the twisting **Mach 5** and **The Storm**, which feels rather like being flushed down the toilet.

WonderWorks

9067 International Drive, at Pointe Orlando · Daily 9am–midnight · $25.99, children 4–12 and seniors over 55 $19.99 · ☎ 407 351 8800, ⓦ wonderworksonline.com

This collection features more than a hundred high-tech interactive gizmos inside an upside-down creaking house. Many of the exhibits rely on simulators to re-create various exciting situations such as landing the Space Shuttle and riding a rollercoaster, while quirkier exhibits let you feel what it's like, for example, to lie on a bed of 3500 nails.

ARRIVAL AND DEPARTURE

ORLANDO

BY PLANE

The region's primary airport, Orlando International (☎ 407 825 2001, ⓦ orlandoairports.net), is 9 miles southeast of downtown Orlando.

By bus to Orlando Shuttle buses will carry you from the airport to any hotel or motel in the Orlando area. The flat rate from the airport to downtown Orlando is $19; to International Drive it's $20; and to Lake Buena Vista or US-192, the fare is $22. Mears Transportation (☎ 407 423 5566, ⓦ mearstransportation.com) is one of the largest and most reliable operators. Lynx Buses (☎ 407 841 5969, ⓦ golynx.com), which serve Orlando and surrounding areas, link the airport with downtown Orlando (#11 or #51, both 40min), International Drive (#42; 1hr), and SeaWorld/ Florida Mall (#111; 45min). All buses depart from Level 1 (on the "A Side" concourse) every 30min between approximately 5.30am and 11.30pm.

By bus to Disney World For those staying at Walt Disney World, Disney's Magical Express Transportation (☎ 407 939 6244 or ☎ 0800 16 90 730 if calling from the UK) provides a free transfer from the airport to your hotel and vice versa, including collecting your luggage and delivering it to your room. Upon arrival at the airport, make your way to the Disney Welcome Center on Level 1 of the airport's Main Terminal (on the "B Side" concourse). Lynx Buses also link the airport with Disney World, but you must transfer to bus #50 at SeaWorld (#111 from Level 1 on the "A Side" concourse; around 1hr 15min).

By taxi A taxi to downtown Orlando, International Drive or the hotels on US-192 will cost from $40 to $70; Walt Disney World is around $70.

By SunRail Although the network is rather limited, Orlando's first light rail opened in April 2014. The trains run north–south from DeBary to Sand Lake Rd Monday to Friday from 6.15am to 10.15pm. Those arriving at the airport can connect to the Sand Lake SunRail station via bus. Buses depart from Level 1 on the A Side concourse. (#11 or #42; around 1hr 15min).

ORLANDO SANFORD INTERNATIONAL

A second airport, Orlando Sanford International (☎ 407 585 4000, ⓦ orlandosanfordairport.com), is a smaller facility 20 miles north of downtown Orlando that receives charter flights from the UK, as well as Allegiant Air (see p.21) flights from a selection of smaller US cities.

BY CAR

Several cross-Florida routes lead to Orlando; see p.260.

BY BUS

Arriving by bus, you'll end up near downtown Orlando at the Greyhound terminal, 555 N John Young Parkway (☎ 407 292 3424); take Lynx #25 (every 30min; 5.30– 1.20am; 10min) into downtown. Buy tickets online at ⓦ greyhound.com for substantial discounts. If you're staying along US-192 in Kissimmee, consider going to the Kissimmee Greyhound terminal (see p.297), which provides easier access to the US-192 hotels.

Destinations Daytona Beach (2 daily; 1hr 5min); Fort Lauderdale (10 daily; 3hr 30min express service); Fort Pierce (5 daily; 2hr express); Gainesville (5 daily; 2hr 35min); Jacksonville (7 daily; 2hr 30min express); Kissimmee (2 daily; 40min); Lakeland (4 daily; 1hr 20min); Miami (10 daily; 4hr 30min express); Ocala (5 daily; 1hr 30min); Panama City (2 daily; 8hr 20min express); Pensacola (4 daily; 9hr 35min express); St Augustine (1 daily; 2hr 15min); Tallahassee (5 daily; 4hr 35min express); Tampa (6 daily; 1hr 40min express); West Palm Beach (6 daily; 3hr 20min express).

BY TRAIN

The Amtrak train station is 1.5 miles south of downtown at 1400 Sligh Blvd (☏ 407 843 7611); take Lynx #40 (hourly 5am–10pm; 10min) to downtown. If you're staying along US-192 in Kissimmee, consider going to the Kissimmee Amtrak station (see p.297), which provides easier access to the US-192.

Destinations DeLand (2 daily; 1hr); Jacksonville (2 daily; 3hr 13min); Kissimmee (2 daily; 25min); Miami (2 daily; 5hr 45min–7hr 35min); Tampa (2 daily; 2hr); Winter Park (2 daily; 20min).

INFORMATION

TOURIST INFORMATION

Masses of brochures and magazines are available almost everywhere you look; leaf through them for the discount coupons. For Disney information, call ☏ 407 939 2273 (see p.284).

Official Visitor Center 8723 International Drive (daily 8.30am–6.30pm; ☏ 407 363 5872 or ☏ 800 972 3304, ⓦ visitorlando.com). The best source of information, and you can also pick up the free *Official Visitor's Guide* here, or download it from their website. Another useful acquisition is the Orlando Magicard (pick it up here, order it in advance or download it for free from the Official Visitor Center website), which offers savings at a range of attractions, accommodation, restaurants and shops. You'll find other information in Kissimmee (see p.297) and Winter Park (see p.300).

LISTINGS

The best entertainment guides to the area are the alternative paper *The Orlando Weekly*, which comes out on Thursday (ⓦ orlandoweekly.com), and the Friday "Calendar" section of the *Orlando Sentinel* newspaper.

GETTING AROUND

BY CAR

All the main car rental firms (see p.22) have offices at or close to Orlando International Airport. Demand is strong throughout the year, but deals can be had if you book online prior to arrival. Expect to pay at least $40 and as much as $75/day for a compact car.

BY LYNX BUS

Local Lynx buses (☏ 407 841 5969, ⓦ golynx.com) converge at the downtown Lynx Central Station, 455 N Garland Ave. Most routes operate from 5am to 9pm on weekdays, and usually the same on weekends for popular routes.

Fares You'll need exact change ($2 one way; $4.50 day pass) if you pay on board; a weekly pass for $16 is available at the central station and online. The single fare includes a free transfer to another Lynx service, valid for travel within 90min of the initial ticket purchase.

Routes The Lynx system comprises roughly 4000 stops in three counties; the Official Visitor Center (see p.284) has a useful handout entitled *Using the Lynx Bus System*, which explains how to get to many points of interest by bus from International Drive.

BY SUNRAIL

Central Florida's first light rail system (☏ 855 724 5411, ⓦ sunrail.com) opened in April 2014, and connects DeBary in the north to Sand Lake Road (near International Drive) in the south, making stops in Winter Park and downtown Orlando along the way. Trains run Monday to Friday from 6.15am to 9.15pm ($2–4 one way).

BY TROLLEY BUS

The I-Ride Trolley (☏ 407 354 5656 or ☏ 866 243 7483, ⓦ iridetrolley.com) serves all points along International Drive (including SeaWorld Orlando), operating roughly every twenty to thirty minutes daily from 8am to 10.30pm, and costing $2 one way (seniors 25¢, children 3–9 $1); exact change is required. One-day passes for unlimited travel are also available for $5.

BY SHUTTLE BUS

Cheaper than taxis, but more expensive and quicker than local buses, are the shuttle buses, minivans or coaches run by private companies connecting the main accommodation areas, such as International Drive and US-192, with Walt Disney World, SeaWorld Orlando, Universal Orlando, and other attractions. Mears Transportation (see p.297) charges $20 for a round-trip ride for one person from International Drive or US-192 to all the major attractions; you can't get this fare online so book via phone at least a day in advance, and confirm a time for your return.

BY TAXI

Orlando taxis are expensive; rates begin at $4.20 for the first mile, plus $2.40 for each additional mile. For non-drivers, however, they're the most convenient way to get around at night – try Yellow Cab/Mears Taxi (☏ 407 422 2222) or Diamond Cab (☏ 407 523 3333).

ACCOMMODATION

Locations In a sprawling city like Orlando, your choice of accommodation will be guided as much by location as by price. If you don't have your own transport, consider staying along or near International Drive, an area with plenty of chain hotels, or in downtown Orlando, where you'll find a few privately owned hotels and bed and breakfasts – both areas have plenty of good local bus connections. You'll also find numerous hotels within Walt Disney World itself (see p.285), dotted around Disney property in an area called Lake Buena Vista (see p.287), and at Universal Orlando (see p.292). Budget hotels line US-192 (see p.297), just south of Disney, where you'll also find campgrounds and a hostel.

Rates Prices at the Disney and Universal resorts (see p.285 & p.292) are generally the highest you'll pay, with some of the fancier places costing over $400 per night. The hotels in Lake Buena Vista, International Drive and downtown Orlando tend to be mid-range, usually not costing more than $200. For the cheapest rates head to US-192, where you can get a room for around $60 per night.

DOWNTOWN ORLANDO

Aloft Orlando Downtown 500 S Orange Ave ☎ 407 380 3500, ⓦ aloftorlandodowntown.com; map p.264. Orlando's newest downtown hotel features modern, stylish rooms with 10ft ceilings, platform beds and gigantic walk-in showers. There's also a lounge, the popular *W XYZ* bar, a pool and 24/7 fitness centre. $152

★**The Courtyard at Lake Lucerne** 211 N Lucerne Circle E ☎ 407 648 5188, ⓦ orlandohistoricinn.com; map p.264. A lush flower garden and four separate buildings, one of which is the oldest house in Orlando, comprise this peaceful B&B nestled right in the busy downtown area. Options range from elegantly furnished Victorian- and Edwardian-era rooms to a suite tucked away in the attic. $110

Embassy Suites Orlando Downtown 191 E Pine St ☎ 407 841 1000, ⓦ embassysuites1.hilton.com; map p.264. A 5min walk from the action on Orange Ave as well as Lake Eola, this comfortable all-suites hotel is a good mid-range choice for visitors who want to see the city and the Mouse. Suites are spacious and comfortable, with all modern amenities. There's also a small swimming pool and cooked-to-order breakfast every morning. $160

★**Eō Inn** 227 N Eola Drive ☎ 407 481 8485, ⓦ eoinn .com; map p.264. Facing Lake Eola, this chic boutique hotel has seventeen stylish rooms with modern furnishings; some of the more expensive ones have lake views. An on-site spa offers a full range of massages and facials, while the hot tub on the rooftop terrace is another good place to unwind. Gay-friendly. $139

Grand Bohemian Hotel Orlando 325 S Orange Ave ☎ 407 313 9000, ⓦ grandbohemianhotel.com; map p.264. Downtown's most luxurious hotel is centrally located and has classy rooms decorated in soothing, earthy

tones. There's a heated outdoor pool, fitness centre and live jazz at weekends in the hotel's chic lounge. $250

INTERNATIONAL DRIVE AND AROUND

Castle Hotel 8629 International Drive ☎ 407 345 1511, ⓦ thecastleorlando.com; map p.264. This theme hotel features castle-inspired touches in its rooms, such as gilded mirrors and carved headboards. *Antlers Lounge* offers fantastic craft cocktails, and the pool area offers quiet respite from the hustle and bustle of I-Drive. $110

Fairfield Inn and Suites at SeaWorld 10815 International Drive ☎ 407 354 1139 ⓦ marriott.com; map p.264. A great-value option for families, this comfortable hotel next to SeaWorld offers free hot breakfast and complimentary shuttles to SeaWorld and Universal. Guests can also enjoy fast-track passes and discounts at SeaWorld. $98

★**Hilton Orlando** 6001 Destination Pkwy ☎ 407 313 4300, ⓦ thehiltonorlando.com; map p.264. One of the newer hotels in the area, this popular place right off International Drive is a hit with the kids for the huge, lushly landscaped pool and lazy river. There's also a nine-hole putting golf course and comfortable rooms with plush beds. $209

Homewood Suites International Drive 8745 International Drive ☎ 407 248 2232, ⓦ homewood suites3.hilton.com; map p.264. Spacious studios and suites with full kitchens provide families with an opportunity to save money by self-catering. The location is great too, around 1.5 miles from the Universal parks and the shopping and dining options on I-Drive. There's also a complimentary hot breakfast, plus light dinner and drinks (Mon–Thurs). $209

★**Ritz-Carlton Orlando** 4040 Central Florida Parkway ☎ 407 206 2400, ⓦ grandlakes.com; map p.264. One of Orlando's most luxurious hotels, this elegant building with an intimate feel and superb rooms shares the 500-acre Grande Lakes Orlando – the hotel's landscaped grounds – with another excellent hotel (the *J.W. Marriott*) and a golf course. The immaculate facilities include several restaurants, a fitness centre, a lazy river and pool, and a full-service spa. $479

Sonesta ES Suites 8480 International Drive ☎ 407 352 2400, ⓦ sonesta.com/orlando; map p.264. Sonesta took over this popular hotel in 2012 and renovated all 146 suites. There's a free shuttle to all the parks, and you'll be in walking distance of the plentiful entertainment options and restaurants on I-Drive. The spacious one- and two-bedroom suites have well-equipped kitchens and free internet access. A buffet breakfast and nightly happy hour are included. $119

EATING

Given the amount of competition among restaurants hoping to attract hungry tourists, eating out in Orlando is never difficult and – if you venture away from the theme parks – it need not be expensive. In **downtown Orlando**, the need to satisfy a regular clientele of office workers keeps prices low during the day, while at night the wide selection of smart restaurants is testament to downtown's status as a destination in itself. With a car, you might also investigate the local favourites scattered in the outlying areas away from downtown, especially the northern suburb of **Winter Park** (see p.297).

Tourist-dominated **International Drive** offers the complete range of restaurants, all easily accessible by foot, while nearby, around the intersection of Sand Lake Road and Dr Phillips Boulevard, a cluster of trendy restaurants known as **Restaurant Row** is very popular with locals.

DOWNTOWN ORLANDO

Ceviche 125 W Church St ☎321 281 8140, ⊛ceviche .com; map p.264. Come with a crowd to this cavernous tapas joint in Historic Church Street Station. There's live flamenco music, great sangria and plenty of plates to choose from for $5–25. Tues–Thurs 5pm–midnight, Fri & Sat 5pm–2am, Sun 5–10pm.

★**Dandelion Communitea Café** 618 N Thornton Ave ☎407 362 1864, ⊛dandelioncommunitea.com; map p.264. Delicious, organic vegan and vegetarian cuisine comes from the kitchen of this former bungalow in Thornton Park; their chilli and hummus are legendary. There's often live music or a drum circle in the garden. Main dishes for under $10. Mon–Sat 11am–10pm, Sun 11am–5pm.

Dexter's of Thornton Park 808 E Washington St ☎407 648 2777, ⊛dexwine.com; map p.264. A young, urban clientele come here for fresh, tasty food priced right – imaginative sandwiches and salads for lunch (around $13) and more gourmet dinner mains such as roasted red pepper pesto mahi-mahi (around $20) – plus an extensive beer and wine list and a hopping brunch. There's also a location in Winter Park at Hannibal Square. Mon–Thurs 7am–10pm, Fri 7am–2am, Sat 11am–2am, Sun 10am–10pm.

★**Maxine's on Shine** 337 N Shine Ave ☎407 674 6841; map p.264. Tucked into the leafy Colonialtown neighbourhood east of downtown, this local favourite offers imaginative dinner items like drunken mussels and brisket burgers, but it really stands out at brunch, with dishes like chicken and waffles, and eggs Benedict with fried green tomatoes. There's also the rollicking 70s-themed Karaoke for Swingers on the last Wednesday of each month. Most dishes under $20. Tues–Thurs 5–10pm, Fri & Sat 11.30am–11pm, Sun 10am–10pm.

Pho 88 730 N Mills Ave ☎407 897 3488, ⊛pho88orlando.com; map p.264. One of the biggest and best of the many economical Vietnamese restaurants on Mills Ave around the intersection with Colonial Drive. Most dishes under $10. Daily 10am–10pm.

Relax Bar and Grill 211 Eola Parkway ☎407 425 8440, ⊛relaxgrill.com; map p.264. A perfect outdoor bar and restaurant to watch the foot traffic amble by on the Lake Eola path, right across from the swan-boat rental facility. The Mediterranean combo and stir-fries are menu standouts. Most dishes under $15. Mon–Wed & Sun 11.30am–9.30pm, Thurs 11.30am–10pm, Fri & Sat 11.30am–10.30pm.

Shari Sushi 621 E Central Blvd ☎407 420 9420, ⊛sharisushilounge.com; map p.264. Fresh sushi and sashimi – using both classic and Western-inspired ingredients – served in a sleek lounge to beautiful people. Most signature rolls around $15. Mon–Wed & Sun 5–10pm, Thurs–Sat 5–11pm.

White Wolf Café 1829 N Orange Ave ☎407 895 9911, ⊛whitewolfcafe.com; map p.264. Down-to-earth café with creative salads and sandwiches for under $15, plus home-made potato chips, and mac and cheese with lobster. Breakfast dishes are a standout as well; don't miss the cinnamon bun or biscuits and gravy. Mon–Sat 8am–9pm, Sun 8am–3pm.

INTERNATIONAL DRIVE AND RESTAURANT ROW

★**Café Tu Tu Tango** 8625 International Drive ☎407 248 2222, ⊛cafetututango.com; map p.266. Original, imaginative dishes ($7–12) such as Cuban sliders featuring capicola, Genoa salami and braised pulled pork and alligator bites are served tapas-style. The popular tu tu hour (Mon–Fri 4.30–6.30) features two-for-one drink specials and $2 off appetizers. The walls are covered in colourful artwork, and it's all for sale. Mon, Wed, Thurs & Sun 11.30am–11pm, Tues, Fri & Sat 11.30am–midnight.

Christini's Ristorante Italiano 7600 Dr Phillips Blvd ☎407 583 4472, ⊛christinis.com; map p.266. One of Orlando's best Italian restaurants, with old-style supper club decor, excellent service and well-prepared dishes including home-made cheese ravioli, and plentiful meat and seafood options. Pasta dishes cost around $20, meat and seafood from $30. Daily 6–11pm.

Ming Court 9188 International Drive ☎407 351 9988, ⊛ming-court.com; map p.266. This long-standing I-Drive favourite delivers flavourful and well-prepared

---

EATING OUT ON A BUDGET

Budget travellers will relish the opportunity to eat massive amounts at one of the local **buffet restaurants** – all for less than they might spend on a tip elsewhere. Buffet eating reaches its ultimate expression along US-192, where virtually every buffet restaurant chain has at least one outlet. It's also worth noting that **discount coupons** in tourist magazines bring sizeable reductions at many restaurants.

ORLANDO SHOW RESTAURANTS

Although they're not as prolific as they once were, Orlando still has a few "Show Restaurants", where you'll be served a multi-course meal and (sometimes) limitless beer, wine and soft drinks while you watch live entertainment ranging from intriguing whodunits to medieval knights jousting on horseback. The all-inclusive **cost** is usually around $60 for adults or $40–50 for children, although discounts are often available if you book online.

Medieval Times Dinner & Tournament 4510 W Vine St, Kissimmee ☎407 396 1518, ⓦmedieval times.com; map p.266. Knights joust on horseback as wenches serve roast chicken and spare ribs inside this replica of an eleventh-century castle. There's a vegetarian alternative, and two rounds of nonalcoholic beverages are included per person. Mon–Fri & Sun shows begin at 7pm, Sat shows begin at 6 & 8pm.

Pirate's Dinner Adventure 6400 Carrier Drive ☎407 248 0590, ⓦpiratesdinneradventure.com; map p.266. Shivering timbers, peg-leg buccaneers, scalawags, cannons, sword fights, and a host of stunts will keep you entertained as you dine on roast chicken,

beef kebabs or a veggie option. Arrive early to take advantage of the free appetizers before the show. Mon–Thurs & Sun shows begin at 7.30pm, Fri & Sat shows begin at 8.15pm.

★**Sleuth's Mystery Dinner Show** 8267 International Drive ☎407 363 1985, ⓦsleuths.com; map p.266. If you know red herring isn't a seafood dish, you're well on the way to solving the whodunit (which changes throughout the week) acted out in the dining room as you eat a Cornish game hen or lasagne dinner. Expect some audience interaction. Shows begin at 7pm nightly, with some additional 10pm show times Fri & Sat.

Chinese, including meticulously prepared dim sum. Given the flash decor, it's less costly than you might expect (around $15). Daily 11am–3pm & 4.30–11pm.

Nile Ethiopian Restaurant 7048 International Drive ☎407 354 0026, ⓦnile07.com; map p.266. Spongy sourdough *injera* bread takes the place of cutlery at this Ethiopian gem in the heart of tourist territory, and dishes are meant to share. Try the beef *gored-gored*, lean chunks of meat served in a spicy red sauce, or sample one of the tasty vegetarian options such as *kik alicha*, yellow split peas cooked with onions, garlic and green peppers. Mon–Fri 5–10pm, Sat & Sun 4–10pm.

★**The Pharmacy** 8060 Villa Dellagio Way ☎407 985 2972, ⓦthepharmacyorlando.com; map p.266. Like a breath of fresh air in the chain-heavy Sand Lake area, speakeasy-cum-bistro *The Pharmacy* offers both diners and drinkers delicious farm-to-table, hand-crafted concoctions like the beet nofFeratu, a creative cocktail featuring Reyka vodka and beet syrup. On the dinner menu, don't miss the fried buttermilk chicken osso buco and the mac and cheese. It's hard to find (ask the valet for directions): to the unsuspecting, the entrance looks like an elevator door. Mon–Thurs 5–10pm, Fri & Sat 5pm–midnight.

The Pub Orlando Pointe Orlando Mall, 9101 International Drive ☎407 352 2305, ⓦexperience thepub.com/orlando; map p.266. Modelled after a traditional (albeit gigantic) English pub, this is the place to catch soccer on TV whilst tucking into well-executed but imaginative bar food such as chicken and chutney flatbread and English pot roast. There's also a "pour your own beer" wall where you pay by the fluid ounce and pull your own pint. Most dishes under $15. Daily 11am–2am.

Rocco's Tacos 7468 W Sand Lake Rd ☎407 226 0550, ⓦroccostacos.com; map p.266. Tasty Mexican food in a trendy *taquería*, 225 tequilas on offer and a lively bar make this hopping spot worth a visit. The signature guacamole is made tableside; the beef *tamales* and *molcajetes* (baked *fajitas*) are other standouts. Most dishes under $20. Mon & Sun 11.30am–11pm, Tues & Wed 11.30am–midnight, Thurs & Fri 11.30am–2am, Sat 11am–2am.

Seasons 52 7700 W Sand Lake Rd ☎407 354 5212, ⓦseasons52.com; map p.266. All items on the seasonal menu contain fewer than 475 calories, a feat achieved by using plenty of chicken, fish and vegetables rather than skimping on quantity. The desserts, meanwhile, come in "four-bite" portions. There are tables outside overlooking a lake, while the busy piano bar is a popular venue for cocktails, particularly on weekends. Most main dishes cost $17–25. Mon–Thurs & Sun 11.30am–11pm, Fri & Sat 11.30am–midnight.

Taverna Opa Pointe Orlando Mall, 9101 International Drive ☎407 351 8660, ⓦopaorlando.com; map p.266. This raucous Greek restaurant is a great spot for a party – servers shout "opa!" at regular intervals and dancing on the tables is practically de rigueur. The food's great too, with plenty of traditional Greek fare like *moussaka* and kebabs ($15–35). Mon–Thurs & Sun noon–11pm, Fri & Sat noon–midnight.

★**Tommy Bahama Restaurant & Bar** Pointe Orlando Mall, 9101 International Drive ☎321 281 5888, ⓦtommy bahama.com; map p.266. This beach-chic clothing and accessories store has spawned a popular restaurant, with island-inspired dishes like coconut-crusted crab cakes and jerk pork tenderloin. Mon–Thurs 11.30am–10pm, Fri & Sat 11.30am–11pm, Sun 11.30am–10pm.

DRINKING AND NIGHTLIFE

Orlando can make a justifiable claim to have Florida's second best **nightlife** after Miami – and many consider Orlando's more casual after-dark scene preferable to the pompous attitudes that often prevail in South Beach. An eclectic and ever-growing collection of bars, lounges and clubs pack the city's **downtown**, with many of the liveliest spots found along Orange Avenue. **International Drive** has a smattering of options; restaurants such as *The Pub Orlando* (see p.271), and *Rocco's Tacos* (see p.271) tend to function more as bars as the night progresses. Elsewhere, Universal Orlando has created its own after-dark entertainment venue in the form of **CityWalk**, but this can seem somewhat artificial in comparison with downtown.

★The Courtesy 114 N Orange Ave ☏ 407 450 2041; map p.264. The craft cocktail craze has hit Orlando, and this classy spot with exposed brick walls and intimate banquettes executes theirs masterfully. Signature cocktails change frequently, and there's a complimentary Sunday BBQ brunch from 3 to 8pm. Mon–Fri 5pm–2am, Sat 7pm–2am, Sun 3pm–2am.

Eola Wine Company 430 E Central Blvd ☏ 407 481 9100, ⓦ eolawinecompany.com; map p.264. Escape the noise and crowds at this laidback wine bar across from Lake Eola, where you can order by the glass or in "flights" (2oz servings of three or four different wines for $11–16). There's another location on Park Ave in Winter Park. Mon–Thurs 4pm–midnight, Fri & Sat noon–2am, Sun noon–midnight.

The Imperial 1800 N Orange Ave ☏ 407 228 4992, ⓦ imperialwinebar.com; map p.264. This eclectic bar is housed in a furniture import store, filled with artsy pieces from Asia, Bali and India. There's an extensive list of microbrews and boutique wines, frequent live music – and all the furniture's for sale. Mon–Thurs 5pm–midnight, Fri & Sat 5pm–2am.

★The Matador 724 Virginia Drive; no phone or website, but they are on Facebook; map p.264. This hipster haven in the Mills 50 neighbourhood offers a sublime gin and tonic on tap – bartenders will grudgingly give you a lime if you ask, but you won't need it. There's also a great beer list as well as rotating cocktails. Mon–Thurs, Sat & Sun 7pm–2am, Fri 5pm–2am.

★Redlight Redlight Beer Parlour 2810 Corinne Drive ☏ 407 893 9832; map p.264. Consistently rated one of the best beer bars in the nation, there's something for everyone among the 26 rotating drafts and 250-plus bottles. Friendly bartenders are happy to walk you through the extensive menu. They've also got a decent selection of wine. Daily 5pm–2am.

The Social 54 N Orange Ave ☏ 407 246 1419, ⓦ thesocial.org; map p.264. Grunge, alternative rock, and everything else non-mainstream is on offer at one of Orlando's best live-music venues, showcasing the talents of bands with local and national followings. Check the website for upcoming events. Typically open at 8pm depending on show.

Walt Disney World

For full details on tickets and opening times see p.284. ⓦ disneyworld.disney.go.com for general information or call ☏ 407 939 2273

Whatever your attitude toward theme parks, there's no denying **WALT DISNEY WORLD** is the pacesetter: it goes way beyond Walt Disney's original "theme park" – Disneyland, which opened in Los Angeles in 1955 – delivering escapism at its most technologically advanced and psychologically brilliant. Here, litter is picked up within seconds of being dropped (by any of the "cast members", as all employees are called, who happen to spy it), subtle mind-games ease the tedium of standing in line, the special effects are the best money can buy, and Disney employees don't break a sweat when confronted with tantrums of epic proportions. It's not cheap, **forward planning** is essential (see p.284), and there are times when you'll feel like a cog in a vast machine – but Walt Disney World unfailingly delivers what it promises.

The whole complex comprises over 39 square miles and is not easy to take in, even if spread over a week. The **four main parks** are quite separate entities. The **Magic Kingdom** is the Disney park everyone imagines, the signature Cinderella's Castle towering over it all, where Mickey Mouse meets the crowds and the emphasis is on fantasy and fun – very much the park for kids. Recognizable for its giant, golfball-like geosphere, **Epcot** is Disney's attempted celebration of science and technology, coupled with a very Disneyfied trip around various countries and cultures; not as compelling for young kids, it's a sprawling area involving a lot of walking. **Disney's Hollywood Studios** suits almost everyone; its special effects are enjoyable even if you've never seen the movies they're derived from, and the fact that this is also a working production studio lends a welcome touch of reality to your Disney experience. The more relaxed **Disney's Animal Kingdom** is part zoo, part theme park, remarkable in bringing an African and Asian feel to the swamplands of southwest Orlando.

Brief history

When brilliant illustrator and animator Walt Disney devised the world's first theme park, California's **Disneyland** – which brought to life his cartoon characters Mickey Mouse, Donald Duck, Goofy and the rest – he had no control over the hotels and restaurants that quickly engulfed it, preventing growth and missing out on profits he felt were rightfully his. Determined this wouldn't happen again, the Disney Corporation secretly began to buy up 25,000 acres of central Florida farmland, and by the late 1960s had acquired – for a comparatively paltry $6 million – a site a hundred times bigger than Disneyland. With the promise of a jobs bonanza for Florida, the state legislature gave the corporation – thinly disguised as the Reedy Creek Improvement District – the rights of any major municipality: empowering it to lay roads, enact building codes, and enforce the law with its own security force.

Walt Disney World's first park, the **Magic Kingdom** (see p.275), opened in 1971; based, predictably, on Disneyland, it was an equally predictable success. The far

---

BEATING THE CROWDS

Provided you **arrive early** at the park (just before opening time is best), you'll get through the most popular rides before the mid-afternoon crush, when lines can become monstrously long. Each park has regularly updated noticeboards showing the latest **waiting times** for each show and ride – at peak times often about an hour and a half for the most popular rides and up to forty minutes for others.

THE FASTPASS

In an effort to keep outrageous waiting times from wiping the smiles off visitors' faces, Disney set up a system to give people the chance to avoid the long lines – provided they are prepared to return to the attraction later in the day. At certain sites you can obtain a **FASTPASS** by simply inserting your ticket into a special FASTPASS ticket station at the entrance. The machine then prints out a slip indicating the time you should return. In effect, you book a time to enter the FASTPASS line, which bypasses the regular line and gets you in with little or no wait. You can save lots of time booking ahead all day long, but remember you can only hold one FASTPASS for one attraction at any one time – unless you use the online **FASTPASS+ service** (go to My Disney Experience at ⓦdisneyworld.disney.go.com/plan), which lets you pre-book up to three FASTPASS selections at any one park. Disney resort guests can book sixty days in advance; non-resort guests can book thirty days in advance.

TIME-SAVING TIPS

Savvy Disney visitors use different **time-saving tactics** depending on the park they're visiting. At the Magic Kingdom most people turn right (counterclockwise) when reaching the Cinderella Castle at the end of Main Street, USA; therefore, consider starting your tour in a clockwise direction, starting at Adventureland and working your way toward Tomorrowland. At Epcot, new arrivals tend to make straight for the geosphere, beside the entrance, to wait in line for Spaceship Earth. Therefore, a sensible plan is to head for Mission: SPACE, Test Track (where there's a single-rider line), or Soarin', the three most popular rides, obtaining a FASTPASS for one and then joining the line for one of the others (which should be short enough if you arrive early). At Disney's Hollywood Studios, the Lights, Motors, Action! Extreme Stunt Show can take as many as five thousand people out of circulation for around thirty minutes, making this a good time to go on the park's two thrill rides, The Twilight Zone Tower of Terror and Rock 'n' Roller Coaster. By far the most popular attraction at Disney's Animal Kingdom is Expedition Everest, so visit this one at off-peak times or use a FASTPASS for it. And finally, it might be worth avoiding a park on days when it opens early for guests of the Disney resorts – when it's sure to be more crowded than usual.

6

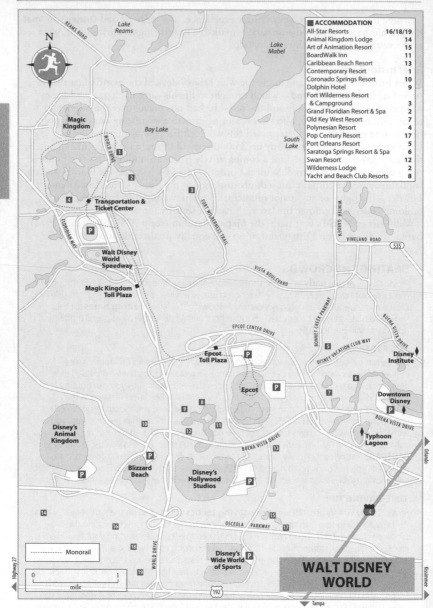

ACCOMMODATION	
All-Star Resorts	16/18/19
Animal Kingdom Lodge	14
Art of Animation Resort	15
BoardWalk Inn	11
Caribbean Beach Resort	13
Contemporary Resort	1
Coronado Springs Resort	10
Dolphin Hotel	9
Fort Wilderness Resort & Campground	3
Grand Floridian Resort & Spa	2
Old Key West Resort	7
Polynesian Resort	4
Pop Century Resort	17
Port Orleans Resort	5
Saratoga Springs Resort & Spa	6
Swan Resort	12
Wilderness Lodge	2
Yacht and Beach Club Resorts	8

WALT DISNEY WORLD

more ambitious **Epcot** (see p.277), unveiled in 1982, represented the first major break from cartoon-based escapism. Millions visited, but the rose-tinted look at the future received a mixed response. Partly because of this reaction, and some cockeyed management decisions, the Disney empire (Disney himself died in 1966) faced bankruptcy by the mid-1980s. Since then, clever marketing has brought the corporation back from the abyss, and it now steers a tight and competitive business ship, and strives to stay ahead of its rivals, notably Universal Orlando. It may trade in fantasy, but, where money matters, the Disney Corporation's nose is firmly in the real world.

The Magic Kingdom

Anyone who's been to Disneyland in California will recognize much of the Magic Kingdom, not least the dramatic Cinderella's Castle sitting smack in the middle of the park, surrounded by several themed sections, each with its own identity. Building facades, rides, gift shops, even the particular characters giving hugs contribute to the distinct feel of each section, while the park as a whole emphasizes fantasy and family fun, as well as offering the greatest number of marquee rides. The areas are called **Main Street USA**, **Adventureland**, **Frontierland**, **Liberty Square**, **Fantasyland** and **Tomorrowland**; Fantasyland completed an expansion in early 2014 to nearly double its size.

The Magic Kingdom is best experienced with enthusiasm: jump in with both feet and go on every ride possible. A warning: don't promise the kids (or yourself) too much beforehand. Even with clever use of the FASTPASS system (see box, p.273), lines are sometimes so long it may be better to pass up some attractions. Although waiting times are posted, lines can be deceiving – Disney masterfully disguises their true length and keeps you cool with shade, fans and air conditioning wherever possible.

Finally, do make an effort to see *Wishes*, held just before the park closes. Of all the imaginative efforts to create an aura of fantasy, this simple but stunning twelve-minute **fireworks display** is the most magical of them all. It's best viewed facing Cinderella's Castle at the end of Main Street USA.

Main Street USA

From the main gates, you'll step into **Main Street USA**, a bustling assortment of souvenir shops selling the ubiquitous mouse-ear hats and other Disney paraphernalia in old-fashioned, town-square stores. Most of the same items are available throughout the park and all over Disney property.

Cinderella's Castle

At the end of Main Street USA you'll see **Cinderella's Castle**, a stunning 189ft pseudo-Rhineland palace that looks like it should be the most elaborate ride in the park. In fact, it's merely a shell that conceals all the electronics and machinery that drive the whole extravaganza. You simply walk through a tunnel in its centre, and use it as a reference point if you lose your bearings.

The rides and attractions

Beat the lines by heading immediately for the popular thrills-and-spills rides, which tend to draw the biggest crowds. The newest is the wildly popular **Seven Dwarves Mine Train** in the revamped Fantasyland area (see p.276), though the park's most nerve-jangling ride is **Space Mountain**, which was renovated in 2009 to include more interactive experiences for guests as they wait in line. In essence it's an ordinary rollercoaster, but the total darkness of the experience makes every jump and jolt unexpected.

Splash Mountain employs water to great effect as the log plumes wind past a cute Br'er Rabbit storyline, leading to a really exciting moment with a 52ft drop down a waterfall that's sure to get you wet.

Big Thunder Mountain Railroad, meanwhile, puts you on board a runaway train, which trundles through Gold Rush California in about three minutes at a modest pace that won't upset too many younger riders.

You don't have to be a rollercoaster junkie to enjoy the Magic Kingdom. Many of the best rides in the park rely on "Audio-Animatronics" characters – impressive vocal robots of Disney invention – for their appeal. Some of the best are seen in **Stitch's Great**

6

Escape, in which the mischievous monster wreaks havoc on the audience, who feel, hear and smell strange things in the dark.

A slew of realistic robots – including Jack Sparrow from the *Pirates of the Caribbean* movies – appear in **Pirates of the Caribbean**, the classic boat ride through a pirate-infested Caribbean island full of drunken debauchery. A large cast of Audio-Animatronics characters is also used to good effect in the **Haunted Mansion**, a mildly spooky ghost ride through a well-devised set, memorable for the ghouls depicted by the clever use of holograms.

The leisurely, if somewhat corny, **Jungle Cruise** is narrated by a pun-loving guide, who takes you down the Amazon, Nile, Congo and Mekong, each river inhabited by the appropriate Audio-Animatronics animals, from crocodiles to elephants, which look slightly less realistic with age.

Finally, the kiddie-friendly **Monsters, Inc. Laugh Floor** is an interactive comedy show in which the Monsters send up members of the audience who are singled out by a roaming camera – amusing enough for extroverts, terrifying for introverts.

Fantasyland

In 2014, the kid-oriented **Fantasyland** completed the park's biggest large-scale renovation since it opened. Additions include new rides and attractions, as well as the extremely popular *Be Our Guest* restaurant, the first in the Magic Kingdom to serve wine and beer with dinner.

Seven Dwarves Mine Train

A roller coaster that transports guests through a day in the life of Snow White and the Seven Dwarves, with a visit from the evil queen at the end, the Magic Kingdom's newest coaster is by far the park's most popular ride, so snag a FASTPASS well in advance online if possible. It's a mostly gentle ride in a mine car up and down a few dips, as well as a slowed-down portion filled with Audio-Animatronic dwarves mining jewels and singing their signature song, *Heigh Ho.*

Under the Sea – Journey of the Little Mermaid

In **Under the Sea – Journey of the Little Mermaid** guests board pastel clam shells for a musical visit to Ariel, Sebastian and the gang from *The Little Mermaid*. The movie's most popular musical numbers are vividly re-created, and the villain Ursula Audio-Animatronic is truly impressive, at over 7ft tall.

The Enchanted Tales of Belle

This guided tour through Belle's cottage and her inventor father's workshop is best for small children, and a lucky one or two (usually a girl) may even be chosen to accompany Belle on stage at the tour's culmination.

Other Fantasyland rides

As for the smaller rides, there's the excellent **Mickey's PhilharMagic**, an enchanting 3-D journey with Daffy Duck and other well-known characters, set to classic Disney soundtracks. **It's a Small World** is a slow, pleasant boat-ride past many ethnic dolls who sing the theme song over and over – and over again. **Peter Pan's Flight**, **Dumbo**

MEETING DISNEY CHARACTERS

Right inside the park entrance, the Town Square Theater is one of the top spots in the park to meet Disney characters. Mickey greets his adoring fans all day, and for the first time, guests can use a FASTPASS to bypass the queue. There's also the new Princess Fairytale Hall in Fantasyland, where guests queue to meet various Disney princesses (also accepts FASTPASS.) Alternatively, there are meet-and-greet locations for various characters around the park, although you will stand in line.

the Flying Elephant and **The Many Adventures of Winnie the Pooh** are low-tech amusements, still very popular with fairytale-loving youngsters and nostalgic adults; **The Barnstormer** is a kid-friendly roller coaster, and **The Mad Tea Party**'s spinning teacups are recommended only for those with strong stomachs.

Epcot

Even before Orlando's Magic Kingdom opened, Walt Disney was developing plans for the Experimental Prototype Community of Tomorrow, or **Epcot**. It was conceived in the 1960s as a real community that would experiment and work with the new ideas and materials of a technologically advancing US. The idea failed to take shape as Disney had envisaged. Epcot didn't open until 1982, when global recession and ecological concerns had put a damper on the belief in the infallibility of science, and the park became a general celebration of human achievement.

A word of warning: be sure to wear comfortable shoes – Epcot is twice as big as the Magic Kingdom and, ironically, given its futuristic themes, can be very tiring on mankind's oldest mode of transport – the feet.

Future World

The **Future World** section of the park keeps close to Epcot's original concept of exploring the history and researching the future of agriculture, transport, energy and communication, and is divided into several pavilions, each corporate-sponsored, and having its own rides, films, interactive computer exhibits and games. There are eight main pavilions in the Future World area, each containing a variety of rides and attractions that are covered below in clockwise order from Spaceship Earth.

Spaceship Earth

Epcot's 180ft-high **geosphere** (unlike a semicircular geodesic dome, the geosphere, invented by futurist Buckminster Fuller, is completely round) sits in the heart of Future World. Inside the geosphere is **Spaceship Earth**, a slow-moving buggy ride through the past, the present, and into the future, with narration by Dame Judi Dench and interactive features such as touch screens in the buggies, which allow you to choose your own vision of the future.

Ellen's Energy Adventure

Dominating the Universe of Energy Pavilion, **Ellen's Energy Adventure,** starring comedienne Ellen DeGeneres, is a celebration of the ways humans have harvested the Earth's energy. Although ultimately educational and with some impressive cinematography on enormous screens, the highlight is a buggy ride through the primeval forests where dinosaurs roamed and today's fossil fuels originated.

Mission: SPACE, Test Track and Captain Eo starring Michael Jackson

Disney worked with NASA advisors, astronauts and scientists to build the eponymously titled ride in the **Mission: SPACE** pavilion, which re-creates as realistically as possible the sensations of being launched in a rocket to Mars, including real G-force on take-off. Opt for the "Orange Team" if you want to experience the ride in all its intensity, or the "Green Team" for a gentler voyage.

The park's only roller-coaster-style ride is **Test Track** in the Test Track Pavilion, where you put a high-performance car through various tests, with only the final thirty seconds or so, when the speed tests are carried out, being truly exciting.

Over in the Imagination! Pavilion is the classic **Captain Eo starring Michael Jackson**, which first premiered in 1986, returned to Epcot in 2010 following the pop legend's death. Prepare yourself for plenty of moonwalking, a strange gerbil-like sidekick, and an appearance by Anjelica Huston as an evil alien queen.

6

BACKSTAGE MAGIC TOUR

There are a variety of backstage tours on offer at Disney, giving a behind-the-scenes look at many aspects of the parks. The best – and most expensive – is the **Backstage Magic Tour** (from outside Epcot main entrance; ☎407 939 8687, ⊕disneyworld.disney.go.com; $249 including lunch), which takes you along the tunnel system beneath the Magic Kingdom and offers a look at some of the backstage goings-on at Epcot and Disney's Hollywood Studios, including the technology required to put on a show such as *The American Adventure* (see opposite) and a peek at the elaborate costumes inside the Disney wardrobe. The tour lasts about seven hours and you must be over 16, not to mention rather dedicated to gaining a greater inside perspective on the parks; it's probably of less interest to first-time visitors trying to bag as many rides as possible. If you're on this tour, there is no admission charge to the three parks. When joining the tour, look for the silver-and-blue "Epcot Guided Tours Meeting Location" sign to the far right of the entrance.

Soarin' and other Land Pavilion attractions

The Land Pavilion holds the park's most popular ride – the superb **Soarin'**, which employs the latest flight-simulator technology to take you on a hang-glider ride over breathtaking California landscapes, the seats banking and turning, and wind blowing through your hair as you soar. Try to sit in the top row on the ride, as otherwise the experience is made slightly less realistic by the dangling feet of those above you.

Also in the Land Pavilion is the rich and informative **Living with the Land**, a boat tour of the world's various biomes and alternative means of food production – including Disney's own successful attempts to produce Mickey Mouse-shaped vegetables (pumpkins and cucumbers among them, if you're wondering). **The Circle of Life** is another worthwhile stop here; this animated fable based on the film *The Lion King* carries a powerful message about keeping the earth a viable habitat for all of its creatures, not just humans. Consider having a bite to eat in the food court, where the options are more varied than the burgers-and-fries found elsewhere in Future World.

The Seas with Nemo & Friends and Innoventions

The vaguely realistic **The Seas with Nemo & Friends**, in the pavilion of the same name, takes you on a terrestrial buggy ride through an aquatic world full of characters from the *Finding Nemo* movie. For real marine life, check out the Pavilion's giant **aquarium**, one of the world's largest artificial saltwater environments, occupied by a multitude of fish, sharks, turtles and other sea creatures – the fish are best viewed at the regular feeding times throughout the day.

The least interesting of Future World's pavilions, **Innoventions** merits only a cursory glance. It's divided into two sections: Innoventions **East** is for the young and old, while Innoventions **West** is mainly for the kids. Both are full of the latest in gizmos and gadgetry, much of which you can fiddle and play with. Note that Innoventions exhibits change regularly.

World Showcase

Opens daily at 11am • During the day, a boat crosses the lagoon at regular intervals, linking the entrance to Future World, Morocco and Germany

Arranged around a forty-acre lagoon, the **World Showcase** section of Epcot attempts to mirror the history, architecture and culture of the eleven nations that responded to Disney's worldwide appeal when the original idea of creating a futuristic ideal community using the latest technology was being developed in the 1970s. Each section features an instantly recognizable landmark – Mexico has a Maya pyramid, France an Eiffel Tower – or a stereotypical scene, such as a British pub or a Moroccan bazaar. The elaborate reconstructions show careful attention to detail, and each country also offers its own cuisine in often excellent restaurants where the decor can be as impressive as the food – notably at the *San Angel Inn* (see p.288) – and the staff are almost all natives of the specific country. The most crowded pavilion is usually **The American Adventure** inside a replica of Philadelphia's Liberty Hall, where Audio-Animatronic versions of Mark Twain and Benjamin Franklin give a somewhat sanitized account of two centuries of US history in under half an hour. As for rides, there's a Mexican version of It's a Small World in the Mexico pavilion – as well as an excellent tequila bar – and a short flume ride in the Norway pavilion. At night, the lagoon transforms into the spectacular sound-and-light show, **IllumiNations: Reflections of Earth**, which starts half an hour before closing. Kids can register for the World Showcase scavenger hunt **Disney Phineas and Ferb: Agent P's World Showcase Adventure** at the main World Showcase entrance.

Disney's Hollywood Studios

When the Disney Corporation began making films and TV shows for adults – most notably *Who Framed Roger Rabbit?* – it also began plotting the creation of a theme park geared as much to adults as kids. After signing an agreement in the 1980s with Metro-Goldwyn-Mayer (MGM) to exploit its many movie classics, Disney had an ample source of instantly recognizable images to mould into rides. The park opened in 1989 as Disney-MGM Studios, but since then, the addition of attractions encompassing music, television and theatre led to the decision to rename the park **Disney's Hollywood Studios** to reflect the broader focus on entertainment. Most of the attractions here take the form of rides or shows, and there are fewer exhibit-style attractions compared with the other Disney parks. This, combined with its relatively small size, makes Disney's Hollywood Studios the easiest park to see in a day.

Hollywood Boulevard

The first of several highly bowdlerized imitations of Hollywood's famous streets and buildings – which cause much amusement to anyone familiar with the seedy state of the originals – **Hollywood Boulevard** leads into the park, its length animated by re-enactments of famous movie scenes, strolling film-star lookalikes and the odd Muppet.

The rides

Avoid a long wait by arriving early and going straight to either of the park's top-notch thrill rides. The better one is **The Twilight Zone Tower of Terror** – arguably the best ride in all of Disney World – which gives you the gut-churning pleasure of experiencing several sudden drops, including moments of weightlessness, on one of four, randomly selected sequences. No matter how many times you ride this one, you'll never quite know what's coming next.

Conveniently located next door to the Tower of Terror, **Rock 'n' Roller Coaster** starts with a breakneck-speed launch and maintains an exhilarating pace through several

---

LIVE SHOWS AT HOLLYWOOD STUDIOS

The park has some very worthwhile **live shows**. Don't miss **The Indiana Jones Epic Stunt Spectacular!**, which re-creates and explains many of the action-packed set pieces from the Steven Spielberg films. In a similar vein, the very noisy **Lights, Motors, Action! Extreme Stunt Show** features equally eye-catching stunts, this time involving cars, motorbikes and jet skis speeding through a Mediterranean village. A welcome addition to the park, the theatre productions of **Beauty and the Beast – Live on Stage** and **Voyage of The Little Mermaid** are live performances of shortened versions of the Disney movies. The wonderful costumes and Broadway-style sets make them worth seeing, in spite of the ham acting. Also check out **Fantasmic!**, the dramatic laser, light and fireworks show that takes place just before the park closes.

loop-the-loops – all done in complete darkness and accompanied by Aerosmith's high-energy music. Lines can get atrocious for this ride, so be sure to pick up a FASTPASS first thing or register for one online.

Within a replica of TCL (formerly Mann's) Chinese Theatre in Hollywood is **The Great Movie Ride**, a nostalgic jaunt through sets from classic movies such as *The Wizard of Oz* and *Public Enemy*, where real-life actors interact entertainingly with the Audio-Animatronics movie stars.

Sharp turns and collisions with asteroids make **Star Tours**, a flight-simulator trip to the Moon of Endor piloted by *Star Wars* characters R2D2 and C-3PO, one of the more physical rides in the park, and it's recently been updated to Dolby 3-D to make it one of the best flight-simulator rides in Orlando. Riders are also treated to one of fifty story combinations, chosen at random, ensuring a new experience every time they ride.

Other attractions
The Magic of Disney Animation lets guests go behind the scenes to see how some of their favourite characters come to life. A Disney animator illustrates basics of the craft, and kids can try their hand at drawing cute mice and ducks.

Finally, you can enjoy laughs courtesy of Kermit, Miss Piggy and the gang at **Muppet Vision 3-D**, a three-dimensional film whose special effects and "feelies" put you right inside the *Muppet Show*. There's an entertaining twelve-minute pre-show before the action starts in the theatre, where film critics Statler and Waldorf mercilessly lampoon their fellow Muppets.

Disney's Animal Kingdom
DISNEY'S ANIMAL KINGDOM was opened in 1998 as an animal-conservation park with Disney's trademark over-the-top twist. The result is a nearly 500-acre theme park, Disney World's largest by far, divided into four major "lands" – **Africa/Rafiki's Planet Watch**, **Asia**, **Discovery Island** and **DinoLand USA** – with Africa and Asia being the most visually impressive, each re-creating the natural landscapes and exotic flavours of these two continents with admirable attention to detail.

The Tree of Life
Upon entering the park, visitors pass through **The Oasis**, with its flamingos and other exotic birds, reptiles and mammals, before crossing a bridge to **Discovery Island**. Here you'll find **The Tree of Life**, a 145ft-high concrete imitation tree with depictions of animals cleverly and intriguingly woven into the trunk and branches. Inside the tree, the amusing 3-D presentation **It's Tough to be a Bug!** shows you what an insect's life is really like, and includes some moments that can be a little intimidating for the very young.

Asia
The park's most exciting ride, in Asia, is **Expedition Everest – Legend of the Forbidden Mountain**, a roller coaster in which a train careers (both forwards and backwards) around a detailed replica of a Himalayan mountain, building up to a memorable encounter with a yeti.

As with most Disney water rides, you'll probably get soaked on **Kali River Rapids**, a river-raft ride on the Chakranadi River in Asia. You can always wear a Disney poncho, but in the Florida heat, getting drenched might be appealing.

Asia's **Maharajah Jungle Trek** gives you an astoundingly up-close look at the healthiest-looking tigers in captivity frolicking amid faux ruins, as well as a host of other creatures from that continent.

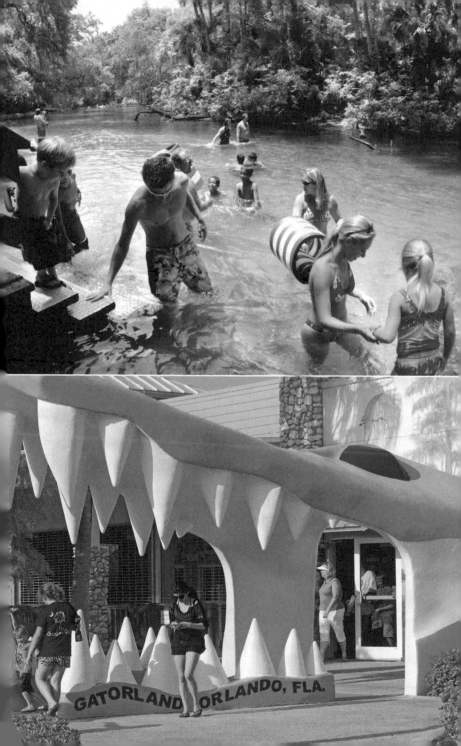

> ### LIVE SHOWS IN ANIMAL KINGDOM
>
> Disney's Animal Kingdom has three live shows, fun for all ages. Head to DinoLand USA for **Finding Nemo – The Musical**, where singing actors armed with piscean puppets on sticks tell the *Finding Nemo* story. In **Africa** you'll find the *Festival of the Lion King*, a Broadway-style production of upbeat music with some nifty acrobatics, loosely based on its namesake film. Asia's charming **Flights of Wonder** animal show sees falcons, vultures, owls and other wonderful birds interacting deftly with the audience.

6

Africa/Rafiki's Planet Watch

In Africa, you'll find one of the most involving and best-realized attractions in the park: **Kilimanjaro Safaris**. Climb into a good jeep facsimile and be swept into what feels very much like a real safari through the African savannah (local oak trees have been trimmed to look like African acacias). Throughout the tour, the driver keeps up a running commentary, pointing out the uncaged animals while helping other park rangers track down make-believe poachers. This ride is best early in the morning or around dusk, when animals are most active.

Saunter along the **Pangani Forest Exploration Trail**, home to Stanley cranes, okapi (the only living known relative of giraffes), a troop of lowland gorillas, hippos (view them underwater at the hippo pool), and innumerable exotic creatures.

Accessible by a ten-minute ride on the **Wildlife Express Train**, Rafiki's Planet Watch features **Conservation Station**, the most educational part of the park. Here you can view interactive exhibits promoting nature conservation and experience **Song of the Rainforest**, a simple yet extremely effective attraction where sounds from screeching birds to buzzing chainsaws come alive as you sit with earphones in a small, dark booth. Rafiki's is also home to **Affection Section**, where kids can pet docile sheep and goats.

DinoLand USA

Fearsome creatures generate the excitement in **DINOSAUR** in DinoLand USA, where your "Time Rover", on a mission to save a friendly Iguanadon from extinction, makes lots of short drops and sudden stops in the dark as beasts spring menacingly from the prehistoric forest, roaring all the while.

The water parks

If you're planning to visit the four main Disney parks, consider splitting your itinerary with a day at either **Blizzard Beach** or **Typhoon Lagoon**. Both water parks follow the fantastical themes typical of Disney, and the thrilling slides, along with artificial white-sand beaches and hundreds of deckchairs, should appeal to kids and worn-out parents alike. You can bring **food** (but no alcohol or glass containers) to both of the Disney water parks; Typhoon Lagoon is the better choice for picnicking, with the Surf Pool's large sandy beach the obvious place to eat.

Blizzard Beach

1534 Blizzard Beach Drive • Daily 9am–8pm • $53, children 3–9 $45, lockers $13–15, towel rental $2

Blizzard Beach is based on the fantasy that a hapless entrepreneur has opened a ski resort in Florida and the entire thing has started to melt. A combination of sand and fake snow surround Melt Away Bay, which lies at the foot of a snow-covered "mountain", complete with a ski lift and water slides. The quickest way down is via **Summit Plummet**, designed to look like a ski jump but in fact an incredibly steep water-slide 120ft high. This ride offers an exhilarating ten-second drop, and there are panoramic views over Disney property as you wait in line. The chairlift transporting you to the starting point of this and most of the park's other rides is really considered an attraction in itself (complete with waiting lines); walking up the stairs is a far quicker option. Alternatively, you can lounge around in deckchairs on the sand and soak up some rays, then cool off in one of the pools rippled by wave machines. Arrive early in summer to beat the inevitable crowds and secure a deckchair.

Typhoon Lagoon

1145 Buena Vista Drive • Daily 9am–8pm • $53, children 3–9 $45 • Lockers $13–15, towel rental $2

Busiest in the summer and on weekends (often reaching full capacity), **Typhoon Lagoon** consists of an imaginatively constructed "tropical island" around a two-and-a-half-acre lagoon called the **Surf Pool**, where a powerful wave machine generates slow-building six-foot waves. The rides are generally less daunting than what's on offer at Blizzard Beach, but exciting enough to justify the price of entrance. **Humunga Kowabunga**, three speed-slides 50ft up the "mountain" beside the lagoon, is the most exhilarating ride, followed by several smaller slides and a saltwater **Shark Reef** where you can snorkel among benign sharks and pretty tropical fish.

Downtown Disney

1780 E Buena Vista Drive (take Exit 26B off I-4) • Most shops and restaurants open daily 9.30am–11pm

Several other Disney-devised amusements exist to keep people on Disney property as long as possible and to offer therapeutic recreation and relaxation to those suffering theme-park burnout. Chief among these is **Downtown Disney**, which is undergoing a multi-year transformation into **Disney Springs**. Bordered by a lake on one side and the I-4 on the other, it's essentially a sprawling shopping mall. Once complete, the area will comprise **West Side**, **Marketplace**, **The Landing** and **Town Center**, where you'll find a good range of shops and restaurants (see p.287), a bowling alley, a Cirque du Soleil show and a complex dedicated to video games. All of Downtown Disney is being reimagined as an early 1900s Florida Town, and as of 2016 will be called Disney Springs. The Landing and Town Center will overtake the area formerly known as Pleasure Island, a six-acre island in the middle of Downtown Disney, which was, until 2008, crowded with nightclubs. However, Disney decided to withdraw from the Orlando nightlife scene, closing all of the clubs and planning instead for expanded shopping and more restaurants, such as the popular *Raglan Road Irish Pub* (see p.288).

West Side

DisneyQuest Mon–Thurs & Sun 11.30am–10pm, Fri & Sat 11.30am–11pm • $43, children 3–9 $37 • ☎ 407 828 4600 **Cirque du Soleil** La Nouba shows Tues–Sat 6pm & 9pm; 1hr 30min • $52–159, children 3–9 $52–133 • ☎ 407 939 1298, ⍾ cirquedusoleil.com

As well as some interesting dining alternatives, **West Side**, occupying the western part of Downtown Disney, has the five-storey, high-tech arcade **DisneyQuest**, full of slightly dated virtual-reality games, including a raft ride where you paddle through digital rapids, getting splashed with real water.

West Side is also the permanent home of the **Cirque du Soleil**'s *La Nouba*, a fascinating and surreal ninety-minute show full of the spellbinding acrobatics for which the company is famed.

Marketplace

On the eastern side of Downtown Disney sits **Marketplace**, a shopping emporium crammed with the world's largest Disney merchandise store, a Disney art gallery and a Lego store where kids can play while adults marvel at the massive creations of robots, dinosaurs and the like outside.

6

DISNEY CRUISES

Disney is solidly in the cruise business. Four ships, the **Disney Dream**, **Disney Fantasy**, **Disney Magic** and **Disney Wonder** ply the Caribbean on three- to seven-day voyages. You can also combine days at sea with days at a Disney resort. The elegant ships – the luxurious decor includes inlaid Italian woodwork – depart from Port Canaveral, an hour from the theme parks (parking between $60 and $120 depending on length of cruise), and sail to Nassau and then Disney's own Bahamian island, **Castaway Cay**. Live shows change nightly and separate entertainment areas are provided for children, adults and families. Prices vary considerably depending on when you go and the cabin (or Disney resort) that you choose. Three-day cruises start at around $1000 per person. For more information, call ☎ 800 951 3532 or visit ✆ disneycruiseline.com.

ESPN Wide World of Sports

Two miles east of Disney's Animal Kingdom off Osceola Parkway at 700 S Victory Way • Hours depend on daily events • $16.50, children 3–9 $11.50 • ☎ 407 939 4263, ✆ espnwwos.com

Professional and amateur sporting events (check the website for schedules) are frequently held at Disney's **ESPN Wide World of Sports**, a 200-acre complex of stadiums, arenas and sports fields bustling on any given day with soccer moms, high-school wrestling teams, or pro baseball players. The complex is only really worth a special trip if you time it to coincide with a particular sporting event. The most publicized of these are the games played by the **Atlanta Braves** during March spring training, which take place in the 9500-seat baseball stadium (tickets $15–50).

Richard Petty Driving Experience

Walt Disney World Speedway (at the south end of the Magic Kingdom car park) • Ride-Along daily 9am–4pm, but call to confirm other experiences vary • Ride-Along $105.44; other experiences range from $449 to $2599 for the Racing Experience • ☎ 800 237 3889, ✆ drivepetty.com

The **Richard Petty Driving Experience** offers NASCAR fanatics multiple ways to get a realistic feel for stock-car racing. Take a three-lap stock-car ride around a one-mile tri-oval track driven by an expert in the "Ride-Along", or choose more intensive experiences ranging from eight to fifty laps you drive yourself. In all cases, a valid driving licence must be presented.

ARRIVAL AND GETTING AROUND

Airport transfer If you're staying on property, Disney's Magical Express Transportation (see p.267) provides a free transfer from the airport to your hotel and vice versa, and will collect your luggage and deliver it to your room.

By car The charge for using the Disney World car parks is $17, which covers you for the whole day. These car parks are enormous, so make a note of exactly where you're parked.

By bus With its multiple attractions and resort hotels, Disney property seems at first glance complicated to get around. In fact, it's quite easy, with Disney's fleet of free buses serving all points of interest. As a general rule, buses to all destinations depart at roughly twenty-minute intervals from

WALT DISNEY WORLD

all of the resorts. Intra-park travel, meanwhile, will sometimes involve changing buses at the Transportation and Ticket Center (near the Magic Kingdom) or another park. For example, to get to Disney's Wide World of Sports, you'll have to catch a bus from Disney's Hollywood Studios. Note that buses to Downtown Disney depart from the resorts only.

By monorail Transport between the Transportation and Ticket Center, the Magic Kingdom and Epcot is via the monorail, which runs every few minutes.

On foot Walking from park to park is not a viable option; distances are deceptively long and there are few pedestrian walkways.

INFORMATION, OPENING TIMES AND TICKETS

Information Although there's no main office for visitor information, each park and Downtown Disney has a guest relations desk or centre; nearly every Disney employee should be able to assist you with basic questions as well.

Opening times vary greatly depending on what park you are visiting and at what time of year. The parks are generally open daily from 9am to around 9pm or 10pm during holidays and in the summer, and from 9am to 6pm or later the rest of the year.

Tickets Ticket costs come as a shock, especially to families (children under 3 are admitted free of charge, though note little is designed specifically for their entertainment), but the basic admission fee allows unlimited access to all the shows and rides in a particular park. A one-day, one-park ticket costs $99 (children 3–9 $93; under-3s free), available from any park entrance. The Magic Your Way ticket saves money if you spread your visit over a number of days; for example, a seven-day ticket would cost $324 (children 3–9 $304). You can buy a Magic Your Way ticket for a maximum of ten days and you can only visit one park per day. If you want to move from park to park in the same day, you must add the Park Hopper option for an additional flat fee of $60 per day. The Water Park Fun & More option allows you to add from two to seven extra admissions (the exact number depends on the length of your basic Magic Your Way ticket) to Blizzard Beach, Typhoon Lagoon, DisneyQuest, Disney's Wide World of Sports, Disney's Oak Trail Golf course or either on-site mini golf course for a flat fee of $60/day. There's also a $634 annual pass.

ACCOMMODATION

Areas If you want to escape the all-pervasive influence of Disney World for the night, refer to the Orlando accommodation listings (see p.268) or opt to stay at one of the hotels around Disney property in the area known as Lake Buena Vista (see p.287), from where it's only a few minutes' drive to any of the parks (most of these hotels offer complimentary shuttles to and from the parks). If you can't bring yourself to leave – and staying within easy access of the parks is, after all, the most convenient way of experiencing Disney World – there are plentiful hotels on Disney property, most of which are fully equipped theme-resorts. Transport between the resorts and the main theme parks is free (see opposite).

Booking At quiet times, rooms may be available at short notice, but with Disney resorts pitching themselves to conference-goers as much as holidaymakers, you may turn up only to find everywhere fully booked. To be assured of a room, reserve as far ahead as possible – nine months is not unreasonable. You can make reservations by phone or online (☎ 407 939 6244 or ☎ 407 939 7639, ⊕ disneyworld .disney.go.com).

Facilities Each resort occupies its own landscaped plot, usually encompassing several swimming pools and a beach beside an artificial lake, and has several restaurants and bars. Resort guests have free use of Disney car parks and free airport transfers (see p.267). Extra Magic Hours (see box below) are a further bonus. The standard of service should be excellent; if it isn't, make a stiff complaint and you'll probably be treated like royalty throughout the remainder of your stay.

Rates You can splurge on rooms running more than $300 per night, or you can opt for budget digs at one of the *All-Star Resorts* or *Pop Century Resort* or the new *Art of Animation Resort* where rates start at $85 a night.

MAGIC KINGDOM RESORT
Contemporary Resort ☎ 407 824 1000; map p.274. The Disney monorail runs right through the centre of this hotel, which takes its exterior design from the futuristic fantasies of the Magic Kingdom's Tomorrowland. All the modern, minimalist rooms have balconies, some affording good views of the Magic Kingdom, especially the evening fireworks. Satellite hotel *Bay Lake Tower* is part of the Disney Vacation Club, a timeshare programme that allows members access to Disney-affiliated properties worldwide. Studios and comfortable one- and two-bedroom villas are available for regular guests. *Contemporary Resort* rooms $336, *Bay Lake Tower* $438

Fort Wilderness Resort & Campground ☎ 407 824 2900, campground ☎ 407 824 2900; map p.274. A 750 acre site where you can pitch your tent or hook up your RV, or rent an a/c six-berth cabin – a good deal for larger groups. Entertainment includes nightly open-air screenings of classic Disney movies. Camping $49, cabins $294

Grand Floridian Resort & Spa ☎ 407 824 3000; map p.274. Gabled roofs, verandas and crystal chandeliers are among the whimsical variations on early Florida resort architecture at Disney's most upmarket hotel, complete with a full-service spa. $488

Polynesian Resort ☎ 407 824 2000; map p.274. Accessible via the monorail, this imitation of a Polynesian beach hotel is getting a facelift in 2014, with updates to both the pool area and the Great Ceremonial House lobby. There's a small lakeside beach where you can sit under the shade of coconut palms before retiring to your brightly coloured, tropically themed room. $476

★ Wilderness Lodge ☎ 407 824 3200; map p.274. This magnificent, oversized replica of National Park lodge is furnished with massive totem poles, a wood-burning fire in

---

EXTRA MAGIC HOURS
One advantage of staying at a Disney resort comes in the shape of the **Extra Magic Hours**, when each day one of the four parks either opens one hour earlier or closes up to three hours later exclusively for resort guests, giving them the opportunity for some quality time with Mickey and relatively unimpeded access to the best rides.

the lobby, and Southern-style rocking chairs, while the welcoming rooms have a back-to-nature motif. $289

EPCOT-DISNEY'S HOLLYWOOD STUDIOS RESORT

★ **BoardWalk Inn** ☎ 407 939 6200; map p.274. Styled after a 1930s mid-Atlantic seaside resort, this place comes complete with a waterfront promenade full of shops and restaurants, worthy of a stop even if you're not staying at the resort. The rooms have a spacious feel and all come with balconies. If you're staying here or at the *Yacht* or *Beach Club* (see below) there's a convenient (and much less busy) EPCOT center entrance within walking distance. $366
Caribbean Beach Resort ☎ 407 934 3400; map p.274. Rooms are located in one of six "island villages", each with its own pool and beach surrounded by nicely landscaped grounds. New additions are the pirate-themed rooms, with beds shaped like galleons. $170
Dolphin Hotel ☎ 407 934 4000, ⊛ swandolphin.com; map p.274. Topped by a giant dolphin sculpture and decorated in dizzying pastel shades and reproduction artwork by the likes of Matisse and Warhol, this hotel has rooms with a fresh, contemporary design. A few good restaurants, like celebrity chef Todd English's *bluezoo*, complete the picture. $235
Swan Hotel ☎ 407 934 4000, ⊛ swandolphin.com; map p.274. Sister hotel to the *Dolphin* (see above), from which it's separated by an artificial lake and beach, and likewise whimsically decorated, though with sharper, more vibrant colours, and equipped with every conceivable luxury. $308
Yacht and Beach Club Resorts ☎ 407 934 7000 (Yacht Club), ☎ 407 934 8000 (Beach Club); map p.274. Late nineteenth-century New England is the cue for these twin hotels, complete with clapboard facades, a miniature lighthouse, and bright, airy rooms inspired by nautical themes. Amusements include the best pool on Disney property, a mini-waterpark reminiscent of a Nantucket beach. $356

DISNEY'S ANIMAL KINGDOM RESORT

All-Star Resorts ☎ 407 939 6000 (Music), ☎ 407 939 5000 (Sports), ☎ 407 939 7000 (Movies); map p.274. The most affordable of Disney's resorts, divided into the *All-Star Music Resort*, which is decorated with giant, brightly

coloured cowboy boots and guitar-shaped swimming pools; the *All-Star Sports Resort*, complete with huge Coca-Cola cups and American football helmets; and the *All-Star Movies Resort*, which is littered with enormous reminders of Disney movies. Each complex has its own pools and nearly two thousand functional and brightly decorated rooms; *All-Star Music Resort* also has family suites (sleeping six) with kitchenettes. $85
★ **Animal Kingdom Lodge and Animal Kingdom Villas** ☎ 407 938 3000; map p.274. One of Disney's most spectacular luxury hotels, where from some of the rooms – all of which are done up in warm colours and decorated with African handicrafts – you can wake up to see wildlife grazing outside your window. The Kidani Villas section of the resort features rooms that include kitchens and multi-bedroom units. Lodge rooms $284, villas $318
Coronado Springs Resort ☎ 407 939 1000; map p.274. Moderately priced resort, which pays homage to the cultures of Mexico and the American Southwest. There are nearly two thousand colourful, Latino-inspired rooms and a pool built around a faux-Maya pyramid. $175

DOWNTOWN DISNEY RESORT

★ **Old Key West Resort** ☎ 407 827 7700; map p.274. Caribbean-style wooden architecture and shaded verandas create a tropical ambience based on a late nineteenth-century Key West resort. Accommodation is in studios or villas with kitchens and washer-dryers. Studios $327, villas $452
Port Orleans Resort ☎ 407 934 5000 (French Quarter), ☎ 407 934 6000 (Riverside); map p.274. This resort combines two Southern themes: the row houses and cobbled streets of New Orleans in the *French Quarter*; and the grandiose manors overlooking the Mississippi River at the *Riverside*. $170
Saratoga Springs Resort & Spa ☎ 407 827 1100; map p.274. Spacious studios or well-equipped villas (complete with whirlpool tubs) are offered at this resort modelled on one of America's first holiday resorts, Saratoga Springs, in the late 1800s. $327

ESPN WIDE WORLD OF SPORTS RESORT

★ **Art of Animation Resort** ☎ 407 938 7000; map p.274. The newest Disney resort opened in summer 2012, and features over a thousand suites designed after *Finding*

MY MAGIC+

It's easy to tell which guests are staying at Disney resorts now; they'll all be wearing a **MagicBand**. The bracelets are mailed to resort guests at home (if they book far enough in advance) or delivered upon check-in, and they're an all-in-one electronic park ticket, FASTPASS and room key. Guests who receive the bands in advance can choose colours or have their names etched on their bands. And, never one to miss a sales opportunity, Disney sells bling for your e-bracelet throughout the park.

Nemo, *Cars* and *The Lion King*, and almost 900 standard rooms inspired by *The Little Mermaid*. Three pools round out the offerings – you'll find the largest resort pool at Disney in the *Finding Nemo* courtyard, naturally. $130, suites $296
Pop Century Resort ☎407 938 4000; map p.274. Devoted to mammoth pop icons from each decade of the second half of the twentieth century, this is Disney's largest hotel, with nearly three thousand budget-priced rooms along the same lines as the *All-Star Resorts* (see opposite). $120

LAKE BUENA VISTA

★**Four Seasons Orlando** 10100 Dream Tree Blvd ☎800 267 3046, ⓦfourseasons.com/orlando; map p.266. The Four Seasons brings its venerable brand to Orlando with this new luxury hotel, opened in August 2014, on Disney property. Rooms are sumptuous, complete with marble bathrooms, and there's a Tom Fazio-designed golf course and a full-service spa as well as Explorer Island, an on-site waterpark offering a lazy river and 242ft waterslide. $545
Hyatt Regency Grand Cypress 1 Grand Cypress Blvd ☎407 239 1234, ⓦgrandcypress.hyatt.com; map p.266. This comfortable hotel offers plentiful amenities, such as a

half-acre, free-flowing lagoon pool with a waterslide, rock climbing walls, golf lessons and paddleboat and kayaking on private Lake Windsong. Rooms are stylish and modern. $149
Nickelodeon Suites Resort 14500 Continental Gateway ☎407 387 5437, ⓦnickhotel.com; map p.266. The leader in kid-friendly resorts, with one-, two- and three-bedroom suites sleeping up to six, two giant swimming pools with water slides and even a spa for the little ones. $109
★**Orlando World Center Marriott Resort** 8701 World Center Drive ☎407 239 4200, ⓦmarriot.com; map p.266. Looking like a small city, the two thousand rooms here are comfortable enough, but it's the recreational activities on offer – a giant lagoon-shaped swimming pool, full-service spa and manicured golf course – that are the main draws. $169
★**Sheraton Vistana Resort** 8800 Vistana Centre Drive ☎407 239 3100, ⓦstarwoodhotels.com; map p.266. With the atmosphere of a small village, this sprawling resort is dotted with swimming pools and restaurants, and has activities for the kids. The attractive one- and two-bedroom villas come with large kitchens and washer-dryers. $137

EATING

Besides the fast-food options available at the theme parks, there are plenty of great places to eat on Disney property. You'll find some upmarket dining opportunities at the **resorts**, while at **Downtown Disney** you can choose from a variety of restaurants. **Epcot's World Showcase**, with its multiethnic cuisines, offers the tastiest food among the theme parks. Note that the only alcohol served in the Magic Kingdom is during dinner service at *Be Our Guest* restaurant. All reservations for Disney dining can be made at ☎407 939 3463.

Artist Point Wilderness Lodge. Tuck into hearty cuisine from the Pacific Northwest – including the recommended house speciality, cedar-plank-roasted salmon – washed down with wines from Oregon and Washington, all served under high wood-beamed ceilings. Most main dishes around $30 and up. Daily 5.30–9.30pm.
★**Be Our Guest** Magic Kingdom. Named for the show-stopping number in *Beauty and the Beast*, this sit-down spot in the new Fantasyland is by far your best choice for grown-up fare in the Magic Kingdom. Guests order on touch screens and take an electronic rose back to their tables, to which waiters whisk trays of covered food. There are three themed rooms, each from the Beast's castle: the Main Ballroom, the haunted West Wing and the Rose Gallery. As for the food, expect tasty French-inspired fare like *croque monsieur* and *coq au vin*. Lunch mains are around $13, dinner mains around $24. Daily 10.30am–2.30pm & 4–9.30pm.
Bongo's Cuban Café Downtown Disney West Side, 1498 E Buena Vista Drive ☎407 828 0999. Created by Gloria and Emilio Estefan, the tasty Cuban cuisine here ($10–30) is complemented by the wildly fabulous decor and lively salsa shows (Fri & Sat). Daily 11am–11pm.

★**California Grill** On the 15th floor of Contemporary Resort. One of Disney's best all-round restaurants, with a pricey menu dominated by fresh sushi ($21–28) and some excellent main dishes like oak-fired fillet of beef (around $35), all prepared in an onstage kitchen and served in a recently redone, airy dining-room. A great selection of Californian wines, as well as impressive views over the Magic Kingdom – try to time your reservation with the nightly fireworks show. Most dishes $34–50, sushi $24–27. Daily 5–10pm.
Crossroads at House of Blues Downtown Disney West Side. Tasty Creole- and Cajun-inspired food ($15–25) with live music inside on Fridays and Saturdays, and nightly on the porch starting at 5pm. Try the popular all-you-can-eat Gospel brunch ($40.50) on Sunday (seatings at 10.30 and 1pm). Daily 11.30am–10pm.
Hollywood Brown Derby Disney's Hollywood Studios. A faithful re-creation of the mythic Hollywood landmark, with famous recipes to match (including Cobb salad, invented by the Derby's original chefs). The relaxing, softly lit dining-room gets you away from the park's general hustle and bustle. Most dinner dishes $30–40. Daily noon–9.30pm.

6

★Jiko – The Cooking Place Animal Kingdom Lodge. Enjoy typical American food such as steaks and ribs with a welcome international flavour of curried sauces and exotic grains and spices, all washed down with no fewer than 65 different choices of exclusively South African wine. Most dishes $28–45. Daily 5.30–10pm.

Kouzzina by Cat Cora Disney BoardWalk. Iron Chef Cat Cora gets into the Disney dining scene with this casual Mediterranean spot on the BoardWalk, one of the main resort and restaurant areas near Epcot. The create-your-own *Kouzzina* trio, with dishes such as Greek-style lasagne, a lamb burger and cinnamon stewed chicken, is a standout. Most dishes $21–35. Daily 7.30am–11am & 5–10pm.

★Les Chefs de France/Monsieur Paul French Pavilion at Epcot's World Showcase. Fresh produce is flown in daily to create authentic, and beautifully presented French cuisine at *Les Chefs de France*, including roasted duck breast and warm goat cheese salad (most dishes around $25). Opened in 2012, the even more upmarket *Monsieur Paul* upstairs serves gourmet French fare such as red snapper with braised fennel and grilled beef tenderloin (most dishes $39–44). Les Chefs de France daily noon–9pm; Monsieur Paul daily 5.30–8.30pm.

Raglan Road Irish Pub Downtown Disney ⓣ 407 938 0300. This Irish-owned and -operated pub offers dishes such as fish and chips, pies and stews (mainly $15–20), as well as live entertainment every night at 6pm and plentiful Guinness. Daily 11am–1.30am.

★Sanaa Kidani Village, Animal Kingdom Resort. The word *sanaa* means work of art in Swahili, and it's an apt description for this great spot, which emphasizes the flavours of East Africa and India. Start with the *chana tikki* (spiced chickpea cakes) and move on to the succulent tandoori lamb. Main courses from $20. Daily 11.30am–3pm & 5–9.30pm.

San Angel Inn Mexican Pavilion at Epcot's World Showcase ⓣ 407 939 3463. Savour adventurous dishes ($24–29 at dinner) using ingredients such as cactus and cocoa at this atmospheric re-creation of a Mexican village on a balmy night. Stop in at *La Cava del Tequila* afterwards for one of over 200 tequilas. Daily 11.30am–9pm.

Splitsville Downtown Disney West Side. A bowling alley may not spring to mind as a viable dinner choice, but this new spot in Downtown Disney offers something for everyone, from well-executed sushi to pizza to Asian-style rice bowls. You can work off some of your dinner with a game on one of the retro-inspired alley's thirty lanes. Most dishes $11–24. Daily 11.30am–9pm.

Victoria & Albert's Grand Floridian Resort & Spa, Magic Kingdom. A menu that changes daily, fine wines and harp music set a refined tone at one of central Florida's top-rated restaurants. Reserve far in advance to sit at the Chef's Table in the kitchen, where the chef himself will attend to you. The seven-course menu costs $135 ($200 with wine), both the ten-course menu and Chef's Table cost $210 ($315 with wine). Two sittings daily, varies by season and which dinner you've chosen. Main dining room 5–6.15 pm & 8.30–9.15pm; Queen Victoria room 5–6.30pm only.

Wolfgang Puck Downtown Disney West Side, 1482 E Buena Vista Drive ⓣ 407 938 9653. Three restaurants in one multi-level location: *The Dining Room* upstairs for upmarket dining (dinner only); *The Café* for casual; and *The Express* for self-service. Meals are moderately priced except at *The Dining Room*, which features the celebrity chef's signature dishes ($35–45). Pizzas, rotisserie chickens and good sandwiches are available at *The Express*, which has another location in Downtown Disney Marketplace. Daily 11.30am–10.30pm.

Universal Orlando

Half a mile north of exits 74B or 75A off I-4 • Daily 8–9am until 6–10pm depending on the season • One-day, one-park ticket $96 adults, $90 children 3–9; one-day, two-park ticket $136 adults, $130 children 3–9; fourteen-day Flexticket available (see box opposite); parking $17/day • ⓣ 407 363 8000, ⓦ universalorlando.com

For some years, it seemed US TV and film production would be shifting away from expensive California to Florida, which, with its lower taxes and cheaper labour, was more amenable, and the opening of Universal Studios Florida in 1990 appeared to confirm that trend. So far, for various reasons, Florida has not proved to be a fully realistic alternative, but that hasn't stopped the Universal enclave here, known as **UNIVERSAL ORLANDO**, from expanding enormously and becoming even more successful.

The sequel to the long-established and immensely popular tour of its studios in Los Angeles, **Universal Studios Florida**, like its rival Disney's Hollywood Studios, is a working studio, filling over a hundred acres with high-tech movie-themed attractions. In addition to Universal Studios Florida there's **Islands of Adventure**, boasting a high concentration of some of the best thrill rides in Orlando as well as the wildly popular Wizarding World of Harry Potter attraction, with new addition Diagon Alley. And with all the nightclubs at Downtown Disney now closed, **CityWalk** has become the main competition to downtown Orlando for nightlife dollars (see p.292). Overall, the mood at Universal Orlando is more hip and the rides more intense than at Disney, but the atmosphere is less magical, service can be variable, and the parks can feel less welcoming – as though almost everything is aimed primarily at hyper-energetic adolescent boys who want things louder, faster and with more attitude. For most visitors, two days will be sufficient.

Universal Studios Florida

The park is arranged around a large lagoon and nominally divided into several areas: **Production Central**, **New York**, **San Francisco**, **The Wizarding World of Harry Potter – Diagon Alley**, **World Expo**, **Woody Woodpecker's Kidzone** and **Hollywood**. There's no real need to follow a particular order in your explorations; listed below are the recommended rides.

Wizarding World of Harry Potter – Diagon Alley

In a stroke of pure genius, the masterminds behind The Wizarding World of Harry Potter at Islands of Adventure have opened the second phase of the wildly popular attraction at Universal Studios, thus ensuring that most guests will visit both parks. As fans of the books know, Diagon Alley – disguised as an ordinary London street – is the main back-to-school shopping area for young witches and wizards, and the Universal Studios version is marvellously realized, filled with shops from the books, such as Borgin and Burkes, which offers dark magic accessories, and Madam Malkin's Robes for All Occasions. Eat lunch at the *Leaky Cauldron* or pop into *Florean Fortescue's Ice Cream Parlour* for a soft-serve scoop. There's also a second outpost of the popular Ollivander's wand shop, where young wizards can procure their own magical prop.

Harry Potter and the Escape from Gringotts

The anchor of the Diagon Alley area is the gigantic Gringotts bank, topped by a fire-breathing dragon. Inside is a multidimensional 3-D simulator thrill ride, where guests career through the goblin-run bank, trapped in the middle of the action as Harry and his friends flee security as well as Harry's arch-nemesis Voldemort and his acolytes. Be warned: queues for this wildly popular attraction can easily top two hours.

TICKETS AND PASSES AT UNIVERSAL ORLANDO

ORLANDO FLEXTICKET

In the hopes of prying tourists from Disney's clutches, competitors have teamed up to offer special multi-park passes. The **Orlando FlexTicket** provides unlimited admission for fourteen days to the two Universal Orlando theme parks, SeaWorld Orlando, and two water parks, Aquatica and Wet 'n' Wild, for $319.95 (adults), $299.95 (children 3–9). For $359.95 (adults) or $339.95 (children 3–9), you can add Busch Gardens in Tampa (see p.359), two hours away, with a free shuttle from Orlando to Busch Gardens included.

UNIVERSAL EXPRESS AND SKIPPING THE LINE

Universal has devised **Universal Express** – a system similar to Disney's FASTPASS (see box, p.273) and which includes virtually every attraction – to help get visitors around long waits in line. Whereas Disney's FASTPASS is free, Universal charges for its pass; guests can hold passes for multiple attractions simultaneously. Passes cost from $34.99 for one park and $39.99 for two parks.

Another good way to **beat the crowds** at Universal is to join the (sometimes) quicker **single rider lines** – where you fill up the odd seat not taken by groups wishing to experience the attraction together. All **guests at deluxe Universal resorts** can join the Express lines simply by presenting their room key-card.

Hogwarts Express

After you've purchased your back-to-school supplies in Diagon Alley, step up to Platform 9¾ at King's Cross Station and catch the *Hogwarts Express* over to Hogsmeade at Islands of Adventure, assuming you've got a multi-park ticket. What's essentially a train ride becomes a whimsical journey with the use of windows that project Harry Potter stories, rather than real-life Florida scenery.

Other rides

6

There are several other worthwhile rides in Production Central. The **Hollywood's Rip Ride Rockit** roller coaster opened in 2009 to much anticipation. Riders choose their own soundtrack accompaniment from classic rock, hip-hop, country, techno or pop music to scream along to as the superb coaster shoots them straight up in the air, and nearly straight back down.

Offering some of the most delightful 3-D graphics in the parks, **Despicable Me Minion Mayhem**, a new simulator ride in Production Central, means to make minions out of the audience, but, predictably, spirals out of control when Gru's yellow minions are themselves in charge. Guests travel through Gru's secret workshop and save the day just in time for an anniversary party for his adopted daughters.

A word to the wise: don't eat lunch until after you've been on the rollicking **Transformers: The Ride-3D** in Production Central. Although the graphics on this 3-D simulator ride aren't as crystal-clear as those on Despicable Me, the sheer amount of action on the screen as the gigantic machines fight for supremacy throughout a city in shambles is more than enough to make up for it, as your cart seems to freefall through it all.

Over at World Expo, **The Simpsons Ride** combines cutting-edge flight-simulator technology with the irreverent humour of the Simpsons cartoon family. Guests take a stomach-turning ride through Krustyland, the low-budget theme park created by the Simpsons' resident huckster, Krusty the Clown.

A worthwhile stop is at **Disaster**, in the San Francisco area, which allows riders behind the scenes to see what it's like to create disaster films. The finale is two minutes of terror as you experience all the bone-shaking sights and sounds of a subway train during an 8.0 Richter-scale earthquake.

Along the same lines, **TWISTER … Ride It Out** in New York is a gripping and frighteningly realistic re-creation of a tornado tearing through a small Oklahoma town, complete with simulated lightning, flying objects, and rain (cover all camera equipment). Also in New York, **Revenge of the Mummy** is a fun indoor roller coaster through scenes from the eponymous movie, combining virtual effects with real ones, such as exploding fireballs, as well as an Audio-Animatronic version of the Mummy himself.

Playgrounds and fairground rides dominate Woody Woodpecker's KidZone, where the best attraction is **A Day in the Park with Barney**, a show involving lots of singing and

---

LIVE SHOWS AT UNIVERSAL ORLANDO

A number of live stage shows are on offer throughout Universal Studios Florida. The best is the **Universal Orlando's Horror Make-Up Show**, where horror-movie special effects are revealed amid amusingly tasteless jokes; **Fear Factor Live!** has contestants confront their worst fears in a series of challenges that mimic, albeit in watered-down form, those of the hit TV show (to register as a contestant for this show, present yourself at the venue 90 minutes in advance); **Animal Actors on Location!** explains some of the tricks used to turn animals into film actors; **Beetlejuice's Graveyard Revue** features high-tempo renditions of catchy tunes and risqué humour; **The Blues Brothers** show offers Jake and Elwood singing high-energy paeans to their native Chicago.

At Islands of Adventure there's one live performance offered throughout the day: **The Eighth Voyage of Sinbad**, an action-packed extravaganza of swashbuckling adventure and great pyrotechnics, where the set, stunts and effects are as good as the jokes are bad.

clapping along with Barney the Dinosaur and friends. A ride on pretend bicycles to ET's home planet, **E.T. Adventure** in Woody Woodpecker's KidZone is good for the nostalgic adults in the group who remember watching the movie as a child. The ride is made somewhat more interesting when ET speaks your name (recorded earlier by a computer) as you leave.

Islands of Adventure

Universal Orlando's other theme park, **Islands of Adventure**, is a five-minute walk from Universal Studios Florida. The park is divided into six sections, each with its own unique character: **Marvel Super Hero Island** has the most exciting rides; **The Lost Continent** is based on ancient myths and legends; **Jurassic Park** goes to town on the well-worn dinosaur motif in a scientific as well as scary way; **Toon Lagoon** uses cartoon characters to get you completely soaked; the garishly eye-catching **Seuss Landing** will delight the toddler set; and finally, the hugely popular **Wizarding World of Harry Potter**.

The park is bursting with excellent thrill rides and outshines anything Disney World has to offer in that department – even though no one has yet equalled Disney for the seamless perfection of its imagined environments made real. There's also a live show (see box opposite), though Disney still holds the edge in this area, and a number of decent hands-on play areas spread throughout.

The Wizarding World of Harry Potter

The thrill of this section of the park isn't in the rides, but rather in the atmosphere, a meticulously re-created street scene from Hogsmeade, the English village nearest Hogwarts, where Harry and his friends attend school. Stop into shops like Honeydukes Sweetshop for your own chocolate frog, and be sure to get some butterbeer from the cask outside.

Of the rides, **Harry Potter and the Forbidden Journey** is a (mostly) virtual reality ride, combining virtual and animatronic effects to create a soaring experience through Hogwarts school, over a Quidditch pitch and through Azkaban prison. The line for the ride winds through Hogwarts, and the details, like spyglasses and visits from Dumbledore, are impeccable. The family-friendly mini roller coaster **Flight of the Hippogriff** takes you on a fanciful flight through a pumpkin patch upon a Hippogriff – which has the head of an eagle and the body of a horse – and swoops past Hagrid's hut; while at Ollivander's Wand Shop guests – in groups of twenty – are ushered into the series' famous wand shop, where they are welcomed by a wandkeeper who guides them through the search for their very own wand. Finally, the twin roller coasters of **Dragon Challenge** amp up the adrenaline; though the ride is not new, it's been repurposed with a Harry Potter theme. With separate waiting lines for each, these coasters are engineered to provide harrowing head-on near-misses with one another – which makes sitting in the front row especially thrilling; the seats also leave your feet dangling in mid-air, adding to the sense of danger.

Marvel Super Hero Island

On **Marvel Super Hero Island**, the **Incredible Hulk Coaster** offers an exciting catapult start (apparently packing the same thrust as an F-16 fighter jet) and plenty of loop-the-loops and plunges. **Storm Force Accelatron** is a good ride for all ages, based on the X-Men movies, wherein visitors sit in tub-like cars that spin and whirl in a domed space enveloped by a noisy light show, creating thunder and lightning to defeat villain Magneto. The imposing twin towers of **Doctor Doom's Fearfall** look frightening enough, and afford good views over the park, but the very short ride – a controlled drop during which you experience a few seconds of weightlessness – is an anticlimax.

The Amazing Adventures of Spider-Man

Long one of the best rides in the park, **The Amazing Adventures of Spider-Man** got even better in 2012 when it was reanimated in high-definition. It employs every trick imaginable – 3-D, sensory stimuli, motion simulation and more – to spirit you into Spider-Man's battles with villains across a high-rise city.

Jurassic Park

The main attraction of this section is **Jurassic Park River Adventure**. This generally tame boat-trip through a primeval zoo is spiced up by special effects, pyrotechnics and an unexpected 85ft drop.

Toon Lagoon

In somewhat less adrenaline-pumping mode than Jurassic Park or Spider-Man, you could try **Dudley Do-Right's Ripsaw Falls**, a flume ride where the final 60ft drop will drench all four passengers in the hollowed-out-log boats (avoid on cooler days). Try **Popeye & Bluto's Bilge Rat Barges** for a raft ride that's only slightly drier.

The Lost Continent

In The Lost Continent section, **Poseidon's Fury** is a show/ride offering a few impressive effects using water and fire as you play your part in an Indiana Jones-style tour of the ancient ruins of Poseidon's temple. The storyline is totally unengaging though, and this ride is best visited for the air conditioning on a hot Florida day.

Seuss Landing

This section has plenty of tame, but enchanting, offerings for the little ones, including **Caro-Seuss-el**, a merry-go-round adorned with Seussian characters; the interactive playground **One Fish, Two Fish, Red Fish, Blue Fish**; a carousel called **Caro-Seuss-el**; and **The Cat in the Hat**, which retells the famous story as you sit in spinning sofas. For an aerial perspective of Seuss Landing's incredibly colourful scenery, take a trip on **The High in the Sky Seuss Trolley Rain Ride! Oh the Stories You'll Hear!** is a musical retelling of some of Dr Seuss's most beloved tales.

ACCOMMODATION   UNIVERSAL ORLANDO

There are four resort hotels on Universal property, three of them luxurious and expensive and one brand-new, value-category hotel. They're all incredibly convenient for visiting Universal Studios Florida, Islands of Adventure and CityWalk (regular complimentary water taxis operate between the resorts and a dock at CityWalk). To make reservations at any of the Universal resorts, call ☎ 888 273 1311 or visit ⓦ universalorlando.com.

Hard Rock Hotel 5800 Universal Blvd ☎ 407 503 7625, ⓦ hardrockhotelorlando.com. Stuffed with rock memorabilia, and with familiar tunes blaring out at poolside, this is the least tranquil of the park's resorts – and the most popular with the younger crowd. The simple yet stylish rooms are equipped with high-quality CD players and flat-screen TVs. **$284**

Loews Portofino Bay Hotel 5601 Universal Blvd ☎ 888 430 4999, ⓦ loewshotels.com. A lavish re-creation of the Italian seaside village of Portofino, complete with vintage scooters parked in the piazza. The luxurious rooms are decorated with marble and Italian furnishings, and there's a full-service spa. **$294**

Loews Royal Pacific Resort 6300 Hollywood Way ☎ 888 430 4999, ⓦ loewshotels.com. The comfortable rooms here are decked out in bamboo to enhance the "tropical" theme, while the kids will enjoy the lagoon-style pool. **$234**

★ **Universal's Cabana Bay Beach Resort** 6550 Adventure Way ☎ 407 503 4000, ⓦ loewshotels.com. This new, retro-styled hotel is inspired by the late 1950s and early 1960s. The whole property, from the brightly coloured rooms to the gigantic zero-entry pool with waterslide and lazy river to the on-site bowling alley and poolside tiki bar is bursting with personality. Rooms can comfortably accommodate a family of six. **$124**

EATING, DRINKING AND NIGHTLIFE

With the closure of the nightclubs at Downtown Disney, **CityWalk** (free with a multi-day theme park ticket, $11.99 for all-night access to every club, $15 if you want to take in a movie, plus parking for $5 after 6pm and free after 10pm;

☎ 407 363 8000), a friendly mix of restaurants, live music, dance clubs, bars and a multi-screen cinema, has become the main after-dark alternative to downtown Orlando (see p.272). However, compared with downtown's extensive and diverse options, CityWalk's clubs can seem a little sterile and monotonous, although the area underwent a major refurbishment in 2014.

RESTAURANTS

Emeril's CityWalk ☎407 224 2424, ⓦemerils.com. CityWalk's most upmarket and expensive dining option, overseen by TV chef Emeril Lagasse, serves gourmet food such as filet mignon and seared sea scallops in a somewhat austere dining room. Main dishes $21–42. Mon–Thurs & Sun 11.30am–3pm & 5–10pm, Fri & Sat 11.30am–3pm & 5–10.30pm.

Emeril's Tchoup Chop 6300 Hollywood Way ☎407 503 2467, ⓦemerils.com. At *Loews Royal Pacific Resort*, this tasty restaurant (pronounced "chop chop", offers a South Pacific-inspired fish-centric menu, from sushi to Hawaiian-style snapper. Mon–Thurs 11.30am–2.30pm & 5–10pm, Fri & Sat 11.30am–2.30pm & 5–11pm.

Hard Rock Café CityWalk ☎407 351 7625. Orlando boasts the world's largest *Hard Rock Café*, known as much for its T-shirts and music memorabilia as for its all-American menu – hamburgers generally cost $10–15, other main dishes up to $35. There's also frequent live music in the large performance space next to the restaurant (see below). Daily 11am–midnight.

Jimmy Buffett's Margaritaville CityWalk ☎407 224 2155, ⓦmargaritavilleorlando.com. Caribbean-style food like fish tacos and Key lime pie served in an appropriately tropical setting, complete with a volcano exploding with margarita mix. Busy and moderately priced, with dishes costing around $20. There's also live entertainment every night (see below). Mon–Thurs & Sun 9am–1am, Fri & Sat 9am–2am.

Nascar Sports Grille CityWalk ☎407 224 7223, ⓦnascarsportsgrille.com. If the idea of watching racing cars drive in very fast circles while you dine appeals, then this lively sports bar is your spot. There are actually all manner of sporting events on the many TVs, as well as a game room to keep the kids busy. Tasty nachos, burgers and the like, and most main dishes cost $15–20. Daily 11am–midnight.

NBA City CityWalk ☎407 363 5919. The moderately priced dishes such as chicken blue-cheese pasta and maple-glazed pork chops are more imaginative than at most themed restaurants. There's also an interactive area where you can test your basketball-shooting skills and see how high you can jump. Mon–Thurs & Sun 11am–10.30pm, Fri & Sat 11am–11.30pm.

BARS AND CLUBS

Bob Marley – A Tribute to Freedom CityWalk ☎407 224 3663. There's an on-site replica of Marley's Kingston home at this restaurant-cum-nightclub, holding artefacts from his prolific reggae career. Dishes such as oxtail stew show a Jamaican influence and there's a live reggae band and DJ in the courtyard every night. Mon–Thurs & Sun 4–10pm, Fri & Sat 4–11pm.

CityWalk's Rising Star CityWalk ☎407 224 2961. This energetic spot is a karaoke bar with a twist – on Tuesday to Saturday nights a live band and backing singers accompany those brave enough to perform; on Monday and Sunday there's a host and backing singers, but no band. Daily 8pm–2am.

the groove CityWalk ☎407 224 2166. If you want to dance, this is the place, with its huge dancefloor, flashing lights and good sound system. There's a DJ every night, as well as a few themed rooms for when you're done dancing. Cover charge is $7. Daily 9pm–2am.

Hard Rock Live CityWalk ☎407 351 5483, ⓦhardrock .com/live. This cavernous venue seats up to three thousand in the auditorium and hosts live performers, both locally and nationally known, almost every evening. Hours depend on show.

★ **Jimmy Buffett's Margaritaville** CityWalk ☎407 224 2155. There's live island-style music almost every night on the main stage starting at 10pm as well as an acoustic guitarist on the "Porch of Indecision". Potent margaritas help capture the famous laidback Florida mood perfectly. Daily 11am–2am.

Pat O'Brien's CityWalk ☎407 224 3663. Home of the famous Hurricane drink, this spot offers an Old New Orleans vibe of duelling pianos and wrought-iron

6

HIKING, BIKING AND PICNICKING

Just north of Universal Orlando, next to Florida's Turnpike, lies **Bill Frederick Park and Pool** at Turkey Lake, 3401 S Hiawassee Rd (daily: Nov–March 8am–5pm; April–Oct 8am–7pm; cars $4, ☎407 246 4486), a quiet place to have lunch by a lake, a swim in the pool, or let the kids run around a terrific playground. Five miles west of downtown Orlando off Hwy-50 (take Hwy-50 towards Clermont and look for the County Line Station on your right) is the start of the **West Orange Trail** (☎407 654 1108), 19 miles of scenic, paved pathways that end in the town of Apopka. You can rent bikes at West Orange Trail Bikes and Blades, located along the trail at 17914 Hwy-438, Winter Garden (☎407 877 0600, ⓦorlandobikerental.com).

balconies, with plenty of Mardi Gras beads to go around. Daily 4pm–2am.

Red Coconut Club CityWalk ✆ 407 224 2425. This self-billed "ultra lounge" has plenty of retro couches, a balcony

that's great for people-watching, live music Thurs–Sat. The bar staff pour a mean martini, too. Mon–Sat 7pm–2am, Sun 8pm–2am.

SeaWorld Orlando

6

Sea Harbor Drive, at the intersection of I-4 and the Central Florida Parkway, or I-4 and the Beeline Expressway • Open daily from 9am to between 6pm and 10pm depending on the season • $80 for a single-day ticket; weekday ticket $65, children under 3 free • ✆ 888 800 5447, ⊕ seaworld.com • Take Exit 71 if you're coming from the west on I-4, Exit 72 if you're coming from the east on I-4

SeaWorld Orlando is the biggest and slickest of Florida's sizeable crop of marine parks and attracts some four million visitors a year, despite being the subject of significant public scrutiny over its use of **captive killer whales** (see box below). If you decide to visit, allocate a whole day and be certain to pick up the free map and show schedule at the entrance. To beat the crowds, try going on the park's thrill rides during one of the live animal shows, when the number of people milling about the park shrinks.

The live shows

SeaWorld's signature event remains its most controversial: **One Ocean** – thirty minutes of tricks performed by killer whales (the first fourteen rows will get drenched during the performance). In a similar vein, **Blue Horizons**, at the Whale and Dolphin Theatre, has dolphins doing the tricks, with trapeze artists, high-divers and even parrots. Perhaps the best show for kids takes place at the **Sea Lion and Otter Stadium**, where the mammals put on a pantomime-style entertainment entitled **Clyde and Seamore Take on Pirate Island**. The Seaport Theater hosts **Pets Ahoy!**, in which animals, many of them rescued from local shelters, do their best to win you over by performing a multitude of routines. The last of the park's live shows, **A'Lure...The Call of the Ocean**, at the Nautilus Theater, has humans rather than animals performing acrobatics, accompanied by music and special effects.

The rides

The park's most thrilling ride is the roller coaster **Manta**, in which riders are strapped into seats in a prone position, head-first and face-down, as the ride soars and loops over some of the park's animal habitats. The "water coaster" **Journey to Atlantis** travels on both water and rails. However, it's not as exciting as it sounds, with the only exhilarating moment being a sheer drop that will soak everyone in the front row. Inside the adjacent gift shop are two **aquariums**: a 25,000-gallon, underfoot aquarium

---

THE BLACKFISH CONTROVERSY

Recently SeaWorld has found itself at the centre of a media storm regarding the ethics of keeping whales and dolphins in captivity. In 2013 the CNN film **Blackfish** told the story of Tilikum, a bull orca that has killed several people at marine parks including SeaWorld trainer Dawn Brancheau. The film also pointed out chronic health problems in captive killer whales. SeaWorld claimed the film was "shamefully misleading" but by early 2015 visitor numbers and stock price had both been hit, and several airlines, tour operators and performing artists such as Willie Nelson had ended their associations with the brand.

Given the global opportunities to **watch whales and dolphins in the wild**, SeaWorld's use of these fiercely intelligent marine mammals for entertainment appears increasingly anachronistic; its recent pledge to invest more money in research and enlarge its orca enclosures is unlikely to see a U-turn in public or corporate opinion any time soon.

filled with stingrays, and another one overhead (6000 gallons) with hammerhead sharks. The **Kraken** is a much better bet for thrills and spills; this incredibly high roller coaster reaches speeds of up to 65mph, performing numerous loop-the-loops as your feet dangle unnervingly in midair. The **Wild Arctic** complex (complete with artificial snow and ice) brings you close to beluga whales, walruses and polar bears, which are accessible by foot or via a bumpy but enjoyable flight-simulator ride, which takes you on a perilous helicopter trip through an Arctic blizzard. With less razzmatazz, plenty of smaller tanks and displays around the park offer a wealth of information about the underwater world. **Shark Encounter** includes a walk through a 60ft-long, acrylic-sided and -roofed tunnel, offering an idea of what swimming with sharks must feel like; at **Manta Aquarium**, visitors are surrounded by hundreds of rays and a giant Pacific octopus; and at **Turtle Trek**, visitors take a turtle's perspective on survival in the modern ocean. Elsewhere, buy plates of fish ($5) to feed to the stingrays at **Stingray Lagoon** or the dexterous sea lions and seals at **Pacific Point Preserve**. Dolphin feeding at **Dolphin Cove** (fish $7) was being phased out at the time of writing, reportedly being replaced with small-group encounters ($15). The area set aside for kids is **Shamu's Happy Harbor**, offering inner tubes, a kiddie coaster, slides and climbing nets.

SeaWorld's newest ride is **Antarctica: Empire of the Penguin**, a family-friendly trackless motion-sensor experience, wherein riders can choose either "mild" or "wild" as they journey through the South Pole in purple eight-seater carriages. You're deposited in the brand-new exhibit of the same name at the end of the ride, where you can view colonies of gentoos, rockhoppers, Adélie and king penguins.

Discovery Cove

Next to SeaWorld Orlando on Central Florida Parkway • Daily 8am–5.30pm • From $259 with the dolphin swim, or $179 without; prices include breakfast, lunch, some snacks and alcoholic drinks, plus unlimited fourteen-day access to SeaWorld Orlando and Aquatica; an extra $25 gets unlimited access to Busch Gardens in Tampa for fourteen consecutive days as well • ☎ 877 557 7404, ⓦ discoverycove.com

Discovery Cove is different from anything else you'll find in Orlando: a theme park without a theme; a water park without the slides; an aquarium without the glass tanks. It's billed as a multi-environment tropical paradise where the star attraction is swimming – or, more accurately, standing waist-deep in water – with captive dolphins in the chilly salt waters of the **Dolphin Lagoon**. On entry to the park you'll be given a time for your dolphin encounter, if you've booked it, which lasts for about half an hour and involves stroking, playing with, and riding on the dorsal fin of the docile creatures. Other attractions in the park include an **aviary** packed with tame exotic birds; the **Grand Reef** where you can snorkel with colourful fish; and a swimmable **Wind-away River** that winds around the Grand Reef and past a sandy **beach**.

Access to Discovery Cove is limited to about 1300 visitors a day, so you must reserve in advance. The high cost of admission does include use of equipment (wet suits, snorkelling gear, towels, lockers, animal-friendly sunscreen), breakfast, lunch, and some snacks and drinks, although once you've done your business with the dolphins and been on a few snorkelling expeditions, there's not much to do other than lounge around on the beach.

South of Orlando

The area **south of Orlando**, stretching fifteen miles or so south and east from Walt Disney World, contains more of the same kind of attractions found in Orlando itself, many of them, such as the venerable **Gatorland**, based on animals. The main towns in these parts are **Kissimmee**, just as sprawling as Orlando to the north, and the smaller, quainter **Celebration**, a more amenable place for a leisurely stroll – although you'll really need your own car to explore this area effectively.

Gatorland

14501 S Orange Blossom Trail • Open daily at 10am; closing times vary by season • $26.99, children 3–12 $18.99; Screamin' Gator Zip Line $69.99, including park admission • ☎ 407 855 5496 or ☎ 800 393 5297, ⓦ gatorland.com

Gatorland has been giving visitors an up-close look at Florida's most iconic animals, alligators, since 1949. The park's inhabitants also include crocodiles (whose noses are more pointed than alligators'), snakes and flamingos, but the undisputed highlight remains the **Gator Jumparoo Show**, in which hunks of chicken are suspended from wires and the largest alligators, using their powerful tail muscles, propel themselves out of the water to ferociously snatch their dinner.

When you arrive, pick up a schedule for the other main shows: along with Gator Jumparoo, there's the ethically dubious **Gator Wrestlin'**, where a 7- to 9ft gator is pinned down and its mouth pried open by a staff member; **Up Close Encounters**, where assorted creepy-crawlies are shared with the most terrified-looking members of the audience; and **Allie's Barnyard Petting Zoo**, which lets kids interact with some of the park's cuddlier creatures. The **Screamin' Gator Zip Line** offers a two-hour guided tour over five zip towers, from 35 to 65ft in the air, and over crocodile and alligator enclosures. Make reservations in advance to guarantee a spot, and wear closed-toe shoes. You can easily manage the whole park, shows and zip line in one day.

Kissimmee and around

Continuing south from Gatorland along Orange Blossom Trail brings you to the downtown portion of **KISSIMMEE**, a town spread across much of the rough acreage south of Orlando.

The Monument of States

300 E Monument Ave, in Lakefront Park

Although easy to walk around, Kissimmee's downtown holds little of interest except for the **Monument of States**, a funky 40ft obelisk comprising garishly painted concrete blocks adorned with pieces of stone and fossil representing all of the American states and 21 foreign countries, erected in 1943 as a symbol of American unity after World War II.

Lake Tohopekaliga

Take a stroll to Lakeshore Boulevard and admire pretty **Lake Tohopekaliga**, headwaters to the Everglades and home to many native birds, as well as alligators and bald eagles. To get a closer look at the wildlife, take a thirty-minute airboat ride with **Boggy Creek Airboat Rides** (daily 9am–5pm; $26.95, children 3–10 $20.95; ☎ 407 344 9550, ⓦ bcairboats.com), which leave from Southport Park, about nineteen miles south from the intersection of Poinciana Boulevard and US-192. Night tours and hour-long tours are also available.

Old Town

5770 W Irlo Bronson Memorial Hwy • Shops daily 10am–11pm, rides daily 2–11pm, but individual ride hours vary • Free to enter; buy individual ride tickets or an all-day pass for $15 weekdays and $20 weekends • ☎ 407 396 4888, ⓦ myoldtownusa.com

Kissimmee's other attractions are spread out along US-192 or just to the south of US-192. **Old Town** is a low-rent throwback to a traditional fairground complete with carousel, bumper cars and go karts. It's not overly exciting, except for the kitsch factor, unless you visit on a Friday or Saturday night at around 8.30pm – on Friday, muscle cars take to the street en masse, and Saturday sees hundreds of classic cars paraded up and down the streets.

Green Meadows Petting Farm and Horse World Riding Stables

Petting Farm 1368 S Poinciana Blvd • Daily 9.30am–4pm • $23; ☎ 407 846 0770, ⓦ greenmeadowsfarm.com • **Riding Stables** 3705 S Poinciana Blvd • Daily 9am–5pm • $45.95–79.95 depending on the ride • ☎ 407 847 4343, ⓦ horseworldstables.com

With a peaceful, rural setting a couple of miles south of Old Town, **Green Meadows Petting Farm** is a refreshing change of pace from the bustle of the major parks. The two-hour guided tour takes in all the usual farm animals, and hands-on experience is encouraged, from simple petting to milking a cow. Kids also enjoy pony- and tractor-drawn hay-rides. Horse rides for adults are offered a little further down the road at **Horse World Riding Stables**.

Reptile World Serpentarium

5705 E Irlo Bronson Memorial Hwy, St Cloud • Tues–Sun 10am–5pm; viewings of the extraction process daily noon & 3pm • $8.75, children 6–17 $6.75, children 3–5 $5.75 • ☎ 407 892 6905, ⓦ reptileworldserpentarium.com

Travelling east from Kissimmee along US-192 brings you to the town of St Cloud, where you'll find the wonderfully offbeat **Reptile World Serpentarium**, presided over by George VanHorn, who has been extracting snake venom for sale to antivenom research laboratories for years. He handles several moody vipers, rattlesnakes and cobras; the stub at the end of one of his fingers is testament to the occupational hazards. You can view the fascinating **extraction process** twice daily; the rest of the place – basically a small collection of snakes in glass tanks and a family of alligators – can be perused quickly.

Celebration

If you just can't get enough of the squeaky-clean Disney concept, head to **CELEBRATION** (ⓦcelebrationfl.com), a 4900-acre town nestled between Kissimmee and Disney's theme parks (off US-192) created by Disney and officially opened in 1996. The Disney people did massive sociological research before settling on the design they believed would capture the American ideal of community: old-fashioned exteriors, homes close to the road so neighbours are more likely to interact, and a congenial old-fashioned downtown area beside a tranquil lake. World-famous **architects** were brought in to design major buildings: Phillip Johnson, Ritchie & Fiore designed the Town Hall; Michael Graves the post office; César Pelli the 1950s-style movie house; and Robert A.M. Stern the health centre.

The first 350 residential sites sold out before a single model was even complete. Enthusiasts applaud Celebration's friendly small-town feel, where town events are well attended and children can walk carefree to school. Detractors use words such as "contrived" and "sterile" to describe the atmosphere. The town, though, is worth a short visit – not least for its good restaurants and virtually traffic-free streets that are ideal for a leisurely stroll. Stop by to determine for yourself whether this homogeneity is an evolutionary stage of the American Dream, a touch of elitist Big Brother, or some sort of smug cult.

ARRIVAL AND DEPARTURE

By bus The flat rate from Orlando International Airport (see p.267) to Kissimmee or Celebration is $22 with Mears Transportation (☎ 407 423 5566, ⓦ mearstransportation .com). Lynx Buses also link the airport with Kissimmee and Celebration (#11 or #42). All buses depart from Level 1 (on the "A Side" concourse) every 30min between approximately 5.30am and 11.30pm. The Kissimmee Greyhound terminal is at 103 E Dakin Ave (☎ 407 847 3911), and is handy if you're staying along US-192.

By train The Kissimmee Amtrak station is at 111 E Dakin Ave (☎ 407 933 1170), and provides easier access to US-192 hotels than its Orlando counterpart.

By car Hwy-192/Irlo Bronson Memorial Hwy is the main east–west artery through the area; it joins up with both I-4 and the 417/Central Florida Greenway toll road.

INFORMATION

Tourist information The well-stocked Kissimmee Convention & Visitors Bureau is at 215 Celebration Place (Mon–Fri 8am–5pm; ☎ 407 742 8200, ⓦ experiencekissimmee.com).

ACCOMMODATION

Many people choose to stay in the budget hotels and motels that line **US-192** (also known as Irlo Bronson Memorial Hwy). Not only do these establishments tend to be cheaper than their Orlando equivalents (you can usually get a room for around $50 per night), but they are also close to Disney World (often with free shuttles to the parks), and are most likely to have rooms available at busy times.

6

KISSIMMEE

★**Comfort Suites Maingate East** 2775 Florida Plaza Blvd ☎ 407 397 7848, ⊕comfortsuitesfl.com; map p.266. This chain motel offers good value for money, comfortable, clean suites and a free deluxe continental breakfast, just a few miles from Disney's main gate. $109

Cypress Cove Nudist Resort & Spa 4425 Pleasant Hill Rd ☎ 407 933 5870, ⊕cypresscoveresort.com. For something a little different, ditch the clothes and head to this full-service resort catering to those who prefer to holiday in the nude. Choose from spacious apartments or smaller hotel rooms, some recently remodelled; camping and RV hook-ups are also available. Camping $81 for full hook-up, rooms $142, apartments $185

Embassy Suites Orlando Lake Buena Vista South 4955 Kyngs Heath Rd ☎ 407 597 4000, ⊕embassysuites3.hilton.com; map p.266. Each of these comfortable suites features a bedroom and separate living

area. There's a free cooked-to-order breakfast and a complimentary happy hour each evening too. $132

Orlando/Kissimmee KOA 2644 Happy Camper Place ☎ 407 396 2400, ⊕koa.com; map p.266. A bit pricey but suited to tents and RVs, and offers a large heated pool as well as a playground and games room for kids. Tent camping $42, RV sites $60, lodges $115

Palm Lakefront Resort & Hostel 4840 W Irlo Bronson Memorial Hwy ☎ 407 396 1759, ⊕orlandohostels.com; map p.266. The obvious choice for backpackers, this hostel has six-bed, single-sex dorms, private rooms, a pool and a pleasant lakefront location. Dorms $19, doubles $40

CELEBRATION

Bohemian Hotel Celebration 700 Bloom St ☎ 407 566 6000, ⊕celebrationhotel.com. The nicest hotel in Celebration is a predictably upmarket and classy place, with elegant rooms overlooking the town's picturesque lake. $152

EATING

Along with a couple of high-profile **dinner shows** (see box, p.271), US-192 is lined with **chain restaurants**, many of them offering cheap and cheerful all-you-can-eat meals. Downtown Kissimmee has a few restaurants catering to lunching office workers, but by far the most appealing selection of restaurants is to be found in Celebration.

KISSIMMEE

Chef John's Place 3753 Pleasant Hill Rd ☎ 407 343 4227, ⊕chefjohnsplace.com. This fantastic spot is a little south of Kissimmee proper, but it's well worth the drive. Chef John Walker's gumbo, smoked chicken and Key lime pie make for a delicious meal you won't soon forget. Most dishes $13–25. Mon–Sat 11.30am–9pm.

CELEBRATION

Café d'Antonio 691 Front St ☎ 407 566 2233, ⊕antoniosonline.com. A good, reasonably priced Italian restaurant, serving predominantly meat and pasta dishes ($12–30) in an upmarket atmosphere. Mon–Fri 11.30am–3pm & 5–10pm, Sat 11.30am–10pm, Sun 11.30am–9pm.

Celebration Town Tavern 721 Front St ☎ 407 566 2526, ⊕thecelebrationtowntavern.com. Specializes in New England seafood – although the barbecued baby back ribs ($22) are possibly the tastiest item on the menu. Light meals are available at the bar until 2am, making this a favourite among Celebration's night owls. Most dishes $15–20. Mon–Sat 11am–2am, Sun 10am–2am.

★**Columbia Restaurant** 649 Front St ☎ 407 566 1505. Famous for high-standard, moderately priced Spanish food, notably paella, eaten appropriately enough in a dining room that looks like something straight out of a luxurious Iberian villa. Live Spanish folk music Friday and Saturday evenings. Most dishes $20–30. Daily 11.30am–10.30pm.

The northern suburbs

Head a few miles north from downtown Orlando for a taste of Florida living without the mouse-ear hats. The northern suburbs are an area of welcoming residential neighbourhoods such as **Winter Park**, **Eatonville** and **Maitland**, adorned by parks, lakes and a smattering of decent museums and art galleries which, for all their varying degrees of quality, offer a refreshing change of pace for those with theme-park fatigue.

Winter Park

A couple of miles northeast of Loch Haven Park (see p.263), **WINTER PARK** has been socially a cut above Orlando since it was launched in 1887 as "a beautiful winter retreat for well-to-do people". For all its obvious money – a mix of new yuppie dollars and old wealth – Winter Park is a very likeable place, with a pervasive sense of community and a touch of New Age affluence.

Rollins College and the Cornell Fine Arts Museum

Fairbanks Ave • Museum: Tues–Fri 10am–4pm, Sat & Sun noon–5pm • Free • ☎ 407 646 2526, ⓦ rollins.edu/cfam

On Fairbanks Avenue stand the Mediterranean Revival buildings of **Rollins College**, the oldest recognized college in the state, boasting a tiny but respected liberal arts faculty. Other than its neat landscaping, the campus has just one point of interest: the **Cornell Fine Arts Museum**, where a few Italian Renaissance paintings brighten the otherwise staid bundle of modest nineteenth-century European and American art. The temporary exhibitions are often more contemporary and vibrant.

Albin Polasek Museum and Sculpture Gardens

633 Osceola Ave • Tues–Sat 10am–4pm, Sun 1–4pm • $5 • ☎ 407 647 6294, ⓦ polasek.org

You'll find a more personal art collection than the Cornell's at the **Albin Polasek Museum and Sculpture Gardens**, the former home of Czech-born sculptor Albin Polasek, who arrived penniless in the US in 1901. He spent most of his time over the next fifty years winning big-money commissions, many of the profits from which have been ploughed back into this museum. The most striking sculptures – technically accomplished, Realist works with classical, mythical and liturgical themes – are on display amid the colourful flowers and plants of the three-acre gardens.

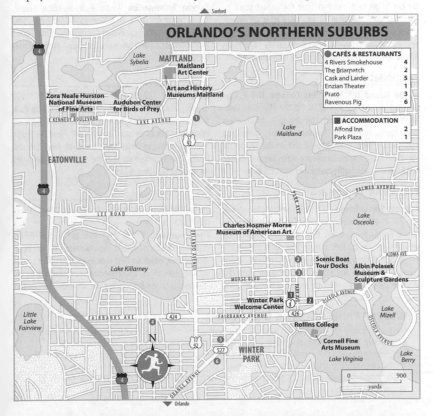

ORLANDO'S NORTHERN SUBURBS

CAFÉS & RESTAURANTS

4 Rivers Smokehouse	4
The Briarpatch	2
Cask and Larder	5
Enzian Theater	1
Prato	3
Ravenous Pig	6

ACCOMMODATION

Alfond Inn	2
Park Plaza	1

Park Avenue

The showpiece of Winter Park is **Park Avenue**, the town's main north–south thoroughfare, which meets Fairbanks Avenue at the gate of Rollins College. This eminently strollable street is lined with chic boutiques, elegant restaurants and diverse art galleries, of which Scott Laurent Collection at no. 348 (daily 11am–7pm; ☎407 629 0278, ⓦscottlaurentcollection.com) is worth a special look for its impressive selection of objets d'art, particularly the colourful glasswork.

6

Charles Hosmer Morse Museum of American Art

445 N Park Ave • Tues–Sat 9.30am–4pm, Sun 1–4pm; Nov–April also Fri 9.30am–8pm • $5 • ☎ 407 645 5311, ⓦ morsemuseum.org

The **Charles Hosmer Morse Museum of American Art** houses the collections of its namesake, one of Winter Park's founding fathers. The major exhibits are drawn from the output of Louis Comfort Tiffany, a legend for his innovative Art Nouveau stained-glass lamps and windows that furnished high-society homes around the turn of the twentieth century. Great creativity and craftsmanship went into Tiffany's work: he was one of the first artisans to use the copper foil method, instead of the centuries-old lead cane method, imbuing it with coloured images of water lilies, leaves and even strutting peacocks. Tiffany's work is so stunning the rest of the museum's admirable possessions, including paintings by Hermann Herzog and John Singer Sargent, pale in comparison.

ARRIVAL AND INFORMATION
WINTER PARK

By car To get to Winter Park from the airport you'll go north on SR436/Semoran Rd and head west on Aloma, which will bring you to the bottom of Park Avenue. To get to Maitland and Eatonville, head north on US 17/92/Mills Ave, which turns into Orlando Ave once it hits Winter Park.

Tourist information Winter Park Welcome Center, 151 W Lyman Ave (Mon–Fri 8.30am–5pm, Sat 9am–2pm; ☎407 644 8281, ⓦcityofwinterpark.org), has good local information and brochures not found at the Official Visitor Center.

ACCOMMODATION

★**The Alfond Inn at Rollins College** 300 E New England Ave ☎407 998 8090, ⓦthealfondinn.com. Winter Park's newest hotel is this chic spot, which offers sleek rooms adorned in chocolate browns, green and aquamarine. There's a lovely pool, and on-site restaurant *Hamilton's Kitchen* serves up creative mains like pan-seared monkfish and fresh truffle mushroom risotto. $249

Park Plaza 307 S Park Ave ☎407 647 1072, ⓦparkplazahotel.com. If you do want to soak up Park Avenue's bustling atmosphere, one of the best (and most affordable) places to stay is the *Park Plaza*, a 1920s "vintage" boutique hotel reminiscent of New Orleans' French Quarter, where some of the rooms have balconies overlooking the street. $149

EATING AND DRINKING

4 Rivers Smokehouse 1600 W Fairbanks Ave ☎407 474 8377, ⓦ4rsmokehouse.com. The best barbecue in central Florida hands down, this place gets wildly busy around prime dining hours, so try to time your visit for early or late. Best dishes include the messy pig sandwich, which comes with coleslaw and a pile of roast pork, all slathered in sauce. Desserts are a must-try as well – if you've saved

room. Main dishes under $15. Mon–Thurs 11am–8pm, Fri & Sat 11am–9pm.

The Briarpatch 252 N Park Ave ☎407 628 8651, ⓦthebriarpatchrestaurant.com. Known for its huge slices of cake, which are best sampled with a coffee on the outside tables. There's also a good brunch menu with mains like raspberry-and-Brie-stuffed French toast for around

---

WINTER PARK'S SCENIC BOAT TOUR

To discover why those who can afford to live anywhere choose Winter Park, take the **Scenic Boat Tour**. The one-hour, narrated voyage of attractive Lake Osceola and adjoining lakes focuses on the rich flora and fauna – including plenty of alligators – although a good part of the fun is in staring enviously at the expensive lakeside homes. Boats leave from the dock at 312 E Morse Blvd, three blocks east of Park Avenue (hourly 10am–4pm; $12; ☎407 644 4056, ⓦscenicboattours.com).

$12. Mon–Sat 7am–5pm, Sun 8am–5pm.

Cask and Larder 565 W Fairbanks Ave ☎ 321 280 4200, ⓦ caskandlarder.com. This immensely popular sister restaurant to *Ravenous Pig* (see below) bills itself as a Southern Public House, and serves creative fare such as a beans and greens salad and Florida frog legs. Menus change seasonally. Most dishes $14–28. Mon–Sat 5–10pm, Sun 10.30am–3pm (brunch) & 5–10pm.

★**Enzian Theater** 1300 S Orlando Ave ☎ 407 629 0054, ⓦ enzian.org. This funky indie movie house also has one of the best outdoor bars in Orlando. There's a full menu, with creative dishes like *carnitas* tacos and quinoa-stuffed peppers. There's a great cocktail menu as well, and free movies on the lawn every Wednesday night, weather permitting. Most dishes under $15. Mon–Thurs & Sun 11am–11pm, Fri & Sat 11am–1am.

★**Prato** 124 N Park Ave ☎ 407 262 0050, ⓦ prato-wp.com. Occupying a prime spot on Park Ave, this convivial Italian restaurant serves creative home-made pasta and pizza, using seasonal, locally sourced ingredients. Standouts include the "widowmaker" pizza, with a fried egg atop the sauce, and truffled potato gnocchi. Most main dishes $30 or under; pastas $9–16. Mon & Tues 5.30pm–11pm, Wed–Sat 11.30am–3pm & 5.30pm–11pm, Sun 11.30am–3pm & 5.30pm–10pm.

★**Ravenous Pig** 1234 Orange Ave ☎ 407 628 2333, ⓦ theravenouspig.com. One of Orlando's best dining spots, this intimate gastropub with exposed brick walls and a rich wood bar brings a bit of casual sophistication to the Winter Park dining scene. The menu changes frequently, but you won't go wrong with favourites like the pub burger with blue cheese or the steak frites. Dinner main courses from $24. Tues–Thurs 11.30am–2pm & 5.30–9.30pm, Fri & Sat 11.30am–2pm & 5.30–10.30pm.

Eatonville

Just to the west of Winter Park lies the small town of **EATONVILLE**, the first incorporated African-American municipality in the United States. Three black men founded the town in 1875 so that, according to an 1889 notice published in the local newspaper, black Americans could "solve the great race problem by securing a home … in a Negro city governed by Negroes", and land was sold for $5–10 an acre to encourage relocation.

The Hurston: Zora Neale Hurston National Museum of Fine Arts

227 E Kennedy Blvd • Mon–Fri 9am–4pm, Sat 11am–1pm • Donation suggested • ☎ 407 647 3307, ⓦ zoranealehurstonmuseum.com

Renowned author Zora Neale Hurston, an Eatonville native, used the town as the setting for novels such as *Their Eyes Were Watching God*. Stop by **The Hurston: Zora Neale Hurston National Museum of Fine Arts**, which features rotating exhibits relating to African-American life. Here you can pick up the pamphlet *A Walking Tour of Eatonville, Florida*, which gives exhaustive historical explanations of every possible point of interest, all of which you can explore on foot in less than an hour.

Maitland

Directly north of Winter Park, **MAITLAND** is a sleepy bedroom community, which nonetheless holds a few attractions for visitors, including a charming arts centre and a beloved farmers' market at Lake Lily every Sunday.

Art and History Museums Maitland at Maitland Art Center

Maitland Art Center 231 W Packwood Ave • Tues–Sun 11am–4pm • $3 • ☎ 407 539 2181, ⓦ artandhistory.org Maitland Historical Museum and Telephone Museum 221 W Packwood Ave • Thurs–Sun noon–4pm • $3 • ☎ 407 644 1364, ⓦ artandhistory.org

The luscious sunsets over Maitland's Lake Sybelia inspired a young artist named Jules André Smith to buy six acres on its banks during the 1930s. With the financial assistance of Mary Bok (wealthy widow of Edward Bok; see p.380), Smith established what is now the **Maitland Art Center**, a collection of stuccoed studios, offices and apartments decorated with Aztec- and Maya-style murals and grouped around garden courtyards. Smith invited other American artists to spend working winters here, but his abrasive personality scared many potential guests away. The colony continued in various forms until Smith's death in 1959, never becoming the aesthetes' commune he'd hoped for. There are temporary exhibitions and a permanent collection of Smith's etchings, paintings and sculpture, but it's the unique design of the place that warrants a visit. A number of local painters and sculptors claim to have felt Smith's presence, his ghost dispensing artistic guidance.

A few steps from the Maitland Art Center sit the **Maitland Historical Museum** and the **Telephone Museum**. The front rooms of the combined museums host rotating exhibits with some bearing on Maitland life – not overly exciting unless you have a particular interest in the area. The back room, on the other hand, is filled with wonderful vintage telephones, commemorating the day in 1910 when a Maitland grocer installed telephones in the homes of his customers, enabling them to order groceries from the comfort of their armchairs.

Audubon Center for Birds of Prey

1101 Audubon Way • Tues–Sun 10am–4pm • $5, children 3–12 $4 • ☎ 407 644 0190, ⓦ fl.audubon.org

The only other reason to linger in Maitland is the **Audubon Center for Birds of Prey**, run by the Florida Audubon Society, the state's oldest and largest conservation organization. The house is primarily an educational centre and gift shop, but the adjacent rehabilitation facility is one of the largest in the southeast US, treating injured and orphaned birds, such as ospreys, owls, hawks, eagles, falcons and the odd vulture, with the aim of returning them to the wild.

North of Orlando

Back-to-back residential areas dissolve into fields of fruit and vegetables **north of Orlando**'s city limits. Around here, farming still has the upper hand over tourism. Although it's easy to skim through on I-4, consider a more leisurely drive along the older local roads.

Sanford and around

Once nicknamed "Celery City" on account of its major agricultural crop, **SANFORD**, fifteen miles north of Maitland on US-92 (also known as US-17 along this section), hasn't had a lot going for it since the boom years of the early twentieth century, but the historic downtown does offer a few hours of antique perusing, as well as a few good restaurants.

Sanford Museum

520 E 1st St • Tues–Fri 11am–4pm, Sat 1–4pm • Free • ☎ 407 688 5198

Visit the **Sanford Museum** for more about the town's history – and Henry Shelton Sanford, the turn-of-the-nineteenth-century lawyer and diplomat who created it – or pick up a self-guided tour map and venture around several buildings of divergent classical architecture in the adjacent old downtown district.

Flea World

On US-17/92 • Fri–Sun 9am–6pm • Free • ⓦ fleaworld.com

As you leave Sanford on US-17/92 to return to Orlando, you'll pass the vast warehouse that is **Flea World**, a massive flea market that's worth a browse for the sheer enormity of it; meticulous browsing is required to find the odd gem.

Mount Dora

To see an authentic Victorian-era Florida village on a pristine lake, feast your eyes on the picket fences, wrought-iron balconies and fancy wood-trimmed buildings that make up **MOUNT DORA**. Antique lovers should check out **Renningers Antique Center**, just east of Mount Dora at 20651 US-441 (Fri 10am–4pm, Sat & Sun 9am–5pm;

☎ 352 383 8393, ⓦ renningers.net), a large weekend market where you'll find most of the area's antique dealers conveniently grouped under one roof.

Cassadaga

A village populated by spiritualists may conjure up images of beaded curtains and crystal balls, but the few hundred residents of **CASSADAGA**, just east of I-4, fifteen miles north of Sanford, are disarmingly conventional citizens in normal homes, offering to reach out and touch the spirit world for a very down-to-earth fee. Cassadaga has been around since 1895, when a young New Yorker bought 35 acres of land here after being told during a séance he would one day be instrumental in founding a spiritualist community.

These days, several **spiritual centres** offer a range of services, from palm and tarot readings to full-blown sessions with a medium. Prices vary little from centre to centre: $60 for thirty minutes, $75 for 45 minutes, and $100 for one hour are the going rates.

Cassadaga Spiritualist Camp
Andrew Jackson Davis Building, on the corner of Rte-4139 (Cassadaga Rd) and Stevens St • ☎ 386 228 2880, ⓦ cassadaga.org

The Cassadaga Spiritualist Camp offers regular seminars and lectures covering topics from UFO cover-ups to out-of-body travel, and also has a well-stocked psychic bookshop staffed by helpful clerks who'll show you everything from the latest spiritualist literature to the store's collection of crystals.

DeLand and around

Intended as the "Athens of Florida" when founded in 1876, **DELAND**, four miles north of Cassadaga, west off I-4, is really just an old-fashioned central-Florida town featuring a domed courthouse, an old theatre, and a welcoming atmosphere.

Stetson University
Woodland Blvd • ☎ 386 822 7100, ⓦ stetson.edu

DeLand boasts the state's oldest private educational centre, **Stetson University**, whose red-brick facades have stood since the 1880s. The school is named after hat manufacturer John B. Stetson, a generous donor to the university and one of its founding trustees. Pick up a free tour map from Griffith Hall for a walk around the vintage buildings.

DeLeon Springs
Ten miles north of DeLand on US-17 • Daily 8am–sunset • Cars $6, pedestrians and cyclists $2 • ☎ 386 985 4212

DeLeon Springs State Park is one of the better-known springs in the area, where thousands of gallons of pure water bubble continuously up from artesian springs. You can swim, canoe and picnic in and beside the spring, and even make your own pancakes at the *Old Spanish Sugar Mill Grill & Griddle House* (see p.305).

Lake Woodruff National Wildlife Refuge
Sunrise to sunset; visitor centre open Nov–March daily 8am–4.30pm • Free • ☎ 386 985 4673

Following US-17 a few miles west to Grand Avenue, you'll come upon the stunning **Lake Woodruff National Wildlife Refuge**, 22,000 acres of untouched wetlands that are home to over 200 species of bird, including the Southern bald eagle, many types of fish and other creatures.

Barberville
1776 Lightfoot Lane • Mon–Sat 9am–4pm • $6, children 6–12 $4 • ☎ 386 749 2959, ⓦ pioneersettlement.org

Seven miles north of Lake Woodruff Wildlife Refuge on US-17, the tiny crossroads community of **Barberville** celebrates rural Florida with its **Pioneer Settlement for the**

Creative Arts, a small collection of turn-of-the-nineteenth-century buildings, including a train station, a log cabin, a turpentine still, a schoolhouse, a bridgehouse and a general store. Here, an assembly of pottery wheels, looms and other tools are put to use during informative **guided tours**, which generally last just under two hours. Tours (included in the admission price) are not scheduled; if you'd like one, just ask once you're in the settlement.

Blue Spring State Park

W French Ave, Orange City, off US-17/92 • Daily 8am–sunset • Cars $6, pedestrians and cyclists $2 • ☏ 386 775 3663

The year-round 22°C (72°F) waters at **Blue Spring State Park**, seven miles south of DeLand, attract **manatees** between mid-November and mid-March. Affectionately known as "sea cows", these best loved of Florida's endangered animals swim here from the cooler waters of the St John's River, so the colder it is there, the more manatees you'll see. Aside from staking out the manatees from several observation platforms (early morning on a cold winter's day is the best time for sightings), you also get the chance to see **Thursby House**, a large frame dwelling built by pioneer settlers in 1872.

Hontoon Island State Park

☏ 386 736 5309 • Ferry daily from 8am to about 1hr before sunset from a landing stage in the park's car parking area

Not far from Blue Spring is **Hontoon Island State Park**, a striking dollop of wooded land set within very flat and swampy terrain. Without a private boat, Hontoon Island is reachable only by a **ferry** that runs on donations. Remarkably, the island once held a boatyard and cattle ranch, but today it's inhabited only by the hardy souls who decide to stay over in one of its cabins or campgrounds (see p.305).

ARRIVAL AND DEPARTURE

NORTH OF ORLANDO

BY PLANE

Orlando Sanford International Airport (☏ 407 585 4000, ⓦ orlandosanfordairport.com) is 20 miles north of downtown Orlando and receives charter flights from the UK, as well as Allegiant Air (see p.21) flights from a selection of smaller US cities.

BY CAR AND SUNRAIL

I-4 passes southwest–northeast through Disney and downtown Orlando to Daytona Beach where it joins up with I-95 N. There are exits for Sanford, Cassadaga and DeLand. Alternatively, you can take US-17/92 to Sanford. To get to Mount Dora, get off I-4 at 46W, or take Hwy 441 (Orange Blossom Trail) all the way from central Orlando. The SunRail also stops in Sanford.

INFORMATION AND TOURS

MOUNT DORA

Tourist information The Chamber of Commerce is at 341 Alexander St (Mon–Fri 9am–5pm, ☏ 352 383 2165, ⓦ mountdora.com).

Tours The Chamber of Commerce has a free brochure containing a walking tour around the old houses of the town's compact centre.

DELAND

Tourist information The Chamber of Commerce, 336 N Woodland Blvd, DeLand (Mon–Fri 9am–5pm; ☏ 386 734 4331, ⓦ delandchamber.org), has brochures on local points of interest.

ACCOMMODATION

SANFORD

Higgins House 420 S Oak Ave ☏ 407 324 9238, ⓦ higginshouse.com. If Sanford's historic buildings, antique shops and quiet charm appeal, stay at this Victorian B&B just a few blocks from downtown, featuring three rooms with antiques and wicker furniture and huge, healthy breakfasts. $150

MOUNT DORA

Lakeside Inn 100 N Alexander St ☏ 352 383 4101, ⓦ lakeside-inn.com. A stay at Mount Dora's genteel *Lakeside Inn* might just transport you to Old Florida, with a long front porch where you can watch sunsets over the lake. $129

Simpson's Bed & Breakfast 441 N Donnelly St

☏352 383 2087, ⊛simpsonsbnb.com. Bed and breakfasts fit in perfectly with Mount Dora's quaintness, and they're not in short supply. This is a good, central option, with six suites, all with kitchenettes, and some eccentrically decorated with palm trees and watering cans on the walls. $115

CASSADAGA
Cassadaga Hotel 355 Cassadaga Rd ☏386 228 2323, ⊛cassadagahotel.net. If you want to stick around for the night, try the *Cassadaga Hotel*. Rooms are vaguely Victorian, and it's said the hotel is (predictably) haunted. There's an on-site psychic centre, and a healing and wellness centre. $55

DELAND
DeLand Artisan Inn 215 S Woodland Blvd ☏386 873 4675, ⊛delandartisaninn.com. This all-suite boutique hotel features comfortable, stylish rooms, all recently redone in greys and oranges. $139

BLUE SPRING STATE PARK
Blue Spring State Park campground Reservations on ☏800 326 3521 or via ⊛floridastateparks .reserveamerica.com. Accommodation in the Blue Spring State Park includes a campground and a/c cabins that sleep up to four people. Camping $24, cabins $95

HONTOON ISLAND STATE PARK
Hontoon Island State Park cabins Reservations on ☏800 326 3521 or via ⊛floridastateparks .reserveamerica.com. In Hontoon Island State Park there are six rustic cabins of various sizes, and some very basic campgrounds. Camping $18, cabins $30

EATING

SANFORD
★**Hollerbach's Willow Tree Café** 205 E 1st St ☏407 321 2204, ⊛willowtreecafe.com. Dine on some of central Florida's most authentic German food at this fun spot, with a large outdoor patio, friendly German waitresses and live polka bands at weekends. There are more than fifty German beers and wines to sample, as well seven preparations of traditional *Schnitzel*. Tues–Thurs & Sun 11am–9pm, Fri & Sat 11am–10pm.

MOUNT DORA
The Goblin Market 330 Dora Drawdy Lane ☏352 735 0059, ⊛thegoblinmarketrestaurant.com. At this popular, mid-priced place, hidden down a quiet side-street, enjoy gourmet food like New Zealand rack of lamb and New York strip with chestnut sage savoury bread pudding; reservations recommended. Dinner mains from $27. Tues–Thurs 11am–9pm, Fri & Sat 11am –10pm, Sun 11.30am–3.30pm.
Pisces Rising 239 W 4th Ave ☏352 385 2669, ⊛piscesrisingdining.com. With a great happy hour and live music four nights a week on the large deck overlooking Lake Dora, you'd be forgiven for thinking this fun spot is more bar than restaurant. But you'd also be missing out on some of the area's best seafood, with dishes like shrimp-n-grits and Caribbean snapper. Dinner mains from $20. Mon–Thurs 11.30–9pm, Fri & Sat 11.30am–10pm, Sun 11am–9pm.
The Windsor Rose Tea Room 142 W 4th Ave ☏352 735 2551, ⊛windsorrose-tearoom.com. It would be sacrilegious to come to Mount Dora and not take tea and scones at one of the many English-inspired teahouses dotted around town. This cute spot serves a full English tea for two for $36, plus other British favourites such as Cornish pasties and bangers and mash. Mon, Tues, Thurs & Fri 11am–4.45pm, Sat & Sun 9am–4.45pm.

DELAND
Santorini Greek Cuisine 210 N Woodland Blvd, ☏386 736 7726, ⊛santoriniindeland.com. Some of the best Greek food you'll enjoy this side of Tarpon Springs (see p.376), you can't go wrong with the *dolmades* or chicken Corfu. Mon–Thurs 11–8.30pm, Fri & Sat 11am–10pm.

DELEON SPRINGS
Old Spanish Sugar Mill Grill In the grounds of DeLeon Springs State Park, at the corner of Ponce de León Blvd and Burt Parks Rd, west of US-17 ☏386 985 5644. You can make your own pancakes at this place, set in a historic sugar mill. Mon–Fri 9am–4pm, Sat & Sun 8am–4pm.

6

The
northeast

DAYTONA SPEEDWAY

The northeast

The roots of modern Florida – and some would argue, the United States itself – can be found in the northeastern part of the state, settled by the Spanish in 1565, some forty years before English colonists arrived in Virginia. This long history colours much of the region, no more so than in St Augustine, the oldest permanent settlement in the nation. Around fifty miles south lies Daytona Beach, a small town with a big-name stretch of sand, and equally famous speedway track. The towns making up the Space Coast, further south, primarily serve the hordes passing through to visit NASA's impressively efficient Kennedy Space Center, birthplace of the nation's outer space exploits.

North of St Augustine and just inland, the city of **Jacksonville** merits more than a cursory glance, especially for its world-class **Cummer Museum of Art**, as you strike out toward the state's northeastern extremity. Here, flirting with the coast of Georgia, slender **Amelia Island** is fringed by gorgeous silver sands and features a quirky, posh Victorian-era main town. Yet, as with much of Florida, it's the **beach** that provides the biggest allure. Substantially free of commercial exploitation, the 190 miles of coastline dominating Florida's northeast may have you feeling like doing nothing more strenuous than settling down beside the ocean.

When planning your trip, remember that, owing to the less tropical climate, the northeast coast's tourist **seasons** are the reverse of those of the southeast coast: the crowded time here is the summer, when accommodation is more expensive and harder to come by than during the winter months.

The Space Coast

The barrier islands that occupy much of the Treasure Coast (see p.203) continue north into what's known as the **SPACE COAST**, the home of NASA's phenomenal **Kennedy Space Center**, which occupies flat, marshy Merritt Island bulging into the Atlantic just fifty miles east of Orlando. Many of the visitors who flock here are surprised to find that the land from which rockets are launched is also a sizeable **wildlife refuge** framed by several miles of rough coastline. Except for the beach-oriented communities on the ocean, the towns of the Space Coast are of little interest other than for low-cost overnight stops or meal breaks.

VISITING THE SPACE COAST

Getting around For most of the Space Coast you'll need a car to get around. The nearest Greyhound bus stops are at Titusville and Melbourne, from where it is possible to take local buses to Cocoa Beach (see p.315).

Tourist information You can get general information about the area by calling the Space Coast Office of Tourism on ☎ 877 572 3224, or by visiting ⊕ visitspacecoast.com.

Highlights

❶ Kennedy Space Center This huge space theme park showcases the NASA space programme through bus tours, exhibits and wildly entertaining simulations. **See p.311**

❷ Daytona Beach The famous beach you can drive on if you watch your speed, and the famous race track where you can drive as fast as you like. **See p.318**

❸ St Augustine North America's oldest city, with Spanish charm, cobbled streets and an entertaining pirate museum. **See p.326**

❹ Crocodile Crossing Fly across St Augustine Alligator Farm on the only zipline to traverse a wildlife park. **See p.337**

❺ Jacksonville food Middle Eastern cuisine with a Floridian twist – feast on "camel riders" and "steak in a sack". **See p.343**

❻ Timucuan Ecological & Historic Preserve Explore untouched forests, old slave plantations, French forts and tranquil beaches, just a short drive from Jacksonville. **See p.344**

❼ Amelia Island A beautifully restored Victorian-era town, a great beach area, and fewer tourists than you'd expect. **See p.347**

HIGHLIGHTS ARE MARKED ON THE MAP ON P.310

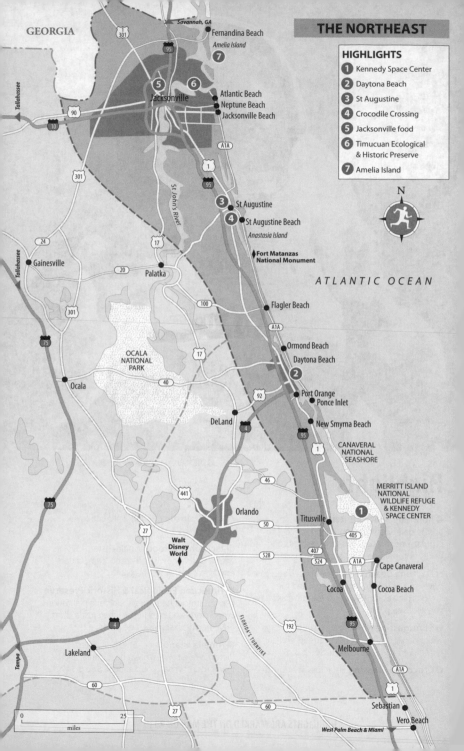

The Kennedy Space Center

Justifiably the biggest draw in the region, the **Kennedy Space Center (KSC)** has been the nucleus of the US space programme since 1958: it's here on Merritt Island and the adjacent Cape Canaveral Air Force Station that NASA's space vehicles are developed, tested and blasted into orbit. With the end of the **Space Shuttle programme** in 2011 it's not clear when human space flights will resume, but the centre's **visitor complex** remains a compelling attraction that can easily fill a whole day.

The Kennedy Space Center Visitor Complex

Hwy-405, Merritt Island • Daily 9am–6pm (July & Aug till 7pm) • $50, children 3–11 $40; parking $10 • ☎ 866 737 5235, ⓦ kennedyspacecenter.com • Take Hwy-405 from Titusville or Hwy-3 off Hwy-A1A between Cocoa Beach and Cocoa

Set up a bit like an Orlando theme park, the vast **Kennedy Space Center Visitor Complex** will enthral anyone with the slightest interest in space exploration, with everything from enormous rockets and the history of the moon landings, to IMAX movies and a space shuttle launch simulation on offer. Regular admission covers the **General Bus Tour** and all the attractions in the complex reviewed below, plus the **Rocket Garden** (where all NASA's major rockets are on show), the **Astronaut Encounter**, a chance to meet and question a real-life astronaut (25min; twice a day), and the **US Astronaut Hall of Fame** across the Indian River in Titusville (see p.314).

IMAX Theater

Daily 10am–5.30pm; shows usually around 45min • Included in Kennedy Space Center entrance price

In the centre of the complex, the **IMAX Theater** shows two 3-D films throughout the day. The films change sporadically, although you can count on both focusing on a space theme and containing at least some footage shot by actual astronauts in space.

Exploration Space

Included in Kennedy Space Center entrance price

NASA won't be getting an astronaut on Mars any time soon, but it's hoping to build a moon base in the 2020s (if Congress ever approves the funding). **Exploration Space** is an absorbing interactive exhibit hinting at what the future of space travel may hold, an educational journey that includes live presentations and movies every thirty minutes.

Shuttle Launch Experience

Every 10min • Included in Kennedy Space Center entrance price

Ever wondered what it's like to blast-off in a rocket? The **Shuttle Launch Experience** is a fun (but bone-shaking) simulation ride where passengers get to experience what it's like

---

KENNEDY SPACE CENTER: THE EXTRAS

With more time and even more cash you can enhance your Space Center experience with additional tours: these often sell out, so reserve in advance online or call ☎ 866 737 5235. Note that the 1hr–1hr 30min General Bus Tour is included with admission.

Cape Canaveral: Then and Now Visits the now retired launch sites of the Mercury, Gemini and Apollo programmes, and the less interesting Air Force Space and Missile Museum. 3hr–3hr 30min; $25, children 3–11 $19.

Up-Close Explore Tour Takes you to NASA's KSC headquarters, the closest possible view of the former Apollo and Space Shuttle launch pads, and the Vehicle Assembly Building. 2–2hr 30min; $25, children 3–11 $19.

Launch Control Center Tour Visit Firing Room 4 to see where all 21 shuttle launches since 2006 were controlled. 2hr 30min; $25, children 3–11 $19.

Lunch with an astronaut There are cafés and snack bars scattered around the complex that provide standard pizza-and-hot-dog fare at just short of stratospheric prices. Instead, you can opt to have lunch with a real astronaut (albeit shared with other tourists). 1hr; $29.99, children 3–11 $15.99.

7

7

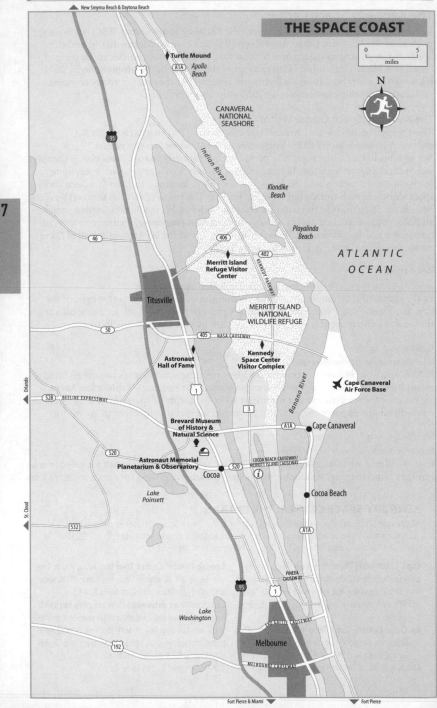

New Smyrna Beach & Daytona Beach

THE SPACE COAST

0   5
miles

N

Turtle Mound
Apollo Beach

CANAVERAL
NATIONAL
SEASHORE

Indian River

Klondike
Beach

Playalinda
Beach

ATLANTIC
OCEAN

Merritt Island
Refuge Visitor
Center

MERRITT ISLAND
NATIONAL
WILDLIFE REFUGE

Titusville

NASA CAUSEWAY

Astronaut
Hall of Fame

Kennedy
Space Center
Visitor Complex

Cape Canaveral
Air Force Base

Orlando

BEELINE EXPRESSWAY

Banana River

Brevard Museum
of History &
Natural Science

Cape Canaveral

Astronaut Memorial
Planetarium & Observatory

COCOA BEACH CAUSEWAY/
MERRITT ISLAND CAUSEWAY

Cocoa

St. Cloud

Lake
Poinsett

Cocoa Beach

PINEDA
CAUSEWAY

Lake
Washington

Melbourne

MELBOURNE CAUSEWAY

Fort Pierce & Miami   Fort Pierce

AMERICANS IN SPACE

The growth of the Space Coast started with the **"Space Race"**, which followed President John F. Kennedy's declaration in May 1961 to "achieve the goal, before the decade is out, of landing a man on the moon and returning him safely to Earth". This statement came in the chill of the Cold War, when the USSR – which had just put the first man into space following its launch of the Sputnik satellite in 1957 – appeared scientifically ahead of the US, a fact that dented American pride and provided great propaganda for the Soviets.

Money and manpower were pumped into the National Aeronautics and Space Administration (**NASA**), and the communities around Cape Canaveral expanded with a heady influx of scientists and would-be astronauts. The much-hyped Mercury programme helped restore prestige, and the later Apollo moonshots captured the imagination of the world. The moon landing by **Apollo 11** in July 1969 not only turned the dreams of science-fiction writers into reality, but also meant that for the first time – and in the most spectacular way possible – the US had overtaken the USSR.

During the 1970s, as the incredible expense of the space programme became apparent and seemed out of all proportion to its benefits, pressure grew for NASA to become more cost-effective. The country entered a period of economic recession and NASA's funding was drastically slashed.

After the internationally funded **Skylab** space station programme (1973–79), NASA's solution to the problem of wasteful one-use rockets was the reusable **space shuttle**, first launched in April 1981, and able to deploy payloads – notably the **Hubble Telescope** – and carry out repairs to orbiting satellites. The shuttle's success silenced many critics, but the **Challenger disaster** of January 1986 – when the entire crew perished during take-off – not only imbued the country with a deep sense of loss but highlighted the complacency and corner-cutting that had crept into the space programme after many accident-free years.

Despite hundreds of successful flights, technical problems were to cause serious delays to the space shuttle programme over the next two decades, as well as another tragedy: the **Columbia shuttle disaster** of 2003, in which the vehicle burned up during re-entry, killing all on board. The subsequent investigation concluded that NASA had failed to learn from its earlier mistakes (and could have given even more consideration to safety controls). Despite the eventual resumption of flights two years later, NASA began to focus more on the **International Space Station** in the Earth's orbit, and its continued (and highly successful) unmanned space probe programme. In 2011, the **Atlantis** made the **last shuttle flight**, ending for the foreseeable future, US manned space flights. The first flight-test of the new Space Launch System (SLS) is scheduled for 2017 (with manned flights to follow in 2021), but though plans to build a permanent moon base in the 2020s, and to even put a man on Mars in 2033 or 2045 have been touted, budget constraints make this seem unlikely. The reality is that unmanned exploration of the solar system, while less glamorous, is far cheaper and less dangerous than sending people into space.

to be an astronaut, vertically "launching" into space, and orbiting Earth aboard the space shuttle.

The Kennedy Space Center General Bus Tour

Daily 10am–4.30pm, every 15min; 2hr • Included in Kennedy Space Center entrance price

The **General Bus Tour** around the rest of the Merritt Island complex provides a dramatic insight into the colossal grandeur of the space programme. After zooming through the main gate and passing countless alligators on the side of the road, you'll pass the **Vehicle Assembly Building** (VAB), where space shuttles, like the Apollo and Skylab spacecraft before them, were put together and fitted with payloads. At 52 storeys and equivalent in volume to three-and-a-half Empire State Buildings, it's the largest single-storey scientific building in the world. The VAB is the first stop for the "crawlerway" – the huge tracks along which space shuttles were wheeled to the launch pad.

The bus doesn't stop at the VAB but continues on to the **LC-39 Observation Gantry**, a vantage point from where you can gaze at the former shuttle **launch pad.** Inside the building, exhibits and a movie focus on the space shuttle missions. The second and final stop is the mind-blowing **Apollo/Saturn V Center**, where besides a nose-to-nozzle inspection of a fantastically big Saturn V rocket (363ft), which produced enough power on blast-off to light up New York City for over an hour, there's a simulated Apollo countdown and take-off, watched from behind the blinking screens of an actual control room. The dramatization of the **Apollo 11 moon landing** brings home how touch-and-go the operation was, with signals crashing, alarms lighting and just 25 seconds of fuel left when the Eagle touched down.

US Astronaut Hall of Fame

6225 Vectorspace Blvd (Hwy-405), Merritt Island Causeway • Daily noon–5pm • $27, children 3–11 $23; also included in the Kennedy Space Center ticket • ☎ 866 737 5235

Six miles west of the KSC Visitor Complex via Hwy-405 is the **US Astronaut Hall of Fame**, one of Florida's most entertaining interactive museums, where in addition to perusing the largest collection of astronaut memorabilia, simulation rides allow visitors to experience stomach-churning G-forces or a ride across the bumpy surface of Mars.

ARRIVAL AND DEPARTURE   KENNEDY SPACE CENTER

By car There is no public transport to the Space Center. The only road access is on Hwy-405 from Titusville, 11 miles east of I-95 exits 215 and 212; from Cocoa Beach you can drive north on Hwy-A1A and Hwy-3 for 10 miles or so, and then bypass the air force base by taking Space Commerce Way to Hwy-405.

By bus The nearest bus stations to the Space Center are in Titusville and Melbourne, but you'll have to continue on via taxi from either place. Greyhound serves the Titusville bus station at 1220 S Washington Ave (☎ 321 267 8760), with two daily buses from Orlando (55min); you have to change buses in Orlando for other destinations.

ACCOMMODATION AND EATING

The most convenient place to stay near the Space Center is the otherwise unexceptional city of Titusville, just off I-95, 10 miles west of the visitor complex. Day-trips from Cocoa Beach, Orlando or Daytona Beach are easy alternatives.

Casa Coquina del Mar 4010 Coquina Ave, Titusville (just off US-1) ☎ 321 268 4653, ⊛ casacoquina.com. With new owners in 2012, this B&B remains laidback and great value. Originally built in 1927, it now offers seven suites, cable TV, free wi-fi, complimentary happy hour each night from 5 to 7pm and views across to the Space Center. **$99**

★**Dixie Crossroads** 1475 Garden St (Hwy-406), Titusville ☎ 321 268 5000, ⊛ dixiecrossroads.com. Local favourite since 1983, best known for corn fritters and

shrimp of every variety but especially its sweet wild ocean shrimp ($18.99 for a dozen large; all-you-can-eat $46.99). Mon–Thurs & Sun 11am–9pm, Fri & Sat 11am–10pm.

Holiday Inn Titusville Kennedy Space Center 4715 Helen Hauser Blvd (I-95 exit 215, Hwy-50), Titusville ☎ 877 859 5095, ⊛ holidayinn.com. This is easily the best of the chain hotels near the Space Center, with an outdoor heated pool, free wi-fi, 24hr gym and spacious rooms decked out in a sleek, contemporary style. **$100**

Merritt Island National Wildlife Refuge

Garden St (Hwy-406, I-95 exit 220) • Daily sunrise–sunset; visitor centre Mon–Sat 9am–4pm • Free; Black Point Wildlife Drive $5 • ☎ 321 861 0667, ⊛ fws.gov/merrittisland

NASA shares its land with the 218 square miles of the **Merritt Island National Wildlife Refuge**, just over the Max Brewer Causeway Bridge from Titusville. Here you'll find alligators, armadillos, raccoons, bobcats and one of Florida's greatest concentrations of birdlife living alongside some of the world's most advanced technology.

Even if you're only coming for a day at the Space Center, it would be a shame to pass up such a spectacular place – though it has to be said that Merritt Island, on first glance, looks anything but spectacular, comprising acres of estuaries and brackish marshes interspersed with occasional hammocks of oak and palm and pine flatwoods where a few bald eagles construct nests ten feet in circumference. Winter (Oct–March) is the **best time to visit**, when the island's skies are alive with thousands of migratory birds from the frozen north, and when mosquitoes are absent. At any other period, and especially in summer, the island's Mosquito Lagoon is worthy of its name; bring ample insect repellent.

Visitor Information Center
Four miles past the refuge entrance on Hwy-402

Start your tour at the **Visitor Information Center**, with a twenty-minute video, wildlife and habitat exhibits and the three-quarter-mile **Oak Hammock Trail** and the two-mile **Palm Hammock Trail**, both accessible from the car park. **Alligators** inhabit the freshwater ponds behind the visitor centre.

Black Point Wildlife Drive
Signposted off Hwy-406, beyond the refuge entrance • Driving time around 40min

The best place to see wildlife, including plenty of alligators, is the seven-mile **Black Point Wildlife Drive**, a one-way dyke road around several shallow marshes and through pine flatwoods. At the entrance you can pick up a highly informative, free leaflet that describes specific stops along the route. One to two hours after sunrise and one to two hours before sunset are the best times to see animals and birds.

Canaveral National Seashore (South District)
Beach Rd (Hwy-406, then Hwy-402; I-95 exit 220) • Daily: 6am–6pm; late May to Aug usually 6am–8pm • $5 per car, bicycles/pedestrians $1 • ☎ 321 267 1110, ⓦ nps.gov/cana

Encompassing the slender, 25-mile-long barrier island dividing Merritt Island's Mosquito Lagoon from the Atlantic Ocean, the **Canaveral National Seashore (South District)** begins at **Playalinda Beach** on Hwy-402, seven miles east of the Merritt Island Refuge visitor centre. Note that the north district of the Canaveral National Seashore is only accessible from New Smyrna Beach (see p.317). The National Seashore's entire length is top-notch beachcombing and surfing territory and also suitable for swimming; note that the road ends at Playalinda and you can only reach tranquil **Klondike Beach** on foot (a back-country permit is required; $2).

Cocoa Beach

Some thirty miles south of the Kennedy Space Center, **Cocoa Beach** encompasses a ten-mile strip of shore that is a favoured haunt of **surfers**, who are drawn here by some of the choicest waves in Florida. Major (and minor) surfing contests are held here during spring and summer, and throughout the year the place has a perky, youthful feel. If you can't find what you want at the vast **Ron Jon's** flagship, 4151 N Atlantic Ave (open 24hr; rentals daily 8am–8pm; surfboard rental $30/day, beach bikes $30/3 days, kayaks $40/day, wetsuits $50/week; ☎321 799 8888, ⓦronjonsurfshop.com), try the **Cocoa Beach Surf Company** next door at 4001 N Atlantic Ave (daily 8am–11pm; ☎321 799 9930, ⓦcocoabeachsurf.com). There's also a big **beach volleyball** contingent, as well as free music around the pier and beachside parks often on weekends.

TURTLES ON THE SPACE COAST

The Space Coast is the second largest **turtle nesting** area in the world and, not surprisingly, turtle-watching is a popular local pastime. **Turtle-watches** (Wed–Sat 8pm–midnight; $14; ages 15 and under free) with a park ranger on Playalinda Beach are offered in June and July (**reserve** one month in advance; ☎386 428 3384, ext. 223, ⓦnps.gov/cana). Children must be 8 years or older to participate. Common turtle species include loggerheads, greens and leatherbacks, with nests along the Canaveral National Seashore currently topping five thousand per year.

ARRIVAL AND INFORMATION

By car Cocoa Beach is separated from the mainland and Cocoa itself (13 miles west) by the Banana River, traversed by Hwy-520: Hwy-A1A runs north–south along the beach, linking it with Titusville (30 miles) to the north and the Treasure Coast to the south (Vero Beach is 52 miles).

By bus At Titusville Greyhound station (see p.314) you can switch to local Space Coast Area Transit buses (☎ 321 633 1878, ⓦ ridescat.com); Route #1 runs hourly Mon–Sat along US-1 to Cocoa Transit Center, where you can change to Route #4 (Mon–Sat every 30min; Sun limited service) to Cocoa Beach. Once here, Route #9 runs up and down the beach itself (Beach Trolley; Mon–Sat every 30min; Sun limited service). Fares are $1.50 per ride.

By shuttle bus Cocoa Beach Shuttle vans (☎ 321 631 4144 or ☎ 888 784 4144, ⓦ cbshuttle.com) run to and from Orlando International Airport for $33 one way for one person (two people $58); call to be collected from any hotel on Hwy-A1A.

Tourist information The local Convention & Visitors Bureau runs a tourist information centre at 8501 Astronaut Blvd (Hwy-A1A), Suite Four (daily 8.30am–6pm; ☎ 321 454 2022, ⓦ visitcocoabeach.com). Alternatively, head to the Cocoa Beach Chamber of Commerce, at 400 Fortenberry Rd (Mon–Thurs 9am–5pm, Fri 9am–4.30pm; ☎ 321 459 2200, ⓦ cocoabeachchamber.com).

ACCOMMODATION

Banana River Resort 3590 S Atlantic Ave (Hwy-A1A) ☎ 321 784 0166, ⓦ bananariverresort.info. Perfect for families, with plenty of on-site activities from yoga and surfing to kayaking and paddleboarding, with Banana River Lagoon on one side and the beach a short walk across the street. Rooms are no-frills but cosy, with two-bedroom apartments and a smaller efficiency. Camping **$20** per person, doubles **$90**

★ **Beach Place Guesthouses** 1445 S Atlantic Ave (Hwy-A1A) ☎ 321 783 4045, ⓦ beachplaceguesthouses .com. Attractive, wildly popular hotel a short walk from the beach, with enticing beach deck areas behind the dunes equipped with hammocks, rocking chairs and loungers. The sixteen cabin-like guesthouses are top-notch, with free wi-fi, one or two bedrooms, separate living/dining areas and fully equipped kitchens. **$210**

Fawlty Towers 100 E Cocoa Beach Causeway (Hwy-520 and Hwy-A1A) ☎ 321 784 3870, ⓦ fawltytowersresort

.com. Nothing like the television show, this friendly, roomy, pink-towered motel near the beachfront has a pool, cable TV, free wi-fi and a popular tiki bar; the rooms are fairly plain, but the prices are a real bargain. **$72**

★ **Inn at Cocoa Beach** 4300 Ocean Beach Blvd ☎ 321 799 3460, ⓦ theinnatcocoabeach.com. The friendly, laidback vibe at this prime beachfront hotel tops all the chain hotels in town; rooms vary in size and style, but all are well maintained and some have ocean views. There's a convenient honour bar, free wine and cheese in the evenings, a superb breakfast and macaws perched outside. **$125**

Jetty Park 400 E Jetty Drive (George King Blvd) ☎ 321 783 7111, ⓦ jettyparkbeachandcampground.com. The most tent-friendly campground in the area, 5 miles north of Cocoa Beach at Cape Canaveral, with its own beach, 1200ft fishing pier, hot showers, free wi-fi, laundry facilities and camp store. Parking is $10/day. Pitches cost $10 less May–Dec. Basic pitches **$37**, full hook-ups **$49**, cabins **$83.25**

EATING AND DRINKING

Atlantic Ocean Grille 401 Meade Ave, Cocoa Beach Pier ☎ 321 783 7549. An enticing dinner option on the pier, with a quality menu especially strong on Florida seafood (mains $11–23), and also a Sunday Champagne brunch. Mon–Sat 5–10pm, Sun 10am–2pm & 5–10pm.

Coconuts on the Beach 2 Minuteman Causeway ☎ 321 784 1422, ⓦ coconutsonthebeach.com. A party-hearty place with bikini contests to accompany the drinking and live music on the beach (with no cover); opt for the tasty Baja fish tacos ($11.50) if you're looking to eat. Daily 11am–2am.

★ **Fat Snook** 2464 S Atlantic Ave ☎ 321 784 1190, ⓦ thefatsnook.com. Top seafood restaurant in town, with locally caught fish and seasonal produce contributing to the modern American- and Caribbean-inspired menu: main courses might include *Cuba libre* braised pork belly with yucca *mofongo* ($30) or goat's cheese lasagne ($22). Daily 5.30–9.30pm.

Florida's Seafood Bar & Grill 480 West Cocoa Beach Causeway ☎ 321 784 0892, ⓦ floridas-seafood.com. Another enticing seafood option – try the shrimp and crab salad ($9.99), fried oyster sandwich ($9) or the creamy clam chowder ($5.25). Daily 11am–10pm.

Green Room Café 222 N 1st St ☎ 321 868 0203, ⓦ greenroomcafecocoabeach.com. Delicious, healthy food and friendly service right off the beach, serving fresh juices, smoothies, sandwiches ($10.25), wraps ($10.75) and salads ($11.25), with plenty of vegetarian and vegan choices. Mon–Sat 10.30am–9pm.

Pelican's Bar & Grill 401 Meade Ave, Cocoa Beach Pier ☎ 321 783 7549. This 2014 re-launch of the old *Marlin's* is a good bet for drinks and snacks, with cold beer, killer cocktails (from $7.95) and the best views of the beach and ocean in town. The food is so-so – stick with bar favourites, like burgers ($11.95) and fried shrimp ($11.95). Daily 11am–9pm.

New Smyrna Beach

After the virgin vistas of the Canaveral National Seashore, the likeable, low-key beach community of **NEW SMYRNA BEACH**, thirty miles north of Titusville on US-1 or I-95, is a gentle reintroduction to tourism along the coast. The coastal section of town fronts a stretch of water that's perfect for **swimming** and **surfing**; to reach the beach – or the northern section of the Canaveral National Seashore (see below) – you have to pass through the inland section of the town, where the **Canal Street Historic District** is a sleepy but attractive collection of old homes, shops and restaurants, with a few reminders of New Smyrna's unusual history.

New Smyrna Museum of History

120 Sams Ave • Tues–Sat 10am–4pm • Free • ☎ 386 478 0052, ⓦ nsbhistory.org

One of the state's best little museums, the **New Smyrna Museum of History** chronicles the town's history from Timucuan times, though the highlight is the special exhibition – enhanced by videos – on the colony founded here in 1768 by wealthy Scottish physician **Andrew Turnbull**. The exhibit tells the story of how Turnbull acquired land at what was called Mosquito Inlet after Florida reverted to the British. He then set about recruiting 1400 Greeks, Corsicans, Italians and Minorcans to work on his indigo plantation in return for fifty acres of land per person (Smyrna was then a Greek city in modern-day Turkey, now Izmir). The colony didn't last long: bad treatment, language barriers, disease and financial disasters hastened its demise, and most of the settlers moved north to St Augustine in 1777 (see p.326).

Old Fort Park

Riverside Drive and Julia St • 24hr • Free

Nothing remains of the original settlement of New Smyrna, founded by Andrew Turnbull and workers from the Mediterranean in 1768, save a half-submerged stone wharf. However, one block north of the New Smyrna Museum of History, **Old Fort Park** preserves the coquina foundations of buildings that may date back to the Turnbull period (their precise origins remain a mystery, with some local historians even suggesting a Spanish link).

Canaveral National Seashore (North District)

7611 S Atlantic Ave • Daily: 6am–6pm; late May to early Sept usually 6am–8pm; Apollo visitor centre daily 9am–5pm • $5 per car, bicycles/pedestrians $1 • ☎ 321 428 3384, ⓦ nps.gov/cana

Seven miles south of central New Smyrna Beach, Hwy-A1A terminates at the northern arm of **Canaveral National Seashore**, an untouched, narrow spit of overgrown sand-bank, known here as **Apollo Beach**, that stretches down to Merritt Island (see p.314). The road continues for another six miles or so beyond the entrance, providing access to the beach, several nature trails and historic Mouton-Wells House, aka **Eldora State House** (Fri–Sun noon–4pm), constructed around 1915 by local homesteaders and containing exhibits on the former community of Eldora. Make time also for the vast **shell midden** known as **Turtle Mound** just beyond the entrance, created by the Timucuan people long before the arrival of Europeans.

Turtle Mound

Daily 6am–6pm • Admission included in park entry • ☎ 321 267 1110, ⓦ nps.gov/cana

Smothered in jungle, it's hard at first to see that **Turtle Mound** is actually a massive two-acre heap of oyster shells and other refuse left by the Timucuan people between 800 and 1400. The 30ft mound became prominent enough over time to be marked on maps by Florida's first Spanish explorers, being visible several miles out to sea. Take a few minutes to walk along the boardwalks, through the dense, fragrant vegetation (and under the huge spiders) to the top of the mound – aside from its historical significance, the observation point provides stellar views of the surrounding parkland and ocean.

ARRIVAL AND INFORMATION

NEW SMYRNA BEACH

By car Hwy-44 provides the main link between New Smyrna and I-95 (Exit 249A); once in the centre Hwy-44 becomes Hwy-A1A and continues past Canal Street and over the causeway to the beach area. You can park along historic Canal Street for free (for two hours), and there are plenty of car parks along the beach.

By bus Getting to New Smyrna is tough without your own

transport. You can take local Votran buses (☎votran.org) from Daytona Beach (see p.323), but you'll have to change in Port Orange.

Tourist information The visitor centre, at 2238 Hwy-44, just off I-95 in a small shopping arcade (Mon–Sat 9am–5pm, Sun 10am–2pm; ☎386 428 1600 or ☎800 541 9621, ☎nsbfla.com), has maps and all the usual local information.

ACCOMMODATION

Night Swan Intracoastal B&B 512 S Riverside Drive ☎386 423 4940, ☎nightswan.com. Luxurious and welcoming, this 1906 gem comes with its own dock and a fabulous location overlooking the Intracoastal Waterway. The antique-filled rooms and suites come in a variety of sizes, with the best deals in the Main House. Free wi-fi. $119

Riverview 103 Flagler Ave ☎386 428 5858, ☎riverviewhotel.com. Romantic, 1885 Victorian-style

hotel on the waterway, oozing historic character, with eighteen small but cosy rooms, all with wooden shutters (the rooms on the third floor are more expensive but not much bigger). The heated pool is open year-round. $122

Seahorse Inn 423 Flagler Ave ☎386 428 8081, ☎seahorseinnflorida.com. Less than a block from the beach and in the heart of the Flagler Ave action is this twenty-unit motel with clean, 1950s-style retro rooms with terrazzo floors and driftwood decor. $80

EATING AND DRINKING

The Breakers 518 Flagler Ave ☎386 428 2019, ☎thebreakersnsb.com. Cosy beachside diner best known for its finely crafted burger menu; the classic beach burger ($7.95) is one of the best on the coast, but the more exotic combos – salsa burger, inferno burger (both $10.25) – are worth sampling. Mon–Thurs & Sun 11am–11pm, Fri & Sat 11am–midnight.

★**JB's Fish Camp** 859 Pompano Ave (Hwy-A1A) ☎386 427 5747, ☎jbsfishcamp.com. Come here to try the justly famous crab cakes ($6.50) and grouper sandwich ($11) on the weathered deck overlooking the Halifax River, or take your dinner inside where bumper stickers behind the bar read, "Finish your beer, there are sober people in China". Daily 11am–10pm.

Norwood's 400 2nd Ave (Hwy-A1A) ☎386 428 4621, ☎norwoods.com. For the area's finest upmarket dining, head to this venerable place opened in 1946; the best time to stop by is on a Friday (5–7pm), when they have one of their popular wine tastings to complement the mouthwatering seafood (mains $15–27). Daily 11.30am–10pm.

Pappa's Drive In 1103 N Dixie Freeway (US-1) ☎386 427 0633, ☎pappasdrivein.com. Heading north from downtown to Daytona Beach, stop by this classic piece of Americana, an old-style diner knocking out gut-busting breakfasts ($2.75–8.95) and tasty burgers ($2.65) since 1970. Daily 5am–9.30pm.

Daytona Beach

The consummate Florida beach town, **DAYTONA BEACH** owes its existence to 23 miles of sugary white sand where the only pressure is to relax and enjoy yourself. Yet Daytona is also synonymous with **car racing**. The world-famous **Daytona 500** stock-car meeting has been held at the Daytona International Speedway since 1959, but cars have been

LEARNING TO SURF AT DAYTONA

Surfing all along Daytona Beach is good for beginners, with long, generally gentle, sandy breaks.

Daytona Beach Surfing School 2424 N Atlantic Ave (Grand Seas Resort) ☎386 441 1110, ☎daytona surfingfirst-best.homestead.com. The ideal place for beginners to start; private lessons are $60/hr.

Mimi Munro Surf Camps Harvard Ave, Ormond Beach ☎386 672 5600, ☎mimimunrosurfs.com.

Lessons with surf legend and former longboard champion Mimi Munro. Lessons $125 9am–noon.

Surfari Surf School 52 Bovard Ave W, Ormond Beach ☎386 299 3609, ☎surfarisurf.com. Runs sociable surf camps for kids, teens and adults. Private lessons are $75/1hr 30min (group sessions $50).

thrashing along the beach since 1903. The land speed record was regularly smashed here, five times by British speedster **Malcolm Campbell** who, in 1935, roared along at 276mph. Even today, driving on the beach (albeit at much reduced speeds) is one of Daytona's trademark attractions. The central section of the beach around the pier at the end of **Main Street** is crammed with amusement arcades, shops, bars and cafés, but you can find much quieter stretches of sand to the north and south.

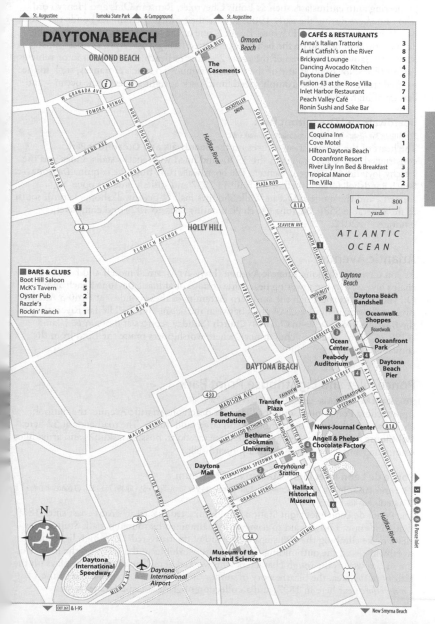

DAYTONA BEACH

St. Augustine | Tomoka State Park | & Campground | St. Augustine

ORMOND BEACH

Ormond Beach

The Casements

CAFÉS & RESTAURANTS	
Anna's Italian Trattoria	3
Aunt Catfish's on the River	8
Brickyard Lounge	5
Dancing Avocado Kitchen	4
Daytona Diner	6
Fusion 43 at the Rose Villa	2
Inlet Harbor Restaurant	7
Peach Valley Café	1
Ronin Sushi and Sake Bar	4

ACCOMMODATION	
Coquina Inn	6
Cove Motel	1
Hilton Daytona Beach Oceanfront Resort	4
River Lily Inn Bed & Breakfast	3
Tropical Manor	5
The Villa	2

7

HOLLY HILL

ATLANTIC OCEAN

0 — 800 yards

Daytona Beach

Daytona Beach Bandshell

Oceanwalk Shoppes

Boardwalk

BARS & CLUBS	
Boot Hill Saloon	4
McK's Tavern	5
Oyster Pub	2
Razzle's	3
Rockin' Ranch	1

Ocean Center

Oceanfront Park

Peabody Auditorium

Daytona Beach Pier

DAYTONA BEACH

Transfer Plaza

Bethune Foundation

Bethune-Cookman University

News-Journal Center

Angell & Phelps Chocolate Factory

Daytona Mall

Greyhound Station

Halifax Historical Museum

N

Museum of the Arts and Sciences

Daytona International Speedway

Daytona International Airport

Halifax River

& Ponce Inlet

EXIT 261 & I-95

New Smyrna Beach

The beach

Without a doubt, the best thing about Daytona Beach *is* the **beach**, a seemingly limitless affair – 500ft wide at low tide and, lengthways, fading dreamily into the heat haze. There's little to do other than develop your tan, take the occasional ocean dip, or observe one of the many pro volleyball tournaments that set up camp during the summer. Even before the students and bikers, the beach was a favourite with pioneering auto enthusiasts such as Louis Chevrolet, Ransom Olds and Henry Ford, who came here during the early 1900s to race their prototype vehicles beside the ocean. As a legacy of these times, Daytona Beach is one of the few Florida towns where the dubious thrill of **driving on the beach** is permitted (daily: Nov–April sunrise–sunset; May–Oct 8am–7pm); eleven of the area's 23 miles of beach are open to motor vehicles. Pay $5 (Feb–Nov only) at any of the officially signposted beach entrances, stick to the marked track, observe the 10mph speed limit, park at right angles to the ocean – and beware of high tide.

Boardwalk and Oceanfront Park

12 N Atlantic Ave • 24hr • Free • ⓦ daytonabeachboardwalk.com

The heart of the beach action centres on the **Boardwalk and Oceanfront Park**, constructed as a WPA project in the 1930s and lined with snacks stalls, shops and the kitschy Joyland Amusement Center. The boardwalk runs from the coquina **Daytona Beach Bandshell** (ⓦbandshell.info), built in 1937 and still a venue for open-air concerts, and the modern Ocean Walk Shoppes mall (ⓦoceanwalkshoppes.com), south to the venerable 858ft **Daytona Beach Pier**, dating back to 1925 and completely renovated in 2012.

Atlantic Avenue

As you travel south along **Atlantic Avenue** (Hwy-A1A), small motels and fast-food chains give way to the towering beachside condos of affluent **Daytona Beach Shores**. On your right as you reach the southern extremity of these condos, at 3140 S Atlantic Ave, you'll spot a large patch of grass between the ocean and the Halifax River; this is the **Daytona Beach Drive-In Christian Church** (Sunday services at 8.30am & 10am; ☎386 767 8761, ⓦdriveinchurch.net), where worshippers praise the Lord from the comfort of their cars.

Ponce Inlet and Lighthouse Point Park

5000 S Atlantic Ave • Daily sunrise–sunset • $5 per vehicle • ☎ 386 756 7488

Approaching **Ponce Inlet**, south of Daytona Beach on Atlantic Avenue, the outlook changes to single-storey beach homes and large sand dunes. The road ends at 52-acre **Lighthouse Point Park**, where you'll often see raccoons, possums, skunks and armadillos scampering along the **nature trails** and boardwalk.

Ponce de Leon Inlet Light Station and Museum

4931 S Peninsula Drive, Ponce Inlet • Daily: June–Aug 10am–9pm; Sept–May 10am–6pm • $5 • ☎ 386 761 1821, ⓦ ponceinlet.org • Bus #17A from Daytona Beach (Transfer Plaza)

The **Ponce de Leon Inlet Light Station** has illuminated this treacherous coast since 1889, though it's now a private aid to navigation maintained by museum staff. Stupendous views make climbing the 203 steps to the top of the rusty-red 175ft-high lighthouse worthwhile, and the outbuildings hold engaging exhibits and a video on the history of the site, as well as the tough characters who worked here. There are also displays on the history of the area, the bizarre story of author **Stephen Crane**, shipwrecked in the *Commodore* near here in 1897, and a collection of giant antique Fresnel lenses.

Marine Science Center

100 Lighthouse Drive, Ponce Inlet • Tues–Sat 10am–4pm, Sun noon–4pm • $5, children 3–12 $2 • ☎ 386 304 5545,
Ⓦ marinesciencecenter.com • Bus #17A from Daytona Beach (Transfer Plaza)

Once you've checked out the Ponce Inlet lighthouse, pop next door to the **Marine Science Center**, where sick and injured sea turtles and sea birds are nursed back to health. The visitor centre is a mini-aquarium, with a touch tank of friendly stingrays, and tanks containing turtles and various types of local fish. Outside you can view the turtle rescue area from a distance, and across the car park visit the sea-bird rehab area, where permanent guests are on display: these injured bald eagles, owls, pelicans, kestrels and hawks will never be able to fend for themselves in the wild again. Birds that are expected to fully recover (and be released) are treated in a restricted area that you can peek into through windows.

Ormond Beach

In 1888, as part of his plan to bring his East Coast railway south from St Augustine, oil baron Henry Flagler bought the local hotel, built a beachside golf course, and helped give **Ormond Beach**, three miles north of Daytona's Main Street, the refined tone it retains to this day. Facing the Halifax River on Granada Boulevard, Flagler's by-now hopelessly ruined **Ormond Hotel** was demolished in 1992 to much public mourning.

The Casements

25 Riverside Drive, Ormond Beach • Mon–Fri 9am–5pm, Sat 9am–noon; tours given according to demand Mon–Fri 10am–3.30pm, Sat
10–11.30am • Free • ☎ 386 676 3216, Ⓦ thecasements.net • Bus #18, #19 from Daytona Beach (Transfer Plaza)

By the early 1970s, the **Casements** was little more than a burnt-out ruin: it was saved from demolition and restored by a group of local women primarily because of the link with **John D. Rockefeller**, America's richest tycoon. Rockefeller bought the three-storey villa in 1918 as a winter retreat in his retirement – he actually died here in 1937. Today the wooden mansion is in fine shape (most of the original furniture, though, was sold; what remains resides in the Rockefeller Room). Guided tours of the house take in the second-floor rooms, restored to how they would have looked in Rockefeller's time, and the third-floor exhibits on the **Boy Scouts of America**, which Rockefeller's money helped to establish.

Mainland Daytona Beach

When you're tired of the sands or nursing your sunburn, cross the river to mainland **Daytona Beach**, where several waterside parks and walkways contribute to a relaxing change of scene, and several museums will keep you out of the sun for a few hours.

DAYTONA SPEED WEEKS AND MORE

The Daytona Speedway hosts several major race meetings each year, starting in late January with the **Rolex 24**, a 24-hour race for GT prototype sports cars. A week or so later begin the qualifying races leading up to the biggest event of the year, the **NASCAR Daytona 500** stock-car race in mid-February. Tickets (see below) for this are as common as Florida snow, but many of the same drivers compete in the **Coke Zero 400**, for which tickets are much easier (and cheaper) to get, held on the first Saturday in July. The track is also used for motorcycle races. **Bike Week**, in early March, sees a variety of high-powered clashes, highlighted by **American Motorcycle Association** championship racing; and the **Fall Cycle Scene**, held the third week in October to coincide with **Biketoberfest**, features the **Championship Cup Series** races (see Ⓦ officialbikeweek.com).

   Tickets for the bigger events sell out well in advance (expect to pay $30–50 for car racing and $32–220 for the Daytona 500; some motorcycle races cost only $10), and it's advisable to book accommodation at least six months ahead. For **information** and ticket details call ☎ 877 306 7223 or check Ⓦ daytonainternationalspeedway.com.

Halifax Historical Museum

252 S Beach St • Tues–Fri 10.30am–4.30pm, Sat 10am–4pm • $5, donation only on Thurs • ☎ 386 255 6976, ⓦ halifaxhistorical.org

At the heart of Daytona's modest historic downtown is the **Halifax Historical Museum**, housed in a stately mural-decorated bank building completed in 1910. Chronological displays chart the area's history from the Timucua and Spanish periods through to the modern day: special exhibits focus on the Daytona races, **Mary McLeod Bethune** (see below) and **Mathias Day**, who established the city in 1870 on an old plantation (the town was named after him six years later). Look out for information on local 1920s rumrunner **Bill McCoy** (seriously, "the real McCoy"), **Brownie**, the "town dog" in the 1940s, and the giant toy giraffe upstairs, its legs damaged by years of hugging (it acted as a sort of mascot for a local toy shop in the 1950s).

Angell & Phelps Chocolate Factory

154 S Beach St • Shop Mon–Sat 9.30am–6pm; hourly tours (20–30min) Mon–Sat 10am–4pm • Free • ☎ 386 252 6531, ⓦ angellandphelps.com

The enlightening tours of **Angell & Phelps Chocolate Factory**, founded in 1925, explain how old-fashioned chocs and candy are made by hand, with windows allowing a glimpse of the process at work. The free samples – chewy caramels, crunchy nut chocolate and the like – and heavenly aromas of roasting cacao will have you loading up with goodies in the factory shop.

Bethune Foundation

640 Mary McLeod Bethune Blvd • Mon–Fri 10am–3pm, Sat by appointment • Free • ☎ 386 481 2122, ⓦ cookman.edu • Free parking in the college lots just in front of the house

The **Bethune Foundation**, a mile or so north of downtown, commemorates Daytona native Mary McLeod Bethune, born in 1875 to freed slave parents and a lifelong campaigner for racial and sexual equality. In 1904, against the odds, she founded Florida's first black girls' school here – with savings of $1.50 and five pupils. **The Retreat**, the white-framed house where Bethune lived from 1915 until her death in 1955, contains scores of awards and citations alongside furnishings and personal effects, and sits within the campus of **Bethune-Cookman University**, which has grown up around the original school and is still primarily an African-American institution. Tours (free) take in the **Eleanor Roosevelt Room**, where the pioneering former First Lady would stay on her visits down here. Mary's final resting place is in the garden outside.

Museum of Arts and Sciences

352 S Nova Rd • Tues–Sat 9am–5pm, Sun 11am–5pm • $12.95, children 6–17 $6.95 • ☎ 386 255 0285, ⓦ moas.org

The family-friendly **Museum of Arts and Sciences** houses an eclectic series of temporary and permanent exhibits ranging from the remains of a million-year-old giant ground sloth to a collection of American quilts, Teddy bears and Coke memorabilia amassed by the **Root family** (responsible for designing the iconic Coca-Cola bottle in 1915). Outside there are two luxurious railroad cars built in 1948, used by the Roots to travel the length and breadth of the country. There's also a collection of African ceremonial objects, Cuban paintings and sculpture spanning two centuries (donated by Cuba's former dictator, Fulgencio Batista, who spent many years of exile in a comfortable Daytona Beach house), and a Chinese gallery containing some fine nineteenth-century Qing Dynasty porcelain and a couple of rare Han Dynasty tomb figures from 100 BC. By the end of 2015 the museum should have opened the **Cici and Hyatt Brown Museum of Art** (housing paintings of Florida), a new **West Wing**, and a new **planetarium**.

Daytona International Speedway

1801 W International Speedway Blvd • **All access tour** Daily 10am–3pm (on the hour); 1hr 30min • $23, children 6–12 $17 • **Speedway tour** Daily 11.30am, 1.30pm, 3.30pm & 4pm; 30min • $16, children 6–12 $10 • ☎ 386 254 2700, ⓦ daytonainternationalspeedway.com • Bus #18 from Daytona Beach (Transfer Plaza)

About three miles west of downtown stands an ungainly configuration of concrete and steel that has done much to promote Daytona Beach's name around the world: the **Daytona International Speedway**, home of the Daytona 500 stock-car rally and a few other less famous but similar events. By the 1950s, beach races were taking place in South Daytona, on an oval course half on the sand and half on Hwy-A1A. When high speeds made racing on Daytona's beaches unsafe, the solution was this 150,000-capacity temple to high-performance thrills and spills, which opened in 1959.

Though it doesn't quite capture the excitement of a race, the guided **all access tour** gives visitors a chance to see the sheer size of the place and the remarkable 31-degree gradient of the curves, which help make this the fastest race track in the world – reaching speeds of 200mph is not uncommon. You'll start by driving around the vast **infield** area, stopping to explore the Drivers' Meeting Room and Fan Zone, where you can look into car garages, watch any activity on the track at the Pit Road, and pretend you're a winner at the Victory Lane. Tours end at the **Sprint Tower** press box followed by a look at the current winning car (by tradition, Daytona keeps it).

Richard Petty Driving Experience

1801 W International Speedway Blvd • Daily 9am–4pm (call in advance to confirm) • ☎ 800 237 3889, ⓦ drivepetty.com • Ride-alongs $144, self-drive from $549 (8 laps)

If taking a guided tour of **Daytona International Speedway** isn't enough, you can actually get behind the wheel of a stock car yourself – for a price – thanks to the **Richard Petty Driving Experience**. You can opt to ride with a professional driver for three laps, or to drive yourself. Buy tickets at the Speedway ticket office.

ARRIVAL AND DEPARTURE
DAYTONA BEACH

By plane Daytona Beach International Airport (ⓦ flydaytonafirst.com) lies 3 miles southwest of downtown at 700 Catalina Drive, next to the Speedway. Currently Delta flies to Atlanta and New York (LGA) and US Airways (under American Airlines) flies to Charlotte. Taxis (around $25), shuttles and local buses (see p.324) are available for transfers to the beach.

By bus The Greyhound bus station (☎ 386 255 7076) is at 138 S Ridgewood Ave (US-1), in the mainland section of the town. To get to the beach you'll have to take a taxi or local bus #18 or #19 (see p.324), which pass the bus station. There are also direct services to Orlando airport from Daytona (see box below).

Destinations Jacksonville (2 daily; 1hr 40min–1hr 55min); Orlando (5 daily; 1hr 5min); St Augustine (1 daily; 1hr).

By car Daytona Beach is easily reached from I-95 Exit 261A, following International Speedway Blvd. As Ridgewood Ave, US-1 steams through mainland Daytona Beach north–south, while Hwy-A1A (known as Atlantic Ave) runs along the beach. Parking near the pier can be tough, but along the rest of the beach you should find plenty of free or cheap spots.

INFORMATION AND TOURS

Tourist information Visit the Halifax Area Advertising Authority at 126 E Orange Ave (Mon–Fri 9am–5pm; ☎ 800 854 1234, ⓦ daytonabeach.com), on the way to the beach. For information on Ormond Beach, drop by its local Chamber of Commerce, 165 W Granada Blvd (Mon–Fri 9am–5pm; ☎ 386 677 3454, ⓦ ormondchamber.com).

Tours and rentals Ponce Inlet Watersports (☎ 386 405 3445, ⓦ ponceinletwatersports.com), 4936 S Peninsula Drive, runs Ecotours by boat ($25; 1hr 30min) around Ponce Inlet; it also offers parasailing ($65–100; ⓦ daytonaparasailing.com) and kayak rentals ($30/hr; $95/8hr). For scenic boat tours of the Indian River, looking for dolphins and manatees, opt for the *Manatee*

DAYTONA BEACH TO ORLANDO AIRPORT

If you're enjoying yourself at the beach but have to fly home from Orlando, you can take advantage of the **Daytona–Orlando Transit Service** (DOTS; ☎ 386 257 5411 or ☎ 800 231 1965, ⓦ dots-daytonabeach.com), whose shuttle buses run daily every ninety minutes (4am–7pm; 1hr 45min) from 1034 N Nova Rd at 11th St in Daytona to Orlando International Airport. The one-way fare is $30 ($55 return), booked at least two days in advance. Call ahead for details and reservations (required).

7

(☎ 800 881 2628, ⊛ manateecruise.com), at 133 Inlet Harbor Rd, Ponce Inlet. Two-hour cruises run at 10am, 1pm and 4pm; sunset cruises depart at 7pm (June–Sept only). All cruises are $25 ($16 for children under 12).

GETTING AROUND

By bus Local buses (Votran: $1.50 a ride; ☎ 386 761 7700, ⊛ votran.org) connect the beaches with the mainland and the Greater Daytona Beach area, and also provide limited night and Sunday services. The main bus terminal, called Transfer Plaza, sits at the junction of Ridgewood Ave and Mary McLeod Bethune Blvd in mainland Daytona Beach. Buses #1, #18 and #19 run from here up and down the Daytona Beach front, while bus #18 and #19 also run in the other direction to the airport and the Speedway. Bus #17A runs south to Ponce Inlet.

By tram (trolley) At the beach, trams ($1.25 a ride) run Mon–Sat noon–midnight (Sun 7am–6pm) along the central part of Atlantic Ave from mid-Jan to early Sept (Labor Day). A $3.50 one-day pass gets you unlimited trips for 24hr including transfers to regular Votran routes.

By taxi Several taxi companies operate in Daytona Beach and the surrounding communities: try AAA Metro Taxi (☎ 386 253 2522) or Daytona Taxi (☎ 386 255 5555). Rides (all use meters, starting at $2.20) from Daytona Beach to Ormond are around $16–21, and around $15–20 for the Speedway. Figure on $29–34 for Ponce Inlet.

ACCOMMODATION

You'll get the lowest rates – motel rooms dip as low as $40–50 – after Labor Day (early Sept) through to the end of January. Prices rise sharply (at least double) during big events, when five- or seven-night minimum stays are often required.

Coquina Inn 544 S Palmetto Ave ☎ 386 254 4969, ⊛ coquinainn.com. This welcoming B&B occupies a grand mansion built in 1912 (with coquina), near the historic district inland, close to the nightlife on Beach St. The four rooms are dressed in a cosy period style, and there's free wi-fi and use of bikes for guests. **$119**

Cove Motel 1306 N Atlantic Ave ☎ 386 252 3678, ⊛ motelcove.com. Family-friendly 38-room motel has some rooms that come with kitchenettes, free wi-fi and private balconies. It's showing its age, but if you're looking for basic and relatively cheap rooms on the water, this is the place. **$65**

Hilton Daytona Beach Oceanfront Resort 100 N Atlantic Ave ☎ 386 254 8200, ⊛ daytonahilton.com. Definitely the biggest and certainly one of the more luxurious options, this 744-room resort right in the centre of Atlantic Ave is hard to miss. Oceanfront rooms have great views over a 3-mile stretch of car-free beach, and all the usual five-star amenities. Extras include the $12/night "resort charge", wi-fi at $5/day and parking $14/day. **$99**

Nova Family Campground 1190 Herbert St, Port Orange ☎ 386 767 0095, ⊛ novacamp.com. Ten miles

south of mainland Daytona Beach (accessible by buses #7, #12 or #17B), with wi-fi, a heated pool and laundry. Basic tent sites **$20**

★ **River Lily Inn Bed & Breakfast** 558 Riverside Drive ☎ 386 253 5002, ⊛ riverlilyinnbedandbreakfast.com. Spotless B&B in a historic 1895 mansion inland from the beach, with six beautifully decorated rooms and incredibly accommodating hosts. The sumptuous breakfasts are supplemented by a fridge of free bottled water, soft drinks and choc ices. **$125**

★ **Tropical Manor** 2237 S Atlantic Ave, Daytona Beach Shores ☎ 386 252 4920, ⊛ tropicalmanor.com. This oceanfront pink motel is a gem, from the personal service to the lovingly maintained rooms to the charming hand-painted flowers, foliage and fish inside and outside the rooms. There's a large pool and the rooms range from standard motel rooms to oceanfront suites. **$65**

The Villa 801 N Peninsula Drive ☎ 386 248 2020, ⊛ thevillabb.com. Situated in an elegant Spanish-style mansion near the Halifax River, this pleasant B&B has opulent rooms, a pool and lush gardens. **$100**

EATING

Anna's Italian Trattoria 304 Seabreeze Blvd ☎ 386 239 9624. If you had an Italian grandma, this is how she'd cook. Home-made pastas like cannelloni and house favourite seafood risotto ensure that you won't leave hungry. Main courses around $20. Tues–Sat 5–10pm.

★ **Aunt Catfish's on the River** 4009 Halifax Drive, Port Orange ☎ 386 767 4768, ⊛ auntcatfishontheriver .com. Mighty portions of ribs and seafood prepared in traditional Southern style. Start with salt & pepper catfish ($8.99) or fried alligator ($10.99), before sampling the

sunburn popcorn rock shrimp ($16.99), or the best shrimp and grits you'll ever taste ($17.99). Mon–Thurs 11.30am–9.30pm, Fri & Sat 11.30am–10pm, Sun 9am–10pm.

Brickyard Lounge 747 W International Speedway Blvd ☎ 386 253 2270, ⊛ daytonabrickyard.com. Best burgers on this stretch of coast, thick wedges of sirloin steak served with fries ($8.99). Being so close to the Speedway there's a racing theme, and it's a big hit with bikers. Mon–Sat 11am–10pm, Sun noon–8pm.

Dancing Avocado Kitchen 110 S Beach St ☎386 947 2022. Health-conscious café serving salads, vegetarian sandwiches and Mexican snacks, including a filling breakfast tofu burrito. Mains average $6.50–12. Mon–Sat 8am–4pm.

Daytona Diner 2043 S Atlantic Ave ☎386 256 2603, ⓦdaytonadiner.com. This 1950s-style diner knocks out huge breakfasts for $5.95–8.45, its justly famed thick and juicy charbroiled burgers for $7.95, and a slice of home-made fruit pie for $3.75. Daily 7am–3pm.

★**Fusion 43 at the Rose Villa** 43 W Granada Blvd, Ormond Beach ☎386 615 7673, ⓦfusion43.com. Exceptional continental cuisine and service make this the best fine-dining in the Daytona area, enhanced by the late nineteenth-century property itself. Feast on cashew butter-crusted pork ribeye ($26) and coconut shrimp stew ($28). Tues–Sat 5–10pm.

Inlet Harbor Restaurant 133 Inlet Harbor Rd, Ponce Inlet ☎386 767 5590, ⓦinletharbor.com. Enjoy shrimp cooked in a number of different ways (try one of the tasty pasta dishes) at this restaurant right on the marina. Live music nightly. Sandwiches $9–13, main courses $17–28. Daily 11am–9pm.

Peach Valley Café 185 E Granada Blvd, Ormond Beach ☎386 615 0096, ⓦpeachvalleyrestaurants.com. Part of the local *Stonewood Grill* stable, this doesn't feel like a chain and serves the best apple fritters ($4.99) you'll ever eat, as well as biscuits and gravy, chicken pot pie, perfect eggs Benedict and excellent Southern-style food. Free wi-fi. Mon–Fri 7am–2.30pm, Sat & Sun 7am–3.30pm.

Ronin Sushi and Sake Bar 111 W International Speedway Blvd ☎386 252 6320, ⓦroninsushiandbar .com. This sushi joint is a local favourite, offering the freshest seafood and sushi rolls and a chic atmosphere. Mon–Thurs & Sun 5–10pm, Fri & Sat 5–11pm.

7

DRINKING AND NIGHTLIFE

Daytona Beach has a varied nightlife, with bikers especially prevalent during the major Speedway events, and US students filling the bars during Spring Break (Feb & March). Main Street has the best biker bars while Seabreeze Boulevard offers Spring Break-style entertainment year-round, with plenty of sports bars and clubs. Buy a copy of the *Daytona Beach News-Journal* (ⓦnews-journalonline.com) for the latest events.

Boot Hill Saloon 310 Main St ☎386 258 9506, ⓦboothillsaloon.com. They say it's "better here than across the street", referring to the neighbouring cemetery, but this slightly rowdy biker bar, with bras dangling from the ceiling, is at least several notches above that, with live rock Thurs–Sun. Daily 11am–3am.

McK's Tavern 218 S Beach St ☎386 238 3321. Boasts a vast range of draft and bottle beers, live Irish music at the weekends and a decent menu featuring juicy burgers, potato pancakes and Guinness stew. Mon–Wed 11am–midnight, Thurs–Sat 11am–2am, Sun 11am–midnight.

Oyster Pub 555 Seabreeze Blvd ☎386 255 6348, ⓦoysterpub.com. Lively sports bar with numerous TVs set up for all the big games, dirt-cheap Apalachicola raw oysters and a loud jukebox. Daily 11.30am–3am.

Razzle's 611 Seabreeze Blvd ☎386 257 6236, ⓦrazzlesnightclub.com. Large disco with headache-inducing light shows and throbbing music for dancers, plus four pool tables and twenty TVs for everyone else. Drink specials every night; cover varies. Daily 8pm–3am.

Rockin' Ranch 801 S Nova Rd, Ormond Beach ☎386 673 0904, ⓦrockinranchnightclub.com. If country is your thing, come here Wednesday, Friday or Saturday for live C&W, or anytime for free line-dancing lessons. Mon–Sat 6pm–2am.

ENTERTAINMENT

Ocean Center 101 N Atlantic Ave ☎386 254 4500, ⓦoceancenter.com. Huge convention and events arena near the pier, host to trade expos and a variety of sports events and shows.

Peabody Auditorium 600 Auditorium Blvd ☎386 671 3460, ⓦpeabodyauditorium.org. Constructed in 1949, this venerable concert venue is the occasional winter home of the London Symphony Orchestra, as well as the Daytona Beach Symphony Society and the Daytona Beach Civic Ballet. Also hosts travelling Broadway shows.

North of Daytona Beach

Leaving Daytona, assuming you don't want to cut inland to Orlando (see p.323), keep on Hwy-A1A **northward** along the coast, where there are a handful of attractions, endless sea views and tranquil beaches all the way to St Augustine. The first community you'll encounter is **Flagler Beach**, 21 miles from Daytona Beach, comprising a few restaurants and shops, a pier ($1.50), and a very tempting beach, far less crowded than its southern neighbour.

Washington Oaks State Gardens

6400 N Oceanshore Blvd (Hwy-A1A), Palm Coast • Daily 8am–sunset • Cars $5 ($4 for single occupant); pedestrians and cyclists $2 •
☎ 386 446 6780, ⓦ floridastateparks.org/washingtonoaks

Twelve miles north of Flagler Beach you'll pass the blazing blossoms of **Washington Oaks State Gardens**, a 425-acre preserve of marshland, coquina rock formations along the coast and **formal gardens**, best in spring and summer when the azaleas, camellias and roses are in bloom. The property was once owned by a distant relative of George Washington, but the gardens were established by rich New Yorkers Louise and Owen Young, who purchased the land in 1936 and built a winter retirement home here.

Marineland

9600 N Oceanshore Blvd (Hwy-A1A) • Daily 8.30am–4.30pm • $11.95, children 3–12 $6.95; experiences: Immersion $229, Touch and Feed $31.95, Discover $169, Designs $99 • ☎ 877 298 5994, ⓦ marineland.net

Opened in 1938, **Marineland** is now managed by Georgia Aquarium, renovated and reloaded as a "**dolphin adventure**". General admission allows you to observe the dolphins playing, but you can also fork out for the "Immersion" experience, a chance to swim with the dolphins for twenty minutes in shallow water, plus another ten minutes with a mask in deep water. You can also opt for more limited "Touch and Feed", "Discover" and "Designs" experiences – this last has you holding a canvas while the dolphins create jarring images using their noses and real paint – despite the whole thing being of questionable conservation/educational value.

Fort Matanzas National Monument

Rattlesnake Island, 8635 Hwy-A1A S • Daily 9am–5.30pm • Free • ☎ 904 471 0116, ⓦ nps.gov/foma • Ferries daily 9.30am–4.30pm every hour on the half-hour

The Spanish garrison at St Augustine (15 miles north) completed what is today **Fort Matanzas National Monument** in 1742 at the southern tip of Anastasia Island (see p.337). The idea was to guard Matanzas Inlet and the southern approaches to St Augustine, but the fort was only attacked once, and by the late nineteenth century had become an abandoned ruin. Today the restored fort – more like a 30ft fortified tower – is accessible only by free **ferry** (you get around 40min to explore the site), but the visitor centre (with a video explaining the history of the fort) lies on land just off Hwy-A1A. The site also commemorates the **massacre of French soldiers** by Spanish general Pedro Menéndez, following his destruction of Fort Caroline in 1565 (see p.344); after being wrecked in a storm and captured by the Spanish, 245 Frenchmen were killed on or near this site for refusing to convert to Catholicism.

St Augustine and around

The oldest permanent settlement in North America, **ST AUGUSTINE** is a small city of eminently strollable streets crammed with museums, restaurants, restored Spanish homes and especially entertaining attractions for families.

The town was founded in 1565 by Spanish general Pedro Menéndez de Aviles, but nothing survived the devastating attacks of Francis Drake in 1586 and the pirate Robert Searle in 1668; only the stone-built **Castillo de San Marcos** escaped further destruction wrought by Carolina governor James Moore in 1702. As a result, most of what you see today dates from the late eighteenth century or the Spanish Revival building boom of the 1880s and 1890s, when tycoon **Henry Flagler** developed the town as his first Florida winter resort. Adding to the architectural mix, many buildings have been renovated or reconstructed completely since the 1930s. Today St Augustine is part historic theme park, part enigmatic memorial to America's oft forgotten Spanish roots – though it was founded

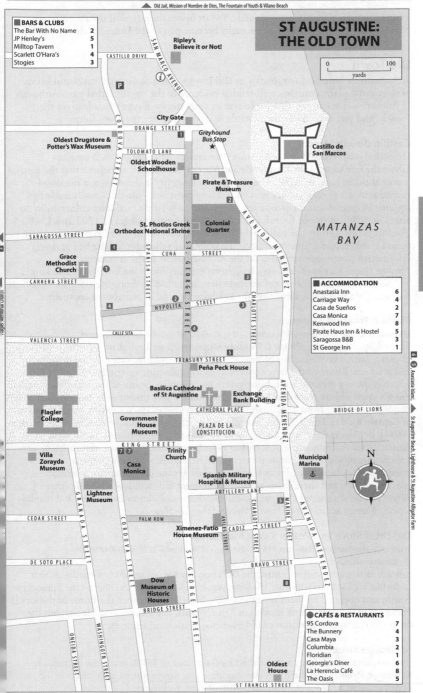

Old Jail, Mission of Nombre de Dios, The Fountain of Youth & Vilano Beach

ST AUGUSTINE: THE OLD TOWN

0   100
yards

BARS & CLUBS

The Bar With No Name	2
JP Henley's	5
Milltop Tavern	1
Scarlett O'Hara's	4
Stogies	3

ACCOMMODATION

Anastasia Inn	6
Carriage Way	4
Casa de Sueños	2
Casa Monica	7
Kenwood Inn	8
Pirate Haus Inn & Hostel	5
Saragossa B&B	3
St George Inn	1

CAFÉS & RESTAURANTS

95 Cordova	7
The Bunnery	4
Casa Maya	3
Columbia	2
Floridian	1
Georgie's Diner	6
La Herencia Café	8
The Oasis	5

Ripley's Believe it or Not!

CASTILLO DRIVE

SAN MARCO AVENUE

CORDOVA STREET

City Gate

ORANGE STREET

Greyhound Bus Stop

Castillo de San Marcos

Oldest Drugstore & Potter's Wax Museum

TOLOMATO LANE

Oldest Wooden Schoolhouse

Pirate & Treasure Museum

St. Photios Greek Orthodox National Shrine

Colonial Quarter

MATANZAS BAY

SARAGOSSA STREET

CUNA STREET

Grace Methodist Church

CARRERA STREET

SPANISH STREET

HYPOLITA STREET

ST. GEORGE STREET

CHARLOTTE STREET

AVENIDA MENENDEZ

CALLE SITA

VALENCIA STREET

TREASURY STREET

Peña Peck House

Basilica Cathedral of St Augustine

Exchange Bank Building

CATHEDRAL PLACE

BRIDGE OF LIONS

Flagler College

Government House Museum

PLAZA DE LA CONSTITUCION

Villa Zorayda Museum

KING STREET

Trinity Church

Casa Monica

Spanish Military Hospital & Museum

Municipal Marina

N

Lightner Museum

ARTILLERY LANE

CEDAR STREET

GRANADA STREET

CORDOVA STREET

PALM ROW

AVILES STREET

CADIZ STREET

CHARLOTTE STREET

MARINE STREET

AVENIDA MENENDEZ

Ximenez-Fatio House Museum

DE SOTO PLACE

BRAVO STREET

Dow Museum of Historic Houses

ST GEORGE STREET

BRIDGE STREET

ONEIDA STREET

WASHINGTON STREET

Oldest House

ST FRANCIS STREET

7

Anastasia Island

St Augustine Beach, Lighthouse & St Augustine Alligator Farm

some forty years before Jamestown and 55 years before the arrival of the Pilgrims in Massachusetts, St Augustine didn't actually become part of the United States until 1821.

Old Town

St Augustine's historic downtown – or **Old Town** – along St George Street and south of the central plaza, contains well-tended evidence of the town's varied past. Although St Augustine is small, there's a lot to see: an early start will give you a lead on the crowds, and you should ideally allow three days to explore the town fully.

Castillo de San Marcos

1 S Castillo Drive • Daily 8.45am–5.15pm • $7, children under 15 free; parking $1.50/hr • ☎ 904 829 6506, ⓦ nps.gov/casa

Given the fine state of the **Castillo de San Marcos**, it's difficult to believe that the fortress was established back in 1672. The secret of its longevity is the design: a diamond-shaped rampart at each corner maximized firepower, and 14ft-thick walls made of coquina (a type of soft limestone found on Anastasia Island) reduced vulnerability to attack – as British troops found when they waged fruitless sieges in 1702 and 1740. The fort is now run by the National Park Service; docents in Spanish uniforms carry period muskets and fire cannon from the walls, and schedules for the free and very informative twenty-minute talks on the fort are posted at the entrance.

Inside, there's a series of exhibits highlighting everyday life in the fort, the British attacks and Native American prisoners of war held here in the 1880s. Venturing along the 35ft-high ramparts gives handsome views over the low-lying city and its waterborne approaches.

Pirate & Treasure Museum

12 S Castillo Drive • Daily 10am–8pm • $12.99, children 5–12 $6.99 • ☎ 877 467 5863, ⓦ thepiratemuseum.com

The wildly entertaining **Pirate & Treasure Museum** opens a window into the golden age of piracy with a combination of interactive exhibits and precious original documents and artefacts. Much of the latter comes from the collection of entrepreneur **Pat Croce**, who has spent a lifetime assembling pirate memorabilia. Some of the highlights include the 400-year-old **treasure chest** of Captain Thomas Tew, one of only two original **Jolly Roger** flags (dating from 1850), and the priceless journal documenting the last journey of **Captain Kidd** in 1699. There's also a rare first English edition of *Bucaniers of America* (1684), by Alexander Esquemelin. Disney designed a three-minute audio show especially for the museum, dramatizing Blackbeard's last moments, and touch-screens present information on famous pirates (Brits be warned – **Francis Drake** is unequivocally one of the pirates here). You even get the chance to fire a cannon (electronically), and there's also a fun treasure-hunt kids will love (as will plenty of adults). Finally, a special Hollywood exhibit chronicles pirates in movies, and displays Johnny Depp's actual sword from *Pirates of the Caribbean*.

Old Drug Store and Potter's Wax Museum

31 Orange St • Mon–Thurs & Sun 10am–5pm, Fri & Sat 10am–7pm • $9.99, children 6–12 $6.99 • ☎ 904 829 9056, ⓦ potterswaxmuseum.com

Just across from the visitor centre, the **Old Drug Store** is a warped clapboard gem that looks like it's about to fall over. The store was established around 1887 by the Speissegger family, and operated by them into the 1960s. Since 2013 it's been the home of the kitsch **Potter's Wax Museum** (think models of Tiger Woods, Halle Berry and Moses), but the front still contains a collection of old medicine bottles and registers.

St George Street

Two coquina pillars, remnants of the **City Gate** built in 1808, mark the entrance to **St George Street**, once the main thoroughfare and now a tourist-trampled pedestrianized strip – but home to plenty of genuine history.

The Oldest Wooden Schoolhouse

14 St George St • Daily 9am–6pm • $4.50 • ☎ 888 653 7245, Ⓦ oldestwoodenschoolhouse.com

Originally the home of Juan Genopoly, a Greek refugee from the failed colony at New Smyrna (see p.317), the weathered **Oldest Wooden Schoolhouse** is wonderfully redolent of the last years of Spanish rule, its original red-cedar and cypress timber walls and tabby floor (a mix of crushed oyster shells and lime) still intact. Whether it really is the oldest school is debatable: though it is likely that there was a much older building on this site when Juan bought it, most experts believe the current structure was built between 1800 and 1804, and later converted into a school (there's a much older school building in Staten Island). The interior has been faithfully decked out in nineteenth-century style, though pupils and teacher are now unconvincingly portrayed by speaking animatronic models.

Colonial Quarter

33 St George St • Daily 10am–6pm • $12.99, children 5–12 $6.99 • ☎ 904 342 2857, Ⓦ colonialquarter.com

Taking up a fair-sized plot along St George Street, the **Colonial Quarter** is an enthusiastic effort to portray life during the Spanish and British colonial periods, with four themed areas of reconstructed homes and workshops running chronologically from the sixteenth to nineteenth centuries. This is a living museum, rather than a series of displays; volunteers dressed as Spanish settlers go about their daily tasks at anvils and foot-driven wood lathes, making candles and the like.

St Photios Greek Orthodox National Shrine

41 St George St • Mon–Sat 9am–5pm, Sun noon–6pm • Free • ☎ 904 829 8205, Ⓦ stphotios.com

An unassuming doorway midway along St George Street leads into the petite **St Photios Greek Orthodox National Shrine**, where Byzantine choral music echoes through the halls, and icons and candles watch over hard-hitting displays and videos depicting the experiences of Greek immigrants to the US – especially those who settled in New Smyrna (see p.317). The small but ornate shrine itself was dedicated in 1982, while a video explains why New Smyrna, and later St Augustine, represent the Greek "Plymouth Rock" in America.

Peña Peck House

143 St George St • Mon–Sat 10.30am–5pm, Sun 12.30–5pm; tours Mon–Fri & Sun 12.30–4pm, Sat 10.30am–4pm • Free, donation requested • ☎ 904 829 5064, Ⓦ penapeckhouse.com

For an intimate look at local life in St Augustine during the early American period, head for the **Peña Peck House**. Thought to have been built for the Spanish city treasurer in 1750, and later home to the British governor, this house was purchased by Dr Seth Peck and his gregarious spouse in 1837 (when Florida was a US territory), and turned into a high-society rendezvous. The Pecks' furnishings and paintings, plus the enthusiastic spiel of the guides (members of the nonprofit Woman's Exchange, which owns the house), make for an enjoyable tour.

Plaza de la Constitución

St George Street runs into **Plaza de la Constitución**, a square and marketplace dating from 1598, dominated by the **cathedral** and the soaring 1928 Moorish Revival skyscraper known as the **Exchange Bank Building** next door.

Government House Museum

48 King St (Plaza de la Constitución) • Daily 10am–5pm • $7.99 • ☎ 904 825 5079, Ⓦ staugustinegovernment.com

The ground floor of **Government House Museum**, on the west side of the Plaza de la Constitución, will be host to the excellent, interactive **First Colony Exhibit** until at least the end of 2015 (from the Florida Museum of Natural History), which tells the story of the early Spanish settlement. Though the stately Georgian-style stone mansion was once home to the Spanish government and incorporates parts of older buildings (the east wing dates from 1710), most of what you see today dates from the 1930s, when it was converted into a post office.

Cathedral Basilica of St Augustine

38 Cathedral Place (Plaza de la Constitución) • Daily 7am–5pm • Donation requested • ☎ 904 824 2806, ⓦ thefirstparish.org

The **Cathedral Basilica of St Augustine** adds a touch of grandeur to the Plaza de la Constitución, though it's largely a 1960s remodelling of the late eighteenth-century original, with grand murals by Hugo Ohlms depicting life in St Augustine framing the entrance, and its distinctive red ceiling and black roof beams beautifully restored.

Spanish Military Hospital & Museum

3 Aviles St • Daily 10am–6.30pm (tours every 30min till 6pm) • $7 • ☎ 904 342 7730, ⓦ spanishmilitaryhospital.com

Reconstructed in 1966, the **Spanish Military Hospital & Museum** was originally a hospital built in 1791, and the museum re-creates the spartan care wounded soldiers received in the 1783–1821 Spanish period. It includes displays of rusty surgical instruments and also the "mourning room", where the priest administered last rites to doomed patients. Access is by guided tour only.

Ximenez-Fatio House Museum

20 Aviles St • Tues–Sat 11am–4pm (hourly tours until 3pm) • $7 • ☎ 904 829 3575, ⓦ ximenezfatiohouse.org

Built around 1798 for a Spanish merchant, the **Ximenez-Fatio House Museum** became a boarding house in the nineteenth century, representing one of the few socially acceptable business ventures for a woman at the time. The museum explores this history, while guided tours of the rickety but wonderfully preserved coquina house itself add illuminating details. Don't miss the rare 1650 **Caravaca Cross** displayed in the museum, discovered on the property in 2002.

Dow Museum of Historic Houses

149 Cordova St • Mon–Sat 10am–5pm, Sun 11am–5pm • $8.95 • ☎ 904 823 9722, ⓦ moas.org/dowmuseum

The **Dow Museum of Historic Houses** is a collection of nine period buildings that have been expertly restored from every period and cultural stripe between 1790 and 1910, not just the Spanish. Particularly fascinating is the **Prince Murat House** (1790), briefly home to Napoleon's nephew (for whom it was named) in 1824, whose main room and upstairs bedroom is graced by ravishing French Empire furniture.

The Oldest House

14 St Francis St • Daily 9am–5pm, last admission 4.30pm; guided tours every 30min • $8 • ☎ 904 824 2872, ⓦ staugustinehistoricalsociety.org

Built in the years after the destruction of St Augustine by the British in 1702, the González-Alvarez House is better known today as the **Oldest House**. The site also includes a small **museum** on the history of the town, the **Edwards Gallery** of historic maps and the **Tovar House** of 1740, home to modest exhibits on local archeology. The Oldest House itself – which really is one of the oldest and most atmospheric structures in town – can be visited by guided tour only, the ground floor furnished in the sparse, rough style of the early 1700s. The second floor was grafted on during the British period in the 1770s, a fact evinced by the bone china crockery belonging to a former occupant, one Mary Peavitt. Her disastrous marriage to a hopeless gambler provided the basis for a popular historical novel, *Maria*, by Eugenia Price (the gift shop has copies).

Flagler College

74 King St • Guided tours daily: May to mid-Aug 10am–3pm (hourly); mid-Aug to April 10am & 2pm • $10 • ☎ 904 819 6400, ⓦ legacy.flagler.edu

A walk west from the Plaza de la Constitución along **King Street** bridges the gap between early St Augustine and its turn-of-the-twentieth-century tourist boom. You'll soon notice, at the junction with Cordova Street, the flowing spires, arches and Spanish Revival red-tiled roof of **Flagler College**. Now a liberal arts campus, it was completed by Henry Flagler in 1888 as the *Ponce de León Hotel*, the cornerstone of his plan to remake St Augustine into a lavish winter retreat of the nation's rich and mighty. As Flagler developed properties further south and extended his railway, the *Ponce de León* fell from favour, and the hotel became a college in 1968. Forty-minute **guided tours** start at the mesmerizing 80ft **Rotunda**, with its Tiffany sunroof, stunning oak carvings, fourteen-carat gold gilding and murals by George Maynard. Tours also take in the incredibly opulent **dining room** with its precious collection of Tiffany stained-glass windows and more dramatic murals by Maynard, as well as the elegant **Grand Parlor**, where female hotel guests would socialize under rare Tiffany Austrian crystal chandeliers and a massive white-onyx fireplace.

Lightner Museum

75 King St • Daily 9am–5pm, last admission 4pm • $10 • ☎ 904 824 2874, ⊕ lightnermuseum.org

After the *Ponce de León Hotel*, Henry Flagler's plan to convert St Augustine into a posh resort continued with the construction of the *Alcazar Hotel* right across the street in 1888. The *Alcazar* closed in 1931 and has served as the **City Hall** since 1973. Fronted by a courtyard of palm trees and fountains, the Spanish Renaissance building also now contains the **Lightner Museum**, a whimsical collection of Victorian cut glass, Tiffany lamps, antique music boxes, an Egyptian mummy and even a fossilized dinosaur egg. Most of the booty was acquired by publishing ace **Otto C. Lightner** (1887–1950) from once-wealthy estates hard hit by the Depression – the tycoon bought the ex-hotel in 1947 and is buried in the courtyard. The opulent interior is more enticing than the collection – the upstairs galleries occupy the former hotel's Turkish and Russian baths, and you can circle the spacious Ballroom Gallery above *Café Alcazar* (daily 11am–3pm).

Villa Zorayda Museum

83 King St • Mon–Sat 10am–5pm, last admission 4.30pm, Sun 11am–4pm • $10, including audio tour; free parking • ☎ 904 829 9887, ⊕ villazorayda.com

Built by eccentric Bostonian architect Franklin W. Smith in 1883, the **Villa Zorayda Museum** was his re-creation of the famed Alhambra. The architect was so impressed by the Moorish architecture he'd seen in Spain that he built a copy of one wing of the thirteenth-century palace here, at a tenth of the original size. The building so dazzled Henry Flagler, he offered to buy it – Smith refused, but shared the secret of his Portland cement/coquina combo building method, inspiring Flagler to embark on the building spree that came to define modern St Augustine.

Today the villa is home to an intriguing collection of Smith's personal belongings and rare antiques owned by one A.S. Mussallem, who purchased the house in 1911 (his family still owns it). The villa is brought to life by a detailed **audio guide** that charts its history and the curios on display. Highlights include a collection of 1881 French watercolours of the Middle East, Smith's original photos of the Alhambra, rare newspaper cuttings from 1888 and a Thomas Cole reproduction of the painting *Youth*. Most remarkable of all is the "**Sacred Cat Rug**", a 2400-year-old carpet made from the hairs of ancient Egyptian cats. It was discovered in 1861 as wrapping for the foot of a looted mummy (also on display here).

Whetstone Chocolate Factory

139 King St • **Shop** Mon–Fri 10am–5.30pm, Sat 9.30am–5.30am, Sun noon–5pm • Free • **Tours** Mon–Fri 11am, 1pm, 2.15pm & 3.30pm, Sat 10am, 11.15am, 1pm, 2.15pm & 3.30pm, Sun 1pm, 2.15pm & 3.30pm • $8 • ☎ 904 217 0275, ⊕ whetstonechocolates.com

Chocoholics should make for the free samples and factory tours at this local chocolatier, based here since the 1970s. Don't leave without sampling their chocolate sea shells (try the Key lime flavour; 7oz bag $8.95), gelato or sumptuous, frozen hot chocolate.

San Sebastian Winery

157 King St • Mon–Sat 10am–6pm, Sun 11am–6pm • Tours and tastings free • ☎ 904 826 1594, ⊚ sansebastianwinery.com

St Augustine wineries were around 150 years before their counterparts in California, and regular guided tours of the **San Sebastian Winery** explain the various stages in the wine-making process. You can taste several of the wines after the tour, mostly of the sweet variety with a very distinctive bouquet guaranteed to divide opinions – some visitors end up buying bottles to take home, others end up comparing them to jet fuel and burnt tyres.

Flagler Memorial Presbyterian Church

32 Sevilla St • Mon–Sat 9am–4pm, Sun services at 8.30am & 11am • Free • ☎ 904 829 6451, ⊚ memorialpcusa.org

In 1890, the Presbyterian community in St Augustine dedicated what would become the **Flagler Memorial Presbyterian Church**, funded by tycoon Henry Flagler (son of a Presbyterian minister) as a memorial to his daughter Jenny (who had died of complications from childbirth). Flagler himself was buried here in 1913, and his tomb is one of the main features of the interior, though it's the ornate Venetian Renaissance exterior and 120ft copper dome that really stand out.

San Marco Avenue

Leading away from the tightly grouped streets of the Old Town, the traffic-bearing **San Marco Avenue**, beginning on the northern side of the City Gate at St George Street, passes the sites of the first Spanish landings and settlements as well as some reminders of the Timucua Indians who greeted them.

Ripley's Believe It or Not!

19 San Marco Ave • Daily 9am–8pm • $12.99, children 6–11 $6.99; free parking • ☎ 904 824 1606, ⊚ ripleys.com/staugustine

Always wanted to see a six-legged cow, a headless chicken and a genuine shrunken human head? Robert Ripley's collections of the weird, wacky and plain gross have been entertaining (and disgusting) the public since he first displayed his "Odditorium" in 1933. Some may roll their eyes at any mention of the ubiquitous **Ripley's Believe It or Not!** but this was the first permanent "museum", opened shortly after Ripley's death in 1950. Housed in a lavish Moorish Revival-style mansion, built in 1887 by millionaire William Warden, the collection here is vast, running over several ornate floors.

Mission of Nombre de Dios

27 Ocean Ave • Mon–Fri 8am–5pm, Sat & Sun 10am–5pm; museum Thurs–Sat 10am–4pm, Sun noon–4pm • Free • ☎ 904 824 2809, ⊚ missionandshrine.org

Pedro Menéndez founded St Augustine in 1565 some five blocks north of the current Old Town, in a rustic setting along the Matanzas Bay now shared between the Fountain of Youth (see p.334) and the Catholic complex known as the **Mission of Nombre de Dios**. Soon after the Spanish arrived, Father Francisco López de Mendoza Grajales celebrated the first official Mass in North America here. The mission that was established on this spot around 1620 was the first of many in the southeast US founded by Jesuit, then Franciscan, priests to convert Native Americans to Christianity; abandoned after 1706, it had little long-term impact on the region.

Nevertheless, a small, ivy-covered 1914 re-creation of the original **Shrine of Our Lady of La Leche** is still revered by pilgrims, while a pathway leads across a nineteenth-century cemetery to the 208ft stainless steel **Great Cross** raised in 1965, glittering in the sun beside the river. The **Mission Nombre de Dios Museum** shows a twelve-minute film dramatizing the Spanish arrival, and houses the actual painted coffin of Menéndez (though he's not inside), a gift from the Spanish city of Avilés in 1929. Next door is the fairly dull and modern **Prince of Peace Church**, built in 1965.

FROM TOP CASTILLO DE SAN MARCOS, ST AUGUSTINE (P.328); JACKSONVILLE (P.338) >

The Fountain of Youth

11 Magnolia Ave, at Williams St · Daily 9am–6pm · $12, children 6–12 $8 · ☎ 904 829 3168, ⓦ fountainofyouthflorida.com

In addition to the prospect of finding gold and silver, it's said that **Ponce de León** was drawn to Florida by the belief that the fabled life-preserving "fountain of youth" was located here. Rather tenuously, this fact is celebrated at a mineral spring touted as **The Fountain of Youth**, very near the point where Ponce de León probably landed in 1513, and where the first Spanish colony was established in 1565. As you enter the site you'll be handed a cup of fresh spring water (with a smelly bouquet of sulphur), but it's the expansive fifteen acres of surrounding park that have far more significance as an archeological site. Beside the remains of the original Spanish settlement, many Timucua relics have been unearthed, including a rare collection of graves, some of which are Christian burials. Menéndez founded his first colony on the site of a Timucua village known as **Seloy** – after just nine months, conflict with the natives forced him to relocate. Exhibits and reproductions explore the history of the Spanish and Timucua here (most of the latter had died out by 1729), while monuments honour Ponce de León. There's also a small **Planetarium** and an authentic Spanish cannon fired at regular intervals. Brilliantly plumed **peacocks** wander the site, an ancient Christian symbol of eternal life.

Old Jail and around

167 San Marco Ave, at Williams St · Guided tours daily 9am–4.30pm, every 20min · $9.50, children 6–12 $5.30 · ☎ 904 829 3800, ⓦ trolleytours.com

The collection of attractions surrounding the **Old Town Trolley** terminus and the **Old Jail**, halfway up San Marco, offer plenty of old-fashioned hokey fun, especially for families. The jail was completed in 1891 and designed by Henry Flagler, apparently without irony, to resemble a Queen Anne-style hotel building. It closed in 1953 and today costumed deputies take you on guided tours through the cell blocks, sheriff's quarters and the old gallows.

Oldest Store Museum

167 San Marco Ave, at Williams St · Guided tours only; daily 8.30am–4.30pm, every 20min · $9.50, children 6–12 $5.30 · ☎ 904 829 3800, ⓦ trolleytours.com

Next to the Old Jail, the **Oldest Store Museum** is crammed with the original inventory of local nineteenth-century storekeeper C.F. Hamblen (the building was actually owned by an old insurance company), with costumed actors playing the roles of sales clerks, butchers and even snake-oil salesmen.

Old St Augustine History Museum

167 San Marco Ave, at Williams St · Daily 8.30am–4.30pm · $6.40, children 6–12 $5.30; free with trolley ticket · ☎ 904 829 3800, ⓦ trolleytours.com

The **Old St Augustine History Museum** charts the impact of Henry Flagler on the town (with special exhibits on the creation of his railway), and displays everything from old dolls to a Spanish sunken treasure room, a replica Timucua village and a Florida "cracker" trading post.

ARRIVAL AND DEPARTURE   ST AUGUSTINE

By bus Greyhound buses will drop you right next to the castle at 1 Castillo Drive, an easy stroll from anywhere in the Old Town. Buy tickets at RJD of St Augustine, 52 San Marco Ave, two blocks north (daily 6am–10pm; ☎ 904 829 6401). Airport Shuttle of St Augustine (☎ 904 825 0004, ⓦ airportshuttlestaugustine.com) runs a shuttle bus to and from Jacksonville Airport (daily 7am–7pm; $60, $5 for each additional person up to six people; door-to-door

service for $75).
Destinations Daytona Beach (2 daily; 1hr 5min); Jacksonville (1 daily; 55min); Orlando (2 daily; 2hr 20min).
By car Driving to St Augustine is straightforward, with several exits from I-95 leading to downtown, sandwiched between US-1 (Ponce de Léon Blvd) and Hwy-A1A (Ocean & San Marco blvds). You should find plenty of signed parking near the centre; if in doubt, aim for the large 24hr

parking garage next to the tourist office (see below): it costs $10 to park there for the day (or $1.50/hr), and it's convenient enough if you're strolling the streets. If you intend to take the Trolley Bus tour, there's free parking at the Old Town Trolley Welcome Center, 27 San Marco Ave.

GETTING AROUND AND INFORMATION

By bus Tickets for the Old Town Trolley Tour (see box, below) include exclusive use of the free Beach Shuttle, which departs hourly from the south side of the Plaza de la Constitución, stopping at the Lighthouse and Alligator Farm on the way to the beach. Exploring beyond the Old Town is otherwise tough without a car. The Sunshine Bus Company (☎904 209 3716, ⓦsunshinebus.net) runs small buses to the beaches (Red Line, then Green Line; $1 per ride; $3 one-day pass), but services are not especially frequent (5–6 daily), so grab a timetable at the visitor centre.

By taxi Try Ancient Cab (☎904 824 8161).

Tourist information The main visitor centre, 10 Castillo Drive (daily 8.30am–5.30pm; ☎904 825 1000 or ☎800 653 2489, ⓦfloridashistoriccoast.com), offers the usual tourist brochures and discount coupons.

ACCOMMODATION

Several chain **motels** line San Marco Ave (Hwy-A1A) and Ponce de León Blvd (US-1) for a mile or two north of the centre, and offer lower rates than the hotels in the Old Town. For a list of 25 gorgeous historic **B&Bs** in town visit ⓦstaugustineinns.com.

Carriage Way 70 Cuna St ☎904 829 2467, ⓦcarriageway.com. Canopy and four-poster beds, clawfoot tubs and antiques add to the period feel of this romantic 1880s B&B. $189

Casa de Sueños 20 Cordova St ☎904 824 0887, ⓦcasadesuenos.com. This sumptuous bed and breakfast, a Mediterranean-style house built in 1904, offers five Spanish-themed rooms and all the amenities (even cream sherry in your room). $159

Casa Monica 95 Cordova St ☎904 827 1888, ⓦcasamonica.com. By far the most elegant, and costly, choice in the heart of Old Town. This magnificently restored, Spanish-style 1888 gem has 138 uniquely furnished rooms and an air of royalty – in fact, the tower suite has hosted the king and queen of Spain. Book well in advance. $199

Kenwood Inn 38 Marine St ☎904 824 2116, ⓦthekenwoodinn.com. Enjoying a peaceful location, this 1880s Queen Anne Victorian gem features gorgeous period rooms, its own pool, and a complimentary cocktail hour every day. Free use of bikes for guests. $159

7

ST AUGUSTINE TOURS

The two major **sightseeing tours** are distinguishable only by their colours: **Ripley's Red Train Tours** (170 San Marco Ave; 3 days for $23.99, children $9.99; ☎904 829 6545 or ☎800 226 6545, ⓦripleys.com/redtrains) and the green-and-orange **Old Town Trolley Tours** (167 San Marco Ave and 27 San Marco Ave; 3 days for $25.75, children 3–12 $10.30; ☎904 829 3800, ⓦtrolleytours.com). They operate daily 8.30am to 5pm (Ripley's Sightseeing Train) or 4.30pm (Old Town Trolley), and make approximately twenty stops during an hour-long narrated circuit; you can hop on and off whenever you like. The Old Town Trolley includes the Beach Shuttle (see above).

The tourist office has recommendations for a variety of other tours, but the following usually offer good value:

City Walks ☎904 825 0087, ⓦstaugcitywalks .com. Offers well-organized and informative walking tours with historic and culinary themes. $15–24

Ghosts & Gravestones ☎888 461 1009, ⓦghostsandgravestones.com. These 1hr 20min ghoulish bus tours reveal local legends, tall tales and haunted and spook-filled sites; tours start at the Old Town Trolley Welcome Center at 27 San Marco Ave. $26.75, children 3–12 $14.40

Pirate Ship Black Raven ☎904 826 0000, ⓦblackravenadventures.com. Kids will love this – a mock pirate ship that turns into a pirate show full of music, hearty singing and lots of "Ahrrrrs", à la *Pirates of the Caribbean*. $34.95, children 3–12 $24.95

Scenic Cruise ☎800 542 8316, ⓦscenic-cruise.com. Offers four to five (depending on the season) daily 1hr 15min guided trips around the bay. $16.75, children 4–12 $7.75

St Augustine Eco-Tours ☎904 377 7245, ⓦstaugustineecotours.com. Guided 2hr kayak tours ($45), 1hr 30min dolphin boat tours ($40) and 2hr sailing adventures ($50).

★**Pirate Haus Inn & Hostel** 32 Treasury St ☎ 904 808 1999, ⓦ piratehaus.com. A renovated pirate-themed hotel and adjacent hostel, with a giant kitchen and a common room stuffed with local guidebooks. All of the private rooms in the hotel have a/c, and there's a free pancake breakfast. Free wi-fi, too. Dorms $22, doubles $90

★**Saragossa B&B** 34 Saragossa St ☎ 904 808 7384, ⓦ saragossainn.com. This lovely little pink cottage began life in 1924 as a prefab bungalow and now holds four comfortable guestrooms and two suites, just a bit west of the beaten path. $104

St George Inn 4 St George St ☎ 904 827 5740, ⓦ stgeorge-inn.com. You can't get much more central than this plush hotel, with many of the 25 luxurious rooms with balconies and views of the Intracoastal Waterway and the Castillo de San Marco. $159

EATING

One item to look out for in St Augustine is the extra hot **datil pepper**, only grown in these parts. Many restaurants use them, but you can also buy them at **Minorcan Datil Pepper Products**, 150 St Johns Business Place (☎ 904 522 0059, ⓦ minorcandatil.com).

95 Cordova 95 Cordova St, at the Casa Monica Hotel ☎ 904 810 6810, ⓦ casamonica.com. You'll need to make reservations to partake of the masterful *nouvelle* Continental cuisine at this opulent bistro. Expect to pay $23–44 for main courses (like coriander-crusted sea scallops) or $9.50–13 for a gourmet lunch sandwich. Mon–Thurs & Sun 7.30am–2.30pm & 5–9pm, Fri & Sat 7.30am–2.30pm & 5–10pm.

The Bunnery 121 St George St ☎ 904 829 6166, ⓦ bunnerybakeryandcafe.com. All the tempting goodies in this old-style bakery are made in-house except the strudel. There's also good coffee and economical breakfasts ($3.25–7.25), plus tempting sandwiches and paninis ($7–8.25). Mon–Fri 8am–4pm, Sat & Sun 8am–5pm.

★**Casa Maya** 17 Hypolita St ☎ 904 823 1739. Didn't expect to find "organic Mayan cuisine" in Florida? Everything on the eclectic menu at this little four-table restaurant is excellent, from the "Apocalypto" breakfast sandwich with chorizo, egg, avocado, beans, tomato and bacon ($9.50) to the marinated "Aztec" pork dinner ($16.95). Mon 8am–3.30pm, Wed & Thurs 10am–3.30pm & 5.30–9pm, Fri–Sun 8am–3.30pm & 5.30–9.30pm.

Columbia 98 St George St ☎ 904 824 3341, ⓦ columbiarestaurant.com. Enjoy traditional Spanish and Cuban food, from tapas to sumptuous paellas, amid splashing fountains, wood beams, candlelight and painted tiles. Dinner mains cost $18–35; wash the meal down with a pitcher of mojito, made tableside ($25.95). Mon–Sat 11am–10pm, Sun noon–10pm.

★**Floridian** 39 Cordova St ☎ 904 829 0655, ⓦ thefloridianstaug.com. Fresh, locally sourced produce and a creative menu, blending Southern classics with lighter options, makes this extra special; think slow-smoked BBQ pulled pork over buttermilk waffles ($16.75) and cheddar and veggie-stuffed cornbread topped with choice of blackened fresh fish or tofu ($13). Mon, Wed, Thurs & Sun 11am–3pm & 5–9pm, Fri & Sat 11am–3pm & 5–10pm, Tues 5–9pm.

Georgie's Diner 100 Malaga St ☎ 904 819 9006. Retro steel dining-car with red booths, chequered floors and a blend of classic diner food and Greek cuisine – try the gyros ($7.50–8.95) or spinach pie ($11.95). Mon, Tues & Sun 7am–9pm, Fri & Sat 7am–10pm.

La Herencia Café 4 Aviles St ☎ 904 829 9487, ⓦ laherenciacafe.com. You'll get some of the best Cuban food in town at this cute little diner, as well as great omelettes like the Tropical, featuring sweet plantain. Excellent lunch specials from $12. Mon–Thurs & Sun 8.30am–8pm, Fri & Sat 8.30am–10pm.

DRINKING AND NIGHTLIFE

The Bar With No Name 16 Castillo Drive ☎ 904 826 1837. Central, laidback, easy to find and with plenty of quality (and varied) live music, this place is a great find – but it really does have no name. Popular with Flagler College students. Daily 11am–2am.

JP Henley's 10 Marine St ☎ 904 829 3337, ⓦ jphenleys .com. Beer and sports lovers should explore this friendly pub, home to around fifty draught brews and six flat-screen TVs for sports events. Also does wine, but no spirits. Daily 11am–1am.

Milltop Tavern 19½ St George St ☎ 904 829 2329, ⓦ milltoptavern.com. Lots of local folk hang out above this old grist mill; there's a terrific, funky atmosphere, live music in the afternoons and evenings, and an open-air view of the Castillo and harbour. Daily 11am–midnight.

Scarlett O'Hara's 70 Hypolita St ☎ 904 824 6535, ⓦ scarlettoharas.net. Tuck into full meals (barbecue is the speciality) and enjoy a variety of live music, including karaoke, at this cedar and cypress building that was once an old Florida "cracker" house, built in 1879. Pitchers of draught beer $11. Mon–Thurs & Sun 11am–1am, Fri & Sat 11am–2am.

★**Stogies** 36 Charlotte St ☎ 904 826 4008. Coolest joint in town, blending quality live jazz bands with excellent draught beers in an old Victorian house with a humidor at the back, where you can smoke big fat cigars all night. Daily 2pm–2am.

World Golf Hall of Fame

1 World Golf Place (I-95 Exit 323) • Mon–Sat 10am–6pm, Sun noon–6pm • $19.50, audio guides $3 • ☎ 904 940 4000,
ⓦ worldgolfhalloffame.org

Even non-golfers will find this lavish tribute to the game intriguing, with the **World Golf Hall of Fame** set within the sprawling World Golf Village complex of condos and golf courses just off I-95, north of St Augustine.

The museum section begins with a surprise – a tribute to **Bob Hope** (1903–2003), in honour of the comedian's famed commitment to golf and charitable causes. Upstairs the history of golf is explored, starting with its ancient Scottish roots and the establishment of the **Royal & Ancient Golf Club** in St Andrews in 1754. The first giants of the game, such as **Tom Morris** (1821–1908), are commemorated and there's a replica nineteenth-century putting green to try. The rest of the complex is jam-packed with golfing memorabilia from almost every major player of the last sixty years, with the 88ft **Wall of Fame** itself in the centre. You can also take an elevator to the top of the 190ft **Trophy Tower**, and have a swing in the state-of-the art drive simulator. Your ticket includes a round on the **18-hole putting course** outside, while **Bill Murray** fans should make a pit stop at *Caddy Shack* across the pond (daily from 11.30am; ☎ 904 940 3673, ⓦ murraybroscaddyshack.com), a restaurant owned by Bill and his five brothers in honour of the eponymous movie.

Anastasia Island

The Bridge of Lions takes Hwy-A1A across the Intracoastal Highway from St Augustine onto **Anastasia Island**, home to fine **beaches** just a couple of miles from the Old Town. **St Augustine Beach** is family terrain, but to the north you'll find the wilder **Anastasia State Park**. At the far southern end of the island lies **Fort Matanzas National Monument** (see p.326).

Anastasia State Park

1340 Hwy-A1A • Daily 8am–sunset • Cars $8 ($4 single occupant), cyclists and pedestrians $2 • ☎ 904 461 2033, ⓦ floridastateparks.org
/anastasia

Offering over 1600 protected acres of dunes, marshes, scrub and a wind-beaten group of live oaks, **Anastasia State Park** is crisscrossed by nature walks – though most people come here to catch a fish dinner from the lagoon or just lounge on the pristine four-mile beach.

St Augustine Lighthouse and Museum

81 Lighthouse Ave • Daily 9am–6pm, or 7pm in summer • $9.95, children 12 and under $7.95 • ☎ 904 829 0745,
ⓦ staugustinelighthouse.org

Scintillating views of St Augustine and the beaches are afforded by the **St Augustine Lighthouse and Museum**, assuming you climb the spiral staircase to the 165ft view deck. Completed in 1874, the elegant tower was restored in the 1990s. Panels on the way up and displays in the surrounding buildings tell the story of the keepers and the lights they tended. Don't miss the intriguing exhibit on the wreck of British transport ship *Industry*, which sank off this coast in 1764.

St Augustine Alligator Farm

999 Anastasia Blvd (Hwy-A1A) • Daily 9am–5pm, 6pm in summer • $22.95, children 3–11 $11.95; Crocodile Crossing $35–65 •
☎ 904 824 3337, ⓦ alligatorfarm.com

Essentially a small zoo set around a wildlife-infested swamp, the **St Augustine Alligator Farm** is the only place in the world where you can meet all 23 members of the crocodilian family, including an Australian saltwater crocodile measuring over fifteen feet. It's also home to thousands of wading birds, which come to roost in the rookery in the late afternoons. From April to July these birds are in full breeding plumage – a great time for budding photographers to snap away. Time your visit to coincide with the alligator, reptile or bird shows (one or two shows daily, call for exact times) or the alligator feeding demonstration – grisly stuff, especially when you're listening to the crunch of bone between reptilian teeth. The newest attraction here is **Crocodile Crossing** – a heart-racing nine-stage zip line that takes you flying across the alligator lagoon (45–90min courses).

ARRIVAL AND DEPARTURE   ANASTASIA ISLAND

By car You'll need a car to explore Anastasia State Park, though there are limited bus services to the other island attractions. Hwy-A1A becomes Anastasia Blvd on the other side of the Bridge of Lions from St Augustine, with all the major sights clearly signposted.
By bus The Sunshine Bus Company (✆ 904 209 3716,

ⓦsunshinebus.net) runs small buses (Red Line; $1 per ride; $3 one-day pass) from downtown St Augustine (Bridge of Lions and the visitor centre) along Hwy-A1A past the Alligator Farm and lighthouse, but services are not especially frequent (5–6 times a day), so grab a timetable at the visitor centre.

ACCOMMODATION AND EATING

Anastasia Inn 218 Anastasia Blvd ✆ 904 825 2879, ⓦanastasiainn.com. Across the bay from the Old Town, on Anastasia Island, well within striking distance of all the sights and the beach, the *Anastasia Inn* has simple, ageing but clean motel rooms; a solid budget choice. **$52**
Anastasia State Park Campground 1340-A Hwy-A1A, Anastasia Island ✆ 904 461 2033, ⓦfloridastateparks.org/Anastasia. Best campground in

the area, where you can pitch a tent for $28. Hot showers, toilets and beach access.
The Oasis 4000 Ocean Trace Rd (at Hwy-A1A) ✆ 904 471 3424, ⓦworldfamousoasis.com. Satiate yourself with excellent burgers ($4.99–9.49), featuring a multitude of toppings, at this fun shack at St Augustine Beach. Daily 6am–11pm.

Jacksonville and around

Founded in 1822, **JACKSONVILLE** was named after Andrew Jackson, the seventh US president and first governor of Florida. Today it is a large, sprawling city with a major seaport on the wide St Johns River, enticing restaurants, an NFL team – the **Jacksonville Jaguars** – and some of the best cultural attractions in the state. Just to the east, the **Timucuan Ecological & Historic Preserve** encompasses old plantations, forts and untouched marshland riddled with birdlife, while **Jacksonville Beach** offers sugary sands and a lively surf scene.

Downtown Jacksonville

Most of Jacksonville was destroyed in the **Great Fire of 1901**, and today's **downtown** is dominated by a forest of shiny modern skyscrapers, with the tallest being the obelisk-like **Bank of America Tower** (617ft), constructed in 1990. While there's only a handful of sights, notably the **Museum of Contemporary Art**, downtown is an increasingly relaxing place to wander, particularly around central **Hemming Plaza** and along the banks of the St Johns River, which snakes through the centre and is lined by the pedestrianized **Riverwalk** on both sides.

ART WALKS, ART MARKETS AND OFF THE GRID

On the first Wednesday of each month, Jacksonville's **Art Walk** sees local galleries and museums open their doors (for free) to celebrate the city's artistic verve. The event is sponsored by **Downtown Vision** (ⓦdowntownjacksonville.org), which has also helped create the **Off the Grid** initiative, where artists are given empty shop spaces to exhibit their work (see the website for details of current galleries). More arts and crafts are on offer (plus food and live music) at the **Riverside Arts Market** held under the Fuller Warren Bridge every Saturday (March–Dec 10am–4pm; ⓦriversideartsmarket.com).

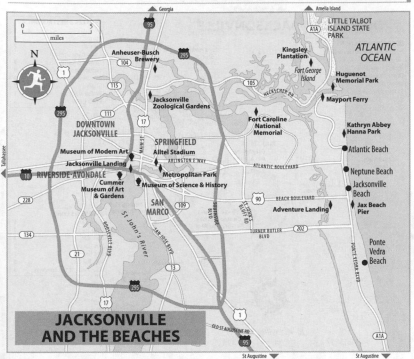

Museum of Contemporary Art

333 N Laura St • Tues, Wed, Fri & Sat 11am–5pm, Thurs 11am–9pm, Sun noon–5pm • $8 • ☎ 904 366 6911, ⓦ mocajacksonville.org

In the heart of downtown on Hemming Plaza, the **Museum of Contemporary Art** contains a refreshingly bright series of galleries displaying a mix of high-quality travelling and permanent exhibits in photography, painting and sculpture from the 1960s on. Highlights from the permanent collection include **Picasso**'s *Imaginary Portrait* series, based on 29 images he created on cardboard in 1969, and works by **Alexander Calder** and **Robert Rauschenberg**.

Jacksonville Maritime Museum

Jacksonville Landing, 2 Independent Drive • Tues–Sat 11am–5pm • Free, donation $3 • ☎ 904 355 1101,
ⓦ jacksonvillemaritimeheritagecenter.org

The city's long and vital relationship with the sea is explored at the **Jacksonville Maritime Museum**, currently housed in the **Jacksonville Landing** mall (Mon–Thurs 10am–8pm, Fri & Sat 10am–9pm, Sun noon–5.30pm) overlooking the river. The museum houses hundreds of ship-related artefacts and permanent exhibits on the aircraft carrier USS *Saratoga* and former governor Napoleon B. Broward's *Three Friends* tugboat, launched in 1895.

Springfield Historic District

After the Great Fire, many of Jacksonville's rich relocated to the **Springfield Historic District**, a compact neighbourhood founded back in 1869. Beginning at State Street and Hogan's Creek, a ten-minute walk north of downtown, most of the homes here date from the 1880s to 1920s, incorporating a variety of lavish styles. After years of steady decline, the area has re-emerged as a trendy arts district attracting, once again, well-off homebuyers and independent stores such as **Sweet Pete's Candy Shop**, 1922 N Pearl St (Mon–Sat 10.30am–7pm, Sun noon–5pm; ⓦ sweetpetescandy.com). Visit ⓦ sambajax.org

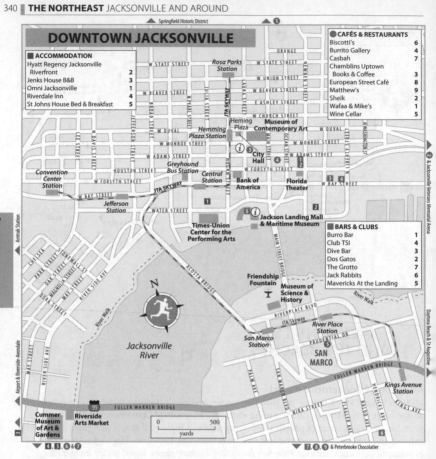

and ⓦmyspringfield.org for more information, and ⓦsustainablespringfield.net for details of the neighbourhood's innovative **community gardens** project.

San Marco

South of downtown and across the St Johns River, the **San Marco** neighbourhood (ⓦmysanmarco.com) is worth a stroll for an hour or two, crammed with laidback boutiques and hip restaurants, particularly along San Marco Boulevard and at the 1920s Mediterranean Revival development known as **San Marco Square** (at San Marco Blvd and Atlantic Blvd). Pop into the heavenly smelling **Peterbrooke Chocolatier**, a local chocolate-maker at 1470 San Marco Blvd (Mon–Fri 9.30am–6pm, Sat 10am–4pm, Sun noon–5pm; ☎904 398 2489, ⓦpeterbrooke.com), where you can watch grinning workers making chocolate behind glass screens.

Museum of Science and History

1025 Museum Circle • Mon–Thurs 10am–5pm, Fri 10am–8pm, Sat 10am–6pm, Sun noon–5pm • $10, children 3–12 $6 (planetarium additional $5) • ☎904 396 6674, ⓦthemosh.org • Take the Skyway (see p.342) or walk across Main Street Bridge

On the south side of the river, just behind the oversized **Friendship Fountain**, the **Museum of Science and History** has educational hands-on exhibits primarily aimed at kids, plus a planetarium offering high-tech virtual trips around the cosmos.

Riverside-Avondale

South of downtown (beyond I-95 and I-10), the pedestrian-friendly neighbourhood of **Riverside-Avondale** was developed along the north bank of the river in the years after the Great Fire, and is home to an eclectic assortment of residential architecture. The **Five Points** (W 5pointsjax.com) area along Park Street between Margaret and Post streets is a good place to wander, with an artsy, alternative vibe and plenty of independent shops, bars and restaurants. The **Riverside Trolley** (see p.342) connects downtown with Riverside-Avondale.

Cummer Museum of Art & Gardens

829 Riverside Ave • Tues 10am–9pm, Wed–Sat 10am–4pm, Sun noon–4pm • $10, free Tues after 4pm • T 904 356 6857, W cummer.org • Riverside Trolley or bus #P4

Just south of the Fuller Warren Bridge (I-95), the **Cummer Museum of Art & Gardens** delivers a carefully curated journey through the history of art from ancient Egypt to Modernism. The museum is the legacy of Arthur and Ninah Cummer, who made a fortune in the timber business. After Ninah died in 1958 she bequeathed her entire art collection to the museum, as well as her former estate; the gardens remain but her house was demolished to make way for a new gallery building (the spirit of the English-style Cummer home is preserved in the museum's **Tudor Room**).

The spacious galleries and sculpture-lined corridors contain works by prominent European masters such as Dürer, Rubens, Vasari and Agnolo Gaddi, but **American art** is the Cummer's strongest feature: Edmund Greacen's smoky cityscape *Brooklyn Bridge East River* (1916) and Norman Rockwell's heart-wrenching *Second Holiday* (1939) are particularly moving, but there is also work from Childe Hassam, William Glackens, John Singer Sargent and Winslow Homer, as well as one of Gilbert Stuart's "Athenaeum" paintings of **George Washington** from 1803. The museum's signature piece is Thomas Moran's *Ponce de León in Florida* (1878), a romantic imagining of the explorer's meeting with local Native Americans (though this event never occurred).

Also worth lingering over is an extensive collection of eighteenth-century **Meissen porcelain**, the first porcelain to be made in Europe after the previously secret Chinese technique was finally cracked in Germany in 1711. If you have young children with you, be sure to check the **Art Connections** section, specially designed with little ones in mind. Afterwards, take a stroll through the flower-packed formal English and Italianate **gardens**, which roll down to the river's edge, providing a view of Jacksonville's sleek office towers.

Anheuser-Busch Brewery

111 Busch Drive (I-95 Exit 360) • Shop open June–Aug Mon–Sat 10am–5pm, Sept–May daily except Wed 10am–4pm; tours 11am, 1pm & 3pm • Free • T 904 696 8373, W budweisertours.com • No public transport

Trekking around Jacksonville you'll inevitably have worked up a thirst, and the local **Anheuser-Busch Brewery**, founded in 1852 (in St Louis, Missouri) and the purveyor of **Budweiser**, would like to quench it for you. After taking the free tour, which charts the Germanic and Czech roots of America's most popular suds, visitors can indulge in the main attraction: free beer.

DOWNTOWN AMBASSADORS

As part of an attempt to rejuvenate Jacksonville's downtown area, in 2001 the city established a team of volunteers known as Downtown Ambassadors. Identifiable by their orange shirts, these men and women are on hand to provide directions, clear litter, and help out in emergencies; some have a good knowledge of local history, which they are happy to share. To contact a Downtown Ambassador, call T 904 634 0303 or T 904 465 7980 (Mon–Thurs 7am–9pm, Fri 7am–11pm, Sat 10am–11pm, Sun 9am–5.30pm; W downtownjacksonville.org).

Jacksonville Zoo and Gardens

370 Zoo Pkwy (off Heckscher Drive, I-95 Exit 358A) • Daily 9am–5pm (till 6pm Sat & Sun March–Aug) • $15.95, children 3–12 $10.95; giraffe feeding $2; stingray pool $2; train rides $4 • ☎ 904 757 4463, ⊛ jacksonvillezoo.org • No public transport

The **Jacksonville Zoo and Gardens**, just off I-95 north of downtown Jacksonville, is one of the better zoos around, affording its inmates plenty of space to prowl, pose and strut. A justifiable source of pride is the "**Range of the Jaguar**", where the majestic big cats roam around a landscape of lush vegetation, waterfalls and pools. Other highlights include the zoo's chilled-out silverback gorillas, the giraffe overlook (feed them for $2), playful penguins and a pool of touch-friendly stingrays. Train rides around the park make negotiating the 110-acre site a bit easier in the summer heat.

ARRIVAL AND DEPARTURE

JACKSONVILLE

By plane Jacksonville International Airport (⊛ flyjacksonville.com) lies 13 miles north of downtown, with numerous connections all over the US (though most flights route through Atlanta). All the major car rental firms have a presence at the airport, while Gator City Taxi (☎ 904 999 9999) provides taxi services. Otherwise, local bus #CT3 (AirJTA) departs for downtown (Jackson Landing) every 1hr–1hr 30min ($1.50), with reduced service Sat & Sun. You can also arrange a pickup with private minivan operators like A9A Airport Transportation (☎ 877 399 8288, ⊛ skyjax.net), who will take you downtown for $35, or to Jacksonville Beach for $60.

By car Driving into downtown Jacksonville is relatively straightforward and the roads are surprisingly uncongested, provided you avoid the rush hour periods: I-95 and I-10 cut right through the centre. Parking is also easy to find, though it can be pricey. The Jacksonville Landing car park during the week costs $2 for any time less than three hours before 4pm (maximum daily rate $10).

By bus The Greyhound bus station is downtown at 10 N Pearl St (☎ 904 356 9976).

Destinations Miami (via West Palm Beach and Fort Lauderdale; 4 daily; 7hr 15min–8hr); Orlando (via St Augustine and Daytona Beach; 5 daily; 2hr 30min–3hr 5min); Tallahassee (3 daily; 2hr 40min–3hr 5min).

By train The Amtrak station lies an awkward 6 miles northwest of town at 3570 Clifford Lane, off US-1. A taxi to the centre will cost around $15. Alternatively, you can hop on local bus #K2 every 30–45min ($1.50).

Destinations Miami (2 daily; 9–11hr); New York (via Charleston, Raleigh and Washington, DC; 2 daily; 18–20hr 20min); Orlando (2 daily; 3hr); Tampa (1 daily; 5hr 20min).

GETTING AROUND AND INFORMATION

By bus The JTA bus system ($1.50 a ride; $2 for the X2 Express to the beaches, exact change only; ☎ 904 630 3100, ⊛ jtafla.com) is comprehensive. In addition, the Riverside Trolley bus (Mon–Fri 10.30am–2.30pm, every 10min; $1.50) links downtown and Riverside-Avondale and Five Points via the Cummer Museum.

By monorail The JTA Skyway monorail (Mon–Fri 6am–9pm; free) links the north bank with the San Marco neighbourhood south of the river every 3–6min.

Tourist information Visit Jacksonville maintains a well-stocked visitor centre at 208 N Laura St, just south of Heming Plaza (Mon–Fri 9am–5pm; ☎ 904 421 9156, ⊛ visitjacksonville.com), and there are affiliated information booths at the airport (daily 9am–10pm; ☎ 904 741 3044) and in the Jacksonville Landing Mall (Mon–Thurs 11am–3pm, Fri & Sat 10am–7pm; ☎ 904 791 4305). For listings and events, grab a copy of monthly newspaper *EU Jacksonville* or visit ⊛ eujacksonville.com.

ACCOMMODATION

Accommodation is concentrated in several neighbourhoods: the business-oriented hotels are in downtown's bustling Riverwalk, while you'll find the best bed and breakfasts in the sleepier Riverside-Avondale area. Most of the (numerous) cheaper chain motels lie near the airport off I-95, while **Jacksonville Beach** offers a more relaxed ocean-side scene (see p.346).

Hyatt Regency Jacksonville Riverfront 225 E Coastline Drive ☎ 904 558 1234, ⊛ jacksonville.hyatt .com. Great riverfront location just a few steps from Jacksonville Landing. Rooms have all the amenities and there's a rooftop pool, hot tub, sauna and fitness centre. Wi-fi is $9.95/day. **$169**

Jenks House B&B 2804 Post St, Riverside-Avondale ☎ 904 387 2092, ⊛ thejenkshouse.com. This cosy bed and breakfast was built in the Prairie School style in 1925,

featuring some Mission and early Art Deco furnishings in just two rooms, both with free wi-fi, ceiling fans and healthy breakfasts. Free parking. **$110**

Omni Jacksonville 245 Water St ☎ 904 355 6664, ⊛ omnihotels.com. The city's most luxurious business hotel, smack in the centre of downtown with large, elegantly furnished rooms and a host of services and facilities; limos will whisk you anywhere downtown for free. Wi-fi is $9.95/day. **$150**

Riverdale Inn 1521 Riverside Ave, Riverside-Avondale ☎904 354 5080, ⓦriverdaleinn.com. Opulent option in the city's old neighbourhood, with ten luxurious rooms in a grand mansion built in 1901 for a local turpentine merchant. Spacious rooms feature original heart-of-pine floors, some with fireplaces, all furnished in an early twentieth-century style. Free wi-fi. **$140**

St Johns House Bed & Breakfast 1718 Osceola St, Riverside-Avondale ☎904 384 3724, ⓦstjohnshouse .com. Spacious rooms and inviting porches are among the draws at this gorgeous Prairie School house built in 1914, close to the river. The three elegant rooms blend antiques with modern amenities (cable TV, free wi-fi), and the breakfast is top-notch. Open Nov–Feb, April & May only. **$99**

EATING

You'll find decent restaurants throughout the city, with the most appealing spots in the San Marco and Riverside-Avondale neighbourhoods. Thanks to a large and dynamic immigrant community, **Middle Eastern food** is a speciality in Jacksonville – pitta-wrapped "steak in a sack", and "the camel rider" (a cold-cut sandwich on pitta bread), have become signature sandwiches (washed down with a cherry limeade).

Biscotti's 3556 St John's Ave, Riverside-Avondale ☎904 387 2060, ⓦbiscottis.net. Part-coffeehouse, part-restaurant, with Mediterranean salads and sandwiches ($10–13.50), nine-inch pizzas ($10.50–12.50), and a superb Sunday brunch; most locals have become addicted to the *crème brûlée* French toast ($9.50). Mon–Thurs 10.30am–10pm, Fri 10.30am–midnight, Sat 8am–midnight, Sun 8am–9pm.

Burrito Gallery 21 E Adams St ☎904 598 2922, ⓦburritogallery.com. Dark, grungy restaurant with no-nonsense large burritos, tacos and wraps for $5.95–8.95. The interior is given a welcome splash of colour by the local artwork on the walls (all of which is for sale) and there's also an outside patio. Mon–Thurs & Sat 11am–10pm, Fri 11am–midnight.

Casbah 3628 St Johns Ave, Riverside-Avondale ☎904 981 9966, ⓦthecasbahcafe.com. While it's true there are cheaper (and less packed) Middle Eastern restaurants in the city, ignore the posers with hookah pipes outside and focus on some of the most authentic Lebanese food in the city. Nightly belly-dancing and delicious meze plates ($3.95–7.95). Daily 11am–2am.

Chamblins Uptown Books & Coffee 215 N Laura St ☎904 674 0868, ⓦchamblinbookmine.com. Quirky neighbourhood favourite in the heart of downtown, with a bookshop blending into a laidback coffee shop at the front. Mon, Tues, Thurs & Fri 8am–5pm, Wed 8am–9pm, Sat 9am–4pm, Sun noon–5pm.

European Street Café 1704 San Marco Blvd, San Marco ☎904 398 9500, ⓦeuropeanstreet.com. Huge sandwich selection ($8–11.95), plus several economical German sausage dishes (from $6), all of which play second fiddle to the unrivalled beer list, which includes brews from Greece, Honduras and China. Daily 10am–10pm.

★**Matthew's** 2107 Hendricks Ave, San Marco ☎904 396 9922, ⓦmatthewsrestaurant.com. One of the finest restaurants in the city, featuring venison, duck and foie gras on changing tasting menus ($70 or $125 with wine pairings) or à la carte (mains $16–45). Reservations recommended. Mon–Sat 5.30–10pm.

★**Sheik** 9720 Atlantic Blvd ☎904 721 2660. One of the earliest creators of the "camel rider" has served the famed sandwich – a stack of ham, salami, bologna, cheese, lettuce, tomato, onions and special sauce ($4.99) – since 1972. You can also try the "steak in a sack" here ($4.99), some addictive fries ($1.49) and the ubiquitous cherry limeade that locals seems to love. Mon–Sat 6am–8pm.

Wafaa & Mike's 1544 N Main St, Springfield ☎904 683 8313. This no-frills place is popular with a local lunch crowd for its excellent chicken kebab platters ($12.99) and the best falafel this side of Beirut ($10.99). Mon–Sat 10am–9pm.

Wine Cellar 1314 Prudential Drive ☎904 398 8989, ⓦwinecellarjax.com. The ambience is rustic French at this local favourite; dine on classic cuisine (steaks, lobster, tuna, salmon) in the attractive garden. Over 200 wines available. Dinner mains range from $24 to $36. Mon–Fri 11am–2.15pm & 5–10.30pm, Sat 5–10.30pm.

DRINKING AND NIGHTLIFE

Jacksonville has a dynamic **nightlife** that easily competes with the beaches, much of it centred around the "Elbow", at the intersection of N Ocean and E Bay streets (ⓦtheelbowjax.com). Though the heyday of "Southern Fried Rock" was the 1970s, local legends Lynyrd Skynyrd (of *Sweet Home Alabama* fame) and 38 Special still perform today. Jackson Landing mall has live acts every week on its riverfront stage, while in May there's the **Jacksonville Jazz Festival** (ⓦmakeascenedowntown.com), the second-largest jazz festival in the nation.

Burro Bar 100 E Adams St ☎904 353 4686, ⓦburrobarjax.com. This artsy dive bar opened downtown in the "Elbow" in 2011, with twenty craft beers on tap and local rock and indie bands livening up the floor. Mon–Fri 4pm–2am, Sat & Sun 6pm–2am.

Club TSI 333 E Bay St ☎904 424 3531, ⓦclubtsi.com.

Hipster hangout, dance club and edgy underground live venue in one, with different themes each night: Bangarang Saturday is the big club-night, while Crunchay Sunday features live jams. Daily 8pm–3am.

Dive Bar 331 E Bay St ☎ 904 359 9090. Nightclub, not really a dive (it has French Renaissance couches for starters), specializing in live indie rock, DJs spinning Top 40 and house music the rest of the time, and cheap drinks. Wed–Sat 8pm–2am.

Dos Gatos 123 E Forsyth ☎ 904 354 0666, ⊛ dosgatosjax .com. Jacksonville's premier downtown cocktail lounge, opposite the Florida Theater. Try the "Shelton", a spicy blend of tequila, ruby-red grapefruit, bitters and King's Ginger. Mon–Fri 4pm–2am, Sat & Sun 6pm–2am.

The Grotto 2012 San Marco Blvd, San Marco ☎ 904 398 0726, ⊛ grottowine.com. Cosy wine and tapas bar with comfy chairs in the back; diverse wines are served by the glass or bottle. Tues & Wed noon–11pm, Thurs–Sat noon–midnight, Sun 4–11pm.

Jack Rabbits 1528 Hendricks Ave, San Marco ☎ 904 398 7496, ⊛ jaxlive.com. A San Marco institution, this dive bar/music venue hosts local bands and national acts. Cover from $10.

Maverick's At the Landing 2 Independent Drive, Jackson Landing mall ☎ 904 356 1110, ⊛ mavericksatthelanding.com. Just in case you've forgotten you're in the Deep South, visit this real country bar; just like the movies, there are tall men in cowboy hats and blue jeans, heartfelt live acts and even a mechanical bull to ride. Yee-haw! Cover from $5. Thurs–Sat 8pm–2am.

ENTERTAINMENT

Florida Theatre 128 E Forsyth St ☎ 904 355 2787, ⊛ floridatheatre.com. Opened in 1927, the interior has been restored with a dazzling gold proscenium arch, and is used for a variety of performances.

Jacksonville Veterans Memorial Arena 300 A. Philip Randolph Blvd ☎ 904 630 3900, ⊛ jaxevents.com. This larger venue (15,000 seats) hosts major events, from Taylor Swift concerts to college basketball matches and home games of the American Basketball Association's Jacksonville Giants.

Times-Union Center for the Performing Arts 300 W Water St ☎ 904 633 6110, ⊛ jaxevents.com/times union.php. Major performance centre opened in 1997, now home to the Jacksonville Symphony Orchestra.

Timucuan Ecological & Historic Preserve

Large tracts of the wild marshland along the St Johns River, dividing Jacksonville from the ocean, are protected within the **Timucuan Ecological & Historic Preserve**. Apart from providing numerous opportunities to hike in semitropical forests and spy a huge variety of birds, from giant herons to pelicans, the preserve contains some lesser-visited historic gems. You'll need a car to explore this area.

Fort Caroline National Memorial

12713 Fort Caroline Rd • Daily 9am–5pm • Free • ☎ 904 641 7155, ⊛ nps.gov/timu

The first European colony in Florida was actually **French**: in 1564, **René Laudonnière** established an outpost of two hundred settlers near the current site of **Fort Caroline National Memorial**. The small visitor centre details the significance of the reconstructed Huguenot (French Protestant) fort, little more than three grassy turf walls surrounded by Spanish moss-smothered trees (the exact location of the original is not known). A short drive along the road there's the poignant **Ribault Monument**, commemorating the French commander who explored the region two years earlier. The establishment of Fort Caroline provoked the Spanish into founding St Augustine in 1565 – what's often glossed over is that the Spanish leader Pedro Menéndez obliterated the French colony in the process, massacring 152 settlers (Laudonnière was one of the few who escaped).

CROSSING THE ST JOHNS RIVER

The best way to travel between the southern and northern sections of the Timucuan Preserve is to cross the St Johns River on the tiny St Johns River Ferry aka **Mayport Ferry** that connects Mayport and Hwy-A1A South with the north bank (Mon–Fri 6am–7pm, Sat & Sun 7am–8.30pm; every half-hour; cars $6, cyclists and pedestrians $1; ⊛ dev.stjohnsriverferry.com). Pelicans tend to hang out around the dock on the Mayport side, seemingly oblivious to the activity below.

Ribault – who had turned up to reinforce the colony – and 245 of his men were similarly massacred a few days later (see p.326), abruptly ending French ambitions in the region. Your sympathy for the French will grow further when you see how voracious the mosquitoes are around here – spray up before you go.

Kathryn Abbey Hanna Park

500 Wonderwood Drive • Daily: April–Oct 8am–8pm; Nov–March 8am–6pm • $1 per person until 10am, then $3 per car • ☎ 904 249 4700

A few miles east of Fort Caroline lies bucolic **Kathryn Abbey Hanna Park**, with a mile and a half of unblemished Atlantic beachfront (home to the premier surf spot known as "the poles"), and 450 acres of woodland surrounding a large lake. Near the lake is a kids' splash park and campground (see p.346).

Kingsley Plantation and around

11676 Palmetto Ave, Fort George Island • Daily 9am–5pm • Free • ☎ 904 251 3537, ⓦ nps.gov/timu

The first site of interest north of the St Johns River in Timucuan Ecological & Historic Preserve is the **Kingsley Plantation** on Fort George Island, the centrepiece of which is the elegant riverside mansion bought in 1814 by Scotsman **Zephaniah Kingsley**. The house and its 1100 acres were acquired as a cotton plantation with proceeds from **slavery**, of which Kingsley was an advocate and dealer, amassing a fortune through the import and export of Africans. The theme of slavery is understandably a major focus of the site, with the remains of the original tabby slave quarters at the entrance and exhibits in the visitor centre, barn and old kitchen (the house itself is closed for a long-term restoration project, but tours sometimes run Sat & Sun at 11am & 3pm). Kingsley's remarkable wife, a Senegalese Wolof woman known as **Anna Jai**, ran the plantation and lived in extravagant style until moving to Haiti in 1837 – perhaps compensating for being sold as a slave at the age of 13 (she was pregnant with Kingsley's child shortly afterwards, and freed in 1811). On the way back to Hwy-A1A, stop off at the **Ribault Club Visitor Center** (Wed–Sun 9am–5pm; free), a former 1920s golf club now housing exhibits on Fort George Island.

Talbot Islands state parks

Little Talbot Island State Park 12157 Heckscher Drive (Hwy-A1A) • Daily 8am–sunset • Cars $5, $4 single occupant, cyclists and pedestrians $2 • **Big Talbot Island State Park** Hwy-A1A North • Daily 8am–sunset • $2 per person to access the George Crady Bridge Fishing Pier; $3 per vehicle to access the Bluffs • ☎ 904 251 2320, ⓦ floridastateparks.org

Heading north from the St Johns River, Hwy-A1A crosses the Fort George River to **Little Talbot Island State Park**, 1900 acres of a thickly forested barrier island inhabited by some 194 species of birdlife. The park has thirteen picnic areas and a superb four-mile **hiking trail**, which winds through a pristine landscape of oak and magnolia trees, wind-beaten sand dunes and a chunk of the park's five-mile-long beach.

Alternatively, carry on across Simpson Creek to **Big Talbot Island State Park**, which contains the **Bluffs Scenic Shoreline** (signposted off the road), where the bluffs have eroded, depositing entire trees on the beach, some of them still standing upright with all their roots intact. There's also the **Blackrock Trail**, a one-and-a-half-mile hike through woods onto the Atlantic coast, to rocks once made from peat.

KAYAK AMELIA

Kayaks are the best way to explore the tranquil salt marshes and creeks of the Talbot Islands, the haunt of egrets, herons and sometimes dolphins and manatees. **Kayak Amelia** (daily 9am–5pm; ☎ 904 251 0016, ⓦ kayakamelia.com) rents canoes and kayaks ($35/4hr) at 13030 Heckscher Drive (Hwy-A1A) on Simpson Creek, the inlet that separates Big and Little Talbot, and also runs **guided tours** of the area (from $65).

ARRIVAL AND INFORMATION

By car You will need a car to explore the Timucuan Preserve. Hwy-A1A links the northern and southern sections, via the Mayport Ferry (see box, p.344).

Tourist information The preserve visitor centre (daily

TIMUCUAN PRESERVE

9am–5pm; ☎ 904 641 7155, ⊛ nps.gov/timu) is at the Fort Caroline site (see p.344), with maps, books, exhibits on the ecosystems in the preserve and information about the weather and the state of local trails.

ACCOMMODATION

Kathryn Abbey Hanna Park Campground 500 Wonderwood Drive ☎ 904 249 4700. This rustic campground offers almost 300 shaded camp sites, a kids'

splash park, two playgrounds, kayak and paddleboat rentals and access to the beach. $20.34

Jacksonville Beach

Some twelve miles east of downtown Jacksonville, **JACKSONVILLE BEACH** is a mini seaside resort that is inexplicably – and refreshingly – neglected by tourists outside of the summer months, when it's as packed as any other Atlantic beach in northern Florida. The enticing white sands here run for miles in either direction, though the centre of the action – shops, bars and restaurants – is at the end of **Beach Boulevard** (US-90). Just to the north (at the end of 4th Ave N) is the 1320ft **pier** (entrance $1), where you can walk out over the ocean for stellar views of the coast. This section of coast is also prime beachcombing terrain – retreating tides often leave **sharks' teeth** among the more common ocean debris. Hwy-A1A runs north–south three blocks inland from the beach; **Atlantic and Neptune beaches** to the north are far less residential, while exclusive **Ponte Vedra Beach** to the south boasts million-dollar homes and world-class golf courses. Indeed, **TPC Sawgrass** (110 Championship Way; ☎ 904 273 3235, ⊛ tpc.com) is home of the Players Championship and the PGA Tour; its famous clubhouse is open to the public daily from 7am to 9pm.

ARRIVAL AND DEPARTURE

JACKSONVILLE BEACH

By bus The #X-2 express (⊛ jtafla.com) runs between downtown Jacksonville and the beach (Mon–Fri 6.30am–6.30pm; $2), while the slower #K2 ($1.50) runs daily.

By car Several major roads connect Jacksonville (and I-95)

with the beaches: from I-95 exit 344, Hwy-202 is the fastest route to the southern section of Jacksonville Beach, while US-90 connects the beach with downtown. Parking is abundant and usually free at the beach.

INFORMATION AND GETTING AROUND

By tram (trolley) Beaches Trolley (daily 4.30am–midnight, every 30min–1hr; $1.50) shuttles between Atlantic Beach, Neptune Beach and Jacksonville Beach.

By bike A good way to get from beach to beach is to rent a bike from Champion Cycling, 1303 N 3rd St (Hwy-A1A) at 12th Ave N (Mon–Fri 10am–7pm, Sat 9am–6pm, Sun

noon–7pm; $7/hr, $20/day; ☎ 904 241 0900, ⊛ championcycling.net).

Tourist information Beaches Visitor Center, 380 Pablo Ave (Tues–Sat 10am–4.30pm; ☎ 904 242 0024, ⊛ jacksonvillebeach.org, ⊛ visitjacksonville.com).

ACCOMMODATION

★**Casa Marina** 691 N 1st St, Jacksonville Beach ☎ 904 270 0025, ⊛ casamarinahotel.com. This

Mediterranean-style hotel first opened in 1925, and still boasts elegant touches like hardwood floors and period

---

SURFING AT JAX BEACH

The **surf scene** is big in Jacksonville Beach, with especially good action around the pier, year-round (see above). The sandy breaks at Atlantic Beach are less crowded and better for beginners. You can check surf reports and information at ⊛ voidlive.com/jacksonville/surf-report, or visit one of the surf shops: Jax Beach Surf Shop, 221 1st St N, facing the beach north of Beach Boulevard (Mon–Wed 10am–7pm, Thurs–Sat 10am–8pm, Sun 11am–6pm; ☎ 904 247 7873, ⊛ jaxbeachboardshop.com), offers lessons for $75/hr, and rents boards from $15/hr to $35/day.

furniture in the rooms, as well as a great rooftop cocktail lounge. **$159**

Fig Tree Inn Bed and Breakfast 185 4th Ave S ☎ 904 246 8855, ⓦ figtreeinn.com. Renovated 1915 beachhouse, with free wi-fi and access to kitchen, laundry, beach chairs and umbrellas, one block from the ocean. The six differently themed rooms are neat and cosy. **$145**

One Ocean Resort 1 Ocean Blvd, Atlantic Beach ☎ 904 247 0305, ⓦ oneoceanresort.com. There's an art gallery in the lobby of this luxury hotel, and each floor has a volunteer eager to escort you to your room. Though the museum/gallery theme is a little over-the-top, you can't argue with the elegant rooms and serene setting. **$179**

EATING

Beach Hut Café 1281 S 3rd St, Jacksonville Beach ☎ 904 249 3516. Popular breakfast spot – as the frequent lines out the door (particularly on Sun) will attest – with generous portions of biscuits and gravy, pancakes, French toast and the like at reasonable prices (from $7.99). Daily 6am–2.30pm.

★**Mojo Kitchen** 1500 Beach Blvd, Jacksonville Beach ☎ 904 247 6636, ⓦ mojobbq.com. If you crave classic Southern barbecue, then make for this friendly spot and order the "whole hawg" sampling of everything ($36) with mac and cheese – the smoked ribs and smoked turkey are especially lip-smacking. Mon & Sun 11am–9pm, Tues–Thurs 11am–10pm, Fri & Sat 11am–11pm.

Ragtime Tavern Seafood Grill 207 Atlantic Blvd,

Atlantic Beach ☎ 904 241 7877, ⓦ ragtimetavern.com. Boasting an extensive seafood menu with dinner mains in the $14.95–28.95 range, this restaurant is a favourite among locals and visitors alike. Enjoy your steak, lobster and shrimp tacos or orange miso salmon alfresco in the garden at the back. Mon–Thurs & Sun 11am–midnight, Fri & Sat 11am–1am.

Sliders Seafood Grille 218 1st St, Neptune Beach ☎ 904 246 0881, ⓦ slidersseafoodgrille.com. It's little more than a shack off the beach, but the fresh seafood is superb; think seafood meatloaf, stuffed flounder and seared sea scallops for $14–17. Mon–Thurs 5–9.30pm, Fri 5–10.30pm, Sat 11am–10.30pm, Sun 11am–9pm.

DRINKING AND NIGHTLIFE

Jacksonville Beach has an especially lively nightlife scene, fed as much by locals from Jacksonville as visitors. "The Strip" is usually considered to be the boardwalk between First Street and Beach Boulevard, and First Street and Sixth Avenue, with numerous clubs and restaurants and live music most nights. If you visit in April, check out **Springing the Blues** (ⓦ springingtheblues.com), a three-day blues festival held in Jacksonville Beach since 1990.

★**Engine 15 Brewing Co** 1500 Beach Blvd ☎ 904 249 2337, ⓦ engine15.com. One of the newer generation of craft brewpubs in the region, with friendly staff, great beers (try the four flight taster for a sample; $5) and large pretzels that come with beer cheese for dipping ($3.50). Mon 4.30pm–midnight, Tues–Sun 11am–midnight.

Freebird Live 200 N 1st St, Jacksonville Beach ☎ 904 246 2473, ⓦ freebirdlive.com. Named for Lynyrd Skynyrd's best-known song (it's owned by Ronnie Van Zant's widow), this concert venue has a slightly rough atmosphere that's softened by the spirited music, from

funk to rock to jazz to bluegrass. Cover varies from $10 to $30. Open show days only, 7pm–2am.

Pete's Bar 117 1st St, Neptune Beach ☎ 904 249 9158. Novelist John Grisham based a bar in his novel *The Brethren* on this pool-hall-cum-local-dive, where a game of pool costs only 25¢ and the drinks are also cheap. It's been here since 1933 and looks it. Cash only. Daily 10am–2am.

The Ritz 185 N 3rd Ave, Jacksonville Beach ☎ 904 246 2255, ⓦ theritzlounge.com. Classic bar open since 1945, with a couple of pool tables and a reputation as one of the beaches' best meeting places for singles. You can also smoke here. Mon–Fri 4pm–2am, Sat & Sun noon–2am.

Amelia Island

Most first-time visitors to Florida would be hard-pressed to locate **AMELIA ISLAND**, at the state's northeastern extremity, which perhaps explains why this finger of land, thirteen miles long and never more than two across, is so peaceful and only modestly commercialized despite the unbroken silver swathe of Atlantic beach gracing its eastern edge. Matching the sands for appeal, **Fernandina Beach**, the island's sole town, was a haunt of pirates before transforming itself into an outpost of Victorian-era high society in the 1880s – a fact proven by its immaculately restored old centre.

Fernandina Beach

Hwy-A1A runs more or less right into the effortlessly walkable town of **Fernandina Beach**, whose Victorian heyday is apparent in the restored, painted wooden mansions alive with turrets, twirls and towers that line the short main drag, **Centre Street**. The English spelling of the street name reflects bygone political tugs-of-war (the Spanish named the town but the British named the streets), but an old-fashioned charm and Southern gentility are still very much in evidence. Well suited to swimming and busy with beach sports, the most active of the island's beaches is **Main Beach** at the eastern end of Fernandina's Atlantic Avenue, a mile from the town centre.

Amelia Island Museum of History

233 S 3rd St • Mon–Sat 10am–4pm, Sun 1–4pm; guided tours Mon–Sat at 11am & 2pm, Sun at 2pm • $7 • ☎ 904 261 7378, Ⓦ ameliamuseum.org

The obvious place to gain insights into the town is the **Amelia Island Museum of History** – which served as county jail from 1878 to 1978. A series of detailed galleries chronicle the island's surprisingly complex history, from when the Timucuan people called the island "Napoyca", through to the Spanish, Civil War and modern-day periods.

Fort Clinch State Park

2601 Atlantic Ave • Daily 8am–sunset; fort daily 9am–5pm; candle-lit tour early May–Aug Fri & Sat at sunset • Cars $6, single occupant $4, pedestrians and cyclists $2; entrance to the fort $2; candle-lit tour $3 • ☎ 904 277 7274, Ⓦ floridastateparks.org/fortclinch

In 1847, the US started to build a fort on Amelia's northern tip, three miles from Fernandina, to protect seaborne access to Georgia – but it wasn't finished when the fort was abandoned in 1867. The fort now forms part of **Fort Clinch State Park** and provides a home for a gang of enthusiasts who pretend they're Union soldiers in the Civil War. The most interesting way to see the fort is with the guided **candle-lit tour** (reservations required). With the faux Civil War garrison moaning about their work and meagre rations, the tour may sound like a ham job, but in fact it is a convincing, informative – and quite spooky – hour-long affair.

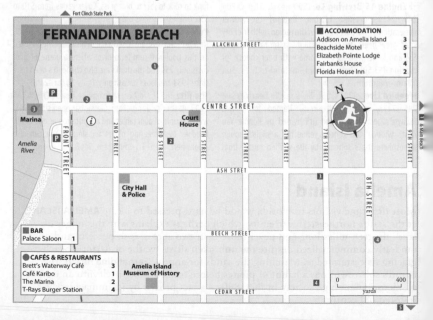

The trails and the beach

You'll see the rest of the 1121-acre park on the three-mile drive en route to the fort, passing an animal reserve (from which overgrown alligators often emerge, so if you do fancy a spot of hiking, stick to the marked 30- and 45min **nature trails**) and a turn-off for the stunning 2.5-mile-long **beach**, where legions of crab catchers cast their baskets off a long fishing jetty. From both jetty and fort there's an immaculate view of **Cumberland Island** (only accessible by ferry from St Mary's, on the Georgia mainland), a Georgian nature reserve famed for its wild horses – if you're lucky, a few will be galloping over the island's sands.

ARRIVAL AND INFORMATION
AMELIA ISLAND

By car You need a car to visit Amelia Island. The fastest way to get here from Jacksonville is to thrash up I-95 then head east on Hwy-A1A, but you can also take the slower Hwy-105 along the north side of the St Johns River and along the coast. On-street parking is fairly easy to find on or off Centre St (3hr max; free).

Tourist information Opposite Amelia Island's marina, at the western end of Centre St you'll spot the useful visitor centre (Mon–Fri 9am–4pm, Sat & Sun 11–4pm; ☎ 904 261 3248, ⓦ ameliaisland.com).

ACCOMMODATION

The best way to savour Fernandina's unique historic atmosphere is by staying in one of the town's antique-filled **bed and breakfasts**, most of them housed in nineteenth-century mansions; but you'll also find more basic **motels** on the way to or on Fletcher Avenue (Hwy-A1A).

★ **The Addison on Amelia Island** 614 Ash St ☎ 904 277 1604, ⓦ addisononamelia.com. Each of the fourteen rooms of this elegantly restored 1876 antebellum bed and breakfast is a study in understated luxury. From the high-quality linens to the rain showerheads, to the breakfast cooked to order, you'll feel pampered within an inch of your life. **$195**

Beachside Motel 3172 S Fletcher Ave ☎ 904 261 4236, ⓦ beachsidemotel.com. Old-style motel right on the beach, with remodelled, contemporary rooms featuring free wi-fi, flat-screen TVs, ocean views and a/c; some have full kitchens. **$130**

Elizabeth Pointe Lodge 98 S Fletcher Ave ☎ 904 277 4851, ⓦ elizabethpointelodge.com. The location alone, right on a gorgeous stretch of sugary beach, would sell this friendly 1890s Nantucket shingle-style bed and breakfast, but the rooms are also lovely, the veranda is wide, and the fresh-baked cookies are available all day. **$245**

Fairbanks House 227 S 7th St ☎ 904 277 0500, ⓦ fairbankshouse.com. At this whimsical 1885 gem, now a twelve-room bed and breakfast, check out the top-floor Grand Tower Suite ($450; sleeps four), with private turret. **$185**

Florida House Inn 20 S 3rd St ☎ 904 261 3300, ⓦ floridahouseinn.com. Sleep where the likes of Ulysses S. Grant and Cuban revolutionary José Martí stayed, at the state's oldest hotel, dating from 1857. Some rooms have working fireplaces and there's also a cosy restaurant and pub. **$140**

EATING AND DRINKING

Brett's Waterway Café 1 S Front St, end of Centre St ☎ 904 261 2660. Generous portions of Florida seafood (low country boil with shrimp, sausage and corn $24; scallops with grits $29), but the real highlight here is the stunning sunset view across the Intracoastal Waterway. Daily 11.30am–2.30pm & 5.30–10pm.

Café Karibo 27 N 3rd St ☎ 904 277 5269, ⓦ cafekaribo .com. Moderately priced salads, sandwiches, decent microbrews and tasty main dishes like Cajun gumbo and "pig & apple" (from $7.99). Eat on the garden patio, shaded by oaks. Mon 11am–3pm, Tues–Sat 11am–9pm, Sun 11am–8pm.

The Marina 101 Centre St ☎ 904 261 5310. One of the island's oldest restaurants, with a convivial atmosphere. Choose from a seafood menu featuring everything that swims (the speciality is the fried seafood platter). They also serve burgers, pork chops, meatloaf and fried chicken. Most mains $15–27. Daily 11am–9pm.

Palace Saloon 117 Centre St ☎ 904 491 3332, ⓦ thepalacesaloon.com. If you're just looking to tip one back, try the *Palace Saloon*, which claims to have the oldest bar in Florida, forty feet of hand-carved mahogany, built in 1878 and opened as a tavern by a German immigrant in 1901. The *Palace* also has live music on weekends. Associated *Sheffield's at the Palace* next door reverts to swanky lounge bar and club (Tues & Wed 4.30–10pm, Thurs–Sat 4.30pm–2am). Daily 11am–2am.

★ **T-Rays Burger Station** 202 S 8th St ☎ 904 261 6310, ⓦ traysburgerstation.com. You can't get more local than this. T-Ray himself mans the grill of this former petrol station, unsigned from the outside, with a classic no-frills canteen interior and delicious home-cooked food. Order the best burger on the island (from $5.25) or the fried bologna sandwich ($5.95). Mon–Fri 7am–2.30pm, Sat 8am–1pm.

7

Tampa Bay and the northwest

ST PETERSBURG

Tampa Bay and the northwest

The diverse and dynamic Tampa Bay area, midway along Florida's three-hundred-mile west coast, is home to buzzing cities, world-class museums and, crucially, miles of beaches with sands and sunset views rivalled only by those of the Florida Keys. Those wanting to get off the beaten track should head north along the coast of the largely beachless northwest or along I-75 toward the Panhandle and Georgia, where placid fishing hamlets, forests, horse ranches and insular villages speak of a Florida largely ignored by the brochures – but one well worth exploring.

The cultural and economic nerve centre of the region, the **Tampa Bay area** comprises Tampa, Clearwater and St Petersburg, with a population greater than Miami's. The wide waters of the bay provide a scenic backdrop for Tampa itself, and the barrier-island **beaches** along the coast let the locals swap metropolitan bustle for luscious sunsets and miles of glistening beaches. **Tampa** boasts a modern art museum and aquarium, while **Ybor City** is Tampa's – and one of the state's – hippest and most culturally eclectic quarters. Directly across the bay, **St Petersburg** is riding high on its major collection of paintings by the Surrealist **Salvador Dalí** and the stunning glasswork of **Dale Chihuly**. For most visitors, though, the Tampa Bay area begins and ends with the **St Petersburg beaches** – miles of sea, sun and sand fringed by condos as far as the eye can see. The beaches are pure vacation territory but are also a good base for exploring the Greek-dominated community of **Tarpon Springs** just to the north.

The coast north of Tampa (known as the **Big Bend** for the way it curves toward the Panhandle) is consumed by flat marshes, large chunks of which are wildlife refuges with little public access. Scattered throughout is evidence of much busier and prosperous times, like the prehistoric sun-worshipping site at **Crystal River**. **Cedar Key**, which was a thriving port in the mid-nineteenth century, is now an enticing remnant of Old Florida. Locals here have preserved a laidback way of life, and the community is a time-warped enclave of excellent restaurants and rewarding sights. The wildlife park at **Homosassa Springs**, fifteen miles south of Crystal River, offers the chance to view some of Florida's endangered animals, like the **manatee**. The alternative route north from Tampa, passing through north central Florida along I-75, is another area of unexpected discoveries – the huge forest and numerous horse ranches around **Ocala**, and the historic villages and natural springs near the lively university town of **Gainesville**.

MANATEE, CRYSTAL RIVER

Highlights

❶ Ybor City This neighbourhood features Tampa Bay's most exciting nightlife and dining; sample the Cuban music and flamenco dancing at the *Columbia*. **See p.357**

❷ Chihuly Collection St Petersburg is also home to a mesmerizing collection of Dale Chihuly glass installations. **See p.365**

❸ The Salvador Dalí Museum View Dalí masterpieces like *The Discovery of America by Christopher Columbus* at St Petersburg's unlikeliest art collection. **See p.366**

❹ Tarpon Springs Shop for high-quality Gulf sponges and enjoy some of the best Greek food in the South. **See p.376**

❺ Child of the Sun Tour Florida Southern College, home to the largest collection of innovative Frank Lloyd Wright buildings anywhere in the world. **See p.379**

❻ Swimming with manatees Don't miss the chance to snorkel with these fascinating, endearing water giants. **See p.384**

❼ Cedar Key Oyster harvesting and an intoxicatingly slow pace of life still hold sway over tourism at this remote and picturesque spot along the northwest coast. **See p.385**

HIGHLIGHTS ARE MARKED ON THE MAP ON P.354

Tampa

TAMPA is a small city with an infectious, upbeat mood. Cradled by Old Tampa and Hillsborough bays, with the Hillsborough River running through downtown, it's surrounded by water – and the Gulf of Mexico lies less than an hour's drive west. You'll only need a day or two to explore the city thoroughly, but you'll depart with a lasting impression of a metropolis on the rise.

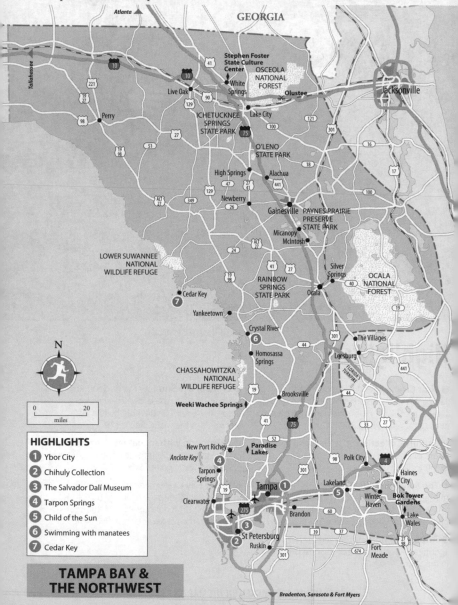

HIGHLIGHTS

1. Ybor City
2. Chihuly Collection
3. The Salvador Dalí Museum
4. Tarpon Springs
5. Child of the Sun
6. Swimming with manatees
7. Cedar Key

TAMPA BAY & THE NORTHWEST

Brief history

Tampa began as a small settlement beside **Fort Brooke** (a US Army base built to keep an eye on local Seminoles in 1824), and remained tiny, isolated and insignificant until the 1880s, when the railway arrived and the Hillsborough River was dredged to allow seagoing vessels to dock. It became a booming port and simultaneously acquired a major **tobacco industry** as thousands of Cubans moved north in 1886 from Key West to the new cigar factories of neighbouring **Ybor City**. Tampa was chosen as an embarkation centre for American troops in the Spanish–American War in 1898, giving a further boost to the economy, while Ybor City flourished during "the Golden Age" of tobacco, 1900 to 1929. The Great Depression ushered in a period of decline in Ybor City that lasted into the 1980s, but thanks to the US military, Tampa itself grew considerably as a result of World War II; MacDill Air Force Base remains a major employer and the influx of people and money that started in the 1960s has never really ended.

Downtown Tampa

Downtown Tampa's prosperity is most evident in its stylish office towers, the tallest of which is the 42-storey **100 North Tampa** (579ft) completed in 1992 (primarily the home of Regions Bank). **Riverwalk** is a pleasant ramble along the Hillsborough River, connecting the major sights and several family-friendly parks.

Tampa Theatre

711 N Franklin St • Guided tours twice monthly (1hr 30min); call for times; $7.50 • Movie tickets $11 • ☎ 813 274 8981, ⓦ tampatheatre.org

The single substantial relic of Old Tampa is the **Tampa Theatre**, erected in 1926 to a design by famed theatre architect John Eberson. When silent movies enthralled the masses, Eberson's cinemas heightened the escapist mood: ceilings became star-filled skies, balconies were chiselled to resemble Moorish arches, gargoyles leered from stuccoed walls, and replica Greek and Roman statuary filled every nook and cranny. Today, the place boasts a full programme of movies (an added bonus – for some – is the Wurlitzer organ that rises from the orchestra pit fifteen minutes before each screening to serenade the crowd) and concerts. Seeing a movie (see p.363) is one way to gain access to the splendidly restored interior, another is the highly entertaining **"Balcony to Backstage" guided tour**.

Tampa Museum of Art

120 W Gasparilla Plaza • Mon–Thurs 11am–7pm, Fri 11am–8pm, Sat & Sun 11am–5pm • $10; free Fri 4–8pm • ☎ 813 274 8130, ⓦ tampamuseum.org

Art fans should make time for the **Tampa Museum of Art**, a small but thoughtfully curated collection of primarily modern artwork overlooking the river at Curtis Hixon Park. The only permanent exhibit – and the only section that offers a complete contrast with the rest of the galleries – is the exceptional ensemble of **Greek sculpture and pottery** from 2500 BC to 500 AD. The bright and spacious galleries on the second floor focus on contemporary, mixed media art that changes three to six times a year. You'll probably see rotating displays from the museum's permanent collection, including work from Photorealist pioneer **Ralph Goings** and various contemporary photographers.

Glazer Children's Museum

110 W Gasparilla Plaza • Mon–Fri 10am–5pm, Sat 10am–6pm, Sun 1–6pm • $15; children 1–12 $9.50 • ☎ 813 443 3861, ⓦ glazermuseum.org

Just next door to the art museum is the **Glazer Children's Museum**, crammed with a vast range of interactive activities and displays designed to excite (and hopefully enlighten) youngsters. Exhibits cover everything from flight and cruise-ship simulations, to areas where you can design and build a house.

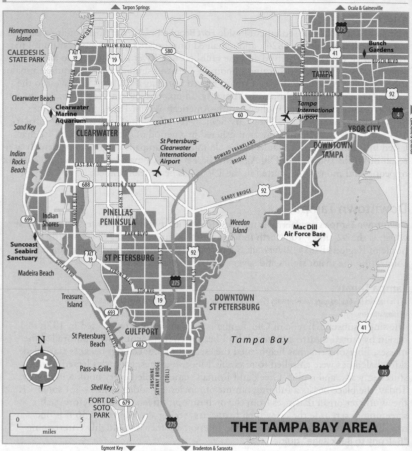

THE TAMPA BAY AREA

Florida Aquarium

701 Channelside Drive • Daily 9.30am–5pm • $23.95, children under 12 $18.95; parking $6 • ☎ 813 273 4000, ⓦ flaquarium.org

The **Florida Aquarium** houses lavish displays of Florida's fresh- and saltwater habitats, ranging from springs and swamps to beaches and coral reefs. What makes this aquarium different (and there are many aquariums along this coast) is that all the exhibits are laid out along an easy-to-follow trail, indoors, and take in a real variety of creatures, from otters, turtles and baby alligators, to manatees, reef fish, sharks and countless species of bird. The real highlight is actually not from around here – it's the special seahorse exhibit that includes the jaw-dropping **leafy sea dragons** from South Australia. Most people organize their time around the roster of **daily shows**, which can include anything from otter experiences to penguin promenades.

American Victory Ship Mariners Memorial Museum

705 Channelside Drive • Mon & Sun noon–5pm, Tues–Sat 10am–5pm • $10, children 4–12 $5 • ☎ 813 228 8766, ⓦ americanvictory.org

Next door to the Florida Aquarium, the **American Victory Ship Mariners Memorial Museum** was established to preserve one of only four fully operational World War II ships in the country. The SS *American Victory* was a naval cargo ship completed in 1945, serving in World War II and also the Korean and Vietnam wars. Today you can explore the surprisingly cavernous interior of the ship, restored to its 1940s heyday.

Tampa Bay History Center

801 Old Water St • Daily 10am–5pm • $12.95, students $10.95, children 4–12 $7.95 • ☎ 813 228 0097, ⓦ tampabayhistorycenter.org •
Free parking in the Amalie Arena Blue Lot (get your parking ticket validated when you buy your admission)

With a picturesque location on the waterfront, the **Tampa Bay History Center** chronicles
the region's past with a series of enlightening displays, from the first Tocobaga and
Calusa inhabitants and the Spanish conquistadors, to the cigar industry (including a
reproduction of a 1920s cigar store) and a restored 1908 REO automobile.

Henry B. Plant Museum

401 W Kennedy Blvd • Tues–Sat 10am–5pm, Sun noon–4pm • $10 • ☎ 813 254 1891, ⓦ plantmuseum.com • Free parking in garage on
North Blvd and North B St

On the east bank of the Hillsborough River, you can't miss the silver minarets, cupolas
and domes of the University of Tampa and the **Henry B. Plant Museum** – formerly the
Tampa Bay Hotel. Built in Moorish Revival style, and financed to the tune of $3 million
by steamship and railway magnate **Henry B. Plant** (aka "the King of Florida"), the
structure is as bizarre a sight today as it was on its opening in 1891, when its 500
rooms looked out on a community of just 700 people.

The museum preserves just one wing of the old building, including an original suite
containing what's left of the hotel's furnishings. The rooms – once guest bedrooms –
are an intriguing clutter of Venetian mirrors, elaborate candelabras, oriental rugs,
Wedgwood crockery and intricate teak cabinets – all the fruits of a half-million-dollar
shopping expedition undertaken by Plant and his wife across Europe and Asia. There
are special displays dedicated to the Spanish–American War and the life of Plant
himself, as well as a short film providing historical context.

Neglect (the hotel was only used during the winter months and left to fester
during the scorching summer) and Plant's death in 1899 hastened the hotel's
transformation into a pile of musty, crumbling plaster. The city authorities bought
the place in 1904 and halted the rot, before leasing the building to the fledgling
University of Tampa in 1933.

8

Ybor City

In 1886, as soon as Henry Plant's ships (see above) ensured a regular supply of
Havana tobacco into Tampa, cigar magnate **Don Vicente Martínez Ybor** cleared a
patch of scrubland three miles northeast of present-day downtown Tampa and laid
the foundations of **Ybor City**. Around 20,000 immigrants – mostly Cubans drawn
from the strife-ridden Key West cigar industry – settled here, creating an enclave
of Latin American life and producing the top-class hand-rolled cigars that made
Tampa the "Cigar Capital of the World" for forty years. Yet mass-production, the
popularity of cigarettes and the Depression proved a fatal combination for skilled
cigar-makers; Ybor City was engulfed by drab and dangerous low-rent
neighbourhoods by the 1950s.

Today, Ybor City has been transformed again; it buzzes with bars, shops and
restaurants (see p.362), and at night the atmosphere can become raucous, especially at
weekends. Don't miss the **Saturday Market** (9am–1pm; ⓦ ybormarket.com) at

TAMPA BASEBALL MUSEUM

The new Tampa Baseball Museum, Ybor City's homage to "America's pastime", should be open
by 2015. Housed in the former home of local baseball legend Al López, the catcher who made
his professional debut with the Brooklyn Dodgers in 1928, the museum will display mementos
from Tampa's long baseball history (a team was first organized here in 1878). The house is at
2003 N 19th St, with admission expected to be $8.95. Visit ⓦ tampabaseballmuseum.org for
the latest.

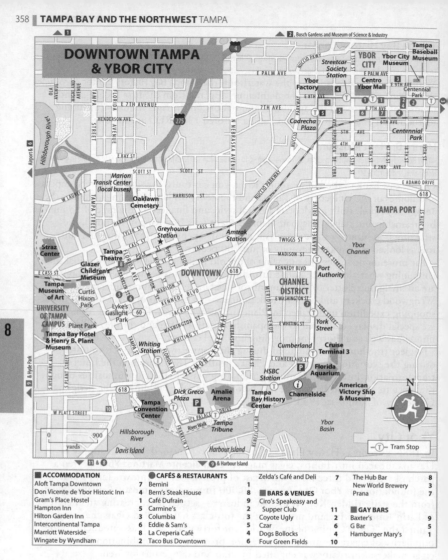

8

Centennial Park, near the trolley terminus, where vendors sell not just cigars but banana bread, jewellery and arts and crafts. The rest of the week the main shopping drag is **Eighth Avenue** just south of here, and at the **Centro Ybor** mall (ⓦcentroybor.com), which includes the restored Centro Español building on Seventh Avenue, an old Cuban clubhouse built in 1912.

Ybor City Museum

1818 E 9th Ave • Daily 9am–5pm • $4 • ☎ 813 247 6323, ⓦ ybormuseum.org • Bus #8

Housed in the old Ferlita Bakery built in 1924, the **Ybor City Museum** charts the neighbourhood's development and its multiethnic make-up; though Cubans are at the forefront, you'll also learn about the non-Cuban immigrant groups who came here, particularly the Sicilians and Italians, and the huge contribution of women, in the factories and in the home.

YBOR'S SOCIAL CLUBS

From the earliest days, each of Ybor City's ethnic communities ran its own **social clubs**. Stepping inside one (opening hours vary wildly) reveals patriotic paraphernalia and lots of old photographs. For a look at Ybor City life most visitors miss, visit the 1917 *The Cuban Club*, 2010 Ave República de Cuba (now an event venue; see ⓦthecubanclub.org), which has retained some of its original features; the 1902 *Centro Asturiano*, 1913 N Nebraska Ave (ⓦcentroasturianotampa.org); or *L'Unione Italiana*, 1731 E 7th Ave (ⓦitalian-club.org).

Ybor Factory Building

1911 N 13th St, at 8th Ave

For a bit more history, stroll over to **Ybor Factory Building**, a red-brick behemoth completed in 1886 by Don Vicente Martínez Ybor as the original cigar factory. In 1893, Cuban Revolutionary leader **José Martí** stood at the entrance, and spoke movingly in favour of Cuban independence. A stone marker at the foot of the steps records the event (the building itself has been Tampa headquarters of the Church of Scientology since 2010).

North Tampa

The suburbs of **north Tampa** contain plenty of attractions, especially for families, though you'll need a car to make the most of them. The top draw is roller-coaster-heavy Busch Gardens, but make some time for the zoo, science museum and bucolic Hillsborough River State Park.

Busch Gardens and Adventure Island

3000 E Busch Blvd • Daily: May–Aug 9.30am–9pm; Sept–April 10am–6pm • $65–95 for everyone over 3, discounts on website and for multi-park packages; parking $17 • ☎ 888 800 5447, ⓦseaworldparks.com • Two miles east of I-275 or 2 miles west of I-75, Exit 54; Bus #5; free Busch Gardens Shuttle runs from Orlando (see website)

It's no surprise that one of Tampa's biggest crowd-pullers is **Busch Gardens**, a vast amusement park with an African theme and some truly mind-blowing **roller coasters**, as well as plenty of interest and entertainment for younger members of the family. Overall it's typical theme-park fare and lots of fun if you approach it in the right way: families especially should plan on spending a whole day here to make the high cost of entry worthwhile; you'll pay $17 just to park your car, and you'll have to store bags in a locker (50¢, nonrefundable) each time you ride a roller coaster. Many locals take advantage of long-term payment and package deals to ease the pain.

Aficionados of roller coasters may pay up just to experience the thrills of the **SheiKra**, a "floorless dive roller coaster" with a 200ft, 90-degree vertical drop, and **Cheetah Hunt**, a 102ft-tall, 60mph steel launched roller coaster; there are four more gut-wrenching rides here, with all the high-speed drops, twists and turns to satisfy the most serious of adrenaline junkies.

Thrills aside, the 335-acre park is divided into nine themed African areas, all smothered in gift shops and places to eat, from Nairobi and Congo to Egypt and the 80-acre **Serengeti Plain**, a fully fledged wildlife park containing elephants, lions, giant tortoises and giraffes viewed by train or skyride – you'll find various other animal enclosures throughout the park, from crocodiles and flamingos, to kangaroos and monkeys.

Just across the street from Busch Gardens is sister park **Adventure Island** (mid-March to early Sept; see website for times; $47 for ages 3 and up; parking $12; ⓦadventureisland.com), a thirty-acre complex of water-soaked rides, slides, waterfalls and a giant wave pool. Get a cheaper joint-ticket if you intend to visit both parks.

8

Lowry Park Zoo

1101 W Sligh Ave (just west of I-275 exit 48) • Daily 9.30am–5pm • $24.95, children 3–11 $19.95; free parking • ☎ 813 935 8552, ⓦ lowryparkzoo.com • Bus #45

Encompassing 56 acres of thoughtfully landscaped animal attractions, **Lowry Park Zoo** is five and a half miles north of downtown Tampa and two miles southwest of Busch Gardens. Highlights include the **Florida Manatee and Aquatic Center**, where you can view manatees from above and under the water thanks to special viewing areas, and the endearing (and endangered) **orangutans**. The **Florida Boardwalk** offers a chance to see native black bears, panthers, alligators and red wolves up close – creatures you're unlikely to see in the wild.

Museum of Science and Industry

4801 E Fowler Ave (I-275 exit 51) • Mon–Fri 9am–5pm, Sat & Sun 9am–6pm • $22.95, children 2–12 $18.95, including admission to Planetarium and a single IMAX screening; parking $5 • ☎ 813 987 6100, ⓦ mosi.org • Bus #6

Two miles northeast of Busch Gardens, the **Museum of Science and Industry** reveals the mysteries of the scientific world, with enough hands-on displays and machines to easily fill half a day. To get the most from your visit, study the programme schedule carefully on arrival: entertaining presentations run at various times throughout the day. The Gulf Coast Hurricane is a convincing demonstration allowing begoggled participants to feel the force of the strongest winds known, while the High Wire Bicycle gives you the somewhat daunting opportunity to pedal a bike 98ft along a one-inch steel cable suspended 30ft above the ground (it's totally safe). After this excitement, relax in the **Planetarium** and gaze at the stars or catch a movie in Florida's first **IMAX theatre** housed in a dome. Extras include a gravity-defying **ropes course**, 36ft high ($7), and a 700ft **zip-line** ride ($10).

Hillsborough River State Park

15402 US-301 N (12 miles north of Tampa) • Daily 8am–sunset • Cars $6, single occupant $4, pedestrians and cyclists $2 • ☎ 813 987 6771, ⓦ floridastateparks.org/hillsboroughriver

Shaded by live oaks, magnolias and sable palms, the **Hillsborough River State Park** contains one of Florida's rare instances of rapids – outside of a theme park. Here, the Hillsborough River tumbles over limestone outcrops before pursuing a more typical meandering course. Rambling or biking the sizeable park's walking trails, and canoeing the gentler sections of the river could easily fill a day; **canoe rentals** are $25 for two hours, or $50 per day (kayaks $15/hr). Bikes are $25 per day. The park **Interpretive Center** (daily 8am–5pm) has exhibits on the Seminole Wars.

Fort Foster State Historic Site

15402 US-301 N • $5 for up to eight people per vehicle • Tours Sat 2pm & 4pm, Sun 11am; $2 per person, children 6–12 $1 • ☎ 813 987 6771, ⓦ floridastateparks.org/fortfoster

Devote part of a weekend to the **Fort Foster State Historic Site** in the eastern section of Hillsborough River State Park, the only standing replica of an 1830s Seminole War fort. The fort – roughly-hewn log barracks, blockhouse and a sharpened timber perimeter fence – can only be seen on **guided tours**. Occasionally, period-attired

---

CANOEING ON THE HILLSBOROUGH RIVER

To spend two hours or a whole day gliding past the alligators, turtles, wading birds, and other creatures that call the Hillsborough River home, contact **Canoe Escape** at John B. Sargeant Park, 17 miles northeast of downtown Tampa (☎ 813 986 2067, ⓦ canoeescape.com), who have devised a series of six novice-friendly routes along the tea-coloured river. Prices range from $46 to $69 depending on length of trip and the type of kayak/canoe, and you should make a reservation at least 24 hours in advance. You can also rent kayaks by the hour ($14). Parking is $2.

enthusiasts occupy the fort and recount historical details – such as the fact that more soldiers died from tropical diseases in the Seminole Wars than in battle.

ARRIVAL AND DEPARTURE TAMPA

By air Tampa International Airport (☎813 870 8700, ⓦ tampaairport.com) is 5 miles northwest of downtown Tampa. Local bus #30 is the cheapest connection (Mon–Fri 6am–8pm, every 15min; Sat & Sun every 30min; $2) to downtown Tampa, while the taxi fare to downtown Tampa is a $25 flat rate. The firms are United (☎813 777 7777) and Yellow (☎813 253 0121). A cheaper option if you're heading straight to the beach is the Super Shuttle (☎800 282 6817, ⓦ supershuttle.com), which runs shared vans for $25 per person (St Petersburg $23; Tampa from $12).

By car If you arrive by car from St Petersburg, the route into Tampa is I-275, which crosses Old Tampa Bay and ends up in the west of downtown. From east or central Florida, you'll come in on the I-4, which intersects with I-75. Be advised that from I-75, it's essential to exit at SR-60 (signposted Kennedy Blvd) for downtown Tampa. There are

seven less convenient exits and if you miss this one and end up in north Tampa, the city's fiendish one-way system could keep you in your car for hours.

By bus Greyhound buses terminate in downtown Tampa at 610 Polk St.

Destinations Gainesville (1 daily; 4hr 50min); Jacksonville (3 daily; 5hr–6hr 25min); Miami (2 daily; 7hr 55min–9hr 5min); Naples (1 daily; 5hr) via St Petersburg (2 daily; 30min), Sarasota (2 daily; 1hr 25min) and Fort Myers (2 daily; 3hr 50min); Orlando (6 daily; 1hr 40min–2hr 5min); Tallahassee (2 daily; 5hr 35min–5hr 45min) via Crystal River (2 daily; 2hr).

By train Amtrak trains terminate at 601 N Nebraska Ave in downtown Tampa.

Destinations Jacksonville (1 daily; 5hr 20min); Miami (1 daily; 5hr 20min); Orlando (1 daily; 1hr 50min).

GETTING AROUND

By bus Although downtown Tampa and Ybor City are easily covered on foot, to travel between them – or to reach Busch Gardens or the Museum of Science and Industry – without a car, you'll need to use local buses (HART ☎813 254 4278, ⓦ hartline.org; one way $2, day-pass $4), whose routes fan out from the Marion Transit Center on Marion St at the northern edge of downtown Tampa. Useful bus numbers are the #8 to Ybor City; #5 to Busch Gardens; #6 to the Museum of Science and Industry; #45 to Lowry Park Zoo; and #30 to the airport. Commuter (express) buses ($3,

day-pass $6) run between Tampa and the coast: #100X to St Petersburg and #200X to Clearwater.

By streetcar Another way to travel between downtown Tampa and Ybor City is on the TECO Line Streetcar System (☎813 254 4278, ⓦ tecolinestreetcar.org), a vintage replica streetcar running daily several times an hour, and until 2am on Fridays and Saturdays. The route takes you via Harbour Island and the Florida Aquarium (see p.356) and costs $2.50 one way. You can buy a $5 souvenir day-pass on the streetcar that works on all public transport.

8

INFORMATION

Downtown Tampa Collect vouchers, leaflets and general information at the Visitors Information Center, 615 Channelside Drive, Suite 108A (Mon–Sat 9.30am–5.30pm, Sun 11am–5pm; ☎813 223 2752, ⓦ visittampabay.com).

Ybor City Ybor City Visitor Information Center, Ybor Centro, 1600 E 8th Ave, Suite B104 (Mon–Sat 10am–5pm, Sun noon–5pm; ☎813 241 8838, ⓦ ybor.org).

ACCOMMODATION

Within Tampa, the cheaper **motels** are all on East Busch Boulevard close to Busch Gardens; you'll find all the major chain motels off I-295 at the western end of the city (exits 39 and 40). Ybor City makes an agreeable alternative to downtown Tampa, with a handful of tempting accommodation options.

TAMPA

★**Aloft Tampa Downtown** 100 W Kennedy Blvd ☎813 898 8000, ⓦ alofthotels.com. One of Tampa's newest hotels features all the boutique chain's signature minimalist style, steps from the Riverwalk, with bright rooms, rainforest showers, outdoor pool and free wi-fi. Parking $20/day. $109

Gram's Place Hostel 3109 N Ola Ave ☎813 221 0596, ⓦ grams-inn-tampa.com. This hip motel-cum-hostel offers both private rooms with bathrooms – all

themed in different musical styles – and rather tatty youth-hostel-style accommodation in a mock sleeper rail car. Free wi-fi, terminal available for $2/hr. Dorms $25, doubles $75

Intercontinental Tampa 4860 W Kennedy Blvd ☎813 286 4400, ⓦ intercontampa.com. Hard to beat this location if you intend to explore the area by car, with easy access to I-275 and routes to downtown Tampa, St Petersburg and the beaches. Rooms are stylish and modern, with free wi-fi and parking. $165

Marriott Waterside 700 S Florida Ave ☎813 221 4900, ⓦmarriott.com. One of downtown Tampa's largest and most luxurious hotels, this waterfront palace towers above the nearby Convention Center and Channelside entertainment complex. Top-notch facilities – spa, health club, and a beautiful pool – and stellar views of the bay. Rates drop by fifty percent off-season. Wi-fi $12.95/day. $329

Wingate by Wyndham 3751 E Fowler Ave ☎813 979 2828, ⓦwingatetampa.com. With a free shuttle bus to Busch Gardens (5min away), small pool, great free breakfast, clean rooms with free wi-fi and a solicitous staff, this is the best of the motels in North Tampa. $109

YBOR CITY

Don Vicente de Ybor Historic Inn 1915 Avenida República de Cuba ☎866 206 4545, ⓦdonvicenteinn .com. Historic B&B option in the heart of Ybor City (dating back to 1895), featuring sixteen beautifully restored suites with four-poster beds and Persian rugs, as well as swing dancing on Tuesday nights; free parking. $139

Hampton Inn 1301 E 7th Ave ☎813 247 6700, ⓦhamptoninn.com. Ybor City's best motel accommodation offers comfortable rooms and suites and includes a free breakfast, free wi-fi, a free shuttle within a 3-mile radius, and a parking garage ($8/day). $129

Hilton Garden Inn 1700 E 9th Ave ☎813 769 9267, ⓦtampayborhistoricdistrict.gardeninn.com. Well-equipped, comfortable digs, even if the decor is a little sterile to be in the heart of Tampa's most historically rich neighbourhood. Free wi-fi and free shuttle to downtown Tampa; parking $9. $239

NORTH TAMPA

Hillsborough River State Park campground 15402 US-301 ☎800 326 3521, ⓦfloridastateparks.org /hillsboroughriver. The nearest campground to downtown Tampa where tents are welcome, this is an enjoyable place to stay, with water, electricity, hot showers and laundry facilities; primitive camping sites also available ($5). $24 per pitch

EATING

DOWNTOWN

★**Bern's Steak House** 1208 S Howard Ave ☎813 251 2421, ⓦbernssteakhouse.com. The most memorable charcoal-grilled steaks you'll ever have, starting from around $32.40 and going up to $245 for the choicest 60oz strip sirloin. Open since 1956, 3 miles southwest of downtown, the restaurant also boasts a huge caviar menu and the largest working wine cellar in the world. Don't leave without sampling the apple pie in the Harry Waugh Dessert Room. Mon–Thurs & Sun 5–10pm, Fri & Sat 5–11pm.

Café Dufrain 707 Harbour Post Drive, Harbour Island, ☎813 275 9701, ⓦcafedufrain.com. This great, moderately priced place overlooking the water on Harbour Island serves a variety of New American cuisine with mouthwatering meat and seafood dishes – try the pomegranate-glazed lamb chops with parsnip purée ($29) or the wood-grilled burgers (from $12.50). Mon–Sat 11.30am–10pm.

Eddie & Sam's 203 E Twiggs St ☎813 229 8500, ⓦeddieandsamspizza.com. Florida isn't known for its pizza, but this joint knocks out a decent New York-style slice (made with imported NYC water no less), with 12-inch pizzas ranging $9–14. Mon–Thurs & Sun 11am–9pm, Fri & Sat 11am–10pm.

★**Taco Bus Downtown** 505 Franklin St ☎813 397 2800, ⓦtaco-bus.com. This beloved local Mexican chain began as a food truck on Hillsborough Ave, and now boasts several truck-themed outlets all over the city. This branch features all the usual options: choose your base (tacos $3, burritos $7.50), then the filling (*carne asada*, fish, veggies) and finally the toppings (home-made salsas and

guacamole). Mon–Thurs & Sun 11am–10pm, Fri & Sat 11am–3am.

Zelda's Café and Deli 1239 E Kennedy Blvd, Channelside Drive ☎813 226 0257, ⓦzeldascafeand deli.com. Great place for breakfast (served all day), with some of the creamiest and tastiest cheese grits in the state ($1.50), and delicious, fresh salads (from $7.50) and sandwiches (from $5.75). Daily 7am–9pm.

YBOR CITY

Bernini 1702 E 7th Ave ☎813 248 0099, ⓦberniniofybor.com. An Italian joint serving up wood-fired pizza ($10–15) and pasta ($18–24) in the lovely old Bank of Ybor City (note the giant-insect door handles). The lunch menu is much cheaper. Mon–Thurs 11.30am–10pm, Fri & Sat 11.30am–11pm, Sun 4–9pm.

Carmine's 1802 E 7th Ave ☎813 248 3834, ⓦcarminesybor.com. This longtime Tampa restaurant, in an airy space with wood tables and exposed brick, offers a variety of hearty pastas as well as the requisite Tampa Cuban sandwich (the local speciality) for $9.50; most regulars also opt for the devil crab ($5), a hunk of blue crab meat mixed with spices. Mon 9am–5pm, Tues–Thurs 9am–10pm, Fri & Sat 9am–11am, Sun 9am–9pm.

Columbia 2117 E 7th Ave ☎813 248 4961, ⓦcolumbiarestaurant.com. Serving refined yet moderately priced Spanish and Cuban food, this is a Tampa institution – it's also Florida's oldest restaurant, founded in 1905. Try its famous salad ($4.95), the bean soup (actually rich in Spanish sausage; $4.95) or the classic Cuban sandwich ($8.95), served strictly with no mayonnaise.

8

Pitchers of mojito are $25.95. Mon–Thurs 11am–10pm, Fri & Sat 11am–11pm, Sun noon–9pm.

La Creperia Cafe 1729 E 7th Ave ☎813 248 9700, ⓦlacreperiacafe.com. Besides offering almost sixty delicious sweet and savoury crêpes, this little gem makes every kind of speciality coffee and has free wi-fi. Crêpes range $9–16.25. Mon 10am–3pm, Tues–Thurs 10am–10pm, Fri 10am–11pm, Sat 9am–11pm, Sun 9am–8pm.

NIGHTLIFE

Ybor City is brimming with **clubs and music bars** that tend to be popular with a younger crowd, especially along East Seventh Avenue, though there are also plenty of options in downtown Tampa. For a list of all things nightlife-related, pick up a copy of the free *Creative Loafing Weekly* (every Thurs; ⓦcltampa.com), or the Friday edition of the *Tampa Tribune* (ⓦtbo.com).

DOWNTOWN

Ciro's Speakeasy and Supper Club 2109 Bayshore Blvd ☎813 251 0022, ⓦcirostampa.com. This dimly lit bar has a cool 1920s theme, a restaurant and a range of classic cocktails. Call in advance for the password – in true Prohibition style there is no sign and you have to whisper the password through a slot in the door to get in. Mon–Wed 5pm–1am, Thurs–Sat 5pm–3am, Sun 5pm–1am.

Four Green Fields 205 W Platt St ☎813 254 4444, ⓦtampa.fourgreenfields.com. This pulls off the Irish theme better than most, with near-perfect Guinness, decent pub food and real Irish music in a thatched cottage just across the river from downtown. Daily 11am–2am.

The Hub Bar 719 N Franklin St ☎813 229 1553, ⓦthehubbartampa.com. Dive bar open since the 1940s with the strongest drinks on the coast (served in plastic cups), a great jukebox and loyal group of regulars. Cash only. Mon–Sat 10am–3am, Sun 1pm–3am.

YBOR CITY

Coyote Ugly 1722 E 7th Ave ☎813 241 8459, ⓦcoyoteuglysaloon.com/tampa. This version of the franchised booze parlour is one of the few places in America you'll see signs encouraging you to "get fxxxed up inside". If you've seen the movie, then you have an idea of what to expect: singing and dancing on the bar, body shots and country music. Wed–Sat 5pm–3am.

Czar 1503 E 7th Ave ☎813 247 2664, ⓦczarnation .com. Tampa's justly popular Russian-themed vodka bar and club features three rooms and dancefloors housed inside the historic Ritz Theatre. Cover charge usually runs $6–8. Fri & Sat 10pm–3am.

Dogs Bollocks 1704 E 7th Ave ☎813 247 764 4509. Can you guess the theme of this bar? Yep, it's a British pub. Bangers and mash, pool tables, darts, lots of karaoke and dangerously potent fireball shots await inside. Tues–Sat 5pm–3am, Sun 3pm–3am.

New World Brewery 1313 E 8th Ave ☎813 248 4969, ⓦnewworldbrewery.net. Best place in Tampa for live music, from the local independent music scene to major national bands. Stocks an extensive selection of craft brews and microbrews (they no longer brew their own). Daily 11am–3am.

Prana 1619 E 7th Ave ☎813 241 4139, ⓦclubprana .com. One of Tampa's most celebrated nightclubs is still going strong, with five dancefloors (featuring different styles of music from hip-hop to house and reggae). Cover normally $10, and no shorts, hats or sandals. Thurs–Sat 9pm–3am.

ENTERTAINMENT

Comedy *Side Splitters*, 12938 N Dale Mabry Hwy (Thurs–Sun; ☎813 960 1197, ⓦsidesplitterscomedy.com) features a line-up of national and regional comedians. The *Improv Comedy Theatre*, 1600 E 8th Ave (Wed–Sun; ☎813 864 4000, ⓦimprovtampa.com), right in the heart of Ybor City, hosts similar-calibre acts. Cover charges range from $10 to $35 at both venues.

Concerts and events Amalie Arena, 401 Channelside Drive (☎813 301 6600, ⓦamaliearena.com), hosts major concerts, shows and sports events.

Film For a full list of films playing around the city, check the Friday edition of the *Tampa Tribune*. Foreign-language, classic or cult films only crop up at the Tampa Theatre, 711 Franklin St, for $11 (see p.355). The multi-screen cinema at

8

NEW YORK YANKEES: SPRING TRAINING IN TAMPA

Every spring you can see one of the world's most famous baseball teams warm up for the season at George M. Steinbrenner Field (☎813 875 7753, ⓦsteinbrennerfield.com), 3802 W Dr Martin Luther King Blvd, off US-92 in Tampa. The **New York Yankees** play games here against the likes of the Phillies and Red Sox from late February through to early April, and the stadium was designed to mimic the old Yankee Stadium in New York. The best place to get tickets is at the stadium or online at ⓦticketmaster.com.

Channelside shows stream movies and IMAX films.

Theatre Regular high-quality shows appear at the Straz Center, 1010 N W.C. MacInnes Place (box office Mon–Sat noon–8pm, Sun noon–6pm; ☎813 229 7827, Ⓦstrazcenter.org), a state-of-the-art performance venue

featuring top American and international names. The Gorilla Theatre (tickets $20–25; ☎813 879 2914, Ⓦgorilla -theatre.com), is a lauded local theatre company with a programme including contemporary comedies and dramas as well as the classics (see website for locations).

GAY AND LESBIAN TAMPA

Tampa is a very gay-friendly city, with a sophisticated gay community (Ybor City is sometimes dubbed "Gaybor"), plenty of bars, clubs, gay-oriented accommodation and male-only spas, as well as a thriving lesbian scene (see Ⓦprosuzy.com). For information on Tampa's gay life, visit Ⓦtampabaygay.com and Ⓦtbglcc.org. Every October, Tampa hosts the International Gay and Lesbian Film Festival; check Ⓦtiglff.com for up-to-date information.

Baxter's 1519 S Dale Mabry Hwy ☎813 258 8830, Ⓦbaxterslounge.com. The clean, dimly lit *Baxter's* is currently enjoying its third reincarnation since 1982 and features pool tables and dancers Friday and Saturday nights from 10pm to 1 or 2am. Happy hour all day till 8pm. Daily noon–3am.

G Bar 1401 E 7th Ave ☎813 247 1019. Current Ybor City hotspot, this huge nightclub features those male dancers in

Speedos, drag queens and a bone-tingling sound system. Tues–Sat 9pm–3am.

Hamburger Mary's 1600 E 7th Ave ☎813 241 6279, Ⓦhamburgermarys.com/tampa. The outrageously over-the-top drag bar and LGBT-friendly burger chain operates a branch in the heart of Ybor, with all the usual fun: "drag bingo", karaoke and popular drag cabaret shows. Mon–Thurs 11am–11pm, Fri & Sat 11am–1am, Sun 11am–9pm.

DIRECTORY

Hospital Tampa General on Davis Island ☎813 844 7000. Emergency room ☎813 844 7100, Ⓦtgh.org.
Police Emergencies ☎911, non-emergency ☎813 231 6130.

Post office 401 N Ashley Ave, downtown (Mon–Fri 8.30am–5.30pm); in Ybor City, at 2000 E 12th Ave (Mon–Fri 8.30am–5pm, Sat 8.30am–noon).

St Petersburg

Sitting on the eastern edge of the Pinellas Peninsula, **ST PETERSBURG** (named by a homesick Russian), holds the world record for the number of consecutive days of sunshine – 768 in total, set in 1967–69 – and enjoys on average 361 days of sunshine a year. By the early 1980s, few people under 50 lived in the city and although it remains a retirement haven, St Petersburg has worked hard to lure young blood and there's a definite hipster vibe along Central Avenue. In addition to the rejuvenated pier, which now offers something for every age, its diverse selection of museums and plethora of art galleries – notably world-class collections of **Salvador Dalí** and **Dale Chihuly** – have contributed to its emergence as one of Florida's richest cultural cities.

The Pier

800 2nd Ave NE • Daily 24hr • Free

The focal point of downtown St Petersburg is its quarter-mile-long pier, which juts from the end of Second Avenue and ends at a five-storey, inverted-pyramid-like building. The pier was closed in 2013 due to structural deterioration, but was reopened again in 2014 solely for pedestrian access, fishing and cycling – the building remains closed. Though it's been dogged by controversy, plans are underway to develop a replacement by 2017.

Museum of History

335 2nd Ave NE • Mon–Sat 10am–5pm, Sun noon–5pm • $15 • ☎727 894 1052, Ⓦspmoh.org

Opposite the entrance to the pier, the **Museum of History** chronicles St Petersburg's early twentieth-century heyday as a winter resort, and the world's first commercial airline flight that took place between St Petersburg and Tampa in 1914. There's documentation, too, on Weedon Island (see p.368).

Museum of Fine Arts

255 Beach Drive NE • Mon–Sat 10am–5pm, Sun noon–5pm • $17, including free guided tours • ☎ 727 896 2667, ⓦ fine-arts.org

One block north of the pier, a group of handsome Mediterranean Revival buildings house the **Museum of Fine Arts**. Opened in 1965, the museum has more than 18,000 works in its collection, and its 26 galleries hold objects from antiquity to the present day. The most inspiring work is in the section on Impressionism, featuring Morisot's *Reading* (1888), Monet's *Houses of Parliament* (1904), and American Impressionist Childe Hassam's *Home, Sweet Home* (1916). The American contemporary room displays include Georgia O'Keeffe's vibrant *Poppy* (1927) and George Luks' *The Musician*.

Chihuly Collection

400 Beach Drive NE • Mon–Sat 10am–5pm, Sun noon–5pm • $14.95 including free guided tours every 30min Mon–Fri till 3.30pm •
☎ 727 822 7872, ⓦ moreanartscenter.org

A short walk north of the Museum of Fine Arts lies one of St Petersburg's great treasures and a major coup for the city – in 2011 lauded American glass artist

Dale Chihuly (b. 1941) presided over the opening of the **Chihuly Collection**, the largest permanent ensemble of his work in the world. Though it's actually not that big – tours take thirty minutes or so – the glass installations here are absolutely mesmerizing.

Start with the fifteen-minute film introducing the artist before moving on to the first gallery housing some of Chihuly's acrylic **drawings**: after accidents in 1976 and 1979, the artist is now unable to physically manipulate the glass himself, and acts as artistic director for "Team Chihuly", using these drawings as inspiration. The **Sunset Persian Wall** in the next gallery is a flaming orange masterpiece, a technique Chihuly used for the ceiling of the *Bellagio* in Las Vegas. More wonders await in the **Chandelier Room**, where his spellbinding *Midnight Blue* chandelier looks like a tower of twisting blue cobras, made up of 375 separate pieces. See also the **Ruby Red Icicle Chandelier**, a mass of red spikes that appear to be dripping with water. In a smaller gallery there's the **Macchia series** of intense, giant clam-like sculptures, while the **Float Boat Room** contains an installation of 150 glass balls of various sizes and colours, tumbling out of a small boat. Walk through a passage sporting the *Persian Ceiling* from here to the climactic **Thousand Flower Garden**, a vast multicoloured glass installation, and the **Blue Room**, containing a neon-inspired **Tumbleweed** installation. If your curiosity has been piqued, you can visit the parent **Morean Gallery**, 719 Central Ave (Mon–Sat 10am–5pm, Sun noon–5pm; ⓦmoreanartscenter.org), and the adjacent glass studio.

Florida Holocaust Museum

55 5th St S • Daily 10am–5pm • $16 • ☏ 727 820 0100, ⓦ flholocaustmuseum.org • Free parking

Dedicated to encouraging public awareness and understanding of the Holocaust, the emotionally wrenching **Florida Holocaust Museum** charts the genocide of Europe's Jewish population, and puts the history of anti-Semitism, from the first anti-Jewish legislation in Europe in 1215 AD, into context. The museum has both permanent and temporary exhibits, including an expansive second-floor gallery focusing on Holocaust art, and eleven eternal flames – symbolizing the eleven million victims of the Nazis – form part of the building's facade.

The brainchild of local businessman and World War II veteran Walter Loebenberg, who escaped Germany in 1939, the museum includes among its exhibits a massive, original boxcar – #1130695-5 – that carried thousands of victims to their deaths and is one of only four in the US. A child's ring, found wedged in the boxcar floor, is displayed alongside it.

Dalí Museum

1 Dalí Blvd • Mon–Wed, Fri & Sat 10am–5.30pm, Thurs 10am–8pm, Sun noon–5.30pm • $21, tours free; parking $5 • ☏ 727 823 3767, ⓦ thedali.org

Few places make a less likely depository for the biggest collection of works by the world's best-known Surrealist than St Petersburg. The **Dalí Museum** displays all 96 Salvador Dalí paintings from the collection of Cleveland industrialist **Reynolds Morse** (1914–2000) and his wife **Eleanor**, who struck up a friendship with the artist in the 1940s (when he was living in the US), bought stacks of his work, and eventually ran out of space to show them – thanks to a wily group of community leaders, they were persuaded to share their treasure with the public in the sunny climes of St Petersburg. While Dalí's own gallery in Figueres, Spain, houses more work, it's not the same – Dalí planned the former, for theatrical and artistic effect, while the Morse collection is a measured, thoughtful view of his whole oeuvre.

The collection

The new, stylish gallery that opened in 2011 on the waterfront is a wonderful space for the collection. The second-floor galleries run chronologically, but you'll appreciate them more if you take a tour or grab one of the **free audio guides** (though the alternative commentary by Dalí's Spanish-accented "moustache" can get a bit wearing).

The collection begins with the first painting bought by Morse in 1943, the jarring *Daddy Longlegs of the Evening*, then continues with Dalí's early experiments with **Impressionism** from 1917. Landscapes of **Cadaqués** (his home town in Catalunya) dominate, but there's also his flamboyant *Self Portrait* of 1921 and *Cadaques* of 1923, which marks his initial forays into **Cubism**. *Girl with Curls* (1926) is regarded as Dalí's first flirtation with **Surrealism**, and beyond here galleries explore Dalí's increasingly intense and bizarre interpretation of dreams in paint. The collection includes some classics of the genre: the dripping watches of *The Disintegration of the Persistence of Memory* (1954) and the dripping eggs of *Eggs on the Plate Without the Plate* (1932). Dalí's cheeky humour, darkness and twisted sense of reality are starkly revealed by works such as *The Average Bureaucrat* (1930), a satiric depiction of his father, and *Atmospheric Skull Sodomizing a Grand Piano* (1934), which leaves little to the imagination. Yet there are also paintings here that are touchingly beautiful – see *Enchanted Beach with Three Fluid Graces* (1939).

Dalí's later works (post-1940s), especially his huge, epic canvases (dubbed "**masterworks**" here) are especially thought provoking: see *Gala Contemplating the Mediterranean Sea* (1976), with its double image of a woman's back and Abraham Lincoln's face, or the overwhelming *Discovery of America by Christopher Columbus* (1959), with Gala (Dalí's wife) playing the role of the Virgin Mary. *The Hallucinogenic Toreador* (1970) is perhaps the most complex of these giant paintings, with multiple double-images of the Venus de Milo and Spain's symbol of virility used to showcase themes of desire and death.

There's also a huge gallery showing Dalí-themed new media (films, prints etc), and photographs of the master by Philippe Halsman.

The Sunken Gardens

1825 4th St N • Mon–Sat 10am–4.30pm, Sun noon–4.30pm • $8 • ☎ 727 551 3102, ✆ stpete.org/sunken • Free parking

If you've had your fill of museums, head for the **Sunken Gardens**, a mile north of the pier. In 1935, a water-filled sinkhole was drained and planted with thousands of tropical plants and trees, forming what is now four acres of shady and sweet-scented gardens, 15ft below street level.

Haslam's

2025 Central Ave • Mon–Sat 10am–6.30pm, Sun noon–5pm • ☎ 727 822 8616, ✆ haslams.com

Though a considerable trek west along Central Avenue, **Haslam's**, Florida's largest bookstore, will keep browsers occupied for hours. Opened in the Depression to provide avid readers with used magazines and books at bargain prices, the store stocks over 300,000 new and used books on all topics.

Weedon Island Preserve

1800 Weedon Drive NE • Preserve: daily 7am–sunset; Cultural & Natural History Center: Thurs–Sat 9am–4pm • Free • ☎ 727 453 6500,
ⓦ weedonislandpreserve.org • From Gandy Blvd (US-92) turn south on San Martin Blvd

Some twelve miles north of downtown St Petersburg, and home to Native American cultures for at least 7000 years, **Weedon Island Preserve** is now a state-protected wildlife refuge. Within the preserve are two miles of boardwalk, hiking trails and a two-mile paddling trail, with kayak rentals available ($17/hr, $40 half-day). The best place to get oriented is the **Cultural & Natural History Center**, which chronicles the long and complicated history of the island – the Weedon Island culture, noted for its pottery, flourished here some 1800 to 1000 years ago, and the island is still sacred to the Seminoles.

ARRIVAL AND DEPARTURE ST PETERSBURG

By plane St Pete-Clearwater International Airport (☎ 727 453 7800, ⓦ fly2pie.com), 6 miles north of downtown at 14700 Terminal Blvd, is served by a handful of charter and budget airlines, notably Las Vegas-based Allegiant Air. A private taxi will cost around $30 to downtown St Petersburg (there is no public transport). If you are arriving at Tampa airport (see p.361) and need to get to St Petersburg or the beaches, Super Shuttle (☎ 800 282 6817, ⓦ supershuttle .com), runs shared vans for $25 per person to the beaches (St Petersburg downtown $23); reservations are recommended.

By car The route by car into St Petersburg is I-275 – don't get off before the "Downtown St Petersburg" exit or you'll face a barrage of traffic lights.

By bus The Greyhound bus station is centrally located at 180 Dr Martin Luther King St N, with services to Tampa (2 daily; 30min) and Naples (1 daily; 4hr 20min) via Fort Myers (2 daily; 3hr 10min). PSTA Bus #32 ($2) runs into downtown from the bus station. The only regular local bus service to Tampa is the #100X commuter service ($3) running between downtown Tampa and the out-of-town Gateway Mall, on Dr Martin Luther King St and 77th Ave, which is both inconvenient to reach (you'll have to transfer to bus PSTA #4 for downtown St Petersburg, or take a taxi), and infrequent between 9am and 4pm.

GETTING AROUND

Downtown buses The Downtown Looper (☎ 727 821 5166, ⓦ loopertrolley.com) runs every 15min Mon–Thurs & Sun 10am–5pm, Fri & Sat 10am–midnight, connecting the pier to major sights downtown, while the Central Avenue Trolley runs from the pier along Central Ave (same times) all the way from the pier to Pass-a-Grille Beach. Both buses cost $0.50 per ride within Downtown (to go all the way to Pass-a-Grille is $2), though rides are free anywhere in the Free Fare Zone (basically Beach Drive Parking Lot to the Museum of Fine Arts).

Buses to the beaches The easiest way to reach St Pete Beach is to take the Central Avenue Trolley from Downtown ($2). Most local bus services to Downtown (☎ 727 540

1900, ⓦ psta.net) arrive at and depart from Williams Park, at the junction of 1st Ave N and 3rd St N, where an information booth (Mon–Sat 7am–5.45pm, Sun 8am–4pm) gives route details. From here, there's a direct connection from Williams Park to Indian Rocks Beach via bus #59, and to Clearwater with bus #18 and bus #52 (where you can make the short bus or taxi ride to Clearwater Beach).

Go Card The best option if you're planning to take several PSTA buses in one day is to purchase a Go Card pass, which allows unlimited travel for a day. It costs $4.50 (or seven days for just $20) and can be purchased on board (exact change only).

INFORMATION

Tourist information St Petersburg Area Chamber of Commerce is at 100 2nd Ave N (Mon–Fri 8am–7pm, Sat 9am–7pm; ☎ 727 821 4069, ⓦ stpete.com).

ACCOMMODATION

★**The Birchwood** 340 Beach Drive NE ☎ 727 896 1080, ⓦ thebirchwood.com. This distinctive white Spanish-mission-style building built in 1922 offers plush rooms with luxury four- or two-poster beds, free wi-fi, iPod docks and excellent views of St Petersburg and the coast from the rooftop bar. Valet parking $18/day. **$205**

★**Dickens House** 335 8th Ave NE ☎ 727 822 8622, ⓦ dickenshouse.com. B&B housed in a beautifully restored 1912 Arts & Crafts cottage with five classically styled rooms within walking distance of downtown. The affable owner serves up delicious gourmet breakfasts. Free wi-fi. **$139**

Larelle House 237 6th Ave NE ☎ 727 490 3575,

ⓦlarellehouse.com. Antique furnishings abound in this charming 1908 Queen Anne-style Victorian home, two blocks from the waterfront. Full breakfast and evening wine and cheese included. Free wi-fi and parking. **$159**

Pier Hotel 253 2nd Ave N ☎727 822 7500, ⓦthepierhotel.com. Bright and tastefully decorated rooms at this shabby-chic hotel, built in 1921, that offers exceptionally cheap deals online (rooms from $61

depending on the season). Free wi-fi; parking $6/day. **$129**

Vinoy Renaissance St Petersburg 501 5th Ave NE ☎727 894 1000, ⓦmarriott.com. If you want to stay in style, try this pink hotel opened in 1925 as a haven for the rich and famous. Now beautifully restored, it offers luxurious rooms, two swimming pools, twelve tennis courts, a golf course, an excellent gym and health spa, grandiose ballrooms and gourmet restaurants. Wi-fi $13/day; parking $15/day. **$254**

EATING

Ceviche 10 Beach Drive ☎727 209 2299, ⓦceviche.com. The tapas are tops at this fun spot inside the *Ponce de León* hotel. You can't go wrong with any of the ceviches or many hot plates and you shouldn't deny yourself the pleasure of the *patatas bravas*, lightly fried potato wedges tossed in home-made *aioli*. Tapas $3.95–19.95, ceviche $9.95–11.95. Live flamenco music Tues–Sat. Mon & Wed 5–10pm, Tues 5–11pm, Thurs 5pm–1am, Fri 5pm–2am, Sat 8am–2am, Sun 8am–10pm.

★**The Chattaway** 358 22nd Ave S ☎727 823 1594, ⓦthechattaway.com. A one-time grocery store opened in 1922, this is now a good-quality, inexpensive American diner, famous for its juicy Original Cheeseburger ($9.10) with all the trimmings. Cash only. Daily 11am–9.30pm.

Marchand's Bar & Grill Vinoy Renaissance, 501 5th Ave NE ☎727 824 8072. The best restaurant in St Petersburg's best hotel boasts well-presented and moderately expensive American and "Floribbean" food

(Gulf grouper, scallops and basil linguini) in a mural-adorned dining room, which frequently reverberates with piano music and occasional live jazz. Mains $28–38. Daily 6.30am–2.30pm & 5–10pm.

Moon Under Water 332 Beach Drive NE ☎727 896 6160, ⓦthemoonunderwater.com. Overlooking the waterfront, this inexpensive British Colonial-style tavern is well known for its cocktails, curries and baked salmon (mains $11–24). Try the killer Key lime pie ($6) for dessert. Mon–Thurs & Sun 11am–11pm, Fri & Sat 11am–midnight.

★**Parkshore Grill** 300 Beach Drive NE ☎727 896 3463, ⓦparkshoregrill.com. Downtown restaurant serving high-quality farm-to-table contemporary American cuisine (all the beef, pork and lamb is sourced from lauded Niman Ranch), with wonderful steaks and seafood (mains $20–42). Mon–Fri 9am–6pm, Sat 9am–2.30pm.

DRINKING AND NIGHTLIFE

★**3 Daughters Brewing** 222 22nd St S ☎727 495 6002, ⓦ3dbrewing.com. One of the region's newest and best craft breweries, with fourteen taps in the tasting room serving such creations as Summer Storm Oatmeal Stout and Biminy Twist IPA. Mon & Tues 2–9pm, Wed & Thurs 2–10pm, Fri 2pm–midnight, Sat noon–midnight, Sun 1–9pm.

Ale and the Witch 111 2nd Ave NE ☎727 821 2533, ⓦthealeandthewitch.com. Justly popular for drinks and bar food (think smoked fish dip and beer cheese dips), with a roster of 32 beers on tap, all American microbrews. Live music most nights (jazz/funk). Daily 3pm–midnight.

Jannus Live 200 1st Ave N ☎727 565 0550, ⓦjannuslive.com. The oldest (and one of the largest) outdoor concert venues in Florida offers a steady procession of DJs and bands playing rock, reggae, folk and the like. Check the weather forecast before you go. Most shows Fri & Sat from 6, 7 or 8pm.

A Taste For Wine Bar and Balcony 241 Central Ave ☎727 895 1623, ⓦtasteforwine.net. Just up the stairs off the main drag you'll find this hidden gem – a chic wine bar with a balcony, comfortable art-filled lounge and live music on weekends. Tues–Thurs 1–9pm, Fri & Sat 2pm–midnight, Sun 4–9pm.

ENTERTAINMENT

American Stage 163 3rd St N ☎727 823 7529, ⓦamericanstage.org. The oldest theatre in the Tampa Bay area runs a programme of high-quality plays and musicals year-round. Tickets $29 to $59. Free parking at 333 3rd Ave N.

Coliseum 535 4th Ave N ☎727 892 5202, ⓦstpete.org/coliseum. Turn up with your own booze (there's no

bar) at this 1924 big-band venue that boasts one of the largest dancefloors in the US; it primarily hosts expos and trade shows these days, but it still runs Wednesday tea dances (Oct–May, first and third Wed of month; 12.30–3.30pm; $7); it's $10 including lessons (11.30am–12.30pm).

8

THE PINELLAS TRAIL

If you're looking for an intriguing alternative to the usual beach-hopping paths of tourists up and down the coast, explore the **Pinellas Trail** (ⓦpinellascounty.org/trailgd), a 37-mile hiking/cycling track that runs between St Petersburg and Tarpon Springs (see p.376). You can pick up a free, informative, and portable guide to the trail at any of the visitor centres between these two destinations, or visit the website. The guide describes the route and picks out points of interest, providing easy-to-manage maps and mileage charts. Numerous exit and entry points encourage a leisurely approach, so allow yourself time to meander off the well-marked confines of the trail and, if you don't feel inclined to tackle its entirety, you can take a bus or drive to selected areas for day-excursions. Despite some uglier sections through urban centres (tricky on a bike), the trail offers enjoyable scenery along its rural portions and a chance for contemplation away from tanning and watersports. Keep in mind that Florida law requires everyone under 16 to wear a helmet when they ride a bike – no matter where they ride.

The St Petersburg beaches

Framing the Gulf side of the Pinellas Peninsula – a bulky thumb of land poking out between Tampa Bay and the Gulf of Mexico – are 35 miles of barrier islands forming the **St Petersburg beaches**, one of Florida's busiest coastal strips. Although each beach area forms part of an individual community, in reality they merge together into one long, built-up strip. The beaches themselves are gorgeous, the sea warm, and the sunsets magical, but in no way is this Florida at its best. That said, staying here can be very cost effective (especially during the summer), and if you're prepared to travel beyond the major built-up areas, you will find quieter strips of sand.

A warning: alcohol is prohibited on all municipal beaches in Florida, and glass containers are also illegal. Police in this area are particularly vigilant in chucking the drunk and disorderly in jail. The following guide is arranged south–north, starting at Fort de Soto Park. Note that **high season** here is usually regarded as February through May; summer rates are much cheaper.

GETTING AROUND   THE ST PETERSBURG BEACHES

By public transport You'll need a car to make the most of this area, but it is possible to get around via public transport. The Suncoast Beach Trolley (daily 5.05am–10.10pm, Fri & Sat till midnight; every 20–30min; $2, day-pass $4.50; ⓦpsta.net/beachtrolley.php) travels along Gulf Blvd and connects all the beaches from Park Street Terminal in downtown Clearwater to 75th Ave in St Pete Beach, where you can continue south to Pass-a-Grille on the Central Avenue Trolley (p.372) – the latter also connects the beaches with St Petersburg itself.

Fort De Soto Park

3500 Pinellas Bayway S, Tierra Verde (Hwy-679) • Sunrise–sunset • Free; parking $5; Pinellas Bayway toll $0.50; Hwy-679 toll $0.35 • ⓣ727 552 1862, ⓦpinellascounty.org/park

On this stretch of coast, the furthest point south you can reach by car is **Fort De Soto Park**, at the end of Hwy-679, made up of five interconnected keys covering 1136 untrammelled acres and some blissfully undeveloped **beaches**. The Spaniard credited with discovering Florida, Juan Ponce de León, is thought to have anchored here in 1513 and again in 1521 when the islands' indigenous inhabitants inflicted on him what proved to be a fatal wound. The islands later became a strategically important Union base during the Civil War, and in 1898 a **fort** was constructed to forestall attacks on Tampa during the Spanish–American War.

The fort

You can wander around the back of what remains of the **fort** (aka Battery Laidley) to view its giant gun batteries, some with the old 12-inch mortars (made in 1901) still in place, before climbing up to the top of the earthworks for views of the beaches. Pick up a leaflet near the entrance, or join a guided walking tour offered on Saturdays at 10am. Construction started in 1898, but the fort was never really finished, and it never saw combat. The adjacent **Fort De Soto Museum** (daily 9am–4pm; free) in the old Quartermaster Storehouse chronicles the history of the site with artefacts and film clips.

The beaches

The park contains almost three miles of white sandy beach, which possess an intoxicating air of isolation during the week – pristine **North Beach** is contender for the best on the Gulf coast. You can **rent bikes** ($8–10/hr) and **kayaks** ($23/hr, $55/day) from the park concession (daily 10am–5pm; bikes ☎727 864 1376, kayaks ☎727 864 1991; ⓦunitedparkservices.com). The best way to savour the area is by **camping** (see p.371).

ACCOMMODATION	FORT DE SOTO PARK
Fort De Soto Park 3500 Pinellas Bayway S, Tierra Verde (Hwy-679) ☎727 582 2267, ⓦpinellascounty .org/park. There are no campsites on St Petersburg	beaches – this is the nearest and nicest spot (with grills, water, electricity, washers, dryers, restrooms, showers and a camp store), and is adjacent to sand and sea. **$37.53**

Egmont Key State Park

Park open daily 8am–sunset • Free • ☎727 893 2627, ⓦ floridastateparks.org/egmontkey • Ferries depart Bay Pier, Fort De Soto Park, March–Aug daily 10am & 11am, return 1.30pm & 2.30pm; Sept–Nov 11am, return 3pm; Dec–Feb 11am, return 2pm; $20, children 11 and under $10

From Fort De Soto Park ferries shoot off to **Egmont Key State Park** to the southwest, a tranquil island wildlife refuge for gopher tortoises, numerous birds and dolphins. The 85ft **Egmont Key Lighthouse** at the north end dates from 1858, while the ruins of **Fort Dade** date back to 1898. You can rent snorkelling gear for $5. Call ahead to make reservations.

Shell Key

Daily 24hr • Free • ⓦ shellkey.org • Ferries depart Merry Pier, 801 Pass-a-Grille Way, St Pete Beach • Daily 10am, noon, 2pm (return 12.15pm, 2.15pm & 4.15pm) • $25, children 12 and under $12.50 • ☎727 360 1348, ⓦ shellkeyshuttle.com

Tiny 195-acre **Shell Key**, in between Pass-a-Grille and Fort De Soto Park, is an enticing undeveloped barrier island, part of the larger Shell Key Preserve. There's little to do here but enjoy the beach, and collect the shells that pile up on the shore – you can take off as many as you can carry. Expect to spy dolphins, manatees and numerous stingrays along the way.

Pass-a-Grille and around

In twenty or so miles of heavily developed coast, just one section of the St Petersburg beaches has the feel of a genuine community with a history attached to it. The slender finger of **PASS-A-GRILLE**, at the southern tip of the barrier island chain, was first settled in the 1880s, though legend has it the name comes from French fishermen who would grill their catch nearby, naming it "*la passe aux grilleurs*". Modern Pass-a-Grille comprises two miles of tidy houses, well-kept lawns, small shops and a cluster of bars and restaurants on one of the area's liveliest stretches of sand. You'll find most of the action at **8th Avenue** and **Gulf Way**.

Gulf Beaches Historical Museum

115 10th Ave • June–Sept Fri & Sat 10am–4pm, Sun 1–4pm; Oct–May Thurs–Sat 10am–4pm, Sun 1–4pm • Free • ☎727 552 1610, ⓦ gulfbeachesmuseum.com

Built in 1917, the **Gulf Beaches Historical Museum** building served as the first church on the barrier islands till 1959, and today traces the history of the islands through photographs, news clippings and artefacts.

Loews Don CeSar Hotel

3400 Gulf Blvd • Rooms from $239 • ☎ 727 360 1881, ⓦ loewshotels.com/Don-CeSar-Hotel

A mile and a half north of central Pass-a-Grille lies the **Don CeSar Hotel**, a lavish pink castle with white-trimmed, arched windows and vaguely Moorish turrets. The hotel fills seven beachside acres and was conceived by 1920s property speculator, Thomas J. Rowe, opening in 1928. Its glamour was short lived; the Depression forced Rowe to use part of the hotel as a warehouse and later to allow the New York Yankees baseball team to make it their spring training base. After decades as a military hospital and then as federal offices, the building received a $1-million facelift during the 1970s and became a hotel again as part of the Loews Group. The current interior bears little resemblance to its original appearance, but even if you don't stay you should check out one of the posh bars or restaurants inside (where you can also validate your parking ticket; otherwise $10–15/day).

ARRIVAL AND INFORMATION   PASS-A-GRILLE

Central Avenue Trolley Pass-a-Grille is connected to St Petersburg and St Pete Beach by the Central Avenue Trolley

($2; p.370), but you'll need a car from anywhere else.
Tourist information ⓦ visitpassagrille.com.

ACCOMMODATION AND EATING

Coconut Inn 113 11th Ave ☎ 727 367 1305, ⓦ pagbeachinns.com. Sleek, modern suites with full kitchens just 200ft from the beach, with a small heated pool in the quiet courtyard garden; wi-fi available in the latter, though not in rooms. **$135**

Island's End Resort 1 Pass-a-Grille Way ☎ 727 360 5023, ⓦ islandsend.com. Five one-bedroom cottages and a three-bedroom cottage with its own private pool, all occupying a tranquil spot at the southernmost tip of Pass-a-Grille. **$204**

★ **Maritana Grille** Don CeSar Hotel, 3400 Gulf Blvd ☎ 727 360 1881, ⓦ loewshotels.com/Don-CeSar-Hotel.

Best fine-dining in the whole beach area; experience New American Cuisine with "Floribbean" accents from Chef Eric Neri. His perfectly seared pan-fried sea scallops ($34) and fabulous spicy coconut bisque ($12) just scrape the surface of the menu. Daily 6–10pm.

The Wharf 2001 Pass-a-Grille Way ☎ 727 367 9469, ⓦ wharfrestaurant.org. Forming part of the marina and a popular place with locals. An enormous bowl of mouthwatering seafood chowder will only set you back around $6; come on Tuesday for the fish fry ($7.95). Mon–Sat 8am–2am, Sun 11am–2am.

St Pete Beach and around

Keeping to Gulf Boulevard north of Pass-a-Grille brings you into **St Pete Beach**, row after row of hotels, motels and restaurants grouped along the road and continuing for several miles. Further north, the community of **Treasure Island** offers abundant watersports for those bored with lying in the sun.

The Suncoast Seabird Sanctuary

18328 Gulf Blvd, Indian Shores • Daily 9am–sunset • Free • ☎ 727 391 6211, ⓦ seabirdsanctuary.com

Nine miles north of St Pete Beach, the **Suncoast Seabird Sanctuary** offers an engrossing break from the sands. The sanctuary is the largest wild-bird hospital in North America, treating between 400 and 600 convalescing birds at any one time, in state-of-the-art facilities. These birds, commonly injured by fishing lines or environmental pollution, are released back into their natural habitat once well.

ARRIVAL AND INFORMATION   ST PETE BEACH AND AROUND

By bus The Central Avenue Trolley runs from the pier in St Petersburg to St Pete Beach ($2). Change here for the Suncoast Beach Trolley (see p.370).
Tourist information In St Pete Beach, visit the Tampa Bay Beaches Chamber of Commerce, 6990 Gulf Blvd

(Mon–Fri 9am–5pm; ☎ 727 360 6957, ⓦ tampabay beaches.com). The Treasure Island Chamber of Commerce is at 245 107th Ave (Mon–Fri 9am–5pm; ☎ 727 360 4121, ⓦ treasureislandchamber.org).

ACCOMMODATION AND EATING

Fetishes 6305 Gulf Blvd ☎727 363 3700, ⓦfetishesrestaurant.com. An intimate fine-dining restaurant with exquisite American cuisine and only eight tables, so reservations are essential. Try the redfish with lobster sauce ($34) or the roast duck *à l'orange* ($32). There's also a good wine selection. Tues–Sat 5–10pm.

Gulf Tides Inn 600 68th Ave ☎727 367 2979 ⓦgulftidesinn.com. This family-owned place is easily the best-value hotel on the beach, with clean, modern apartment-sized suites and rooms, a large heated pool and free wi-fi. **$89**

Madfish 5200 Gulf Blvd ☎727 360 9200, ⓦmadfishonline.com. While it's true they do deep-fry Snickers and Twinkie bars ($4.95), this diner is all about burgers, oysters, the justly famed 60oz grilled prime rib and the irresistible house doughnuts ($6.95). Mon–Thurs & Sun 4–10pm, Fri & Sat 4pm–1am.

Plaza Beach Resort 4506 Gulf Blvd ☎727 367 2791, ⓦplazabeachresorts.com. Smack-dab on the sand, this friendly, comfortable resort hotel is decent value for the money, and a step up in comfort and amenities from *Gulf Tides*. There's also a large pool, free mini-golf and beach cabanas. **$155**

DRINKING AND NIGHTLIFE

★**Caddy's on the Beach** 9000 Gulf Blvd, Treasure Island ☎727 360 4993, ⓦcaddysotb.com. Pick of the beach bars around here, with big-screen TVs, live music, chilli cheese dogs, cold draft beers and lounge chairs on the beach provided for free. Daily 8am–11pm.

Drunken Clam 46 46th Ave, St Pete Beach ☎727 360 1800, ⓦdrunkenclambar.com. Genuine, local dive bar: it's grimy, the bar smells of smoke and beer, the food comes on paper plates (it tastes good though), and the drinks are served in plastic cups – it's excellent. Daily 11am–2am.

Sloppy Joe's on the Beach 10650 Gulf Blvd, Bilmar Beach Resort, Treasure Island ☎727 367 1600, ⓦsloppyjoesonthebeach.com. This outpost of the Key West legend boasts a two-tiered deck, the ideal place to enjoy a sundowner and live music day and night. Daily 11am–10pm.

Gulfport

Absent from most tourist brochures and unseen by the thousands of visitors who hustle between downtown and the St Petersburg beaches, **GULFPORT** is a charming enclave of peaceful restaurants, eclectic art galleries and independent shops, all shaded by oak trees dripping with Spanish moss. It's one of the best places to stay in the area if you want to get off the tourist trail.

ARRIVAL AND DEPARTURE GULFPORT

By car From downtown St Petersburg, travel a few miles south on I-275 to Exit 6, then turn right at the bottom of the exit onto Gulfport Blvd (22nd Ave S), which, after about 2 miles, serves as the central axis for the town; look for Beach Blvd on the left, which becomes the town's main street near the water, where it meets the casino and Shore Drive.

By bus PSTA bus #23 ($2; ⓦpsta.net) from the Williams Park terminal (downtown St Petersburg) takes you into central Gulfport.

ACCOMMODATION AND EATING

O'Maddy's 5405 Shore Blvd ☎727 323 8643, ⓦomaddys.com. Perfect place to soak up the artsy vibes of Gulfport, with great views over the bay thrown in; happy hour usually runs all day till 8pm, and there's karaoke every night. Mon–Sat 8am–3am, Sun 11am–3am.

Peg's Cantina & Brewery 3038 Beach Blvd ☎727 328 2720, ⓦpegscantina.com. Huge range of microbrews, including excellent "GOOD" beers made on-site. Also serves fresh and delicious Mexican food. Tues & Wed 5–10pm, Thurs & Fri 5–11pm, Sat noon–11pm, Sun noon–10pm.

Peninsula Inn & Spa 2937 Beach Blvd ☎727 346 9800, ⓦinnspa.net. A comfortable place with British Colonial-style decor, just twelve luxurious rooms, Indonesian hand-crafted furniture, full-service spa and two restaurants. Free wi-fi. **$139**

Sea Breeze Manor 5701 Shore Blvd ☎727 343 4445, ⓦseabreezemanor.com. A gloriously restored Tudor-style seaside house built in 1923, with sumptuous beds, antique furnishings and home-baked breakfasts that makes a great alternative to staying in St Petersburg proper. **$155**

★**Ted Peters' Famous Smoked Fish** 1350 Pasadena Ave ☎727 381 7931, ⓦtedpetersfish.com. Local icon since 1951, where you can indulge in hot smoked-fish dinners with all the trimmings, including German potato salad (smoked mullet $13.99), or catch your own fish and have it cooked in the restaurant's red oak smoker to go. 11.30am–7.30pm; closed Tues.

8

CLEARWATER: THE HOME OF SCIENTOLOGY

Two miles east of the beach, the city of **Clearwater** is the spiritual headquarters of the **Church of Scientology**, the controversial religion founded by science-fiction writer L. Ron Hubbard in 1954 (celebrity Scientologists include John Travolta and Tom Cruise). The church started buying properties in the area in the 1970s, including the historic 1926 **Fort Harrison Hotel**, which is now linked by a 124ft bridge to the vast **Flag Building** (aka Super Power Building), housing churches, stores and a public information centre. The Clearwater complex, dubbed Flag Land Base, now spans some fifty buildings over a nine-mile grid, with an estimated 12,000 Scientologists living in the area. See ⓦscientology .org for more information.

Clearwater Beach and around

North of St Pete Beach, Gulf Boulevard (Hwy-699) continues to follow the coast along a wall-to-wall line of condos and time-share apartments through Indian Shores, Indian Rocks Beach and Belleair Beach, though things tend to be fairly quiet until you reach **CLEARWATER BEACH**, another full-scale resort community popular with students and families alike, with a carnival atmosphere throughout the summer. Just to the south lies pretty 65-acre **Sand Key Park**, 1060 Gulf Blvd, where tall palm trees frame a scintillating strip of sand. This classic beach vista is a good spot to watch dolphins, though the view is marred by the nearby high-rises. Beyond lounging on its belt of sparkling white sands, enjoying the daily sunset festivities at **Pier 60** (see opposite) and visiting the world's most famous dolphin (see below), you can also make a day-trip to **Caladesi Island**, a few miles north.

Clearwater Marine Aquarium

249 Windward Passage (Winter's Dolphin Tale Adventure at 300 Cleveland St) • Daily 9am–6pm; Winter's Dolphin Tale Adventure daily 10am–6pm • $21.95, children 3–12 $16.95 • Free parking at both locations • ☎ 727 441 1790, ⓦ seewinter.com

Home to the world's best-known dolphin, the **Clearwater Marine Aquarium** on Pasadees Key rescues and rehabilitates injured marine mammals and sea turtles. In 2006 the aquarium rescued a 3-month-old dolphin they named "**Winter**", badly injured by a crab trap line. Winter subsequently lost her whole tail, and the remarkable story of how she learned to survive with a prosthetic was made into a Hollywood movie (*Dolphin Tale*) in 2011. General admission gets you in to the **Winter's Dolphin Tale Adventure** (two miles away, on the mainland), where Winter now resides along with a plethora of dolphin-related exhibits, as well as the main aquarium – the free "Jolley Trolley" shuttle bus runs between the two locations throughout the day. You can also opt for an illuminating **Sea Life Safari Cruise** in the bay ($25.95; 1hr 30min) or a "Behind the Scenes Tour" ($16.95, with general admission).

Caladesi Island State Park

1 Causeway Blvd, Dunedin • Daily 8am–sunset • Entry via Honeymoon Island State Park: $8 per car, single occupant $4; pedestrians, cyclists, kayakers $2 • ☎ 727 469 5918, ⓦ floridastateparks.org/caladesiisland • Ferry from signposted landing stage beside Hwy-586 on Honeymoon Island; daily 10am–5pm (mid-Feb to mid-Sept every 30min, mid-Sept to mid-Feb every hour); $14, children 6–12 $7 round trip

For a glimpse of what these islands must have looked like before the onset of mass tourism, make for **Caladesi Island State Park**, just to the north of Clearwater Beach. The **Caladesi Island Ferry** (☎ 727 734 1501, ⓦ caladesiferry.org) departs from **Honeymoon Island State Park** daily. Once ashore at Caladesi's mangrove-fringed marina, boardwalks lead to a beach of unsurpassed tranquillity that's perfect for swimming, sunbathing and shell collecting. While here, try and summon the strength to tackle the three-mile **nature trail**, which cuts inland through saw palmetto and slash pine. Bring food and drink to the island, as the poorly stocked snack bar at the marina is the sole source of sustenance.

ARRIVAL AND INFORMATION

CLEARWATER BEACH

By car Driving to Clearwater Beach is easy enough via Hwy-60 and the causeway from Clearwater proper, but parking around Pier 60, in the heart of the action, can be tough in peak season: metered parking ($1.25/hr) is available (bring a roll of quarters), or you can try the Pier 60 Lot, 160 S Gulfview Blvd (7am–1am; $3; maximum stay 5hr), or the *Hyatt Regency* parking garage, 301 S Gulfview Blvd, with public parking available even if you're not a guest ($16/day).

By bus With the closure of Clearwater bus station in 2013, the nearest Greyhound stations are in Tampa (p.361) and St Petersburg (p.368). From St Petersburg, PSTA (wpsta .net) bus #18 and bus #52 run to the Park Street terminal in downtown Clearwater; bus #66 also runs here from Tarpon Springs and #200X (weekdays and rush hours only) from Tampa. The Suncoast Beach Trolley ($2; see p.370) connects

the Park Street Terminal with Clearwater Beach and points south to St Pete Beach.

By Jolley Trolley Once at the beach, the Jolley Trolley (☎727 445 1200, wclearwaterjolleytrolley.com) runs daily (Mon–Thurs & Sun 10am–10pm, Fri & Sat 10am–midnight) between Sand Key (from the *Sheraton Sand Key Resort*) and the north end of Clearwater Beach; fares are $2, with an unlimited daily pass $4.50. On Fridays to Sundays the trolley runs as far as Tarpon Springs.

Tourist information The Clearwater Beach Visitor Information Center booth is at Pier 60, 1 Causeway Blvd (daily 10am–7pm; ☎727 442 3604, wvisitclearwaterflorida .com), or try the Clearwater Beach Chamber of Commerce Welcome Center, 333C S Gulfview Blvd (Mon–Fri 9am–5pm; ☎727 726 1547, wbeachchamber.com).

ACCOMMODATION

Barefoot Bay 401 E Shore Drive ☎727 447 3316, wbarefootbayresort.com. This small, family-owned motel, perched on Clearwater Bay, offers a variety of brightly painted rooms with fridge and microwave, pool, free wi-fi and free parking. **$105**

★**East Shore Resort Apartment Motel** 473 E Shore Drive ☎727 442 3636, weastshoreresort.com. These tranquil rental apartments near the beach are spacious, spotlessly clean and incredibly good value for stays of one week or more (kitchens included). Also has a decent pool and laundry facilities. Weekly rates (Dec–April) from **$865**

Hyatt Regency Clearwater Beach Resort and Spa 301 S Gulfview Blvd ☎727 373 1234, wclearwater beach.hyatt.com. This giant pink pile dominates the beach, an all-suite hotel with luxurious amenities (plus large pool, sunset views and good restaurants) and free

wi-fi (there's a mandatory $25/day resort fee, however). Parking $16/day. **$235**

Sea Captain Resort 40 Devon Drive ☎727 446 7550, wseacaptainresort.com. Small 1950s motel offering comfortable rooms and suites with fridges, microwaves and kitchenettes for reasonable rates just off the beach. There's a heated pool and you can fish from the dock. Free parking and free wi-fi. **$135**

Sheraton Sand Key 1160 Gulf Blvd, Sand Key ☎727 595 1611, wsheratonsandkey.com. One of the best and most popular hotels (especially for conferences) on the St Petersburg beaches, with standard five-star rooms. There's an attractive poolside area with pleasant gardens, a great restaurant and the best-equipped gym hereabouts. Parking is free, but wi-fi is $9.95/day (free in lobby). **$149**

EATING

Clear Sky Beachside Café 490 Mandalay Ave ☎727 442 3684, wclearskycafe.com. Especially good bet for breakfast (big plates from $7.95), but knocks out tasty seafood and diner classics all day; think half-pound burgers (from $9.50), lobster mac and cheese ($18.95) and grouper sandwich ($12.95). Mon–Fri 7am–1am, Sat & Sun 7am–2am.

★**Frenchy's Café** 41 Baymont St ☎727 446 3607, wfrenchysonline.com. This 1981 original beach dive has a funky, casual vibe and features favourites such as the smoked fish spread and crackers ($7.95), boiled shrimp ($9.95) and the "super grouper" sandwich ($13.50), best served fried. Be warned – it is a very small space. Daily 11am–11pm.

★**Rusty's Bistro** Sheraton Sand Key, Sand Key ☎727 595 1611, wsheratonsandkey.com. Seafood dishes like eastern spice-seared tuna are as good as the choice steaks and the prime rib buffet ($22.95) at this contemporary American gourmet restaurant. Dinner mains range $17–30. Daily 7am–11.30am & 6–10pm.

Shephard's Ocean Flame 619 S Gulfview Blvd ☎727 441 6875, wshephards.com. Huge but relatively cheap buffet breakfasts (Mon–Fri 8–11pm; $7.95), lunches (from $10.95) and dinners ($26.95 including crab legs and prime rib) are available at this waterfront resort. Sunday champagne brunch is $24.95 (just one glass of champagne). Daily 8am–10.30pm.

NIGHTLIFE AND ENTERTAINMENT

Sunsets at Pier 60 Pier 60, Clearwater Beach ☎727 434 6060, wsunsetsatpier60.com. This free daily street

festival celebrates the area's famed sunsets with street entertainers and live music of all kinds on offer around Pier

8

60 in the heart of Clearwater Beach. Daily 6.30–10.30pm.

Tiki Beach Bar 601–619 S Gulfview Blvd, Shephard's Beach Resort ☎727 441 6875, ⊛shephards.com. Features live reggae and rock music, bikini contests and loads of people looking for a good time. Also has a grill if you're looking for a quick sandwich snack. Daily 4pm–2am.

The Wave 601–619 S Gulfview Blvd, Shephard's Beach Resort ☎727 441 6875, ⊛shephards.com. This two-level nightclub is one of the more popular of the beaches' partying spots. Its massive sound system and light show attract a youngish crowd. Cover from $10. Wed–Sun 9pm–3am.

Tarpon Springs

The condos and time-shares continue for ten miles north of Clearwater all the way to **TARPON SPRINGS**, a Greek enclave that makes an intriguing cultural and gastronomic interlude from the beach resorts. **Sponge farming** developed here in the 1890s, soon bolstered by Greek sponge-divers who introduced modern diving equipment in 1905. These early migrants established what has become a sizeable Greek community in a town previously the preserve of wealthy wintering northerners. Demand for sponges was unprecedented during World War II (among other attributes, sponges are excellent for mopping up blood), but the industry was devastated by a marine blight (1947–57), and the subsequent development of synthetic sponge. The Greek presence in Tarpon Springs remains strong, however, and is most evident every January 6 when around 30,000 participate in the country's largest **Greek Orthodox Epiphany** celebration.

Today there are two key areas worthy of exploration: the **historic downtown** area centred on Tarpon Springs Avenue, where you'll find several old houses that have been converted into curio-filled antique shops; and the **sponge docks** area along Dodecanese Boulevard, with its carnival seaside-like atmosphere at weekends and holidays, and some genuinely good food and bargain sponges in between the tack.

Historic Train Depot Museum

160 E Tarpon Ave • Wed 11am–3pm, Thurs–Sat 11am–4pm • Free • ☎727 943 4624, ⊛tarponspringsareahistoricalsociety.org

While downtown, check out the **Historic Train Depot Museum**, housed in the old train station built in 1909 and in use until 1985. Now part of the **Pinellas Trail** (see box, p.370), it displays old photos of residents and other historic bric-a-brac relating to Tarpon Springs, as well as serving as a welcome centre for the town. Note the two ticket windows near the entrance: up to the 1960s, the larger, nicer of the two was for white passengers, the smaller for black travellers.

St Nicholas Orthodox Cathedral

36 N Pinellas Ave, at Orange St • Daily 9am–5pm • Free • ☎ 727 937 3540, ⓦ epiphanycity.org

In the heart of town, on Pinellas Avenue, you'll see the strongest symbol in this Greek community: the resplendent Byzantine Revival **St Nicholas Orthodox Cathedral**. Partly funded by a half-percent levy on local sponge sales, the cathedral was finished in 1943. The full significance of the cathedral's ornate interior will inevitably be lost on those not of the faith, though the icons, three massive Czech chandeliers and slow-burning incense create an intensely spiritual atmosphere.

The George Innes Junior Collection

230 Grand Blvd, at Read St • Tues 10am–2pm or by appointment • Donations suggested • ☎ 727 937 4682, ⓦ uutarpon.org

The otherwise plain **Unitarian-Universalist Church** is known for its collection of whimsical paintings by the early twentieth-century landscapist **George Innes Junior** (1854–1926), who wintered in Tarpon Springs between 1902 and 1926. To mark what would have been the 100th birthday of his late father (a much more celebrated painter), Innes painted a delicate rendition of *Spring Bayou* (a crescent-shaped lake at the western end of Tarpon Ave), now a centrepiece of the church's collection. Innes spent much of his career mired in depression and mediocrity, but this particular work seemed to ignite a creative spark and prompted the series of hauntingly beautiful paintings (two of which once hung in the Louvre) created between 1918 and 1926 dominating the church's walls today.

Shrine of St Michael Taxiarchis

113 Hope St • Open 24hr

Just a few minutes' walk from the Universalist church, the simple **Shrine of St Michael Taxiarchis** was erected by a local woman in gratitude for the unexplained miracles provided by an icon of the saint she'd obtained in Greece, including the recovery of her "terminally ill" son in 1939. Numerous instances of the blind regaining their sight and the crippled throwing away their walking sticks after visiting the shrine (in the 1950s and 1960s) have been reported, all detailed in a free pamphlet. You can view the miraculous icon inside the shrine, and whatever you believe, it's a beautiful example of Greek Orthodox artistry.

Heritage Museum

100 Beekman Lane, off Spring Blvd • Tues & Fri noon–4pm • $3 • ☎ 727 942 5605, ⓦ tarponarts.org

Walking west along Tarpon Avenue takes you downhill to **Spring Bayou**, a crescent-shaped lake ringed by the opulent homes of Tarpon Springs' pre-sponge-era residents, and to the **Heritage Museum**, which chronicles the history of the town. It also has a special exhibition on the Greek community, and the large-scale murals of local artist Christopher Still.

The sponge docks

Along Dodecanese Boulevard, on the banks of the Anclote River, the **sponge docks** are a slightly down-at-heel conglomeration of one-time supply stores turned into restaurants and gift shops touting cassettes of Greek "belly-dancing music" and, of course, **sponges**. Only a few sponge boats still operate commercially today, but the tacky atmosphere, especially at the weekend, is strangely infectious. Suitably intrigued, take a half-hour **sponge-diving trip** from the St Nicholas Boat Line, 693 Dodecanese Blvd (daily 11am–4.30pm; $8; ☎ 727 942 6425). The trip includes a cruise through the sponge docks, a talk on the history of sponge diving, and a demonstration of harvesting performed in a traditional brass-helmeted diving suit.

Sponge Factory

15 Dodecanese Blvd • Mon–Fri & Sun 10am–7pm, Sat 10am–10pm • Free • ☎ 727 938 5366, ⊛ thespongefactory.com

Learn more about the local community and sponge diving at the **Sponge Factory**, a sponge shop that includes the slightly run-down Museum of Sponge Diving and an informative half-hour film detailing where sponges grow and how they are harvested. It also traces the history of Tarpon Springs' Greek settlers and shows the primitive techniques still used in the industry.

Konger Tarpon Springs Aquarium

850 Dodecanese Blvd • Mon–Sat 10am–5pm, Sun noon–5pm • $7.75, children 3–11 $5.75 • ☎ 727 938 5378,
⊛ tarponspringsaquarium.com

Once you've had your fill of sponges and tourist shops, the small **Konger Tarpon Springs Aquarium** has a simulated coral reef in a 120,000-gallon tank, home to nurse sharks, bonnet head sharks, snook, tarpon and protected jewfish, and the obligatory touch tank, where you can safely pet and feed stingrays and small sharks.

Anclote Key Preserve State Park

Anclote Key • Daily 8am–sunset • Free • ☎ 727 469 5942, ⊛ floridastateparks.org/anclotekey

For a really lazy and very pleasurable half-day, you can take a **boat tour** to nearby **Anclote Key Preserve State Park**, four miles of dazzling sandy beach with an 1887 lighthouse at its southern end. **Sun Line Cruises**, 18 Dodecanese Blvd, offers a variety of trips, from environmentally themed journeys to Anclote Key sightseeing cruises (Mon–Fri 12.30pm & 2.30pm, Sat & Sun 1pm & 3pm; $20; ☎ 727 944 4468, ⊛ sunlinecruises.com). **Sponge-O-Rama**, 510 Dodecanese Blvd (☎ 727 943 2164, ⊛ spongeoramacruiselines.com), offers a similar line-up of cruises and trips to the island for $18.95 (usually daily noon, 2pm & 4pm).

ARRIVAL AND INFORMATION   TARPON SPRINGS

By bus From St Petersburg, PSTA (⊛ psta.net) bus #19 runs frequently to the Tarpon Mall at the junction of Tarpon Ave and US-19; #66 runs direct to the sponge docks from downtown Clearwater. For both buses, frequency reduces to hourly services on Sundays and holidays. Fares are $2.

Tourist information Visit the Chamber of Commerce at the sponge docks, 100 Dodecanese Blvd (daily 10.30am–3.30pm; ☎ 727 937 6109, ⊛ tarponspringschamber.com).

ACCOMMODATION

Ashley's Victorian Haven Bed & Breakfast 313 N Grosse Ave ☎ 727 505 9152, ⊛ ashleysvictorianhaven .com. Perfect B&B; a charming house built in 1894, friendly owners, tasty breakfasts and two cosy suites, a short walk from downtown. Free wi-fi. **$129**

Hampton Inn & Suites Tarpon Springs 39284 US-19 N ☎ 727 945 7755, ⊛ hamptoninn.hilton.com. Best of the chain hotels in the area, offering great service, luxurious rooms, decent outdoor pool and breakfast included. Free wi-fi and parking. **$105**

EATING

Costas 521 Athens St ☎ 727 938 6890, ⊛ costascuisine .com. For authentic Greek food, sample the offerings at local favourite *Costas*, which specializes in seafood, salads and *souvlaki*. Dishes start at around $11. Mon–Fri 11am–10pm, Fri & Sat 9am–10pm.

★**Mykonos** 628 Dodecanese Blvd ☎ 727 934 4306. Some of the best Greek food in the country is knocked up at this no-frills family diner, everything from a classic *moussaka* ($10.95), to wonderfully fragrant lamb shank ($12.95), home-made *taramasalata* ($6.25) and superb desserts like *baklava* ($3.50). Daily 11am–10pm.

Plaka 769 Dodecanese Blvd ☎ 727 934 4752,

⊛ plakatarponsprings.com. This is the place for gyros ($7) – the meat is tender, the *tzatziki* tasty and the pitta bread always fresh. Huge portions, and usually not as busy as the other restaurants along here. Mon–Thurs & Sun 10.30am–8pm, Fri & Sat 10.30am–9pm.

Zánte Cafe 13 N Safford Ave ☎ 727 934 5558. An eclectic downtown café that resembles a grandmother's overstuffed attic. The Cajun-Greek cuisine includes such delicious dishes as the Louisiana crab cakes ($10.99) and roasted eggplant pasta for $8.99. Tues–Sat 11.30am–9pm.

8

Lakeland and around

LAKELAND, thirty miles east of Tampa, plays the suburban big brother to its more rural neighbours and provides sleeping quarters for Orlando and Tampa commuters, who emerge on weekends to stroll the edges of the town's numerous lakes. Aided by its busy railway terminal, Lakeland's fortunes rose in the 1920s, and a number of its more important buildings have been preserved as the **Munn Park Historic District**. A stronger draw, and something of a surprise in such a tucked-away community, is the largest single grouping of buildings by **Frank Lloyd Wright**, who redefined American architecture in the Twenties and Thirties.

Florida Southern College

111 Lake Hollingsworth Drive • Campus daily 8am–sunset • Free • Education centre daily 9.30am–4.30pm • Tours (reserve in advance) $20–55 • ☎ 863 680 4597, ⓦ flsouthern.edu

Maybe it was the rare chance to design an entire communal area that appealed to Frank Lloyd Wright – the fee he got for converting an orange grove into **Florida Southern College**, a mile southwest of Lakeland's centre, certainly didn't; the financially strapped college paid on credit and got its students to provide the labour. Established here in 1922, today the 100-acre campus is the home of the largest collection of Frank Lloyd Wright architecture in the world, dubbed "Child of the Sun". Wright completed the buildings between 1941 and 1958, and though much of the integrity of his initial concept has been lost, the campus remains a startlingly inventive statement. Start at the **Sharp Family Tourism and Education Center** at 750 Frank Lloyd Wright Way, which displays photographs, furniture and exhibits related to the site. The centre occupies the **Usonian House** (tours $7), designed by Wright in 1939, but only completed in 2013. Various tours begin here (the **In-Depth Tour**, at $35, is the best, with access inside most of the buildings), but self-guided visits around the campus are free.

Most of the Wright buildings are best appreciated from the outside, beginning with the starkly geometric **Annie Pfeiffer Chapel**, completed in 1941 and Wright's first structure on the campus. Other highlights include the curving **Buckner Building**, a library completed in 1946, and the **Water Dome**, a sleek, Modernist fountain-cum-installation, restored in 2007 to Wright's original plans (the fountains turn on daily 9.45–11.30am, 12.30–2pm, 2.30–3.30pm & 4.30–5.30pm). You can usually take a peek inside the **Danforth Chapel**, completed 1955, with its crisp, jagged lines and red cypress interior. As you walk around, take time also to admire the **Esplanades**, covered walkways with a decidedly futuristic look.

8

ARRIVAL AND INFORMATION   LAKELAND

By bus Greyhound buses arrive at 303 N Massachusetts Ave in the historic district, and run from Orlando (3 daily; 1hr 20min) and Tampa (3 daily; 45min). You'll need to take a taxi to Florida Southern College.

By train The Amtrak train station is near the bus station at 600 E Main St, with daily services to Tampa, Orlando,

Jacksonville and all points north.

Tourist information Get a descriptive walking-tour map of the Munn Park Historic District from the Chamber of Commerce, 35 Lake Morton Drive (Mon–Fri 8.30am–5pm; ☎ 863 688 8551, ⓦ lakelandchamber.com).

ACCOMMODATION AND EATING

Harry's Seafood Bar & Grille 101 N Kentucky Ave ☎ 863 686 2228, ⓦ hookedonharrys.com. Great bar that also serves up New Orleans Cajun- and Creole-inspired food amid lots of dark wood and exposed brick. Dinner mains $13–18. Mon–Thurs & Sun 11am–10pm, Fri & Sat 11am–11pm.

Reececliff Family Diner 940 S Florida Ave ☎ 863 686 6661. A spartan diner in business since 1934, offering cheap breakfasts ($6–7) and mains like chicken and waffles and country fried steak ($9–12); justly celebrated for its home-made sweet potato pies ($3). Mon–Sat 7am–9pm, Sun 8am–3pm.

★**Terrace Grille** Terrace Hotel, 329 E Main St ☎863 688 0800, ⓦterracehotel.com. If you're in the mood for a posh meal, try this chic option in the historic hotel (see opposite), where you can tuck into superb dishes, such as herb-crusted rack of lamb ($38) and jumbo lump crab cakes ($21). Daily 7am–10pm.

The Terrace Hotel 329 E Main St ☎863 688 0800, ⓦterracehotel.com. This plush hotel nestled between the main drag and Mirror Lake was built in 1924 and is loaded with historic charm, though the rooms are comfy and modern. Free valet parking and free wi-fi. $109

Bok Tower Gardens

1151 Tower Blvd, Lake Wales • Daily 8am–6pm, last admission 5pm • $12, children 5–12 $3; $18/$8 with Pinewood Estate • ☎863 676 1408, ⓦboktowergardens.org

"A more striking example of the power of beauty could hardly be found, better proof that beauty exists could not be asked for," rejoiced landscape gardener William Lyman Phillips in 1956 on visiting **Bok Tower Gardens**, a rolling park of greenery two miles north of Lake Wales on Hwy-17A. As sentimental as it may sound, Phillips' comment was, and is, accurate. Whether it's the effusive entanglements of ferns, oaks and palms; the bright patches of magnolias, azaleas and gardenias; or just the sheer novelty of a hill (this being the highest point in peninsular Florida, at 298ft), Bok Tower Gardens is one of the state's loveliest places.

Not content with winning the Pulitzer Prize for his autobiography in 1920, Dutch-born office-boy turned author and publisher **Edward Bok** resolved to transform the pine-covered Iron Mountain (as this red-soiled hump is named) into a "sanctuary for humans and birds", hiring famed architect Frederick Law Olmsted Jr in 1922.

The Singing Tower

Marvellous though they are, these 250 acres would be just a glorified botanical garden were it not for the awe-inspiring **Singing Tower**, 205ft of marble and coquina rising steeply above the foliage, poetically mirrored in a swan- and duck-filled lily pond. Originally intended to conceal the garden's water tanks, the tower features finely sculpted impressions of Florida wildlife on its exterior and fills its interior with a sixty-bell carillon: richly toned chimes resound through the garden every half-hour and during two recitals at 1pm and 3pm every day (the interior is closed to the public). The tower was completed in 1929, and when Edward Bok died one year later, he was interred at its base.

Pinewood Estate

Mon–Sat 11am–4pm, Sun noon–4pm (May–Sept closes at 3pm)

The twenty-room Mediterranean-style **Pinewood Estate**, occupying eight acres of the gardens, was completed in 1932, and has been artfully restored to reflect the period. The lavish house was the winter home of tycoon Charles Austin Buck, vice president of Bethlehem Steel, and was acquired by the Gardens in 1970.

The Big Bend

Popularly known as the **BIG BEND** for the way it curves toward the Panhandle, Florida's **northwest coast** is one of its best-kept secrets. Far from the tourist beaches and theme parks, this sparsely populated coastline offers thousands of mangrove islands and marshlands, wide spring-fed rivers and quiet roads leading to small communities. Here you will find some of the best wildlife Florida has to offer and an outstanding Native American ceremonial site.

Weeki Wachee Springs State Park

6131 Commercial Way (US-19), Weeki Wachee • Daily 9am–5:30pm, show times vary seasonally • $13, children 6–12 $8 •
☎ 352 596 2062, Ⓦ weekiwachee.com

Some thirty miles north from Tarpon Springs on US-19, the first attraction of
note is **Weeki Wachee Springs State Park**, an old-fashioned roadside attraction that
opened in 1947. The park is actually a theatre built into an underwater spring,
and has attracted numerous celebrities over the years – including Elvis – to its
thoroughly kitsch underwater shows performed by "mermaids" (actually highly
skilled female swimmers who take surreptitious breaths through an air hose while
performing). Your ticket also allows access to the slides and rides of **Buccaneer Bay
Water Park** (swimming area daily 9am–5.30pm; water slides and rides late March to
mid-June Sat & Sun 10am–5pm; mid-June–Aug daily 10am–5pm; Sept Sat & Sun
10am–4pm; entry to the water park is via the Springs State Park – no separate
admission).

Homosassa Springs and around

Twenty miles north of Weeki Wachee is **HOMOSASSA SPRINGS**, the first community of
any size on US-19, but also an enticing introduction to the natural wonders of the Big
Bend. It's one of the best places anywhere in the world to see **manatees**, and to catch
tarpon (May and June are the prime fishing months).

Homosassa Springs Wildlife State Park

4150 S Suncoast Blvd (visitor centre and entrance) • Daily 9am–5.30pm, last ticket sold at 4.45pm • $13; children 6–12 $5 •
☎ 352 628 5343, Ⓦ floridastateparks.org/homosassasprings

Though **Homosassa Springs Wildlife State Park** is really just a small zoo, it's a marvellous
showcase of Florida's native wildlife, offering a chance to see animals, birds and plants
in their natural setting. If you park at the visitor centre on US-19 you'll be whisked to
the park entrance proper via a twenty-minute boat ride along the turtle-rich **Pepper
Creek** (free; every 30min) – you can also walk or take a trolley bus back. Inside the park
the highlight is the spring-fed lake containing six or so **manatees**; you can view them
and hordes of fish from the underwater observatory (aka **Fishbowl**) built on top of the
spring – it's the closest you'll get to these strange, gentle giants without getting into the
water. From here trails circle the lake passing compounds of bobcats, cougars and
wolves, with the central area swamped by all manner of squawking birds and nasty-
looking black vultures.

Monkey Island

Homosassa Riverside Resort, 5297 S Cherokee Way • ☎ 352 628 2474, Ⓦ riversideresorts.com

Monkeys in Florida? Once just a pile of stones in the river, man-made "**Monkey
Island**" was created out of dirt and rocks in the 1960s, and houses a family of **spider
monkeys** brought from Africa for a research project. Today the island is owned by the
Riverside Resort (see p.383), which maintains it as a giant play area for the monkeys.
Though the island is strictly off limits, the monkeys are fed by the hotel twice a day,
their playful antics amusing guests and onlookers from the river bank – all slightly
bizarre but kooky fun.

Withlacoochee State Forest

Visitor centre 15003 Broad St, Brooksville (US-41) • $2 • Mon–Fri 8am–noon & 1–4.30pm • ☎ 352 797 4140, Ⓦ freshfromflorida.com

The area around Homosassa Springs contains many parks and preserves, most with
opportunities for hiking, kayaking and birdwatching. One of the largest is
Withlacoochee State Forest, actually divided into several distinct tracts of land; the
Homosassa Tract is the closest to the springs (access on US-19), but for details of
trails and current conditions, stop by the visitor centre near Brooksville.

Separately, the **Withlacoochee State Trail** runs for 46 miles along an old rail line, cutting through the forest between Citrus Springs and Owensboro Junction near Dade City, east of Homosassa. The trail can be hiked or biked – see ⓦrailstotrailsonline.com.

Chassahowitzka National Wildlife Refuge

US-19 • Daily sunrise–sunset • Free • ☎ 352 563 2088, ⓦ fws.gov/chassahowitzka

South of Homosassa Springs on US-19 you'll pass the entrance to **Chassahowitzka National Wildlife Refuge**, a 31,000-acre reserve of pristine saltwater bays, estuaries and brackish marshes at the mouth of the Chassahowitzka River. The refuge is accessible only by boat; rental boats are available in Homosassa, but the easiest way is on a cruise organized by **River Safaris**, 10823 W Yulee Drive, Homosassa (prices range $35–120; ☎ 352 628 5222, ⓦ riversafaris.com), or **Chassahowitzka River Wildlife Tours** (☎ 352 382 0837, ⓦ chassahowitzkariverwildlifetours.com) departing the Chassahowitzka Public Boat Ramp ($5 parking) at 8600 W Miss Maggie Drive, two miles west of US-19. Tours cost $25–35 for two or three hours.

ARRIVAL AND INFORMATION   HOMOSASSA SPRINGS

By car You'll need your own transport to visit Homosassa Springs; the nearest Greyhound bus station is at Crystal River, 7 miles north (see p.385).

Tourist information Citrus County Visitors & Convention

Bureau, next to the wildlife park entrance at 9225 W Fishbowl Drive (Mon–Fri 8am–5pm; ☎ 352 628 9305, ⓦ visitcitrus.com), has details on boat tours, manatees, kayaking and local sights.

ACCOMMODATION

Chassahowitzka River Campground 8600 W Miss Maggie Drive ☎ 352 382 2200, ⓦ chassahowitzka florida.com. Twenty-eight primitive tent sites, plus 53 full hook-up RV sites, within walking distance of the Chassahowitzka River, convenient for canoeing ($35/day). Parking is $5/day extra. Basic pitch $\underline{23}$

Homosassa Riverside Resort 5297 S Cherokee Way ☎ 352 628 2474, ⓦ riversideresorts.com. No frills but great-value standard rooms on the river opposite Monkey

Island, and larger suites with kitchens (it's worth the extra for a riverside room). Boat rental is available ($50/half-day). $\underline{105}$

MacRae's 5300 S Cherokee Way ☎ 352 628 2602, ⓦ macraesofhomosassa.com. The place of choice for fishermen for kicking back in a rocking chair on the porch, with simple but clean and comfy cabins. Boat rental is available ($30/hr or $100/day), and there's free wi-fi. $\underline{75}$

8

MANATEES

Manatees are one of Florida's most beloved creatures, but sadly also one of its most endangered. More closely related to elephants and aardvarks than to other sea life, it's hard to believe these large animals – they can grow up to 13ft long and weigh up to 3500 pounds – are the source of the mermaid myth. Manatees are harmless and love to graze on seagrasses in shallow water, surfacing every three to four minutes to breathe. They have been on the endangered species list since 1973, and there are only a few thousand left in Florida waters. With no natural predators, a third of manatee deaths have human-related causes, such as accidents with boats, pollution and flood control gates that automatically close. Although scientists believe manatees can live to 60 or longer, their slow development to sexual maturity and low birth-rate do little to compensate for their disproportionately high death-rate.

Manatees may be endangered, but Florida law prohibits breeding them; resources, they say, are better spent on the care and rehabilitation of wild manatees that have suffered the blows of ship's propellers or river poisoning. You should never approach, feed or touch manatees in the wild and if you see an injured or dead one, a calf with no adult around, or see anyone harassing one, call the Florida Fish and Wildlife Conservation Commission on ☎ 888 404 3922. To learn more about manatees and their conservation, read **Manatees: An Educator's Guide** produced by the Save the Manatee Club, 500 N Maitland Ave, Maitland (☎ 800 432 5646, ⓦ savethemanatee.org), available as a pdf online. Most of the dive shops in Crystal River offer snorkelling trips geared to **swimming with the manatees** (see p.384).

Nature's Resort 10359 W Halls River Rd ☎352 628 9544, ⓦnaturesresortfla.com. This well-equipped RV resort, with shop, restaurant, pool and a host of activities, allows camping and also rents comfy chalets. Free wi-fi. Basic pitches $33, chalets $120

EATING

★**Freezer** 5590 S Boulevard Drive ☎352 628 2452. Cheap and fresh seafood, especially crab, crawfish, chowder, shrimp (2.5 pounds for $22) and scallop, served in no-frills styrofoam trays overlooking the water (cold pitchers of beer from just $7). Classic place to chill out with the locals. Cash only. Daily 11am–10pm (call in advance to confirm).

Neon Leon's Zydeco Steakhouse 10350 W Yulee Drive ☎352 621 3663, ⓦneonleonszydecosteakhouse.com. Good ol' Southern dining (created by the family of the late Leon Wilkeson, bass player with rock band Lynyrd Skynyrd), with an extensive menu of fresh seafood and Creole and Cajun dishes (think gator tails, jambalaya and seafood gumbo). Mains average $15–16. Tues–Sun 11am–9pm.

Riverside Crab House Homosassa Riverside Resort ☎352 628 2474, ⓦriversideresorts.com. The best spot to consume your blue crabs ($20), grouper sandwiches ($12) and fried shrimp ($10–15) is at a table overlooking the river and Monkey Island. Mon–Thurs 11am–9pm, Fri–Sun 11am–10pm.

Crystal River and around

Seven miles north of Homosassa Springs, **CRYSTAL RIVER** is among the region's larger communities, with a population topping a whopping four thousand. **Manatees** take a shine to the sedate beauty of the clear river from which the town takes its name, and the adjacent **Kings Bay**, home to around forty freshwater springs. The manatees can be seen all year round, but in greater numbers during the winter – the best way to see them is to join one of many **tour boat** operators, rent a kayak or even swim or dive with them (see below).

Crystal River State Archaeological Park

3400 N Museum Point • Daily 8am–sunset; visitor centre Mon & Thurs–Sun 9am–5pm • Cars $3, pedestrians and cyclists $2 • ☎352 795 3817, ⓦfloridastateparks.org/crystalriverarchaeological • Take State Park Rd off US-19 just north of the town

Crystal River's present dwellers are by no means the first to have lived by the waterway – it provided a source of food for Native Americans from at least 9000 BC. To gain some insight into their culture, head to the **Crystal River State Archaeological Park**, where large temple, burial and shell midden mounds are still visible dating back to the period 500 BC to 900 AD. Inside the **visitor centre** there is a short video and an enlightening assessment of finds (arrowheads, pottery and the like) from the 450 graves discovered here, indicating trade links with tribes far to the north. More fascinating, however, are the connections with the south. The site contains two *stelae*, or ceremonial stones, much more commonly found in Mexico, and the engravings – thought to be faces of sun deities – suggest large-scale solar ceremonies were conducted here. The sense of the past and the serenity of the setting – the grounds are studded with Spanish-moss-smothered oak and palmetto – make wandering the site a highly evocative experience.

SWIMMING WITH THE MANATEES

Crystal River is the only place in Florida where you are permitted to swim with **manatees** – snorkelling or diving with these tranquil creatures is a magical experience.

American Pro Diving Center 821 SE US-19 ☎352 563 0041 or ☎800 291 3483, ⓦamericanprodiving .com. Offers all kinds of guided dives and snorkel trips from $29.50 to $69.50.

Captain Mike's Sunshine River Tours 1 SW 1st Place ☎352 628 3450, ⓦsunshinerivertours.com. Tours on the Crystal River and King's Bay from $45. Also does scalloping tours for $75 (season is July–Sept).

Crystal River Manatee Tour and Dive 267 NW 3rd St ☎888 732 2692, ⓦmanateetoursusa.com. Offers a similar range of dive and snorkelling trips (scalloping from $75, manatee trips $39–49), as well as air-boat tours of the Crystal River.

Crystal River Preserve State Park

3266 N Sailboat Ave • Visitor centre Mon–Fri 9am–5pm, park open 8am–sunset • Free • Heritage-Eco River Tour Mon, Wed & Fri 10.30am & 1.30pm; $15 • ☎ 352 563 0450, ⓦ floridastateparks.org/crystalriverpreserve

Covering twenty miles of Gulf coast, the **Crystal River Preserve State Park** contains tranquil islands, inlets, backwaters and subtropical forests. The park offers fishing at the "mullet hole", a canoe and kayak launch, and seven miles of nature trails that can be hiked or biked. Pick up a trail map in the **visitor centre**, where you can also view movies, aquariums, two snake exhibits and a diamondback terrapin enclosure. On the ninety-minute **Heritage-Eco River Tour** a guide discusses the ways pre-Columbian Indians may have used the abundant marine resources and gives an ecological interpretation of plants and wildlife. Tickets are sold on a first come, first served basis one hour prior to boat trips, and often sell out fast.

Crystal River National Wildlife Refuge

1502 SE Kings Bay Drive, at Paradise Point Rd (west off US-19) • Refuge daily sunrise–sunset; visitor centre Mon–Fri 8am–4pm; mid-Nov to March also open weekends 8am–4pm • Free • ☎ 352 563 2088, ⓦ fws.gov/crystalriver

At the visitor centre of the **Crystal River National Wildlife Refuge** – set up specifically for the protection of the endangered West Indian manatee, and part of the larger **Chassahowitzka National Wildlife Refuge** (see p.383) – you can gather information on swimming with manatees (see box opposite), snorkelling, scuba diving and boat trips in the area.

ARRIVAL AND INFORMATION	CRYSTAL RIVER	**8**

By bus The Greyhound bus station is at 640 SE 8th Terrace, just off US-19 in the centre of town. Buses run from here to Tallahassee (2 daily; 3hr 40min) and Tampa (2 daily; 1hr 40min–2hr).

Tourist information Crystal River's helpful Chamber of Commerce Welcome Center is right on US-19 (no. 28) in the centre of town (Mon–Fri 9am–5pm; ☎ 352 795 3149, ⓦ citruscountychamber.com). You'll have to park around the corner; the car park adjacent to the chamber is private property.

ACCOMMODATION

Crystal Manatee Extended Stay Suites 310 N Citrus Ave ☎ 352 586 1813, ⓦ crystalmanateesuites.com. Solid economical choice in the older part of town and close to the bay, with simple but clean and comfy rooms with kitchens, cable TV, free wi-fi and hospitable staff. $75

Holiday Inn Express 1203 NE 5th St ☎ 877 859 5095, ⓦ hiexpress.com. Newest and certainly the best of the chain motels in town, with spotless rooms, LCD TVs, free wi-fi, decent breakfast and free cookies. $90

Plantation on Crystal River 9301 W Fort Island Trail (Hwy-44) ☎ 352 795 4211, ⓦ plantationoncrystalriver .com. The most luxurious accommodation in town, with an on-site dive shop and a golf course nearby; the modern rooms and bigger villas feature contemporary decor, free wi-fi and flat-screen TVs. $119

EATING AND DRINKING

Crystal River Ale House 1610 SE Paradise Circle ☎ 352 795 3113, ⓦ porthotelandmarina.com/dining .html. Casual dining right on the water, with a pub menu of fresh seafood, pasta, burgers and steak, and live music and cocktails at the Tiki Bar (most mains $10–23). Mon–Thurs & Sun noon–8pm, Fri noon–10pm, Sat 11am–10pm.

★**Dan's Clam Stand** 2315 N Sunshine Path (Hwy-44) ☎ 352 795 9081. No-frills dive serving fresh clams (from Massachusetts) and oysters, but also fish baskets and burgers, and a luscious peanut-butter pie. Most orders under $10. Cash or debit only. Mon–Fri 11am–9pm.

★**Seafood Seller & Café** 1801 US-19 (Crystal River Mall) ☎ 352 228 4936. Popular Cajun joint in the local strip mall, with excellent fresh fish, chicken and steaks – think fried green tomatoes ($4), hefty grouper sandwiches ($11) and authentic gumbo ($7). Mon–Sat 11am–9pm.

Cedar Key

Whatever you do on your way north, spend a day or two at the splendidly isolated **CEDAR KEY**, an intriguing remnant of Old Florida. In the 1860s, the railroad from

ROSEWOOD

Little remains of **Rosewood**, a once thriving African-American community that lies on Hwy-24 just northeast of Cedar Key. A small historical marker on the side of the road commemorates the **massacre** that occurred here in 1923, though even today, no one knows exactly how many people died. The town was attacked by whites from nearby Sumner after a white female accused a black man of assaulting her. Days of terror and fear ensued as armed mobs looted and burned Rosewood. At least six blacks were tortured and killed, and two whites died. Dubbed a "race riot" at the time, no arrests were made, the town was never reoccupied and the true events only came to light in the 1980s. In 1994 nine survivors filed a lawsuit for compensation from the state (they won $150,000 each). The massacre was also the subject of a 1997 **film**, *Rosewood*, directed by John Singleton, which suggested that many more died: some survivors claimed there may have been up to 27 black residents killed.

Sadly, Rosewood was merely one of many such incidents in Florida; in 1920 a white mob destroyed Ocoee's black community, causing as many as 30 deaths. A travelling display of what happened in Rosewood goes on tour internationally; a permanent display is housed in the library of Bethune-Cookman University in Daytona Beach (p.322).

Fernandina Beach (see p.348) ended its journey here, turning the community – which occupies one of several small islands – into a thriving port. When ships got bigger and moved on to deeper harbours, Cedar Key began cutting down its cypress, pine and cedar trees to fuel a pencil-producing industry. Inevitably, the trees were soon gone, and by 1900 Cedar Key was all but a ghost town. The few who stayed eked out a living from fishing and harvesting oysters, as many of the thousand-strong population still do. Cedar Key has, however, undergone a revival, with many decaying timber-framed homes becoming restaurants and shops. With its rustic, ramshackle galleries, old wooden houses on **2nd Street**, the bars and restaurants on **Dock Street**, and the glittering waters of Cedar Key's unspoiled bay, the area makes for a beguiling target, though happily, it is never likely to be deluged with visitors.

Cedar Key State Museum

12231 SW 166th Court • Thurs–Mon 10am–5pm • $2 • ☎ 352 543 5350, ⊚ floridastateparks.org/cedarkeymuseum

The modest **Cedar Key State Museum** is primarily a tribute to **Saint Clair Whitman**, a long-time Cedar Key inhabitant who amassed a vast collection of seashells and Native American artefacts until his death in 1959. Today the museum displays his collection along with information on naturalist John Muir, who came here in 1867, Rosewood (see box above), and the Key's overall history from the 1840s. The 1880 shingle cottage just outside is part of the museum and has been restored to its appearance when Whitman purchased it in the 1920s – stacks of his seashells are displayed inside. The museum is tucked away in what's known as Way Key – follow the signs from the main road.

Cedar Key Historical Museum

7070 D St (Hwy-24), at 2nd St • Mon–Fri & Sun 1–4pm, Sat 11am–5pm • $2 • ☎ 352 543 5549

For another perspective on the history of these islands, visit the **Cedar Key Historical Museum**, housed in the handsome 1871 Lutterloh Building in the heart of town. Small exhibits throw light on the Seminole Wars, Cedar Key's seafood and lumber industries and the Civil War, while the **Andrew's House** annex is dedicated to the Florida Peninsula Railroad, which operated from 1861 to 1932 between here and Fernandina Beach.

ARRIVAL AND INFORMATION
CEDAR KEY

By car Turn west off US-19 onto Hwy-24 at the hamlet of Otter Creek and drive for 24 miles until the road ends. There's no public transport.

Tourist information The Welcome Center, next to the library on 2nd St (Mon & Thurs–Sun 10am–3pm; ☎ 352 543 5600, ⊚ cedarkey.org), has all the usual information.

ACCOMMODATION

★ **Cedar Key Bed & Breakfast** 810 3rd St ☎ 352 543 9000, ⊚ cedarkeybedandbreakfast.com. Relax on the back porch of this romantic wooden house built in 1880, with a garden dominated by a 400-year-old oak tree. Choose from eight comfortable, cosy rooms or a more private "Honeymoon Cottage". Free wi-fi, complimentary bikes and free home-made cookies. $120

★ **Cedar Key Harbour Master Suites** 390 Dock St ☎ 352 543 9320, ⊚ cedarkeyharbourmaster.com. Amazing views right in the heart of the action, with nine modern suites with wraparound balconies and kitchenettes in one of the old wooden buildings over the water. Free wi-fi in courtyard only. $90

Dockside Motel 491 Dock St ☎ 352 543 5432. You won't find anything cheaper or as centrally located as this motel,

which sits on the dock a few steps away from the fishing-friendly pier. Ten well-furnished suites, one with a full kitchen, are also available. Call between 9am and noon to reserve. Free wi-fi. $60

Island Hotel 373 2nd St, at B St ☎ 352 543 5111, ⊚ islandhotel-cedarkey.com. Built in 1860, this hotel is full of character, with sloping wooden floors, overhanging verandas and sepia murals. Ask about the ghosts that supposedly haunt three of the rooms. No TVs or phones, but free wi-fi and breakfast included. $80

Pirates' Cove Hwy-24 ☎ 352 543 5141, ⊚ piratescovecottages.com. The location about half a mile from the town centre results in cheaper rates and views of the bayou, with its diverse birdlife. Accommodation is in six modern cottages with kitchens and free wi-fi. $69

EATING AND DRINKING

★ **Black Dog Bar & Tables** 360 Dock St ☎ 352 325 0050, ⊚ cedarkeybar.com. Sample the huge selection of quality beers (around 160 types of bottled beer) and wines at this friendly local bar on the water, which also boasts a cigar humidor. Wed–Sun 3pm–midnight.

Blue Desert Café 12518 SR-24 ☎ 352 543 9111. The food – all of it cooked from scratch, so be patient – includes

fine pizzas, *bruschette* and a salsa dip to die for. A friendly ambience and thirty different types of beer add to the appeal. It also does breakfast. Mains range $12–17. Tues–Thurs 5–9pm, Fri & Sat 5–10pm.

The Island Room 192 E 2nd St, at Cedar Cove Resort ☎ 352 543 6520, ⊚ islandroom.com. Cedar Key's most elegant restaurant, boasting a justly famous crab bisque

8

TOURING THE OUTER CEDAR KEYS

To really appreciate the isolation and untrammelled beauty of this stretch of coast, you'll need to take a boat trip out to the twelve islands within a five-mile radius of Cedar Key – set aside in 1929 as the **Cedar Keys National Wildlife Refuge** (☎ 352 493 0238, ⊚ fws.gov/cedarkeys). Atsena Otie Key was the island first settled in the 1800s, and contains a nature trail and the ruins of Faber Mill, built in 1868. Most tours also take in views of Seahorse Key and its pretty 52ft lighthouse built in 1851, now used by the University of Florida as a marine laboratory (note that landing is prohibited on Seahorse Key between March and June when the island becomes a sanctuary for nesting birds).

Cedar Key Boat Rentals and Island Tours East end of Dock St, at A St ☎ 352 231 4435, ⊚ cedarkey boatrentalsandislandtours.com. Daily 2hr cruises (11am–2hr before sunset) to Atsena Otie and Seahorse keys for $25. They'll drop you off for the day on Atsena for $15, and also rent out boats (from $80/3hr).

Tidewater Tours City Marina, 4 Dock St ☎ 352 543 9523, ⊚ tidewatertours.com. Offers the Island Tour (daily 11am & 2pm; $26), but also Suwannee River ($45) and Coastal Marsh ($35) tours where you're likely

to spot a spectacular variety of bird including nesting bald eagles, manatees and dolphins.

Wild Florida Adventures Williston ☎ 352 528 3984, ⊚ wild-florida.com. Also worthwhile are these kayak tours, which explore much of the Big Bend as well as the lower Suwannee River. The half-day tours cover the Lower Suwannee National Wildlife Refuge, which fronts 26 miles of the Gulf of Mexico and is an ideal place to see the nesting grounds of the white ibis, egret, blue heron, osprey, and brown pelican. All tours $50; by reservation only.

ON THE TRAIL OF THE SEMINOLE WAR

Today the Seminole tribe calls southern Florida home (see p.162), but they were once lords of the northern and central parts of the state. Little remains of their presence, but there are a few intriguing monuments to the **Second Seminole War** (see p.450) between Tampa and Gainesville.

Dade Battlefield State Park 7200 Hwy-603, Bushnell (daily 8am–sunset, visitor centre 9am–5pm; $3 per car, $2 per pedestrian; ☎ 352 793 4781, ⓦ dadebattlefield.com). This poignant 80-acre park commemorates the event that sparked the Second Seminole War. Here in 1835 a band of Seminoles destroyed a column of US troops marching to Ocala – only three men survived out of 108. A 12-minute documentary-style video and a series of exhibits add context (including a sword and red leather belt dug up from the battlefield). Each year on the weekend following Christmas the battle is re-enacted.

Fort Cooper State Park 3100 S Old Floral City Rd, Inverness, off US-41 (daily 8am–sunset; $3 per car, $2 per pedestrian; ☎ 352 726 0315, ⓦ floridastateparks.org/fortcooper). There's no visitor centre here, just a small section of timber wall that recalls the US Army stockade that was attacked for sixteen days by Seminole leader Osceola in 1836.

Fort King National Historic Landmark 3925 E Fort King St, Ocala. Built in 1827 and active throughout the Second Seminole War, Fort King was eventually deconstructed by local townspeople – a historical marker stands at the site, which was developed into a historical park in 2014 (open Mon & Fri–Sun noon–7pm; free; ⓦ fkha.org) with interpretive trails and the small Fort King Heritage Center.

Micanopy Town named after famous Seminole chief and located near the site of the Seminole village of Cuscowilla (see p.392).

8

($5.75) and great home-made linguini with scampi ($15), Cedar Key seafood boil ($16) and desserts. Dinner mains $12–24. Mon–Thurs 5–9pm, Fri 5–10pm, Sat 8am–10pm, Sun 8am–9pm.

★ **Kona Joe's Island Cafe** 4051 D St ☎ 352 543 9898.

Best place on the island for breakfast, with a back deck overlooking the bayou. Feast on "shrimp-n-grits" ($2), lip-smacking blue crab quiche ($7), scrumptious bacon cheeseburgers ($6.50) and home-made Key lime pie. Free wi-fi. Wed–Sat 7am–4pm, Sun 7am–3pm.

North central Florida

The alternative and quicker option to taking US-19 from the Tampa Bay area to the Panhandle is to follow I-75 up through **north central Florida**, then, instead of continuing north into Georgia, turn west onto I-10 to Tallahassee. As unrelentingly ordinary as I-75 is, just a few miles to the east of the interstate are the villages and small towns that typified Florida before the arrival of mass tourism. The region has just two appreciably sized towns, one of which, **Ocala**, is the access point to a sprawling national forest. The other, **Gainesville**, holds a major university and a terrain that varies from rough scrub to resplendent grassy acres lubricated by dozens of natural springs.

Ocala and around

Florida's version of the Kentucky Downs, **OCALA** is known throughout the US for the champion horses bred and trained at the farms occupying its green and softly undulating surrounds. Horse lovers and horse riders will find plenty to do here (see box, p.391), while the pristine **natural springs** nearby make for a more languid day out. **Downtown Ocala** itself is hemmed in on all sides by vast strip malls, a small oasis of historic buildings dating back to the period after the great fire of 1883 – because the post-fire buildings were constructed of solid materials (not wood), Ocala became known as "**Brick City**".

Don Garlits Museum of Drag Racing

13700 SW 16th Ave (I-75 Exit 341) • Daily 9am–5pm • $20 • ☎ 877 271 3278, ⓦ garlits.com

Drag racing – high-speed car racing – was born in 1930s California, but the undisputed grandfather of the modern sport is a Floridian. The **Don Garlits Museum of Drag Racing** contains dozens of low-slung drag-racing vehicles, including the "Swamp Rat" machines that propelled local legend "Big Daddy" **Don Garlits** to 270mph over the drag tracks during the mid-1980s (Don still gives private tours for $200). Yellowing press cuttings and grainy films chart the rise of the sport, while a subsidiary **Museum of Classic Automobiles** displays Chevys, Buicks and Fords – and classic hits pumped out by a Wurlitzer jukebox – to evoke an *American Graffiti* atmosphere.

Appleton Museum of Art

4333 E Silver Springs Blvd (Hwy-40) • Tues–Sat 10am–5pm, Sun noon–5pm • $8 • ☎ 352 291 4455, ⓦ appletonmuseum.org

Where the strip malls on the eastern edge of Ocala fade into forest seems an unlikely place for an art museum, but the **Appleton Museum of Art** at the College of Central Florida contains a rich permanent collection of 16,000 objects from Europe, Africa, Asia and the Americas. Though the museum continues to buy contemporary art, the core was created by businessman Arthur Appleton (1915–2008), who had the building purpose-built from Italian marble in 1986 before donating it to the city. The first floor contains Appleton's **Asian statuary and art**, including a fine Tang Dynasty ceramic horse from the eighth century. Don't miss the Japanese *netsuke* here, delicate miniature figures carved from ivory. There's also a rare collection of medieval Persian ceramics, some Mesoamerican idols and a large cache of West African carvings – the "fire spitter masks" are exceptional.

The paintings on view upstairs are nicely curated, but the focus is primarily early **nineteenth-century French** canvases – Appleton had a penchant for Romanticism and Orientalism, movements that today compare poorly with the Impressionism that followed. Look out for a minor *Landscape* by Constable, and *General Miles Indian Campaign* by Wild West romancer Frederic Remington.

Silver Springs State Park

River entrance 1425 NE 58th Ave (Hwy-35); Spring entrance 5656 E Silver Springs Blvd (Hwy-40) • **Park** Daily 8am–sunset • $8 per car, single occupant $5; cyclists and pedestrians $2 • ☎ 352 236 7168, ⓦ floridastateparks.org/silversprings • **Silver River Museum** Sat & Sun 9am–5pm, also Tues–Fri 10am–4pm in July • $2 • ☎ 352 236 5401

Silver Springs has been winning admirers since the 1860s, when Florida's first tourists came by steamboat to stare into the spring's deep, clear waters. During the 1930s and 1940s, six of the original *Tarzan* films, starring Johnny Weissmuller, were shot here. Today, the **Silver Springs State Park** is a reserve of tranquil woodland that encompasses all of the upper Silver River, and since 2013, the famous headsprings themselves (the state took over the tacky zoo and theme park that had previously stood here).

On the spring side of the park you can view the headspring from a viewing deck; take a **glass-bottom-boat ride** (daily 10am–6pm, every 30–45min; $11), given a certain

---

JOHN TRAVOLTA AND AMERICA'S "FLY-IN" COMMUNITY

Those travelling with their own jet planes should be pleased to learn that Ocala is home to **Jumbolair** (ⓦjumbolair.com), the nation's largest and most exclusive "fly-in community", using the old Greystone air strip as its own private runway. **John Travolta** and his wife Kelly Preston were some of the first land purchasers here, and they remain by far the most famous (and conspicuous) residents – the eccentric airport-like Travolta home, and the two airliners often parked outside it, has become something of an architectural icon. Spend enough time in Ocala and you may well see the Travoltas, who are known to frequent local restaurants and shops.

8

OCALA'S ZIP

One of Ocala's most popular attractions is **Canyons Zip Line and Canopy Tours**, 8045 NW Gainesville Rd (daily during daylight hours; ☎352 351 9477, ⊛zipthecanyons.com), where you whisk past giant cliffs, over lakes and through the trees. The whole circuit includes nine zip lines, two rope bridges and a rappel, all within a beautiful, wilderness setting. Full tours from $96 (3hr).

---

historical resonance by the fact the glass-bottom boat was invented here in 1878; and rent **canoes and kayaks** ($35/day) on the crystal-clear river.

On the river side you can hike, camp, and visit the excellent **Silver River Museum**, with exhibits highlighting the cultural and natural history of the area: a 12,000-year-old mammoth, the giant jaws of a prehistoric shark, and Seminole canoes and artefacts. There's also a reproduction of a late 1800s "cracker" village, and a circa 1930 one-room schoolhouse used by African-American students during segregation.

If you feel like cooling off, or have kids in tow, visit the adjacent **Wild Waters** (June to early Sept Mon–Thurs 10am–6pm, Fri–Sun 10am–10pm; $10, children 11 and under $5; ☎352 877 2267, ⊛silversprings.com/wild-waters), a water park with slides, wave pools and amusement arcades.

Rainbow Springs State Park

19158 SW 81st Place Rd, Dunnellon (US-41) • Daily 8am–sunset • $2 per person (head springs entrance), plus $5 per vehicle; tubing fee $11 per person (includes shuttle bus and tube) • ☎ 352 465 8555, ⊛ floridastateparks.org/rainbowsprings

Twenty miles west of Ocala, a soothing setting for a walk and a swim is **Rainbow Springs State Park**, containing the headsprings of the Rainbow River. From 1890 until the 1960s, this 1472-acre park was managed as a commercial venture, but has thankfully been allowed to return to its natural state. A popular haunt for locals, it's busy on weekends (when the park can reach maximum capacity and close by noon), with families picnicking on the grass and splashing around in the springs. You can also explore woodland **trails** in peace and quiet, keeping an eye out for bobcats, raccoons, wild pigs, otters and a great variety of birdlife, then have a swim in the cool, crystal-clear waters. Day-trippers to the park can take advantage of **tubing** (April–Sept; ⊛rainbowspringspark.com) and canoe and kayak rentals ($22 first hr, $11/hr thereafter; ☎352 465 3211).

ARRIVAL AND INFORMATION
OCALA AND AROUND

By bus Greyhound buses stop inconveniently at 4032 W SR-326 (at Reds Transportation), just off I-75 and some 8 miles northwest of the town centre. You'll have to call a taxi to get anywhere else (☎352 207 2008).
Destinations Gainesville (4 daily; 40min); Miami (2 daily; 8hr–9hr 10min); Orlando (5 daily; 1hr 35min); Tallahassee (4 daily; 2hr 50min–3hr 20min); Tampa (1 daily; 4hr 35min).

By train Amtrak stopped running trains to Ocala in 2004; connecting buses run once a day from the old station at 531 NE 1st Ave to Lakeland train station (3hr 10min) for train services to Miami (4hr 44min).

Tourist information Visitors & Convention Bureau Welcome Center, 112 N Magnolia Ave, off Silver Springs Blvd (Mon–Fri 9am–5pm; ☎352 438 2800, ⊛ocalamarion .com), has maps and information on local horse farms.

ACCOMMODATION

Rainbow Springs State Park 19158 SW 81st Place Rd, Dunnellon (US-41) ☎352 465 8550, ☎800 326 3521 for reservations, ⊛floridastateparks.org/rainbowsprings. You can camp in this tranquil park (see above) with pitches including water and electricity. Amenities include showers, store, laundry and pool. Basic pitch $30

★**Seven Sisters Inn** 828 SE Fort King St ☎352 433 0700, ⊛sevensistersinn.org. An ideal place to rest your saddle-sore butt after a hard day's horseriding, set in a magnificent 1895 mansion in Ocala's historic district. There are five unique, luxurious bedrooms, all with historical city themes ranging from nineteenth-century Paris to the pharaonic-themed Cairo suite. Fresh-baked cookies and delicious breakfast included. **$189**

Silver Springs Motel 4121 E Silver Springs Blvd ☎ 352 236 4243, ⓦ silverspringsmotel.com. Ocala is well serviced by the big national chain motels, but this old-fashioned 1950s motel is a decent budget alternative, with a lot more atmosphere. Simple but spacious and clean rooms, with retro furniture, Italian terrazzo floors, newish TVs and free wi-fi. **$50**

Silver Springs State Park 1425 NE 58th Ave (Hwy-35) ☎ 352 236 7148, ⓦ floridastateparks.org/silversprings. Get the most out of the state park with a restful stay at one of its rustic cabins, all with two bedrooms, bathroom, full kitchen, living room and dining area – all linens and utensils are included, but there are no TVs or phones. The wraparound front porch (screened in, with fans) is the perfect place to relax. Camping **$24** per pitch, cabins **$110**

EATING AND DRINKING

★ **Cuvée Wine & Bistro** 2237 SW 19th Ave ☎ 352 351 1816, ⓦ cuveewineocala.com. This restaurant in a former bank building blends fine dining with a cool concept: to complement the artful continental small-plates menu, each dining room is surrounded by rows of wine dispensers; the wines are available in small pours to facilitate sampling. Most steaks and mains run $24–30. Mon–Thurs 5–10pm, Fri & Sat 5–11pm.

Harry's Seafood Bar & Grille 24 SE 1st Ave ☎ 352 840 0900, ⓦ hookedonharrys.com. This local chain brings the tastes of New Orleans to Ocala, with big bowls of gumbo ($8), crab cakes ($17) and jambalaya ($16). Mon–Thurs 11am–10pm, Fri & Sat 11am–11pm, Sun 11am–9pm.

Latinos Y Mas Spanish Cuisine 2030 S Pine Ave ☎ 352 622 4777, ⓦ latinos-mas.com. This Latin fusion restaurant offers a bit of zest for lunch and dinner. The menu features a range of authentic home-cooked Spanish and Latin American dishes from ceviche ($9) to Cuban *ropa vieja* ($12.95) and classic *arroz con pollo* (chicken rice; $11.95). Mon–Thurs 11am–9pm, Fri & Sat 11am–10pm.

Ocala National Forest

☎ 352 625 2520, ⓦ fs.usda.gov/main/ocala

Translucent lakes, bubbling springs and a shady 65-mile hiking trail bring weekend adventurers to the 600-square-mile **OCALA NATIONAL FOREST**. For swimming, canoeing, gentle hiking and lots of other people – especially on weekends and holidays – the forest boasts three warm-water springs, each of them with a campground. If you only have time for a quick look, take a spin along Hwy-19 (meeting Hwy-40, 22 miles into the forest) running north–south in the shade of overhanging hardwoods near the forest's eastern edge.

Juniper Springs

Hwy-40 • Daily 8am–8pm • $5 per person • ☎ 352 625 3147

The easiest of the springs to reach from Ocala is **Juniper Springs**, fifteen miles into the forest, particularly suited to hassle-free canoeing with a seven-mile marked course. The **Juniper Springs Nature Trail** starts opposite the old mill house, a short 0.4-mile interpretive hike along Juniper Run to Fern Hammock Springs.

A ROUGH GUIDE TO OCALA'S HORSE FARMS

A visit to the Ocala area isn't really complete without seeing one of its numerous **horse ranches**, but you'll need a car to reach them.

Chasin' a Dream Farm 3930 NW 110th Ave ☎ 352 208 3012, ⓦ chasinadream.com. Farm tours offered daily (2hr), by appointment, for $25.

Farm Tours of Ocala 801 SW 60th Ave ☎ 352 895 9302, ⓦ farmtoursofocala.com. Join Karen Grimes on an illuminating tour behind the scenes of local working horse farms. Mon–Sat 8.30–11.30am

($35 per person), but call one day in advance.

★ **Gypsy Gold** 12501 SW 8th Ave ☎ 866 497 7982, ⓦ gypsygold.com. Home of America's first gypsy vanner horses (like Shire horses, with woolly flanks). Open Wed & Sat at 10am for excellent tours (2hr; call ahead; $25 online, $30 on-site).

8

Alexander Springs

Hwy-445 off Hwy-19 • Daily 8am–8pm • $5.50 per person, $6.50 scuba diving fee • ☎ 352 669 3522

The freshwater **Alexander Springs**, about ten miles southeast of Juniper Springs, pumps out 70 million gallons a day and has good canoeing, too; its see-through waters are also perfect for snorkelling and even **scuba diving**. The **Alexander Springs Timucuan Trail** is a 1.1-mile interpretive path that leads off from here along the Alexander Run.

Salt Springs

14100 Hwy-19 • Daily 8am–8pm • $5.50 per person, $6 parking fee (marina only) • ☎ 352 685 2048

To the north of the forest, the most developed site – it even has a petrol station and laundry – is **Salt Springs**. Despite the name, the springs here flow with 52 million gallons of water a day with only a slight salinity, and the steady 72°F temperature stimulates a semitropical landscape of vividly coloured plants and palm trees. One mile south of the recreation area, the **Salt Springs Trail** is an easy 1.5-mile loop to a wildlife observation platform on Salt Springs Run.

INFORMATION AND GETTING AROUND   OCALA NATIONAL FOREST

Tourist information Visitor centres are located at three forest entrances, but thanks to funding cuts tend to be open only when volunteers are available – officially daily 9am–5pm, but often closing completely between August and October. The Pittman Visitor Center, 45621 Hwy-19 (☎ 352 669 7495), in the south near Altoona, is most likely to be open. Other locations include the Ocklawaha Visitor Center, 3199 Hwy-315 (☎ 352 236 0288), near Ocala, and the Salt Springs

Visitor Center, 14100 Hwy-19 (☎ 352 685 3070).

Boat and canoe rentals Alexander Springs (☎ 352 669 3522): canoes $16/2hr or $38/day; Juniper Springs (☎ 352 625 2808): canoes $33/day; Salt Springs Marina (☎ 352 685 2255): canoes $10/half-day, $20/full day, motorboats from $27.50/half-day, plus petrol and parking. You'll need a $20 cash deposit for canoes (and $40 for boats), but you can pay the rental with a credit card.

ACCOMMODATION

Ocala National Forest campgrounds You can camp at Juniper Springs ($21 per primitive tent site, plus overnight parking $12.72 per vehicle), Alexander Springs ($21 per tent site) and Salt Springs ($18.50 per primitive tent site,

$26 for full hook-ups). Make reservations at ⓦ recreation .gov or ☎ 877 444 6777. Very primitive campsites (free) appear at regular intervals along the Ocala Hiking Trail (closed mid-Nov to early Jan), and cannot be reserved.

Micanopy and around

The atmosphere of **MICANOPY**, just off I-75 exit 374, is most evocative of the slowed-down pace of the Old South, with its enormous moss-draped live oaks and century-old brick buildings converted into a small collection of intriguing antique and craft shops. Everything of note lies on sleepy **Cholokka Boulevard**, where you'll find the welcoming **Gallery Under the Oaks**, a log cabin built in 1930 that doubles as the Chamber of Commerce (see below).

THE FLORIDA NATIONAL SCENIC TRAIL IN OCALA

The **Florida National Scenic Trail** runs through the Ocala forest for 66 miles between Rodman Dam and Clearwater Lake, traversing many remote, swampy areas, and passing the three major spring areas. At the visitor centres (see above), pick up the excellent leaflet describing the trail.

However keen you might be, you're unlikely to have the time or stamina to tackle the entire trail, though one exceptional area that merits the slog required to get to it is **Big Scrub**, an imposingly severe, semi-arid landscape with sand dunes – and sometimes wild deer – moving across it. The biggest problem at Big Scrub is lack of shade from the scorching sun, and the fact that the nearest facilities of any kind are miles away – don't come unprepared. Big Scrub is in the southern part of the forest, seven miles along Forest Road 573, off Hwy-19, twelve miles north of Altoona.

The town is thought to lie close to the site of the old Seminole village of **Cuscowilla**, visited by naturalist William Bartram in 1774. During the Seminole Wars of the 1830s and 1840s, timber-built Fort Micanopy was the scene of several skirmishes, and it wasn't until the 1850s that white settlers began to arrive in numbers. The town later flourished thanks to the citrus fruit and turpentine trades, and has gained a modicum of fame thanks to *Cross Creek* (see below), and the movie *Doc Hollywood*, filmed here in 1991.

Micanopy Historical Society Museum

607 NE Cholokka Blvd, at Bay St • Daily 1–4pm • $2 • ☎ 352 466 3200, ⓦ micanopyhistoricalsociety.com

The history of the area is chronicled in the suitably rustic **Micanopy Historical Society Museum**, housed in the creaky wooden Thrasher Warehouse built around 1890. Exhibits shed light on William Bartram's expedition, the Seminole Wars and the town's connection with Seminole chief Micanopy. Items displayed include rare Timucuan artefacts, a Seminole canoe (1700–1800), a moonshine still and a cannonball thought to have been fired during the Battle of Micanopy in 1836.

Marjorie Kinnan Rawlings Home

18700 S CR-325, Cross Creek • Tours on the hour Oct–July Thurs–Sun 10–11am & 1–4pm; grounds daily 9am–5pm • Tours $3, children 6–12 $2; park entrance $3 per vehicle • ☎ 352 466 3672, ⓦ floridastateparks.org/marjoriekinnanrawlings

The restored 1880s **Marjorie Kinnan Rawlings Home** offers an eye-opening insight into the harshness of the "cracker" lifestyle in the early twentieth century. Older Floridians often wax lyrical about **Marjorie Kinnan Rawlings** (1896–1953), author of the international classic *The Yearling* (1937), the Pulitzer Prize-winning tale of the coming of age of a Florida farmer's son, and *Cross Creek* (1942), which describes the daily activities of country folk in the eponymous hamlet, five miles north of Micanopy. Leaving her husband in New York in 1928, Rawlings spent her most productive years writing and tending a citrus grove here – her experience being faithfully re-created in the 1983 film *Cross Creek*.

Paynes Prairie Preserve State Park

100 Savannah Blvd, US-441 (10 miles south of Gainesville) • Daily 8am–sunset; visitor centre daily 9am–4pm • Cars $6, single occupant $4; cyclists and pedestrians $2 • ☎ 352 466 3397, ⓦ floridastateparks.org/paynesprairie

The Great Alachua Savannah stretches between Micanopy and Gainesville, a low-lying, swampy plain that is partly contained within the 22,000-acre wilderness of **Paynes Prairie Preserve State Park**. This is one of the oldest and best-organized state parks, with a modern **visitor centre** tucked away in a grove of live oaks a mile or so from the entrance (it's only a short walk from the car park). Exhibits provide a detailed history of the area, and outline some of the wildlife you might spot on the many hiking trails: cranes, hawks, otters, turtles, white-tailed deer and various wading birds all make homes here, as do many alligators. The nearby 50ft **observation tower** affords the best views of the preserve.

ARRIVAL AND INFORMATION

MICANOPY

By car Micanopy is easily accessible from I-75, exit 374, while US-441 provides a more leisurely route to Gainesville, which lies 12 miles to the north. Park for free along Cholokka Blvd. There's no public transport to Micanopy.

Tourist information The Micanopy Chamber of Commerce (☎ 352 466 9229, ⓦ micanopychamber.com) is at 205 NE Cholokka Blvd in the Gallery Under the Oaks and is usually open daily 10am–5pm.

ACCOMMODATION AND EATING

Coffee n' Cream 201 NE Cholokka Blvd ☎ 352 466 1101, ⓦ micanopycoffeeshop.com. Local café in the centre of the historical strip, serving decent coffee, muffins, brownies and light meals (think chicken and dumplings,

home-made chilli from $4.95). Mon–Thurs, Sat & Sun 9am–5pm, Fri 9am–9pm.

Herlong Mansion Inn 402 NE Cholokka Blvd ☎ 352 466 3322, ⓦ herlong.com. The top choice in Micanopy

8

would certainly be this glorious Greek-Revival place dating back to 1910, whose facade of Corinthian columns and elegant Victorian rooms will make you feel you've just stepped onto the set of *Gone With The Wind*. **$119**

Gainesville and around

Without the University of Florida, **GAINESVILLE**, 35 miles north of Ocala, would be just another slow-paced rural community nodding off in the Florida heartland. As it is, the daintily sized place, once called Hogtown, is given a boost by its 50,000 students, who bring a lively, liberal spirit and account for the only decent **nightlife** in central Florida outside Orlando. Historic downtown Gainesville lies around the intersection of Main Street and University Avenue, but the heart of the action these days is a couple of miles west around the university's sprawling 2000-acre campus, home to a couple of enticing museums and the enchanting Butterfly Rainforest.

The University of Florida: the Gators

If you've been in Florida for a while you've probably seen several "Gators" bumper stickers – if not, you will now. Gainesville is the home of the **University of Florida**, whose football team the **Gators** evokes fanatical support from locals as well as current and former students. University sports are taken very seriously in the US: the 83,000-seat **Ben Hill Griffin Stadium**, nicknamed "The Swamp", is home of the Gators football team and a monument to the popularity of college sports in Florida. To see a game visit ⓦgatorzone.com or the ticket office on the west side of the stadium, on the northern edge of campus (Mon–Fri 8.30am–5pm; ☎800 344 2867). The university itself was founded in 1905, but was only integrated in 1958 and is now one of the largest in the nation.

Florida Museum of Natural History

3215 Hull Rd, at SW 34th St • Mon–Sat 10am–5pm, Sun 1–5pm • Free, parking $4 (cash only) • ☎ 352 846 2000, ⓦ flmnh.ufl.edu

Part of the **University of Florida Cultural Complex**, the **Florida Museum of Natural History** provides an enlightening view of Florida's prehistory and wildlife. The museum is much bigger than it looks – you could easily spend half a day here. The exhibition on the **Calusa** people is especially eye-opening, detailing their complex canal building, fishing and trading cultures, and is certainly the best on early Native American history in the state. The acclaimed **Florida Fossils** section covers every prehistoric period of the last 65 million years in fascinating detail. You'll also see giant mammoth and mastodon skeletons and a replica life-size limestone cave, but the real highlight is the **Butterfly Rainforest**, which has separate admission.

Butterfly Rainforest

3215 Hull Rd at SW 34th St • Mon–Sat 10am–4.30pm, Sun 1–4.30pm • $10.50, children 3–17 $6 • ☎ 352 846 2000, ⓦ flmnh.ufl.edu

Housed in the **Butterfly Rainforest**, a 6400-square-foot tropical enclosure, are hundreds of fluttering **butterflies** of all sizes, seemingly oblivious to the admiring humans traipsing through. It's a magical experience, with around 60 to 80 species at any one time on view, and thousands of preserved Lepidoptera species mounted on the "Wall of Wings" outside.

PUTTING THE GATORS IN GATORADE

These days **Gatorade** is one of PepsiCo's largest soft-drink brands, but it was actually developed in 1965 by researchers at the University of Florida – and it really was named after "the Gators" sports teams. Sadly, the drink is no cheaper in Gainesville than anywhere else in the US.

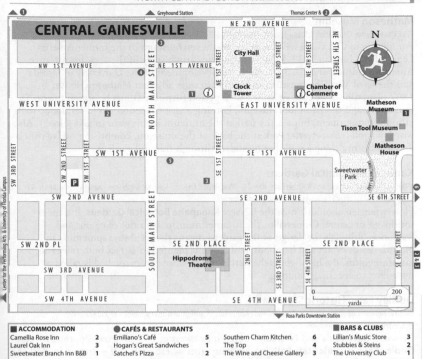

CENTRAL GAINESVILLE

■ ACCOMMODATION			● CAFÉS & RESTAURANTS				■ BARS & CLUBS	
Camellia Rose Inn	2		Emiliano's Café	5		Southern Charm Kitchen	6	Lillian's Music Store	3
Laurel Oak Inn	3		Hogan's Great Sandwiches	1		The Top	4	Stubbies & Steins	2
Sweetwater Branch Inn B&B	1		Satchel's Pizza	2		The Wine and Cheese Gallery	3	The University Club	1

Harn Museum of Art

3259 Hull Rd, at SW 34th St • Tues–Fri 11am–5pm, Sat 10am–5pm, Sun 1–5pm • Free, parking $4 (free Sat & Sun) • ☎ 352 392 9826, ⦿ harn.ufl.edu

Much of the elegant **Harn Museum of Art** is given over to travelling or rotating exhibits in the fields of photography or contemporary art, but there are also exceptional permanent collections on show. The stylish **Asian Art Wing** has a focus on Chinese and Japanese carvings, ceramics, jades, statuary and paintings going back to the Shang Dynasty (c.1600–1100 BC), while the museum's **African collection** is similarly extensive. The Harn also has a world-class collection of art photography by the likes of **Jerry Uelsmann** and Brazilian artist **Sebastião Salgado**, examples of which will be on display somewhere, and a respectable painting collection: highlights include the dreamy *Champ d'avoine* (Oat Field) by **Monet**, the dramatic *Déclaration* by **Toulouse-Lautrec** and the vibrant imagining of *Gloucester* by American Impressionist **Childe Hassam**.

Thomas Center

302 NE 6th Ave • Mon–Fri 8am–5pm, Sat 1–4pm • Free; free parking • ☎ 352 334 5064

Make time to visit the palm-fronted **Thomas Center**, a beautifully restored Mediterranean Revival mansion completed in 1910. Built as a private home for local businessman William Thomas, it was later a posh hotel then community college; it now acts as a venue for events and meetings, but you can visit several rooms set aside for small-scale art exhibits and displays on the history of the city. The **Gallery** inside offers eight to ten shows a year featuring Florida artists, while three rooms (including the Thomas bedroom upstairs) have been restored to their 1920s appearance. Everything revolves around the bright **Spanish Court** in the centre, with its glass roof and sparkling terrazzo floor.

Matheson Museum

513 E University Ave • Mon–Thurs 9.30am–3.30pm • Free • ⓣ 352 378 2280, ⓦ mathesonmuseum.org

For a taster of Old Gainesville, visit the **Matheson Museum** in the former American Legion Hall, built in 1932. Exhibits cover the early history of the area, from Native American cultures and the Spanish, to the development of the University of Florida and the Civil War. The museum also looks after the adjacent **Matheson House**, an 1867 plantation-style cottage loaded with period furniture (tours by appointment; $5 donation), and the **Tison Tool Museum**, housing a vast collection of old-fashioned tools (also by appointment, but ask the staff at the museum if you want to take a look). Also worth a stroll is **Sweetwater Park** at the back of the museum, comprising twelve panels on local history along a trail that meanders through tranquil gardens.

Kanapaha Botanical Gardens

4700 SW 58th Drive (entrance on SW Archer Road, Hwy-24) • Mon–Wed & Fri 9am–5pm, Sat & Sun 9am–sunset • $7, children 6–13 $3.50 • ⓣ 352 372 4981, ⓦ kanapaha.org • Bus #75 from Gainesville

Flower fanciers shouldn't miss the 62-acre **Kanapaha Botanical Gardens**, five miles southwest of central Gainesville. The summer months are a riot of colour and fragrance, although the design of the gardens means there's always something in bloom. Besides vines and bamboos, and sections planted to attract butterflies and hummingbirds, the highlight is the **herb garden**, whose aromatic bed is raised to nose-level to encourage sniffing.

8

Dudley Farm Historic State Park

18730 W Newberry Rd • Wed–Sun 9am–5pm (last entry 4pm) • Cars $5, pedestrians and cyclists $2 • ⓣ 352 472 1142, ⓦ floridastateparks.org/dudleyfarm

Between Gainesville and Newberry, seven miles west of I-75 off Hwy-26, the 325-acre **Dudley Farm Historic State Park** is a working farm where park staff – dressed in clothes the Dudley family would have worn in the late 1800s – perform daily chores and allow visitors to feed the chickens and try their hand at harvesting and other rural activities. There's also a ten-minute video at the **visitor centre** chronicling the history of the family.

Devil's Millhopper Geological State Park

4732 Millhopper Rd (off NW 53rd Ave) • Wed–Sun 9am–5pm • Cars $4, pedestrians and cyclists $2 • ⓣ 352 955 2008, ⓦ floridastateparks.org/devilsmillhopper

Of the thousands of sinkholes in Florida, few are bigger or more spectacular than the one at the **Devil's Millhopper Geological State Park**, seven miles northwest of downtown Gainesville. Formed by the gradual erosion of limestone deposits and the collapse of the resultant cavern's ceiling, the lower reaches of this 120ft-deep bowl-shaped dent have a temperature significantly cooler than the surface, allowing species of alpine plant and animal life to thrive. A steep 0.6-mile boardwalk delivers you down into the thickly vegetated depths, where dozens of tiny waterfalls trickle all around you. A small **visitor centre** at the rim provides exhibits and a video about the site.

ARRIVAL AND DEPARTURE — GAINESVILLE

By bus The Greyhound bus station is relatively central at 101 NE 23rd Ave (ⓣ 352 376 5252), but you'll need a taxi to get to your hotel.

Destinations Miami (3 daily; 7hr 55min–10hr 20min); Ocala (4 daily; 40min); Orlando (5 daily; 2hr–2hr 45min); Tallahassee (3 daily; 2hr 30min); Tampa (1 daily; 5hr 40min).

GETTING AROUND AND INFORMATION

By bus RTS buses (ⓦ go-rts.com) cover most of Gainesville, but have limited use for visitors. The Rosa Parks RTS Downtown Station, 700 SE 3rd St, at Depot Ave, acts as a central hub (with maps), with buses running every 10–15min Mon–Fri (limited Sat & Sun), but travelling between the main sights involves multiple changes. Fares

are $1.50 per ride, or $3 for a day-pass (correct change only).
Tourist information Visitors and Convention Bureau, 30 E University Ave at E 1st St (Mon–Fri 8.30am–5pm; ☎352 374 5260 or ☎866 778 5002, ⓦvisitgainesville.com).

ACCOMMODATION

Although Gainesville has rows of low-cost **motels** a couple of miles outside the centre, along SW 13th Street, and plenty of chain spots at the I-75 exits, note that these fill quickly when the University of Florida Gators are playing at home.

Camellia Rose Inn 205 SE 7th St ☎352 395 7673, ⓦcamelliaroseinn.com. Charming B&B in the centre of town in an elegant Queen Anne home dating back to 1903, with six spacious, comfortable rooms and period furnishings. Huge breakfast and free wi-fi included. **$135**
★**Laurel Oak Inn** 221 SE 7th St ☎352 373 4535, ⓦlaureloakinn.com. Relatively small, five-room B&B in a quiet part of town littered with historic homes; this 1885 Victorian building stands out as one of the more beautiful, with smaller rooms but a few more extras than *Camellia* (free drinks 5–6pm). **$125**
Sweetwater Branch Inn B&B 625 E University Ave ☎352 373 6760, ⓦsweetwaterinn.com. Spacious, beautifully laid out rooms, and convenient to everything the town has to offer, housed in two gracefully restored period homes dating from 1895; the cottages, with kitchens, are especially good value (from $159). **$139**

EATING

Emiliano's Café 7 SE 1st Ave ☎352 375 7381, ⓦemilianoscafe.com. Come here for pan-Latin cuisine, from a full tapas menu to Jamaican jerk pork loin and the signature *chipotle* brownie cake. They also serve a hearty Sunday brunch and the best mojitos in town. Mains range $14.75–19.55. Mon–Thurs 11am–10pm, Fri & Sat 11am–10.30pm, Sun 10am–4pm.
Hogan's Great Sandwiches Albertson's Plaza, 2327 NW 13th St ☎352 376 6224, ⓦhogans83.com. Locals claim these huge sandwiches are the best in the world, and while that might be overdoing things, the stacked meat and cheese subs with tasty toppings are phenomenal value. Twelve-inch subs from $6.45. Cash only. Mon–Sat 10am–midnight, Sun 10am–9pm.
★**Satchel's Pizza** 1800 NE 23rd Ave ☎352 335 7272, ⓦsatchelspizza.com. Hipster pizza joint, served in a shack decorated with stained glass and local art. Cheese slices ($3) and a variety of pizzas (from $12.50) are served with craft beers and handmade bonbons ($1). Cash only. Tues–Sat 11am–10pm.
★**Southern Charm Kitchen** 1714 SE Hawthorne Rd ☎352 505 5553. Excellent Southern food – think watermelon fish, addictive cornbread (smothered in a caramel glaze), black-eyed pea fritters and finger-licking chicken and waffles. Finish off with an apple dumplin'. Lunch for around $16–18. Daily 11am–10pm.
The Top 30 N Main St ☎352 337 1188. Young, arty and hip – a good choice if all you want is a pleasant spot to refuel on salads or sandwiches for about $5. They also serve Sunday brunch. Tues–Sat 5pm–2am, Sun 11am–11pm.
The Wine and Cheese Gallery 113 N Main St ☎352 372 8446, ⓦwineandcheesegallery.com. An amazing selection of International wines and cheeses, plus fresh breads, hors d'oeuvres and *crudités* in a warm, inviting setting. Most sandwiches $6.49, salads $6.95. Mon–Fri 11am–2.15pm, Sat noon–3pm.

NIGHTLIFE AND ENTERTAINMENT

Center for the Performing Arts 315 Hull Rd ☎352 392 1900, ⓦperformingarts.ufl.edu. This University of Florida venue brings in travelling Broadway plays, symphonies, popular music, family entertainment and educational programmes.
Hippodrome Theatre 25 SE 2nd Place ☎352 375 4477, ⓦthehipp.org. This grandiose building dominating the town centre (built in 1911 as the main post office) hosts contemporary plays, films and exhibits by local artists.
Lillian's Music Store 112 SE 1st St ☎352 372 1010. A Gainesville institution since 1974, featuring live bands that play grunge, indie, Southern, and acoustic rock. More of a local dive bar than a student hangout. Some of Gainesville's finest musicians turn out for the Monday jam nights. No cover. Mon–Sat 2pm–2am, Sun 3–11pm.
★**Stubbies & Steins** 9 W University Ave ☎352 384 1261, ⓦstubbiesandsteins.com. Beer drinkers' paradise, with 400 bottles and 24 drafts, great fries and full German food menu in a Bavarian beer-hall-like pub. Mon–Sat 4pm–2am.
The University Club 18 E University Ave ☎352 378 6814, ⓦucnightclub.com. Downtown's no. 1 gay venue, with three levels (a bar, club and disco). Always crowded and lively, with a deck out back. Mon–Fri & Sun 5pm–2am, Sat 9pm–2am.

8

THE FRESHWATER SPRINGS TOUR

Just **north of Gainesville**, close to the town of **High Springs**, you'll find yourself in the heart of some of the most pristine natural-spring parks in the state – waters that lend themselves to leisurely kayaking, canoeing or inner-tube rafting. You can rent **canoes** in most of the parks for $15–25 a day. Weekdays, when beavers, otters and turtles sometimes share the river, are the best time to come to the area; weekend crowds scare much of the wildlife away.

Blue Springs 7450 NE 60th St, High Springs ☎ 386 454 1369, ⓦ bluespringspark.com. Daily 9am–7pm; $10, children 5–12 $3; camping $15 per person, children 5–12 $6.

Ginnie Springs 7300 NE Ginnie Springs Rd, High Springs ☎ 386 454 7188, ⓦ ginniespringsoutdoors .com. Hours vary; $12, children 7–14 $3; camping $20.40 per person, children 7–14 $6; cottage $175 per night for up to four adults.

Ichetucknee Springs State Park 12087 SW US-27, Fort White ☎ 386 497 4690, ⓦ floridastateparks.org /ichetuckneesprings. Daily 8am–sunset; cars $6 (single occupant $4), pedestrians and cyclists $2, another $5 per person for river use.

O'Leno State Park 410 SE O'Leno Park Rd (off US-441), High Springs ☎ 386 454 1853, ⓦ floridastateparks.org/oleno. Daily 8am–sunset; cars $5 (single occupant $4), pedestrians and cyclists $2.

White Springs and around

The small town of **WHITE SPRINGS** was a major resort in the nineteenth century, thanks to the supposed medicinal value of its freshwater sulphur springs on the banks of the languid **Suwannee River**. Today little remains of that period, though the dilapidated 1908 **Spring House** along the river may be restored in future. Instead, it's the musical associations of the river that provide the attraction today, in the form of monuments to **Stephen Foster**, as well as some no-nonsense **whitewater kayaking**.

Stephen Foster Folk Culture Center State Park

11016 Lillian Saunders Drive (US-41) • Daily 8am–sunset; museum and tower daily 9am–5pm • Cars $5, single occupant $4, pedestrians and cyclists $2 • ☎ 386 397 2733, ⓦ floridastateparks.org/stephenfoster

In 1950, much of the old White Sulphur Springs resort area on the banks of the Suwannee River was converted into the **Stephen Foster Folk Culture Center State Park**, a tribute to the man who made the river famous. Foster (1826–64) was actually born in Pennsylvania and never came to Florida, but after he wrote *Old Folks At Home* ("Way down upon the S'wanee river …") in 1851, tourism boomed in the area and 84 years later it became Florida's state song. The tune remains popular, despite criticism that its lyrics mimicking accented Black English and references to "darkies" is racist.

Wisely avoiding discussion of such controversies, the elegant **Stephen Foster Museum** was purpose-built to resemble a plantation house, and contains a collection of old pianos and rudimentary but painstakingly accurate dioramas representing Foster's classic songs: his other hits include *Camptown Races*, *My Old Kentucky Home* and *Oh! Susanna*. These instantly familiar melodies are not just played in the museum – they are actually rung through the oak-filled park from the 200ft-high, 97-bell **Carillon Tower**. A small craft village and gift shop round off a very old-fashioned experience, the whole thing seemingly unchanged since it was put together in the 1950s. There's always the river itself, a mellow tannin-stained stream easily accessible from several points in the park.

Big Shoals State Park

11330 SE Hwy-135 • Daily 8am–sunset • Cars $4, pedestrians and cyclists $2 • ☎ 386 397 4331, ⓦ floridastateparks.org/bigshoals

The Suwannee River may be the subject of a corny song, but it's also the home of Florida's only **Class III whitewater rapids**, protected in the **Big Shoals State Park** near the centre of White Springs. Most of the year the river is too low to create rapids – it's at its best in autumn and winter. The park is a tranquil place for hiking and bike riding year-round, but if you want to get on the water you'll need a kayak: contact **American Canoe Adventures** in White Springs (☎386 397 1309, ⓦaca1.com).

ARRIVAL AND INFORMATION   WHITE SPRINGS

By car White Springs is 3 miles east of I-75 (Exit 439) on Hwy-136, and 60 miles north of Gainesville. There's no public transport.

Tourist information In the centre of the village is the Florida Nature & Heritage Tourism Center (daily 9am–5pm; ☎386 397 0921), with information on the whole state.

ACCOMMODATION

Grady House B&B 420 NW 1st Ave ☎386 454 2206, ⓦgradyhouse.com. Top choice for a few nights in White Springs is this B&B, where the owners have poured their hearts into creating a gorgeous gazebo garden to go with the comfortable rooms (some have antique iron beds). __$130__
High Springs Country Inn Along US-441, 520 NW Santa Fe Blvd ☎386 454 1565, ⓦhighspringscountryinn .com. Excellent budget option, with scrubbed wood furniture that gives the motel-style rooms a homely feel. Free wi-fi, microwaves and mini-fridges in every room. __$42__

Spirit of the Suwannee Music Park 3076 95th Drive, Live Oak (I-75 Exit 451) ☎386 364 1683, ⓦmusic liveshere.com. If you just haven't got enough of the Old Swannee River, this should sate your appetite – a giant campground and RV site, with live music venues sprinkled throughout. In the summer months top country, blues and folk acts perform here weekly, there are daily campfire jam sessions and you can rent kayaks to explore the river. Primitive campsites __$20__, hook-ups __$25__

8

The Panhandle

THE FAMU MARCHING BAND

9

The Panhandle

Butting up against the southernmost borders of both Alabama and Georgia, the long, narrow Panhandle has more in common with the Deep South than it does with the rest of Florida. Though undeniably rural and down-to-earth, the Panhandle has plenty to offer. You certainly won't get a true picture of Florida without seeing at least some of it, and its pristine beaches, forests and parks offer a taste of real untouched wilderness.

A century ago, the Panhandle actually *was* Florida. When Miami was still a swamp, **Pensacola**, at the Panhandle's western edge, was a busy port. Fertile soils lured wealthy plantation owners south and helped establish **Tallahassee** as a high-society gathering place and administrative centre – a role it retains as the state capital.

Today, much of the inland Panhandle consists of small farming towns that see few visitors, despite their friendly rhythm, fine examples of Old South architecture, and proximity to springs, sinkholes and the **Apalachicola National Forest** – perhaps the best place in Florida to disappear into the wild. The coastal Panhandle, on the other hand, is inundated with tourists who flock in from the southern states and wreak havoc during the riotous student Spring Breaks. Much of the coastline is marked by rows of hotels and condos, but there are also protected areas that are home to some of the finest stretches of unspoiled white sand anywhere in the US.

Tallahassee and around

Foreign visitors are often bemused to learn that **TALLAHASSEE**, a provincial city of oak trees and soft hills, and not Miami, is the state capital of Florida. There are no beaches here, and the atmosphere is more Savannah than South Beach, but around its small grid of central streets – where you'll find plenty of reminders of Florida's formative years – briefcase-clutching bureaucrats mingle with some of **Florida State University**'s 40,000 students, who brighten the mood considerably and keep the city awake late into the night.

Downtown Tallahassee

The soul of Tallahassee is the mile-square downtown area, where the premier attractions – the two Capitol buildings, the Museum of Florida History and the two universities – are within walking distance of Adams Street, the sleepy main drag. A unique and charming feature of downtown Tallahassee is the **canopy roads**, thoroughfares lined with oak trees, whose branches, heavy with Spanish moss, arch across the road. If you're after shops, aim instead for the **Market District**, off Thomasville Road north of I-10.

WAKULLA SPRINGS

Highlights

❶ The FAMU Marching Band See Florida A&M University's "Marching 100" in Tallahassee, a scintillating musical sensation. **See p.407**

❷ Wakulla Springs Swim or take a boat across the biggest and deepest natural springs in the world. **See p.412**

❸ Florida Caverns State Park The deep caves here, used by the Seminoles to hide from Andrew Jackson's army, hold enchanting calcite formations. **See p.416**

❹ Forgotten Coast Tour this untouched slice of Old Florida, and feast on Apalachicola oysters, the finest in the US. **See p.418**

❺ St Andrews State Park Enjoy some of the best stretches of sugary white sands on the Gulf coast, and take the boat to untouched Shell Island. **See p.426**

❻ Pensacola Old Spanish town with one of the nation's biggest and best aviation museums, enticing restaurants and nightlife, and silky white sands. **See p.434**

❼ Diving the Oriskany Diving down to this 911ft aircraft carrier, the world's largest artificial reef, is a mesmerizing experience. **See p.441**

HIGHLIGHTS ARE MARKED ON THE MAP ON P.403

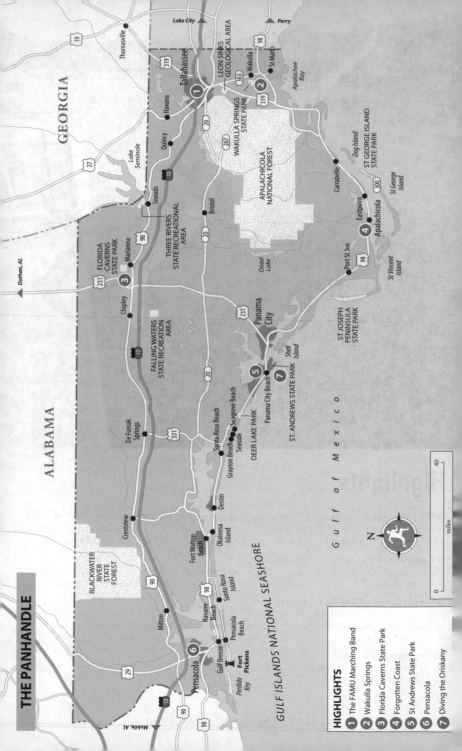

THE PANHANDLE

GEORGIA

ALABAMA

Gulf of Mexico

0   miles   40

N

Lake City
Perry
Thomasville
19
Tallahassee
319
LEON SINKS GEOLOGICAL AREA
98
Wakulla
St Marks
Apalachee Bay
363
319
WAKULLA SPRINGS STATE PARK
Havana
20
Quincy
Lake Seminole
27
267
APALACHICOLA NATIONAL FOREST
Dog Island
ST GEORGE ISLAND STATE PARK
St George Island
Sneads
10
Bristol
20
Carrabelle
300
Eastpoint
Apalachicola
St Vincent Island
THREE RIVERS STATE RECREATIONAL AREA
90
Marianna
FLORIDA CAVERNS STATE PARK
231
Dead Lake
Port St Joe
98
Chipley
FALLING WATERS STATE RECREATION AREA
231
Panama City
ST JOSEPH PENINSULA STATE PARK
Dothan, AL
De Funiak Springs
331
20
Shell Island
Panama City Beach
ST. ANDREWS STATE PARK
Crestview
DEER LAKE PARK
Santa Rosa Beach
Seagrove Beach
Seaside
Grayton Beach
Destin
Fort Walton Beach
Okaloosa Island
10
Milton
Navarre Beach
Santa Rosa Island
Pensacola Beach
90
98
Pensacola
Gulf Breeze
Fort Pickens
Perdido Key
GULF ISLANDS NATIONAL SEASHORE
BLACKWATER RIVER STATE FOREST
29
Mobile, AL

Florida Historic Capitol Museum

400 S Monroe St • Mon–Fri 9am–4.30pm, Sat 10am–4.30pm, Sun noon–4.30pm • Free • ☎ 850 487 1902, ⓦ flhistoriccapitol.gov

The best place to begin a tour of downtown Tallahassee is the **Florida Historic Capitol Museum** in the Old Capitol Building, an elegant Greek Revival structure now standing in the shadow of the towering complex that replaced it in the 1970s. Built in 1845 and remodelled in 1902, the interior has been restored to its appearance in the latter year. Wander the rooms that once echoed with the decisions that shaped modern Florida: the old Supreme Court, the Governor's Suite, and the former House and Senate chambers upstairs. Other rooms are crammed with exhibits exploring not just the history of the state but also its politics in surprisingly rich detail, lifting the lid on Florida's juiciest scandals and controversies. There are sections on campaigning, corruption, and even a ballot used for the contested 2000 Presidential election – with all of its chads successfully punched out.

Florida State Capitol

402 S Monroe St • Mon–Fri 8am–5pm • Free • ☎ 850 488 6167, ⓦ myfloridacapitol.com

Dominating central Tallahassee, the 345ft **Florida State Capitol** was completed in 1977 in a blunt, Modernist style completely at odds with the Old Capitol it now overshadows. Its redeeming feature is the **22nd-storey observation floor**, which provides an unobstructed view over Tallahassee and its environs; from here you can appreciate the relatively small size of the downtown area, as well as the ocean of trees surrounding it, carpeting the landscape to the horizon. If you're visiting in March or April (the annual legislative session only lasts sixty days), stop off at the **fifth floor** for a glance at state government in action. Note that to enter the building you must go through a security check.

Southeastern Regional Black Archives Research Center and Museum

Carnegie Library, Florida A&M University campus, 445 Gamble St • Mon–Fri 9am–5pm • Free • ☎ 850 487 3803, ⓦ amu.edu/index
.cfm?BlackArchives • Drivers must get a visitors parking decal from Parking Services at 2400 Wahnish Way

Located in the 1908 Carnegie Library, the oldest brick building on the campus of **Florida A&M University (FAMU)**, the **Black Archives Research Center and Museum** chronicles the history and persecution of Florida's black community. The first black Floridians arrived with Spanish explorers in the sixteenth century, and many more came as runaways in the early nineteenth century, taking refuge among the Creek and Seminole Indians.

Museum of Florida History

500 S Bronough St • Mon–Fri 9am–4.30pm, Sat 10am–4.30pm, Sun noon–4.30pm • Free • ☎ 850 245 6400,
ⓦ museumoffloridahistory.com

For a well-rounded history – easily the fullest account of Florida's past anywhere in the state – visit the **Museum of Florida History**. Detailed accounts of Paleo-Indian settlements and the significance of their burial and temple mounds – some of which have been found on the edge of Tallahassee (see p.410) – provide valuable insights into Florida's pre-Columbian history. There's also a giant **mastodon skeleton** found at Wakulla Springs, dubbed "Herman" by museum staff. The colonialist crusades of the Spanish, both in Florida and across South and Central America, are also explored, with an intriguing new exhibit dubbed "**Forever Changed: La Florida, 1513–1821**", and a special section of gold and silver treasure recovered from eighteenth-century Spanish shipwrecks. However, other than portraits of hard-faced Seminole chiefs, there's disappointingly little on the nineteenth-century Seminole Wars – one of the sadder and bloodier skeletons in Florida's closet. There's plenty, though, on the Civil War, the citrus industry, the railroads that made Florida a winter resort for wealthy northerners around the turn of the twentieth century, and on the subsequent arrival of the "tin can tourists", whose nickname refers to the rickety Ford Model-T camper vans (forerunners

CENTRAL TALLAHASSEE

■ ACCOMMODATION

Aloft Tallahassee Downtown	3
Doubletree Hotel Tallahassee	4
Governors Inn Hotel	5
Little English Guesthouse	1
Staybridge Suites	
Tallahassee I-10 East	2

■ BARS & CLUBS

American Legion Hall	
Post 13	1
Bird's Aphrodisiac	
Oyster Shack	3
Bradfordville Blues Club	3
Bullwinkle's	4
Clyde's & Costello's	7
Fermentation Lounge	9
Level 8 Lounge	2
The Moon	8
Potbelly's	6

● CAFÉS & RESTAURANTS

Andrew's Capital Grill & Bar	7
Bada Bean	8
Barnacle Bill's	1
Cypress	3
Goodies	5
Jimmy John's	4
Kool Beanz Café	2
Mom and Dad's	9
Po' Boys Creole Café	6

of the modern RV) they drove. The museum ends with an exhibit on World War II and the dramatic, booming impact it had on the state's economy.

Challenger Learning Center

200 S Duval St • Mon–Sat 10am–5pm, Sun 1–5pm • IMAX $5.50–10; Digital Dome Theatre and Planetarium $5, children 12 and under $4.25 • ☎ 850 645 7827, Ⓦ challengertlh.com

The innovative **Challenger Learning Center** is squarely aimed at getting kids interested in space and science, but its state-of-the-art **Space Mission Simulator**, **Digital Dome Theatre and Planetarium** and **IMAX 3D Experience** are great fun for everyone – check the website for the current show times.

Knott House Museum

301 E Park Ave • Wed–Fri 1–3pm, Sat 10am–3pm; closed Aug; guided tours on the hour • Free • ☎ 850 922 2459

Another important landmark in Florida's black history, the **Knott House Museum** is also one of the city's best-restored Victorian homes. Built in 1843, probably by George Proctor, a free black man, the building later became home to Florida's first black physician. It takes its name, however, from the Knott family who bought it in 1928 – the interior has been restored to reflect this time period.

William Knott, the state treasurer, became one of Florida's most respected and influential politicians until his retirement in 1941. His wife, Luella, meanwhile, devoted her energies to the temperance movement (partly through her efforts, alcohol was banned in Tallahassee for a fifty-year period) and to writing moralistic poems, many of which you'll see attached to the antiques and furnishings filling this intriguing relic, and which give it the nickname of "the house that rhymes". The absence of intrusive ropes cordoning off the exhibits allows for an unusually intimate visit.

Mission San Luis

2100 W Tallahassee St (US-27) • Tues–Sun 10am–4pm • $5, children 6–17 $2 • ☎ 850 245 6406, ⓦ missionsanluis.org • Bus A or C from downtown Tallahassee

One of the most awe-inspiring reconstructions of a Native American village in the country, the **Mission San Luis** lies about three miles west of downtown Tallahassee. In 1656 Spanish Franciscans built a church here; their settlement of San Luís de Talimali soon flourished into a town of some 1400 people, mostly Apalachee converts, and became the hub of the entire seventeenth-century Spanish mission system, second only to St Augustine and the capital of western Florida. The settlement was abandoned in 1704 before a marauding British army from Georgia arrived to destroy it, and was never reoccupied. Its story, and especially the fascinating interaction of Spanish and Apalachee cultures that took place here, is told at the **Visitor Center**. Exhibits, artefacts found on site and a video add context and describe how the Apalachee tribe was dispersed (a small group still lives in Louisiana today).

What makes this site different is that the settlement has been rebuilt around the main plaza in the precise locations identified by archeologists: wander the grounds outside to see the jaw-dropping **Council House**, a vast wood-and-thatch circular edifice that would have been the seat of the Apalachee chief, with raised platforms and a giant opening to the sky inside. The thatched **Franciscan Church** opposite is almost as grand, while other buildings include a Spanish house and Friary. There's also an authentic replica timber fort and blockhouse, while the **Messer House** in the middle of the site dates from 1938 and serves as administrative offices. Most of the replica buildings feature period-attired docents who explain what would have been happening here in the 1680s.

ARRIVAL AND DEPARTURE
TALLAHASSEE

By plane Tallahassee Regional Airport (☎ 850 891 7802, ⓦ talgov.com/airport) is 12 miles southwest of downtown Tallahassee at 3300 Capital Circle SW; no public transport services link to the city. A taxi from the airport to the centre will cost around $18–20 on the meter (try City Taxi ☎ 850 562 4222, or Yellow Cab ☎ 850 999 9999).

By car I-10 cuts across Tallahassee's northern perimeter; turning off along Monroe St takes you into downtown Tallahassee. US-90 (known as Tennessee St) and US-27 (Apalachee Parkway) are more central – arriving in or close to downtown. Parking is easy downtown: on-street metered parking is $0.50/hr, while the centrally located Kleman Plaza parking garage (enter at Jefferson St and

Bronough St; ☎ 850 561 3066) is open 24hr and charges $2 for up to 2hr, then $0.50/hr thereafter (maximum $6/day).

By bus The Greyhound terminal is at 112 W Tennessee St, within walking distance of downtown and opposite the local bus station.

Destinations Jacksonville (3 daily; 2hr 40min–3hr); Miami (1 daily; 11hr 45min) via Gainesville (3 daily; 2hr 30min) and Orlando (4 daily; 4hr 20min–5hr 40min); Pensacola (4 daily; 3hr 15min–5hr 30min) via Panama City (3 daily; 2hr 15min); and Tampa (3 daily; 5hr 15min–8hr 20min). Red Coach (ⓦ redcoachusa.com) runs buses from Tallahassee to Gainesville (4 daily; 3hr), Orlando (3 daily; 5hr 20min) and Miami (4 daily; 10hr).

GETTING DOWN WITH THE FAMU MARCHING BAND

Calling them the "Greatest Marching Band in the world" doesn't really do it justice: think of a vast, mega-decibel jazz, rhythm and blues and funk band, grooving to their music in perfect time. If you get the chance to see Tallahassee -based **Florida A&M University**'s "Marching 100", do so – the experience is mesmerizing, inspirational and a vivid expression of African-American culture at its most creative and dynamic. A hazing scandal suspended all band activities between 2011 and 2013, but everything is now back on track. See ⓦ famu.edu for their rehearsal/performance schedule. The pre-term bandcamp takes place the first two weeks of July.

9

PANHANDLE PLANTATIONS

The largest concentration of old cotton plantations in the US lies between Tallahassee and the Georgia town of Thomasville, 28 miles to the northeast. Several of the more notable addresses have been preserved for public viewing (don't expect to hear much about slavery at either place):

Goodwood 1600 Miccosukee Rd, Hwy-146, 2 miles northeast of downtown Tallahassee (tours Tues–Fri 10am–2.30pm, Sat 10am–1pm; $12; gardens open Mon–Fri 9am–5pm, Sat 10am–2pm; free; ☎850 877 4202, ⓦgoodwoodmuseum.org). One of the finest mansions, dating from around 1840. All of the antiques on display were actually in use at one point or another during the 130-year period when the house was occupied, and they range from stately mirrors to a bath painted with flowers, reflecting the diverse tastes of the various owners.

Pebble Hill Plantation 1251 US-319, Thomasville, Georgia (Tues–Sat 10am–5pm, Sun noon–5pm, 1hr guided tour; last tour leaving at 4pm; $15, grounds only $5; ☎229 226 2344, ⓦpebblehill.com). Much of the original Pebble Hill (dating from 1851) burned down in 1934 and what you see now is a fairly faithful rebuilding of the sumptuous main house completed two years later, complete with the extensive fine art, antique, crystal and porcelain collections that belonged to the house's final owner, Elisabeth "Pansy" Ireland Poe, and which were rescued from the fire.

INFORMATION AND GETTING AROUND

On foot Downtown Tallahassee can easily be explored on foot, but you'll need a car to explore the outlying areas.
By bus Tallahassee is served by StarMetro buses fanning out from CK Steele Plaza, 111 W Tennessee St, across from the Greyhound station (☎850 891 5200, ⓦtalgov.com /starmetro), but other than buses A (Azalea) and C (Canopy), which pass Mission San Luis, they are not much use for tourists. Rides cost $1.25 per journey. Route maps and timetables are available online or from CK Steele Plaza.
By bike Despite the area's hills, there is plenty of good cycling terrain. You can rent a bike from The Great Bicycle

Shop, 1909 Thomasville Rd, from $35/day (Mon–Fri 10am–6pm, Sat 10am–5pm, Sun noon–4pm; ☎850 224 7461, ⓦgreatbicycle.com).
Tourist information The Tallahassee Welcome Center, 106 E Jefferson St (Mon–Fri 8am–5pm; ☎850 606 2305 or ☎800 628 2866, ⓦvisittallahassee.com), stocks large numbers of leaflets and guides for the city. While there, be sure to pick up the engaging *Walking Guide to Historic Downtown Tallahassee* booklet, a free, comprehensive guide to the buildings and history of the area.

ACCOMMODATION

Finding accommodation in Tallahassee is only a problem during two periods: the sixty-day sitting of the state legislature beginning with the first Tuesday in March, and on autumn weekends when the Seminoles (Florida State University's immensely popular football team) are playing at home. The cheapest hotels and motels are on N Monroe Street (US-27) about 3 miles north of downtown, near I-10 Exit 199.

Aloft Tallahassee Downtown 200 N Monroe St ☎850 513 0313, ⓦalofttallahassee.com. This refreshingly hip hotel has a great location downtown, with club-like atmosphere in the lobby, pool table, free shuttle bus (2-mile radius) and swimming pool, and rooms with huge wall-mounted flat-screen TVs and Bliss amenities. Parking is $5/day. **$105**
Doubletree Hotel Tallahassee 101 S Adams St ☎850 224 5000, ⓦdoubletree1.hilton.com. Large, business-oriented luxury hotel in the middle of downtown. Spacious rooms come with views of Ponce de León Park or the Capitol Building and Crabtree & Evelyn bath products. Complimentary airport shuttle; parking $8/day and wi-fi $9.95/day. **$128**
★**Governors Inn Hotel** 209 S Adams St ☎850 681 6855, ⓦthegovinn.org. This luxurious downtown inn,

formerly a livery stable, is well worth splurging on. The rooms are decorated with antique furniture, reflecting the period of the governor each is named for. Free cocktails, breakfast, wi-fi and newspapers are also included. Valet parking only ($10/day). **$149**
Little English Guesthouse 737 Timberlane Rd ☎850 907 9777, ⓦlittleenglishguesthouse.com. Another charming alternative to the chain motels just a 10min drive from downtown, this friendly B&B is run by long-term British expats, offering three rooms furnished with English antiques, free wi-fi and fluffy European duvets. **$99**
★**Staybridge Suites Tallahassee I-10 East** 1600 Summit Lake Drive ☎850 219 7000, ⓦstaybridge.com /tallahassee. Just off the interstate (exit 209), but 8 miles from downtown, this is still one of the best places to stay in

the area – you get a spacious suite with kitchenette overlooking a tranquil lake, and in addition to breakfast most weekday nights feature free buffet dinners (and free beer and wine) 5.30–7.30pm. Free wi-fi. $139

Tallahassee East KOA 346 KOA Rd, just off the I-10,

Monticello ☎ 850 997 3890, ⓦ koa.com/campgrounds /tallahassee. Although it's 20 miles east of Tallahassee, this campground offers complimentary home-made cakes and cookies (3–8pm), and a free continental breakfast. Primitive sites $26, sites with electricity $35, cabins $46

EATING

Andrew's Capital Grill & Bar 228 S Adams St ☎ 850 222 3444, ⓦ andrewsdowntown.com. A great lunch option with plenty of seating indoors and out. Choose from burgers and various chicken and pasta dishes, as well as a weekend brunch buffet (sandwiches and burgers around $10–12). Mon–Thurs 11.30am–10pm, Fri & Sat 11.30am–11pm, Sun 11am–2pm.

The Bada Bean 2500 Apalachee Pkwy ☎ 850 562 2326, ⓦ thebadabean.com. Excellent café that serves gourmet coffee, great-value breakfasts and lunches; everything from a hefty Bada cheesesteak sandwich to salads, melts and pancakes (tall stacks $7). Mon–Fri 6.30am–3pm, Sat & Sun 7.30am–3pm.

Barnacle Bill's 1830 N Monroe St ☎ 850 385 8734 ⓦ barnaclebills.com. Reasonably priced dive-bar serving up fabulous fresh oysters and Florida fish (grouper, mahi-mahi), a raucous atmosphere and occasional live music on the deck. Fish dinners range $13–20. Mon–Thurs & Sun 11am–11pm, Fri & Sat 11am–midnight.

Cabo's Island Grill & Bar 1221 Apalachee Pkwy ☎ 850 878 7707, ⓦ cabosgrill.com. No-frills restaurant with a beach shack theme – surfboards hanging from the ceiling, tropical fish tanks and large-screen TVs for sports events. Lunch specials are just $7.50, with a choice of soup, tacos, burritos or burgers (the burritos are huge). Sandwiches are otherwise around $7–12, with a range of Tex-Mex favourites from $2–7 (tacos, enchiladas and the like). Mon–Thurs 11am–midnight, Fri & Sat 11am–2am, Sun

9am–midnight.

Cypress 320 E Tennessee St ☎ 850 513 1100, ⓦ cypressrestaurant.com. This small and chic option offers a Southern take on upmarket dining, with Gulf Coast oysters and biscuits replacing the more conventional side items. Mains range $18–32. Tues–Sat 5–10pm, Sun 10.30am–2pm.

Donut Kingdom 685 W Tennessee St ☎ 850 668 3663, ⓦ donutkingdomtallahassee.com. Incredibly addictive doughnuts, just across from FSU, with every type from standard glazed and strawberry frosted ($1), to jelly filled ($1) and apple fritters ($1.80). Mon, Tues & Sun 10.30am–8pm, Wed & Thurs 10.30am–9pm, Fri 10.30am–10pm, Sat 10.30am–10.30pm.

★ **Kool Beanz Café** 921 Thomasville Rd ☎ 850 224 2466, ⓦ koolbeanz-cafe.com. Original starters, such as fried oysters and cheese grits ($12), are followed by quality mains ($17–24) like pecan-crusted mahi-mahi and crawfish tacos. Be warned – the spice levels are set on hot. Mon–Fri 11am–2.30pm & 5.30–10pm, Sat 5.30–10pm, Sun 10.30am–2pm.

★ **Shell Oyster Bar** 114 E Oakland Ave ☎ 850 224 9919. Local favourite since 1945, in a former petrol station – it looks rough from the outside, but the oysters are local, fresh and delicious (just $8 per dozen). The home-made coleslaw and cheese grits are excellent sides. Cash only and despite the name, no alcohol (you can BYOB). Mon–Sat 11am–6pm.

DRINKING AND NIGHTLIFE

American Legion Hall Post 13 229 Lake Ella Drive ☎ 850 222 3382, ⓦ floridalegionpost13.org. For a taste of the past, try this venue, which hosts the Tallahassee Swing Band every Monday ($5) and Tuesday ($6), 7.30–10pm, and Sue Boyd's country dance lessons Wed (6.30–9.45pm; $8).

Bird's Aphrodisiac Oyster Shack 325 N Bronough St ☎ 850 222 1075, ⓦ birdsoystershack.com. Freshly shucked oysters from Apalachicola ($13 per dozen) accompany a full roster of entertainment at this amiable bar with the cool name: live music (Fri & Sat), karaoke (Thurs) and comedy (Wed). Tues–Fri 11am–2am, Sat noon–2am.

★ **Bradfordville Blues Club** 7152 Moses Lane ☎ 850 906 0766, ⓦ bradfordvilleblues.com. Drive down a rutted dirt road to this hole-in-the-wall club about 10 miles north of downtown. You can enjoy live blues every

weekend and the band's second set will most likely be played outside around a bonfire. Tickets $12–25. Fri & Sun 8pm–close.

Bullwinkle's 620 W Tennessee St ☎ 850 224 0651, ⓦ bullwinklessaloon.com. Rock and blues dominate in this log-cabin-like setting popular with FSU students, which also features DJs mixing the favourite dance music of the moment. Cover $10 Fri & Sat. Wed 10pm–2am, Thurs–Sat 9pm–2am.

Clyde's & Costello's 210 S Adams St ☎ 850 224 2173. Pulls a mix of locals, students and politicos (aides and staffers), who grow a bit rowdy during the early-evening happy hours. Mon–Sat 4.30pm–2am.

★ **Fermentation Lounge** 113 All Saints St ☎ 850 727 4033. Cool bar boasting over 100 craft beers and artisan wines, and a large screen that features a weekly rotation of vintage ads and film clips from the late 1940s to mid-1960s

9

to match the themed decor. Mon–Thurs 5pm–1am, Fri & Sat 4pm–2am, Sun 4–11pm.

★**Level 8 Lounge** Hotel Duval, 415 N Monroe St ☎850 224 6000, ⓦhotelduval.com. This classy rooftop lounge shines in a college town better known for dive bars and cheap drinks. Sip cocktails or glasses of wine, laze on the pillow-laden couches and soak up the views of the city. Mon, Tues & Thurs 4pm–midnight, Wed, Fri & Sat 4pm–2am.

The Moon 1105 E Lafayette St ☎850 222 6666, ⓦtallahassee.moonevents.com. Come for the indie bands, Ladies nights (Wed; cover $10, free till midnight), or Friday night's "Stetsons on the Moon" – a country music extravaganza with line dancing and much thigh slapping – and free drinks for the girls till midnight ($5 cover). Wed 10pm–2am, Fri 8pm–2.20am, Sat 10pm–3am.

Potbelly's 459 W College Ave ☎850 224 2233, ⓦpotbellys.net. On the frat-house-filled approach to the FSU campus, this rather grubby bar – with a stage for live music – is a major student watering-hole. Watch out for drink specials like $4 pitchers of beer. Tues, Thurs & Sat 10pm–2am, Fri 3pm–2am.

ENTERTAINMENT

FSU School of Theatre (Richard G. Fallon Theatre) 540 W Call St ☎850 644 6500, ⓦtickets.fsu.edu. The student productions on the FSU campus tend to be high quality, with several venues hosting productions most of the year, notably the Richard G. Fallon Theatre. Box office Tues–Sat 11am–4pm.

Tallahassee Symphony Orchestra Ruby Diamond Concert Hall, 222 S Copeland St ☎850 224 0461, ⓦtallahasseesymphony.org. Delivers a season of classical music (Oct–April) at the Ruby Diamond Concert Hall, which also hosts FSU's **Seven Days of Opening Nights** arts festival in February (ⓦsevendaysfestival.org). Box office Mon–Fri 10am–4pm (also Sat 9am–4pm on concert days).

Theatre Tallahassee 1861 Thomasville Rd ☎850 224 8474, ⓦtheatretallahassee.org. There's a fair amount of theatre in Tallahassee, headed by this local group founded in 1949. Their venue was renovated in 2013, with several productions each season ranging from *Evita* to Agatha Christie. Box office Mon–Fri noon–4pm.

Around Tallahassee

Scattered around the fringes of Tallahassee are half a dozen enticing sights that could easily fill up a couple of days, among them a remarkable antique car museum, giant sinkholes, lakeside gardens and more remnants of Florida's Spanish past. All are easily accessible by car, but much harder to reach by bus.

Tallahassee Automobile Museum

6800 Mahan Drive (US-90) • Mon–Fri 8am–5pm, Sat 10am–5pm, Sun noon–5pm • $17.50, children 5–8 $8 • ☎850 942 0137, ⓦtacm.com

The Southeast's finest collection of rare cars is on display at the **Tallahassee Automobile Museum**, a few miles west of downtown. The biggest crowd-pleasers in the collection are three **Batmobiles**, including the gleaming 21ft-long incarnation from the Tim Burton movie *Batman Forever* (1995), bought for $500,000 and complete with Batman's suits and gloves and a flame-thrower attachment. While the most valuable car

---

TALLAHASSEE'S MOUND BUILDERS

Tallahassee lies at the heart of a series of **ancient Native American settlements** that once featured giant mounds and sophisticated societies. Today, there's not much left besides the mounds, but the sites are tranquil, enigmatic places. The parks are usually open sunrise to sunset and cost $3 per car.

Lake Jackson Mounds Archaeological State Park 3600 Indian Mound Rd (off US-27, 2 miles north of I-10). One of the most important archeological sites in Florida, a former chiefdom and ceremonial centre of the Fort Walton Culture (1100–1550). Three large mounds are clearly visible (you can climb up two of them).

Letchworth Mounds Archaeological State Park 4500 Sunray Rd S, 14 miles east of Tallahassee off US-90. Preserves the state's tallest Native American ceremonial earthwork mound, 300ft wide and 46ft high. It is estimated to have been built 1100 to 1800 years ago by the Weedon Island Culture. An interpretive trail and boardwalk add context to the site.

in the collection is a $1.2 million 1931 Duesenberg Model J, the most intriguing specimen is an 1860-built horse-drawn hearse believed to have carried Abraham Lincoln to his final resting place.

9

Alfred B. Maclay Gardens State Park

3540 Thomasville Rd • **Park** Daily 8am–sunset • Cars $6, single occupant $4, pedestrians and cyclists $2 **Gardens** Daily 9am–5pm • Jan–April $6, May–Dec free • ☎ 850 487 4115, ⓦ floridastateparks.org/maclaygardens

For a lazy half-day, head four miles northeast of downtown Tallahassee to **Alfred B. Maclay Gardens State Park**, set in a lakeside park north of I-10, Exit 203. New York financier and amateur gardener Alfred Maclay bought this large piece of land in 1923 and planted flowers and shrubs in order to create a blooming season from January to April. It worked: for four months each year the gardens are alive with the fragrances and fantastic colours of azaleas, camellias, pansies and other flowers, framed by dogwood and redbud trees and towered over by huge oaks and pines. The gardens are worth visiting at any time, if only to retire to the lakeside pavilion for a snooze as lizards and squirrels scurry around your feet.

The admission fee to the gardens also gets you into the **Maclay House Museum** (open Jan–April only), which is filled with the Maclays' furniture and countless books on horticulture.

Tallahassee Museum

3945 Museum Drive • Mon–Sat 9am–5pm, Sun 11am–5pm • $9, children 4–15 $6 • ☎ 850 575 8684, ⓦ tallahasseemuseum.org

Some five miles southwest of downtown, on the shores of Lake Bradford, the **Tallahassee Museum** is a sprawling showcase of northern Florida's history and wildlife; with a little bit of everything, it's an especially fun spot for families. Much of the site is given over to **Big Bend Farm**, a re-creation of rural Floridian life circa 1880, and **Wildlife Florida**, a zoo containing black bears, white-tailed deer, red wolves and Florida panthers. Also on the grounds is the graceful 1837 **Bellevue Plantation** (the home of Catherine Murat in the 1850s, a relative of George Washington), replete with slave cabin, the 1937 **Bethlehem Missionary Baptist Church** (founded by Rev James Page, a slave preacher), and the 1897 one-room **Concord schoolhouse**. More exhibits can be found in the **Fleischmann Natural Science Building** (containing a small aquarium), the **Phipps Gallery** with changing exhibits of local art, and the **Discovery Center**, with family-friendly interactive exhibits on the natural history and culture of northern Florida.

Natural Bridge Battlefield State Historic Site

7502 Natural Bridge Rd, off Hwy-363 at Woodville (15 miles southeast of Tallahassee) • Daily 8am–sunset • $3 per car, $2 pedestrians and cyclists • ☎ 850 922 6007, ⓦ floridastateparks.org/naturalbridge

At the **Natural Bridge Battlefield State Historic Site**, on March 4, 1865, a motley band of Confederate soldiers saw off a much larger force of Union troops, preventing Tallahassee from falling into Yankee hands. Not that it made much difference – the war ended a couple of months later – but the victory is celebrated by a monument and an annual re-enactment on or close to the anniversary involving several hours of shouting, loud bangs and smoke.

San Marcos de Apalache Historic State Park

148 Old Fort Rd, St Marks • Mon & Thurs–Sun 9am–5pm • Grounds free, museum $2 • ☎ 850 925 6216, ⓦ floridastateparks.org/sanmarcos

Twenty miles south of Tallahassee, Hwy-363 expires at the hamlet of **St Marks**, where the **San Marcos de Apalache Historic State Park** preserves more of Florida's oft forgotten **Spanish roots** in the form of the second-oldest surviving Spanish fortification in the state. Exhibits and a twenty-minute video in the **museum** throw light on the fort's complex and turbulent history: early wooden incarnations dating from 1679 were destroyed by hurricanes or just abandoned to pirates and the Seminoles. A more determined effort to occupy the site was made by the Spanish in 1787, when it also became the base of

9

English traders Panton, Leslie & Co. Andrew Jackson took the fort in 1818 – the cemetery where most of his men were buried, victims of disease, is still there. The fort was occupied by US troops again between 1821 and 1824, and apart from the Civil War, has been largely abandoned since then. The grounds contain scattered remnants of the fort, principally old stone foundations, the eighteenth-century Spanish bombproof (redoubt), and more substantial Confederate earthworks from 1861.

St Marks National Wildlife Refuge

1255 Lighthouse Rd (Hwy-59) • Daily sunset–sunrise; visitor centre Mon–Fri 8am–4pm, Sat & Sun 10am–5pm • Cars $5, pedestrians and cyclists $1 • ☎ 850 925 6121, ⓦ fws.gov/refuge/st_marks

Encompassing around 106 square miles spread out along the Gulf coast south of Tallahassee, the **St Marks National Wildlife Refuge** is best approached from the main entrance on Hwy-59, off US-98 at Newport. The refuge is home to bald eagles and black bears, though from the various roadside lookout points and observation towers you're more likely to spot otters, white-tailed deer, raccoons and a wealth of birdlife. Just inside the main entrance, a **visitor centre** doles out useful information. Apart from the natural attractions, a drive to the end of Hwy-59 will bring you to the picturesque 73ft **St Marks Lighthouse**, completed in 1842 and still active.

Wakulla Springs State Park

465 Wakulla Park Drive, Hwy-267 (just off Hwy-61) • Daily 8am–sunset • Cars $6, $4 single occupant; pedestrians and cyclists $2 • ☎ 850 561 7276, ⓦ floridastateparks.org/wakullasprings

Fifteen miles south of Tallahassee, **Wakulla Springs State Park** contains what is believed to be one of the biggest and deepest natural springs in the world, pumping up half a million gallons of crystal-clear water from the bowels of the earth every day – difficult to guess from the calm surface. In summer it's refreshing to **swim** in the cool waters here, but to learn more about the spring, you should take a boat tour. Thanks to increasing run-off in recent years, it's rarely clear enough for the 25-minute narrated **glass-bottom boat tour** (noon, 1pm & 2pm, conditions permitting; $8). If you're lucky (usually in late winter or early spring), from the boat you can peer down to the shoals of catfish hovering around the 120ft-deep cavern through which the water comes. Otherwise year-round you can join the 45-minute **river cruise** (9.40am–5pm; $8) for glimpses of some of the park's other inhabitants: deer, turkeys, turtles, herons and egrets – and the inevitable alligators. If déjà vu strikes, it may be because a number of films have been shot here, including several of the early *Tarzan* movies and parts of *The Creature from the Black Lagoon*.

You shouldn't leave without strolling through the **Wakulla Lodge** (see below), a hotel built beside the spring in 1937 and retaining many of its original features: Moorish archways, stone fireplaces and fabulous hand-painted Toltec and Aztec designs on the lobby's wooden ceiling. You can also pay your respects to the stuffed carcass of "**Old Joe**", one of the oldest and largest alligators ever known. Joe was mysteriously killed in 1966, measuring 11ft long and supposedly aged 200; he's in a glass case by the reception desk.

ACCOMMODATION   WAKULLA SPRINGS STATE PARK

Wakulla Lodge 550 Wakulla Park Drive ☎ 850 926 0700, ⓦ wakullaspringslodge.com. Located in the middle of the state park (see above), overlooking the springs, this 1930s lodge retains a relaxing ambience that can prove quite soothing. Its 27 rooms are simply but authentically furnished in Art Deco style, with phones but no TVs. **$95**

Havana

Sixteen miles northwest of Tallahassee, tiny **HAVANA** (pronounced "Hey-vannah") provides an authentic dose of Americana, just before the Georgia border. Officially chartered in 1906, this little town takes pride in its history and, although it has a number of shops catering to the tourist trade, this seems only to have strengthened the community's sense of identity. Havana's name came from its **tobacco** plantations, which once supplied cigar-making factories in Cuba. Following the embargo against Cuba in 1958, the town could no longer sell tobacco leaves to Havana and went into decline, only to be rejuvenated again in the 1980s when the first **antique shops** opened and the community discovered history can mean business. Most of the action takes place on Seventh Avenue and First and Second streets, just off Hwy-27 as it passes through the centre of town. Note that shops tend to open Wednesday to Sunday 10am to 6pm; almost everything is closed Monday and Tuesday.

One of the most captivating examples of early Havana architecture is the 1860s **McLauchlin House**, at 201 NW 1st St at the corner of Seventh Avenue, with a beautiful wraparound porch, sloping floors and uneven doors. Today it serves as **Weezie's Cottage Living** furniture store (Wed–Sat 11am–6pm, Sun 1–5pm; ☏850 539 9001). Nearby sits the 1928 **Planter's Exchange**, 204 NW 2nd St (☏850 539 6343; Wed–Fri 10am–5pm, Sat 10am–5.30pm, Sun noon–5pm), a renovated former tobacco warehouse, now home to over thirty antique dealers.

ARRIVAL AND DEPARTURE   HAVANA

By car Havana lies 16 miles north of Tallahassee, some 12 miles north of I-10 along Monroe St (US-27). There is no public transport.

EATING

Magnolia Cafe & Coffee House 310 N Main St ☏850 539 3737. Feast on Belgian waffles or home-made scones with jam for breakfast, or a selection of sandwiches and chicken, shrimp and tuna salads for lunch. Tues–Fri 9am–3pm, Sat 9am–4pm, Sun 11am–3pm.

Tomato Café & Tea Room 107 W 7th Ave ☏850 539 2285. This charming place serves afternoon tea, including scones and Devonshire cream, as well as soups and sandwiches (and delicious tomato pie). Wed 11am–4pm, Thurs–Sun 11am–8pm.

Apalachicola National Forest

With swamps, savannahs and springs dotted liberally about its 900 square miles, the **Apalachicola National Forest** is the inland Panhandle at its natural best. Several roads enable you to drive through a good-sized chunk and multiple spots provide opportunities for a rest and a snack; the **Apalachee Scenic Byway** runs along 35 miles of surfaced roads (Hwy-12 and Hwy-65) that traverse the western end of the forest, passing Fort Gadsden (see p.414), Hickory Lake and Wright Lake (see p.415). But to see more of the forest than its picnic tables, you'll have to make an effort. Leave the periphery and delve into the pristine interior to explore at a leisurely pace, following 85 miles of hiking trails, taking a canoe on one of the rivers, or simply spending a night under the stars at one of the basic campgrounds. The only place to rent a canoe or kayak near the forest is **TNT Hideaway** (☏850 925 6412, ⊕tnthideaway.com), at 6527 Coastal Hwy (US-98), two miles west of St Marks on the Wakulla River. Prices range from $25 (single kayaks) to $35 (two-person canoes).

Leon Sinks Geological Area

US-319 • Daily 8am–8pm • $3 • ☏850 926 3561

Seven miles south of Tallahassee on US-319 lies the **Leon Sinks Geological Area**, a tantalizing karst landscape (terrain altered by rain and ground water dissolving underlying limestone bedrock). It contains several prominent **sinkholes**, numerous depressions, a natural bridge and a disappearing stream, all of which give a unique glimpse of the surrounding area before human interference. There are three manageable trails of between half a mile and three miles, cutting through the most scenic areas.

DEEPER INTO THE FOREST: HIKING AND CANOEING

Several short, clearly marked **nature walks** lie within the forest, but the major **hiking trail**, strictly for ardent and well-equipped backpackers, is the former **Apalachicola Trail**, now part of the state-wide 1400-mile **Florida National Scenic Trail** which begins close to Crawfordville, on US-319. Around 74 miles of the trail passes through the forest and includes a memorable (and sometimes difficult, depending on the weather conditions and water level) leg across an isolated swamp, the Bradwell Bay Wilderness. After this, the campground at Porter Lake, just to the west of the wilderness area, with its toilets and drinking water, seems the epitome of civilization.

The trail leads on to **Camel Lake**, whose campground has drinking water and toilets, and the less demanding nine-and-a-half-mile **Trail of Lakes**. By vehicle, you can get directly to Camel Lake by turning off Hwy-20 at Bristol and continuing south for twelve miles, watching for the signposted turn-off on the left.

Although there are numerous places to put in along its four rivers, **canoeists and kayakers** can paddle right into the forest from the western end of Lake Talquin (close to Hwy-20), and continue for a sixty-mile glide along the Ochlockonee River – the forest's major waterway – to the Ochlockonee River State Park, close to US-319. The length of trip means that to do it all you'll have to use the riverside **campgrounds**. You can pick up info on these from any of the forest ranger offices (see below).

Lost Lake and Silver Lake recreation areas

Lost Lake Lost Lake Rd, off Springhill Rd (Hwy-2203) • Daily: April–Oct 8am–8pm; Nov–March 8am–6pm • Free **Silver Lake** Silver Lake Rd (off Hwy-20) • Daily: April–Oct 8am–8pm; Nov–March 8am–6pm • $3 per car

One of the closest attractions in the Apalachicola National Forest to Tallahassee, seven miles from downtown along Hwy-2203, **Lost Lake Recreation Area** offers a few shady picnic tables beside a small lake (though it's not really suitable for swimming), as well as a trailhead for the forest's motorcycle and horse trails. If you fancy a swim, aim for the enticing white-sand beach at nearby **Silver Lake Recreation Area**, where you can also stroll along a one-mile loop trail.

Fort Gadsden Historical Site

Forest Rd 129-B (off Hwy-65) • Daily 8am–sunset • Free

The remote outpost along the Apalachicola River now known as the **Fort Gadsden Historical Site** dates back to the War of 1812, when the British constructed a fort here to encourage the local Seminole tribes to attack the US (the territory was officially Spanish at the time). When the Brits departed in 1815 they left their Seminole allies in charge, their ranks swollen by fugitive slaves from the Southern US states. This rag-tag force began raiding Georgia from what was now known as **Negro Fort**; in 1816 US forces obliterated the fort, in part thanks to a lucky cannon shot that ignited the fort's gunpowder store, killing most of the defenders. In 1818, a second fort was built nearby by US Lieutenant James Gadsden. Today the ruins of both forts can be seen from an interpretive trail along the banks of the Apalachicola River.

ARRIVAL AND INFORMATION

APALACHICOLA NATIONAL FOREST

By car You'll need a car to explore the forest. The northeast corner of the forest almost touches Tallahassee's airport, fanning out from there to the edge of the Apalachicola River, about 35 miles west. Most of the northern edge is bordered by Hwy-20, the eastern side by US-319 and US-98, while to the south lies US-98 and St George Sound.

Tourist information The Ochlockonee River divides the forest into two administrative districts and the following offices are responsible for the west and east sides, respectively: Apalachicola Ranger District, 11152 Hwy-20, near Bristol (☎ 850 643 2282); Wakulla Ranger District, 57 Taft Drive near Crawfordville (☎ 850 926 3561). Both open Mon–Thurs 8am–4.30pm, Fri 8am–4pm.

ACCOMMODATION

Apalachicola campgrounds Accommodation is limited to camping; backcountry camping is free, but even the five designated campgrounds have just basic facilities – usually just toilets and drinking water. For more information, call ☎ 850 643 2282 or ☎ 850 926 3561. The five are *Camel Lake* ($10), *Mack Landing* ($3), *Wright Lake* ($10), *Whitehead*

Landing ($3) and *Hickory Landing* ($3). There is no backcountry camping allowed in the park during deer hunting season from mid-November through mid-February, unless you're part of a deer hunting camp. Campsites are available on a first-come basis; there are no reservations.

Heading west: the inland route

To discover the real character of the inland Panhandle, take I-10 or US-90 **west from Tallahassee** towards **Pensacola** and the Alabama border. This stretch is 180 miles of forest, rural landscapes and time-locked farming towns that have been down on their luck since the demise of the timber industry fifty or so years ago, but the compensations are the endless supply of rustic eating places, low-cost accommodation, several appealing natural areas – and a chance to see a part of Florida travel brochures rarely mention. You'll need a car to explore this route, as there is no public transport.

Quincy

Twenty miles west of Tallahassee, and just two miles north of I-10 Exit 181, **Quincy** looks like a typical Panhandle small town, but it's actually one of the first communities to strike it rich because of **Coca-Cola**. In the early 1920s, at the urging of a local banker, Quincy's tobacco farmers bought shares in the Atlanta-based company. The pay-off was spectacular, with the funding of lavish public facilities and a stable economy even during the Great Depression and the collapse of the tobacco industry in the 1960s – many residents still own stock today. On the other hand, most of the grandiose villas sprinkled throughout the town were built before the Coke investment, and despite the wealth of some residents, the surrounding area remains overwhelmingly black and poor.

From the square on **Madison Street** and US-90, observe the immaculate **Gadsden County Court House**, surrounded by topiaries, and a small marble pillar commemorating slain Confederate soldiers at the back. Just across US-90, on East Jefferson Street, the wall of **Padgett's jewellery store** is covered with the original Coke ad. Painted here in 1905, it espouses Coke as "delicious and refreshing, five cents at fountains and bottles". Take time to explore the **Gadsden Arts Center**, 13 N Madison St (Tues–Sat 10am–5pm; ☎ 850 875 4866, ⓦ gadsdenarts.org). One of the finest art galleries in the area, it hosts major travelling exhibitions as well as the work of local and regional artists.

ARRIVAL AND INFORMATION   QUINCY

By car Quincy is an easy 26-mile drive along I-10 (to exit 181) from Tallahassee (35min).
By bus The commuter-oriented Gadsden Express (☎ 850 574 6064) provides a bus service between Quincy and Tallahassee (CK Steele Plaza bus station; p.408) for just $1, but only four times daily Mon–Fri (to Quincy 7am, 11.30am,

4pm & 6pm, returning 6am, 8am, 12.30pm & 5pm; 1hr).
Tourist information The Gadsden County Chamber of Commerce is just north of the square at 208 N Adams St (Mon–Fri 9am–12.30pm & 1.30–5pm; ☎ 850 627 9231, ⓦ gadsdencc.com). You can park around the square for free (2hr maximum).

CROSSING THE TIME ZONE

Crossing the Apalachicola River, which flows north–south across the inland Panhandle, roughly 45 miles west of Tallahassee, takes you into the **Central Time Zone**, an hour behind Eastern Time and the rest of Florida. In the coastal Panhandle, the time shift occurs about ten miles west of Port St Joe, on the boundary between Gulf and Bay counties.

9

ACCOMMODATION AND EATING

Allison House Inn 215 N Madison St ☎888 904 2511, ⓦallisonhouseinn.com. A lovely English-style bed and breakfast in one of the oldest houses in town (circa 1843), with six Victorian-themed rooms and a Laura Ashley feel. Free wi-fi. **$95**

Mainstreet Café 112 E Washington St ☎850 627 2226. Next door to the Quincy Music Theatre in the centre of town, this local café offers a bit more character for lunch than the usual range of fast-food options that line US-90 on the outskirts. Great lunch deals for $5–8. Mon–Sat 10am–3pm.

McFarlin House 305 E King St ☎850 875 2526, ⓦmcfarlinhouse.com. The finest of all Quincy mansions also happens to be a bed and breakfast, an exquisite, turreted pile whose sumptuous bedrooms and 42-pillar porch were created for John McFarlin, Quincy's richest tobacco planter, in 1895. Free wi-fi. **$109**

Florida Caverns State Park

3345 Caverns Rd, Marianna (off Hwy-166) • Daily 8am–sunset; hourly tours 9am–4pm Thurs–Mon • Cars $5, single occupant $4; pedestrians and cyclists $2; tours $8 • ☎850 482 9598, ⓦfloridastateparks.org/floridacaverns

The main attraction on the I-10 corridor, some fifty miles west of Quincy, the **Florida Caverns State Park** encompasses a series of dazzling 65ft-deep caves filled with wildly twisted calcite formations, flowstones and draperies. **Guided tours** (45min) venture through some of the most spellbinding caverns. Back in the sun, the park has a few other features to fill a day comfortably. From the **visitors centre** at the caverns' entrance, a **nature trail** leads around the flood plain of the Chipola River, which dips underground for several hundred feet as it flows through the park. Rent a canoe ($15/4hr, $20/8hr) and bunk at its **campground** ($20 with electricity; reservations ☎800 326 352).

Falling Waters State Park

1130 State Park Rd, Chipley • Daily 8am–sunset • Cars $5, $4 for single occupant; pedestrians and cyclists $2 • ☎850 638 6130, ⓦfloridastateparks.org/fallingwaters

Accessible from I-10 Exit 120 (follow the signs), the **Falling Waters State Park** lies three miles south of the highway and is the home of Florida's only **waterfall**. The fall is in fact a 73ft drop into a tube-like sinkhole smothered in fern and moss and topped by a viewing platform. The waterfall can be spectacular after heavy rain; the flipside is that at times of drought or dry weather (which happens a lot in summer), it can completely dry up. The park is worth a visit regardless, a tranquil reserve of pine forest pitted with sinkholes, a two-acre lake where you can swim and an abandoned oil well – remnant of an unsuccessful attempt to strike black gold in 1919.

DeFuniak Springs

A real jewel of the inland Panhandle, **DeFuniak Springs**, forty miles west of Falling Waters on I-10, was founded as a fashionable stop on the newly completed Louisville–Nashville railroad in 1882. Drawn to the large, naturally circular **Lake DeFuniak** (which is still spring-fed), nineteenth-century socialites built fairy-tale villas to fringe the waters here. In 1886 the **Florida Chautauqua Alliance**, a benevolent religious society espousing free education for all, made the town its winter base. The alliance's headquarters was at the grandiose **Hall of Brotherhood**, which still stands on one-mile **Circle Drive** – an ideal cruising lane to view the splendid villas, all painted in gingerbread-house style with white or wedding-cake blue trim. With the death of its founders the Florida meetings ended in the 1920s, and in 1975 the main auditorium was demolished by Hurricane Eloise. Don't leave town without checking out the **Little Big Store**, 35 S 8th St (☎850 892 6066), just off the lake, an old-fashioned country store loaded with old-fashioned snacks, toys and souvenirs.

Chautauqua Hall of Brotherhood
95 Circle Drive • Chamber of Commerce Mon–Fri 9am–5pm

Built around 1909 to replace tents and temporary buildings, the stately **Chautauqua Hall of Brotherhood** is all that remains of the Chautauqua complex after the 1975 hurricane, its dome dominating the surrounding lake. In 1996 the Florida Chautauqua Assembly was re-established, and a **Chautauqua Assembly Revival** is now held nearby at 1290 Circle Drive around the end of January or the beginning of February (see ⓦfloridachautauquaassembly.org). In addition to holding workshops on whatever is the featured topic that year and craft activities, the town also opens up its historic houses at this time. Today the Chautauqua Hall of Brotherhood is occupied by the Walton Area Chamber of Commerce (see p.417).

Walton-DeFuniak Library
3 Circle Drive • Mon & Wed–Sat 9am–5pm, Tues 9am–8pm • Free • ☎ 850 892 3624

The only building on Circle Drive regularly open to the public is the **Walton-DeFuniak Library**, which has been lending books since 1887 and has a small stash of medieval European weaponry on display.

Walton County Heritage Museum
1140 Circle Drive • Tues–Sat 1–4pm • Free • ☎ 850 951 2127, ⓦwaltoncountyheritage.org

The old 1882 train station on the lake (trains haven't stopped here for years) has been converted into the **Walton County Heritage Museum**, an enthusiastic attempt to chronicle the area's history with heaps of bric-a-brac and artefacts from the Civil War through to the later twentieth century. Outside there's a fully refurbished **caboose** (a carriage used as living quarters by the train crew), built in 1968 (tours on Sat only, one week's notice required).

ARRIVAL AND INFORMATION | DEFUNIAK SPRINGS

By car DeFuniak Springs is 120 miles west of Tallahassee, an easy drive along I-10 (around 2hr); Pensacola is 80 miles in the other direction. There is no public transport.

Tourist information The Walton Area Chamber of Commerce (☎850 892 3191, ⓦwaltonareachamber.com)

is at 95 Circle Drive (at the Chautauqua Hall of Brotherhood), open Mon–Thurs 8.30am–5pm. The DeFuniak Springs Visitors Center at 1162 Circle Drive (next to the old station; ⓦdefuniakspringsvisitorsbureau.com) takes up the slack Sat & Sun 11am–3pm.

ACCOMMODATION AND EATING

Bogey's Bar and Restaurant Hotel DeFuniak ☎850 951 2233, ⓦbogeysrestaurant.net. Serves breakfast, lunch and dinner, as well as a variety of speciality coffees and desserts; dishes include stuffed shrimp ($18) and chicken Marsala ($16). Tues–Fri 11am–2pm & 5–9pm, Sat 5–9pm.

★**H&M Hot Dog** 43 N 9th St ☎ 850 892 9100. This local institution has been knocking out Chicago-style hot dogs since 1947 (opened by Harley and Margaret Broxson, it's

now owned by the former mayor). Expect succulent boiled hot dogs on steamed buns, chilli dogs and freshly made burgers. Just a handful of stools and standing room inside. Cash only. Mon–Fri 9am–5pm, Sat 10am–4pm.

Hotel DeFuniak 400 E Nelson Ave ☎850 892 4383, ⓦhoteldefuniak.com. Built in 1920 and charmingly restored right in the centre of town, offering singles as well as standard doubles and suites, with free wi-fi and breakfast included. **$105**

The Blackwater River State Forest
Blackwater River State Forest 11650 Munson Hwy, Milton • Free • ☎ 850 957 6140 Blackwater River State Park 7720 Deaton Bridge Rd • Daily 8am–sunset • Cars $4, pedestrians and cyclists $2 • ☎ 850 983 5363, ⓦfloridastateparks.org/blackwaterriver

Between the sluggish towns of Crestview and Milton, thirty miles west of DeFuniak Springs, the creeks and slow-flowing rivers of **Blackwater River State Forest** are jammed each weekend with waterborne families enjoying what's officially dubbed "**the canoe capital of Florida**". In spite of the crowds, the forest is by no means over-commercialized, being big enough to absorb the influx and still offer peace,

9

isolation and unruffled nature to anyone intrepid enough to hike through it. If you're not game for canoeing or hiking, but just want a few hours' break, the **Blackwater River State Park** within the forest, four miles north of Harold off US-90, has some easy walking trails.

Hiking and canoeing

Hardened **hikers** carrying overnight gear can tackle the 21-mile **Jackson Trail**, named after Andrew Jackson, who led his invading army this way in 1818, seeking to wrest Florida from Spanish control. On the way, two very basic shelters have hand pumps for water. The trail runs between Karick Lake, off Hwy-189, fourteen miles north of US-90, and the Krul Recreation Area. The shorter **Sweetwater Trail** is a good substitute if your feet aren't up to the longer hike. An enjoyable four-and-a-half-mile walk, it leaves the Krul Recreation Area and crosses a swing bridge and the Bear Lake Dam before joining the Jackson Trail.

Canoeing on the Coldwater River is offered by Adventures Unlimited (see below) and Bob's Canoes on Hwy-191 (daily 8.30am–6pm; ☎850 623 5457; canoes from $21 for 5 miles). You can also rent tubes ($18) and kayaks for $25 (both 5-mile trips), while Adventures Unlimited also operates a **zipline** that soars over the river ($89–129; ⓦfloridaziplineadventures.com).

ACCOMMODATION	BLACKWATER RIVER STATE FOREST
Accommodation in the state park is limited to camping (☎850 983 5363 for information, ☎800 326 3521 for reservations; $20). There are also five fully equipped campgrounds within the state forest (☎850 957 6140; $10–20), offering amenities including swimming, hiking trails and boat ramps. Free basic sites intended for hikers are dotted along the main trails. **Adventures Unlimited** 8974 Tomahawk Landing Rd	☎850 623 6197, ⓦadventuresunlimited.com. Offers restored "cracker" and other nineteenth-century-style cabins in a variety of sizes along Coldwater Creek and in the forest (most have a/c, kitchens and bathrooms), as well as eight rooms in the *Old School House Inn* (no TVs or phones). Rustic cabins with basic amenities are just $69, while camping prices begin at $25 for a pitch with hook-ups. Cabins **$129**

The Forgotten Coast

Time-consuming to reach and oft ignored, the aptly named **Forgotten Coast** offers a taste of Old Florida blissfully free of major development and tourist crowds. The architecture and pace of life here sometimes resembles Cajun Louisiana more than the rest of Florida, with little **Apalachicola** and **Port St Joe** anchoring the region with fine fishing, seafood and especially **oysters**. Just offshore lie beautiful unspoiled sands and **barrier islands** where people are a rarer sight than wildlife. With no public transport, you'll need a car to explore this area.

Apalachicola

A few miles south of the Apalachicola National Forest (see p.413), **APALACHICOLA** is the first substantial settlement on the Forgotten Coast from Tallahassee. Now a tiny port with an income largely derived from harvesting **oysters** (ten percent of the nation's oysters come from here), the town once rode high on the cotton industry, which kept its dock busy and its populace affluent until the 1850s. Visit the **Chamber of Commerce** (see p.420) to pick up a walking-tour map of the town's stock of captivating historic buildings.

CLOCKWISE FROM TOP LEFT SEASIDE HOUSE (P.429); APALACHICOLA NATIONAL FOREST (P.413); PERDIDO KEY (P.443) >

9

John Gorrie Museum State Park

6th St, at Ave D • Mon & Thurs–Sun 9am–noon & 1–5pm • $2 • ☏ 850 653 9347, ⓦ floridastateparks.org/JohnGorrieMuseum/default.cfm

The one-room **John Gorrie Museum State Park** is a tribute to the man who invented air conditioning, as well as charting the general history of Apalachicola. Arriving in the town in 1833, John Gorrie was seeking a way to keep malaria patients cool when he devised a machine to make ice (previously transported in large blocks from the North). He died here (and is buried across from the museum), however, before the idea took off and became the basis of modern refrigerators and air conditioners. The museum contains a replica of his cumbersome ice-making device (the original is in the Smithsonian Institution in Washington, DC).

Apalachicola Maritime Museum

103 Water St • Daily 10am–5pm • $5 (boat tour prices include entry) • ☏ 850 653 2500, ⓦ ammfl.org

The **Apalachicola Maritime Museum** is a modest attempt to chronicle the importance of the sea in the town's history, with a collection of artefacts, vintage black-and-white photos, and boat building clinics on the dock. It's worth taking one of its enlightening **boat tours** from here, ranging from historic waterfront cruises ($15; 3hr) to more extensive estuary ecotours ($40; 3hr). You can also take kayak and canoe trips ($10–20).

The museum is hoping to expand considerably in the next few years, with a historic boat building operation dating from 1920 just down the road, and a second museum in the town of Chattahoochee, a hundred miles north.

ARRIVAL AND INFORMATION

APALACHICOLA

By car Apalachicola lies around 76 miles southwest of Tallahassee via US-319 S (1hr 40min). There is no public transport.

Tourist information The Chamber of Commerce Visitor Center is at 122 Commerce St (Mon–Sat 10am–4pm; ☏ 850 653 9419, ⓦ apalachicolabay.org).

ACCOMMODATION

Apalachicola River Inn 123 Water St ☏ 850 653 8139, ⓦ apalachicolariverinn.com. The 26 modern rooms here all have river views, full tile bathrooms and ceiling fans, close to downtown. Rates include breakfast and free wi-fi. **$149**

Consulate Suites 76 Water St ☏ 850 927 2282, ⓦ consulatesuites.com. These luxury suites are housed in the venerable Grady Market building, rebuilt after a 1900 fire – the French really had a consulate here in the early 1900s. All the suites have kitchens, cable TV with VCRs, laundry facilities and balconies. **$185**

Coombs House Inn 80 6th St ☏ 850 653 9199, ⓦ coombshouseinn.com. B&B housed in a lovely Queen Anne-style mansion built in 1905, filled with antiques and oriental carpets, with bicycles available for guests' use. **$109**

Gibson Inn 57 Market St ☏ 850 653 2191, ⓦ gibsoninn .com. A beautiful wooden hotel built in 1907 with a wraparound veranda, four-poster beds and Victorian claw-foot tubs. Offers murder-mystery weekends and a full dinner menu in its own restaurant. **$125**

EATING AND DRINKING

Apalachicola Chocolate Company 75 Market St ☏ 850 370 6937. Handmade fudge, caramel with walnuts, bittersweet chocolate, almond rocky-road clusters, caramel turtles, French pudding truffles and luscious gelato (chocolates sold by the pound from $10–14). Cash only. Daily 10am–6pm.

Apalachicola Seafood Grill & Steakhouse 100 Market St ☏ 850 653 9510. Open since 1903, this still knocks out decent lunch and dinner specials, as well as its huge fried-fish sandwiches ($11), though you are paying for the history as much as the food (half-dozen oysters $8, fish from $12). Mon–Sat 11am–9pm, Sun 11.30am–4pm.

Boss Oyster 125 Water St ☏ 850 653 9364, ⓦ bossoyster.com. Though this is no longer the best

seafood joint in town, *Boss* remains a classic Old Florida experience, its fresh Apalachicola oysters prepared in thirty-plus different ways, as well as blue crabs and a range of seafood (mains $15–25). Mon–Fri & Sun 11.30am–9pm, Sat 11.30am–10pm.

Hole In The Wall Seafood 23 Ave D ☏ 850 653 3222. Genuine oyster shack with seafood and Apalachicola oysters (around $10/dozen) at reasonable prices (the shrimp, celebrated fried grouper sandwich and home-made gumbo are all excellent). Limited seating inside (four big tables and the bar). Mains $14.95–19.95. Tues–Sat 11.30am–9pm.

Owl Café 15 Ave D ☏ 850 653 9888, ⓦ owlcafeflorida .com. Fresh seafood and friendly service on a second-floor porch overlooking the time-warped downtown make this one of the most popular restaurants in Apalachicola. Famed fried oysters ($11) and blue crab dip ($9), but also top-quality steaks and salads (dinner mains $20–28). Craft beers on draft in the *Tap Room* next door. Mon–Sat 11am–9pm.

ENTERTAINMENT

Dixie Theatre 21 Ave E ☎850 653 3200, ⓦ dixietheatre.com. Built in 1912 and restored in 1997, this theatre hosts all sorts of acts, from tribute bands to flamenco, and folk to jazz (the season runs Jan–March only). Box office Wed & Sat noon–5pm.

The barrier islands

A few miles off the coast, framing Apalachicola Bay and the broad, marshy outflow of the Apalachicola River, the Apalachicola **barrier islands** are well endowed with beaches and creatures – including thousands of birds that use them as resting stops during migration – while two of them hold what must be among the most isolated communities in Florida. It's worth seeing one of the islands if you have the chance, but only the largest island, St George, is accessible by road – Hwy-300, which leaves US-98 at Eastpoint. Once here you can visit the rest with Journeys of St George's Island, 240 E 3rd St (☎850 927 3259, ⓦsgislandjourneys.com; closed Jan–Feb), which provides a variety of instructional, guided canoe trips and hikes.

St George Island

St George Island State Park 1900 E Gulf Beach Drive • Daily 8am–sunset • Cars $6, single occupant $4, pedestrians and cyclists $2 • ☎ 850 927 2111, ⓦ floridastateparks.org/stgeorgeisland

Twenty-seven miles of powdery white sands and Gulf vistas are not the only reason to come to **St George Island**, where shady live-oak hammocks and an abundance of osprey-inhabited pine trees add colour to a day's lazy sunning. Occupying the island's central section are a few restaurants and beach shops, as well as the elegant *St George Inn* (see below) and the **Cape St George Light** (Mon–Wed, Fri & Sat 10am- 5pm, Sun noon–5pm; $5; ⓦstgeorgelight.org), a replica 1852 lighthouse with a small museum and spectacular views spanning miles along the coast. The eastern sector is dominated by the raccoon-infested **St George Island State Park**, with nine miles of pristine beach and where a three-mile **hiking trail** leads to a very basic **campground** (see p.421).

INFORMATION ST GEORGE ISLAND

Tourist information Stop by the St George Island Visitor Center, 2 E Gulf Beach Drive (☎850 927 7744, ⓦseestgeorgeisland.com), next to the lighthouse, open Mon–Thurs noon–5pm, Fri & Sat 9am–5pm, Sun 1–5pm. Tours of the lighthouse are $5.

ACCOMMODATION

St George Inn 135 Franklin Blvd ☎850 927 2903, ⓦ stgeorgeinn.com. A beautiful wooden motel with a wraparound veranda, steps from the beach. Free wi-fi. **$120**
St George Island State Park Campground ☎800 326 3521. Well-equipped site (with electricity and water hook-ups), a quarter-mile from the beach, and primitive camping at Gap Point accessible only by foot, via the 2.5-mile Gap Point Trail. Main site **$24**, primitive camping **$5** (per person)

St Vincent Island

Daily sunrise–sunset • Free • ⓦ stvincentfriends.com

The freshwater lakes and saltwater swamps of the eighteen-square-mile **St Vincent Island**, almost within a shell's throw of St George's western end, form a protected refuge for endangered red wolves, Sambar deer, loggerhead turtles and bald eagles, among many other creatures. Trips to the island are available year-round with **St Vincent Island Shuttle Services** (☎850 229 1065, ⓦstvincentisland.com) from $10 (from 690 Indian Pass Rd in Port St Joe, p.422); they also organize bike rentals but you need to call in advance. You

9

can also kayak to the island, or take a cruise from the Apalachicola Maritime Museum (Thurs & Sun 7am; 4hr; $50; see p.420). For more information, visit the **St Vincent Wildlife Refuge Office** at 479 Market St in Apalachicola (Mon–Fri 8am–4pm). Note that the only facilities on the island are basic toilets, and there is no overnight camping.

St Joseph Peninsula State Park

8899 Cape San Blas Rd · Daily 8am–sunset · Cars $6, single occupant $4, pedestrians and cyclists $2 · ☎ 850 227 1327,
ⓦ floridastateparks.org/stjoseph

For a final taste of virgin Florida coast before hitting more commercial waters, take Hwy-30 – eighteen miles from Apalachicola, off US-98 – to the **St Joseph Peninsula State Park**. A long finger of sand with a short **nature trail** at one end and a spectacular nine-mile **hiking route** at the other, the park has rough **camping** with no facilities ($5) at its northern tip and better-equipped sites ($24 with electricity) and **cabins** ($100; ☎ 800 326 3521) about halfway along near Eagle Harbor.

Port St Joe

The St Joseph Peninsula wraps a protective arm around **PORT ST JOE** on the mainland, another dot-on-the-map fishing port that has an eventful history. Founded as **St Josephs** in 1835 by settlers disgruntled with the leaders of Apalachicola, just three years later the town managed the incredible coup of hosting the conference called to draw up **Florida's first constitution**, a legislative feat that took just 34 days. Despite the construction of an early railroad, devastating hurricanes and a nasty outbreak of yellow fever destroyed the town, and by the mid-1840s it was abandoned. New settlers arrived in 1905, and today Port St Joe is a sleepy fishing town, with a small downtown area of shops and restaurants along Reid Avenue (just off US-98).

Constitution Convention Museum State Park

200 Allen Memorial Way · Thurs–Mon 9am–noon & 1–5pm · $2 · ☎ 850 229 8029, ⓦ floridastateparks.org/constitutionconvention

At the **Constitution Convention Museum State Park**, signposted from US-98 as you enter the town, you'll find battery-powered mannequins that re-enact the great debate held here 1838–39 to create **Florida's first constitution**. There are also more credible mementos of the town's colourful past, starting with various Spanish attempts to settle here from 1701, and the brief French incursion at **Fort Crevecoeur** in 1718 (now Beacon Hill).

ARRIVAL, INFORMATION AND ACTIVITIES

PORT ST JOE

By car Port St Joe is just 24 miles west (30min) from Apalachicola via Hwy-30/US-98, and 46 miles southeast of Panama City Beach (around 1hr 15min). There is no public transport.

Information Gulf County Welcome Center is at 150 Captain Fred's Place, just off US-98 in the centre of town (Mon–Fri 8am–5pm, Sat 10am–2pm; ☎ 850 229 7800, ⓦ visitgulf.com).

Dive tours Daly's Dock & Dive Center, US-98 (☎ 850 229 6330, ⓦ dalysdock.com). Open daily 8am–6pm for PADI Discover Scuba ($140), dive trips ($140), snorkelling trips

($50), rental kayaks ($50/day) and paddleboards ($50/day).

Fishing Fish'n Xpress at 340 Marina Drive (☎ 850 227 8200, ⓦ tightlinesgoodtimes.com) runs fun fishing trips and cruises from $43–107, including a shark-fishing excursion.

Horseriding Broke a Toe (☎ 850 899 7433, ⓦ brokeatoe .com) on Cape San Blas Rd (on the road to the St Joseph Peninsula) offers horseriding lessons and guided rides along the beach from $50 for 1hr ($70 for 1hr 30min). Rides normally run daily 8am and 9am, and 5pm, 6.30pm and 7.45pm.

ACCOMMODATION

Port Inn 501 Monument Ave ☎ 850 229 7678, ⓦ portinnfl.com. St Joe's central hotel, with plenty of clapboard charm, 21 comfy rooms, a great little bar and

top-notch Southern hospitality. Free wi-fi. **$110**

Turtle Beach Inn 140 Painted Pony Rd ☎ 850 229 9366, ⓦ turtlebeachinn.com. Wonderful wooden beach-house with sea views, large shaded porches and sundecks. The four rooms are brightly decorated in a simple, modern style, with access to shared kitchen and lounge with DVD player and wi-fi. **$190**

EATING

Indian Pass Raw Bar 8391 Indian Pass Rd, Hwy-30A (just south of Port St Joe) ☎850 227 1670, ⓦindian passrawbar.com. A casual local favourite dating back to a wooden store in the 1930s, justly renowned for its Old Florida roadhouse atmosphere, raw oysters ($14.95 per dozen), Key lime pie and stuffed shrimp ($15.95 per dozen). Pitchers of beer from $7.50. Tues–Sat noon–9pm.

★**Joe Mama's Wood Fired Pizza** 406 Reid Ave ☎850 229 6262, ⓦjoemamaspizza.com. Hard to believe you'd find quality pizzas down here, but Joe's Tuscan hearth-fired creations do the business; their 12-inch classics include the tasty Quattro (San Marzano tomatoes, fresh mozzarella, prosciutto and basil; $15.50) but you can create your own from $11.50. Mon–Sat 4.30–9pm.

Panama City Beach and around

With its spectacular 27-mile-long strip of sugary-white sands and family-oriented attractions, **PANAMA CITY BEACH** attracts some six million visitors every year. It's a full-scale resort of motels, condos, go-kart tracks, mini-golf courses and amusement parks, but with the shops, bars and restaurants all trying to undercut one another, there are some great bargains to be found – from airbrushed T-shirts and cut-rate sunglasses to some of the best **restaurants** on the Gulf. With everybody out to have a good time, there's some fine carousing to be done, too; not least during the Spring Break month of March, when thousands of students arrive to drink and dance themselves into oblivion.

Throughout the lively summer, accommodation costs are high and advance bookings essential; the best time to come is autumn or early winter, when prices drop and visitors are fewer. Although most of the attractions off the beach, such as the wacky science at **WonderWorks** and aquariums at **Gulf World Marine Park**, attract primarily families with kids – indeed, even the Obama family holidayed here in 2010 – the balmy waters, bone-white sands and untouched landscapes of **St Andrews State Park** and **Shell Island** are pristine natural wonders that will appeal to anyone looking for a slice of Old Florida, and well worth exploring on foot or in a kayak.

The beach

Whatever your feelings about the development behind it, there's little debate that the **beach** here is one of the finest in the world, a silky-soft wedge of white sands bookended by the unspoiled reserves at Camp Helen and St Andrews state parks.

Front Beach Road is the main drag, a two-lane highway running along the main eight-mile segment of the beach, from **Pier Park** at the west end (see box, p.425), to the **Grand Lagoon** in the east. There are two, rather similar landmarks: **City Pier** at 16201 Front Beach Rd (daily 24hr; ☎850 233 5080), and **County Pier** (daily 24hr; ☎850 236 3035), two miles to the east at 12213 Front Beach Rd (both are around 1500ft long and charge $3 entrance). When judging distances, count on having to go about a mile to get from, say, number 15,000 to 16,000 Front Beach Road.

Other than the beach-based activities, you can try your hand at a variety of waterborne pastimes such as jet-skiing, parasailing, fishing, snorkelling and scuba diving (see box, p.426), while go-kart rides and amusement parks are fodder for landlubbers.

WonderWorks

9910 Front Beach Rd • Mon–Thurs & Sun 9am–9pm, Fri & Sat 9am–10pm • $23.99, children 4–12 $18.99 • ☎850 249 7000, ⓦwonderworkspcb.com

The whimsical upside-down building at the junction of Front Beach and Hutchinson roads is the Panama City outpost of **WonderWorks**, four storeys of

9

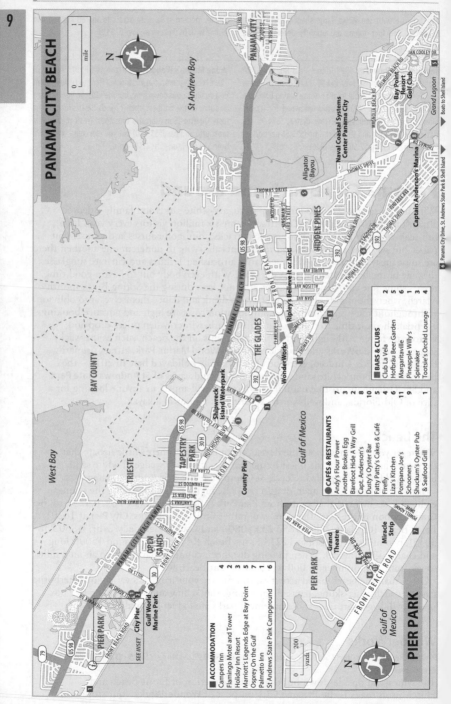

PANAMA CITY BEACH

St Andrew Bay

PANAMA CITY

Gulf of Mexico

West Bay

BAY COUNTY

TRIESTE

TAPESTRY PARK

THE GLADES

HIDDEN PINES

Naval Coastal Systems Center Panama City

Captain Anderson's Marina

Bay Point Resort Golf Club

Grand Lagoon

▶ Boats to Shell Island

▶ 6: Panama City Drive, St. Andrews State Park & Shell Island

Alligator Bayou

Ripley's Believe It or Not!

WonderWorks

Shipwreck Island Waterpark

County Pier

OPEN SANDS

PIER PARK

City Pier

Gulf World Marine Park

SEE INSET

■ ACCOMMODATION

Campers Inn	4
Flamingo Motel and Tower	2
Holiday Inn Resort	3
Marriott's Legends Edge at Bay Point	5
Osprey On the Gulf	7
Palmetto Inn	1
St Andrews State Park Campground	6

● CAFÉS & RESTAURANTS

Andy's Flour Power	7
Another Broken Egg	3
Barefoot Hide A Way Grill	2
Capt. Anderson's	8
Dusty's Oyster Bar	10
Fatty Patty's Cakes & Café	5
Firefly	4
Liza's Kitchen	6
Pompano Joe's	11
Schooners	9
Shuckum's Oyster Pub & Seafood Grill	1

■ BARS & CLUBS

Club La Vela	2
Hofbräu Beer Garden	5
Margaritaville	6
Pineapple Willy's	3
Spinnaker	1
Tootsie's Orchid Lounge	4

PIER PARK

Pier Park

Grand Theatre

Miracle Strip

Gulf of Mexico

0 | 200 yards

0 | 1 mile

PIER PARK TOP 10

The giant **Pier Park** development at the western end of the beach, a blend of shops, restaurants and bars, has rapidly become the de facto **"downtown"** of Panama City Beach. The initial Boardwalk section runs inland from Front Beach Road at City Pier along Pier Park Drive, while the more standard Town Center shopping mall lies a short walk behind this. Parking (free) is easy on all sides of the complex. This list is arranged heading inland from Front Beach Road. Regular mall hours are Mon–Sat 10am–9pm and Sun noon–6pm, though bars and restaurants stay open later.

Pompano Joe's 16202 Front Beach Rd ☎850 233 1790, ⓦpompano-joes.com. Beach shack restaurant with a Caribbean theme and plenty of seafood. Daily 11am–10pm.

Margaritaville 16230 Front Beach Rd ☎850 235 7870, ⓦmargaritavillepanamacitybeach .com. Jimmy Buffet's empire comes to Panama City – it's a bit cheesy, but after a few cocktails it's a lot more fun, and the sea views are exceptional. Daily 11am–11pm.

Del Sol 801 S Pier Park Drive ☎850 234 1000, ⓦdelsol.com. The Caribbean's largest clothing retailer, best known for clothing that changes colour in the sun. Daily 10am–9pm.

Earthbound Trading 800 Pier Park Drive ☎850 234 6631, ⓦearthboundtrading.com. Slightly hippy, multicultural merchandise. Mon–Sat 10am–9pm, Sun 10am–6pm.

Hofbräu Beer Garden 701 Pier Park Drive ☎850 235 4632, ⓦhofbraupcb.com. Bavarian-style brewpub, with high-quality beers and food on offer. Mon–Wed 11am–10pm, Thurs & Fri 11am–2am, Sat 10am–11pm, Sun 10am–10pm.

Tootsie's Orchid Lounge 700 Pier Park Drive ☎850 236 3459, ⓦtootsies.net. This huge purple-painted bar is part of the Nashville chain founded in 1960, featuring live country music and staple bar food. Daily 11am–3am (reduced hours Nov–Feb).

Peace Frog 701 Pier Park Drive ☎850 230 3964, ⓦpeacefrogs.com. Cool clothes shop selling line of T-shirts and ecofriendly clothing. Mon–Sat 10am–9pm, Sun noon–6pm.

Déjà Vu 700 Pier Park Drive ☎850 267 0293, ⓦshopdejavu.com. Boutique fashion store from Southern designer Stephanie Carter. Mon–Sat 10am–9pm, Sun noon–6pm.

Grand Theatre 500 South Pier Park Drive ☎850 233 4835, ⓦthegrandtheatre.com. Huge Cineplex and IMAX complex. Tickets $6.50–7. Movies daily from 12.30pm.

Miracle Strip 284 Powell Adams Rd (adjacent to Pier Park) ⓦms-pp.com. Old-style funfair rides rescued from a much-loved but now-defunct 1960s theme park, including a Ferris wheel and carousel (one ride $4, twelve rides $40). April to mid-Aug Mon–Fri 4pm–midnight, Sat & Sun noon–midnight; Sept & Oct Fri 5–10pm, Sat noon–10pm, Sun noon–7pm.

high-tech games, hands-on exhibits and simulations that will keep kids enthralled for half a day. The activities are designed as a fun way to introduce scientific principles – a simulation of 74mph winds to mimic hurricanes, a gallery of paintings that contain optical illusions and a tank of freezing cold water you can test with your hand, to experience what the Atlantic was like the day the *Titanic* sank. The displays end with a ropes course ($9.99) and a good old-fashioned video arcade (you need coins for the latter). Opposite, it's hard to miss the mock *Titanic* housing the ubiquitous **Ripley's Believe It or Not!** (daily 10am–6pm; $17.99; ⓦripleyspanamacitybeach.com), offering more family fun, with the emphasis on the weird and wacky rather than the educational.

Gulf World Marine Park

15412 Front Beach Rd · Daily 9.30am, closing times vary throughout the year · $28, children 5–11 $18 · ☎850 234 5271, ⓦgulfworldmarinepark.com

Allow about three hours to wander around **Gulf World Marine Park**, a 20,000-square-foot open-air aquarium, where you can see dolphin, sea lion and tropical bird shows, as well as view sharks and giant turtles being fed (most are rescued animals), alligators and a touch tank full of friendly stingrays.

9

SCUBA DIVING AT PANAMA CITY BEACH

While not as warm as the waters farther south, the Gulf of Mexico around Panama City Beach offers a greater variety of dive sites than is typically found elsewhere in Florida. Besides the natural reefs that lie a few miles offshore at depths of between eighty and a hundred feet, the coastal waters include some fifty artificial reefs created by the Panama City Marine Institute as an aid to marine research. Known as the "Wreck Capital of the South", Panama City Beach also offers divers the opportunity of poking around a number of sunken ships, including a 441ft World War II Liberty ship, a 160ft coastal freighter and, most famously, the 465ft **Empire Mica**, a large freighter that was torpedoed and sunk in World War II.

The best time for diving in Panama City Beach is from April to September, when water temperatures are at their warmest. Of the several **dive shops** along the beach, try Panama City Dive Center, 4823 Thomas Drive (☎850 235 3390, ⊕pcdivecenter.com), for dive packages, courses and equipment rental (day-dives from $85).

Shipwreck Island Waterpark

12201 Hutchison Blvd · Daily late April to mid-Aug 10.30am–4.30pm (5pm June & July) · $33.99; $28.99 35–50 inches in height; free for under 35 inches · ☎850 234 3333, ⊕shipwreckisland.com

Gambling on the notion people would pay for the privilege of being tossed and turned in water (when they could get it for free in the Gulf of Mexico over the road), this water park built its reputation around a pool that produces 3ft waves roughly every ten minutes. So far at least, the venture appears to have paid off, and the wave pool, thrilling slides, and a play area for the kids make this a good break from a day on the beach.

St Andrews State Park

4607 State Park Lane · Daily 8am–sunset · Cars $8, single occupant $4, pedestrians and cyclists $2; bike rentals $18/day · ☎850 233 5140, ⊕floridastateparks.org/standrews

One of the region's real highlights, spend at least one day enjoying the pristine waters and 1000 acres of untrammelled wilderness at **St Andrews State Park**, right at the eastern end of Panama City Beach. The brilliant white beaches here are wild and undeveloped gems, while a further 800 acres of untouched **Shell Island**, across the inlet, is also part of the reserve. The **beach** is the main focus, running from the 500ft **Gulf Pier**, popular with fishermen, to the **Jetties** area, popular with surfers on the seaward side. Families make for the inlet-side of Jetties, where the namesake stone walls have created a safe, calm swimming lagoon perfect for snorkelling and observing the flocks of pelicans offshore.

On the lagoon-side side of the park you can rent boats, jet skis and kayaks ($35/half-day) from the concession stand, or take the pontoon boat across to Shell Island (see below).

To make the most of the inland areas, visit in the early morning or late afternoon (or camp here): **coyotes** stalk the plentiful **white-tailed deer** that live in the woods (and keep clear of humans), while the whole park is a magnet for birdlife, including **osprey**. The island in man-made **Gator Lake** is smothered in nesting **egrets** February to May, while the resident **alligators** get frisky during the May-to-June mating season (you'll see them all year). Trails also lead around the **Buttonwood Marsh** at the centre of the park, especially colourful when the trees bloom in spring. Take advantage of the campground (see opposite) to enjoy the quietest times in the park.

Shell Island

Daily 8am–sunset · Ferries depart every 30min, daily 9am–5pm May–Aug · Round-trip $16.95, children 2–12 $8.95 · ☎850 233 0504, ⊕shellislandshuttle.com

Just a short pontoon-boat ride across from the main section of St Andrews State Park, **Shell Island** is a dazzling seven-mile strip of sand and a haven for shell collectors and sun worshippers alike. As there's no shade on the island, sunglasses and hats are essential; the glare off the sands can be blinding. There's also nothing in the way of facilities – bring all food and plenty of water with you. **Shell Island Shuttle** ferries run through the summer, every thirty minutes or so, but you can visit any time if you rent a pontoon boat ($285/day) or kayak. Snorkelling ($24.95) and kayak ($55/day) packages, which include the ferry ride, are available from St Andrews park concessions. There are also numerous boat trips to Shell Island from Captain Anderson's Marina (ⓦcaptandersonsmarina.com) back in Panama City Beach. Prices vary wildly among tour operators, so shop around.

ARRIVAL AND DEPARTURE
PANAMA CITY BEACH

By plane Most flights to Northwest Florida Beaches International Airport, 6300 West Bay Pkwy (ⓣ850 763 6751, ⓦiflybeaches.com), 13 miles north of the beach, route via larger hubs such as Atlanta. All the major car rental companies have desks at the airport, but you'll have to take a taxi otherwise.

By bus Greyhound buses only go as far as Panama City (917 Harrison Ave ⓣ850 785 6111). To get to the beach

you'll have to take a taxi, or bus #4, then change to bus #7 (Mon–Sat 6am–8pm; hourly, Sat every 2hr; $1.50).
Destinations Gainesville (2 daily; 5hr 40min–6hr 10min); Miami (1 daily; 14hr 55min); Orlando (3 daily; 8hr 10min–9hr); Pensacola (3 daily; 3hr) via Fort Walton Beach (3 daily; 1hr 50min); Tallahassee (3 daily; 2hr 15min); Tampa (1 daily; 12hr).

INFORMATION AND GETTING AROUND

By bus Bay Town Trolley (ⓣ850 769 0557, ⓦbaytown trolley.org) provides bus services year-round Monday through Saturday in Panama City itself and the beach: buses #7 and #8 (Mon–Sat 6am–8pm; hourly, Sat every 2hr) run along the beachfront, meeting at the Panama City Beach Senior Center. One-way fares are $1.50; day-passes are $4.

By scooter If you don't have a car, you can rent a scooter

(around $45/day; driving licence necessary) from any of the myriad beach shops; try Classic Rentals (ⓣ850 230 5187, ⓦclassicrntlsinc.com) at 13226 or 17280 Front Beach Rd.
Tourist information Visitor Information Center at 17001 Panama City Beach Pkwy (daily 8am–5pm; ⓣ800 722 3224, ⓦvisitpanamacitybeach.com). The airport information desk opens daily at 8am until the last flight arrives.

ACCOMMODATION

Campers Inn 8800 Thomas Drive ⓣ866 872 2267, ⓦcampersinn.net. Offers camping close to the beach (and nightlife, so can be noisy), as well as on-site amenities including fishing supplies, laundry and grocery stores. Suitable for RVs and tents, but also features basic log cabins with electricity and a/c. Camping from $27.95, cabins $64.95

Flamingo Motel and Tower 15525 Front Beach Rd ⓣ850 234 2232, ⓦflamingomotel.com. It's not fancy and can get noisy in the summer, but this large beach motel, half a mile east of City Pier, is superb value ($49 in winter): it features a tropical garden on the beach and kitchen-equipped rooms in the tower. The cheaper rooms are on the non-beach side of the road. Free but weak wi-fi. $99

Holiday Inn Resort 11127 Front Beach Rd ⓣ850 230 4080, ⓦhipcbeach.com. One of the most centrally located and comfortable hotels on the beach. All 340 rooms have balconies overlooking the palm-fringed cascading pool – a useful aid to socializing for the young crowd that tends to congregate here. Free wi-fi. $119

Marriott's Legends Edge at Bay Point 4000 Marriott Drive ⓣ850 236 4200, ⓦmarriott.com. This is one of the

more luxurious condo resort options around, with two-bedroom villas, balconies overlooking the pool (it's not on the beach, though higher floors have sea views), fully equipped kitchens and free wi-fi. $219

Osprey On the Gulf 15801 Front Beach Rd ⓣ850 234 0303, ⓦospreymotel.com. This family-friendly, large beachfront motel offers heated pool, hot tub and beach bar, and guests can also use the shuffleboard and volleyball facilities at the nearby Driftwood Lodge. Rooms are simply furnished but clean and have full kitchens. $125

★**Palmetto Inn** 17255 Front Beach Rd ⓣ850 234 2121, ⓦpalmettomotel.com. This modern, friendly, family-owned motel on the beach offers spacious suites with kitchens, heated pool (open late), a full range of beach activities and a free airport shuttle. Limited parking. No under-25s (unless part of a family) allowed. $95

★**St Andrews State Park Campground** 4607 State Park Lane ⓣ800 326 3521, ⓦreserveamerica.com. If you like camping right on the water, then this is the spot for you. The 176 sites include electricity and water hook-ups, and there are showers and toilets on-site. The Camp Store provides groceries. Sites from $28

9

EATING AND DRINKING

★**Andy's Flour Power** 3123 Thomas Drive (north of Grand Lagoon) ☎850 230 0014, ⌨andysflourpower.com. This local favourite is a real gem, with outstanding, fresh ingredients and all cakes, muffins and breads made in-house: the spinach, feta and tomato rolled omelette ($6.45) is a perfectly seasoned treat, while the French toast ($6.95), made with baguette and topped with strawberries is exquisite. Try to squeeze in a bowl of the exceptional cheese grits ($1.95), made with Vermont cheddar. Mon–Sat 7am–2pm, Sun 8am–2pm.

Another Broken Egg 11535 Hutchison Blvd ☎850 249 2007, ⌨anotherbrokenegg.com. For something different for breakfast make for this Louisiana chain, which serves exceptional omelettes (try the lobster and brie; $15), a sensational crab-cake eggs Benedict ($14) and specials such as blackberry grits ($3.30) and addictive biscuit beignets ($5). Daily 7am–2pm.

Barefoot Hide A Way Grill 15405 Front Beach Rd ☎850 249 2031, ⌨bythesearesorts.com/barefoot-beach-club. Beachfront bar and restaurant where you could happily spend a lazy afternoon soaking up the views and the beers or cocktails. The fish taco ($9.95) is a great choice for lunch. Daily 11am–10pm.

Capt. Anderson's 5551 N Lagoon Drive, Captain Anderson's Marina ☎850 234 2225, ⌨captandersons.com. Since 1967, this stalwart has offered fresh seafood dishes (around $19–29) including grilled bay shrimp ($18.95), and a good enough selection of steaks to satisfy meat eaters. It also doubles as a top-quality seafood market, and sells amazing Key lime pie. Mon–Fri 4.30–9pm, Sat 4.30–10pm; closed mid-Nov to Jan.

★**Dusty's Oyster Bar** 16450 Front Beach Rd ☎850 233 0035. The world's fastest oyster shuckers rule at this no-frills oyster emporium, where pitchers of beer ($5) come with plastic cups and oysters served on trays. Be prepared for long waits to be seated at dinner. Mon–Sat 11am–11pm.

Fatty Patty's Cakes & Café 948 Thomas Drive ☎850 236 9276, ⌨fattypattys.com. Fabulous home-cooked breakfasts ($6.50–10.50), as well as tasty burgers ($10), salads ($6–11) and crab cakes ($9). Cakes are made to order. Mon–Sat 6am–2pm.

★**Firefly** 535 Richard Jackson Blvd (in the Edgewater Shoppes) ☎850 249 3359, ⌨fireflypcb.com. Panama City's best fine-dining restaurant offers an eclectic and well-executed menu with standouts like a perfectly seasoned "she crab soup" ($8), a superb avocado Caprese salad ($9) and local snapper ($30), as well as extensive sushi, wine and martini lists. The Obamas dined here in 2010. Mains $23–43. Daily 5–10pm.

Liza's Kitchen 7328 Thomas Drive (Mirabella Square) ☎850 233 9000, ⌨lovelizas.com. Great spot for a light lunch or takeaway picnic, build your own sandwiches ($5–8.50) and weekend brunch items like chicken biscuit ($5.95). Mon–Fri 11am–4pm, Sat & Sun 9am–3pm.

Schooners 5121 Gulf Drive ☎850 235 3555, ⌨schooners.com. It may not be the "last local beach club", but it's been open since the late 1960s and you can enjoy fresh seafood (try the grilled grouper sandwiches; $15) and listen to live music – plus they shoot off a cannon every night at sunset. Dinner mains range $17–27. Mon–Fri 11am–late, Sat & Sun 8.45am–late.

Shuckum's Oyster Pub & Seafood Grill 15614 Front Beach Rd ☎850 235 3214, ⌨shuckums.com. Cheap, fresh Apalachicola oysters raw, baked and fried since 1967, with delicious oyster poboy sandwiches ($15). Daily 11am till the oysters run out.

NIGHTLIFE AND ENTERTAINMENT

Club La Vela 8813 Thomas Drive ☎850 235 1061, ⌨clublavela.com. Complex featuring dozens of bars, several dancefloors, live bands and a predominantly under-25 clientele eagerly awaiting the bikini and wet T-shirt contests and "hunk shows". During the day, the action is by the clubs' open-air pools. Cover charges vary nightly (generally $10–15). Wed, Fri & Sat 11am–4am, Sun 11am–5pm; open daily during Spring Break.

Pineapple Willy's 9875 S Thomas Drive ☎850 235 1225, ⌨pwillys.com. Legendary sports bar on the beach, with a newer pier bar right over the water, finger-licking ribs ($24) and the "Pineapple Willy" cocktail (Myer's rum, pineapple juice and coconut cream; $15), invented here in 1985. Daily 11.30am–midnight.

Spinnaker 8795 Thomas Drive ☎850 234 7882, ⌨spinnakerbeachclub.com. This beach club (next door to *Club La Vela*) has been rockin' since the 1970s, famous for its "takes two hands to hold 'em burgers" ($10–14) and barbecue during the day (at the *Paradise Grill*), as well its boisterous club nights. Cover charges vary nightly (usually $5–15). Paradise Grill daily 11am–2am; club open Fri–Sun 10pm–4am; daily during Spring Break. Closed Nov–Feb.

The South Walton beaches

West of Panama City Beach, the motels eventually give way to the more rugged and less developed **beaches of South Walton County**: fifty miles of some of Florida's best-kept coastline. With some notable exceptions, accommodation here is in resort complexes with sky-high rates, but it's a gorgeous area to spend a few days. **Hwy-30A** (far superior to US-98, which takes an inland route) links the region's small Gulf-coast communities starting at **Rosemary Beach** (⊕rosemarybeach.com) and **Alys Beach** (⊕alysbeach.com), both "New Urbanist" resort towns just off US-98 designed in the late 1990s.

Deer Lake State Park and Seagrove Beach

6721 Hwy-30A • Daily 8am–sunset • Cars $3, pedestrians and cyclists $2 • ☎ 850 267 8300, ⊕ floridastateparks.org/deerlake

Ten miles west of Panama City Beach, **Deer Lake State Park** is a dramatic stretch of creamy-white sand dunes on a coastline studded with driftwood. The best beach of the South Walton bunch, it somehow goes almost without mention in the area's tourist brochures. The road signposted "Deer Lake Park" ends at a car park, and a five-minute walk through scrubland leads to the beach, a favourite hideout for nude sunbathing – officially, it's forbidden, but the rules are enforced infrequently.

A few miles west, the community of **SEAGROVE BEACH** shares the same attractive shoreline as Deer Lake Park. If you're keen to **cycle** or **paddle** around, **Butterfly Bike & Kayak**, 3657 Hwy-30A (daily 8am–6pm; ☎850 231 2826, ⊕butterflybikeandkayakrentals .com), is a good place to start.

Eden Gardens State Park

181 Eden Gardens Rd (Hwy-395) • Daily 8am–sunset • Cars $4, pedestrians and cyclists $2; tours $4 • ☎ 850 267 8320,
⊕ floridastateparks.org/edengardens

Away from the coast road, only 115-acre **Eden Gardens State Park**, reached by Hwy-395 from Seagrove Beach, is worth a detour. The gardens, now disturbed only by the buzz of dragonflies, were once the base of the Wesley Lumber Company, which helped decimate Florida's forests during the 1890s timber boom. Impressed with the setting of moss-draped live oaks, William Henry Wesley pinched some of the wood to build himself a grandiose two-storey plantation-style home in 1897, the **Wesley House** (guided tours on the hour Mon & Thurs–Sun 10am–3pm). After the death of the last Wesley in 1953, the house stood empty for ten years until Lois Maxon, a journalist with an interest in antiques, bought it in 1963 as a showcase for her collections, which include a Chippendale cabinet and a Louis XV mirror.

Seaside and Watercolor

⊕ seasidefl.com

An exception to the casual, unplanned appearance of most South Walton beach towns, **SEASIDE**, just west of Seagrove Beach, is an experiment in urban architecture (aka "New Urbanism") begun in 1981 by a rich, idealistic developer named Robert Davies. The theory was that Seaside's pseudo-Victorian cottages, all in gleaming pastels and incredibly well kept, would foster village-like neighbourliness and instil a sense of community. In reality, they did nothing of the sort, and it's basically a wealthy and sterile resort these days, blurring into the similarly designed enclave of **WATERCOLOR**. Still, there's no escaping the unique appeal of the streets and the half-moon curve of Central Square on Hwy-30; the shops are interesting and unusual, offering high-quality arts and crafts, gourmet food and expensive clothing, and the beach is fantastic.

Grayton Beach

Grayton Beach State Park 357 Main Park Rd • Daily 8am–sunset • Cars $5, single occupant $4, pedestrians and cyclists $2 •
☎ 850 267 8300, ⊕ floridastateparks.org/graytonbeach

An utter contrast to Seaside lies just a few miles further along, off Hwy-30A on Hwy-283 (DeFuniak St), at **GRAYTON BEACH**, whose secluded position and ramshackle

9

wooden dwellings have taken the fancy of a number of artists who now reside here. Many who visit Grayton skip straight through to **Grayton Beach State Park**, just east of the village. The park is walled by sand dunes and touches the banks of a large, brackish lake – you can also camp here (see below).

Blue Mountain Beach and Santa Rosa Beach

Just west of Grayton Beach, the relatively undiscovered **BLUE MOUNTAIN BEACH** is a welcome escape from the Spring Break crowds. The quiet beach here is an expanse of creamy white sand bordered by vacation homes.

A mile further west is **SANTA ROSA BEACH**. Slightly more developed than Blue Mountain, Santa Rosa pads out its beach life with shopping- and leisure-focused attractions, as well as some good eating options. Beyond Santa Rosa, Hwy-30A swings north and rejoins US-98.

ARRIVAL AND INFORMATION

By car With no public transport to the area, you'll need a car to get here: Seagrove Beach is around 25 miles (40min) along the coast from Panama City Beach, and 5 miles from Blue Mountain Beach – the latter is around 20 miles (and 35min) from Destin via Hwy-30 W/US-98 W.

Tourist information Stop by the Visitor Information Center (daily 8.30am–5pm; ☎ 800 822 6877, ⓦ visitsouthwalton.com), at 23777 US-331 at the junction with US-98, 20 miles west of Panama City Beach (10 miles east of Destin) in Santa Rosa Beach.

SOUTH WALTON BEACHES

GETTING AROUND

By bus Though you'll have a lot more freedom with a car, Sunshine Turtle Express (ⓦ sunshineshuttle.com) offers free trolley bus rides between Blue Mountain Beach and Seagrove (via Seaside, Watercolor and Grayton Beach). The

bus runs daily (hourly), but only in the summer (11am–midnight; late May to Aug). The scheme was launched on a trial basis in 2014, so check the website to see if it's still operating.

ACCOMMODATION

SEAGROVE BEACH

Lisbeth's Bed & Breakfast By The Sea 3501 Hwy-30A ☎ 850 231 1577, ⓦ lisbethsbb.com. Good old-fashioned Southern hospitality (from owners Lisbeth and Tom) in a lovely antebellum-style house just across the road from the beach with beautifully decorated rooms and delightful breakfasts. Over-25s only. Free wi-fi. **$199**

GRAYTON BEACH

Grayton Beach State Park Campground 357 Main Park Rd ☎ 800 326 3521, ⓦ reserveamerica.com. This rustic campsite off the beach is quiet (at night) and well

maintained. The cabins are basic but clean, with screened porch, BBQ grill and rocking chairs. No TVs or wi-fi. Pitches **$24–30**, cabins from **$110**

★ **Hibiscus Coffee & Guesthouse** 85 DeFuniak St ☎ 850 231 2733, ⓦ hibiscusflorida.com. Unusual option on this stretch of coast, which serves up a delicious (vegetarian) breakfast and also offers accommodation in nine eclectic and comfortable rooms – four in the coffeehouse building and five in Bert's Barn, a renovated 1904 house, as well as a standalone cottage and two luxury flats. Doubles **$125**, flats **$235**, cottage **$155**

EATING AND DRINKING

SEAGROVE BEACH

Café Thirty-A 3899 Hwy-30A ☎ 850 231 2166, ⓦ cafethirtya.com. You'll find upmarket dining at this stylish place, with wood oven-fired pizzas ($14–15) and bar serving mainly fish and meat dishes in a casual atmosphere. Mains $28–38. Daily 5–9pm.

SEASIDE

Bud and Alley's 2236 Hwy-30A ☎ 850 231 5900, ⓦ budandalleys.com. Offers a variety of high-quality seafood dishes (try the steamed Cedar Key clams; $13) and

sandwiches ($11–15), overlooking the bay and those spectacular sunsets. Dinner mains $25–34. Daily 11.30am–3pm & 5.30–9.30pm.

★ **The MeltDown on Hwy-30A** 2235 Hwy-30A ☎ 850 231 5686. Reasonably priced (for Seaside) food truck (one of several Airstream trailers in the square), with justly celebrated grilled-cheese sandwiches (from $5) and hefty Cubans ($8). Try the bacon jam grilled biscuit ($5) for breakfast. Daily 8am–8pm.

Modica Market 109 Central Square ☎ 850 231 1214, ⓦ modicamarket.com. For luscious cakes (including the legendary chocolate cake) and gourmet picnic supplies, head for this well-stocked grocery store (they also serve draft beer and lunch specials from $11). Daily 7am–7pm.

GRAYTON BEACH

Borago 80 Hwy-30A ☎ 850 231 9167. Head here for a delicious Italian dinner, with a tasty antipasti menu including Parmesan-fried oysters and pan-seared scallops. Pastas range $15–22, mains $25–35. Daily 6–9pm; closed Sun Jan & Feb, and two weeks after Thanksgiving.

★**The Red Bar** 70 Hotz Ave ☎ 850 231 1008, ⓦ theredbar.com. If all the relaxing on the beach has you itching for a night out, pop by *The Red Bar*, formally the old Grayton Store built in 1937. Open for breakfast, lunch and dinner, this funky restaurant serves a variety of fresh salads and mains before morphing into a live music venue that stays hopping into the night. Daily 11am–3pm & 5–11pm (bar open till midnight Fri & Sat).

BLUE MOUNTAIN & SANTA ROSA BEACH

Blue Mountain Beach Creamery 2129 S Hwy-83 (at Hwy-30), Blue Mountain ☎ 850 278 6849. Take a break at this strategically located ice-cream specialist (think toasted coconut and pineapple, coffee toffee); they also sell home-made frozen yoghurt and sorbet (single cone or dish $3.95). Daily noon–10pm.

Café Tango 14 Vicki St, Santa Rosa Beach ☎ 850 267 0054. Serves some of the best food in the area including the shrimp and crab gnocchi ($14) and excellent pistachio-crusted grouper, which you can pair with any of eighty choices on the extensive wine list. The intimate dining room is in a little red-and-green cottage dating from 1945. Mains $28–38. Daily 6–10pm.

Stinky's Fish Camp 5960 Hwy-30A ☎ 850 267 3053, ⓦ stinkysfishcamp.com. Don't be fooled by the wacky name – this is a high-quality fish shack, with crawfish pie, grilled shrimp with pasta, catfish, fish stew and fresh fish of the day (mains $18–35). Mon–Sat 11am–10pm, Sun 10am–10pm.

Destin and around

Some 47 miles northwest of Panama City lies **DESTIN**, once a small fishing village and a cult name among anglers for the fat marlin and tuna lurking in an undersea canyon a few miles offshore. The resort town now boasts towering condos, glimmering in the heat haze as you approach, bearing witness to more than two decades of unrestrained exploitation that have stripped away much of the town's character – the beach retains its Gulf-coast charm, though, and the fishing is still exceptional. Destin has no public transport, so you'll need a car to get here.

Destin History and Fishing Museum

108 Stahlman Ave • Tues–Sat 10am–4pm • $5 • ☎ 850 837 6611, ⓦ destinhistoryandfishingmuseum.org

Evidence of Destin's sudden expansion can be found amid the fading photos in the **Destin History and Fishing Museum**, with over sixty mounted record-breaking catches and thousands of pictures of landed fish with their grinning captors, offering proof of Destin's high esteem among hook-and-line enthusiasts. The museum also includes the town's first post office building.

The beach

The enticing white sands just east of downtown Destin provide an escape from the condo overkill. The **beach** here is family territory, but it offers relaxation, excellent swimming and classic Gulf-coast sunsets. To reach it, take **Hwy-2378** (Scenic Gulf Drive), which makes a coast-hugging loop off US-98, starting about four miles east of Destin.

ARRIVAL AND DEPARTURE	DESTIN

By car Destin is easily accessible via Hwy-30/US-98, some 8 miles east of Fort Walton Beach, and 47 miles northwest of Panama City Beach (1hr 10min). There is no public transport.

9

ACCOMMODATION

Henderson Beach State Park 17000 Emerald Coast Pkwy ☎800 326 3521, ☜floridastateparks.org /hendersonbeach. This park of pristine beachfront, sand pines and scrub oaks has sixty campsites for tents or RVs, with water, electricity, picnic tables, ground grills and clothesline posts. The restrooms have showers, coin-operated washers, dryers and vending machines. **$30**

Henderson Park Inn 2700 US-98 ☎888 836 1105, ☜hendersonparkinn.com. Destin's most luxurious and romantic hotel, right on the water on the edge of Henderson State Park. Most rooms come with kitchenette, DVD player and free wi-fi, and everyone gets a bottle of wine, fresh grapes and flowers on arrival. **$169**

Hidden Dunes Beach & Tennis Resort 65 Pompano St ☎800 225 7652, ☜hiddendunesdestin.com. This 27-acre resort feels less commercial than the other Destin hotels, with a long strip of beach, six tennis courts and a choice of three- to four-bedroom beach villas, beach condos and Carolina-style cottages, perfect for families. **$227**

EATING AND DRINKING

The Back Porch 1740 US-98 ☎850 837 2022, ☜theback-porch.com. Destin's oldest seafood and oyster house (since 1974), serving celebrated smoked tuna dip ($10), fresh Apalachicola oysters and char-grilled amberjack ($13). Daily 11am–11pm.

Beach Walk Café Henderson Park Inn, 2700 US-98 ☎850 650 7100, ☜beachwalkhendersonpark.com. This oceanfront place offers award-winning fine dining in one of Destin's best hotels: think shrimp and grits ($27), New Zealand venison ($36) and grilled local grouper with melted leek-potato hash and mushrooms ($33). Daily 5.30–10pm.

★ **Buck's Smokehouse** 303 Harbor Blvd ☎850 837 3600, ☜bucksbarbq.com. This no-frills BBQ joint has garnered a loyal following for its sumptuous dry-rubbed meats served on butcher's paper ($12–14), oak-smoked turkey platters ($13.79), beans, rich sauces and home-made banana pudding ($3.75). Mon–Sat 11am–8pm.

Dewey Destin's Seafood 9 Calhoun Ave ☎850 837 7575, ☜destinseafood.com. Local favourite managed by the family of town founder Leonard Destin, where you can sit on a weathered dock overlooking Crab Island (actually an underwater sandbar). If you feel like sharing some of your terrific stuffed shrimp ($18.95) or soft shell crabs, there are plenty of pelicans nearby to take leftovers off your hands. Mains $13–20. Daily 11am–9pm.

Okaloosa Island and Fort Walton Beach

US-98 leaves Destin by rising over the **Destin Bridge**, offering towering views of the two-tone ocean and intensely white sands, before hitting the crazy-golf courses and amusement parks of **OKALOOSA ISLAND**. The island's spectacular sugary-white **beaches** are more enticing, kept in their unspoiled state by their owner – the US Air Force – and making a lively weekend playground for local youths and high-spirited beach bums.

Some seven miles west of Destin, the neon motel signs greeting arrivals to **FORT WALTON BEACH** offer no indication this was the site of a major religious and social centre during the Paleo-Indian period – so important were the finds made here that the place came to be associated with a rigid form of tribal society, the so-called "**Fort Walton Culture**" (see below). These days it's military culture that dominates, as the town is home to Hurlburt Field and Eglin, the country's biggest Air Force base. Aside from a few crewcuts and topless bars, however, you'll see little evidence of the bases close to US-98, and much of Fort Walton Beach has a more downbeat and homely feel – and slightly lower prices – than Destin.

Heritage Park & Cultural Center

139 Miracle Strip Pkwy (US-98) • Indian Temple Mound Museum June–Aug Mon–Sat 10am–4.30pm; Sept–May Mon–Fri noon–4.30pm, Sat 10am–4.30pm; other museums open Mon–Sat noon–4pm (Sept–May 1–3pm) • $5 • ☎850 833 9595, ☜fwb.org/museum

Now virtually hidden beneath a thick canopy of palm trees and tropical foliage beside the busy highway into Fort Walton Beach, **Fort Walton Temple Mound** is preserved within the **Heritage Park & Cultural Center** complex. Built between 800 and 1400 AD, the earth mound is thought to have served as a religious centre and what remains is 12ft tall and 223ft across. Get oriented at the **Indian Temple Mound Museum**, where over a thousand stone, bone, shell and clay Native American artefacts are displayed, with a fine collection of prehistoric ceramics. Adjacent buildings include the

Camp Walton Schoolhouse Museum (the old pine and oak schoolhouse opened in 1912), the **Garnier Post Office Museum**, dating back to 1918, and the **Civil War Exhibit Building**, a relatively new addition charting Florida's experience in the US Civil War.

Gulfarium Marine Adventure Park

1010 Miracle Strip Pkwy (US-98), Okaloosa Island • Daily 9am–4.30pm (3.30pm Oct–April) • $19.95, children 3–12 $11.95 • ☏ 850 243 9046, ⓦ gulfarium.com

The most popular attraction in the area is the world's oldest marine show and aquarium: **Gulfarium Marine Adventure Park**. Opened in 1955, it's still one of the best aquariums in the area, with all kinds of sea life on display. Sharks, moray eels and sea turtles cruise around relatively natural habitats and other exhibits include penguins, otters and stingrays. A programme of dolphin and sea lion shows, each lasting about twenty minutes, is scheduled throughout the day.

ARRIVAL AND INFORMATION   FORT WALTON BEACH

By bus Fort Walton Beach is one of the few towns on this stretch of coast served by Greyhound buses. The bus station is at 101 Perry Ave SE, a 15min walk from the bay and the bridge to Okaloosa Island.
Destinations Panama City (3 daily; 1hr 30min); Pensacola (3 daily; 1hr 10min); Tallahassee (3 daily; 3hr 55min–4hr

10min).
Tourist information Emerald Coast Convention & Visitors Bureau, 1540 Miracle Strip Pkwy (US-98), Fort Walton Beach (Mon–Fri 8am–5pm, Sat & Sun 9am–4pm; ☏ 850 651 7131, ⓦ emeraldcoastfl.com).

ACCOMMODATION

Aunt Martha's Bed and Breakfast 315 Shell Ave SE ☏ 850 243 6702, ⓦ auntmarthasbedandbreakfast .com. A little gem right off US-98. Rooms are comfortable (all have waterfront views) and the full, hot breakfasts are delicious. **$105**
The Breakers 381 Santa Rosa Blvd, Okaloosa Island ☏ 850 244 9127, ⓦ breakersfwb.com. Spacious one-, two- or three-bedroom beachfront condos with full

kitchens and access to two pools, tennis court and the beach. Free wi-fi throughout. Rates drop by fifty percent off season. **$252**
Venus Condos 885 Santa Rosa Blvd, Okaloosa Island ☏ 850 301 9600, ⓦ venuscondos.com. This more affordable condo-style rental offers ageing but comfy one- to three-bedroom units, with rates dropping to just $101 in winter. Free wi-fi. **$151**

EATING AND DRINKING

Old Bay Steamer 102 Santa Rosa Blvd, Okaloosa Island ☏ 850 664 2795, ⓦ oldbaysteamerfwb.com. Delicious fresh seafood and pasta dishes served in a no-frills dining room just off the beach; piles of steamed lobster, snow crab, king crab, shrimp, oysters, mussels and clams are on offer ($17–29). Daily 4–11pm.
Pandora's 1226 Santa Rosa Blvd, Okaloosa Island ☏ 850 244 8669, ⓦ pandorassteakhouse.com. This 1970s throwback remains a top-notch steakhouse, with a classic mahogany interior and perfectly cooked slabs of

meat over a wood-fired grill – no wonder Bob Hope used to dine here. Steaks range $25.95 to $43.95 for the rib-eye. Tues–Thurs & Sun 5–10pm, Fri & Sat 5–10.30pm.
Props Brewery & Grill 255 Miracle Strip Pkwy ☏ 850 586 7117, ⓦ propsbrewery.com. Best burgers (from $9) on the coast and tasty craft beers make this a local favourite, with brews such as Flying Coffin IPA made on-site (inside the Publix shopping centre). Daily 11am–midnight.

Fort Walton to Pensacola: Hwy-399

If you're heading **west from Fort Walton**, branch off Hwy-30/US-98 along **Hwy-399**. The road runs sixty scenic miles along **Santa Rosa Island** to Pensacola Beach (see p.441), cutting through a stunning landscape of untouched beach and scrub reminiscent of a desert.

Navarre Beach

Navarre Beach, just beyond where Hwy-399 curves north to cross the Pensacola Sound, is one of the loveliest stretches of reef dunes and sand on the Panhandle coast. In some places along this stretch there are no lifeguards, so swim in the sea at your own risk.

★ **Juana's Pagodas/Sailors' Grill** 1451 Navarre Beach Causeway ☎ 850 939 2130, ⊚ juanaspagodas.com. Two *palapa*-style thatch huts at the end of the causeway mark these sister joints, serving the best food in Navarre Beach. *Sailor's* is the main restaurant (the breakfasts are scrumptious and the Key lime pie is legendary), while *Juana's* is the beach bar. Live music Thurs–Sun. Juana's daily 11am–late; Sailor's daily 8am–9pm.

Pensacola and around

Tucked away at the western end of the Panhandle, **PENSACOLA** offers an enticing dose of immaculate beaches, early Floridian history and attractions associated with the huge naval base here, not least the **National Naval Aviation Museum** and the **Blue Angels**. Built on the northern bank of the broad Pensacola Bay, five miles inland from the coast, the city also makes a good base for exploring one of the prettiest and least-spoiled parts of the Panhandle. Just across the Bay Bridge to the coast you'll find **Pensacola Beach** neighbouring the wild, protected beaches of the **Gulf Islands National Seashore**.

Brief history

In 1559, Spanish soldiers and colonists led by **Don Tristán de Luna y Arellano** established a settlement at Pensacola that lasted two years before being destroyed by a hurricane. A permanent Spanish settlement was established here in 1698, when **Santa María de Galve** was built on the site of the naval air base today. The colony was briefly occupied by the French before the Spanish moved the city to the location of today's downtown in 1752; it was the British, who arrived eleven years later, who expanded the fort and created the town plan that exists today. In 1821 Pensacola became the venue where Florida was officially ceded by Spain to the US. Pensacola was already a booming port at the turn of the nineteenth century, and the opening of the Panama Canal in 1914 was expected to further boost the city's fortunes. The surge in wealth never came, but the optimism of the era is apparent in the delicate ornamentation and detail of the buildings downtown.

The Palafox Historic District

Much of downtown Pensacola is preserved within the **Palafox Historic District**, easily explored on foot. Take a look first at the grand **Old Escambia County Court House**, at the junction of Palafox and Government streets, which was completed in 1887 as the customs house. Opposite at 226 S Palafox, the slender form and vertically aligned windows of the 141ft **Seville Tower** (aka Empire Building) exaggerate the height of what, in 1910, was the tallest building in Florida (built as a bank, it's office space today). The building overlooks shady **Plaza Ferdinand VII**, where a bust of Andrew Jackson marks the spot where he was inaugurated as Florida governor in 1821.

Quayside Art Gallery

17 E Zaragoza St • Mon–Sat 10am–5pm, Sun 1–5pm • Free • ☎ 850 438 2363, ⊚ quaysidegallery.com

One of Florida's most respected galleries, the artist-owned **Quayside Art Gallery** is always worth perusing, even if you don't intend to buy. The gallery occupies the pale pink former headquarters of the Germania Steam Fire Engine & Hose Company, constructed in the 1870s, and hosts shows of fine arts and crafts from the west Florida region.

Pensacola Museum of Art

407 S Jefferson St • Tues–Sat 10am–5pm • $7 • ☎ 850 432 6247, ⊚ pensacolamuseum.org

Cleverly incorporated into the old jailhouse, the **Pensacola Museum of Art** was built in 1906 on what was once the shoreline of Pensacola Bay (after ships started dumping

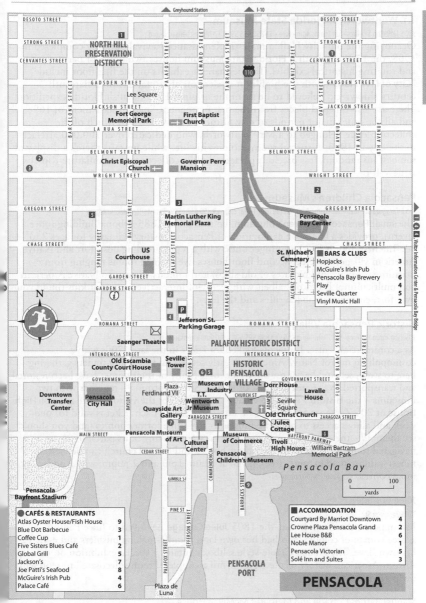

PENSACOLA

BARS & CLUBS
Hopjacks	3
McGuire's Irish Pub	1
Pensacola Bay Brewery	6
Play	4
Seville Quarter	5
Vinyl Music Hall	2

CAFÉS & RESTAURANTS
Atlas Oyster House/Fish House	9
Blue Dot Barbecue	3
Coffee Cup	1
Five Sisters Blues Café	2
Global Grill	5
Jackson's	7
Joe Patti's Seafood	8
McGuire's Irish Pub	4
Palace Café	6

ACCOMMODATION
Courtyard By Marriot Downtown	4
Crowne Plaza Pensacola Grand	2
Lee House B&B	6
Noble Manor	1
Pensacola Victorian	5
Solé Inn and Suites	3

their ballast stones, the shoreline was pushed out by half a mile). The temporary exhibits (major shows last around three months) are a mixed bag, with anything from the abstract work of Joan Miró to Japanese kimonos on display, but the building itself is worth exploring: old prison cells have been preserved as exhibition space and classrooms for children now occupy the former cell blocks.

9

T.T. Wentworth Jr Florida State Museum

330 S Jefferson St • Tues–Sat 10am–4pm • Free • ☎ 850 595 5990, ⓦ historicpensacola.org

Occupying the old City Hall, a majestic Renaissance Revival building completed in 1908, the **T.T. Wentworth Jr Florida State Museum** houses two floors of permanent and rotating historical exhibits. The permanent exhibits on the first floor include "**City of Five Flags**", with the highlight a selection of artefacts from a sixteenth-century shipwreck, believed to be from the original 1559 Spanish Florida expedition. There are also bits and pieces from the first permanent Spanish settlement of 1698, and all the other major periods of city history to the Civil War. Much of the collection once belonged to a Mr Wentworth, who dedicated over 100,000 artefacts to the city in 1983. A special room explores his life, while upstairs there's a display of some of his random, less precious garage-sale-like collections – a miniature Ripley's Believe It or Not.

Pensacola Children's Museum

115 E Zaragoza St • Tues–Sat 10am–4pm • $3 (all over 1 year old) • ☎ 850 433 1559, ⓦ historicpensacola.org

The small **Pensacola Children's Museum**, housed in the 1885 Arbona Building (once a tavern), provides a hands-on exploration of Pensacola history primarily for ages 2 to 13. The first floor is for the younger ones, with a replica trading post, fort and Native American village, while the second floor houses five themed rooms ranging from maritime (displays and pictures of old ships) and military history, to Native American and multicultural Pensacola, albeit with plenty of interactive games for kids (build your own fort, costumes, wooden rifles and the like).

Historic Pensacola Village

205 E Zaragoza St • Tues–Sat 10am–4pm • $6 • ☎ 850 595 5985, ⓦ historicpensacola.org

As a commercial centre, Pensacola kicked into gear in the late 1700s with a cosmopolitan mix of Native Americans, early settlers and seafaring traders gathering here to swap, sell and barter on the waterfront. Many of their homes have been restored and transported to the area just east of Palafox Street, forming – together with two museums – the **Historic Pensacola Village**. Buy tickets at the visitor centre at **Tivoli High House** at 205 Zaragoza St, just east of Tarragona Street. Each ticket is valid for one week and allows access to both the museums and three former homes (and you should see them *all* – the effect of the whole is far greater than any of its parts) in an easily navigated four-block area. Another three houses and the old church can be viewed on ninety-minute **guided tours** (free), given at 11am, 1pm and 2.30pm, which adds a lot more context to the experience.

Julee Cottage

210 E Zaragoza St

Just opposite the Tivoli house, the 1805 **Julee Cottage** belonged to Julee Panton, a "freewoman of colour" who had her own land, candle-making business and even her own slave. The French Creole-style saltbox contains a special exhibition on the African-American history of the region, with a couple of rooms decorated to represent the period 1865–77.

Manuel Barrios Cottage and Margaret McMillan House

207 E Zaragoza St & 209 E Zaragoza St

Next door to the Tivoli house, the tiny **Manuel Barrios Cottage** was constructed around 1888 in typical Gulf Coast style, and contains a display on Pensacola in the 1920s. Next door again is the similar **Margaret McMillan House**, dedicated to Pensacola in the 1940s and World War II.

Museum of Commerce and Museum of Industry
201 E Zaragoza St & 200 E Zaragoza St

Occupying a nineteenth-century warehouse, the **Museum of Commerce** is an entertaining indoor re-creation of Palafox Street in its turn-of-the-twentieth-century heyday, displaying many of the original storefronts, shop fittings and a collection of antique printing presses. Much of the prosperity of Pensacola was based on the timber industry, a point celebrated by a noisy, working sawmill in the **Museum of Industry**, just across Zaragoza Street, housed in another old warehouse. Exhibits also highlight other early money-makers – fishing, brick-making and the railroad.

Tours

Guided tours are designed to walk you through several generations of Pensacola history, starting with the 1805 **Lavalle House** at 205 E Church St, a French Creole home furnished in the style of the 1820s. The 1871 **Dorr House** at 311 S Adams St is a stately two-storey Greek Revival mansion, ornately restored with period furniture and wallpaper – watch out for the wreath made out of human hair. You'll also visit the 1890 **Lear-Rocheblave House** at 214 E Zaragoza St, a pristine example of Victorian Folk architecture, and the venerable **Old Christ Church** on tranquil Seville Square, built in 1832 and one of the oldest churches in Florida.

North Hill Preservation District

Between 1870 and 1930, Pensacola's professional classes took a shine to the area now known as the **North Hill Preservation District**, north of the Palafox District, and commissioned elaborate homes in a plethora of fancy styles. Strewn across the tree-studded fifty-block area are pompous Neoclassical porches, cutesy Tudor Revival cottages, low-slung California-style bungalows, and rounded towers belonging to fine Queen Anne homes. These are private residences not open to the public, and the best way to see them is by walking or driving around Palafox, Spring, Strong and Baylen streets. Note especially the ornate Spanish Revival **Christ Episcopal Church** at Wright and Palafox, built in 1903, and the 1867 **Governor Perry Mansion** opposite, now part of the First United Methodist Church.

Naval Air Station Pensacola

The vast **Naval Air Station Pensacola** (NAS) covers nine square miles along the bay, six miles southwest of downtown. One of America's largest military training facilities, it's also the home of the **Blue Angels**, the nation's oldest flying aerobatic team (you can see them practice in the skies above the naval base on various days between April and October, at 11.30am – on Wednesdays the pilots show up at the aviation museum afterwards for autographs; see ⍟blueangels.navy.mil). The base contains a trio of enticing attractions and its main roads are open to the public, but you'll need to show your **driving licence** (or some kind of photo ID) to get in: the main entrance lies at the end of Navy Boulevard, while the back entrance is on Blue Angel Parkway.

Fort Barrancas

901 Taylor Rd • Daily: March–Oct 9.30am–4.45pm; Nov–Feb 8.30am–3.45pm • Free • ☎ 850 455 5167, ⍟ nps.gov/guis • Bus #57 (no Sun service)

The first sight you'll pass inside the base is **Fort Barrancas** overlooking the bay, part of the National Seashore area (see p.441) and a rare remnant of Spanish Pensacola. The original fort was built in 1698, but nothing remains of that structure: instead you can explore the half-moon **Spanish Water Battery**, a low-lying gun emplacement built in 1797, and the bulking main fort itself, its 20ft walls built by slaves for the American army 1839–44. The fort was part of a series designed to protect the US navy base in

9

Pensacola, with the main section linked to the water battery by a 45ft underground tunnel. In the main fort you can explore the fascinating system of connecting interior vaults known as the **Scarp Gallery**, while the tiny **visitor centre** has a twelve-minute video and exhibits that shed light on the complex history of the site. Guided tours of the complex run daily at 2pm (June–Aug only).

National Naval Aviation Museum

1750 Radford Blvd • Daily 9am–5pm • Free • ☎ 850 452 3604, ⓦ navalaviationmuseum.org • Bus #57 (no Sun service)

You don't have to be a military fanatic to enjoy the **National Naval Aviation Museum**, a mind-blowing assembly of planes from every era, history displays and some wildly entertaining simulation rides (and it's free). The museum underscores Pensacola's role as the home base of US naval aviation, where thousands of new pilots are trained each year. Get a taste of that experience by climbing into one of the **3-D flight simulators** on the second floor. The museum's collection of US naval aircraft, from the first flimsy seaplane acquired in 1911 to the Phantoms and Hornets of more recent times, are displayed in two massive halls and in Hangar Bay One. Highlights include the **NC-4 Flying Boat**, the first plane to cross the Atlantic (in 1919), and special sections on America's giant **aircraft carriers**, "four-and-a-half acres of sovereign US territory, anytime, anywhere". There's also a seven-storey-tall **IMAX theatre**, on which a pilot's-eye-view of flight makes for quite a visual sensation (tickets $8.75).

Pensacola Lighthouse & Museum

2081 Radford Blvd • Mon–Sat 10am–5.30pm, Sun noon–5.30pm • $6 • ☎ 850 393 1561, ⓦ pensacolalighthouse.org • Bus #57 (no Sun service)

On the other side of the road from the aviation museum, the **Pensacola Lighthouse & Museum** includes a climb up the landmark 1859 lighthouse (159ft), said to be the most haunted in America. Assuming you survive the ghosts and make it to the top (177 steps), you'll be able to view the stunning beaches on nearby Perdido Key. The museum in the restored 1869 keeper's quarters contains exhibits on the Native American Weedon Island culture, the first permanent Spanish colony of 1696, and the first Pensacola Lighthouse of 1824.

ARRIVAL AND DEPARTURE

PENSACOLA

By plane Pensacola International Airport, 2430 Airport Blvd (☎ 850 436 5005, ⓦ flypensacola.com), is 5 miles and a 15min drive or taxi ride ($15–17) from downtown, with most flights going through Atlanta, Dallas or Houston. Bus #63 serves the airport, but to get to downtown you need to change to Bus #41 at the PSC Transfer Center.

By bus Unfortunately, the Greyhound bus station is far from central, being 7 miles north of the city centre at 505 W Burgess Rd (☎ 850 476 8199); bus #60 links it to Pensacola proper.

Destinations Fort Walton Beach (3 daily; 1hr 10min); Mobile (4 daily; 1hr 5min); Orlando (4 daily; 9hr 40min–12hr 10min); Panama City (2 daily; 2hr 50min); Tallahassee (4 daily; 3hr 5min–5hr 30min).

By car Access to downtown Pensacola is made easy via I-110 from I-10, exit 12. You should find plenty of parking; meters and most lots charge 50¢/hr (free Sat & Sun), with the Jefferson Street Parking Garage, 53 S Jefferson St, charging a maximum $6 for the day ($2 after 6pm and on Sun).

PITCHER PLANT PRAIRIES

The closest thing in the real world to a triffid, the rare and carnivorous **white-topped pitcher plant** is preserved at the 4200-acre **Tarkiln Bayou Preserve State Park** (daily 8am–sunset; $3 per car; ☎ 850 492 1595, ⓦ floridastateparks.org/tarkilnbayou), just west of Pensacola on Hwy-293 (aka Bauer Rd). The best times to visit are the spring and autumn, when the flowers are in bloom and you'll see great clusters poking out between the long grass, with that distinctive tubular "mouth" drawing in unfortunate insects.

INFORMATION AND GETTING AROUND

By bus Escambia County Area Transit buses (☎ 850 595 3228 ext 30, ⓦ goecat.com) serve the city; bus #61 goes to Pensacola Beach three times daily (Mon–Sat); Beach Jumper (#64) runs more regularly, but just Fri–Sun. Bus #57 connects downtown with the attractions in the navy base, but only runs 6am–4pm every 90min or so (Mon–Sat). Fares to the beach are $2.35; elsewhere fares are $1.75. The Downtown Transfer Center is at the junction of Reus and Government streets.

By taxi Getting from the city centre to the beach by taxi will cost roughly $20–30 (and at least $25 to the National Naval Aviation Museum); try Yellow Cab (☎ 850 456 8294).

Tourist information At the foot of the Bay Bridge, on the city side, the Pensacola Bay Area Convention & Visitors Bureau Welcome Center, 1401 E Gregory St (Mon–Fri 8am–5pm, Sat 9am–4pm, Sun 10am–4pm; ☎ 850 434 1234 or ☎ 800 874 1234, ⓦ visitpensacola.com), is packed with the usual worthwhile handouts.

ACCOMMODATION

The main approach roads from I-10 – N Davis Boulevard and Pensacola Boulevard – are both lined with billboards advertising budget chain **motels** for $50–75 a night. The closest campgrounds are on Pensacola Beach, Perdido Key and Santa Rosa Island (see p.442).

Courtyard By Marriot Downtown 700 E Chase St ☎ 850 439 3330, ⓦ courtyardpensacoladowntown .com. Modern chain hotel with all the usual business amenities, comfortable, if a bit sterile, rooms and a nice pool if you can't be bothered to go to the beach. **$149**

Crowne Plaza Pensacola Grand 200 E Gregory St ☎ 850 433 3336, ⓦ pensacolagrandhotel.com. This hotel, incorporating the old 1912 train station, oozes character, though freight trains still pass by – ask for a high floor if the noise will bother you. The stylish rooms include free wi-fi and large flat-screen TVs. **$125**

Lee House B&B 400 Bayfront Pkwy ☎ 850 912 8770, ⓦ leehousepensacola.com. This dazzling replica of a plantation house with wraparound porches features eight elegant suites, all with free wi-fi and iHome audio system. **$165**

★**Noble Manor** 110 W Strong St ☎ 850 434 9544, ⓦ noblemanor.com. This charming 1905 bed and breakfast sits in the peaceful North Ilill District, with six cosy rooms. Breakfast is served in either the formal dining room or front porch, and, unusually for a B&B, there is a pool, hot tubs, and koi pond. **$145**

Pensacola Victorian 203 W Gregory St ☎ 850 434 2818, ⓦ pensacolavictorian.com. This charming bed and breakfast is in a ravishing Queen Anne-style home, with rooms decked out in late Victorian style, and home-baked cookies. Free wi-fi. **$95**

★**Solé Inn and Suites** 200 N Palafox St ☎ 850 470 9298, ⓦ soleinnandsuites.com. This centrally located 1950s-style motel has been given a funky boutique makeover, with stylish rooms, free breakfast, wi-fi and use of coin laundry – a real bargain. **$109**

EATING

Atlas Oyster House/Fish House 600 S Barracks St ☎ 850 470 0003, ⓦ atlasoysterhouse.com, ⓦ fishhouse pensacola.com. These two popular sister restaurants sit side by side on the waterfront: *Atlas* features fresh Apalachicola Bay and East Bay oysters, locally caught fish, famous Key lime pie ($6) and half-price sushi on Tuesdays. *Fish House* features steaks, sushi and signature dish "Grits à Ya Ya" (smoked Gouda cheese grits covered with grilled mushrooms and shrimp; $20). Atlas Mon–Sat 5–10pm, Sun 11am–10pm; Fish House daily 11am–10pm.

★**Blue Dot Barbecue** 310 N DeVilliers St ☎ 850 432 0644. Open since 1947, it's easy to miss this no-frills diner with just two items on the menu: burgers their way (no cheese, no pickles, but diced onions, salt and pepper, mayonnaise and barbecue sauce) for around $4, and (sometimes) delectable rib sandwiches for $7.50, with meat sizzled on a venerable grill that looks 100 years old. Cash only. Mon–Thurs 11.30am–2.30pm, Fri & Sat 11.30am–5pm.

Coffee Cup 520 E Cervantes St ☎ 850 432 7060. Lines form at the weekends to eat at this classic 1945 diner,

---

THE NUT HOUSE

J.W. Renfroe Pecan Company has been selling Florida pecans since 1957; visit its "Nut House" to sample the product and numerous other varieties of nuts, fudge, sumptuous pecan pie, "Southern Pecan Coffee" and their famous New Orleans-style pralines. Harvesting begins in October, so the freshest pecans are on sale at the end of the year. You'll find Renfroe at 2400 W Fairfield Drive (Mon–Fri 8.30am–5pm; ☎ 800 874 1929, ⓦ renfroe-pecans.com).

9

whose motto "no grits no glory" is taken seriously; the Nassau grits, served with tomatoes ($3), are a creamy treat. Mon–Fri 6am–2pm, Sat 6am–1pm.

Five Sisters Blues Café 421 W Belmont St ☎850 912 4856, ⓦfivesistersbluescafe.com. Genuine soul food enhanced with regular live blues music; staples include the addictive Aunt Sara's Southern fried chicken and the blueberry bread pudding. Mains $12–16. Tues–Thurs 11am–9pm, Fri & Sat 11am–2am, Sun 11am–5pm.

★**Global Grill** 27 S Palafox Place ☎850 469 9966, ⓦglobalgrillpensacola.com. Chef Frank Taylor brings tapas to Pensacola, blending Mediterranean and traditional Southern flavours; think lamb lollipops with Israeli couscous cake ($14), yellowfin tuna, seared with coriander and fennel ($15) and scallops with savoury goat cheese cheesecake ($13). Tues–Thurs 5–9pm, Fri & Sat 5–10pm.

Jackson's 400 S Palafox St ☎850 469 9898, ⓦjacksonsrestaurant.com. This elegant steakhouse occupies a restored 1860 building overlooking Plaza Ferdinand VII. The dinner menu includes steaks from $29 and open-fired yellowedge Gulf grouper ($34). Tues–Fri 11am–2pm & 5–10pm, Sat 5–10pm.

★**Joe Patti's Seafood** 524B St, at Main St ☎850 432 3315, ⓦjoepattis.com. Open since the 1930s, this seafood market offers a huge range of fresh seafood, but also has a sushi bar and deli, serving bread pudding ($3.80), cakes, gelato and coffee; you can also ask them to steam fresh shrimp for a picnic (from $6.69 per pound). Mon–Sat 7.30am–7pm, Sun 7.30am–6pm.

McGuire's Irish Pub 600 E Gregory St ☎850 433 6789, ⓦmcguiresirishpub.com. While the atmosphere here in this old 1927 firehouse is very Irish (see below), it's daubed with over $1 million in dollar bills left by patrons, and the food menu ranges from down-to-earth corned beef and cabbage to excellent steaks and some hefty burgers, from the $100 "Grand" Filet Mignon burger, to the famed Garbage burger ($11), and even a Skippy peanut burger ($10). The bean soup is just 18 cents (as it was in 1977). Daily 11am–2am.

Palace Café Seville Quarter, 130 E Government St ☎850 434 6211, ⓦsevillequarter.com. The Quarter is best known for its bars, but the local secret is this café, open for breakfast: the coffee ($1.50) is excellent, but it's the New Orleans-style beignets ($3–5) that make a visit worthwhile. Mon–Sat 7am–3am.

NIGHTLIFE AND ENTERTAINMENT

Hopjacks 10 Palafox Place ☎850 497 6073, ⓦhopjacks.com. Main anchor of the Palafox Place scene, this popular bar gets kudos for the vast range of beers on tap, and their perfectly paired Belgian fries, which are cooked in duck fat ($6); the rest of the menu (and the pizza, from $4) is hit and miss though. Daily 11am–3am.

McGuire's Irish Pub 600 E Gregory St ☎850 433 6789, ⓦmcguiresirishpub.com. This lively pub brews its own ales and features nightly entertainment in each of its nine dining rooms. Beware: kissing the moose head above the fireplace may be the price you pay for refusing to sing along to the Irish folk music. It's also a great place to eat (see above). Daily 11am–2am.

Pensacola Bay Brewery 225 E Zaragoza St ☎850 434 3353, ⓦpbbrew.com. Pensacola's own microbrewery

knocks out some inventive craft beers: the seasonal and extremely potent Conquistador Dopple Bock and Treasure Grove citra pale ale are good examples (samplers for $5.50). Tours run Sat at 3pm; $5. No food. Mon–Thurs noon–9pm, Fri & Sat noon–11pm, Sun noon–6pm.

Pensacola Little Theatre 400 S Jefferson St ☎850 432 2042, ⓦpensacolalittletheatre.com. Also home of Ballet Pensacola, this theatre gem is housed in the Pensacola Cultural Center (Mon–Fri 9am–10pm, Sat 9am–4pm), and even if you don't see a production here, it's worth going inside just to look around (it's the old 1911 jail). Box office Mon–Fri 10am–5.30pm and 1hr before curtain; tickets from $15.

Play 2/F, 16 S Palafox Place ☎850 466 3080, ⓦiplaypensacola.com. This place is a real treat,

---

THE GAY MEMORIAL DAY WEEKEND PARTY

For a city with a conservative reputation, Pensacola has a surprisingly lively gay scene and a wild gay Memorial Day celebration (ⓦmemorialweekendpensacola.com). Every year between the Friday and Monday of the last week of May, Pensacola is consumed by a **gay and lesbian party**, which began when a 20-year-old local, Dickie Carr, threw a party at the **San Carlos Hotel** (demolished to build the courts of law). Dickie's father, who managed the hotel in the 1970s, said he would foot the bill for any of the five hundred rooms that weren't taken. They all were. The party took place on Memorial Day and has become an annual event involving most of the town and drawing large numbers of outsiders. The daytime festivities are mainly at the beach, while at night the partying shifts to the Pensacola nightclubs; **Emerald City**, 406 E Wright St (☎850 433 9491, ⓦemeraldcitypensacola.com), is the biggest dance club for gays and lesbians all year round.

DIVING THE ORISKANY

Largely a well-kept secret since the 1960s, the dive scene in Pensacola took off in 2006 after the sinking of the retired 911ft aircraft carrier USS **Oriskany**, creating the **world's largest artificial reef**, starting some 84ft down at the former bridge tower. Technical divers hang out on the actual deck (around 146ft), but assuming visibility is good, just peering down from the tower is a mind-blowing experience.

The other famous wreck out here is battleship USS **Massachusetts**, which attracts moray eels, nurse sharks, rays, red snapper, grouper and amberjack in just 25ft of water. Contact H2O Below Scuba Diving Charters (☎850 291 3501, ⓦussoriskanydiver.com) to arrange a trip ($150).

---

combining microbrews with vintage arcade games, pool tables and skee-ball machines. Mon–Fri 4pm–2.30am, Sat & Sun noon–2.30pm.

Saenger Theatre 118 S Palafox Place ☎850 595 3880, ⓦpensacolasaenger.com. This spectacular 1925 historic theatre puts on plays and operas in a season running from October to April. Box office Mon–Fri 10am–5pm and 2hr before curtain.

Seville Quarter 130 E Government St ☎850 434 6211, ⓦsevillequarter.com. A local and tourist favourite, offering seven venues decked out to reflect Pensacola's history; step from *Apple Annie's* courtyard to *Lili Marlene's*

karaoke bar and then *Rosie O'Grady's* for its Flaming Hurricane drinks and duelling piano shows; *Fast Eddie's* offers pool tables; *Phineas Phogg's* is more like a club; and *End O' the Alley* is the place for live music. The *Palace Café* is a great place for breakfast (see opposite). Mon–Sat 11am–3pm, Sun 5pm–3am.

Vinyl Music Hall 2 S Palafox Place ⓦvinylmusichall .com. Live music now rings out in this old Masonic temple, a major venue for rock and indie bands on the Gulf coast. Cover usually ranges $15–20; check the website for the latest schedule of shows. Box office Mon–Fri noon–5pm.

Pensacola Beach

From downtown Pensacola, US-98 leads over the three-mile-long Pensacola Bay Bridge to Gulf Breeze, where Hwy-399 continues across 3/4-mile Pensacola Beach Bridge ($1 toll, southbound only) to Santa Rosa Island and the epitome of a Gulf-coast strand, **PENSACOLA BEACH**. Featuring mile after mile of fine white sands, rental outlets for beach and watersports equipment, the 1471ft **Pensacola Beach Gulf Pier** ($1.25; ⓦfishpensacolabeachpier.com), and beachside bars and restaurants, it's hard to beat for uncomplicated seaside recreation. With its sprinkling of motels and hotels (see p.442), Pensacola Beach also makes an alternative – if pricier – base to mainland Pensacola.

Gulf Islands National Seashore

☎850 934 2600, ⓦnps.gov/guis

The **Gulf Islands National Seashore** is a collective name for several national parks, each with a specific point of natural or historical interest, stretching 160 miles along the coast from here to Mississippi. In Florida it includes the Naval Live Oaks Area, where the main visitor centre is located (see p.442), Fort Barrancas (see p.437), and the eastern section of Perdido Key (see p.443). The section at Pensacola Beach covers the entire western half of Santa Rosa Island, an untrammelled landscape of white sand and scrub ending at Fort Pickens.

Naval Live Oaks Area

1801 Gulf Breeze Pkwy • Reservation daily 8am–sunset; visitor centre daily 8.30am–4.30pm • $8 per car, $3 for pedestrians and cyclists • ☎850 934 2600, ⓦnps.gov/guis

Midway between Pensacola and Pensacola Beach you'll pass through the wealthy community of **Gulf Breeze**, gateway to the **Naval Live Oaks Area**. In the 1820s, part of this live-oak forest was turned into a tree farm, intended to ensure a supply of shipbuilding material for years to come. Problems were plentiful: the oak was too heavy for road transport, wood rustlers cut down trees and sold them to foreign navies, and the final blow for the farm was the advent of iron-built ships.

9

The National Seashore **visitor centre** has exhibits and explanatory texts on this intriguing forest, where fragments from Native American settlements from as far back as 1000 BC have been found. To escape the glare of the sun for an hour or so, take one of the short but shady **forest trails**, which include a two-mile section of what was, in the early 1800s, Florida's major roadway, linking Pensacola and St Augustine.

Fort Pickens

Fort Pickens Rd • Daily 7am–sunset; visitor centre daily: March–Oct 9.30am–5pm; Nov–Feb 8.30am–4pm • Fort tours Fri–Sun 2pm • $8 per car; $3 for pedestrians and cyclists • ☎ 850 934 2600, ⓦ nps.gov/guis

A near impregnable mass of brick and stone, **Fort Pickens** lies on the barren eastern tip of Santa Rosa Island, surrounded by pristine waters and white-sand beaches. It's the largest of the four forts built to protect the bay, completed by slaves for the US military in 1834. Grab a self-guided tour leaflet at the tiny visitor centre and wander the battlements and the old officers' quarters, where Apache leader **Geronimo** was kept prisoner in 1887.

ARRIVAL AND INFORMATION   PENSACOLA BEACH

By bus Escambia County Area Transit (☎ 850 595 3228 ext 30, ⓦ goecat.com) bus #61 ($2.35) connects Pensacola with Pensacola Beach three times daily (Mon–Sat); the Beach Jumper (#64; $2.35) runs more regularly, but just Fri–Sun. Once here, the free Beach Trolley bus runs along the beach (late May to early Sept daily 4pm–midnight; every 45min).

Tourist information The Visitors Information Center is opposite the pier at 735 Pensacola Beach Blvd (daily 9am–5pm; ☎ 800 635 4803, ⓦ visitpensacolabeach.com).

ACCOMMODATION

Fort Pickens Campground ☎ 877 444 6777, ⓦ recreation.gov. Camping is possible at the Fort Pickens section of the National Seashore, with water, electricity, grills and picnic tables. Nov–Feb first-come first-served only. $26

Hilton Pensacola Beach Gulf Front 12 Via de Luna Drive ☎ 850 916 2999, ⓦ hiltonpensacolabeach.com. One of the beach's most luxurious properties, geared to business guests as much as to vacationing families. Here you'll find Pensacola's largest convention space, the city's only indoor heated pool, and a "Kid's Club" with various activities to keep the youngsters entertained. Wi-fi $3/day. $340

Holiday Inn Resort 14 Via de Luna Drive ☎ 850 932 5331, ⓦ holidayinnresortpensacolabeach.com. Flashy resort hotel with large, stylish rooms, huge outdoor pool

and 250ft lazy river, and even "kids suites" designed for families with children, featuring PlayStation 3. Free wi-fi. $270

Margaritaville Beach Hotel 165 Fort Pickens Rd ☎ 850 916 9755, ⓦ margaritavillehotel.com. Jimmy Buffett's empire expands to hotels, but unlike the eponymous restaurants, the hotel is elegantly furnished, with spacious suites overlooking the Gulf. It's a lot cheaper off season. Free wi-fi. $299

SpringHill Suites 24 Via de Luna Drive ☎ 850 932 6000, ⓦ marriott.com. All rooms are suites in this comfortable, Gulf-facing hotel, with refrigerators, microwaves and coffee makers. There are also three pools, one of them heated, and a complimentary buffet breakfast. Free wi-fi. $249

EATING

Flounder's Chowder House 800 Quietwater Beach Rd ☎ 850 932 2003, ⓦ flounderschowderhouse.com. This alehouse serves hearty seafood dinners such as shrimp Caesar salad ($14), and of course, flounder chowder ($5) and stuffed flounder ($24). Oct–April Mon–Thurs 11am–10pm, Fri & Sat 11am–11pm, Sun 10.30am–midnight; May–Sept Mon–Wed 11am–midnight, Thurs–Sat 11am–2.30am, Sun 10.30am–midnight.

★ **Grand Marlin** 400 Pensacola Beach Blvd ☎ 850 677 9153, ⓦ thegrandmarlin.com. Best fine-dining restaurant on the beach, with half a dozen fresh oysters

from $7.25 and mains ranging $18.95 (wild American shrimp and grits) to $34.95 (grilled lobster tail). Mon–Thurs 11am–10pm, Fri & Sat 11am–11pm, Sun 10am–10pm.

Peg Leg Pete's 1010 Fort Pickens Rd ☎ 850 932 4139, ⓦ peglegpetes.com. Known for its Cajun food (mains $12.95–19.95) and excellent raw bar, where you can slurp down oysters with various tasty accompaniments. The outdoor playground in the sand makes this a good place to bring the kids. Mon–Thurs & Sun 11am–10pm, Fri & Sat 11am–10.30pm.

NIGHTLIFE AND ENTERTAINMENT

Bamboo Willie's 400 Quietwater Boardwalk ☎850 916 9888, ⓦbamboowillies.com. This lively spot has a long bar on the beach lined with machines churning Technicolor frozen cocktails and enough space for a live band and the attendant dancing. Mon–Thurs & Sun 11am–11pm, Fri & Sat 11am–2am.

The Dock 4 Casino Beach Boardwalk ☎850 934 3625, ⓦthedockpensacola.weebly.com. Packed every Friday and Saturday night when DJs set the mood, this club is also a venue for touring bands, local acts and karaoke nights. Margaritas are just $3 on Tuesdays. Daily 11am–2.30am.

Sandshaker Lounge 731 Pensacola Beach Blvd ☎850 932 2211, ⓦsandshaker.com. The self-professed birthplace of the Bushwacker, an "adult milkshake" consisting of Kahlua, coconut, rum and other ingredients, served in a Styrofoam cup ($3–4) – a popular tipple in these parts since 1975, and still done very well at this bar. Daily 10am–3am.

Perdido Key

The barrier island to the west of Santa Rosa is sixteen-mile **Perdido Key**, lined with spectacular unspoiled, bone-white beaches. Though there has been some development in the centre, large swathes of beach and the island are protected within **Perdido Key State Park** (daily 8am–sunset; $3 per vehicle) and **Gulf Islands National Seashore** (see p.441), which here covers **Johnson's Beach**, the last five miles of the eastern part of the island, untouched by roads. A one-and-a-quarter-mile nature trail allows you to explore the area, and if you're smitten with the seclusion, stick around to swim or pitch your tent at one of the primitive **campgrounds** here (free with National Seashore entrance fee; $3 per person or $8 per vehicle). Keep driving west on Hwy-292 and you'll soon cross the Perdido Pass Bridge to Orange Beach in **Alabama**, where the city of **Gulf Shores** is a hotbed of sport, drinking, and suntanning rituals.

ARRIVAL AND INFORMATION
PERDIDO KEY

By car Perdido Key lies an easy 17-mile drive (30min) southwest from Pensacola via Hwy-292. There is normally no public transport, but in July and August the Big Lagoon Connector (#65) bus runs between the National Naval Aviation Museum in Pensacola and Perdido Key daily 11am–6pm (hourly; $2.35).

Tourist information Perdido Key Visitor Center is halfway along the island at 15500 Perdido Key Drive (Mon–Fri 8.30am–4.30pm, Sat & Sun 10am–4.30pm; ☎850 492 4660, ⓦvisitperdido.com).

EATING AND DRINKING

★**Flora-Bama Lounge & Oyster Bar** 17401 Perdido Key Drive ☎850 492 0611, ⓦflorabama.com. Legendary roadhouse bar established here in 1964 on the state line between Florida and Alabama (the line actually runs through the bar). Known for Cajun steamed oysters ($15/dozen), crawfish in season, and live music every night from 5pm. Daily 11am–3am.

Jellyfish 13700 Perdido Key Drive ☎850 332 6532, ⓦthejellyfishbar.com. If a steady diet of fried fish and burgers is wearing thin, aim for this superb seafood restaurant, which knocks out decent sushi (samplers $18–20) and fresh fish ($13–24) In addition to the usual Florida menu, and well-mixed martinis and cocktails ($8–10). Daily 11am–3am (food till 10pm).

Shrimp Basket 14600 Perdido Key Drive ☎850 492 1970, ⓦshrimpbasket.com. It's a Southern chain but this is the place to come for no-frills seafood: fried shrimp baskets ($12), poboys ($8) and steamed catfish platters ($13). Monday and Thursday is all-you-can-eat fried whitefish ($10); Sunday and Wednesday is all-you-can-eat fried popcorn shrimp ($12). Daily 11am–10pm.

MAP OF FLORIDA C.1591

Contexts

History

Contrary to popular belief, Florida's history goes back far beyond Walt Disney World and beach resorts. For thousands of years, its aboriginal inhabitants lived in organized towns and villages with contacts across a large section of the Americas. In the sixteenth century it became a Spanish colony long before the establishment of Virginia and Massachusetts, and only in 1821 did Florida become part of the US. Hard to believe today, but large parts of the state remained isolated frontier country until the early 1900s.

First peoples of Florida

Florida's **first human inhabitants** most likely arrived from Siberia, crossing North America and reaching northern Florida around 12,000 to 14,000 years ago. These **Paleo** (or "Early") **Indians** lived hunter-gatherer existences – the spear tips they used are widely found across the central and northern parts of the state.

Around 5000 BC, social patterns changed: settlements became semipermanent and diet switched from meat to shellfish, snails and molluscs, which were abundant along the rivers. Travelling was done by dugout canoe and, periodically, a community would move to a new site, probably to allow food supplies to replenish themselves. Discarded shells and other rubbish were piled onto the **midden mounds** still commonly seen in the state.

Though pottery began to appear around 2000 BC, not until 1000 BC was there another big change in lifestyle, as indicated by the discovery of **irrigation** canals, patches of land cleared for **cultivation**, and cooking utensils used to prepare grown food. Around two thousand years ago, the erection of **burial mounds** – elaborate tombs of prominent tribespeople, often with sacrificed kin and valuable objects also placed inside – became common. These suggest strong religious and trading links across an area stretching from Central America to the North American interior.

Native American cultures

Around two thousand years ago, sophisticated Native American cultures began to develop in northern Florida, beginning with the **Weedon Island Culture** (200–800 AD) of Tampa Bay. Spreading east from the Georgian coastal plain, the **Fort Walton Culture** became prevalent from around 1100 AD, dividing society into a rigid caste system and forming villages and towns planned around a central plaza. The Fort Walton peoples were probably the ancestors of tribes encountered by early Spanish explorers in the sixteenth century, when an estimated 350,000 Native Americans inhabited the region.

1513	1521	1528
Spanish conquistador Juan Ponce de León makes the first European landing in Florida.	Ponce de León makes his second landing in Florida – he is injured in a fight with local Native Americans, and dies shortly afterwards.	Pánfilo de Narváez lands near Tampa; within a few months most of his expedition is dead.

European discovery

After Christopher Columbus discovered the "New World" in 1492, the **Spanish** began to carve out a vast empire in Central America and around the Caribbean. Conquistador **Juan Ponce de León**, governor of Puerto Rico, made the **first European landing** in Florida in 1513; legend has it he was searching for Bimini, home of the mythical fountain of youth (he was more likely searching for the usual – gold). Ponce de León sighted land during Pascua Florida, the Spanish Easter "Festival of the Flowers", and named what he saw **La Florida** – or "Land of Flowers". After coming ashore somewhere between the mouth of the St Johns River and present-day Melbourne Beach, Ponce de León sailed on around the Florida Keys, naming them Los Martires, for their supposed resemblance to the bones of martyred men, and Las Tortugas (now the Dry Tortugas), named after the turtles he saw around them.

Sent to deal with troublesome natives in the Lower Antilles, it was eight years before Ponce de León returned to Florida, this time with a mandate from the Spanish king to **conquer and colonize** the territory. Landing on the southwest coast, probably somewhere between Tampa Bay and Fort Myers, Ponce de León met a hostile reception from the Calusa and was forced to withdraw, eventually dying from an arrow wound received in the battle.

Narváez and De Soto

Rumours of **gold** hidden in Apalachee, in the north of the region, stimulated several Spanish incursions into Florida, all which the organization and power of the Native American tribes, and the ferocity of the terrain and climate, drove back. First up was conquistador **Pánfilo de Narváez**, who landed near Tampa in 1528. His mission soon became a nightmare; after being ravaged by disease, starvation and deadly attacks by various tribes as they marched north, the Spaniards sailed out into the Gulf of Mexico. Eight years later, only four survivors made it back to Spanish territory.

Far more successful – even though it ended in death for its leader – was the **Hernando de Soto** expedition, a thousand-strong band of war-hardened knights and treasure seekers, which landed at Tampa Bay in May 1539. Recent excavations in Tallahassee have located the only confirmed site of one of De Soto's camps, established before the expedition continued north and eventually made the first European crossing of the Mississippi River – for a long time marking Florida's western boundary. With De Soto's death in 1542, the destruction of numerous Native American villages and no sign whatsoever of gold or riches, the remaining Spanish returned to Mexico. In 1559 **Tristán de Luna y Arellano** established a colony near modern-day Pensacola, but this too was abandoned within two years – the Spanish seemed doomed to failure in Florida.

1539	1562	1564
Hernando de Soto leads another Spanish expedition to Florida and west towards the Mississippi, leaving a trail of devastation in his wake.	French explorer Jean Ribault charts the coast of Florida.	French Huguenots led by René Goulaine de Laudonnière establish Fort Caroline near modern-day Jacksonville.

The French and St Augustine

Spain wasn't the only European nation looking to exploit the riches of the New World. France's first colony in North America was **Fort Caroline**, a settlement near the mouth of the St Johns River near present-day Jacksonville. Naval officer **Jean Ribault** visited the site in 1562, and two years later a small group of **French Huguenots** led by René Goulaine de Laudonnière established a permanent presence here.

The French move forced the Spanish to make a more determined effort at settlement. Already commissioned to explore the Atlantic coast of North America, **Pedro Menéndez de Aviles** (1519–74) was promised the lion's share of whatever profits could be made from Florida. Landing south of the French fort on August 28, 1565, the day of the Spanish Festival of San Augustin, Menéndez named the site **St Augustine** – founding what was to become the longest continuous site of European habitation on the continent. Ribault sailed down the coast to attack the Spanish, but his ships were scattered by a hurricane; Menéndez marched north, destroyed Fort Caroline and massacred most of the male inhabitants. A few days later the Spanish rounded up Ribault and his surviving soldiers, massacring some 350 Frenchmen in the process – the site of the killing is still known as Matanzas, or "Place of Slaughter".

The first Spanish period (1565–1763)

Only the enthusiasm of Menéndez held Florida together during the early decades of Spanish rule, and the colony remained dependent on an annual subsidy sent from Mexico City. It was a far from harmonious setup: homesick Spanish soldiers frequently mutinied and fought with the Native Americans, and even St Augustine was a lifeless outpost unless a ship happened to be in port. Despite sinking all his personal finances into the colony, Menéndez was unable to make Florida prosper, and he left in 1571, after the king ordered him to help plan the Spanish Armada's attack on Britain.

Bent on Christianizing the local tribes, the Spanish built a string of **Franciscan missions** along the coast and into the Panhandle from 1606, around which a few small and insecure settlements were established; besides seeking to earn the loyalty of the natives, these were intended to provide a defensive shield against attacks from the north. The chief mission was **San Luis de Apalachee**, founded in 1656 near present-day Tallahassee, while **Pensacola** was founded in 1698, becoming the de facto capital of west Florida (St Augustine remained in control of the east).

This expansion came to an end between 1702 and 1704, when the **British governor of South Carolina** and his Yamassee allies led two devastating raids into Florida, enslaving the local Timucua people and destroying almost all the missions. The survivors withdrew to St Augustine and Pensacola, and only the timely arrival of Spanish reinforcements prevented the fall of St Augustine to the British in 1740. By this time war and disease had virtually wiped out all the Native American tribes in Florida – displaced Creek peoples from the north moved in, gradually forming the **Seminole** tribes that exist today.

In 1763, the **Treaty of Paris**, concluding the Seven Years' War in Europe, ceded Florida to the British – the Spanish deserted St Augustine en masse for Cuba.

1565	1586	1606
Spanish commander Pedro Menéndez de Aviles founds St Augustine; he destroys Fort Caroline and massacres a French force ed by Jean Ribault a few days later.	English privateer Sir Francis Drake plunders St Augustine.	Spanish Franciscans begin to expand the Catholic mission system across northern Florida.

PIRATES OF LA FLORIDA

Lightly garrisoned, St Augustine was always vulnerable to attack. In 1586 the town was sacked by an English force led by **Sir Francis Drake**, and the surviving Spanish settlers chased out into the jungle. In 1668 St Augustine was again plundered by notorious English buccaneer **Robert Searle**, who was later slapped on the wrist for his action by the governor of Jamaica. The Spanish regarded Drake and Searle unequivocally as pirates; you'll see them described that way in St Augustine today. To the English of course they were heroic seamen, privateers labouring – at least in part – for the British Crown. Either way, in the aftermath of the Searle raid the Spanish began construction of the Castillo de San Marcos, America's oldest fort, ensuring that the town would never again be taken by force.

The British period (1763–83)

Despite their two centuries of occupation, the Spanish failed to make much impression on Florida. It was the British, already developing the colonies further north, who grafted a social infrastructure onto the region.

Like the Spanish, the British acknowledged the numerical importance of the Seminoles and sought good relations with them. In return for goods, the British took Native American land around ports and supply routes, but generally left the Seminoles undisturbed in the inland areas.

Despite attractive grants, few settlers arrived from Britain. Those with money to spare bought Florida land as an investment, never intending to develop or settle on it, and only large holdings – **plantations** growing corn, sugar, rice and other crops – were profitable. Charleston, in South Carolina to the north, dominated sea trade in the area, though St Augustine was still a modestly important settlement and the gathering place of passing British aristocrats and intellectuals. West Florida, on the other hand, was driven by political factionalism and was also often the scene of skirmishes with the Seminoles, who received worse treatment than their counterparts in the east.

The American Revolutionary War (1775–83)

Being a new and sparsely populated region, Florida was barely affected by the discontent that fuelled the **American Revolutionary War** in the 1770s, except for St Augustine, which served as a haven for British Royalists fleeing the war, many of whom moved on to the Bahamas or Jamaica. Pensacola, though, was captured in 1781 by the Spanish hero **Bernardo de Gálvez**, who had won back West Florida for Spain under the guise of helping the American rebels defeat the British. Within two years, diplomacy confirmed what was already a reality on the ground and signalled the end of British rule in Florida.

The second Spanish period (1783–1821)

The **1783 Treaty of Paris**, under which Britain recognized American independence, not only returned Florida to Spain but also gave it Louisiana and the prized port of New Orleans. Spanish holdings in North America were now larger than ever, but with Europe in turmoil and the Spanish colonies in Central America agitating for their own independence, the country was ill-equipped to capitalize on them. Moreover, the

1698	1702–04	1763	1775
Pensacola established.	South Carolina governor James Moore and his Yamassee and Creek allies raid Florida and destroy the Spanish missions.	Florida is ceded to Great Britain; the British divide the territory into East and West Florida.	American Revolutionar War begins; Florida remains loyal to Britain

complexity of Florida's melting pot, comprising the British, smaller numbers of ethnically diverse European settlers, and the increasingly assertive Seminoles (now well established in fertile central Florida, and often joined by Africans escaping slavery further north), made it impossible for a declining colonial power to govern.

As fresh European migration slowed, Spain was forced to **sell land to US citizens**, who bought large tracts, confident that Florida would soon be under Washington's control. Indeed, in gaining Louisiana from France in 1803 (to whom it had been ceded by Spain), and moving the Georgia border south, it was clear the US had Florida in its sights. During the **War of 1812** (fought between the US and Britain), Britain landed troops at Pensacola, with the Spanish powerless bystanders; in response, a US militia general, **Andrew Jackson**, marched south, eventually removing the British and scoring a famous victory at the Battle of New Orleans in 1815.

The First Seminole War (1814–18)

Jackson's campaigns of 1814–15 were the initial acts of the **First Seminole War**. As international tensions heightened, Seminole raids into Georgia were commonly used as excuses for US incursions into Florida. In 1816 a US force destroyed the "**Negro Fort**", aka Fort Gadsden, base of escaped slaves and Seminole warriors, before heading back to US territory. In 1818, Jackson finally received what he took to be presidential approval (the "Rhea Letter", thought to have been authorized by President Monroe) to march again into Florida on the pretext of subduing the Seminoles but with the actual intention of taking outright control.

While US public officials were uneasy with the dubious legality of these events, the American public was firmly on Jackson's side. The US government issued an ultimatum to Spain, demanding it either police Florida effectively or relinquish its ownership. With little alternative, Spain formally **ceded Florida to the US** in 1819, in return for the US assuming the $5 million owed by the Spanish government to American settlers in land grants. The treaty was finally ratified in 1821, and Andrew Jackson was sworn in as Florida's first American governor.

US territory (1821–42)

Under American rule it was soon evident the East and West divisions of Florida were unworkable, and a site midway between St Augustine and Pensacola was selected as the new administrative centre in 1824: **Tallahassee**, an abandoned Apalachee settlement.

Under Spanish and British rule, the Seminoles, notwithstanding some feuding among themselves, lived peaceably on the productive lands of northern central Florida. These, however, were precisely the agriculturally rich areas US settlers coveted. Under the **Treaty of Moultrie Creek** in 1823, most of the Seminole tribes signed a document agreeing to sell their present land and resettle in southwest Florida. Neither side was to honour this agreement: no time limit was imposed on the Seminole exodus, and those who did go found the new land to be unsuitable for farming. The US side, meanwhile, failed to provide promised resettlement funds.

Andrew Jackson spent only three months as territorial governor, though his influence on Florida continued from the White House when he became US president in 1829. In 1830 he approved the **Act of Indian Removal**, decreeing all Native Americans in the

1781	1783	1812–15
The Spanish – temporarily allies of the Americans – capture Pensacola from the British.	Treaty of Paris ends the Revolutionary War; all of Florida returned to Spain.	War of 1812. British troops occupy Pensacola; US forces under Andrew Jackson invade Florida and expel the Brits.

eastern US should be transferred to reservations in the open areas of the Midwest. Two years later, James Gadsden, the newly appointed Indian commissioner, called a meeting of the Seminole tribes at Payne's Landing on the Oklawaha River, near Silver Springs, urging them to cede their land to the US and move west. Amid much acrimony, a few did sign the **Treaty of Payne's Landing**, which provided for their complete removal within three years.

The Second Seminole War (1835–42)

A small number took what monies were offered and resettled in the west, but most of the Seminoles were determined to stay in Florida. The **Second Seminole War** ensued in 1835, with the Native Americans repeatedly ambushing US militiamen; 110 soldiers under the command of Major Francis Dade were wiped out between Tampa and Ocala by a force led by Chief Micanopy. The Seminoles also ransacked the plantations of white settlers, many of whom fled and never returned. Trained for set-piece battles, the US troops were rarely able to deal effectively with the guerrilla tactics of the Seminoles. Colonel Zachary Taylor led the US to rather pyrrhic victories at the **Battle of Lake Okeechobee** in 1837 and at the **Battle of Loxahatchee** in 1838, but it was apparent the Seminoles were unlikely to be defeated by conventional means. In October 1837 their leader, **Osceola**, was lured to St Augustine with the promise of a truce – only to be arrested and imprisoned, eventually to die in jail. This treachery failed to break the spirit of the Seminoles, though a few continued to give themselves up and leave for the west, while others were captured and sold into slavery.

It became the policy of the US to drive the Seminoles steadily south, away from the fertile lands of central Florida and **into the Everglades**. There, the Seminoles raided the Cape Florida lighthouse and destroyed the white colony on Indian Key in the Florida Keys in 1840. With the remaining Seminoles confined to the Everglades, the US formally **ended the conflict** in 1842, when the Seminoles agreed to stay where they were – an area earlier described by an army surveyor as "fit only for Indian habitation".

The war crippled the Florida economy but stimulated the growth of a number of new towns around the army forts. Several of these, such as Fort Brooke (Tampa), Fort Lauderdale, Fort Myers and Fort Pierce, have survived into modern times. Conflict erupted yet again during the **Third Seminole War** of 1855–58, after which only a handful of Seminoles remained in Florida, deep in the Everglades.

Statehood and secession (1842–61)

The Second Seminole War forestalled the possibility of Florida **attaining statehood** – which would have entitled it to full representation in Washington and to appoint its own administrators. Influence in Florida at this time was split between two camps. On one side were the wealthy slave-owning plantation farmers, concentrated in the "cotton counties" of the central section of the Panhandle, who enjoyed all the traditions of the upper rungs of Deep South society. They were eager to make sure the balance of power in Washington did not shift toward the non-slave-owning "free" states, which would inevitably bring a call for the abolition of slavery. Opposing statehood were the smallholders scattered about the rest of the territory – many of whom were Northerners, already ideologically against slavery and fearing the imposition of federal taxes.

1817–18	1821	1823
Andrew Jackson leads punitive campaign against the Seminoles in Florida, part of the First Seminole War.	US formally takes control of Florida from the Spanish; Andrew Jackson is first governor.	Treaty of Moultrie Creek establishes a Seminole reservation in the middle of the state; the treaty is annulled in 1830 when Congress passes the Indian Removal Act

One compromise mooted was a return to a divided Florida, with the West becoming a state while the East remained a territory. Eventually, based on a narrowly agreed upon **constitution** drawn up in Port St Joseph on the Panhandle coast in 1838 (on the site of present-day Port St Joe), Florida **became a state** on March 3, 1845. The arrival of statehood coincided with a period of material prosperity: the first **railroads** began spidering across the Panhandle and central Florida; an organized school system became established; and Florida's population of 60,000 doubled within twenty years.

Nationally, the issue of slavery was to be the catalyst that led the US into civil war, though it was only a part of a great cultural divide between the rural Southern states – to which Florida was linked more through geography than history – and the modern industrial states of the North. As federal pressure intensified for the abolition of slavery, Florida formally **seceded from the Union** on January 10, 1861, aligning itself with the breakaway Confederate States in the run-up to the Civil War.

The Civil War (1861–65)

Inevitably, the **Civil War** had a great effect on Florida, although most Floridians conscripted into the Confederate army fought far away from home, and rarely were there more than minor confrontations within the state. The relatively small number of Union sympathizers generally kept a low profile, concentrating on protecting their families. At the start of the war, most of Florida's **coastal forts** were occupied by Union troops as part of the blockade on Confederate shipping. Lacking the strength to mount effective attacks on the forts, those Confederate soldiers who remained in Florida based themselves in the interior and watched for Union troop movements, swiftly destroying whatever bridge, road or railroad lay in the invaders' path – in effect creating a stalemate, which endured throughout the conflict.

Away from the coast, Florida's primary contribution to the war effort was the **provision of food** – chiefly beef and pork reared on the central Florida farms – and the transport of it across the Panhandle toward Confederate strongholds further west. Union attempts to cut the supply route gave rise to the only major battle fought in the state, the **Battle of Olustee**, just outside Live Oak, in February 1864: 10,000 participated in an engagement that left nearly 3000 dead or injured and both sides claiming victory.

The most celebrated battle from a Floridian viewpoint, however, happened in March 1865 at **Natural Bridge**, when a youthful group of Confederates defeated the technically superior Union troops, preventing the fall of Tallahassee. As events transpired, it was a hollow victory: following the Confederate surrender, the war ended a few months later.

Reconstruction (1865–76)

Following the cessation of hostilities, Florida was caught in an uneasy hiatus. In the years after the war, the defeated states were subject to **Reconstruction**, a rearrangement of their internal affairs determined by, at first, the President, and later by a much harder-line Congress intent on ensuring the Southern states would never return to their old ways.

1824	1832	1835–42	1845
Tallahassee founded as state capital.	Treaty of Payne's Landing; the US promises Seminoles land west of the Mississippi River if they agree to leave Florida voluntarily.	Second Seminole War.	Florida becomes the 27th state of the US.

The Northern ideal of free-labour capitalism was an alien concept in the South, and there were enormous problems. Of paramount concern was the future of the **freed slaves**. With restrictions on their movements lifted, many emancipated slaves wandered the countryside, often unwittingly putting fear into all-white communities that had never before had a black face in their midst. Rubbing salt into the wounds, as far as the Southern whites were concerned, was the occupation of many towns by black Union troops. As a backlash, the white-supremacist **Ku Klux Klan** became active in Tennessee during 1866, and its race-hate, segregationist doctrine soon spread into Florida.

Against this background of uncertainty, Florida's **domestic politics** entered a period of unparalleled chicanery. Suddenly, not only were black men allowed to vote, but there were more African-American voters than white. The gullibility of the uneducated blacks and the power of their votes proved an irresistible combination to the unscrupulous and power-hungry. Double-dealing and vote-rigging were practiced by diverse factions united only in their desire to restore Florida's statehood and acquire even more power. Following a constitution written and approved in controversial circumstances, Florida was **readmitted to the Union** on July 21, 1868.

Eventually, in Florida as in the other Southern states, an all-white, **conservative Democrat government** emerged. Despite emancipation and the hopes for integration outlined by the Civil Rights Act passed by Congress in 1875, African-Americans in Florida were still denied many of the rights reasonably regarded as basic. In fact, all that distanced the new administration from the one that led Florida into secession was awareness of the power of the federal government and the need to at least appear to take outside views into account. It was also true that many of the former slave-owners were now the employers of freed blacks, who remained very much under their white masters' control.

A new Florida (1876–1914)

Florida's bonds with its neighbouring states became increasingly tenuous in the years following Reconstruction. A fast-growing population began spreading south – part of a gradual diminishing of the importance of the Panhandle, where ties to the Deep South were strongest. Florida's identity was forged by a new **frontier spirit**. Besides smallholding farmers, loggers came to work the abundant forests, and a new breed of wealthy settler started putting down roots, among them Henry DeLand and Henry S. Sanford, who each bought large chunks of central Florida and founded the towns still bearing their names.

As northern speculators invested in Florida, they sought to publicize the region, and a host of articles extolling the virtues of the state's climate as a cure for all ills began to appear in the country's newspapers. These early efforts to promote **Florida as a tourist destination** brought the wintering rich along the new railroads to enjoy the sparkling rivers and springs, along with naturalists keen to explore the unique flora and fauna.

With a fortune made through his partnership in Standard Oil, **Henry Flagler** (1830–1913) opened luxury resorts on Florida's northeast coast for his socialite friends in the 1880s, and gradually extended his Florida East Coast Railway south (see box opposite), giving birth to communities such as **Palm Beach** and making the remote trading post of **Miami** an accessible, expanding town. Flagler's friendly rival **Henry Plant** (1819–1899) connected his railroad to **Tampa**, turning a desolate hamlet into a

1855–58	1861–65	1888
Third Seminole War; less than two hundred Seminoles remain in Florida in the aftermath.	Civil War: Florida secedes from the Union.	Oil tycoon Henry Flagler opens the *Ponce de León Hotel* in St Augustine, the first step in developing his new "American Riviera".

FLAGLER'S FLORIDA EAST COAST RAILWAY

Henry Flagler first visited Florida in 1878, and five years later he gave up his day-to-day responsibilities at Standard Oil to focus on his ambitious plan to develop the east coast of Florida for tourism. As his railroad inched south, hotels and commerce followed.

1885 Flagler purchases the Jacksonville, St Augustine and Halifax River Railway.
1886 Railway extended to Ormond Beach and Daytona.
1892 Railway reaches New Smyrna.
1894 Railway extends to West Palm Beach.
1895 Flagler formally names his railroad the Florida East Coast Railway.
1896 Railway reaches the site of today's Miami.
1904–12 Flagler builds railway extension to Key West.
1913 Flagler dies.
1935 Key West extension destroyed by hurricane; it is reopened as highway US-1 in 1938.

thriving port city and a major base for cigar manufacturing. The **citrus industry** also revved into top gear: Florida's climate enabled oranges, grapefruits, lemons and other citrus fruits to be grown during the winter and sold to an eager market in the cooler north. The **cattle farms** went from small to strong, with Florida becoming a major supplier of beef to the rest of the US: cows were rounded up with a special wooden whip that made a gunshot-like sound when used – hence the nickname "**cracker**" that was applied to rural settlers.

One group that didn't benefit from the boom years was the African-Americans. Many were imprisoned for no reason, and found themselves on chain gangs building the new roads and railroads; punishments for refusing to work included severe floggings and hanging by the thumbs. There was, however, the founding of **Eatonville** in 1887, just north of Orlando, which was the first town in Florida – and possibly the US – to be founded, governed and lived in by African-Americans.

The Spanish–American War (1898)

By the 1890s, the US was a large and unified nation itching for a bigger role in the world, and as the drive in **Cuba** for independence from Spain gathered momentum, an opportunity to participate in international affairs presented itself. Florida already had long links with Cuba – the capital, Havana, was just ninety miles from Key West, and several thousand Cuban migrants were employed in the Tampa cigar factories. During 1898, tens of thousands of US troops arrived in the state after the **Spanish–American War** was declared on April 25. As it turned out, the fighting was comparatively minor. Spain was defeated relatively quickly, and on January 1, 1899, Cuba attained independence (and the US a big say in its future). But the war was also the first of several major conflicts that were to prove beneficial to Florida. Many of the soldiers would return as settlers or tourists, and improved railroads and strengthened harbours at the commercially significant ports of Key West, Tampa and Pensacola did much to boost the economy.

The Broward era (1905–10)

The early years of the 1900s were dominated by the progressive policies of **Napoleon Bonaparte Broward** (1857–1910), who was elected state governor in 1905. Broward

1896	1898	1910–40	1912
Flagler's Florida East Coast Railway reaches Biscayne Bay. Miami is formally established.	Spanish–American War.	Great Migration sees 40,000 African-Americans move from Florida to northern cities.	Flagler's railroad reaches Key West.

championed the little man against corporate interests, particularly the giant land-owning railroad companies. Among Broward's aims were an improved education system, a state-run commission to oversee new railroad construction, a tax on cars to finance road building, better salaries for teachers and the judiciary, a state-run life insurance scheme and a ban on newspapers – few of which were well disposed toward Broward – knowingly publishing untruths. Broward also enacted the first **conservation laws**, protecting fish, oysters, game and forests; but at the same time, in an attempt to create new land to rival the holdings of the rail barons, he conceived the drainage programme that would cause untold damage to the Everglades.

By no means did all of Broward's policies become law, and he departed Tallahassee for a US Senate seat in 1910, dying shortly afterwards. Nonetheless, the forward-thinking plans of what became known as the **Broward era** were continued through subsequent administrations – a process that went some way toward bringing a rough-and-ready frontier land into the twentieth century.

World War I and the 1920s

World War I continued the tradition of the Spanish–American War by giving Florida an economic shot in the arm, as the military arrived to police the coastline and develop sea-warfare projects. Despite the influx of money and the reforms of the Broward years, there was little happening to improve the lot of Florida's African-Americans. The Ku Klux Klan was revived in Tallahassee in 1915, and the public outcry following the beating to death of a young African-American on a chain gang was answered only by the introduction of the sweatbox as punishment for prisoners considered unruly.

The coast so vigilantly protected from advancing Germans during the war was left wide open when **Prohibition** was introduced in 1919; the many secluded inlets became secure landing sites for shipments of spirits from the Caribbean. The illicit booze improved the atmosphere in the new resorts of **Miami Beach**, a picture-postcard piece of beach landscaping replacing what had been a barely habitable mangrove island just a few years before. Drink was not the only illegal pleasure pursued in the nightclubs: gambling and prostitution were also rife, and were soon to attract the attention of big-time **gangsters** such as Al Capone, initiating a climate of corruption that was to scar Florida politics for years.

The lightning-paced creation of Miami Beach was no isolated incident. Throughout Florida, and especially in the southeast, new communities appeared almost overnight. Self-proclaimed architectural genius **Addison Mizner** (see box, p.194) erected the "million-dollar cottages" of Palm Beach and began fashioning **Boca Raton** with the same mock-Mediterranean excesses, on the premise "get the big snob and the little snob will follow". Meanwhile, visionary **George Merrick** plotted the superlative **Coral Gables** – now absorbed by Miami – which became the nation's first preplanned city and one of the few schemes of the time to age with dignity.

In the rush of prosperity following the war, it seemed everyone in America wanted a piece of Florida, and chartered trains brought in thousands of eager buyers. The spending frenzy soon meant that for every genuine offer there were a hundred bogus ones: many people unknowingly bought acres of empty swampland.

1923	1925–26	1926	1929
Massacre of African-Americans at Rosewood.	Property bust in Florida; economy collapses.	Hurricane devastates Miami.	Great Depression begins.

Although millions of dollars technically changed hands each week during the peak year of 1925, little hard cash actually moved. Most deals were paper transactions with buyers paying a small deposit into a bank. The inflation inherent in the system finally went out of control in 1926. With buyers failing to keep up payments, banks went **bust** and were quickly followed by everyone else. A **hurricane** devastated Miami the same year, and an even worse hurricane in 1928 caused Lake Okeechobee to burst its banks and flood surrounding communities.

With the Florida land boom well and truly over, the **Wall Street Crash** in 1929 proceeded to make paupers of the millionaires, such as Sarasota's **John Ringling**, whose considerable investments had helped to shape the state, and who would later found the **Ringling Brothers Barnum and Bailey Circus**.

The Depression and World War II

At the start of the 1930s, even the major railroads that had stimulated Florida's expansion were in receivership, and the state government only avoided bankruptcy with a constitutional escape clause. Due to the property crash, Florida had a few extra years to adjust to grinding poverty before the whole country experienced the Depression, and a number of recovery measures – making the state more active in citizens' welfare – pre-empted the national New Deal legislation of President Roosevelt.

No single place was harder hit than **Key West**, which was not only suffering the Depression but hadn't been favoured by the property boom either. With a population of 12,000, Key West was an incredible $5 million in debt, and had even lost its link to the mainland when the Overseas Railroad – running across the Florida Keys between Key West and Miami – was destroyed by the 1935 Labor Day hurricane.

What saved Key West, and indeed brought financial stability to all of Florida, was **World War II**. Once again, thousands of troops arrived to guard the coastline – off which there was an immense amount of German U-boat activity – while the flat inland areas made a perfect training venue for pilots. Empty tourist hotels provided ready-made barracks, and the soldiers, and their visiting families, got a taste of Florida that would bring many of them back.

In the immediate **postwar period**, the inability of the state to plan and provide for increased growth was resoundingly apparent, with public services – particularly in the field of education – woefully inadequate. Because of the massive profits being made through illegal gambling, corruption became endemic in public life. State governor **Fuller Warren**, implicated with the Al Capone crime syndicate in 1950, was by no means the only state official suspected of being in cahoots with criminals. A wave of attacks against African-Americans and Jews in 1951 caused Warren to speak out against the Ku Klux Klan, but the discovery that he himself had once been a Klan member only confirmed there was poison flowing through the heart of Florida's political system.

A rare upbeat development was a continued commitment to the conservation measures introduced in the Broward era, with $2 million allocated to buying the land that, in 1947, became **Everglades National Park**.

1935	1941–45	1959	1962
Flagler's Key West railway destroyed by a hurricane – it is eventually rebuilt as a road.	US involved in World War II; Florida booms.	The Cuban Revolution leads to a large wave of Cuban immigration into south Florida.	Work starts at the Kennedy Space Center.

The 1950s

Cattle, citrus and tourism continued to be the major components of Florida's economy as, in the ten years from 1950, the state soared from being the twentieth to the tenth most populous in the country, home to some five million people. While its increased size raised Florida's profile in the federal government, the demographic changes within the state – most dramatically the shift from rural life in the north to urban living in the south – went unacknowledged, and **reapportionment** of representation in state government became a critical issue. It was only resolved by the **1968 constitution**, which provided for automatic reapportionment in line with population changes.

The fervent desire for growth and the need to present a wholesome public image prevented the state's conservative-dominated assembly from fighting as hard as their counterparts in the other southern states against **desegregation**, following a ruling by the federal Supreme Court on the issue in 1956. Nonetheless, African-Americans continued to be banned from Miami Beach after dark and from swimming off the Palm Beach coast. In addition, they were subject to segregation in restaurants, buses, hotels and schools – and barely represented at all in public office.

The 1960s

As the **Civil Rights** movement gained strength during the early 1960s, bus boycotts and demonstrations took place in Tallahassee and Daytona Beach, and a march in St Augustine in 1964 resulted in the arrest of the movement's leader, Dr Martin Luther King Jr. The success of the Civil Rights movement in ending legalized discrimination did little to affect the deeply entrenched racist attitudes among much of Florida's longer-established population. Most of the state's African-Americans still lived and worked in conditions that would have been intolerable to whites: a fact that, in part, accounted for the **Liberty City riot** in August 1968, which was the first of several violent uprisings in Miami's depressed areas. The area would see its worst rioting over a decade later, on May 18, 1980, after an all-white jury acquitted four white police officers of the beating to death of an African-American citizen, Arthur MacDuffie. Eighteen people died, 400 were injured and damage to property was estimated at over $200 million.

The ideological shift in Florida's near-neighbour, **Cuba** – declared a socialist state by its leader Fidel Castro in 1961 – came sharply into focus with the 1962 **missile crisis**, which triggered a tense game of cat and mouse between the US and the USSR over Soviet missile bases on the island. After world war was averted, Florida became the base of the US government's covert anti-Castro operations. Many engaged in these activities were among the 300,000 **Cuban immigrants** who had arrived following the Castro-led revolution. The Bay of Pigs fiasco in 1961 proved there was to be no quick return to the homeland, and while not all of the new arrivals stayed in Florida, many went no further than Miami, where they were to change completely the social character – and eventually the power balance – of the city.

Another factor in Florida's expansion was the basing of the new civilian space administration, **NASA**, at the military long-range missile-testing site at Cape Canaveral. The all-out drive to land a man on the moon brought an enormous influx of space industry personnel here in the early 1960s – quadrupling the population of the region soon to become known as the **Space Coast**.

1968	1971	1972	1977
Liberty City riot.	Disney's Magic Kingdom opens in Orlando.	The Miami Dolphins under Don Shula complete the first full undefeated season in the NFL (aka the "Perfect Season").	Gloria Estefan and Miami Sound Machine start making records; Estefan goes on to become the "Queen Of Latin Pop".

The 1970s to the 1990s

Florida's tourist boom truly began with the opening of **Walt Disney World** in 1971, which had actually been in development since the mid-1960s. The state government bent over backwards to help the Disney Corporation turn a sizeable slice of central Florida into the biggest theme-park complex ever known, even though throughout its construction debate raged over the commercial and ecological effects of such a major undertaking on the rest of the region. Undeterred, smaller businesses rushed to the area, eager to capitalize on the anticipated tourist influx, and the sleepy cow-town of **Orlando** suddenly found itself the hub of one of the state's fastest-growing population centres – soon to become one of the world's best-known holiday destinations.

Time, plus Disney's success and Miami's rise to prominence, had only helped solidify Florida's place in the **international tourist market** by the 1990s. Directly or indirectly, one in five of the state's twelve million inhabitants was making a living from tourism. At the same time, the general swing from heavy to **high-tech industries** had resulted in many American corporations forsaking their traditional northern bases in favour of Florida, bringing their white-collar workforces with them. Yet the lack of state spending, due in part to low **taxes** intended to stimulate growth, reduced funding for public services, leaving the apparently booming state with high levels of adult illiteracy, infant mortality and crime.

Natural resources and challenges

Increased protection of the state's **natural resources** was a more positive feature of the 1990s. Impressive amounts of land were now under state control and, overall, wildlife was less threatened than at any time since white settlers first arrived. Most spectacular of all was the revival of the state's alligator population.

Behind the optimistic facade, however, lay many problems. For starters, much of southern Florida's resurgent landscape – and its dependent animals – could still be destroyed by south Florida's ever-increasing need for land and drinking water. And **nature** itself often posed a serious threat. In August 1992, **Hurricane Andrew** brought winds of 168mph tearing through the southern regions of Miami, blowing down the

---

THE DRUG TRADE

In the 1980s Florida's other multi-billion-dollar business – the **drug trade** – began taking off. Indeed, Florida's proximity to various Latin and South American countries with large drug production operations perfectly positioned the state as a gateway for drug smuggling and money-laundering; estimates suggest at least a quarter of the cocaine entering the US still arrives through the state. The inherent violence of the drug trade, along with lax Florida gun laws, helped Miami earn the unflattering designation "murder capital of the US" in the late 1980s, a label it has largely shaken off, though some incidents of **violence against tourists** in the early 1990s resullied its reputation. Despite the social problems engendered, much money was being made by the US–Latin American trade – both legal and contraband – and poured into the coffers of a burgeoning **banking** industry, which set up shop in gleaming high towers just south of downtown Miami. Ironically, the switch in Florida's "war on drugs" from capturing dealers to clamping down on **money-laundering** began to threaten many of these financial institutions, built on – and it's an open secret – the drug trade.

1984–89	1992	1997	2000
Miami Vice TV show runs on NBC.	Hurricane Andrew leaves forty people dead, 100,000 homes affected and damage of $20–30 billion.	Florida Marlins win the baseball World Series for the first time; they win again in 2003.	Florida becomes the battleground of the controversial US presidential election contest between Al Gore and George Bush.

radar of the National Hurricane Center in the process and leaving an estimated $30 billion worth of damage in its wake. In the summer of 1999, another storm, **Hurricane Floyd**, came blowing through, leading to the evacuation of millions of residents all along the southeast US coast and causing considerable damage, though fortunately less than was feared.

Florida today

Today Florida is the fourth most populous state in the US, with just under twenty million people and a GDP of around $800 billion, bigger than most European countries. Yet the last ten years has been rough for the Sunshine State: tourism has been battered by a series of domestic and international economic downturns, and the **US mortgage crisis** has hit Florida very hard. Since 2008, the state has posted some of the highest mortgage delinquency and foreclosure rates in the country. And with the NASA Space Shuttle programme shut down in 2011, thousands of formerly well-paid engineers and other workers were still looking for jobs two years later.

Considerable environmental challenges also persist; the state was pummelled by six major **hurricanes** in the 2004 season alone (see box, p.461), while the **BP oil spill** of 2010 wreaked havoc on Florida's Gulf coast. On a positive note, the state purchased 187,000 acres of land abutting the **Everglades** from the US Sugar Corporation in June 2008, ostensibly to help restore water flow to the imperilled ecosystem; it's still too soon to determine whether this will work. In 2009 the state received $96 million in stimulus funds to replace a one-mile stretch of the **Tamiami Trail**, north of Everglades National Park, which should allow more water to flow south; in 2014 governor Rick Scott earmarked $250 million for further Everglades restoration.

In 2013 the nation was riveted by the trial of **George Zimmerman**, a neighbourhood watch coordinator who had shot and killed unarmed teenager **Trayvon Martin** in Sanford, just north of Orlando. Zimmerman's eventual acquittal of murder angered the

---

THE 2000 ELECTION

The political manoeuvring by which **George W. Bush** became the 43rd president of the US in 2000 cast a shadow over the Sunshine State, as well as the entire country. The election itself was a virtual dead heat: **Al Gore**, the Democratic Party's nominee, won the country's **popular vote** by around half a million, but Bush led in the **electoral college** tally – with Florida too close to call. Bush's margin was so narrow – he led by less than 1000 votes out of a total of nearly six million cast – that a recount was called for. And although Bush's brother, **Governor Jeb Bush**, officially recused himself during the controversy, his Secretary of State – and Bush's campaign chairman for the state – **Katherine Harris**, didn't. Instead, she disallowed a full count, shutting down normal recount operations while her man was leading by only a few hundred votes and calling him the winner. Thousands of Floridians protested amid accusations of illegal police roadblocks that kept African-Americans – who overwhelmingly supported Al Gore – from even getting to the polls. Attempts by the **Florida Supreme Court** to overturn the Harris decision were summarily quashed by the right-leaning **US Supreme Court**, which allowed the peremptory decision to stand.

2003	2006	2008	2010
Tampa Bay Buccaneers win the Super Bowl.	Miami Heat win the NBA championship for the first time; they win again in 2012 and 2013.	Housing mortgage crisis begins – it is still affecting Florida in 2014.	BP oil spill threatens the Gulf coast.

FLORIDA TERMS

Barrier island A long, narrow island of the kind protecting much of Florida's mainland from coastal erosion, comprising sandy beach and mangrove forest – often blighted by condos.

Condo Short for "condominium", a tall and usually ugly block of (normally) expensive apartments.

Cracker Nickname given to Florida settlers and farmers from the 1800s, stemming from the sound made by the whip used in cattle round-ups (or possibly from the cracking of corn to make grits – a hot cereal).

Crackerbox Colloquial architectural term for the simple wooden cottage early crackers lived in, ingeniously designed to allow the lightest breeze to cool the whole dwelling.

Florida ice Potentially hazardous mix of oil and water on a road surface following a thunderstorm.

Hammocks Not open-air sleeping places but patches of trees. In the south, and especially in the Everglades, hammocks often appear as "tree islands" above the flat wetlands. In the north, hammocks are larger and occur on elevations between wetlands and pinewoods. All hammocks make excellent wildlife habitats and those in the south are composed of tropical trees rarely seen elsewhere in the US.

Intracoastal Waterway To strengthen coastal defences during World War II, the natural waterways dividing the mainland from the barrier islands were deepened and extended. The full length, along the east and southwest coasts, is termed the "Intracoastal Waterway".

Key Derived from the word "cay" – an island or bank composed of coral fragments.

No see'ums Tiny, mosquito-like insects; near-impossible to spot until they've already bitten you.

Snowbird Term applied to a visitor from the northern US or Canada coming to Florida during the winter to escape sub-zero temperatures – usually recognized by their sunburn.

African-American community, raising questions about just how far race relations had progressed in the state.

When it comes to **politics**, Florida has generally leaned to the right in recent years, though Barack Obama did win the state in 2008 and 2012 (by 0.88 percent). Republicans have been firmly in charge of the state legislature since 2008, and the governorship since 1999; Republican governor **Rick Scott** began his four-year stint in 2011. In a bizarre twist, his opponent in the 2014 election was former Republican governor **Charlie Crist** – now representing the Democratic Party.

2011	2012	2014
Space Shuttle programme formally ends.	George Zimmerman kills Trayvon Martin, an African-American teenager, in Sanford, and is later (controversially) acquitted of murder.	Flooding devastates the Panhandle after the heaviest rains in 130 years.

Natural Florida

The biggest surprise for most people in Florida is the abundance of undeveloped, natural areas throughout the state and the extraordinary variety of wildlife and vegetation within them. From a rare hawk that eats only snails to a vine-like fig that strangles other trees, natural Florida possesses plenty you've probably never seen before, and which – due to drainage, pressures from the agricultural lobby, and the constant need for new housing – may not be on view for very much longer.

Many factors contribute to the unusual diversity of **ecosystems** found in Florida, the most obvious being **latitude**: the north of the state has vegetation common to temperate regions, which is quite distinct from the subtropical flora of the south. Another crucial element is **elevation**: while much of Florida is flat and low-lying, a change of a few inches in elevation drastically affects what grows, due in part to the enormous variety of soils.

Forests and woodlands

Forests and woodlands aren't the first thing people associate with Florida, but the state has an impressive assortment, ranging from the great tracts of upland pine common in the north to the mixed bag of tropical foliage found in the southern hammocks.

Pine flatwoods

Covering roughly half of Florida, **pine flatwoods** are most widespread on the southeastern coastal plain. These pine species – longleaf, slash and pond – rise tall and straight like telephone poles. The Spanish once harvested products such as turpentine and rosin from Florida's flatwood pines, a practice that continued during US settlement, and some trees still bear the scars on their trunks. Pine flatwoods are airy and open, with abundant light filtering through the upper canopy of leaves, allowing thickets of shrubs such as saw palmetto, evergreen oak, gallberry and fetterbrush to grow. **Inhabitants** of the pine flatwoods include white-tailed deer, cotton rat, brown-headed nuthatch, pine warbler, eastern diamondback rattlesnake and oak toad. Many of these creatures also inhabit other Florida ecosystems, but the **fox squirrel** – a large and noisy character with a rusty tinge to its undercoat – is one of the few mammalian denizens more or less restricted to the pine flatwoods.

THE ROLE OF FIRE

Florida has more thunderstorms than any other part of the US, and the resulting lightning frequently ignites **fires**. Many Florida plants have adapted to fire by developing thick bark or the ability to regenerate from stumps. Others, such as cabbage palmetto and sawgrass, protect their growth bud with a sheath of green leaves. Fire is necessary to keep a natural balance of plant species – human attempts to control naturally ignited fires have contributed to the changing composition of Florida's remaining wild lands.

Human intervention was desperately needed in July 1998, when Florida suffered one of its most severe summer droughts. In an instant, devastating wildfires roared out of control in Volusia County, and raged on a head-on course for downtown Daytona and the beaches. Over 140,000 acres of forested lands were destroyed – approximately ten percent of the land in Volusia County. The total loss attributed to the fires was estimated at $379 million. The positive aspect of this destruction was that the fire promoted a healthy rejuvenation of the forest floor.

HURRICANES

Florida has long taken a perverse pride in its ongoing battle with the weather but as tropical storms have grown more frequent and severe, that pride has proved rather misplaced. Weather forecasters say that in 2004, the Caribbean and its environs came out of a 25-year calm period; experts predict more frequent and more intense hurricanes in the next few decades, though between 2006 and 2013 direct hits on Florida were mercifully rare.

Florida's **storm season** officially spans from June to November, but most storms froth up in August or September, and last around ten days. The modern **naming system**, introduced in 1953, originally only used female names; it wasn't until 24 years later it began to alternate between men's and women's (the letters Q, U, X, Y and Z are not used). Names are chosen from French, English and Spanish to reflect the languages across the Caribbean. These days, to keep it manageable, the list repeats every six years; an exception is when a hurricane is especially deadly or causes major damage. In such cases – Jeanne, for example – the name is officially retired and replaced with a new one. If there are more than 21 storms in any season, as happened in the especially tumultuous 2005, Greek letters are used; the last storm to form, the harmless Epsilon, astonished weather-watchers when it swirled to life on December 30 (proving the idea of a hurricane season is at best a man-made guess).

Hurricanes all turn in a counter-clockwise direction around an eye – as a rule, the tighter the eye, the fiercer and more dangerous the storm – and because of this rotation pattern, the areas to the north and east of landfall are often most badly damaged by its leading edge. A hurricane's intensity is graded on what's known as the **Saffir-Sampson scale**: category 1 (sustained winds 74–95mph) will cause cosmetic problems like downed trees or broken windows while a category 5 (sustained winds 156mph and up) will level almost anything in its path, whether natural or man-made. Both Hurricane Charley, which killed 27 and caused $6.8 billion of damage to Florida's southwest coast in 2004, and Katrina, which hit New Orleans a year later, were only category 4 storms when they made landfall (winds 131–155mph). The sole category 5 to hit at full force since modern records began is Camille, which tore into Mississippi's Gulf coast in 1969 and left destruction so severe observers likened it to an atomic bomb.

Florida's emergency management system has been tested, and taxed, by the onslaught of such severe storms; but although no one can predict when a devastating storm like Camille will whip up in the Atlantic again, advanced computer modelling to gauge its probable path – and so prepare people and property accordingly – is growing ever more sophisticated. For more information go to Ⓦ hurricanes.noaa.gov.

Upland pine forests

As the name suggests, **upland pine forests** – or high pinelands – are found on the rolling sand ridges and sandhills of northeastern Florida and the Panhandle, conditions that tend to keep upland pine forests drier and therefore even more open than the flatwoods. Upland pine forests have a groundcover of wiregrass and an overstorey of (mostly) longleaf pine trees, which creates a park-like appearance. Redheaded woodpeckers, eastern bluebirds, Florida mice, pocket gophers (locally called "salamanders", a distortion of "sand mounder") and gopher tortoises (amiable creatures often sharing their burrows with gopher frogs) all make the high pine country their home. The latter two, together with scarab beetles, keep the forest healthy by mixing and aerating the soil. The now-endangered red-cockaded woodpecker is symbolic of old-growth upland pine forest; logging and repression of the natural fire process have contributed to its decline.

Hammocks

Wildlife tends to be more abundant in hardwood **hammocks** than in the associated pine forests and prairies (see opposite). Hammocks consist of narrow bands of (non-pine) hardwoods growing transitionally between pinelands and lower, wetter vegetation. The make-up of hammocks varies across the state. In the south, they chiefly comprise tropical hardwoods; in the north, they contain an overstorey of oak, magnolia and beech, along with a few smaller plants. Red-bellied woodpeckers, red-tailed and red-shouldered hawks and barred owls nest in them, while down below you can also find eastern wood rats, striped skunks and white-tailed deer.

Scrubs and prairies

Scrub ecosystems once spread to the southern Rocky Mountains and northern Mexico, but climatic changes reduced their distribution and remnant stands are now found only in northern and central Florida. Like the high pines, scrub occurs in dry, hilly areas. The vegetation, which forms an impenetrable mass, consists of varied combinations of drought-adapted evergreen oak, saw palmetto, Florida rosemary and/or sand pine. The **Florida bonamia**, a morning glory with pale blue funnel-shaped blossoms, is one of the most attractive plants of the scrub, which has more than a dozen plant species officially listed as endangered. Scrub also harbours some unique animals, including the Florida mouse, the Florida scrub lizard, the sand skink and the Florida **scrub jay**. The scrub jay has an unusual social system: pairs nest in cooperation with offspring of previous seasons, who help carry food to their younger siblings. Although not unique to scrub habitat, other inhabitants include black bear, white-tailed deer, bobcats and gopher tortoises.

Some of Florida's inland areas are covered by **prairie**, characterized by love grass, broomsedge and wiregrass – the best examples surround Lake Okeechobee. Settlers destroyed the bison that roamed here some two hundred years ago, but herds are now being reintroduced to some state parks. A more diminutive prairie denizen is the **burrowing owl**: while most owls are active at night, burrowing owls feed during the day and, equally unusually, live in underground dens and bow nervously when approached, earning them the nickname the "howdy owl". Eastern spotted skunks, cotton rats, black vultures, eastern meadowlarks and box turtles are a few other prairie inhabitants. Nine-banded **armadillos** are also found in prairie habitats and in any non-swampy terrain. Recent invaders from Texas, the armadillos usually forage at night, feeding on insects. As they have poor eyesight, they often fail to notice a human's approach until the last minute, when they will leap up and bound away noisily.

The south Florida rocklands

Elevated areas around the state's southern tip – in the Everglades and along the Florida Keys – support either pines or tropical hardwood hammocks on limestone outcrops collectively known as the **south Florida rocklands**. More jungle-like than the temperate hardwood forests found in northern Florida, the **tropical hardwood hammocks** of the south tend to occur as "tree islands" surrounded by the sparser vegetation of wet prairies or mangroves. Royal palm, pigeon plum, gumbo limbo (one of the most beautiful of the tropical hammock trees, with a distinctive smooth red bark), and ferns form dense thickets within the hammock. The **pine forests** of the south Florida rocklands largely consist of scraggly-looking slash pine and are similarly surrounded by mangroves and wet prairies.

Epiphytic plants

Tropical hammocks contain various forms of **epiphytic plant**, which use other plants for physical support but don't depend on them for nutrients. In southern Florida, epiphytes include orchids, ferns and bromeliads; **Spanish moss** is one of the most widespread bromeliads, hanging from tree branches throughout the state and forming the "canopy roads" in Tallahassee (see p.402). Seemingly the most aggressive of epiphytes, **strangler figs**, after germinating in the canopy of trees such as palms, cut off their host tree from sunlight. They then send out aerial roots that eventually reach the soil and then tightly enlace the host, preventing growth of the trunk. Finally, the fig produces so many leaves that it chokes out the host's greenery and the host dies, leaving only the fig.

Other plants and vertebrates
The south Florida rocklands support over forty plants and a dozen vertebrates found nowhere else in the state. These include the crenulate lead plant, the Key tree cactus, the Florida mastiff bat, the Key deer, and the Miami black-headed snake. More common residents include **butterflies and spiders** – the black-and-yellow yeliconia butterflies, with their long paddle-shaped wings and a distinctive gliding flight pattern, are particularly elegant. Butterflies need to practise careful navigation as hammocks are laced with the foot-long webs of the banana spider. Other wildlife species include sixty types of land snail, green tree frogs, green anoles, cardinals, opossums, raccoons and white-tailed deer. Most of these are native to the southeastern US, but a few West Indian bird species, such as the mangrove cuckoo, grey kingbird and white-crowned pigeon, have colonized the south Florida rocklands.

Swamps and marshes
Although about half have been destroyed due to logging, peat removal, draining or sewage outflow, **swamps** are still found all over Florida. Trees growing around swamps include pines, palms, cedars, oaks, black gum, willows and bald cypress. Particularly adapted to aquatic conditions, the bald cypress is ringed by knobby "knees" or modified roots, providing oxygen to the tree, which would otherwise suffocate in the wet soil. Epiphytic orchids and bromeliads are common on cypresses, especially in the southern part of the state. Florida's official state tree, the **sabal palm**, is another swamp/hammock plant: "heart of palm" is the gourmet's name for the vegetable cut from its insides and used in salads.

Florida swamps also have many species of **insectivorous plants**; sticky pads or liquid-filled funnels trap small insects, which are then digested by the nitrogen-hungry plant. The area around the Apalachicola National Forest has the highest diversity of carnivorous plants in the world, among them pitcher plants, bladderworts and sundews.

Wetlands with relatively few trees, **freshwater marshes** range from shallow wet prairies to deep-water cattail marshes. **The Everglades** form Florida's largest marsh, most of which is sawgrass. On higher ground with good soils, sawgrass (actually a sedge) grows densely; at lower elevations it's sparser, and often an algae mat covers the soil between its plants.

Wetlands wildlife
Swamp-dwellers include dragonflies, snails, clams, fish, bird-voiced tree frogs, limpkins, ibis, wood ducks, beavers, raccoons and the elusive **Florida panther**. With luck, you might see a **snail kite**: a brown or black mottled hawk with a very specialized diet, entirely dependent on large apple snails. Snail and snail kite numbers have drastically fallen following the draining of marshes for agriculture and flood control, which so far

---

ALLIGATORS
Alligators are one of the most widely known inhabitants of Florida's wetlands, lakes and rivers. Look for them on sunny mornings when they bask on logs or banks. If you hear thunder rumbling on a clear day, it may in fact be the bellow of territorial males. Alligators can reach 10ft in length and primarily prey on fish, turtles, birds, crayfish and crabs. Once overhunted for their hides and meat, alligators have made a strong comeback since **protection** was initiated in 1973; by 1987, Florida had up to half a million of them and another fifteen years later, the number was estimated to be 1.5 million. They are not usually dangerous – around twenty fatal attacks have been registered in the past 55-plus years. Most at risk are people who swim at dusk and small children playing unattended near water. To many creatures, however, alligators are a life-saver: during the summer, when the marshes dry up, they use their snouts, legs and tails to enlarge existing pools, creating a refuge for themselves and for other aquatic species. In these **"gator holes"**, garfish stack up like piles of logs, snakes search for frogs, and otters and anhingas forage for fish.

> **WALKING CATFISH**
>
> Some native Florida fish species are threatened by the introduction of the **walking catfish**, which has a specially adapted gill system enabling it to leave the water and take the fish equivalent of cross-country hikes. A native of India and Burma, the walking catfish was released into southern Florida canals in the early 1960s and within twenty years had "walked" across twenty counties, disturbing the indigenous food chain. A freeze eliminated a number of these exotic fish, though enough remain to cause concern.

has irreversibly drained over sixty percent of the Everglades. **Wading birds** are conspicuous in the wetlands. Egrets, herons and ibis, usually clad in white or grey feathers, stalk frogs, mice and small fish. Plume-hunters in the early 1900s decimated these birds to make fanciful hats, and during the last few decades habitat destruction has caused a ninety-percent reduction in their numbers. Nonetheless, many are still visible in swamps, marshes and mangroves. **Cattle egrets**, invaders from South America, are a common sight on pastures, where they forage on insects disturbed by grazing livestock. Pink waders – roseate spoonbills and, to a much lesser extent, **flamingos** – can also be found in southern Florida's wetlands.

Lakes, springs and rivers

Florida has almost eight thousand freshwater **lakes**. Game fish such as bass and bluegill are common, but the waters are too warm to support trout. Most Florida **springs** release cold fresh water, but some springs are warm and others emit sulphur-, chloride- or salt-laden waters. Homosassa Springs (see p.382), for example, has a high level of chloride, making it attractive to both freshwater and marine species of fish.

Besides fish, Florida's extensive **river** system supports snails, freshwater mussels and crayfish. Southern river-dwellers also include the lovable **manatee**, which inhabits bays and shallow coastal waters. The only totally aquatic herbivorous mammal, manatees sometimes weigh almost a tonne but only eat aquatic plants. Unable to tolerate cold conditions, manatees are partial to the warm water discharged by power plants, taking some of them as far north as North Carolina. In Florida during the winter, the large springs at Crystal River (see p.384) attract manatees, some of which have become tame enough to allow divers to scratch their bellies. Although they have few natural enemies, manatees are on the decline, often due to powerboat propellers injuring their backs or heads when they feed at the surface.

The coast

There's a lot more than sunbathing taking place around Florida's **coast**. The sandy beaches provide a habitat for many species, not least sea turtles. Where there isn't sand, you'll find the fascinating mangrove forests or wildlife-filled salt marshes and estuaries. Offshore, coral reefs provide yet another exotic ecosystem, and one of the more pleasurable to explore by snorkelling or diving.

Sandy beaches

Waves bring many interesting creatures onto Florida's **sandy beaches**, such as sponges, horseshoe crabs and the occasional sea horse. Florida's **shells** are justly famous; fig shells, moon snails, conches, whelks, olive shells, red and orange scallops, murex, cockles, and pen and turban shells are a few of the many varieties. As you beachcomb, beware of stepping barefoot on purplish fragments of **man-of-war** tentacles: these jellyfish have no means of locomotion, and their floating, sail-like bodies often cause them to be washed ashore – their tentacles, which sometimes reach to 60ft in length, can deliver a painful sting. More innocuous beach inhabitants include wintering birds such as black-bellied plovers and sanderlings, and nesting black skimmers.

Of the seven species of **sea turtle**, five nest on Florida's sandy beaches: green, loggerhead, leatherback, hawksbill and Olive Ridley. From February to August, the female turtles crawl ashore at night, excavate a beachside hole and deposit a hundred-plus eggs inside. Not many of these will survive to adulthood; raccoons eat a lot of the eggs, and hatchlings are liable to be crushed by vehicles while attempting to cross the coastal highways. Programmes to hatch the eggs artificially have helped offset some of the losses, however. The best time to view sea turtles is during June – peak nesting time – with one of the park-ranger-led walks offered along the southern portion of the northeast coast (see p.315).

Mangroves
Found in brackish waters around the Florida Keys and the southwest coast, Florida has three species of **mangrove**. Unlike most plants, mangroves bear live young, as the "seeds" or propagules germinate while still on the tree; after dropping from the parent, the young propagule floats for weeks or months until it washes up on a suitable site, where its sprouted condition allows it to put out roots rapidly. Like bald cypress, mangroves have difficulty extracting oxygen from their muddy environs and solve this problem with extensive aerial roots, which either dangle finger-like from branches or twist outwards from the lower trunk. **Mangrove inhabitants** include various fish species that depend on mangroves as a nursery, such as the mangrove snapper, as well as frogs, crocodiles, brown pelican, wood stork, roseate spoonbill, river otter, mink and raccoon.

Salt marshes and estuaries
Like the mangrove ecosystem, the **salt marsh and estuary habitat** provides a nursery for many fish species, which in turn serve as fodder for larger fish, herons, egrets and the occasional dolphin. **Crocodiles**, which have narrower and more pointed snouts than alligators, are seldom sighted and are confined to saltwater at the state's southernmost tip. In a few southern-Florida salt marshes, you might find a **great white heron**, a rare and handsome form of the more common great blue heron. Around Florida Bay, great white herons have learned to beg for fish from local residents, with each of these massive birds "working" a particular neighbourhood – striding from household to household demanding fish by rattling window blinds with their bills or issuing guttural croaks. A less-appealing salt marsh inhabitant is the **mosquito**: unfortunately, the more damaging methods of mosquito control, such as impounding salt water or spraying DDT, have inflicted extensive harm on the fragile salt marshes and estuaries.

The coral reef
A long band of living **coral reef** frames Florida's southeastern corner. Living coral comes in many colours: star coral is green, elkhorn coral orange and brain coral red. Each piece of coral is actually a colony of hundreds or thousands of small, soft animals called **polyps**, related to sea anemones and jellyfish. The polyps secrete limestone to form their hard outer skeletons, and at night extend their feathery tentacles to filter seawater for microscopic food. The filtering process, however, provides only a fraction of the coral's nutrition – most is produced via the photosynthesis of algae living within the polyps' cells. In recent years, influxes of warmer water, possibly associated with global warming, have killed off large numbers of the algae cells. The half-starved polyp then often succumbs to disease, a phenomenon known as "bleaching". Although this has been observed throughout the Pacific, the damage in Florida has so far been moderate; the impact of the tourist industry on the reef has been more pronounced, though reef destruction for souvenirs is now banned.

FLORIDA LOBSTERS

Though the Maine coast may be the better-known source of **lobsters**, Florida boasts its share of these crustaceans, which differ from their northern counterparts by having a broad, flat tail, as opposed to the Maine variety's large, meaty claws. And while lobsters are prized as a delicacy, they're vital to the undersea ecosystem. As predators, lobsters are the custodians of the coral reefs: they gorge on the sea snails that aggressively graze the coral and keep the population in check. As prey, species like the spiny Florida lobster are a staple in the diet of many larger creatures – the jewfish, for example, feeds almost exclusively on them – and make a tasty treat for octopus, rays and eels as well.

In recent years, **lobster fishing** has had a catastrophic effect on the underwater ecosystem around southern Florida, decimating the supplies of a key member of the food chain; at the same time, **pollution** has diminished the oxygen content of the sea to such an extent that even hardy crustaceans suffer. To stem the losses, fishermen have agreed to take part in a government programme that would reduce the number of **traps** left out each year. In recreational fishing, too, there are now **strict regulations** on the lobster's size (the carapace or body must be at least three inches long), the length of the season (Aug 6–March 31), and the number that can be caught (six lobsters per person per day). Meanwhile, locals grumble that opportunistic tourists have less respect for supplies than fishermen who rely on the lobsters for their livelihood, especially during the two-day **Sport Lobster season** (starting at 12.01am on the last Wednesday in July), when you're most likely to hear amateurs bragging about their sizeable catches with little regard for the environmental consequences. Only time will tell whether the government's actions are enough to bolster the lobster supplies, or whether the crustacean's fate will mirror that of the **conch** – once so abundant in the Keys but now mainly farmed in the Caribbean.

Coral reefs are home to a kaleidoscopic variety of brightly coloured fish – beau gregories, porkfish, parrot fish, blennies, grunts and wrasses – which swirl in dazzling schools or lurk between coral crevices. The **damselfish** is the farmer of the reef: after destroying a polyp patch, it feeds on the resultant algae growth, fiercely defending it from other fish. Thousands of other creatures live in the coral reef, among them sponges, feather-duster worms, sea fans, crabs, spiny lobsters, sea urchins and conches.

Florida on film

The silver screen and the Sunshine State have one vital thing in common: escapism. Both on film and off, Florida has always represented the ultimate getaway. For nineteenth-century homesteaders, Cuban refugees, New York retirees, libido-laden college kids or criminals on the lam, the state has always beckoned as some kind of paradise. Hollywood has also used Florida as an exotic backdrop for everything from light-hearted holiday flicks to black-hearted crime yarns, and the state has made the most of its movie-land charms. Henry Levin's phenomenally successful teen flick *Where the Boys Are* (1960), for instance, not only spawned a cinematic sub-genre, but also made Fort Lauderdale the country's top Spring Break resort. And Miami's rejuvenation in the 1980s can be attributed at least in part to the glamour imparted by filmmaker Michael Mann's TV series *Miami Vice*.

To immerse yourself in Florida's cinematic history, where images of palm trees, beaches and luxury hotels predominate, is to take a virtual holiday. And though there are plenty of mediocre Florida flicks (most of them sun-addled Spring Break romps or Elvis Presley showcases), there are many conveying the unique and varied qualities of the state. Here are some of the best, of which those tagged with the ★ symbol are particularly recommended.

DRAMA AND HISTORY

Beneath the 12-Mile Reef (Robert Webb, 1953). In this beautiful travelogue, Greek sponge fishermen from Tarpon Springs venture south to fish the "Glades" and tangle with the Anglo "Conchs" of Key West. Robert Wagner plays a young Greek Romeo named Adonis, who dares to dive the "12-mile reef" for his sponge-worthy Juliet.

Distant Drums (Raoul Walsh, 1951). One of many movies that have focused on Florida's Seminole (the first was made by Vitagraph in 1906), *Distant Drums*, set in the midst of the Second Seminole War in 1840, stars Gary Cooper as a legendary US Army captain who finds himself and his men trapped in the Everglades. Cooper and his band encounter snakes, alligators and hordes of Seminole braves as they attempt to reach dry land.

Dolphin Tale (Charles Martin Smith, 2011). Heart-warming family drama inspired by the true story of Winter, a dolphin that was rescued in 2005 off the Florida coast and raised by the Clearwater Marine Aquarium, where most of the movie was filmed. *Dolphin Tale 2* was released in 2014.

Great Expectations (Alfonso Cuarón, 1998). This contemporary re-telling of the Dickens classic has become something of a cult hit, with lead performances from Ethan Hawke, Gwyneth Paltrow, Robert De Niro, Anne Bancroft and Chris Cooper. Locations include the opulent Ca d'Zan mansion in Sarasota, and the city of Bradenton.

Reap the Wild Wind (Cecil B. De Mille, 1942). A stirring account of skulduggery in the Florida Keys of the 1840s.

Spunky Paulette Goddard vacillates between sea salt John Wayne and landlubber Ray Milland while trying to outwit pirates, gangs and a giant squid off the deadly coral reefs.

Rosewood (John Singleton, 1997). Fictionalized but thought-provoking account of the harrowing Rosewood massacre of 1923, when an African-American community near Cedar Key was effectively destroyed by lynch mobs from a neighbouring white town.

Ruby in Paradise (Victor Nuñez, 1993). Ashley Judd plays Ruby, who leaves her home in the Tennessee mountains and hitches a ride south to taste life in the Florida Panhandle. Settling in Panama City, Ruby finds work in a tourist shop selling tacky souvenirs. She fends off the boss's son and finds herself along the way. The film was sensitively directed by Florida's own Victor Nuñez, a true regional independent who has been making movies in northern Florida since 1970.

Salesman (Albert and David Maysles, 1968). The second half of this brilliant and moving documentary follows four Bible salesmen to Opa-Locka on the outskirts of Miami. It's not a tale of beaches and luxury hotels, but rather low-rent apartments, cheap motels, and the quiet desperation of four men trying to sell overpriced illustrated Bibles door to door.

Seminole (Budd Boetticher, 1953). Set five years before *Distant Drums* (see above) and far more sympathetic to the Seminoles' plight, this Western stars Rock Hudson as a US dragoon and Anthony Quinn as his half-breed childhood friend who has become the Seminole chief Osceola.

Attempting to claim even the swamps of Florida for white settlers, a power-hungry general sends a platoon into the Everglades to flush out the Seminole and drive them out west.

Ulee's Gold (Victor Nuñez, 1997). Twenty-two years after *92 in the Shade*, Peter Fonda gave the best performance of his career as Florida beekeeper Ulee, a stoical Vietnam vet raising his granddaughters while his son is in jail. Local auteur Nuñez (*Ruby in Paradise*) knows and captures northern Florida better than any filmmaker, and despite a strained plot about a couple of ne'er-do-wells and a stash of money, this meditative, measured movie is a triumph.

Vernon, Florida (Errol Morris, 1981). This documentary lovingly – if a little mockingly – captures every foible of the Florida eccentrics who fill the small town of Vernon in the Panhandle. Standout is the turkey hunter, memorable for his hushed and reverential attitude toward the birds he hunts and kills.

The Yearling (Clarence Brown, 1946). A classic about a family struggling to eke out a living in the scrub country of northern Florida (in the vicinity of Lake George and Volusia) in 1878. Oscar-winner Claude Jarman Jr plays the son of Gregory Peck and Jane Wyman who adopts a troublesome fawn. The movie was shot on location and based on Floridian Marjorie Kinnan Rawlings' Pulitzer Prize-winning novel of the same name.

CRIME STORIES

Blood and Wine (Bob Rafelson, 1997). Jack Nicholson plays a dodgy Miami wine dealer with access to the cellars of southern Florida's rich and famous in this underrated thriller. He enlists a wheezy expat safe-breaker (Michael Caine) and a savvy Cuban nanny (Jennifer Lopez) in his scheme to snag a million-dollar necklace. When the jewels end up in the hands of his jilted wife (Judy Davis) and perpetually pissed-off stepson (Stephen Dorff) the action heads south to the Florida Keys.

Body Heat (Lawrence Kasdan, 1981). Filmed just south of Palm Beach in the small coastal town of Lake Worth, Kasdan's directorial debut makes the most of the sweaty potential of a southern Florida heat wave. Shady lawyer William Hurt falls for the charms of wealthy Kathleen Turner and plans to bump off her husband for the inheritance.

Illtown (Nick Gomez, 1995). Depending on whom you ask, Nick Gomez's movie is either a stylish, strange and ambitious achievement or a pretentious mess. Either way, it's hard to ignore Tony Danza as a gay mob boss, and a gaggle of familiar indie stars (including Michael Rapaport and Lili Taylor) playing an unlikely bunch of Miami drug dealers.

Key Largo (John Huston, 1948). Though shot entirely on Hollywood sets, Huston's tense crime melodrama about an army veteran (Humphrey Bogart) and a mob boss (Edward G. Robinson) barricaded in a Key Largo hotel during a major hurricane has the credible feel of a muggy summer in the Florida Keys.

Miami Blues (George Armitage, 1990). This quirky crime story about a home-loving psychopath (Alec Baldwin), the naive hooker he shacks up with (Jennifer Jason Leigh) and the burnt-out homicide detective who's on their trail (Fred Ward) is set in a seedy backstreet Miami that glitters with terrific characters, gritty performances and delicious offbeat details.

Miami Vice (Michael Mann, 2006). Glossy, big-budget remake of the 1980s TV show that heralded South Beach's renaissance, this time starring Jamie Foxx and Colin Farrell as pastel-suited crime-fighting duo Crockett and Tubbs.

Night Moves (Arthur Penn, 1975). In one of the great metaphysical thrillers of the post-Watergate era, Gene Hackman plays a weary LA private eye with marital problems who is hired to track down a young and underdressed Melanie Griffith in the Florida Keys.

★**Out of Sight** (Steven Soderbergh, 1998). Flip-flopping between past and present and between a jazzy, sun-drenched Florida and a snow-peppered Detroit, Soderbergh's movie is a hugely satisfying adaptation of Elmore Leonard's novel of the same name. The action is set in motion when George Clooney's urbane bank-robber tunnels out of a Pensacola penitentiary and into the life of Federal Marshal Jennifer Lopez.

Palmetto (Volker Schlondorff, 1998). Woody Harrelson returns from jail to the Sarasota beach town of Palmetto and becomes Florida's number-one patsy when a bleach-blonde Elisabeth Shue walks into his life and proposes a little fake kidnapping. Perfectly exploiting Florida's sultry charms, *Palmetto* lapses into neo-noir cliché at times, but the twisty plot keeps things interesting.

★**Scarface** (Brian De Palma, 1983). Small-time Cuban thug Tony Montana arrives in Miami during the 1980 Mariel boatlift and murders, bullies and snorts his way to becoming the city's most powerful drug lord. One of the great Florida movies, De Palma's seductive and shocking paean to excess and the perversion of the American dream stars Al Pacino in a legendary, go-for-broke performance.

Tony Rome (Gordon Douglas, 1967). Wise-cracking, hard-living private eye Frank Sinatra tangles with pushers, strippers, gold diggers and self-made millionaires on the wild side of Miami. The movie is a run-of-the-mill detective yarn, but Frank was entertaining enough to warrant a sequel: *Lady in Cement*.

Wild Things (John McNaughton, 1997). A convoluted, noirish thriller about handsome high-school counsellors, lubricious schoolgirls and wealthy widows in a well-heeled community in the Everglades. Beautifully shot and played to the hilt by Matt Dillon, Kevin Bacon, Denise Richards and Neve Campbell, the plot corkscrews with twists until the final frame.

COMIC CAPERS

92 in the Shade (Thomas McGuane, 1975). A nutty, laidback comedy about rival fishing guides in Key West, starring a potpourri of Hollywood's greatest oddballs: Peter Fonda, Harry Dean Stanton, Warren Oates, Burgess Meredith and William Hickey. Ripe with local colour but somewhat lacking in effect, the movie was based on Thomas McGuane's acclaimed novel of the same name (see p.473).

Ace Ventura, Pet Detective (Tom Shadyac, 1994). The movie that launched Jim Carrey's thousand faces. He stars as a bequiffed investigator on a quest to recover Snowflake, the Miami Dolphins' kidnapped mascot, on the eve of the Super Bowl. The Miami Dolphins and their quarterback Dan Marino appear as themselves.

Adaptation (Spike Jonze, 2002). Susan Orlean's bestseller (see p.471) serves as the springboard for this entertaining, fictionalized version, in which the film's screenwriter (Nicolas Cage) struggles to adapt the book, undermined all the while by his twin brother (also played by Cage). Meryl Streep's Orlean pursues orchid-poacher Chris Cooper to the Loxahatchee National Wildlife Refuge.

The Bellboy (Jerry Lewis, 1960). This movie was shot almost entirely within Miami Beach's ultra-kitsch pleasure palace *The Fontainebleau* (the same hotel where James Bond is meant to be sunbathing at the beginning of 1964's *Goldfinger*). Jerry Lewis, in his debut as writer-director, plays Stanley, the bellhop from hell, and cameos as vacationing movie star Jerry Lewis in one of the most site-specific movies ever made.

The Birdcage (Mike Nichols, 1996). Nichols' Miami remake of *La Cage Aux Folles* makes lighthearted use of South Beach's burgeoning gay scene, portraying the rejuvenated Art Deco playground as a bright paradise of pecs, thongs and drag queens – the opening scene plays as a love letter to Ocean Drive. Impresario Armand (Robin Williams) and reigning *Birdcage* diva Albert (Nathan Lane) are happily cohabiting in kitsch heaven until the day Armand's son brings his ultra-conservative future in-laws to dinner.

The Cocoanuts (Joseph Santley & Robert Florey, 1929). Set during Florida's real-estate boom, the Marx Brothers' first film stars Groucho as an impecunious hotel proprietor

attempting to keep his business afloat by auctioning off land (with the usual interference from Chico and Harpo) in Cocoanut Grove, "the Palm Beach of tomorrow". Groucho expounds on Florida's climate while standing in what is really a sand-filled studio lot.

A Hole in the Head (Frank Capra, 1959). Frank Sinatra plays an irresponsible Miami Beach hotel owner who has dreams of striking it rich by turning South Beach into "Disneyland". The breezy opening titles in this musical comedy are pulled on airborne banners across the Miami Beach skyline.

Moon Over Miami (Walter Lang, 1941). Gold-digging, Texas-hamburger-stand waitress Betty Grable takes her sister and aunt to Miami, where "rich men are as plentiful as grapefruit, and millionaires hang from every palm tree". Grable has little trouble snagging herself a couple of ripe ones in this colourful, sappy musical comedy. On-location shooting took place in Winter Haven and Ocala, a few hundred miles north of Miami.

The Palm Beach Story (Preston Sturges, 1942). In this madcap masterpiece, Claudette Colbert takes a train from Penn Station to Palm Beach ("the best place to get a divorce", a cabbie tells her) to free herself from her penniless dreamer of a husband and find herself a good millionaire to marry.

★ **Some Like It Hot** (Billy Wilder, 1959). Wilder's classic farce sees jazz musicians Tony Curtis and Jack Lemmon escape retribution for witnessing the 1929 Chicago St Valentine's Day massacre by disguising themselves as women and joining an all-girl jazz band on a train to Miami. Though *Some Like It Hot* could be a candidate for the best movie ever set in Miami, it was actually shot at the *Hotel del Coronado* in San Diego.

There's Something About Mary (Peter and Bobby Farrelly, 1998). Years after a heinous pre-prom disaster (involving an unruly zipper), Rhode Island geek Ben Stiller tracks down Mary (Cameron Diaz), the eponymous object of his affection, to her new home in Miami. Once there he finds he's not the only one suffering from obsessive tendencies. The Farrelly brothers have created a hysterical, gross-out masterpiece.

FANTASY LANDS

★ **Cocoon** (Ron Howard, 1985). Even extraterrestrials holiday in Florida. This charming fantasy centres on residents of a Florida retirement community who discover a local swimming pool with alien powers of rejuvenation. Nearly half a century after appearing in *Moon Over Miami*, Don Ameche won a Best Supporting Actor Oscar for this film.

Dumbo (Ben Sharpsteen, 1941). In the opening sequence of this Disney animated classic there is a wonderful stork's-eye view of the entire state of Florida, where the circus has hunkered down for the winter. Though the show eventually goes on the road, this eyeful of Florida seems prescient considering Disney's role in the state some quarter of a century later.

Escape from Tomorrow (Randy Moore, 2014). This accomplished fantasy horror follows what appears to be a normal family vacation at Orlando's Walt Disney World Resort – but something sinister is going on beneath the smiles and rides. Shot on location, without Disney's permission.

The Truman Show (Peter Weir, 1998). The picture-perfect, picket-fence community of Seahaven that Jim Carrey's Truman Burbank calls home turns out to be nothing more than a giant television studio, where Truman is watched every minute of the day in the world's longest-running soap opera. The false paradise of Seahaven is actually the real, but equally artificial, Florida Gulf-coast town of Seaside.

Books

Florida's perennial state of social and political flux has always promised rich material for historians and journalists eager to pin the place down. Rarely have they managed this, though the picture of the region's unpredictable evolution that emerges can make for compulsive reading. Many established fiction writers spend their winters in Florida, but few have convincingly portrayed its characters, climate and scenery. Those who have succeeded, however, have produced some of the most remarkable and gripping literature to emerge from any part of the US. Books tagged with the ★ symbol are particularly recommended, and o/p denotes out of print.

HISTORY

Edward N. Akin *Flagler: Rockefeller Partner and Florida Baron*. Solid biography of the man whose Standard Oil fortune helped build Florida's first hotels and railroads.

Willie Drye *Storm of the Century*. Astonishing account of the Labor Day Hurricane in 1935, which tore across – and decimated – the Upper Keys. Provides a chilling foreshadowing of the potential dangers from current extreme weather patterns.

John J. Guthrie Jr, Philip Charels Lucas and Gary Monroe *Cassadaga: The South's Oldest Spiritual Community*. A look at the history, people and religious beliefs of the "metaphysical mecca" of Cassadaga, a small town between Orlando and Daytona Beach established more than a hundred years ago on the principle of continuous life.

★**Carl Hiaasen** *Team Rodent*. A native of Florida, Hiaasen has been a first-hand witness to Disney's domination of Orlando, and this book is a scathing attack on the entertainment conglomerate, exposing Disney for what Hiaasen thinks it is: evil. "Disney is so good at being good that it manifests an evil", he writes, "so uniformly courteous, so dependably clean and conscientious, so unfailingly entertaining that it's unreal, and therefore is an agent of pure wickedness." Like Hiaasen's fiction work (see p.472), the prose is a mix of sharp wit, informed research and a lot of humour.

Robert Kerstein *Politics and Growth in Twentieth Century Tampa*. A history of the politics and growth in Tampa from the coming of the railroads and cigar industry to the mid-1990s.

Howard Kleinberg *Miami: The Way We Were*. Oversized overview of Miami's history; colourful archival photos accompany text by a former editor-in-chief of the now defunct newspaper, *The Miami News*.

Stuart B. McIver *Dreamers, Schemers, and Scalawags*. An intriguing mix of biography and storytelling that tells Florida's history through its mobsters and millionaires. This is volume one of a continuing series.

Jerald T. Milanich *Florida's Indians, from Ancient Times to the Present*. A comprehensive history spanning 12,000 years of Indian life in Florida.

Gary R. Mormino and George E. Pozzetta *The Immigrant World of Ybor City*. Flavourful accounts of the Cuban, Italian and Spanish immigrants who built their lives around Ybor City's cigar industry at the turn of the twentieth century.

Helen Muir *Miami, USA*. An insider's account of how Miami's first developers gave the place shape during the land boom of the 1920s; a little toothless, but a fair overview.

John Rothchild *Up for Grabs: A Trip Through Time and Space in the Sunshine State*. An irreverent look at Florida's chequered career as a vacation spa, tourist trap and haven for scheming ne'er-do-wells.

Les Standiford *Last Train to Paradise*. Miami-based novelist Standiford turns his storytelling eye to the twisty tale of Flagler's railroad; it's a rollicking narrative, but Standiford's tendency to digress into minutiae does drag it down somewhat.

Charlton W. Tebeau *A History of Florida*. The definitive academic tome, but not for casual reading.

Victor Andres Triay *Fleeing Castro*. An emotional account of the plight of Cuba's children during the missile crisis. With their parents unable to obtain visas, 14,048 children were smuggled from the island; many never saw their families again.

Garcilaso de la Vega *The Florida of the Inca*. Comprehensive account of the sixteenth-century expedition led by Hernando de Soto through Florida's prairies, swamps and aboriginal settlements. Extremely turgid in parts, but overall an excellent insight into the period.

David C. Weeks *Ringling*. An in-depth work chronicling the time spent in Florida by circus guru John Ringling.

Patsy West *The Enduring Seminoles*. A history of Florida's Seminole Indians, who, by embracing tourism, found a means to keep their vibrant cultural identity alive.

Lawrence E. Will *Swamp to Sugarbowl: Pioneer Days in Belle Glade* (o/p). A "cracker" account of early times in the state, written in first-person redneck vernacular. Variously oafish and offensive but never dull.

NATURAL HISTORY

Mark Derr *Some Kind of Paradise*. A cautionary history of Florida's penchant for mishandling its environmental assets, from spongers off the reefs to Miami's ruthless hotel contractors.

★**Marjory Stoneman Douglas** *The Everglades: River of Grass*. Concerned conservationist literature by one of the state's most respected historians (who died in 1998 at the age of 108), describing the nature and beauty of the Everglades from their beginnings. A superb work that contributed to the founding of Everglades National Park.

David McCally *The Everglades: An Environmental History*. For both general readers and environmentalists, this book examines the formation, development and history of the

Everglades – believed to be the most endangered ecosystem in North America.

National Geographic Society *Field Guide to the Birds of North America* (4th ed). The best countrywide guide, with plenty on Florida, and excellent illustrations throughout.

Bill Pranty *A Birder's Guide to Florida*. Detailed accounts of when and where to find Florida's birds, including maps and charts. Aimed at the expert but excellent value for the novice birdwatcher.

Glen Simmons with Laura Ogden *Gladesmen*. Entertaining accounts of the "swamp rats": rugged men and women who made a living wrestling alligators and trekking the "Glades".

TRAVEL IMPRESSIONS

★**William Bartram** *Travels*. The lively diary of an eighteenth-century naturalist rambling through the Deep South and on into Florida during the period of British rule. Outstanding accounts of the indigenous people and all kinds of wildlife.

Edna Buchanan *The Corpse Had a Familiar Face*. Sometimes sharp, often sensationalist account of the author's years spent pounding the crime beat for the *Miami Herald*: five thousand corpses and gore galore. The subsequent *Vice* is more of the same.

Joan Didion *Miami*. Didion's bony prose is hard going but it's worth persevering, at least in the early chapters, to understand the complex relationship between Cuban expats and the US government. Midway, though, she's derailed into musings on the minutiae of Washington politics, and the book rapidly loses focus.

Lynn Geldof *Cubans*. Passionate and rambling interviews with Cubans in Cuba and Miami, which confirm the tight bond between them.

Herbert Hiller *Highway A1A*. Hiller uses a trip along the road that rims the length of Florida's Atlantic coast as a framework to look at the emergence of tourism, development and the myth of sunny, worry-free Florida. An insightful, offbeat read.

Henry James *The American Scene*. Interesting waffle from the celebrated novelist, including written portraits of St Augustine and Palm Beach as they thronged with wintering socialites at the turn of the twentieth century.

Norman Mailer *Miami and the Siege of Chicago*. A rabid study of the American political conventions of 1968, the

first part frothing over the Republican Party's shenanigans at Miami Beach when Nixon beat Reagan for the presidential ticket.

Kevin McCarthy *Alligator Tales*. This intriguing collection of both actual and slightly overblown encounters with alligators is illustrated with the photographs of John Moran.

Michele McPhee *Mob Over Miami*. Gripping, exhaustively researched true-crime tale, focusing on Staten Island mobster turned South Beach nightlife mogul Chris Paciello.

Susan Orlean *The Orchid Thief*. New Yorker staff writer Orlean immerses herself in the orchid-fancying subculture of South Florida, following an eccentric gardener on his illegal gathering trips in the wild. The basis for Spike Jonze's film *Adaptation* (see p.469).

Roxanne Pulitzer *The Prize Pulitzer: The Scandal that Rocked Palm Beach*. A small-town girl who married into the jet-set lifestyle of Palm Beach describes the mud-slinging in Florida's most moneyed community when she seeks a divorce.

Alexander Stuart *Life on Mars*. "Paradise with a lobotomy" is how a friend of the author described Florida. This is an often-amusing series of vignettes about the empty lives led by the beautiful people of South Beach and the redneck "white trash" of upstate.

John Williams *Into the Badlands: A Journey through the American Dream*. The author's trek across the US to interview the country's best crime writers begins in Miami, "the city that coke built"; its compelling strangeness is all too briefly revelled in.

ARCHITECTURE

Barbara Baer Capitman *Deco Delights*. A tour of Miami Beach's Art Deco buildings by the woman who championed their preservation, with definitive photography.

Laura Cerwinske *Miami: Hot & Cool*. Coffee-table tome with text on high-style South Florida living and glowing, colour photos of Miami's beautiful homes and gardens. By the same author, *Tropical Deco: The Architecture & Design of Old Miami Beach* delivers a wealth of architectural detail.

Donald W. Curl *Mizner's Florida: American Resort Architecture*. An assessment of the life, career and designs of Addison Mizner, the self-taught architect responsible for the "Bastard Spanish Moorish Romanesque Renaissance Bull Market Damn the Expense Style" structures of Palm Beach and Boca Raton.

★**Hap Hatton** *Tropical Splendor: An Architectural History of Florida*. A readable, informative and well-illustrated account of the wild, weird and wonderful buildings that have graced and disgraced the state over the years.

Nicholas N. Patricios *Building Marvelous Miami*. The architectural development of Florida's favourite city documented by 250 photos.

ART AND PHOTOGRAPHY

Todd Bertolaet *Crescent Rivers*. Ansel Adams-style photos of the dark, blackwater rivers that wind through Florida's Big Bend.

Anne Jeffrey and Aletta Dreller *Art Lover's Guide to Florida*. A comprehensive guidebook featuring 86 of the most dynamic and exciting art galleries in Florida, including museums and art centres.

Gary Monroe *Life in South Beach*. A slim volume of black-and-white photos showing Miami Beach's South Beach before the restoration of the Art Deco district and the arrival of globetrotting trendies.

★**Tom Shroder and John Barry** *Seeing the Light:* *Wilderness and Salvation: A Photographer's Tale*. An attractive book describing the story of photographer Clyde Butcher's long connection with the Everglades and showcasing his wonderful pictures of the area.

Woody Walters *Visions of Florida*. Black-and-white photos, but ones that convey the richness and beauty of Florida's terrain, from misty mornings in Tallahassee to bolts of lightning over the Everglades.

Millard Wells *Florida Key Impressions*. An illustrated journal describing a journey through the Florida Keys, highlighted by the author's original watercolour paintings.

FICTION AND POETRY

Pat Booth *Miami*. Miami's South Beach is used as a backdrop for this pot-boiling tale of seduction and desire.

Liza Cody *Backhand*. London's finest female private investigator, Anna Lee, follows the clues from Kensington to the west coast of Florida – highly entertaining.

Harry Crews *Florida Frenzy*. A collection of tales relating macho outdoor pursuits like 'gator poaching and cockfighting.

Kate Di Camillo *Because of Winn-Dixie*. When a stray dog appears in the midst of the produce section of the Winn-Dixie grocery store, it leads 10-year-old India Opal Buloni from one new friend to the next in a small Florida town. The stories India gathers in this award-winning children's book help her to piece together a new definition of family.

Tim Dorsey *Triggerfish Twist*. The standout novel in Dorsey's ongoing saga of psycho Florida eccentric Serge A. Storms takes in homicidal Little League parents, predatory real estate agents, and a mild-mannered corporate cog. Try also his *Torpedo Juice*, where Serge – in his own crackpot way – decides to find himself a wife.

Edward Falco *Winter in Florida*. Flawed but compulsive story of a cosseted New York boy seeking thrills on a central Florida horse farm.

Connie May Fowler *Before Women Had Wings*. Set in and around Tampa in the 1960s, this powerful novel tells the story of the youngest daughter of a family crippled by poverty and the effects of alcohol, violence and broken dreams.

James Hall *Under Cover of Daylight; Squall Line; Hard Aground*. Taut thrillers with a cast of crazies that make the most of the edge-of-the-world landscapes of the Florida Keys.

Ernest Hemingway *To Have and Have Not*. Hemingway lived and drank in Key West for years but set only this moderate tale in the town, describing the woes of fishermen brutalized by the Depression.

★**Carl Hiaasen** *Double Whammy*. Ferociously funny fishing thriller that brings together a classic collection of warped but believable Florida characters, among them a hermit-like ex-state governor, a cynical Cuban cop and a corrupt TV preacher. By the same author, *Skin Tight* explores the perils of unskilled plastic surgery in a Miami crawling with mutant hitmen, bought politicians, and police on gangsters' payrolls, and *Native Tongue* delves into the murky goings-on behind the scenes at a Florida theme park. Anyone with a passing interest in Florida should read at least one of these.

Carl Hiaasen (ed) *Naked Came the Manatee*. Thirteen of Miami's best-known novelists teamed up to pen this caper, which centres on the discovery of Fidel Castro's dismembered head. Full of in-jokes, this broad satire is good, if uneven, fun.

Zora Neale Hurston *Their Eyes Were Watching God*. Florida-born Hurston became one of the bright lights of the Harlem Renaissance in the 1920s. This novel describes the founding of Eatonville – her home town and the state's first all-black town – and the labourer's lot in Belle Glade at the time of the 1928 hurricane. Equally hard to put down are *Jonah's Gourd Vine* and the autobiography *Dust Tracks on a Road*.

Elmore Leonard *Stick*; *La Brava*; *Gold Coast*. The pick of this highly recommended author's Florida-set thrillers, respectively detailing the rise of an opportunist ex-con through the money, sex and drugs of Latino Miami; lowlife on the seedy South Beach before the preservation of the Art Deco district; and the tribulations of a wealthy gangster-widow alone in a Fort Lauderdale mansion.

Peter Matthiessen *Killing Mister Watson*. The first in a thoroughly researched trilogy on the early days of white settlement in the Everglades. Slow-paced but a strong insight into the Florida frontier mentality.

Thomas McGuane *Ninety-Two in the Shade*. A strange, hallucinatory search for identity by a young man of shifting mental states who aspires to become a Key West fishing guide – and whose family and friends are equally warped. McGuane directed the film version (see p.469).

Theodore Pratt *The Barefoot Mailman*. A 1940s account of the long-distance postman who kept the far-flung settlements of pioneer-period Florida in mail by hiking the many miles of beach between them.

Marjorie Kinnan Rawlings *Short Stories*. A collection of 23 of Rawlings' most acclaimed short pieces, which draw heavily on Florida's natural surroundings for inspiration.

John Sayles *Los Gusanos*. Absorbing if long-winded novel set around the lives of Cuban exiles in Miami at the time of the Mariel boatlift – written by the indie movie director.

Edmund Skellings *Collected Poems: 1958–1998*. A "best of" collection of work by Florida's poet laureate.

Patrick D. Smith *A Land Remembered*. This historical novel is an epic portrayal of the lives of an American pioneering family, set against the rich and rugged history of Florida.

Randy Wayne White *Sanibel Flats*. First in a series of Doc Ford detective novels, this book tells the story of a murder committed on a deserted mangrove island on Florida's west coast.

★**Charles Willeford** *Miami Blues*. Thanks to an uninspired movie, the best-known but not the best of a highly recommended crime fiction series starring Hoke Mosely, a cool and calculating, but very human, Miami cop. Superior titles in the series are *The Way We Die Now*, *Kiss Your Ass Goodbye* and *Sideswipe*.

COOKERY

Linda Gassenheimer *Keys Cuisine*. A collection of recipes that captures the flavour of the Florida Keys.

Sue Mullin *Nuevo Cubano Cooking*. Easy-to-follow instructions and mouthwatering photographs of recipes fusing traditional Cuban cooking with *nouvelle cuisine*.

Small print and index

Rough Guide credits

Editor: Ann-Marie Shaw
Layout: Jessica Subramanian
Cartography: Swati Handoo
Picture editor: Michelle Bhatia
Proofreader: Diane Margolis
Managing editors: Mani Ramaswamy, Andy Turner
Assistant editor: Payal Sharotri
Production: Janis Griffith

Cover design: Nicole Newman, Dan May,
Jessica Subramanian
Photographers: Dan Bannister; Anthony Pigeon;
Dan Oborn
Editorial assistant: Rebecca Hallett
Senior pre-press designer: Dan May
Programme manager: Helen Blount
Publisher: Joanna Kirby
Publishing director: Georgina Dee

Publishing information

This tenth edition published July 2015 by
Rough Guides Ltd,
80 Strand, London WC2R 0RL
11, Community Centre, Panchsheel Park,
New Delhi 110017, India
Distributed by Penguin Random House
Penguin Books Ltd,
80 Strand, London WC2R 0RL
Penguin Group (USA)
345 Hudson Street, NY 10014, USA
Penguin Group (Australia)
250 Camberwell Road, Camberwell,
Victoria 3124, Australia
Penguin Group (NZ)
67 Apollo Drive, Mairangi Bay, Auckland 1310,
New Zealand
Penguin Group (South Africa)
Block D, Rosebank Office Park, 181 Jan Smuts Avenue,
Parktown North, Gauteng, South Africa 2193
Rough Guides is represented in Canada by Tourmaline
Editions Inc. 662 King Street West, Suite 304, Toronto,
Ontario M5V 1M7
Printed in Singapore

Help us update

We've gone to a lot of effort to ensure that the tenth
edition of **The Rough Guide to Florida** is accurate and up-
to-date. However, things change – places get "discovered",
opening hours are notoriously fickle, restaurants and
rooms raise prices or lower standards. If you feel we've got
it wrong or left something out, we'd like to know, and if
you can remember the address, the price, the hours, the
phone number, so much the better.

Please send your comments with the subject line
"Rough Guide Florida Update" to mail@uk
.roughguides.com. We'll credit all contributions and
send a copy of the next edition (or any other Rough Guide
if you prefer) for the very best emails.
 Find more travel information, connect with fellow
travellers and plan your trip on roughguides.com.

ABOUT THE AUTHORS

Sarah Hull has been a contributor to Rough Guides since 2005, writing about New England, Canada and the South. Her first visit to Florida was a childhood trip to Disney World; now, Miami and South Florida live deep in her heart. When she's not on the road, she's in New York Supreme Court reporting on corporate shenanigans and celebrity lawsuits.

Stephen Keeling has been travelling to Florida since 1991 and covering the state for Rough Guides since 2008. He worked as a financial journalist for seven years before writing his first travel guide and has written several titles for Rough Guides, including books on Puerto Rico, Colombia, New England, Mexico and Canada. Stephen lives in New York City.

Rebecca Strauss fled colder climes for sunny central Florida in 2008. She's worked as a travel writer and editor ever since, contributing to magazines such as *Caribbean Travel + Life* and *Florida Travel + Life* and updating the last four editions of *The Rough Guide to Florida*.

Acknowledgements

Sarah Hull Thanks to Stephen Keeling for the mental health meet-ups, his dedication to the cause and his restorative sense of humour. Annie Shaw deserves ten high fives for her kindness, patience and editing dexterity. Jennifer Haz, the patron saint of Miami, gave me the keys to the city and worked tirelessly to provide me with area information. I couldn't have done it without Heidi Barfels, Stephan Ginez, Hilary Saunders, Julia Axelrod, Dario Arana, Christine Corson, Laura Cotter and Shazeen Shah. Finally, a huge thank you to Julia McBee, ally, DP, road companion, and great friend – you turn even the world's worst breakfast into a sunny experience. I would like to dedicate my work this round to my nephew, Henry DelGreco, who is visiting Disney for the first time this year.

Stephen Keeling Thanks to Tangela Boyd in Daytona Beach, Dena Bush and Laura Lee in Pensacola, Kari Cobham, Cindy Stavely and Jay Humphreys in St Augustine, fellow troopers Sarah Hull and Rebecca Strauss, Annie Shaw for doing such a fabulous editing job, and Tiffany Wu, whose love and support, as always, made this possible.

Rebecca Strauss Special thanks to tourism boards in Naples, Orlando and Fort Lauderdale, as well as the Disney and Universal public relations teams.

Readers' updates

Thanks to all the readers who have taken the time to write in with comments and suggestions (and apologies if we've inadvertently omitted or misspelt anyone's name):

Dominique Ebbeng; Tobin Fricke; Jessie Gilmartin; Robert Modderman & Helena Janatova; Matthew Smith; Jo Thomas.

Photo credits

All photos © Rough Guides except the following:
(Key: b-below/bottom; c-centre; l-left; r-right; t-top)

Index

Maps are marked in grey

Map symbols

The symbols below are used on maps throughout the book

	Freeway		Point of interest		Garden		Church (regional map)
	Main road		Post office		Tower		Church (town map)
	Minor road	@	Internet		Stately home		Market
	Pedestrianized road		Hospital		Fortress		Building
	Railway	(i)	Information office		Museum		Stadium
	Path	P	Parking		Statue		Park
	Wall	★	Bus stop		Observatory		Cemetery
	Ferry		Battlefiled		Lighthouse		Beach
	International airport		Campsite		Bridge		Gate
	Air force base		Golf course		Swamp		

Listings key

- Accommodation
- Café/restaurant
- Bar/club/live music venue/ gay/lesbian bar
- Shop